PHILOSOPHY AND
HUMANISM

PHILOSOPHY AND HUMANISM

*Renaissance Essays in Honor of
Paul Oskar Kristeller*

EDITED BY

EDWARD P. MAHONEY

LEIDEN
E. J. BRILL
1976

Associate Editors

ELIZABETH STORY DONNO
JOHN CHARLES NELSON

Editorial Board

F. EDWARD CRANZ
ELIZABETH STORY DONNO
PHYLLIS GOODHART GORDAN
JOAN KELLY-GADOL
EDWARD P. MAHONEY
JOHN CHARLES NELSON
EUGENE F. RICE, Jr.
CHARLES TRINKAUS

ISBN 90 04 04378 0

Copyright 1976 by E. J. Brill, Leiden, Netherlands

All rights reserved. No part of this book may be reproduced or translated in any form, by print, photoprint, microfilm, microfiche or any other means without written permission from the publisher.

PRINTED IN BELGIUM

CONTENTS

Tabula gratulatoria VII
Preface XXI
Acknowledgments XXV

Paul Oskar Kristeller and His Contribution to Scholarship . . . 1
EUGENE F. RICE, Jr., The *De magia naturali* of Jacques Lefèvre d'Etaples 19
DONALD R. KELLEY, Louis Le Caron Philosophe 30
RICHARD H. POPKIN, The Pre-Adamite Theory in the Renaissance 50
RICHARD LEMAY, The Fly against the Elephant: Flandinus against Pomponazzi on Fate 70
MARTIN PINE, Pietro Pomponazzi and the Medieval Tradition of God's Foreknowledge 100
F. EDWARD CRANZ, Editions of the Latin Aristotle Accompanied by the Commentaries of Averroes 116
JOSEF SOUDEK, A Fifteenth-Century Humanistic Bestseller: The Manuscript Diffusion of Leonardo Bruni's Annotated Latin Version of the (Pseudo-) Aristotelian *Economics* . . . 129
EDWARD P. MAHONEY, Nicoletto Vernia on the Soul and Immortality 144
JOAN KELLY-GADOL, Tommaso Campanella: The Agony of Political Theory in the Counter-Reformation 164
CHARLES TRINKAUS, Protagoras in the Renaissance: An Exploration 190
MARISTELLA DE PANIZZA LORCH, *Voluptas, molle quodam et non invidiosum nomen*: Lorenzo Valla's Defense of *voluptas* in the Preface to his *De voluptate*. 214
NEAL W. GILBERT, Richard de Bury and the "Quires of Yesterday's Sophisms" 229
MALCOLM BROWN, A Pre-Aristotelian Mathematician on Deductive Order 258
JOHN H. RANDALL, Jr., Paduan Aristotelianism Reconsidered 275
WILLIAM F. EDWARDS, Niccolò Leoniceno and the Origins of Humanist Discussion of Method 283

C. DORIS HELLMAN, A Poem on the Occasion of the Nova of
1572 306
EDWARD ROSEN, Kepler's Mastery of Greek 310
W. T. H. JACKSON, The Politics of a Poet : The Archipoeta as
Revealed by his Imagery 320
JOHN CHARLES NELSON, Love and Sex in the *Decameron* . . 339
GEORGE B. PARKS, Pico della Mirandola in Tudor Translation. 352
RICHARD HARRIER, Invention in Tudor Literature : Historical
Perspectives 370
HELENE WIERUSZOWSKI, Jacob Burckhardt (1818-1897) and
Vespasiano da Bisticci (1422-1498) 387
MORIMICHI WATANABE, Gregor Heimburg and Early Humanism
in Germany 406
RAYMOND DE ROOVER, Cardinal Cajetan on "Cambium" or
Exchange Dealings 423
JULIUS KIRSHNER, Conscience and Public Finance : A *Questio
disputata* of John of Legnano on the Public Debt of Genoa 434
JOHN MUNDY, The Origins of the College of Saint-Raymond at
the University of Toulouse. 454
CHARLES B. SCHMITT, Girolamo Borro's *Multae sunt nostrarum
ignorationum causae* (Ms. Vat. Ross. 1009) 462
GUIDO KISCH, An Unpublished *Consilium* of Johannes Sichardus 477
PATRICIA H. LABALME, The Last Will of a Venetian Patrician
(1489) 483
FELIX GILBERT, The Last Will of a Venetian Grand Chancellor. 502
HERBERT S. MATSEN, Giovanni Garzoni (1419-1505) to Alessandro Achillini (1463-1512) : An Unpublished Letter and
Defense 518
THEODORE E. JAMES, A Fragment of *An Exposition of the
First Letter of Seneca to Lucilius* Attributed to Peter of
Mantua 531

Bibliography of the Publications of Paul Oskar Kristeller for
the Years 1929-1974 543

Index 591

TABULA GRATULATORIA

Roberto Abbondanza, University of Perugia
Robert P. Adams, University of Washington, Seattle
Danilo Aguzzi-Barbagli, University of British Columbia
András Alföldi, Institute for Advanced Study, Princeton
Elisabeth Alföldi-Rosenbaum, University of Toronto
Marie-Thérèse d'Alverny, Centre National de la Recherche Scientifique, Paris
Milton V. Anastos, University of California, Los Angeles
Gertrude L. Annan, New York Academy of Medicine
Ruth Nanda Anshen, New York
John P. Anton, Emory University
Rudolph Arbesmann, O.S.A., Fordham University
†Hannah Arendt, New School for Social Research
James I. Armstrong, Middlebury College
Klaus Arnold, University of Würzburg
Frederick B. Artz, Oberlin College
Gabriel Austin, Sotheby Parke-Bernet, New York
Rino Avesani, University of Macerata
Renato Badalì, University of Bologna and University of Rome
Josip Badalić, University of Zagreb
Roland H. Bainton, Yale University
Fernando Bandeira Ferreira, Ministry of National Education, Lisbon
Luisa Banti, University of Florence
Moshe Barasch, Hebrew University, Jerusalem
Hans Baron, Newberry Library, Chicago
Salo W. Baron, Columbia University
Jacques Barzun, Columbia University
Marcel Bataillon, Collège de France, Paris
Albert C. Baugh, University of Pennsylvania
Joseph P. Bauke, Columbia University
J. M. W. Bean, Columbia University
Theodore S. Beardsley, Jr., Hispanic Society of America
Guy Beaujouan, École Pratique des Hautes Études, Paris
Luisa Becherucci, University of Pisa
James H. Beck, Columbia University
Marvin B. Becker, University of Michigan
Jean-Albert Bédé, Columbia University
Elmer Belt, M.D., Elmer Belt Medical Group, Los Angeles
Josephine Waters Bennett, Hunter College, City University of New York
Thomas G. Bergin, Yale University
Isaiah Berlin, Wolfson College, Oxford University
Elena V. Bernadskaja, Saltykov-Chtchedrine Library, Leningrad
Aldo S. Bernardo, Verrazzano College
Frederick A. Bernett

Ilse B. Bernett
Margarete Bieber, Columbia University
Ludwig Bieler, University College, Dublin
Peter G. Bietenholz, University of Saskatchewan
Giuseppe Billanovich, Catholic University of the Sacred Heart, Milan
Bernhard Bischoff, University of Munich
Jan Bistřický, Palacky University, Olomouc, Czechoslovakia
Franz Blatt, Carlsberg Foundation, Copenhagen
Morton W. Bloomfield, Harvard University
Emilie Boer, Akademie der Wissenschaften, East Berlin
Helmut Boese, Württembergische Landesbibliothek, Stuttgart
Pere Bohigas, R. Academia de Buenas Letras, Barcelona
Tristano Bolelli, University of Pisa
Giuliano Bonfante, University of Turin
William H. Bond, Houghton Library, Harvard University
Seeger A. Bonebakker, University of California, Los Angeles
William J. Bouwsma, University of California, Berkeley
Marjorie Nice Boyer, York College, City University of New York
Leicester Bradner, Brown University
Vittore Branca, University of Padua and Fondazione Cini, Venice
Tilo Brandis, Staatsbibliothek Preussischer Kulturbesitz, West Berlin
†Quirinus Breen, University of Oregon
Alison Brown, London
Julian Brown, King's College, University of London
Virginia Brown, Pontifical Institute of Mediaeval Studies, Toronto
Gene A. Brucker, University of California, Berkeley
Robert S. Brumbaugh, Yale University
Teddy Brunius, Royal University of Copenhagen
Justus Buchler, State University of New York, Stony Brook
Hugo Buchthal, Institute of Fine Arts, New York University
August Buck, University of Marburg/Lahn
Curt F. Bühler, Pierpont Morgan Library, New York
Marie Luise Bulst
Walther Bulst, University of Heidelberg
Frederick Burkhardt, American Council of Learned Societies
Douglas Bush, Harvard University
Gisela von Busse, Deutsche Forschungsgemeinschaft, Bonn/Bad Godesberg
František Čáda, University of Brno
Lelia Caetani, Fondazione Camillo Caetani di Sermoneta, Rome
Herbert Cahoon, Pierpont Morgan Library, New York
William M. Calder III, Columbia University
Augusto Campana, University of Rome
Harry Caplan, Cornell University
Luciano Capra, Biblioteca Comunale Ariostea, Ferrara
Giuseppe Cardillo, Istituto Italiano di Cultura, New York
Enzo Carli, University of Siena
Emmanuele Casamassima, University of Trieste
Florindo Cerreta, University of Iowa

TABULA GRATULATORIA

André Chastel, Collège de France, Paris
Harold Cherniss, Institute for Advanced Study, Princeton
Monsignore Luigi Chiodi, Biblioteca Civica Angelo Mai, Bergamo
Lucia A. Ciapponi, Chapel Hill
Angelo Ciavarella, Biblioteca Palatina, Parma
Marshall Clagett, Institute for Advanced Study, Princeton
Peter Classen, University of Heidelberg
Robert J. Clements, New York University
Cecil H. Clough, University of Liverpool
Eric Cochrane, University of Chicago
Tristano Codignola, La Nuova Italia Editrice, Florence
Gerson D. Cohen, Jewish Theological Seminary of America
Antonio Colombis, Biblioteca Provinciale, Salerno
Giles Constable, Harvard University
W. G. Constable, Museum of Fine Arts, Boston
Gianfranco Contini, University of Florence
Carlo Cordié, University of Florence
Beatrice Corrigan, University of Toronto
James A. Coulter, Columbia University
Lawrence A. Cremin, Columbia University
Klara Csapodi-Gárdonyi, National Széchényi Library, Budapest
Mark H. Curtis, Scripps College, Claremont
Arthur C. Danto, Columbia University
Charles T. Davis, Tulane University
Howard McP. Davis, Columbia University
Hugh H. Davis, Le Moyne College, Syracuse
John Day, Centre National de la Recherche Scientifique, Paris
Ruth J. Dean, University of Pennsylvania
Herbert A. Deane, Columbia University
Maddalena de Luca, Edizioni di Storia e Letteratura, Rome
Enrico de Negri, University of Rome
Roger A. Desmed, Ecole Normale, Brussels
James A. Devereux, S. J., University of North Carolina
†Carlo Diano, University of Padua
Herbert Dieckmann, Cornell University
Liselotte Dieckmann, Washington University, St. Louis
Carlo Dionisotti, University of London
Vladislav Dokoupil, University Library, Brno
Sergio Donadoni, University of Rome
E. Talbot Donaldson, Indiana University
Elizabeth Story Donno, Columbia University
Alain Dufour, Librairie Droz, Geneva
Douglas M. Dunlop, Columbia University
A. J. Dunston, University of Sydney
R. J. Durling, Christian-Albrechts University, Kiel
Colin Eisler, Institute of Fine Arts, New York University
J. P. Elder, Harvard University
William R. Elton, Graduate Center, City University of New York

Reinhard Elze, Deutsches Historisches Institut, Rome
Charles J. Ermatinger, Saint Louis University
Cornelio Fabro, University of Perugia
Alfred Fairbank
Arthur B. Ferguson, Duke University
Wallace K. Ferguson, University of Western Ontario
Joan M. Ferrante, Columbia University
Giorgio E. Ferrari, Biblioteca Nazionale Marciana, Venice
Lena M. Ferrari, St. John's University, Jamaica, New York
Luigi Ferrarino, Istituto Italiano di Cultura, Madrid
Arnolfo B. Ferruolo, University of California, Berkeley
Luigi Firpo, University of Turin
Massimo Fittipaldi, Ministero di Pubblica Istruzione, Naples
Enrico Fiumi, Consolo, Accademia dei Sepolti, Volterra
Donald Fleming, Harvard University
Thomas P. Fleming, Columbia University
Tino Foffano, Catholic University of the Sacred Heart, Milan
Gianfranco Folena, University of Padua
Elliott C. Forsyth, La Trobe University, Bundoora, Australia
George Bingham Fowler, University of Pittsburgh
Donald M. Frame, Columbia University
Ezio Franceschini, Catholic University of the Sacred Heart, Milan
Charles Frankel, Columbia University
Hugo Friedrich, University of Freiburg/Breisgau
Horace L. Friess, Columbia University
Kurt von Fritz, University of Munich
Horst Fuhrmann, Monumenta Germaniae Historica, Munich
Astrik L. Gabriel, University of Notre Dame
F. L. Ganshof, University of Ghent
Luciano Gargan, Catholic University of the Sacred Heart, Milan
Eugenio Garin, University of Florence
Gino Garosi, Biblioteca Comunale degli Intronati, Siena
Deno J. Geanakoplos, Yale University
Federico Gentile, Casa Editrice G.C. Sansoni, Florence
Rachel Giese, University of British Columbia
James F. Gilliam, Institute for Advanced Study, Princeton
Myron Piper Gilmore, Harvard University
Monsignore Martino Giusti, Archivio Segreto Vaticano
V. R. Giustiniani, University of Freiburg
Hannelore Glasser, Wells College
Jean Glénisson, Institut de Recherche et d'Histoire des Textes, Paris
John D. Goheen, Stanford University
Hermann Goldbrunner, Deutsches Historisches Institut, Rome
Martin P. Golding, John Jay College of Criminal Justice, City University of
    New York
Thomas E. Goldstein, City College, City University of New York
Richard A. Goldthwaite, The Johns Hopkins University
E. H. Gombrich, Warburg Institute, University of London

L. Carrington Goodrich, Columbia University
Aleksandr Gorfunkel, University of Leningrad
Eugenia Govi, Biblioteca Nazionale Marciana, Venice
Otis H. Green, University of Pennsylvania
Henry Guerlac, Cornell University
Hans R. Guggisberg, University of Basel
Werner L. Gundersheimer, University of Pennsylvania
James Gutmann, Columbia University
Augusto Guzzo, University of Turin
John R. Hale, University College, London
Jerome Hall, Hastings College of the Law, University of California
O. B. Hardison, Jr., Folger Shakespeare Library
William E. Harkins, Columbia University
Evelyn B. Harrison, Institute of Fine Arts, New York University
Erich Hassinger, University of Freiburg/Breisgau
Frank-Rutger Hausmann, University of Freiburg
Denys Hay, University of Edinburgh
William H. Hay, University of Wisconsin
John Miles Headley, University of North Carolina
Martin Heidegger, University of Freiburg/Breisgau
Julius S. Held, Barnard College, Columbia University
Carl G. Hempel, Princeton University
Charles W. Hendel, Yale University
Paul Henry, S.J., Leuven-Heverlee, Belgium
Peter Herde, University of Frankfurt
Otto Herding, University of Freiburg/Breisgau
J. H. Hexter, Yale University
Ludwig H. Heydenreich, Zentralinstitut für Kunstgeschichte, Munich
Gilbert Highet, Columbia University
Juliana M. S. Hill
Elisabeth F. Hirsch, Trenton State College
Felix Hirsch, Trenton State College
Rudolf Hirsch, University of Pennsylvania
Sidney Hook, New York University
Nancy Lenkeith Horneffer, Hunter College, City University of New York
Henry Hornik, Queens College, City University of New York
Hubert Howard, Fondazione Camillo Caetani di Sermoneta, Rome
Richard William Hunt, Bodleian Library, Oxford University
James Hutton, Cornell University
Robert B. C. Huygens, University of Leiden
Arthur Hyman, Yeshiva University and Columbia University
Jozef Ijsewijn, University of Louvain
Vincent Ilardi, University of Massachusetts, Amherst
Johannes Irmscher, Akademie der Wissenschaften, East Berlin
H. W. Janson, New York University
Hans Robert Jauss, University of Constance
Sears Jayne, Brown University
Hubert Jedin, University of Bonn

James J. John, Cornell University
Hans Jonas, New School for Social Research
Res Jost, Eidgenössische Technische Hochschule, Zurich
Rosario Jurlaro, Biblioteca De Leo, Brindisi
Werner Kaegi, University of Basel
Thomas Kaeppeli, O. P., Istituto Storico Domenicano, Rome
Henry Kahane, University of Illinois, Urbana
Renée Kahane, University of Illinois, Urbana
Charles H. Kahn, University of Pennsylvania
Oliver L. Kapsner, O.S.B., St. John's Abbey, Collegeville, Minn.
Joseph Katz, State University of New York at Stony Brook and William James Center, Wright Institute, Berkeley
Rita G. Keckeisen, Columbia University Libraries
Neil R. Ker, Oxford University
Eckhard Kessler, University of Munich
Adele Kibre
Pearl Kibre, Hunter College and Graduate Center, City University of New York
Margaret Leah King, Brooklyn College, City University of New York
Robert M. Kingdon, University of Wisconsin
Grayson Kirk, Columbia University
Elfriede Regina Knauer
Georg Nicolaus Knauer, Free University, West Berlin
Hermann Knaus, Staatsbibliothek Preussischer Kulturbesitz, West Berlin
Miloš Kouřil, State Archives, Olomouc
H. P. Kraus, New York City
Richard Krautheimer, Institute of Fine Arts, New York University
Konrad Krautter, University of Constance
Oluf Krückmann, University of Freiburg/Breisgau
K. Kumaniecki, University of Warsaw
Marion L. Daniels Kuntz, Georgia State University
Paul G. Kuntz, Emory University
Otto Kurz, Warburg Institute, University of London
Stephan Kuttner, University of California, Berkeley
George Labalme, Jr., New York Public Library
Vera R. Lachmann, Brooklyn College, City University of New York
Gerhart B. Ladner, University of California, Los Angeles
Albert M. Landry, O.P., University of Montreal
Irving Lavin, Institute for Advanced Study, Princeton
Brian Lawn, London
Raymond Lebègue, Institut de France, Paris
Jean Leclercq, O.S.B., St. Anselm and Gregorian University, Rome
Rensselaer W. Lee, Princeton University
Claudio Leonardi, University of Perugia
G. I. Lieftinck, University of Leiden
John L. Lievsay, Duke University
Kenneth A. Lohf, Columbia University Libraries
Dorothy Bethurum Loomis, Connecticut College
Erich Loos, Free University, West Berlin

Robert S. Lopez, Yale University
Edward E. Lowinsky, University of Chicago
Alexandra Lublinskaya, Institute of History, Leningrad
Walther Ludwig, Columbia University
Hans Lülfing, Deutsche Staatsbibliothek, East Berlin
Robert M. Lumiansky, University of Pennsylvania
Stuart MacClintock, Washington, D.C.
George McCully, Yale University
Alexander Hugh McDonald, Clare College, Cambridge University
Richard McKeon, University of Chicago
Domenico Maffei, University of Siena
Giuseppe Mainardi, Scuola Media "Vergilio," Cremona
Ernst Moritz Manasse, North Carolina Central University
Berta Maracchi Biagiarelli, Biblioteca Medicea Laurenziana, Florence
Giovanni Mardersteig, Verona
Jean-Claude Margolin, Centre d'Études Supérieures de la Renaissance, Tours
Scevola Mariotti, University of Rome
Thomas Carson Mark, University of California, San Diego
Dora Beth Marra, Biblioteca Benedetto Croce and Biblioteca dell'Istituto Italiano per gli Studi Storici, Naples
Thomas E. Marston, Yale University Library
Guido Martellotti, Scuola Normale Superiore, Pisa
Berthe M. Marti, University of North Carolina
Francis X. Martin, O.S.A., University College, Dublin
Lauro Martines, University of California, Los Angeles
François Masai, University of Brussels
Eugenio Massa, University of Pisa and Edizioni di Storia e Letteratura, Rome
Armand A. Maurer, Pontifical Institute of Mediaeval Studies and University of Toronto.
Joseph Anthony Mazzeo, Columbia University
†Millard Meiss, Institute for Advanced Study, Princeton
Benjamin Dean Meritt, University of Texas
Lucy Shoe Meritt, University of Texas
Anne Marie Meyer, Warburg Institute, University of London
Otto Meyer, University of Würzburg
Paul J. Meyvaert, Mediaeval Academy of America
Ulrich Middeldorf, Istituto Longhi, Florence
†Bruno Migliorini, University of Florence
Lorenzo Minio-Paluello, Oriel College, Oxford University
James V. Mirollo, Columbia University
Charles Mitchell, Bryn Mawr College
Arnaldo Momigliano, University College, London
John Monfasani, State University of New York, Albany
Jacques Monfrin, Ecole des Chartes, Paris
†Ernest A. Moody, University of California, Los Angeles
Edouard Morot-Sir, University of North Carolina
Robert J. Mulvaney, University of South Carolina
Franco Munari, Free University, West Berlin

†A. N. L. Munby, King's College, Cambridge University
Charles T. Murphy, Oberlin College
Roger A.B. Mynors, Corpus Christi College, Oxford University
Ernest Nagel, Columbia University
Milton C. Nahm, Bryn Mawr College
Monsignore Giovanni Di Napoli, Lateran University, Rome
Charles G. Nauert, Jr., University of Missouri, Columbia
Benjamin Nelson, New School for Social Research
William Nelson, Columbia University
O. Neugebauer, Brown University
Helaine Newstead, Graduate Center, City University of New York
Marjorie Hope Nicolson, Columbia University
Carl Nordenfalk, University of Pittsburgh
Heiko A. Oberman, University of Tübingen
J. Reginald O'Donnell, Pontifical Institute of Mediaeval Studies, Toronto
Klaus Oehler, University of Hamburg
Alf Önnerfors, University of Cologne
Bernard O'Kelly, University of North Dakota
Revilo P. Oliver, University of Illinois
Alessandro Olschki, Casa Editrice Leo S. Olschki, Florence
John W. O'Malley, S.J., University of Detroit
John J. O'Meara, University College, Dublin
Walter Jackson Ong, S.J., Saint Louis University
K.E.H. Oppenheimer, University of Leiden
Jean d'Ormesson, Member, Académie française; International Council for Philosophy and Humanistic Studies, Paris
G. N. Giordano Orsini, University of Wisconsin
Martin Ostwald, Swarthmore College and University of Pennsylvania
Erwin Walter Palm, University of Heidelberg
Guido Pampaloni, University of Florence
Giovanni Papuli, University of Lecce
Ettore Paratore, University of Rome
Angelo Paredi, Biblioteca Ambrosiana, Milan
John A. Passmore, Australian National University, Canberra
Wilhelm Pauck, Stanford University
Ramón Paz y Remolar, Biblioteca Nacional, Madrid
Lawton Peckham, Columbia University
Letizia Pecorella, Biblioteca Nazionale Braidense, Milan
Carlo Pedretti, University of California, Los Angeles
Bernard M. Peebles, Catholic University of America
Daniel F. Penham, Columbia University
Alessandro Perosa, University of Florence
Agostino Pertusi, Catholic University of the Sacred Heart, Milan
Giorgio Petrocchi, University of Rome
Armando Petrucci, University of Salerno
Ray C. Petry, Duke University
Henri Peyre, Graduate Center, City University of New York
Dayton Phillips, Vanderbilt University

Celestino Piana, O.F.M., Catholic University of the Sacred Heart, Milan
Maria Picchio Simonelli, Boston College
Riccardo Picchio, Yale University
Jan Pinborg, University of Copenhagen
Rainer Pineas, York College, City University of New York
Shlomo Pines, Hebrew University, Jerusalem
David Pingree, Brown University
Emma Pirani, University of Milan
Adolf Placzek, Columbia University
Julian G. Plante, Monastic Manuscript Microfilm Library, St. John's University, Collegeville, Minnesota
John H. Plummer, Pierpont Morgan Library, New York
Viktor Pöschl, University of Heidelberg
Brayton Polka, York University, Toronto
Antonino Poppi, University of Padua
Howard Porter, Columbia University
Gaines Post, Princeton University
Robert A. Pratt, University of Pennsylvania
Sesto Prete, University of Kansas
Giuseppe Prezzolini, Columbia University
Frederick Purnell, Jr., Queens College, City University of New York
Edwin A. Quain, S.J., Fordham University
Andre Racz, Columbia University
Giorgio Radetti, University of Rome
Alfonso Raes, S.J., Biblioteca Apostolica Vaticana
Olga Raggio, Metropolitan Museum of Art
Olga Ragusa, Columbia University
Francis B. Randall, Sarah Lawrence College
John H. Randall III, Boston College
Gian Albino Ravalli Modoni, Biblioteca Estense, Modena
Gordon N. Ray, John Simon Guggenheim Memorial Foundation
Luciano Rebay, Columbia University
C. Reedijk, Royal Library, The Hague
Gustave Reese, New York University
James P. Reilly, Jr., Yale University
Lincoln Reis, Long Island University
Dennis E. Rhodes, British Library (formerly British Museum)
J. F. C. Richards, Columbia University
Cyril C. Richardson, Union Theological Seminary
Peter Riesenberg, Washington University
Max Rieser, American Council for Nationalities
Wilhelm Risse, University of Saarbrücken
Juan Francisco Rivera, Biblioteca de la Catedral, Toledo
Dorothy M. Robathan, Wellesley College
Teresa Rogledi Manni, Ministero della Pubblica Istruzione, Milan
Aurelio Roncaglia, University of Rome
Helmut Roob, Gotha, Thüringen, East Germany
Florence Edler de Roover, Florence

Ernst Rose, New York University
Bernard M. Rosenthal, San Francisco, California
Franz Rosenthal, Yale University
Nathan Rotenstreich, Hebrew University, Jerusalem
Antonio Rotondò, University of Turin
Nicolai Rubinstein, Westfield College, University of London
Jordi Rubió, R. Academia de Buenas Letras, Barcelona
Walter Rüegg, University of Berne
Monsignore José Ruysschaert, Biblioteca Apostolica Vaticana
Lawrence V. Ryan, Stanford University
William Granger Ryan, Seton Hill College
H.D. Saffrey, Centre National de la Recherche Scientifique, Paris
Morris H. Saffron, M.D., College of Medicine and Dentistry, New Jersey
William Salloch, Ossining, New York
Mario Salmi, Istituto Nazionale di Studi sul Rinascimento, Florence
Charles Samaran, Institut de France
Paolo Sambin, University of Padua
Giuseppe E. Sansone, University of Bari
Mario Santoro, Istituto Universitario Orientale, Naples
Hans J. Sarre, University of Freiburg
Willibald Sauerländer, Zentralinstitut für Kunstgeschichte, Munich
Jason L. Saunders, Graduate Center, City University of New York
Giancarlo Savino, Biblioteca Comunale Forteguerriana, Pistoia
Aldo Scaglione, University of North Carolina
Fritz Schalk, University of Cologne
Meyer Schapiro, Columbia University
A. Arthur Schiller, Columbia University
Giancarlo Schizzerotto, Biblioteca Comunale, Mantua
Wolfgang O. Schmitt, Deutsche Akademie der Wissenschaften, East Berlin
Herbert W. Schneider, Columbia University and Claremont Graduate School
Jean-Pierre Schobinger, University of Zurich
Richard J. Schoeck, University of Maryland
Gershom Scholem, Hebrew University, Jerusalem
Dorothy M. Schullian, Cornell University
Hans-Rudolf Schwyzer, Zurich
Harry Sebastian, Monastic Manuscript Microfilm Library, St. John's University, Collegeville, Minnesota
Giovannangiola Secchi Tarugi, Centro Studi Umanistici "Angelo Poliziano," Montepulciano
Jerrold E. Seigel, Princeton University
Karl Ludwig Selig, Columbia University
Gilberta Serlupi Crescenzi, Florence
Kenneth M. Setton, Institute for Advanced Study, Princeton
Ihor Ševčenko, Harvard University
Herman Shapiro, San José State University
Eugene P. Sheehy, Columbia University Libraries
Martin Sicherl, University of Münster
David Sidorsky, Columbia University

Paul N. Siegel, Long Island University
Edmund T. Silk, Yale University
Luis Silveira, Ministry of National Education, Lisbon
Theodore Silverstein, University of Chicago
Franco Simone, University of Turin
Otto von Simson, Free University, West Berlin
Keith Val Sinclair, University of Connecticut
Beryl Smalley, Oxford University
John E. Smith, Yale University
Morton Smith, Columbia University
Rudolf Sobernheim, D.C. Commission on the Arts and Humanities, Washington, D.C.
Friedrich Solmsen, University of Wisconsin
Robert Somerville, Columbia University
Frederick Sontag, Pomona College
Andrés Soria, University of Granada
John Sparrow, All Souls College, Oxford University
Lewis W. Spitz, Stanford University
Rosamond Kent Sprague, University of South Carolina
Philip A. Stadter, University of North Carolina
†Wolfgang Stechow, Oberlin College
André Stegmann, Centre d'Etudes Supérieures de la Renaissance, Tours
Friedrich Stegmüller, University of Freiburg/Breisgau
Kate T. Steinitz, Elmer Belt Library of Vinciana, University of California, Los Angeles
Alfons Stickler, S.D.B., Biblioteca Apostolica Vaticana
Leon Stilman, Columbia University
Gerald Strauss, Indiana University
Joseph R. Strayer, Princeton University
Anselm Strittmatter, O.S.B., St. Anselm's Abbey, Washington, D.C.
Alfred A. Strnad, University of Innsbruck
McKay Sundwall, Columbia University
Patrick Suppes, Stanford University
Robert Dale Sweeney, Vanderbilt University
Richard S. Sylvester, Yale University
Takeshiro Takada, Doshisha University, Kyoto
C. H. Talbot, Wellcome Historical Medical Museum and Library, London
Leonardo Tarán, Columbia University
Wladyslaw Tatarkiewicz, University of Warsaw
Francesco Tateo, University of Bari
John Tedeschi, Newberry Library, Chicago
H. S. Thayer, City College, City University of New York
John Theodorakopoulos, University of Athens
Marcel Thomas, Bibliothèque Nationale, Paris
Craig R. Thompson, University of Pennsylvania
Homer A. Thompson, Institute for Advanced Study, Princeton
F. Allan Thomson, Stockholm, Sweden
S. Harrison Thomson, University of Colorado
S. E. Thorne, Harvard University

E. N. Tigerstedt, Stockholm University
Giuseppe Toffanin, University of Naples
Charles de Tolnay, Casa Buonarroti, Florence
Giorgio Tonelli, State University of New York, Binghamton
Amadeo Tortajada, Consejo Superior de Investigaciones Cientificas, Madrid
Antonio Tovar, University of Tübingen
Richard C. Trexler, University of Illinois, Urbana
Robert G. Turnbull, Ohio State University
Alexander Turyn, University of Illinois, Urbana
Franz Unterkircher, Österreichische Nationalbibliothek, Vienna
K. G. van Acker, State University of Ghent Library
James Grote VanDerpool, Columbia University
Hugh Van Dusen, Harper & Row Publishers, New York
Sofia Vanni Rovighi, Catholic University of the Sacred Heart, Milan
Giuseppe Velli, Smith College
Gerard Verbeke, University of Louvain
Jeanne Vielliard, Institut de Recherche et d'Histoire des Textes, Paris
Gregory Vlastos, Princeton University
Cornelia J. de Vogel, State University of Utrecht
Tamara P. Voronova, Saltykov-Chtchedrine Library, Leningrad
Daniel Pickering Walker, Warburg Institute, University of London
John Walker, National Gallery of Art, Washington, D.C.
Hans Wallach, Swarthmore College
Luitpold Wallach, University of Illinois, Urbana
Clarence C. Walton, Catholic University of America
†Richard Walzer, Oxford University
Paul L. Ward, American Historical Association, Washington, D.C.
Larissa Bonfante Warren, New York University
Jan H. Waszink, University of Leiden
Sister Agnes Clare Way, Our Lady of the Lake College, San Antonio
Rembert G. Weakland, O.S.B., Collegio S. Anselmo, Rome
Herman J. Weigand, Yale University
Donald Weinstein, Rutgers University
Herbert Weisinger, State University of New York, Stony Brook
Kurt Weitzmann, Princeton University
René Wellek, Yale University
Suzanne Fonay Wemple, Barnard College
Siegfried Wenzel, University of North Carolina
W. H. Werkmeister, Florida State University, Tallahassee
Richard Lawrence Wertis, Columbia University
Sandra Karaus Wertis
L. G. Westerink, State University of New York, Buffalo
Virgil K. Whitaker, Stanford University
Lynn White, Jr., University of California, Los Angeles
Morton White, Institute for Advanced Study, Princeton
Harold C. Whitford, Manhattan School of Music
Josephine C. Whitford, Manhattan School of Music
B. J. Whiting, Harvard University

Philip P. Wiener, Temple University and City University of New York
Henry H. Wiggins, Columbia University Press
Curtis A. Wilson, St. John's College, Annapolis
Constance M. Winchell, Columbia University Libraries
Emanuel Winternitz, Metropolitan Museum of Art and City University of New York
Chaim Wirszubski, Hebrew University, Jerusalem
Ronald G. Witt, Duke University
Martin Wittek, Bibliothèque Royale, Brussels
†H. A. Wolfson, Harvard University
Cyril Ernest Wright, British Museum
Elizabeth S. Wrigley, The Francis Bacon Foundation, Claremont
Dieter Wuttke, University of Göttingen
Bernhard Wyss, University of Basel
Frances Yates, Warburg Institute, University of London
John K. Yost, University of Nebraska
Paola Zambelli, University of Florence
Jerzy Zathey, Biblioteka Jagiellońska, Cracow
Silvio Zavala, El Colegio Nacional, Mexico City

PREFACE

This volume of essays has been prepared as a tribute to honor a great scholar, Paul Oskar Kristeller. Its genesis dates back to a meeting of several members of the Columbia University Seminar on the Renaissance in the Spring of 1969. They resolved to undertake the preparation of a Festschrift with the initial intention of presenting it to Professor Kristeller on the occasion of his retirement as a full-time faculty member in the Spring of 1973. After considering long lists of names of American and European scholars who would have to be invited, the group realized that a multi-volume work would be required. It therefore acceded to the wise counsel of Charles Trinkaus, who suggested that the proposed Festschrift be limited to scholars who had some connection with Columbia University, Paul Kristeller's intellectual home in the United States for three decades. The group decided, though reluctantly, that only thus would the task be manageable, and it had hopes, subsequently fulfilled, that others might prepare separate volumes in Kristeller's honor. However, in order that the proposed Festschrift should not remain exclusively a Columbia tribute, it was also decided to include a *Tabula Gratulatoria* in which all the many friends of Paul Kristeller, both in the United States and in Europe, might express their personal good wishes to him on the magnificent accomplishments of his scholarly career. Phyllis Goodhart Gordan generously assumed the unenviable and herculean task of the enormous correspondence necessary to compile the impressive *Tabula* to be found in this volume. Professors Felix Gilbert and Myron P. Gilmore also aided the group by advice provided during this early stage of planning.

Invitations signed by Professors Nelson, Rice and Trinkaus in the name of the committee were sent out on November 3, 1969, and a deadline of December 31, 1970, was set for submission of manuscripts. Not surprisingly, only about ten of the essays in this volume had been received by January 1971, though many who wanted to be included expressed their concern that the pressure of academic duties, both teaching and administrative, made it impossible for them to finish their essays according to schedule. During this early period of the gestation of the work, Professor John Charles Nelson handled the ever-growing correspondence and the manuscripts. At a meeting of the committee on January 29, 1972, he asked to be relieved of the task of editing the volume by reason of the press of his administrative and other university duties. Acceding to his request, the editorial committee expressed their thanks to him for the burden which he had so obligingly borne. Edward P. Mahoney was then asked to assume the major role as editor, and the committee wisely counseled him to draw upon the talents and experience of Professor Donno, well known for her efficiency and success as editor of *Renaissance Quarterly*. The committee examined not only the articles already submitted but also the first draft that Professor Mahoney had prepared of the Bibliography of Paul Kristeller's many publications. It was suggested that the Bibliography be revised so as to include not simply an occasional indication that a particular article had been given previously as a lecture but a complete and thorough chronicle of all the lectures which Professor Kristeller had given. Although this meant a dramatic increase in its length, the effect has been to make much more evident Paul Oskar Kristeller's extraordinary activities as traveler and lecturer, activities which had as their purpose the stimulation of interest in Renaissance studies both in the United States and in Europe.

During the Spring of 1972, additional articles were submitted to the judgment of one and often two scholars, who included both the members of the committee and others. Several close friends of Paul Kristeller with whom the committee had lost contact were also reinvited by the editor to submit contributions. Professors Neal W. Gilbert, Richard Lemay and Helene Wieruszowski happily accepted the invitation and finished their fine contributions during the following several months. In June, 1973, the manuscript was submitted to Columbia University Press and E. J. Brill for evaluation, and their decision to publish the volume jointly was announced the following October. Professor Eugene F. Rice, Jr. graciously agreed to secure the necessary subvention. The names of those individuals and institutions, to whom the committee is deeply grateful, are to be found in a separate list of Acknowledgments. The completely edited manuscript was sent to Brill in June, 1974. Once the manuscript was in proof, the secretarial staff of the Duke Department of Philosophy provided valuable assistance in the handling of correspondence and proof corrections of the more than thirty contributors. My gratitude to them is herewith expressed.

I should like also to express my obligation to members of the editorial board and the many anonymous scholars who graciously served as readers. The suggestions which they made and the high standards of scholarship which they followed have added to the quality of this volume. More than one contributor expressed gratitude for the improvements which they were able to make in their essays by reason of these suggestions. However, I must single out for special praise Professor Elizabeth S. Donno, to whom I am especially indebted. Without her constant advice and encouragement over the last few years, I could not have brought this work to completion. My friends and colleagues at Duke, Professors Francis Newton and Ronald Witt, and Professor F. Edward Cranz of Connecticut College gave an extraordinary amount of their time to study and edit essays, offered advice about the inevitable problems that arose, and made valuable suggestions regarding the Latin texts contained in this volume. I am grateful to them for sacrificing time from their own very active research projects to aid in the completion of a Festschrift for a scholar whom they admire. Professor Martin Pine on more than one occasion did editing and offered advice. I must also thank Professors F. Edward Cranz, Ernst Manasse and Charles Trinkaus for their valuable contributions and suggestions which were incorporated into the essay in Professor Kristeller's honor. All members of the editorial board read a first draft and made useful suggestions for its improvement. I am, however, indebted in a special way to Professor Donno and Professor Joan M. Ferrante who were kind enough to edit the essay and make valuable suggestions for its stylistic improvement. Some of the preparatory work on the index was done by Kenneth Guilmart, Gwen Kincaid and Hilary Smith, to whom I am grateful. But I must thank in a special way Professor Frederick Purnell who not only did some editing but also aided in the compilation of the index in its final stage. His willingness to assume the burdensome task of analyzing the Bibliography for the index was particularly helpful. The Duke University Research Council generously provided grants for some typing done outside the Department of Philosophy and also for the large amount of photo-copying required by a work of this nature. The continuing support it has provided me for this and other projects is appreciated. The reference librarians of Perkins Library at Duke solved many problems with their usual skill and determination.

Professor Eugene F. Rice, Jr. is owed the thanks of the editorial committee, the contributors and the editor for his labor in making arrangements with the Columbia University Press regarding financing of the volume and for securing the subvention. It is fitting that the publishers of Paul Oskar Kristeller's *The Philosophy of Marsilio Ficino*

(New York: Columbia University Press, 1944) and the *Iter Italicum* (Leiden: E. J. Brill, 1963 - -), perhaps his two greatest scholarly accomplishments, are jointly publishing this Festschrift. Mr. John D. Moore of the Columbia University Press provided good advice and aided the arrangements for joint publication with Brill. Mr. T. A. Edridge, his counterpart at Brill, was uniformly helpful in correspondence and most diligent in overseeing the printing and production of the book in Europe. I am thankful to them for their constant interest and patience as well as for their sound judgments.[1]

Finally, I must thank all members of the editorial committee for their support and encouragement. Mrs. Gordan has my special thanks for her dedication to and labors with the *Tabula*. I should also like to thank the contributors, especially those who made the first deadline, for their patience while awaiting the publication of their papers. It is my hope that the volume will be judged worthy of Paul Oskar Kristeller, to whom it is offered as a token of the affection and esteem of his many friends, both at Columbia and elsewhere.

EDWARD P. MAHONEY

---

[1] I must thank Mr. J. Samuel Hammond, Music Librarian at Duke, who played a major role in the final preparation of the index for publication.

ACKNOWLEDGMENTS

The following institutions and individuals helped make possible publication of this Festschrift.

Institutions

Columbia University
Columbia University, Department of Philosophy, Anonymous Gift Fund; Department of History, Dunning Fund; Department of Greek and Latin, Stanwood Cockey Lodge Fund
Columbia University, Casa Italiana
University of California, Berkeley, Institute of Canon Law

Individuals

Professor Roland Bainton
Dr. Elmer Belt
†Professor Josephine Waters Bennett
Mrs. Constance T. Blackwell
Mr. Curt Bühler
Mr. Frederick Burkhardt
Professor Ruth Dean
Professor Wallace K. Ferguson
Professor Felix Gilbert
Mrs. Phyllis Goodhart Gordan
Mr. O. B. Hardison, Jr.

Professor and Mrs. Felix Hirsch
Professor Stephan Kuttner
Mr. and Mrs. George Labalme, Jr.
Professor Rensselaer W. Lee
Mr. R. M. Lumiansky
†Professor Millard Meiss
Professor Walter J. Ong, S.J.
Professor Carlo Pedretti
Professor Gustave Reese
Mr. Bernard Rosenthal
Dr. Morris Saffron
Mr. William Salloch

PAUL OSKAR KRISTELLER
AND HIS CONTRIBUTION TO SCHOLARSHIP

Paul Oskar Kristeller has unquestionably been one of the most productive scholars in Renaissance studies in this century. He has also been one of the most active and influential individuals in the advancement of scholarship in the United States during the last three decades. Born in Berlin on May 22, 1905, he was a student there at the Mommsen-Gymnasium from 1911 to 1923. He received a good background in the classics, studying Latin for nine years and Greek for six. Among his Greek teachers was Ernst Hoffmann. While at the Gymnasium, Kristeller tutored younger students in Greek and Latin, a practice he was to continue as a university student. His interest in two of his favorite philosophers also developed at this time, for he studied Plato with Ernst Hoffmann and read Kant on his own. Hoffmann was also to be his first philosophy teacher at the University of Heidelberg, in a seminar on Aristotle's *Nicomachean Ethics* given in the Spring of 1923, the year of Kristeller's entrance to the University.

It was during these university years that Kristeller was to show that great breadth of intellectual interest which has so markedly characterized his subsequent career. He studied not only medieval history with Karl Hampe and Friedrich Baethgen but also mathematics, and he followed lectures in German literature, linguistics, musicology, and physics as well as in art history, an area of cultural interest which has fascinated him ever since. Four professors of philosophy who taught him during his university years had a major influence on his intellectual outlook: Ernst Hoffmann and Karl Jaspers at Heidelberg, Richard Kroner at Freiburg in 1924, and Martin Heidegger at Marburg in 1926.

Kristeller's interest in philosophy was always central to his intellectual activities. He thus chose to write his dissertation in ancient philosophy with Hoffmann and received his doctorate from Heidelberg in 1928 with his dissertation *Der Begriff der Seele in der Ethik des Plotin*, which was published the following year. This book, representing only a portion of a projected comprehensive study of Plotinus —parts of which were written but never published—was favorably reviewed and has gained a lasting place among the most important monographs on Plotinus written during this century. It is also especially important for tracing Kristeller's career, since some of the themes which he emphasized for the first time in Plotinus, especially that of interior experience, he was later to stress in his work on Ficino. He sent a copy of the dissertation to Ernst Cassirer, from whom he received encouragement. This interchange led to a long, friendly relationship with the celebrated philosopher and historian of philosophy.

Both Cassirer and his philosophical associate, Hoffmann, belonged to the tradition of the German Historical School, which can perhaps be considered Kristeller's "ancestry" in the history of ideas. But it was the personal influence of Hoffmann during those years that should be underscored, since he was both a classical scholar and a historian of philosophy. Kristeller's "inheritance" from him included not only his admiration for Kant but also his method as an historian of philosophy and of ideas : an insistence on philological exactness and an unbiased examination of the texts, an emphasis on precise philosophical analysis, and a comprehensive view of the philosophical tradition of the Western world since classical antiquity. Hoffmann also evinced a special interest in the Platonic tradition in later antiquity and in the Middle Ages and directed the first critical edition of the works of Cusanus. Kristeller's own interest in the Platonic tradition, both in late antiquity and in the Renaissance, as well as his early involvement in editing Renaissance texts should perhaps be seen against the background of Hoffmann's interests and activities.[1]

While writing his dissertation on Plotinus, Kristeller decided that he should undertake formal studies in classical philology in order to broaden his training and prepare himself for further research in ancient philosophy. After he received his doctorate, he studied classics at Berlin with Werner Jaeger and Eduard Norden [2]. In 1929, he took a Proseminar with Jaeger on Cicero's *Orator*. He was then admitted to the Philological Seminar of the University of Berlin, whose leading spirit at the time was Jaeger, on the basis of a research paper entitled "The History of the Concept of Idea from Plato to Plotinus," which was never published. His interest in rhetoric, which was to be lifelong, is revealed in the Latin essay which he wrote at Berlin in the winter of 1930-31 for the Staatsexamen für das höhere Lehramt,

---

[1] For references to Hoffmann, See Paul O. Kristeller, *The Philosophy of Marsilio Ficino* (New York, 1943), xi; *Journal of Philosophy* 48 (1951), 619-21; and *Journal of the History of Philosophy* 1 (1963), 99-102.

[2] See *The Philosophy of Marsilio Ficino*, xi.

namely, "Pericles' First Speech in Thucydides." In this unpublished paper, which presents the history of the "hortatory speech" from Homer to late antiquity (Procopius), he applied Jaeger's concept of "Formgeschichte," a concept which much influenced his later work on the Renaissance.

From 1931 to 1933 Kristeller pursued postgraduate studies in philosophy at Freiburg with Martin Heidegger, who discouraged his entering secondary school teaching despite the fact that a university post did not seem promising. In 1931, Heidegger approved Kristeller's proposal of a study of Ficino for his Habilitationschrift; Kristeller held a fellowship from the Notgemeinschaft der deutschen Wissenschaft of Berlin in 1932-33 to work on the project. He wrote about one third of the book (up to and including the chapter on causality) in Berlin in 1933, continuing the writing in the summer of 1934, by which time he had completed the first half of the important chapter on *Primum in aliquo genere*.[3]

Having spent about a month in Italy in 1933 working on books and manuscripts related to Ficino in libraries in Rome, Florence and Milan, he returned to Italy in 1934, this time with the intention of staying. He had already begun to publish the results of his research on Ficino. He was a teacher at a high school for German Jewish students in Florence in 1934-35 and at the same time was also a lecturer in German at the Istituto Superiore di Magistero. Through the support of Giovanni Gentile, he secured a post as a lecturer in German at the Scuola Normale Superiore and the University of Pisa, and he held this position from 1935 to 1938. Gentile was his major backer in Italy and supported the publication both of his *Supplementum Ficinianum*, for which he wrote a preface, and his book on Ficino. Despite his deep involvement with the Fascist regime, Gentile personally aided Kristeller after he lost his position at Pisa because of the anti-Semitic laws, and he also helped him to emigrate to the United States soon after this. It should be noted that Kristeller has retained a close and warm relationship with the Scuola Normale, its faculty, and its students. He was to return as a visiting professor in 1949 and in 1952, the latter year as a Fulbright fellow, and he was to be a visiting professor again in 1974 under the auspices of the Accademia Nazionale dei Lincei.

Kristeller's five years in Italy were extremely productive and satis-

---

[3] Kristeller recounts the various stages of the writing of the book in *Die Philosophie des Marsilio Ficino* (Frankfurt am Main, 1972), vii.

fying ones, and they influenced the rest of his scholarly career. He made many close and lasting friendships in the Italian academic community, especially at Pisa and Florence, which he has cherished ever since—one thinks of friends like Augusto Campana and Eugenio Garin as well as younger ones like Giuseppe Billanovich and Vittore Branca. In Italy, Kristeller turned once again to his book on Ficino, which he had worked on sporadically after leaving Germany. He took up serious writing at Pisa in the spring of 1936 and concluded the work at Sangodenzo in August of 1937. With the aid of his good friend Alessandro Perosa, the Italian version was finished the following year and accepted for publication by Sansoni, though it was not actually published until after the war.[4] Since he was now aiming at an academic career in Italy, his Italian friends advised him to seek an Italian degree. He had to submit his dissertation, diploma, and course books from Heidelberg in order to have his German degree legally recognized, and in 1937 he was awarded a laurea "per titoli" from Pisa.

It was during this Italian sojourn that Kristeller developed his great interest in and extraordinary gifts for manuscript research as well as his talents for organizing cooperative projects. He explored the manuscript collections not only in Florence and Rome but also in many other Italian cities such as Modena, Parma, Bergamo, Milan, Naples and Venice, seeking whatever unpublished manuscripts of Ficino or related authors he could find. Moreover, he visited libraries outside of Italy, namely, in Berlin, Munich, Wolfenbüttel and Zurich. Hans Baron generously contributed some texts for the project. The result was the impressive two volumes published at Florence in 1937 under the auspices of the Scuola Normale, *Supplementum Ficinianum* : *Marsilii Ficini Philosophi Platonici Opuscula Inedita et Dispersa*. These researches made him keenly aware of the large number of unpublished writings of philosophers and humanists which existed in Italian libraries. He therefore proposed that the more interesting texts be edited and published in a special series, and this plan received the backing of Gentile and Leo S. Olschki. The result was the *Nuova Collezione di Testi Umanistici Inediti o Rari*, which was published by Olschki under the auspices of the Scuola Normale. Perosa dedicated his edition of Cristoforo Landino's poems, which was the first volume of the series, to Kristeller in 1938.[5] Kristeller was reponsible for giving out the first

---

[4] See *Il pensiero filosofico di Marsilio Ficino* (Florence, 1953), xv, xviii-xix.
[5] The work appeared after Kristeller had left Italy. See *Christophori Landini Carmina*

assignments in the series, which now numbers sixteen volumes, and he is still a co-editor, working in cooperation with several close Italian friends. He has himself paid homage in print to three distinguished scholars who served during this period as his "teachers" in manuscript research though never in a formal school or university setting. They are Giovanni Cardinal Mercati, Monsignor Auguste Pelzer, and Ludwig Bertalot.[6] In the summer of 1938, having lost his post at Pisa, where he was to be detained briefly, he was allowed to go to Rome. While he was awaiting permission to enter the United States, he spent the winter working on manuscripts in the Vatican Library as the personal assistant of Bertalot.[7]

Paul Oskar Kristeller arrived in the United States at New York on February 23, 1939 through the good offices of various American friends, among them Dean P. Lockwood and Dom Anselm Strittmater, O.S.B. but especially through the aid of Roland H. Bainton and also Herman J. Weigand and the late Albrecht Goetze of Yale University. He spent the spring term of that year at Yale as a Fellow in Philosophy, where he taught a seminar on Plotinus.

Through the efforts of the Department of Philosophy, Kristeller was invited to come to Columbia for the fall term to join the depart-

---

Omnia, ed. Alessandro Perosa, Nuova Collezione di Testi Umanistici Inediti e Rari, 1 (Florence, 1939), v and ix.

[6] See Paul O. Kristeller, *Iter Italicum* I (London and Leiden, 1963), xxvi.

[7] Kristeller has prepared an edition of Bertalot's collected studies. See now Ludwig Bertalot, *Studien zum Italienischen und Deutschen Humanismus*, ed. Paul Oskar Kristeller, 2 vols., Storia e Letteratura, 129 and 130 (Rome, 1975). In his "Vorrede" to the first volume, Kristeller recounts (pp. viii-ix) how he came to know Bertalot on a personal basis and how there gradually developed a close bond of friendship. Kristeller remarks: "Ich gewann sein Vertrauen und lernte viel von ihm, so dass ich mich in der Handschriftenkunde wohl als seinen Schüler betrachten darf." He then relates that after losing his lectureship at Pisa Bertalot made him his assistant for four months until it was possible to depart for America. Bertalot also sought to aid Kristeller's parents in Berlin during the war. Kristeller considers him to have been one of his German friends who remained loyal during persecution and who thus made possible his own personal reconciliation with Germany after the war. When Mons. Giuseppe De Luca, who was Kristeller's own friend and publisher, suggested that he undertake editing Bertalot's papers, the proposal was gladly accepted. Despite the deaths of De Luca and Bertalot in the early nineteen-sixties and many difficulties involved in the project, Kristeller continued to work on the edition with his characteristic determination. This rich collection of some fifty papers and reviews will stand as a testimony to Kristeller's sense of gratitude to a close and loyal friend. See also the Bibliography of Kristeller's Minor Publications, entries 145-147 and 151.

ment as an Associate, that is, as an adjunct faculty member. He held this rank until he was appointed a regular faculty member in 1948 with the rank of Associate Professor of Philosophy. His first graduate course was on "Philosophy of Humanism and the Renaissance in Italy" and it was given in 1939-1940 under the auspices of the Italian Department. It should be remembered that Dino Bigongiari also took a warm personal interest in his coming to Columbia—Kristeller had met Bigongiari in Italy in the summer of 1938. But it was his association with two members of Columbia's Department of Philosophy, namely, John H. Randall, Jr., and Ernest A. Moody, both of whom were to become his close friends, that was to have the most significant influence on his scholarly interests. Soon after his arrival, that is, in 1940-1941, he began to give a joint seminar with Moody in research techniques in late medieval and Renaissance philosophy, a seminar that he continued to conduct in later years. With Randall, who had spent a sabbatical year in Italy during 1933-1934 studying Italian Aristotelianism of the fifteenth and sixteenth centuries, Kristeller gave graduate seminars in Plato, Aristotle, Plotinus, as well as in the modern philosophers.[8] It is not surprising that the strong interests of Moody and Randall in late medieval and Renaissance Aristotelianism aroused Kristeller's interests in these areas and in Pietro Pomponazzi in particular. As early as 1940 he and Randall coauthored their classic programmatic paper, "The Study of the Philosophies of the Renaissance"; this was delivered as a lecture that year to the New England Renaissance Conference and published the following year. With Ernst Cassirer and Randall he coedited *The Renaissance Philosophy of Man* (1948), a text which has perhaps been the most influential single volume in Renaissance thought to be used in American colleges and universities.[9]

Kristeller's interest in Pomponazzi is evidenced in a paper published in 1944 in which he compares him with Ficino and in articles in 1951 and 1955 which present new material on his psychology based on manuscript discoveries. His growing interest in the various Aristotelian traditions of the Renaissance led to articles on Petrarch's relation to the "Averroists" (1952) and scholasticism and humanism (1955); a

---

[8] For Randall's own estimate of the impact of Kristeller on the Department of Philosophy, see his remarks in *A History of the Faculty of Philosophy, Columbia University* (New York 1957), 135-136.

[9] For Kristeller's evaluation of Randall's contribution to the study of Renaissance philosophy, see his article in *Naturalism and Historical Understanding : Essays on the Philosophy of John Herman Randall, Jr.* (Albany, 1967), 35-41.

survey of scholarship on Paduan Averroism and Alexandrism (1960); *La tradizione aristotelica nel Rinascimento* (1962); the study of Vincenzo Bandello's Thomist critique of Ficino (1965); and above all *Le Thomisme et la pensée italienne de la Renaissance* (1967). In order to understand Pomponazzi better, Kristeller decided that he had to examine and determine the place of philosophy in the university curriculum during the Renaissance. Since this meant that he had to learn the historical background of the curriculum, he proposed to review the intellectual histories of the major Italian universities. The essay on "The School of Salerno" (1945) is the only chapter written of what was to be a general study; Kristeller still hopes to complete the work.[10] He also published a brief survey of the Italian universities (1953) and an essay on the University of Bologna (1957), Pomponazzi's intellectual home during the last part of his life.

The essays on Salerno (1945, 1957) should also be seen in the context of Kristeller's interest in medieval history, an interest dating back to his days at Heidelberg. From his first years in the United States he concerned himself with determining the medieval origins of Renaissance ideas and traditions. His still instructive essay on Augustine and the Renaissance (1941) and his rich study on the scholastic background of Ficino (1944) are among the best examples of his early publications in this vein, but one should also recall his studies on *ars dictaminis* (1951, 1961). His more general statements on medieval origins are to be found in the essay, "The Medieval Antecedents of Renaissance Humanism" (1964), in the Wimmer Lecture, *Renaissance Philosophy and the Medieval Tradition* (1966), and in his recent book, *Medieval Aspects of Renaissance Learning* (1974).

However, the major focus of Kristeller's historical interests in philosophy continued to center on Ficino and Renaissance Platonism. Indeed, the first article that he published in an American journal was on Florentine Platonism (1939). With the aid of various American friends, he set out to prepare an English translation of his book on Ficino, and in 1943 *The Philosophy of Marsilio Ficino* was published by the Columbia University Press. Though the Italian version of 1938 was brought up to date and published in 1953, the original German

---

[10] Kristeller is presently working on a paper which will disclose for the first time the texts and manuscripts of several twelfth-century commentaries on the *Articella*. The manuscript discoveries which it contains rank with those of Ficino's early treatises and should be of interest not only for the history of medicine but also for the history of philosophy and literature.

manuscript was published only in 1972, thirty-five years after its completion. This work is surely Kristeller's most important single scholarly contribution to the study of Renaissance philosophy, and it has succeeded to a remarkable degree in drawing the attention of English-speaking scholars to the thought of Ficino and Florentine Platonism. His analyses of the doctrines of *primum in aliquo genere*, *appetitus naturalis* and internal experience represented a major breakthrough in Ficino studies. Even more revolutionary was his 1944 study, "The Scholastic Background of Marsilio Ficino," which presented manuscript evidence for Ficino's early interest in the medieval philosophers. Two years later he was to publish a long study of Ficino's disciple, Francesco da Diacceto. These and other studies of Ficino and his circle bulk large in the magisterial collection of Kristeller's articles published at Rome in 1956, *Studies in Renaissance Thought and Letters*. Since then he has published further general essays on Ficino (1964, 1965, 1966), on Renaissance Platonism (1959, 1961, 1966, 1968), and on the Platonic Academy and its individual members (1959, 1961, 1967). Ficino and Florentine Platonism also serve as a major point of focus in the Albert le Grand lecture on Thomism and the Italian thought of the Renaissance (1967, 1974).

Kristeller has also written on Ficino's younger friend, Giovanni Pico della Mirandola. Besides the essay for *The Renaissance Philosophy of Man* (1948), he wrote a long and rich study of Pico's sources (1963, 1965) and presented a general examination of his thought in *Eight Philosophers of the Italian Renaissance* (1964). The latter work, which also contains fundamental chapters on Petrarch, Ficino, and Pomponazzi, is certainly the best general analysis of Renaissance philosophy that has been published in English.

The area of historical interpretation in which Kristeller has gained his greatest renown is that of Renaissance humanism. His fascination with its history, developed during his Italian sojourn, continued to grow after he came to the United States. In a crucial and seminal paper, "Humanism and Scholasticism in the Italian Renaissance" (1944-1945), he opposed two prevalent interpretations of Italian humanism, the first that it was simply the rise of classical scholarship and the second that it was a new philosophy which rose to challenge scholasticism and comprehended all the philosophy and thought of the period. He showed that the first view failed to take account of the ideal of eloquence presented in the writings of the humanists and that the second could not explain the persistent survival of scholastic philosophy. He pointed out that the humanists were not philosophers, though they did study moral philosophy and they did influence, at least indirectly through their various translating activities, the development of philosophy during the sixteenth century, and he also emphasized the Renaissance meaning of *humanista*—a term applied to someone who taught one of the *studia humanitatis*, that is, grammar, rhetoric, history, poetry and moral philosophy, a meaning still carried over in our contemporary use of the term "humanities." Thus Renaissance humanism was to be seen both in terms of the professional role of the humanists and in terms of the context of the rhetorical tradition of the West.[11] The humanists, Kristeller pointed out, were the successors to the professional practitioners of *ars dictaminis*, the Italian grammarians and rhetoricians of late medieval Italy. What they added to the latter was the belief that in order to write and speak well, one must study and imitate ancient models: the program of the *studia humanitatis* itself implicitly placed an emphasis on man and his special position in the universe, and this concept was, in turn, to influence philosophical thought during the Renaissance. Instead of asserting its lack of philosophical and cultural consequences, Kristeller stressed that humanism involved no common philosophical doctrine other than this belief in the value of man and in the humanities, coupled with a belief in the value of reviving ancient learning and thereby finding models for expression. He continued his discussion of the nature of humanism and its significance for Renaissance philosophy in *The Classics and Renaissance Thought* (1955), which was republished in 1961 along with "Humanism and Scholasticism" in *Renaissance Thought* (1961). Three further important essays on Renaissance humanism, "Humanist Learning in the Italian Renaissance" (1960), "The Moral Thought of Renaissance Humanism" (1961) and "The European Diffusion of Italian Humanism" (1962), were to be included in Kristeller's *Renaissance Thought II* (1965). More recently he has studied the Byzantine background of humanism (1964), reviewed the relationship of philosophy and humanism (1966), and re-examined the cultural impact of early Italian humanism (1969, 1972).

One of the themes on which Kristeller's study of Renaissance phi-

---

[11] Kristeller's conception of the relation of rhetoric and humanism has been accepted and developed by many younger historians, including many who were not his students. See also the remarks of Charles Trinkaus, *In Our Image and Likeness: Humanity and Divinity in Italian Humanist Thought*, I (Chicago and London, 1970), xiv and xxiv-xxv.

losophers has centered is that of the problem of the human person. The most mature expression of his views can be found in *Renaissance Concepts of Man* (1972). But several of his own favorite papers in other areas of Renaissance studies also deserve special mention, since they reveal the wide range of his research and interests: the paper on the origin and development of Italian vulgar prose, which appeared in both English and Italian versions (1946, 1950); an essay on music and learning in the early Italian Renaissance (1947); and by far the most influential, "The Modern System of the Arts: A Study in the History of Aesthetics" (1952), which has had some influence among art historians as well as among philosophers. All three of these papers were reprinted in *Renaissance Thought II* (1965).

The commitment to manuscript research and to cooperative enterprises with scholars involved in textual studies, a commitment first established in Italy, has led to his involvement in two most important and ambitious projects. The first, a cooperative publication, the *Catalogus Translationum et Commentariorum: Mediaeval and Renaissance Latin Translations and Commentaries, Annotated Lists and Guides*, makes known by systematic listing and description all the Latin translations and commentaries, through 1600 A.D., of Greek and Latin works written before 600 A.D. The material is arranged by individual authors, with each article including a *fortuna* of the author in question, and for each translator or commentator there is a short bio-bibliography. In the conception and planning of the project Professor Kristeller has acted as the leading spirit. He was a member of the ACLS Renaissance Committee which first discussed the project; he chaired the Planning Conference of 1946 which gave it formal organization; and he served through 1969 as the first Secretary of the Executive Committee for the *Catalogus*. He was also Editor-in-Chief of the first two volumes (1960; 1971) which have won wide critical acclaim, especially for the extraordinary completeness and exactness of the bibliographical material. The Associate Editor of volume II was Kristeller's friend and colleague, F. Edward Cranz, who has assumed the editorship for the project. Kristeller's vision of the *Catalogus* met considerable doubts and scepticism when it was first articulated; now, thanks in no small measure to his own Herculean labors, the vision is well on the way to realization. Scholars have come to recognize the central role that such a publication can play in making available for study the all-important classical inheritance of both medieval and Renaissance culture.

The second project can only be called monumental. In 1945 Kristeller met the late Fritz Saxl and described the material on Italian and also some German manuscript collections which he had gathered during his years in Italy. Saxl invited Kristeller to publish under the auspices of the Warburg Institute a descriptive account of Renaissance manuscripts which had not yet been described in printed catalogues. The invitation was accepted. Regular trips to Europe from 1949 onwards, not only during sabbaticals and leaves but also during summer visits, enabled him to add dramatically to his notes on humanistic manuscripts of the Renaissance in Italy and Germany and also to study for the first time manuscript collections in England, France, Spain, and elsewhere. In his determined and stubborn aim to achieve an exhaustive coverage, he visited most European countries including Russia, and he undoubtedly has been in more small and difficult to reach European libraries than any scholar alive today. Because of the unusual diversity of his scholarly training and interests, perhaps he alone possessed the ability and the knowledge required to produce the work that eventually resulted. In 1963 the Warburg Institute and Brill published the first volume of *Iter Italicum* : *A Finding List of Uncatalogued or Incompletely Catalogued Humanistic Manuscripts of the Renaissance in Italian and Other Libraries*. This volume covered Italy, from Agrigento to Novara, while the second volume (1967) covered Italy, from Orvieto to Volterra, as well as Vatican City. Two further volumes are projected to complete the survey of Europe and America. The *Iter Italicum* can truly be said to represent a major change in Renaissance studies insofar as it has made scholars realize much more fully the richness of European manuscript collections. As Kristeller himself observed in the preface to Volume I (p. xxi) : "there is an enormous wealth of unpublished and unstudied source material whose very existence is hardly known to the majority of historians working in this period." Although he can only give a selection of major and minor Renaissance texts, of a host of authors, both Renaissance and also medieval and classical (when there is a connection to Renaissance philosophy, humanism, or literature), no scholar could have been more comprehensive in his selection and more open-minded as to what falls under the rubric of "humanism" and "Renaissance." The *Iter Italicum* opens up resources to contemporary scholars and to future generations of scholars in the way that the Italian humanists themselves evoked the classical revival of the Renaissance by their own search for manuscripts of classical authors.

One of the by-products of the *Catalogus* and the *Iter Italicum* was the publication of another reference tool. As a result of checking manuscript collections both in Europe and in the United States Kristeller became aware of the crucial need for a descriptive guide to the sources as an essential aid in the organizing of manuscript research. As a result, he published in *Traditio* in 1948 and 1953 a two-part bibliographical listing of both printed and unprinted catalogues of Latin manuscript books. This listing was republished in two later revised editions as *Latin Manuscript Books before 1600 : A List of the Printed Catalogues and Unpublished Inventories of Extant Collections* (1960, 1965) and it has become a valuable reference tool for scholars.

Perhaps the most striking aspect of Paul Oskar Kristeller's academic career has been the manner in which he has been able to maintain a high level of personal research and publication while simultaneously engaging in a host of professional activities along with a busy teaching and lecturing schedule. Accepting an invitation from Leicester Bradner, he became in 1944 a member of the ACLS Renaissance Committee, which began to publish *Renaissance News* and which organized the Renaissance Society of America in 1953; he has played a major role in the Society ever since, serving as member of the Executive Board since 1954, as President in 1957-59, and as delegate to the ACLS since 1962.[12] He also helped in organizing the International Federation of Renaissance Studies and then served as secretary until 1960. In 1945, together with other faculty members, he and Randall were active participants in founding the University Seminar on the Renaissance at Columbia. The Seminar has flourished for the last thirty years and Paul Kristeller's devotion to it has been one of the causes of its success.

Since 1959 Kristeller has been a Fellow of the Medieval Academy of America and served as Vice President in 1965-68 and again in 1974-75, and as President in 1975-76. He also served as member of the executive bureau of the Société Internationale pour l'Étude de la Philosophie Médiévale in 1967. He served as book editor of the *Journal of Philosophy* from 1940 to 1951, and he has been an active member of the editorial boards of the *Journal of the History of Ideas* (since 1943), *Studies in the Renaissance, Manuscripta, Journal of the History of Philosophy, International Archives of the History of Ideas, Viator* and *Revue d'histoire des textes*. He is still one of the editors of the *Nuova Collezione di Testi Umanistici*. He has been generous to a fault in giving

---

[12] See the annual reports to the Renaissance Society of America listed in the Bibliography of Kristeller's Minor Publications.

an editorial reading to manuscripts of books and articles of friends and colleagues, and he has maintained a prolific correspondence with scholars all over the world in which he has selflessly provided manuscript references and information, often to people whom he has never even met. He gave full and active support to CRIA, the American Committee to Rescue Italian Art that was established after the Florence flood of 1966, and he was one of those who argued that funds should also be used for the repair and restoration of books and manuscripts. Through these varied activities he has been able to develop a large number of friendships in the American and European scholarly communities, and he has gained stimulation and profit from these contacts for his own projects and research.

All of these activities went on while Kristeller was teaching a wide range of courses in the Department of Philosophy, from seminars in Plato, Aristotle, Plotinus, Descartes, Spinoza, Leibniz, Kant, and Hegel to lecture courses on Late Ancient and Renaissance Philosophy, as well as a special seminar on Research Techniques in Late Medieval and Renaissance Philosophy. Not surprisingly, he attracted graduate students from other departments of the university to his courses, and he played a role on doctoral committees in a wide range of scholarly fields, not only in the Department of Philosophy but also in a number of other departments. In every respect he has been a major force in the heightened interest in the Renaissance at Columbia and in the choice of Renaissance topics for many dissertations, and he has always been eager to aid in the publication of good scholarship by younger unrecognized scholars in the field even when they have not been Columbia students. He played an important role in the Department of Philosophy, being a mainstay not only in the areas of ancient and Renaissance philosophy but also in the areas of modern philosophy, particularly German philosophy from Kant onwards. In classes, he was a model of clarity in explicating texts, and his tenacious commitment to standards of scholarship and rigor of thought have always impressed graduate students. Yet he has always been known too for his kindness and helpfulness to students, for his quick wit and good humor, for his interest in all students, not simply his own doctoral candidates, and for loyalty to his colleagues. Despite the many scholarly areas that he entered and mastered after he received his doctorate in philosophy at Heidelberg, he never surrendered his basic commitment to philosophy and its history, and he has on occasion reaffirmed this commitment in his publications.[13] Kristeller has indeed been an important influence in the growth of serious historical scholarship within the American philosophical community.

Kristeller began to give public lectures to scholarly audiences from the first year of his arrival in the United States, and he has maintained a busy schedule of lecturing ever since. Once the war ended, he lectured and published in Italian and in French as well as in his native German. For him, lecturing has not been an unfortunate nuisance that interfered with his scholarship. On the contrary, it has enabled him to share his scholarly discoveries and to promote interest in Renaissance scholarship, while giving him an opportunity to reconsider major themes in Renaissance thought and culture. Under the pressure of invitations to speak on set themes he has had to think in broad terms about major questions and to consider the interrelationship of different topics. From lectures delivered at Oberlin College, Stanford University, St. Vincent Archabbey, the University of Montreal, and Claremont Graduate School would come several of his most influential and provocative works, namely, *The Classics and Renaissance Thought* (1955), *Eight Philosophers of the Renaissance* (1964), *Renaissance Philosophy and the Medieval Tradition* (1966), *Le Thomisme et la pensée italienne de la Renaissance* (1967), and *Renaissance Concepts of Man* (1972).

As a result of his productivity and the high quality of his published works, Kristeller has received many academic honors. He is a Corre-

---

[13] "Moreover, since many of the subjects with which I deal in these papers do not seem to fall within the province of philosophy as now understood, I should like to emphasize the fact that the history of philosophy has always been the center of my interest, and that all other problems have attracted my curiosity only on account of their direct or remote relationship with that subject" (*Renaissance Thought II* [New York, 1965], viii). At the very beginning of the *Iter Italicum* I (p. xi), he takes pains to explain why "a student of philosophy and its history" undertook such a project. For a clear and forceful statement of his conception of the task of the historian of philosophy, of how the history of philosophy differs from the history of ideas, and of why the history of philosophy must be the concern of the philosopher, see his "History of Philosophy and History of Ideas," *Journal of the History of Philosophy* 2 (1964), 1-14, reprinted in *Renaissance Concepts of Man and Other Essays* (New York, 1972), 156-175. More recently he has observed in *The Pursuit of Holiness*, ed. Charles Trinkaus (Leiden, 1974), 369-370: "I happen to be a philosopher, and hence I cannot ignore these distinctions (to offer a variation on a remark recently made by one of our friends and colleagues, the history of philosophy is too important a subject to be left entirely to the non-philosophers)." For an earlier statement of the position that history of philosophy is a necessary part of philosophy itself and should play an essential role in philosophical education, see the Bibliography of Kristeller's Major Publications, entry 27.

sponding Fellow of various learned academies and institutes in Europe, including Monumenta Germaniae Historica (Munich 1962), Académie des Inscriptions et Belles-Lettres (Paris 1965), Accademia Patavina (Padua 1967), Istituto Veneto (Venice 1968), Accademia Toscana La Colombaria (Florence 1968), Accademia degli Intronati (Siena 1968), Akademie der Wissenschaften und der Literatur (Mainz 1973) and the British Academy (London 1973). He is also a Fellow of the American Academy of Arts and Sciences (1955), and he was made a member of the American Philosophical Society in 1974. For his great contribution to Italian studies he has received the Serena medal of the British Academy (1958), citations of the Society for Italian Historical Studies (1964) and the Associazione Internazionale per gli Studi di Lingua e Letteratura Italiana (1973), and the Premio Internazionale Forte dei Marmi-Galileo Galilei (1968). In 1971, the Italian government named him a Commendatore nell'Ordine al Merito della Repubblica Italiana. He has received honorary doctorates from both the University of Padua (1962) and Middlebury College (1972), but he was especially pleased to receive the degree of Doctor of Humane Letters which he was awarded *honoris causa* by Columbia University on May 15, 1974.

Paul Oskar Kristeller was one of many scholars who were forced to emigrate from their native land during the thirties. Denied the opportunity of an academic post in Germany, he was also to lose the post which he had gained at Pisa. Here in America he was to find an intellectual home at Columbia, where he has pursued a rich career of scholarship and teaching for over thirty years, a career that his colleagues, friends, and students intend to honor with this volume.

About a year after his arrival in the United States Paul Kristeller married Edith Lewinnek, who has herself had a highly successful career as physician and hospital administrator. She has been personally involved in his scholarly work, and she has frequently accompanied him on his research trips to Europe, where they pursue together in spare moments their common interest in art history. Her companionship and the recognition he has received for his scholarly accomplishments have no doubt made up for the setbacks in his early career and for some of the personal loss suffered by reason of "the reign of evil in Europe, 1933-1945." [14] The American academic community has been much richer for his vital presence both as a model of the highest scholarship and as an active participant in the many cooper-

---

[14] See the dedication in *Il pensiero filosofico di Marsilio Ficino,* vii.

ative projects in which he has been involved. As his close friend and long-time colleague, John Herman Randall, Jr., once remarked of him: "He is a living witness to the creative fruits when the best German and the best American thought and scholarship find happy and fruitful union."

ESSAYS

THE *DE MAGIA NATURALI*
OF JACQUES LEFÈVRE D'ETAPLES

EUGENE F. RICE, JR.

Lefèvre did not publish his book on magic and it has remained little read.[1] Until recently the only known manuscript, apart from a fragment in the Bibliothèque Royale in Brussels,[2] was one formerly in the collection of Queen Christina of Sweden and now in the Vatican Library.[3] This is a manuscript copied in Cracow about 1568 for the Hungarian humanist Andreas Dudith. It bears the title *Iacobi Fabri Stapulensis de magia naturali ad clarissimum virum Germanum Ganaum regium gubernatorem libri sex*.[4] It contains only Books I through IV of the promised six; and because the ink has badly discolored the paper is in places difficult to read.

It was therefore a special pleasure to learn from Professor Paul Oskar Kristeller that he had discovered another manuscript of the *De magia* in Czechoslovakia.[5] The Olomouc manuscript begins, *Jacobi*

---

[1] On Lefèvre see A. A. Renaudet, *Préréforme et Humanisme à Paris pendant les premières guerres d'Italie (1494-1517)*, 2nd ed. (Paris, 1953) and E. F. Rice, *The Prefatory Epistles of Jacques Lefèvre d'Etaples and Related Texts* (New York : Columbia University Press, 1972) and the literature there cited. Renaudet read the *De magia*, and so did Lynn Thorndike. The fullest account is Thorndike's, *A History of Magic and Experimental Science*, IV (New York, 1934), 512-516.

[2] Ms. lat. 10875.

[3] Regin. lat. 1115, ff. 1-96.

[4] Pierre Costil, *André Dudith, humaniste hongrois (1533-1589). Sa vie, son œuvre et ses manuscrits grecs* (Paris, 1935), 294-295. Dudith's manuscript was copied from an earlier one possibly brought to Cracow by one of Lefèvre's pupils. A plausible candidate is Jan Schilling of Cracow who worked closely with Lefèvre from as early as February 1504 until at least the end of 1512. See *Prefatory Epistles*, 186.

[5] Olomouc, Universitni Knihovna, ms. M I 119, ff. 174-342. Lefèvre had at least one friend who may plausibly have brought a manuscript of the *De magia* to Bohemia, Stephanus Martini de Tyn. Stephanus, from the diocese of Prague, matriculated at Cologne in April 1477, arrived at the University of Paris during the academic year 1479-1480 and received the M.A. in 1481—that is, he was an almost exact contemporary of Lefèvre at the university. Later he studied medicine, and in 1492 Lefèvre dedicated to him two dialogues on Aristotle's *Physics* (*Prefatory Epistles*, p. 15). All further references to the *De magia* are to this manuscript.

fabri Stapulensis Magici naturalis Liber primus ad clarissimum virum Germanum Ganaium regium senatorem; it is dated 1538, two years after Lefèvre's death; it contains all six books (and is therefore the only presently known source for Books V and VI); and it is easily legible. With his customary generosity Professor Kristeller has allowed me to use his microfilm of this manuscript.

The *De magia naturali* is one of Lefèvre's earliest works, though he was not a young man—at least by Renaissance standards—when he wrote it. Born about 1460, Lefèvre matriculated at the University of Paris, possibly in 1474 or 1475; received the B.A. in 1479; and the licentiate and M.A. probably in 1480. The next ten years are blank. But by 1490 he had chosen an academic career, begun to teach philosophy and the liberal arts at the Collège du Cardinal Lemoine, and written at least one of his Aristotelian textbooks, an *Introduction to the Metaphysics* (which he published only in 1494). During the winter of 1491-1492 he travelled in Italy, drawn there especially, he wrote a few years later, by his wish to meet Pico della Mirandola and Ermolao Barbaro. On his return to Paris, he resumed his lectures at Cardinal Lemoine and before the end of the year published his first book, paraphrases of Aristotle's works on natural philosophy, dedicated to the Chancellor of the university and designed for beginning students in the faculty of arts. He followed it, during the next three years, with an edition of the *Arithmetic* of the thirteenth-century mathematician Jordanus Nemorarius, an introduction to Aristotle's *Ethics*, *argumenta* or summary commentaries on Ficino's *Pimander* ("moved," as he said, "by love for Marsilio, whom I venerate as a father, and by the greatness of Mercurius's wisdom"),[6] and in 1495 a commentary on the *Sphere* of Sacrobosco. The *De magia* dates from these same years.[7]

---

[6] *Mercurij Trismegisti Liber de Potestate et Sapientia Dei per Marsilium Ficinum traductus ad Cosmum Medicem*, ed. Lefèvre d'Etaples (Paris : Wolfgang Hopyl, 31 July 1494), eiii : "... tum amore Marsilii (quem tanquam patrem veneratur), tum Mercurii sapientiae magnitudine promotus". Lefèvre's *argumenta* passed into editions of Ficino's works in the sixteenth century and were long thought to be by Ficino himself. P.O. Kristeller made clear their real author in his *Supplementum Ficinianum*, I (Florence, 1937), cxxx-cxxxi, 97.

[7] An epigram by Lèfevre in Book III, ch. 18 in praise of the dauphin and beginning *Gallia Delphinum nutri felicibus astris* (*De magia*, f. 252ᵛ) fixes the date of composition within the brief lifetime of Charles-Orland, eldest son of Charles VIII and Anne of Brittany. He was born in the château of Montils-lez-Tours on 10 October 1492 and died at Amboise 6 December 1495. See Le Roux de Lincy, *Vie de la reine Anne de Bretagne* (Paris, 1860-

Lefèvre dedicated the treatise to Germain de Ganay, his principal patron before he entered the orbit of the Briçonnet family in 1504; and it reflects not only some of Lefèvre's own early interests—his admiration for Ficino and Pico, for example—but no doubt those of his patron as well. Germain de Ganay, who was to die in 1520 as bishop of Orleans, was in 1493 a "conseiller-clerc" in the Parlement of Paris, canon of Notre-Dame of Paris and of Saint-Etienne of Bourges and dean of Beauvais. The circle of his patronage and correspondence was wide; while the fame of his literary parties, where Parisian lovers of the good arts ate well, drank well, and sometimes spoke Greek, has left attractive traces in the sources. He was particularly devoted to the esoteric. He corresponded with Ficino about the *prisca theologia*. He queried Trithemius about magic. Bovillus explained Lull's number symbolism to him, and Josse Clichtove dedicated to him a book on the secret meaning of numbers. Lefèvre's dedication to him of a book on natural magic fits neatly into this pattern of intellectual interests and patronage.[8]

Lefèvre's definition of magic was both up to date and respectable. He took for granted the common distinction between natural and daemonic magic and wrote about natural magic only. His conception of natural magic owed much to Pico, whom he had so recently met; but he emphasized more carefully that magic was simply a useful, practical branch of natural philosophy. The Chaldeans called *magi*, he tells us, the same sort of persons the Greeks called philosophers. The difference between philosophers and magicians is that philosophers devote themselves primarily to contemplation and speculation, while magicians explore the secret effects or "miracles" of nature. Natural philosophy, therefore, has two divisions : one theoretical, science; the other practical, natural magic.[9]

1861), I, 113-117, 131-133 and *Lettres de Charles VIII, roi de France*, ed. P. Pélicier (1898-1905), III, 304-305. Renaudet, who first used this passage to date the work, conjectured plausibly that Lefèvre wrote the *De magia* in the early months of 1493.

[8] For the literature on Germain de Ganay see my article on "The Patrons of French Humanism, 1492-1520," in *Renaissance Studies in Honor of Hans Baron*, ed. A. Molho and J. Tedeschi (Florence, 1971), 692. At times the *De magia* almost takes the form of a dialogue between author and patron. Parts of the argument are put into the mouth of Germain de Ganay (ch. 7 of Book II) or explicitly attributed to him (for example, at f. 201v).

[9] *De magia*, f. 174. "Apud Chaldaeos magi dicti sunt fere qui apud Graecos philosophi. Hoc tamen discrimen esse videtur quod philosophi magis contemplationi speculationique addicti, minus ad philosophiae secretos effectus probandos sese committunt. Magi

The practical magician may be professionally an astronomer, an astrologer, a physician, or an alchemist, or all of these at once. What are the secret effects of nature he studies or manipulates? They are of two kinds: the attraction or repulsion that produces either friendship or aversion between objects; and, second, the transformation of one object into another object. The transformations Lefèvre had in mind were those of the alchemist. He mentioned them, but he did not discuss them, preferring to devote his exclusive attention to effects of the first kind, to the magic which studies the mutual attractions and repulsions that knit together heavenly and terrestrial things.[10]

The assumption of a sympathetic relationship between things heavenly and earthly, the one agent, the other patient, was for Lefèvre—as it had been for his ancient and medieval predecessors—the guiding principle of natural magic. The basic analogy is sexual. The celestial bodies are masculine; the world is feminine, passively receptive to heavenly influence.[11] The *mundus inferior* is as straitly linked to the *superior mundus* as Juno, the female principle, is joined to Jupiter, the male.[12] Between the two worlds the attentive magician discerns a dense and subtle network of correspondences and "secret" effects, simple in principle, enormously complex in detail.

The secret effects Lefèvre attributed to the constellations will sufficiently illustrate the anecdotal absurdity of his method. Like his

---

vero contra naturae miracula tentant, ita ut bono iure Chaldaeorum orientaliumque magia nihil nisi quaedam naturalis philosophiae practica, operis executiva disciplina fuisse videatur. Quo fit ut magia potissimum ea contempletur quae nos ad occultos naturae eventus perducunt." Cf. Pico in the *Apologia*, for example : "Vocabulum enim hoc Magus, nec Latinum nec Graecum sed Persicum, et idem lingua Persica significat quod apud nos sapiens. Sapientes autem apud Persas idem sunt qui apud Graecos philosophi dicuntur" (*Opera* [Basel, 1601], 112); among the *Conclusiones magicae* : "Magia est pars practica scientiae naturalis" (*ibid.*, 71); or in the *De hominis dignitate* : "haec [magia naturalis] altissimis plena mysteriis, profundissimam rerum secretissimarum contemplationem, et demum totius naturae cognitionem complectitur. Haec, inter sparsas Dei beneficio et inter seminatas mundo virtutes, quasi de latebris evocans in lucem, non tam facit miranda quam facienti naturae sedula famulatur" (ed. Garin, p. 152).

[10] *Ibid.*, f. 174v. "Occulti enim sunt rerum attractus qui per amicitiam fiunt, occultae rerum fugae quae sunt per odia. Occultae inquam et rerum transmutationes [*in margine*: hoc est, res alchimicas], quas naturales magiae beneficio et solerti quadam indagine perficiunt. *De mutuo caelestium et terrenorum consensu, caelo quidem agente, terrenis vero patientibus. Caput secundum.* Proinde magi aut astronomi, aut medici, aut transmutatores [*in margine* : Alchimici], aut haec olim simul fuere."

[11] *Ibid.*, f. 174v-175.

[12] *Ibid.*, f. 178.

predecessors, he associated the *caelestis influxus* or astral influence of the constellation Pegasus with medical skill and the art of prophecy. He ransacked his ancient sources for corroborative evidence. From the *Metamorphoses* he quoted the story of Ocyrhoë, daughter of Chiron the centaur and the nymph Chariclo. She possessed the gift of prophecy and had once foretold the future of Apollo's baby son Esculapius : "You will be the salvation of all the world. Mortal bodies will owe their health to you. It will even be accorded you to raise them from the dead. You yourself will die; though once a god, become a lifeless corpse; but then revive and become again a god." So entirely commanded was she on this occasion by the vatic *furores* of Pegasus that she was transformed into a mare.[13] The meaning of the fable, according to the *magi*, is that divination and sound medical judgment are the special gifts of men and women born under Pegasus. The effect of the waters of Hippocrene, called by Persius the *fons caballinus* because Pegasus produced it by striking the ground with his foot, is equally probing. Those who drank "chastely" from the fountain foretold the future and, when its virtue had a little worn away, became poets.[14] And can one doubt the strength and virtue of this equine *influxus* after learning from Pliny that even terrestrial horses predict the outcome of a battle and the fates of their riders, foretelling victory by their eager high spirits and defeat by their reluctance to receive the bridle?[15] Heaven imprints on the minds of those influenced by Pegasus a true outline of future events. Just as the architect, before he puts up a building, makes preparatory drawings from which he can visualize the structure that his fellow citizens will eventually see in reality, so heaven can instruct the eye of the mind to see past, present and future.[16]

The effects of the constellation Dolphin are even more explicitly deduced from the supposed characteristics of the animal which gave the constellation its name. Dolphins are swift; so humans born under this sign are good runners. Dolphins are intelligent and lovers of music (a dolphin after all carried Arion on its back); so humans influenced by the constellation Dolphin are sharp of wit and lovers of harmony. Dolphins are not afraid of humans. They dote especially on small boys, like the dolphin who made friends with a school-boy he found

---

[13] *Ibid.*, f. 254; Ovid, *Meta.* II, 642-654.
[14] *Ibid.*, f. 253ᵛ; Persius, *Sat.*, prol. 1.
[15] *Hist. Nat.* VIII, 64, 157.
[16] *De magia*, f. 255.

playing on the shore near Baiae. Fish and boy met daily. The dolphin took the boy riding through the waves. One day the boy failed to appear at the rendezvous; he had died of smallpox. His friend was inconsolable and died of frustrated love soon after. The *magi* take Pliny's story to mean that both humans and beasts born under Dolpin have special inclinations to love and friendship, a conclusion further supported by the well-known fecundity of dolphins—the bellies of females are permanently filled with innumerable eggs—and by the fact that they live in the sea, the birthplace of Venus.[17]

The shape of a constellation also determines the character of its influence. Lefèvre found in Deloton, the Triangle, an especially congenial subject for a fanciful essay packed with historical exempla, quotations from the poets, and Christian analogies. He reviewed the mystical significance of the number three (God delights in odd numbers and especially in the number three), and associated the triangle with the Trinity. From the triangle all things come; it is beginning, middle and end. The effects of the constellation are marvellous and beneficent. Triangle arouses admiration for geometry and astronomy. Pythagoras and Archimedes were born under it. It inspires love of justice and equity, for the equilateral triangle is the figure of *aequalitas*. By analogy with the creative power of the Trinity, it stimulates artistic creation in humans. A host of great Greek painters, sculptors, and architects—Apelles, Pyrgoteles, Aristides of Thebes, Praxiteles, Lysippus, Protogenes, Timanthes, and Phidias—were born under Triangle.[18]

Among the principal areas in which the magician manipulates nature's secret effects and the mutual attractions and repulsions that link terrestrial to celestial things is medicine. Following the example of Ficino and a hundred others, Lefèvre devoted a large part of his treatise to the relation of astrology and medicine, *cum astrologia copulans medicinam*.[19] A detailed system of correspondence between parts of the body and signs of the zodiac relates the *inferius animal*, the human body, to the *magnum animal*, the sky. The head of the *magnum animal* is Aries; the neck Taurus; the arms and shoulders, Gemini; breast and lungs, Cancer; back, sides and loins, Leo; stomach and intestines, Virgo; the genitals, Scorpio; the legs and knees, Aquarius; the feet, Pisces.[20] Around this fundamental correspondence,

---

[17] *Ibid.*, ff. 249-253; Pliny, *Hist. Nat.* IX, 8, 25.
[18] *Ibid.*, ff. 257v-260.
[19] Ficino, *Opera*, I (Basel, 1576), 573.
[20] *De magia*, f. 178v.

Lefèvre embroidered—with a perfectly conventional and stereotyped ingenuity—a host of others, connecting with the planets and signs of the zodiac the four elements, the four humors, and the secret properties of plants and animals, colors, stones and drugs.

It is a principal function of the magician to manipulate these correspondences in order to protect the health of his patients. From the earliest times magicians were both doctors and astronomers. Indeed they discovered medicine.[21] So today the competent physician must practice natural magic. There will be nothing profane in this; he will of course have no commerce with demons. (Lefèvre deliberately refrains from mentioning talismans, *imagines*, letters or characters engraved on stones, invocations or incantations.) Knowing the secret effects of nature, he will use the principles of attraction, friendship or *concordia* to maintain the health of organs already healthy and the principle of aversion or *dissentio* or *discordia* to fight with their opposites the pains, diseases, noxious humors and vices of his clients.[22] The *magus* must therefore have an encyclopaedic knowledge of natural things, both terrestrial and heavenly.[23] He will know, for example, that the deer, since it is associated with Saturn, is long lived; and he will put this "secret" knowledge to practical advantage by including in his receipts portions of a deer's heart. This will lengthen his patients' lives. Since the dove is the bird of Venus, a drop of its blood eases inflammation of the eye. If the physician-magician prescribes plants or herbs associated with Saturn, he will stimulate the black bile. Plants associated with Mars activate the flow of yellow bile and make us bold in the face of danger; plants associated with Jupiter purify the blood and dispose us to joy and just dealing; those associated with Venus prompt naturally to lust and luxury; with Mercury to calculation and an aptitude for geometry.[24]

A multitude of phenomena of this sort would no longer seem miraculous to the vulgar if they understood the secret effects of nature.[25] People are amazed that the cramp fish can paralyze sailors. They

---

[21] *Ibid.*, f. 193ᵛ. "Magi quemadmodum iam diximus fuerunt primi quique medicinae repertores."

[22] *Ibid.*, ff. 196ᵛ-197.

[23] *Ibid.*, f. 191. "Quo fit ut magus quispiam esse non possit qui universam naturam non habuerit exploratam, caelestem videlicet pariter et terrenam."

[24] *Ibid.*, f. 190ᵛ.

[25] *Ibid.*, f. 192ᵛ. "Si rerum amicitiae notae essent, multa miracula rerum cessarent multorumque admiratio."

should realize that the cramp fish is under Saturn; that *stupor* and *pigritia* are secret natural effects of Saturn's influence; that the cramp fish produces Saturnian rays which, when they strike a fisherman's hand, paralyze him. In this context the function of the magician is a double one: on the one hand, he understands as natural effects phenomena ordinarily considered miraculous by the simple-minded; on the other hand, he himself produces natural miracles (*naturae miracula*) by putting into practice his knowledge of those same effects.

The magician does not only study the influence of heavenly bodies on earthly bodies. His knowledge of the arcane correspondences between earth and heaven makes him unusually skillful in the ascent from human to divine things, from the world of sense experience to the archetypes in the mind of God. In this perspective, the *magus* is not only a philosopher, physician or astronomer, but a theologian as well.

The knowledge on which he will especially rely to ascend to a knowledge of divine things is mathematics, more especially the mystical significance of numbers. Lefèvre's own liveliest interests emerge from the book he devoted to number mysticism or, as he preferred to call it, "Pythagorean philosophy."[26] Lefèvre's emphasis on mathematics was part of a wider effort to reform the curriculum of the Faculty of Arts. Mathematical studies had flourished at the University of Paris in the thirteenth and fourteenth centuries. The fifteenth century was entirely barren. The university produced not a single mathematical work of consequence, and mathematical instruction, although required by the statutes, was in practice ignored.[27] One of Lefèvre's major achievements was the revival of mathematical instruction and research, both through his own work and through his influence on associates like Josse Clichtove, Charles de Bovelles and Gérard Roussel. At the same time, Lefèvre's mathematical interests were closely related to other philosophical and religious enthusiasms. Before he wrote the *De magia* he had discovered the twelfth-century specialist in number mysticism Odo of Morimond. He had mastered the theological numerology of Ramon Lull and Cusanus. He had learned from Ficino that a mathematical *modus philosophandi* had been propagated by Hermes Trismegistus, Zalmoxis, Zoroaster, Pythagoras, the Egyptian *magi*,

---

[26] *Ibid.*, f. 198. The first chapter of Book II is entitled "De Pythagorica philosophia quae ad magiam introducit."

[27] Richard Ross, *The Mathematical Works of Oronce Finé* (Ph. D. diss., Columbia University, 1971), ch. 1.

Plato and the Cabalists. (His reference to the Cabala in the *De magia* appears to be the earliest yet recorded in France).[28] He concluded that numbers and figures are the most adequate *imagines, signa* or *symbola* of the divine mysteries; that they are the best expressions of the love and harmony that link created things with their divine *paradigmata*; and that they therefore provide human beings with the best possible means of rising from the many to the One, from the composite to the simple, sensible to intelligible, motion to rest, inequality to equality, finite to infinite, feminine to masculine, vestige to truth, shadow to light, time to eternity. In passages more deeply dyed with Neo-Platonism and Neo-Pythagoreanism than anything else he wrote, Lefèvre spoke of the emanation of all things from the One and of how the human mind, using arithmetical or geometrical symbolism, can ascend golden chains from the alterity and diversity of the world to a vision of the Ideas, of the One, and ultimately of the Trinity.[29]

This numerical ascension was for Lefèvre the most ancient teaching of the *magi*, and from it he derived the most profound lesson of natural magic: the correspondence of the planets and fixed stars with the first nine numbers, the association of the hierarchies of angels with the planets, and the harmony of natural magic, understood now as

---

[28] *De magia*, Book II, ch. 14, f. 217 ff. "Nam contendunt secretiores Hebraei ex divinorum nominum elementis cum [*malim* : eum] qui arcanam eorum Cabalam profunde calleret posse omnis sapientiae secreta elicere et omnia miracula supra magos operari. [*In margine* : De Iudaeorum arte Cabalistica praecipua non indigne quidem notetur id.] At vicenarius senarius Tetragrammaton implet : per coniunctionem aut compositionem omnia operari miracula et credunt et hactenus crediderunt, quattuorque his implent numeris. [Illustrated by a small vertical rectangle containing from top to bottom, the numbers 10, 5, 6, and 5, numerical equivalents of YHWH, the ineffable name, whose sum is 26.] Quod Pythagoras ad Aegyptios peregrinus vicinosque Syros studio cognoscendi flagrans profectus cognoscens, numeros ex eorum arcanis elicuit, per quos suo more omnia posse cognosci condendit. Voluntque Cabalam litterariam in numerorum secretam philosophiam magicumque traducere. Hinc pendet secreta Pythagorae philosophia, hinc arcana numerorum singula in solo silentio discenda. Et quemadmodum verba vana putas nullaque probari virtutis efficacia quae divinum nomen non formant, ita quoque numeri qui ex divinis non eliciuntur numeris ad secretam magiae operationem inefficaces esse probantur. Divinos ergo numeros prophetae vatesque quaerunt, sectantur per quos prophetant, et tempora longo post ventura digerunt et rimantur." Cf. F. Secret, *Les kabbalistes Chrétiens de la Renaissance* (Paris, 1964), 151, whose earliest references to the Cabala in France date from 1508 (François Tissard) and 1516 (Symphorien Champier).

[29] *Ibid.*, ff. 201v, 202, 217, 219v.

a form of *prisca theologia*, with Christianity.[30] For the ascent to the Idea is the familiar journey of the Christian mystic; and its goal is the same: a brief and rapturous moment of contemplation in which the mind sees God face to face. It is the journey of St. Paul when he was lifted to the third heaven and saw arcana about which he spoke to no man. Those who recognize the power of his name will become sons of God. More than this : those who properly understand how the inferior world is coupled in love to the heavenly, will recognize that the fundamental link between them, the nexus from which flows all the harmony in the universe, is Jesus Christ. And they will recognize that magic is ultimately reducible to the Christian sacrament whereby man puts on Christ and emerges reformed and repaired by love—*amore divino reformatus atque recuperatus*.[31]

Lefèvre's opinion of magic was clearly a high one. Everyone should realize, he said, "how holy and venerable is the name of magic, for magic so puts to flight all evil things and draws the good to itself in a loving embrace that even the creator and governor of the world wished to reveal his coming by a heavenly sign to *magi*, lovers of heavenly things, and wished to be worshipped by them."[32] On the other hand, he chose not to publish the *De magia*; while in 1504, in the preface to his edition of the Pseudo-Clementine *Recognitiones Petri apostoli*, a work whose most frequently quoted and illustrated episodes were Peter's disputes with Simon Magus, he publicly repudiated his earlier views and attacked even natural magic as a dangerous delusion. After pointing out that the *Recognitiones Petri* contains "apostolic doctrine," Lefèvre emphasized what he took to be the chief profit to be got from it : we should all especially admire this book "because it attacks every sort of vanity. To begin with, it refutes the deceptions of magic, so that no one may henceforth find refuge from his own errors under the cover of magic of any sort; I say of any sort, because no magic is good magic. It is nonsense to believe that any magic is natural or good, for natural magic is a wicked deception practiced by men who seek to hide their crimes under a respectable name."[33] The shift is typical of his intellectual development, and parallels his

---

[30] *Ibid.*, f. 213. Ch. 10 of Book II is entitled "Priscae velatae theologiae ad Christianam theologiam affinis vicinaque concordia."

[31] *Ibid.*, ff. 220-221.

[32] *Ibid.*, f. 192.

[33] *Prefatory Epistles*, 118.

growing disenchantment with Hermes Trismegistus, Pythagoras and the Platonici, a shift the easier to make because virtually all the ideas he had come to disapprove of when they were called "magical" seemed to him as admirable as ever when he found them in the Dionysian corpus, the Fathers of the church, Ramon Lull or Cusanus.

Columbia University

LOUIS LE CARON PHILOSOPHE

DONALD R. KELLEY

"To jurisprudence," Giambattista Vico liked to point out, "the Romans gave the same name as the Greeks gave to wisdom, 'the knowledge of things divine and human.'"[1] In this celebrated formula, repeated hundreds of times over the preceding fifteen centuries, we have a statement both of the significance of jurisprudence for the history of thought in general and of the theme of this essay in particular. Too often legal scholarship has been regarded as a forbiddingly technical and professional subject without redeeming intellectual value, but such was by no means always the case, especially not in antiquity and again, at least in some circles, in the Renaissance. As a result largely of the humanist movement and the revival of classical ideals the study of law in many schools became less technical and more immediately meaningful than philosophy. In several senses jurisprudence was "humanized" : it combined with the *studia humanitatis* in the curriculum (and in sixteenth-century France was often little more than a major subject within the liberal arts course), it was normally taken to be a part of moral philosophy, and according to several classifications of learning it was incorporated into the humanist "encyclopedia."[2] It is in such terms that jurisprudence has, from Valla to Vico, had a significant, though not always immediately apparent impact upon history of ideas.

What made this impact especially deep and enduring is the historical fact that the study of law, mainly civil law, provided a major source—perhaps the major source—of secular, higher education for European

---

[1] *De Universi juris uno principio et fine uno*, ed. F. Nicolini (Bari, 1936), "Proloquium." See n. 9.

[2] Budé, *Annotationes ... in quatuor et viginti Pandectarum libros* (Paris, 1535), f. III, "... studium nunc iuris prorsus ab antiquo veroque degenerasse, nisi vero arbitrabimur philosophiam, id est studium sapientiae ..." Alciato, *Praetermissa*, in *Opera omnia* (Basel, 1582), IV, 250 : "Cum enim in jure multa sint quae sine cognitione studiorum humanitatis percipi nequeant ..." Cf. Poliziano, *Panepistemon*, in *Opera omnia* (Basel, 1553), 428. See also diagram of Le Caron.

society as a whole. "The prime role of lawyers in starting humanism in Italy" was pointed out by Roberto Weiss;[3] it should be added that they played a role also in extending and preserving humanism outside of Italy. In sixteenth-century France no other professional group is anywhere near so well represented among publishing authors, and perhaps among readers as well. There was a whole class of lay intellectuals, especially office-holders, who had studied law mainly as a branch of literature or philosophy, but who had little to do with it in a professional way. Through such men law helped to shape the language and the thought of society in general, though again the detection and tracing of such influence would be a challenging and Herculean labor, and indeed has never been seriously attempted.

More obvious and accessible is the subject defined by Prof. Kristeller as "the philosophical significance of the legal tradition."[4] Yet this topic is also one which has never been fully appreciated, it seems to me, except perhaps in the field of political thought. For within the study of law there were various powerful philosophical impulses: toward the discovery of a useful "method," toward the establishment of a suitable epistemology, toward the rational understanding of social behavior, and in general toward a structured view of the world. Civil law was a "science" by definition, since it tried "to understand things in terms of causes,"[5] and at the same time it made a fundamental distinction between the world of nature (which was eternal and where general rules applied) and the world of society (which was mutable and where positive law applied). What is more, civil law furnished the motive and even the model for a number of encyclopedic schemes, notably those of Barthélemy de Chasseneux, Grégoire de Toulouse, Jean Bodin, and Le Caron himself.[6] It was not only Plato and Aristotle, in other words, not only Descartes and his contemporaries, who encouraged the philosophical system-building of modern times. Legal scholarship contributed in particular to the early creations of social science, from Bodin to Vico and Montesquieu, and in general helped to preserve a continuity between the "encyclopedic" thought of the

---

[3] *The Dawn of Humanism in Italy* (London, 1947), 5.

[4] *Renaissance Philosophy and the Medieval Tradition* (Latrobe, Penn., 1966), 43.

[5] Barthélemy de Chasseneux, *Catalogus gloriae mundi* (Geneva, 1617), 359, proving (with reference to Aristotle) that law, both civil and canon, was a *scientia* : "scire est per causas cognoscere"; and "legistae et canonistae cognoscunt per causas et rationes."

[6] Most ambitious, though least known, are Grégoire de Toulouse, *De Republica libri sex* (Frankfurt, 1609), and especially *Syntagma iuris universi* (Geneva, 1623).

Enlightenment and that of the Renaissance and medieval period, a continuity which the "new philosophy" of the seventeenth century has somewhat obscured.

It is in order to throw some small light upon these themes—the relationship of jurisprudence to the history of ideas, the intellectual role of the lawyer in society, and especially the philosophical significance of law—that I offer this discussion of the thought of Louis Le Caron. No author better exemplifies the compatibility and essential congruity of jurisprudence and philosophy.

"The divine Plato has elegantly declared that true philosophy concerns itself with the life and customs of men."[7] So the nineteen-year-old Louis le Caron expressed what was at once the point of departure, the central premise, and the binding principle of his intellectual development. Although his thought was eclectic and undiscriminating even by the standards of sixteenth-century humanism and although his achievement spanned a wide variety of disciplines, Le Caron remained true to this youthful vision of philosophy, to "cette noble science des choses divines et humaines."[8] What he found most vital in Platonism as he understood it was the fusion between systematic philosophy and the welfare of the community; that is, the organization of all knowledge around a single "idea" which could be identified with the "souverain bien" of the state. Le Caron's own career exemplified this same combination of fascination with system and attention to public service. In this sense he remained throughout his life a "philosophe."

The very same ideal seemed to Le Caron also to be embodied in his chosen profession, and and he was fond of citing the classic formulas of Ulpian to the effect that jurisprudence was literally a form of wisdom and that its practitioners were veritable "priests of the laws."[9]

---

[7] Πειθανῶν, seu verisimilium libri tres priores (Paris, 1553), "De restituendo et in artem redigenda iurisprudentia, praefatio" : "... ut non ineleganter divinus ille Plato eam veram philosophiam dixerit quae in hominum vita et moribus tota est."

[8] La Philosophie (Paris, 1555), dedication to Marguerite de France, and a quarter of a century later, in Questions diverses et discours (Paris, 1583), dedication to Barnabé Brisson, he referred to "la philosophie, à laquelle des ma jeunesse je me suis voué."

[9] Pandectes ou Digestes du droict françois (Paris, 1587), I, 3. "La Jurisprudence est (dit il) la cognoissance des choses divines et humaines, la science du juste et injuste et les Jurisconsultes sont les Pontifes et Prelats (ains j'ayme mieux interpreter sacerdotes) de la Justice"; citing Digest 1, 1, 10, 2, "Iuris prudentia est divinarum atque humanarum rerum notitia, iusti atque iniusti scientia," and 1, 1, 1, 1, "Cuius merito quis nos sacer-

Following his mentor François Baudouin then, Le Caron did not hesitate to identify jurisprudence with the highest kind of knowledge. "I say that true philosophy is contained in the books of law and not in the useless and inarticulate libraries of philosophers, who in effect are men of great learning but incapable in matters of public administration... Wherefore jurisprudence may indeed by called the true philosophy."[10]

For Le Caron the identity of jurisprudence and Greek philosophy had a historical as well as a logical basis. Like most other humanist lawyers he believed that the legal wisdom of Rome was the product of Hellenic philosophy. He accepted, in other words, the story told by the classical jurist Pomponius in his textbook on the origin of laws, that the *decemviri* had prepared for their work on the Twelve Tables by journeying to Attica to consult with the law-givers of Greece. In this way, as Baudouin taught, echoing the famous words of Thucydides, Athens was the school of all Greece, and beyond. It was only natural that Le Caron, following the trail blazed by Baudouin, should have devoted one of his first legal monographs to a reconstruction, out of classical sources, of the Twelve Tables. For this monument, this "image of antiquity," in the words of Cicero cited by both Le Caron and Baudouin, "surpasses the libraries of all the philosophers."[11]

Perhaps the most conspicuous sign of Le Caron's attempt to bring together jurisprudence and Hellenic philosophy was the literary name under which he published most of his works: "Charondas." Le Caron claimed to be descended from a Greek who had migrated in the train of Cardinal Bessarion (another great syncretist) and this could be taken as the original form of his name. But Le Caron was surely inspired

---

dotes appellet." Substituting "scientia" in the first part of this formula for "notitia" transforms it into the standard definition of "sapientia," a parallel idea whose career has been traced by Eugene Rice, *The Renaissance Idea of Wisdom* (Cambridge, Mass., 1957), including some discussion of Le Caron himself.

[10] *La Claire, ou de la prudence du droit* (Paris, 1554), ff. 23-24. See also *Veresimilis*, f. 2. Also see diagram *in calce*; and cf. Baudouin, *Commentarius in quatuor libros institutionum iuris civilis* (Paris, 1554), in tit. : "Perspicuum est leges quae ad publicas actiones pertinent veram et summam philosophiam continere." The ultimate source of this identification is Ulpian in *Digest*, I, 1, 1, which declares the study of law to be "veram (nisi fallor) philosophiam, non simulatam adfectantes," to which Accursius' gloss adds, "nam civilis sapientia vera philosophia dicitur, id est amor sapientiae."

[11] *Ad leges duodecim tabularum liber singularis* (Paris, 1554), citing Cicero, *De Oratore*, 1, 193, 195; *Digest* 1, 2, 2; and referring to the laws "a Balduino ... eleganter restitutas et explicatas," i.e., to Baudouin's *Libri duo in leges Romuli et leges XII tabularum* (Paris, 1554); passages cited in *Tractatus universi juris* (Venice, 1584), I, f. 268 and f. 225.

by the fact that the original Charondas—"who lived not many years before the decemvirs," as Baudouin remarked—was both a law-maker, and, according to a commonly accepted legend, a disciple of Pythagoras, as Le Caron himself was.[12]

Le Caron's account of his intellectual development is a love story—a Platonic love story. His lifelong search for truth and beauty began, he tells us, when he was sixteen years old (in 1550). His discovery of philosophy was so moving that he regarded it more as a passion than as a conversion, and in conventional poetic fashion he embodied his new love in the person of the lady "Claire." To her he dedicated two major books which are all the more interesting in that they were published without his consent.[13] The first of these was a little volume of poems, the second a pretentious set of neo-Platonic dialogues on jurisprudence. In the first of these Claire appears as an ideal of love, beauty, and moral perfection; in the second as intellectual enlightenment and the summit of jurisprudence. "Claire! Claire!" exclaimed Solon, the principal speaker of one dialogue, "You are the law which my eager mind seeks, the law which rules my heart and is obeyed as a sovereign..."[14] From every point of view she was the hypostasis of the Platonic *Idee*.

According to Le Caron's allegorical autobiography, he had been occupied with his college work when he became enamored of Claire and indeed a slave to her.[15] That is, while spending a conventional

---

[12] A new study of Le Caron's career is needed. Still the best is F. Gohin, *De Lud. Charondae vita et versibus* (Paris, 1902); also Lucien Pinvert, "Louis le Caron, dit Charondas (1536 [sic]-1613)," *Revue de la Renaissance* 2 (1902), 1-9, 69-76, 181-88; Anicet Digard, "Etudes sur les jurisconsultes du seizième siècle. Louis le Caron, dit Charondas," *Revue historique de droit français et étranger* 7 (1861), 177-92; Louis Carolus-Barré, "Le Contrat de mariage de Loius le Caron dit Charondas avec Marie de Hénault," *Bibliothèque d'Humanisme et Renaissance* 7 (1945), 252-57. That Le Caron was born in 1534, not 1536, appears from the engraving in the Paris, 1607 edition of his *Pandectes*.

[13] *La Poesie* (Paris, 1554), dedicated "à la Claire"; *La Claire* (n. 10), followed by "la Clairté amoureuse" and likewise dedicated "in Claram"; and "Claire, ou de la beauté," *Les Dialogues* (Paris, 1556), f. 149. In his *Panegyrique, ou Oraison de loüange au roy Charles VIIII* (Paris, 1566) Le Caron says that the first two were published "contre ma volonté."

[14] *La Claire*, f. 9.

[15] *La Claire*, "A tres excellente et tres vertueuse damoiselle cousine de sa Claire" : "... je tombai es retz de la clairté, laquelle ravit mon entendement des premiers desseings douteusement pour-pensez en plus asseuré conception. Car de cette splendeur je me trouvai si ardemment epris, qu'en mes estudes ne voulois suivre autre guide que l'escorte du clin de ses celestes yeus. Ainsi n'aiant attaint l'an de mon eage dixeseptiesme,

youth in the study of the trivium (*la bienparlante literature, biendisante faconde, et subtile dispute*), he came into contact with "la clairté," the splendor of philosophy, in the form of the dialogues of the "divine Plato," as he always called him. Having completed his course in the liberal arts, Le Caron was given leave by Claire to move on to the study of law, on condition that he would remain faithful to her. It was while at Bourges that he received the terrible news of her death. Henceforth he would not be able to gaze upon her face, but he would always keep her memory : though now he was committed to the profession of law, in other words, he would always retain his original philosophical ideals.

The University of Bourges was the center not only of the "reformed jurisprudence" established by Andrea Alciato but also of the "so-called reformed religion" established by his one time student Jean Calvin. By the first of these (commonly referred to as the *mos gallicus*) Le Caron was profoundly and favorably impressed. Although he arrived too late to study with Alciato's first disciple, Eguinaire Baron (who died in 1550), he did work with two of the most distinguished legal humanists, François le Douaren and François Baudouin. By the new religion, on the other hand, though it was closely bound up with the new jurisprudence, he was wholly disgusted. He complained to his uncle Philip Valton about those "evil spirits" who "abandoned themselves to their furious passions" instead of working for the progress of knowledge.[16] This conflict claimed the life of at least one student besides dividing the faculty and causing friction between Le Douaren and Baudouin, who was forced to leave as a result. Characteristically, Le Caron refused to take sides; his syncretism extended also to his private life.

From his years at Bourges Le Caron derived a great familiarity with the techniques and goals of legal humanism, though as always within the framework of his Platonic vision. For a time at least he adopted all the views of this school. He lamented the brutal editorial policy

---

je feus d'une vaine et douteuse liberté, en utile et constante servitude transformé. Mais l'echange me feut heureuse, que l'excellent esprit de si divine Claire ne m'enflamoit que de plus en plus à la connoissance des artz dignes d'un noble cœur ... Elle me permit voir les academies de la plus civile prudence, sous condition de retourner à son premier mandement. Depuis elle m'appella de la fameuse université de Bourges et lors desolee pour la mort d'un tressavant et renommé Docteur [Baron]."

[16] "Philippo Valtono, avunculo suo," prefacing his edition of Ulrich Zasius, *Catalogus legum antiquarum* (Paris, 1555). In general, see Louis Raynal, *Histoire du Berry* (Bourges, 1844), III, 372 ff.

of the Byzantine editor of the texts of civil law, Tribonian, who left only "torn and mutilated fragments of ancient jurisprudence"; and he devoted himself to such tasks of historical restoration as his studies of the Twelve Tables, the Digest, and a recently published manuscript of Ulpian.[17] He attacked the unhistorical and unphilosophical obfuscations of such "scholastic doctors" as Bartolus, while praising the work of the humanists, including Budé, Alciato, Cujas, Le Douaren, Baudouin, and Zasius, whose catalogue of ancient Roman laws he edited. Throughout his life he would retain a deep interest in the newly emerging field of legal history.

Yet unlike such humanists as Baudouin and Cujas, Le Caron was really not interested in history and philology for their own sake. He accepted the view of Ulpian that the rules of grammar did not necessarily apply to legal terms, and he endorsed the conventional derivation of *jus* from *justitia*, for example, on grounds of logical and legal priority. Similarly, he was unable to take their complacent attitude toward the so-called "antinomies" in civil law. To him these contradictions were not so much instances of historical change as departures from the legal ideal, and so almost in scholastic fashion he offered a "rule for the resolving of antinomies found in legal authorities." *Doctrina multiplex, veritas una* held for law as well as for philosophy : "As there were various sects of philosophers in Athens, so there were among jurisconsults in Rome," Le Caron declared, and he deplored such discord in both cases.[18] For him as for Plato, reality was both transverbal and suprahistorical.

What is more, Le Caron was attracted to a branch of the new jurisprudence which inclined rather toward logical reorganization of civil law than toward philological and historical exegesis. Like Le Douaren, Hugues Doneau, François Connan, and to some extent Jean Bodin, he wanted not only to restore the law to its original state but also re-form it in a more systematic way. Such was the theme of his first

---

[17] *Versimilis*, "De Restituendo" referring to "haec abscissa et mutila veteris iurisprudentiae fragmenta quae sic a Triboniano disposita sint"; *Tituli xxviii. ex corpore Ulpiani* ... (Paris, 1554); his edition of the *Digest* (Antwerp, 1575), dedicated to the Parlement of Paris and discussion (p. 2) of the most controversial of the interpolations in the *Digest* (1, 2, 2) : "Sunt qui non sine iudicio hoc caput a Triboniano ex diversis auctoribus sub Pomponii nomine compositum esse existiment, aut certe multa ab illo addita."

[18] *Veresimilis*, f. 82ᵛ; cf. I, 1, and II, 1 : "Dissolvendarum antinomiarum quae in iuris authorum libris inveniuntur ratio." On the problem of *antinomiae*, see Le Douaren's commentary on Justinian's prefaces to the *Digest* in his *Opera omnia* (Lucca, 1765-68), I, 2.

work, a discussion of that well known humanist topic, derived from Cicero, concerning the restoration of jurisprudence and its reduction to an "art" (*de restituendo et in artem redigenda jurisprudentia*), and such would be the intent of a number of later works.[19] In this way, too, Le Caron showed his fundamentally philosophical cast of mind.

In one important respect Le Caron differed from his mentors at Bourges and indeed from all of the established "legal humanists" of his day, and this was in his attitude toward vernacular culture. From the beginning he was a great enthusiast for the French language and indeed a kind of minor satellite of the Pléiade. He particularly admired his friend Pierre Ronsard and indeed credited him with "the renaissance of true poetry."[20] Le Caron's "vernacular humanism" was displayed most conspicuously in two of his earlier books: one his poems (surely among the most tedious of that epoch) dedicated to Claire, Ronsard, "the demon of love," and others; the other a set of neo-Platonic dialogues on philosophical subjects. Although he never completed the dialogues, he planned to honor a number of literary friends, including Claude Fauchet and "the great Pasquier, who puts Plato to shame."[21] Later Pasquier returned the compliment, though a bit less hyperbolically, by recalling Le Caron as one of that vernacularist avant-garde which had fought for the French language.[22] With Pasquier, too, Le Caron shared the fashionable *gaulois* interests of the 1550's, and later joined him, Fauchet, Antoine Loisel, the brothers Pithou, and others in a concentrated assault upon "French antiquities."[23]

---

[19] Cicero, *De Oratore*, I, 42; cf. Quintilian, *De Oratore*, XII, 3, 10, and Aulus Gellius, I, 22, 7; see also n. 41.

[20] *La Claire*, ff. 4v-5, referring to "ce divin Pindare François Pierre Ronsard auquel à bon droit j'attribue la renaissance de la vraie poësie, sans frauder du Bellai, de Thiart et autres ..." Le Caron's poetical work is discussed in various works devoted to the Pléiade such as M. Raymond, *L'influence de Ronsard sur la poésie française (1550-1585)* (Geneva, 1965), 249-54.

[21] *La Poesie*, f. 67, "Au Seigneur Pasquier :
"Le grand Pasquier, qui à Platon fait honte,
Le plus divin des immortelz esprits
Philosophant au giron de Cypris
Par son amour, Amour mesme surmonte."
Les Dialogues, including "Ronsard, ou de la poesie"; according to the table of contents, Book II was to include "Pasquier, ou l'orateur," "Fauchet, ou de l'utilité qu'apporte la congnoissance des choses naturelles," and others.

[22] *Les Recherches de la France* (Paris, 1621), VII, 11.

[23] On this aspect of Le Caron's work, see my *Foundations of Modern Historical Scholarship* (New York, 1970), 241 ff.

Yet in Le Caron's linguistic nationalism there was very little nostalgia. In that endless "quarrel of ancients and moderns" he stood very definitely on the side of youth. "I say and always have said," he wrote, "not only that our language is not poor but that it is richer than Greek, Latin, or any other foreign tongue."[24] A generation before the great humanist Guillaume Budé had conceded this for such barbaric pastimes as the hunt, but Le Caron would recognize no such qualifications. In particular he agreed with the thesis which, contradicting Budé, had been offered just a few years before by Joachim du Bellay in his classic defense of the vernacular : "that the French language is not unsuited to philosophy." Nor was it, of course, to jurisprudence : the old view, shared by Budé and most philologists, that philosophy was a peculiar possession of the Greeks (as law was of the Romans) was quite unacceptable to an idealist—and a Frenchman—like Le Caron.

It may be true to say that Le Caron, like Pico, found the true source of wisdom in history, and it is certainly true that he had a deep interest in the history of philosophy.[25] Yet again his attitude was essentially unhistorical—or rather his perspective was that of sacred not human history. The vehicle of philosophical tradition, Le Caron suggested, following St. Ambrose, was the Holy Spirit;[26] Plato was indeed "divine," beyond time as well as criticism; and as for himself, Le Caron was a kind of Plato redivivus (*à la française*). Conceptually, then, Le Caron's attitude was just the same as that of Luther, Melanchthon, Calvin, and other Protestants toward religious "tradition" : just as they affected to trace the anticipations and doctrinal continuity of the *vera ecclesia*, so he tried to trace the anticipations and doctrinal continuity of the *vera philosophia*, or "La Philosophie chrestienne," as he sometimes called it. Like Pico, in short, Le Caron aimed

---

[24] *Les Dialogues*, f. 2 : " ... je ne suis ne trop serf admirateur, ne trop arrogant despriseur de l'antiquité." *La Philosophie*, dedication : "Je di, et l'ai tousjours soustenu, que nostre langue non seulement n'est pauvre mais aussi plus riche que La Grecque, Latine, ou autre estranger, tant brave soit elle." See also *La Claire*, f. 9. Cf. Budé, *De Philologia* (Paris, 1532), p. 186. And Du Bellay, *La Défense et illustration de la langue française*, ed. L. Séché (Paris, 1905), ch. X, "Que la langue française n'est incapable de la philosophie." Le Caron was responsible for the coining of many new terms; e.g., "droitconseillant," "avant propos," "humaniser."

[25] Rice, *Renaissance Idea of Wisdom*, 100, n. 27; cf. the remarks of Ernst Cassirer, "Giovanni Pico della Mirandola," *Journal of the History of Ideas* 3 (1942),123-44,319-46.

[26] *Discours philosophiques* (Paris, 1583), p. 34 (revised ed. of *La Philosophie*), and *Pandectes*, I, 1; in general, P. Fraenkel, *Testimonia Patrum* (Geneva, 1961).

not at the establishment of a new philosophy but rather at the recovery of a *philosophia perennis*.

The career of philosophy, as described by Le Caron, began with Moses and passed on, by way of Egypt (through Hermes Trismegistus), to the pre-Socratic philosophers of Greece (Le Caron calls them "ancients"), culminating finally in the vision of Plato. Thereafter, though preserved to some extent by Aristotle ("Stagyrite le plus subtil des Platoniciens" is the highest praise Le Caron can find for him), this tradition was corrupted into various sects.[27] Finally, revived and perfected by Christianity, it passed on to the European nations, or more specifically, according to the old conceit, by the "translation of studies" from Athens to Rome to Paris.[28] And at the end of this tradition stood none other than Louis le Caron, called Charondas : *sic transit sapientia mundi*. A very contrived story, but perhaps not so different, after all, from the way in which the history of philosophy has usually been written.

The cultural imperialism inherent in the notion of *translatio studii*, which was an inseparable companion of the *translatio imperii*, is quite in keeping with Le Caron's general view; for philosophy itself, he believed, had an *imperium*. Several times he referred to philosophy as the "sovereign science," and it was his intention to declare the "sovereignty of philosophy" over all other disciplines.[29] Thus he hoped to impose some order upon that unwieldy "encyclopedia" of humanist learning. This purpose was also reflected in his philosophical method, which likewise moved from the top down in legislative fashion : his preference was to proceed not from particulars to universals, or as he put it, from things perceived to things hidden, but rather from first principles to particulars.[30] Such was the flexibility of this method,

---

[27] *La Philosophie*, ff. 22 and 17^v : "Je dirai ... que nul plus gravement, amplement, philosophiquement, et divinement a traicté la philosophie que Platon, mais les autres l'ont plustost corrumpue et obscurcie que descrite." This pioneering contribution to the history of philosophy may be compared to the contemporary sketch by another French Platonist, Louis le Roy, "L'Origine, progres et perfection de la philosophie, avec la comparaison de Platon et Aristote," prefacing his translation, *La Phedon de Platon* (Paris, 1553).

[28] *Nouveau commentaire ... sur la coustume de ... Paris, ou droit civil Parisien* (Paris, 1613), "avant propos."

[29] *Discours philosophiques*, f. 16^v ("la souveraineté de la Philosophie"), f. 12 ("la souveraine sagesse"), f. 9 ("la souveraine science").

[30] *La Philosophie*, f. 40, and diagram. Le Caron's intense belief in sorcery appears in a curious "Discours sur le proces criminel faict à une sorciere condamnee à mort ...," in *De la Tranquillité d'esprit* (Paris, 1588), 159.

so ecumenical, omnivorous, and amorphous was his thought, so "neo-" his Platonism, that he was able to accommodate to it learning of every variety and of every age. From this kingdom of philosophy not even magic was excluded.

In general Le Caron accepted the conventional division of philosophy into things divine and things human, corresponding to wisdom and prudence. From this he drew an epistemological distinction very similar to that made by Vico between the *verum* and the *factum* : that is, between being, "which is without beginning, one, eternal, and immeasurable," and non-being, "which has been created from being, but which is mutable, in motion, and subject to corruption."[31] The first can be comprehended only by divine intelligence, but the second, emerging and disappearing in time, is accessible to human sense perception, and so represents in effect the historical forms of human culture. So philosophy comprehended the entire range of human behavior and indeed was the principal sign of "the dignity of man."

Le Caron was concerned more with the structure than with the substance of philosophy, but more than either he was interested in the "office of the philosopher." In another early dialogue between a "courtier" and himself he discussed the value and purpose of philosophy. The courtier stated all the standard skeptical objections : philosophy had no practical use, its conclusions had never been agreed on by its professors, and it was at bottom nothing more than a pedantic game.[32] In answering these objections Le Caron returned to his central thesis concerning the social basis of philosophy. In the first place he agreed completely with the critique of scholastic philosophy and resumed the line of argument established by such earlier humanists as Ermolao Barbaro and Melanchthon, that true philosophy was inseparable from eloquence. "One who divorces eloquence from wisdom, which are closely bound together," Le Caron said, "seems to me to be

---

[31] *Discours philosophiques*, f. 10ᵛ : "... il faut premierement distinguer ce qui EST, lequel sans commencement est toujours UN, Eternal et immesurable, de ce qui a esté crée n'estant jamais. Au Permenide, il [Plato] monstre que l'ESTANT ne differe de l'UN... Mais ce qui n'est à la verité (lequel imitans les Grecs et Latins, nous appellons NON ESTANT) a esté crée d'iceluy ESTANT ; toutesfois il est muable, mortel et suiect à corruption ... Et ce qui N'EST, peut estre touché de la pensée irraisonable, puis qu'il naist, et perist n'estant jamais à la verité."

[32] *Dialogues*, f. 48ᵛ ff.

throwing society into a wretched state of disorder." [33] The companion of philosophy, in short, should be not dialectic but rhetoric. And in the second place, as Plato himself taught, philosophy was not a simply private pursuit but the very foundation of public life. The achievement of the Platonic tradition, in his view, was to bring philosophy down from the heavens, from "contemplation," not only into the households of men (as Cicero had said of Socrates) but also into the forum, the council chamber, and even the law courts.

The "office of the philosopher," then, was not merely to follow the ancient precept, "know thyself," as Le Caron's disillusioned contemporary Montaigne was teaching.[34] Nor was it to determine the "souverain contentement" of the individual, which implied the still more reprehensible hedonism of Rabelais. True philosophy was aimed rather at "public utility" and the "sovereign good" of the whole community. In short, this "royal philosophy," prescribed by Le Caron for the education of the prince and indeed of any "politic," was equivalent to "la science politique." [35] For Le Caron, of course, the term "politique" had very different connotations than it did for many of his contemporaries, who were beginning to use it in a derogatory way, often as a synonym for "Machiavellian" or even atheist or as a party label. He accepted the rather old-fashioned usage which included also the notions of legality, morality, and public welfare, and which is perhaps best expressed in the remark of Baudouin : "Homo politicus, hoc est, juriconsultus." That is, Le Caron would add, *philosophe*, for

---

[33] *Dialogues*, f. 64 ("Oraison pour la philosophie"), f. 64v. On this controversy in general, see A. Bernardini and G. Righi, *Il concetto di filologia e di cultura classica* (Bari, 1953), ch. II, and Q. Breen's translation of the essential documents in *Journal of the History of Ideas* 13 (1952), 384-426.

[34] *La Philosophie*, f. 15v ("office du philosophe"), f. 12, discussion of the Apollonian precept "COGNOI TOI-MESME," and again in *Questions diverses et discours*, f. 62v : "Mais je diray que la trop grand recherche de soy-mesme n'est que vaine et inutile curiosité." *La Philosophie*, f. 7v : "J'ai dict parcidevant le philosophe (lequel justement merite tel nom) estre celui qui d'une amore de sagesse recherche la verité, estudiant à l'utilité publique." Cf. f. 113v, on the "souveraine contentement" or "volupté" of Rabelais.

[35] *Dialogues*, f. 3, "Le Courtisan, que le Prince doit philosopher, Ou, de la vraie sagesse et Roiale philosophie"; *Panegyrique*, Biv ("la science Royale"); and Eiiiv ("la science politique"); *La Philosophie*, f. 69, "Le Philosophe, Ou, que la philosophie est toute roiale." There are other questions relating to the "institution du prince" in *Questions diverses*.

as Ulpian said, "jurisconsults desired and professed, or rather taught, the true philosophy."[36]

In several respects Le Caron's political position was markedly different from that of most of his colleagues in the French magistracy. Not that he rejected any part of royalist ideology : he rehearsed the old Gallican formulas that the king was the "image of God" and "emperor in his kingdom" and of course attributed to him the *merum imperium*, or sovereignty.[37] But for Le Caron reason was enshrined not in monarchy but in law, and the true "mark of sovereignty" was not the legislative power, as Jean Bodin argued, but justice itself.[38] Le Caron placed great emphasis upon the role of magistrates and the judiciary and upon their discretionary judgment. The delegation of *haute justice* in particular he found "very *politique* and in accord with the opinion of our Plato."[39] What is more, he did not hesitate to associate the notion of justice as much with custom as with formal laws and indeed argued that time and experience operated as a corrective upon the inequities of legislation : *usus legum corrector* was the old precept he cited.[40] The legislator had an important function, of course, but it was rather that of a doctor prescribing for health than that of a ruler trying to control the behavior of his subjects.

Equally unorthodox were Le Caron's views about the historical foundations of the French "chose publique." He offered an even more fundamental rebuke to Bodin by endorsing the argument for "mixed monarchy," regarded as treasonable in some circles. "I accept the opinion of Polybius," he wrote, "that of the three types of government, that is, monarchy, aristocracy, and democracy, one cannot exist alone; rather the three together, organized and balanced, form a true

---

[36] *Pandectes*, I, 3. Cf. Baudouin, *Commentarius de jurisprudentia Muciana* (Halle, 1729), 31.

[37] *Au Roy nostre souverain prince et seigneur* (Paris, 1588) and *Pandectes*, I, 18, "Le Roy est Empereur de France." On the *merum imperium*, see Le Caron's edition of [Jacques d'Ableiges'] *Grand Coustumier de France* (Paris, 1598), p. 531; *Responses et decisions du droict françois* (Paris, 1637), p. 574; and *De Iurisdictione et imperio*, in *Ad Tit. de verborum obligat.* (Paris, 1553), f. 46 ff. There are discussions of Le Caron's political thought in M.P. Gilmore, *Argument from Roman Law in Political Thought 1200-1600* (Cambridge, Mass., 1941), 82-85, and in Vittorio de Caprariis, *Propaganda e pensiero politico in Francia durante le guerre di religione* (Naples, 1959), 214-24.

[38] *Pandectes*, I, 1. (Cf. Bodin's famous remarks in his *Republic*, III, 8.) *Dialogues*, f. 46ᵛ : "... la loi ... est la raison universelle de tout le peuple."

[39] *Les Dialogues*, f. 29.

[40] *Memorables observations du droict françois* (Paris, 1637), 34, and *Pandectes*, I, 3.

republic..., such as that of France."[41] Le Caron also showed a certain sympathy with the general idea of popular sovereignty. It certainly applied to Rome, according to the famous *lex regia*, one of his favorite texts. "As for the French government," he wrote, "it was established not by force but by election." [42] Finally, Le Caron was an admirer of the Estates General and argued that, like the English Parliament, they had once enjoyed a much greater authority than recently.[43]

These were dangerous opinions and in fact resembled nothing so much as the treasonable views spread by the Huguenot propagandist François Hotman. Yet in Le Caron's case they stemmed from no real sympathy for resistance; even as a deputy of the third estate at Blois in 1588 his political position was positively obsequious. As always the shaping force was his oecumenical and neo-Platonic cast of mind and his professional commitment to jurisprudence. As a result of the first he attached more importance to justice than to authority in his republic, and as a result of the second he attached more importance to private than to public law. According to Le Caron, discord was the product not merely of resistance of subjects to oppressive rulers (though there was certainly an excess of that at this time) but more fundamentally of the conflict between "mien et tien," which has always disrupted human tranquillity.[44] The remedy for this was a kind of harmonic justice which Le Caron described in elaborate, neo-Pythagorean terms. This "eunomia" was two-fold, depending both upon a justice that was general and common to all, and a justice that was particular and proportionate to one's individual status, and also upon a sovereign who respected this harmony, whether or not he was a philosopher-king.[45]

---

[41] *Responses et decisions*, "Response politique" : "Je cognois l'opinion de Polybe estre veritable, que les trois especes de Republique qu'on estime les meilleures, à savoir, Monarchie, Aristocratie, et Democratie, l'une ne peut estre seule, ains de trois ensemble composees et temperees se forme une vraye Republique ... Comme est celle de France, en laquelle y a un Roy, qui se gouverne par le conseil des Pairs de France..., et la peuple obeyssant volontairement ... C'est ceste belle et excellent harmonie qui entretient la societé politique..."

[42] *Pandectes*, I, 1 : "La Republique françoise ... n'a esté establie par force, ains par election du peuple ..." On the *lex regia*, see I, 4, and "Leges ... additae" in *Catalogus legum*, f. 142ᵛ.

[43] *Pandectes*, I, 15.

[44] *La Philosophie*, f. 70.

[45] *Panegyrique*, Hiii.

Many traditions went into the making of Le Caron's political views: the ancient notion of the mixed constitution, medieval and modern writings on German history, the mirror-of-the-prince genre, civil law and its various schools of commentary, feudal law, especially those who wrote on the French *coutumes*, movements of legal reform in the sixteenth century (ordinances and the "reformation of customs"), the venerable tradition of French legists, including writings about the estates as well as the sovereign courts, and above all that antiquarian renaissance of the later sixteenth century to which Le Caron himself made important scholarly contributions.[46] Yet even in his political thought Le Caron remained constant to the memory of the lady Claire and to the abstract *idee* of justice, so much so that it is hardly an exaggeration to regard Le Caron as in effect a philosophical constitutionalist—even a Platonic constitutionalist.

The final proof of this observation is Le Caron's lifelong fascination with the idea of a universal system of laws. The ultimate source of this idea as far as law was concerned was of course Roman law itself, especially the plan of Justinian, though of more immediate importance was the contemporary movement toward reforming or systematizing civil law sponsored by such French jurists as Le Caron's teacher Le Douaren, Hugues Doneau (another contemporary at Bourges), François Connan, and to some extent Jean Bodin.[47] These attempts

---

[46] *Grand Coustumier*, preface to son : "Ceux qui de nostre eage ont travaillé et travaillent encores à retirer des tenebres d'oubliance les escrits des anciens Grecs et Latins, et les illustrer d'observations et annotations, ont merité grandement des sciences, n'estans moins loüables que ceux qui publient des nouveaux livres de leur façon. A leur example les François amateurs de leur patrie se doivent dedier à rechercher et remettre en lumiere les anciens livres de leur langue pour la decoration d'icelle. J'en ay veu de diverses sciences, d'histoires, de poësie et d'oraison soluë, qui ne cedent en rien aux Grecs et Latins..." Of Le Caron's fellow researchers, those he cites include Pasquier, Fauchet, Pithou, Choppin, Du Tillet, Du Haillan, Dumoulin, Brisson, Argentré, Bacquet, as well as L'Hôpital and Christofle de Thou.

[47] The tradition of legal system-building from the sixteenth to the eighteenth century, especially in its relations to philosophy, needs further investigation. In general, see R. Stintzing, *Geschichte der deutschen Rechtswissenschaft* (Munich, 1880), I, 139 ff; A. Eyssell, *Doneau* (Dijon, 1860); C. Bergfeld, *Franciscus Connanus (1508-1551)* (Cologne, 1968); F. Ebrard, "Über Methoden, Systeme, Dogmen in der Geschichte des Privatrechts," *Zeitschrift für schweizerisches Recht* 67 (1948), 95-136; Aldo Mazzacane, *Scienza, logica e ideologia nella giurisprudenza tedesca del sec. XVI* (Milan, 1971); Hans Troje, "Arbeitshypothesen zum Thema 'Humanistische Jurisprudenz'," *Tijdschrift voor Rechtsgeschiedenis* 38 (1970), 519-63; and my "The Development and Context of Bodin's Method," in *Jean Bodin : Verhandlungen der internationalen Bodin Tagung in München*, ed. H. Denzer (Munich, 1972).

to rationalize civil law, to find a *ius perennis*, were very obviously grounded in philosophical motives and are linked historically with the grander designs of the seventeenth and eighteenth centuries, such as those of Domat, Pufendorf, Vico, and Montesquieu, for systems of universal law.

But once again Le Caron was diverted by his vernacularist bias and his professional commitments. He came to doubt whether classical antiquity was any more relevant to modern French society than classical languages were to French literature. "Frenchmen," he declared, "you have enough examples in your histories without inquiring into those of Greece and Rome." [48] This was even more obvious in the case of law, since Le Caron shared the growing hostility of many of his colleagues toward the substance, if not the form, of Roman law, both civil and canon. He accepted and indeed insisted upon the conventional Gallican doctrine that, as he declared to King Charles IX, "You are not subject to the laws of the Greeks and the Romans, nor are your magistrates bound by them, except to the extent that they are in accord with reason."[49] Le Caron joined in the growing chorus of complaints by Pasquier, Hotman, and others about the evil effects of Roman law, which in France had brought about a lapse from "the simplicity of ancient manners," and had turned the country into a veritable paradise for litigators. The problem was to find the original tradition of French law.

Thus Le Caron, in the company of many fellow legists, turned from civil law back to the customs of the French countryside. What began as a plan to translate the Digest into French ended up twenty years later as Le Caron's masterpiece, the *Digest of French Law*, which preserved the form of the Digest but concentrated on the substance of French law, institutions, and history. This work was the descendant of a long series of feudist compilations, including those of Philippe de Beaumanoir (a thirteenth-century forerunner of Le Caron as royal official in Clermont in Beauvaisis), Jacques d'Ableiges (whose *Grand Coustumier de France* Le Caron edited), and Charles Dumoulin (like Le Caron a commentator on the Parisian *coutume* and a promoter of a native French code of laws), and various collections of judicial decisions and royal legislation (Le Caron himself

---

[48] *Responses et decisions*, "Avant-propos." "Vous avez, hommes François, assez d'exemples en vos Histoires sans en rechercher aux Grecques et Romaines…"

[49] *Panegyrique*, Dii. Cf. *Pandectes*, I, Juvenal, *Satire*, VII, 148.

produced several of these, as well as an edition of Barnabé Brisson's famous *Code of Henry III*).[50] The work was also among the first in a series of attempts, including those later made by his friends Pasquier and Loisel, to bring some order into the chaos of French customary law by fashioning a system out of medieval history, classical jurisprudence, and philosophy.[51]

In general this work, technical and overloaded with other people's erudition as it is, may be taken as the fulfillment of Le Caron's original philosophical ideal: for here philosophy could exercise its "sovereignty" not only over fields of learning but over "the life and customs of men in general." Into the vulgar and vernacular field of French law, moreover, Le Caron brought all of his general assumptions about jurisprudence. "French law," he wrote, "is composed of all the parts of universal law, the science of which is called jurisprudence, civil science or wisdom, referred to as 'royal' by some. It is the major part of moral as well as political philosophy, which is most useful to human society."[52] So Le Caron brought together, as he believed, all the materials necessary for the formation of an ideal republic in France. So he continued to carry on the task of the jurisconsult as defined by Ulpian and the "office of the philosophe" as conceived by Plato.

---

[50] *Responses de droict françois* (Paris, 1583); also a manuscript (Paris, BN, Fonds français, 21,569), "Responses et arrests de la cour de parlement remarquez par Charondas Iurisconsulte Parisien"; *Ordonnance du domain, et droicts de la couronne de France* (Paris, 1637); *Coustumes ... de Paris* (Paris, 1595); Brisson, *Le Code du Roy Henry III* (Paris, 1609); and n. 31.

[51] *Panegyrique*, Diii : "... ains comme vos sujects vous emportent et appartient tous autant les uns que les autres, aussi doit avoir entre eux une communauté des loix que soyent toutes escriptes en langue François, pour estre entendues non moins de ceux qu'on appelle rustiques et paysans que de plus subtils practiciens... à fin qu'ils cognoissent tous que c'est que vostre Majesté leur command pour vivre politiquement en vostre Royaume." Cf. Loisel, *Institutes Coustumieres* (Paris, 1607), and Pasquier, *L'Interpretation des Institutes de Justinian*, ed. M. le duc Pasquier (Paris, 1847), approximately contemporaneous.

[52] *Pandectes*, I, 3 : "Le droict François est composé de toutes les parties du droict universel, duquel la science est appellee Iurisprudence, science ou sagesse civile, et par aucuns Royal, laquelle est la principale partie de la Philosophie morale, d'autant que c'est la politique qui est la plus utile à la societé humaine. La Philosophie consiste ou en la recherche des secrets ou en l'institution des mœurs; l'une se propose une contemplation et l'autre s'exerce en action; toutes les deux loüables et qui se doivent estre embrassees par les grands et nobles esprits, mais l'action est plus necessaire à la vie commune."

The general effect of jurisprudence upon philosophy, to judge from Le Caron's work, was to shift emphasis from "theoretical" to "practical" knowledge, from the *vita contemplativa* to the *vita activa*, and so from natural to social science. This tendency, so characteristic of Renaissance humanism as a whole, may be seen in a longer perspective and suggests in particular a link with eighteenth-century thought. Clearly, one of the agents of this shift was jurisprudence, which combines, at least potentially, the cultural values of humanism with the systematizing features of formal philosophy. This combination is obviously present in the work of Vico and Montesquieu, who were both, like Le Caron and Bodin, educated in the law and authors of quasi-legal systems of thought. Both sought above all the "spirit of the laws," and it is significant that this concept (*mens legum*), meaning intention or reasonableness as distinct from the letter of the law and implying a moral or philosophical standard transcending the accidents of history and the particularity of specific texts, was itself derived from civil law.[53]

There are other such parallels with the same provenance. It has been noted, for example, that Le Caron's discussion of the origins of society, likewise based on civil law, seems "strangely like eighteenth-century thinking on the subject."[54] Various assumptions crucial for political thinking from the sixteenth to the eighteenth century were preserved in civil law, such as the distinctions between private and public law, between civil society and a pre-legal state of nature, and at least implicitly between the methods of natural and of social philosophy. So were certain interpretations of historical development (from barbarism and oral tradition, corresponding to unwritten custom, to a literate and enlightened society based upon rational and perhaps codified laws) and the endless search for a universal "law of nations" (the *jus gentium* inspired not only Grotius' contributions to international law but also one aspect of Vico's "new science"). Most important, jurisprudence contained what is perhaps the ultimate ideal of a social science, that is, a rational system of understanding human behavior in terms of cause and effect on the basis of accumulated human experience.

---

[53] Alciato, *Parerga*, in *Opera*, IV, 323 : "... quod ipsi [*grammatici*, such as Lorenzo Valla] scilicet ad sola verba attenderent, mentem legum ignorarent." See Vicenzo Piano Mortari, "Il problema dell'interpretatio iuris nei commentatori," *Annali di storia del diritto* 2 (1958), 29-109.

[54] M. P. Gilmore, *Argument from Roman Law*, 83.

In these and other ways Le Caron may, like Bodin, be regarded as a "predecessor of Montesquieu" and, since he combined the ideals of Roman law with Platonic philosophy, even more conspicuously of Vico. Although there is no evidence of direct influence, the parallels are striking. Both men stand in the mainstream of the humanist tradition; both linked their philosophic vision with a formative personal experience and turned to autobiography to express it; both looked to jurisprudence as a source of inspiration and as a conceptual model; both chose Plato as their first authority; and finally, both represent a kind of latter day Socratic revolution—a shift of focus from the "secrets of nature," as Le Caron put it, to the "life and customs of men."

In conclusion, then, we may place Le Caron between two enlightenments—that emanating from the "divine Plato" and that of the eighteenth century. In style and superficiality of thought Le Caron seems to stand closer to the latter, for his interest in philosophy was not really professional, and he was in his own words an "amateur de sagesse."[55] Yet like many eighteenth-century thinkers, and for the same reasons, he regarded himself as the best of all possible philosophers. He, too, found in history some of the most essential lessons about human behavior. He, too, wanted to apply the "knowledge of things divine and human" to problems of government and society for purposes of reform. Though a good Catholic, he, too, attacked papal usurpation and championed ecclesiastical reform. And finally, he, too, hoped to accomplish these things through education and above all through legislation. So it seems appropriate to bestow upon Le Caron the title by which he referred to his own calling, and at the same time to extend to him the observation once made about his more famous colleague Bodin—that he was at once one of the last of the legists and first of the *philosophes*.[56]

University of Rochester

---

[55] *La Philosophie*, f. 8ᵛ. In his *The Enlightenment : An Interpretation* (New York, 1966-69) Peter Gay argues for the exclusive application of "philosophe" to eighteenth-century thinkers; I would not want to stretch the meaning further but only to point out the historical background of the usage he discusses. I make the connection more directly in "Vico's Road," in *Giambattista Vico's Science of Humanity*, ed. G. Tagliacozzo and D. Verene (Baltimore, 1976), 16-29.

[56] Etienne Fournol, *Bodin prédécesseur de Montesquieu* (Paris, 1896), especially p. 27, and most recently, G. Cotroneo, "A Renaissance Source of the *Scienza nuova* : Juan Bodin's *Methodus*," in *Giambattista Vico, An International Symposium*, ed. G. Tagliacozzo and H. White (Baltimore, 1969), 51-59.

APPENDIX

Organization of Knowledge

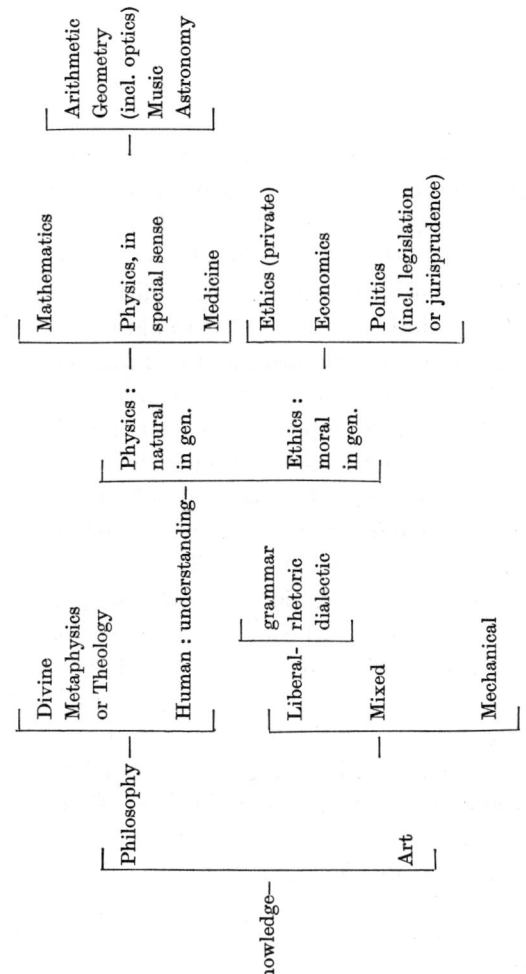

Louis le Caron, *Discours philosophiques* (Paris, 1583), f. 35.

THE PRE-ADAMITE THEORY
IN THE RENAISSANCE*

RICHARD H. POPKIN

The pre-Adamite theory that was to play so great a role in reshaping man's conception of his own nature and destiny went through a major transformation during the late Renaissance. This transformation changed the theory from being either a reinforcement or embellishment of the Judeo-Christian-Islamic religious framework, to one containing the revolutionary seeds that would flower in later centuries as bases for rejecting the revealed picture of man in Scripture. In this paper, dedicated to one of my most important teachers, and one who has greatly influenced my intellectual career, I shall try to show that certain Renaissance developments, principally the humanist restudying of the pagan past, and the Voyages of Discovery, led to new forms of the pre-Adamite theory fraught with dangerous implications for the accepted religious world view. These were welded together in the mid-seventeenth century, via a new religious perspective emerging from certain novel theological concerns of the sixteenth century, into a most powerful theoretical tool by Isaac La Peyrère, a tool that was to be used by Hobbes, Spinoza, Richard Simon, Vico, the English Deists, among others, as a basis for developing Bible criticism, the secularization of human history, and the bases for anthropology. La Peyrère's strange completion of certain lines of Renaissance thought was to have almost as far-reaching an effect as the work of the new astronomers from Copernicus onward. Not only was the conception of the world transformed from a finite to an infinite universe in terms of space, it was transformed into one of enormous or indefinite temporal duration.

---

* Part of the research for this paper was done with the assistance of fellowships from the ACLS and the Guggenheim Foundation. I should like to thank them both for their generosity. I should also like to thank Professor Herman P. Saloman of the State University of New York at Albany for his most helpful critical reading of this paper, and for his suggestions and corrections.

The pre-Adamite theory, that there were human beings prior to Adam, was evidently common in ancient times. Pagans, confronted with Judaism and Christianity, saw that their own historical-mythological accounts of the origins of mankind went back long before the Scriptural one. Theophilus of Antioch around 170 A.D. was debating the claim of Apollonius the Egyptian that the world was 153,075 years old.[1] Two chapters in St. Augustine's *City of God* indicate that a running argument had been going on between those who accepted Egyptian, Greek and Roman accounts, and those who accepted the Bible. St. Augustine's chapter titles, "Of the falsenesse of the History that the world hath continued many thousand yeares," and "The Aegyptians abbominable lyings, to claime their wisdom the age of 100,000 yeares," show his attitude.[2] In these chapters. St. Augustine stated the party-line that was held to by most of the rabbis and Church Fathers, namely, that the pagan views were fables and myths, and the Biblical one was revealed truth :

> For seeing it is not yet sixe thousand yeares from the first man *Adam*, how ridiculous are they that over-runne the truth such a multitude of yeares ? whom shall wee believe in this, so soone as him that fore-told what now we see accordingly effected ? The dissonance of histories, giveth us leave to leane to such as doe accorde with our divinitie. The citizens of Babilon indeed, being diffused all the earth over, when they read two authors of like (and allowable) authority, differing in relations of the eldest memory, they know not which to beleeve. But we have a divine historie to under-shore us, and wee know that what so ever seculer author he bee, famous or obscure, if hee contradict that, hee goeth farre astray from truth. But bee his words true or false, they are of no valew to the attainment of true felicitie.[3]

---

[1] Cf. Paul H. Kocher, *Christopher Marlowe, A Study of his Thought, Learning and Character* (New York, 1962), 44, n. 11, cited from *Theopilus to Autolycus* in the *Ante-Nicene Christian Library*, III (Book III, chap. XVI), 120. Kocher here also gives various ancient pagan figures for the length of human history, far exceeding Biblical ones, from Herodotus, Diodorus Siculus, Pomponius Mela, Plato, Diogenes Laertius, Alexander Polyhistor and Abydenus. Ancient theories about human origins are treated at length in Arthur O. Lovejoy and George Boas, *Primitivism and Related Ideas in Antiquity* (New York, 1965).

[2] These are the titles as given in the Renaissance English edition, which may have played some role in the pre-Adamite theorizing of the time. Cf. St. Augustine, *Of the Citie of God : with the Learned Comments of Io. Lod. Vives*, Englished by J.H., (n. p., 1610), Book XII, chap. 10 and Book XVIII, chap. 40. (The British Museum Catalogue, VIII, col. 518, identifies J.H. as John Healey and gives London as the place of publication). For the Latin text of these passages, see *De Civitate Dei : Libri XI-XXII*, Corpus Christianorum, Series Latina, vol. 48 (Turnhout, 1955), 364-365 and 635.

[3] St. Augustine, *Of the Citie of God*, Book XVIII, chap. 40, p. 729. Cf. *De Civitate Dei : Libri XI-XXII*, 635.

Another version of this view, which probably influenced La Peyrère, is presented very forcefully in Judah Halevi's *The Kuzari*, written between 1130-1140 in Spain. Early in the work, the King of the Khazars asks the Rabbi : "Does it not weaken thy belief if thou art told that the Indians have antiquities and buildings which they consider to be millions of years old ?" And the answer is given, "It would, indeed, weaken my belief had they a fixed form of religion, or a book concerning which a multitude of people held the same opinion, and in which no historical discrepancy could be found. Such a book, however, does not exist. Apart from this, they are a dissolute, unreliable people, and arouse the indignation of the followers of religions through their talk, whilst they anger them with their idols, talismans, and witchcraft."[4] Judah Halevi then went on to attack the pre-Adamite claims in the work that Maimonides later cited, *The Nabatean Agriculture*, the Greek philosophical views that the world is eternal, the claims of the Chaldaeans; all on the grounds that these writers and thinkers did not know the Revelation in Scripture. Finally, apparently influenced by forms of pre-Adamism we will consider next, Judah Halevi concluded the discussion of the matter saying, "If, after all, a believer in the Law finds himself compelled to admit an eternal matter and the existence of many worlds prior to this one, this would not impair his belief that *this* world was created at a certain epoch, and that Adam and Noah were the first human beings."[5]

Judah Halevi's discussion, with the details of the theories he dismissed, probably played an important role later on. His work appeared in three Latin editions in the sixteenth century. His own historical-theological theory and the historical details he dealt with are both very close to La Peyrère's statements in the seventeenth century.[6]

A counter-tendency also developed in the medieval Judeo-Christian-

---

[4] Judah Halevi, *The Kuzari*, intro. by Henry Slonimsky (New York, 1964), Part I, sec. 60-61, p. 52.

[5] *Ibid.*, sec. 61-67. The quotation is from sec. 67, p. 54. Judah Halevi mentioned three people listed in *Nabatean Agriculture* who were supposed to have lived before Adam. La Peyrère became interested in these alleged cases later on.

[6] Brunet's *Manuel du Librairie* lists three editions of *Jehudae levitae liber cozri vel Cuzari seu Cosrois (ex. arab. latine vertit Jehuda ben Saul Tibbon)* : Fani, 1506; Venice, 1547; and Venice, 1594. The last has a commentary of R. Jehudae Muscati. I have not seen this, and do not know if it discusses Judah Halevi's attack on pre-Adamism. In a study now in preparation, I will show the affinities between La Peyrère's theology and Judah Halevi's, and that the former's theory is a modernized and revised version of Judah Halevi's Jewish nationalistic interpretation of world history.

Islamic traditions, working out some forms of pre-Adamism. Some of these were slight embellishments of the Biblical story of Adam, or amalgamations of other Near Eastern legends with the story of Adam. The great Bible scholar, Father Richard Simon, had to explain to La Peyrère, who was always looking for evidence of the existence of men before Adam, that the tales that Adam had a teacher, or that there were three wise men before Adam, were Persian, Arabic or Jewish legends of no authenticity. The alleged teacher of Adam was an angel, named Raziel, hence not a man. The rest, Simon told La Peyrère, is just Mohammedan or Cabalistic nonsense, of no serious historical validity.[7]

In the Midrash and in some of the Cabalistic literature a different kind of pre-Adamism was offered. Pondering the wonders and values of this world, Jewish scholars presented views that God had created other worlds prior to this one, worlds containing human beings. These worlds had been destroyed by God because they were not virtuous enough. Finally this world was created. A lesser version of this kind of pre-Adamism is an attempt to account for why *Genesis* begins with a *Beth* instead of an *Aleph*. A previous Bible must have existed describing a previous world, now completely gone.[8]

These types of pre-Adamism do not pose the possibility of any human beings having existed in *this* world prior to Adam. However, in a crucial chapter of Maimonides' *Guide for the Perplexed*, chap. 29, Book III, just such a possibility is mentioned. In discussing the views of the Sabians, Maimonides reported that "They deem *Adam* to have been an individual born of male and female like any other human individuals, but they glorify him and say that he was a prophet, the

---

[7] Cf. Richard Simon, *Lettres Choisies de M. Simon*, 4 vols. (Rotterdam, 1702; repr. Frankfurt, 1967), Lettre I, Tome II, p. 5; Lettres VII and VIII, Tome II, pp. 36-43. Many of the Persian and Islamic speculations and legends are cited in a forthcoming work of Léon Poliakov on "L'anthropologie des Lumières, Prelude, Les Préadamites," first page.

[8] These Jewish possibilities are discussed in Hans Joachim Schoeps, *Philosemitismus im Barock* (Tübingen, 1952), 15-16. Schoeps also shows how some of these enter into seventeenth-century discussions, and that La Peyrère could have learned of some of them from Manasseh ben Israel's *Problemata de Creatione* of 1635. The Midrash Rabba, in discussing Genesis, says: "The Holy One Blessed be He, created many worlds, and destroyed them one after the other until He consulted the Torah, and created this that endured." Some of the Moslem versions of this kind of pre-Adamism are cited in Arno Borst, *Der Turmbau von Babel*, I (Stuttgart, 1957), 338-39.

envoy of the moon."[9] Maimonides also reports that Sabians believed Adam came from India and went to Babylon. These views are offered without much criticism as the beliefs held by the Sabians according to a work entitled *The Nabatean Agriculture*, translated or written by Ibn Wahshiyya in 904.[10] This work apparently contains a description of Sabean beliefs. Maimonides, by concentrating on the role given to Adam in this work, indicated a slight pre-Adamite possibility, that Adam had had parents; that could easily grow into a larger one, that there were many people before Adam. As a result, this chapter in the *Guide* was to play a significant role in the seventeenth century, when a full-blown pre-Adamite theory was advanced.

Zöckler, in his study of the antecedents of La Peyrère's theory, showed that in the medieval discussions about the existence and nature of the Antipodes, the possibilities of pre-Adamite humans living there was raised, as well as the theory that Paracelsus was to raise, double Adamism : that is, that God created two Adams, one as father of this side of the world and the other as father of the Antipodes.[11] Some of these speculations were seen as heretical suggestions. A canon, Zaninus

---

[9] Moses Maimonides, *The Guide of the Perplexed*, translated with an Introduction and Notes by Shlomo Pines, with an introductory essay by Leo Strauss (Chicago, 1964), 515.

[10] Cf. Pines' n. 25, p. 518 of Maimonides' *Guide*. I am grateful to Dr. G. A. Salinger of the University of California, San Diego Library for further information about this work. There is some dispute about the authorship and original intent of *The Nabatean Agriculture*. T. Fahd, in the article on Ibn Wahshiyya in *The Encyclopedia of Islam*, new edition (Leiden and London, 1969), 964, discusses the various theories and interpretations and gives references to the scholarly literature on the subject. Some interpreters have argued that the work is a forgery intended to criticize Mohammedanism and to glorify the Nabateans over the Arabs.

The Nabatean Agriculture has never been published. Dr. Salinger is preparing a translation of a large section. A description of another part, (Daniel Chwolson, "Über die Überreste der Altbabylonischen Literatur in Arabischen Übersetzungen," *Academie Impériale des Sciences de St. Petersbourg*, Mémoires des savants étrangers, VIII, 2, [repr. Amsterdam, 1968], 158-159, and 173-174), indicates that there is a full-blown pre-Adamic theory in the work : Adam is the one who brought civilization and genuine agriculture to Babylonia, but he is far from being the first man; other religious leaders came before him and innumerable people. One wonders, then, why both Judah Halevi and Maimonides drew such restricted pre-Adamite views from the work.

Some discussion of the significance of *The Nabatean Agriculture* and its effect on Maimonides and Judah Halevi appears in Leo Strauss' *Persecution and the Art of Writing* (Glencoe, 1952), 123-125.

[11] O. Zöckler, *Geschichte der Beziehungen zwischen Theologie und Naturwissenschaften*, I (Gütersloh, 1877), 340.

de Solcia, at Bergamo, went too far, and was condemned in 1459 for holding that Adam was not the first man. The condemnation indicates that he held that God had created other worlds in which many other men and women existed before Adam came on the scene, and that this raised the question of whether Jesus was the saviour of all mankind. (Zaninus de Solcia was accused of being a follower of Epicurus in his many world theory.)[12] A more heretical case is reported by Menéndez Pelayo of one Father Tomás Scoto, who was arrested sometime in the fourteenth century. His opponent, Alvaro Pelagio, gave a list of Scoto's errors, which seem to include a pretty total rejection of Judaism and Christianity. One of the errors of Scoto cited is "Item dixit dictus Thomas Haereticus quod ante Adam fuerunt homines et per illos homines fuit factus Adam et sic infert quod semper fuit mundus, et in eo homines semper fuerunt..."[13] Nothing in the document cited by Menéndez Pelayo indicates the basis of Scoto's pre-Adamism. Since all that seems to exist is the attack on Scoto, one cannot judge how real the case was, and whether it genuinely represented an early case of atheism. Menéndez Pelayo was unable to find any further details about Scoto, but suspected his heresies came from Averroism.[14] A Jew named Samuel Sarsa is reported to have been burned at the stake in 1463 "because he asserted the great antiquity of the world,"[15] but it is not clear if this claim was based on pre-Adamism.

These medieval pre-Adamite theories do not seem to have raised any real stir, or to have raised basic challenges to the Judeo-Christian picture of the world. A few individuals may have had irreligious or

---

[12] O. Zöckler, "Peyrère's (gest. 1676) Präadamiten-Hypothese nach ihren Beziehungen zu den anthropologischen Fragen der Gegenwart," *Zeitschrift für die gesammte lutherische Theologie und Kirche* 39 (1878), 38, where the charges against Zaninus de Solcia are given in n. 2, including "et per consequens Adam primum hominem non fuisse."

[13] Marcelino Menéndez Pelayo, *Historia de los Heterodoxos Españoles*, I (Madrid, 1956), 593; and *Historia de los Heterodoxes Españoles*, VII, ed. E. Sanchez Reyes (Santander, 1948), Apendice I, 324-235, where extracts of Alvaro Pelagio's *Collyrium contra haereses* are given from the Biblioteca San Marco, Venice, cod. lat. III-VI. Cf. J. Valentinelli, *Bibliotheca manuscripta ad S. Marci Venetiarum*, II (Venice, 1869), 126-127.

[14] Menéndez Pelayo could not find the date of Scoto's birth but only that he had been a Dominican and a Franciscan and was jailed in Lisbon. In the citation of the text against Scoto, Menéndez Pelayo added a note : "Se deduce que Scoto era aristotélico, probablemente averroísta, y admitía la eternidad nel mundo" (p. 325, n. 1).

[15] Cited in James Sydney Slotkin, *Readings in Early Anthropology* (Chicago, 1965), 38. The source given is W. Schickard, *Tarich* (Tübingen, 1628), 175-76.

bizarre views, but they hardly damaged the official Biblical theory, or caused serious controversies. In the sixteenth century, however, certain data came to light that made the pre-Adamite theory a live option, as well as a genuine and serious threat to Western religion. The transformation of earlier speculations and legends into a radical alternative to the Scriptural picture of man grew, I believe, out of two Renaissance developments, the humanistic rediscovery of the pagan past, and the expansion of Europe through the voyages of discovery. The study of the pagan historians of antiquity revealed that much data existed which conflicted with the Biblical account of human origins. The great Spanish humanist, Juan Luis Vives, in his edition of St. Augustine's *City of God*, carefully noted cases in ancient literature of people who were reported as living long before Adam and Eve.[16] Although St. Augustine said that when he was writing his masterpiece, the world was not yet 6,000 years old, Vives mentioned that Chaldean figures went back 470,000 years and Egyptian ones over 50,000 years. Vives, whose own religious views are in some doubt, did not press the point, and took the accepted way out, suggesting that the pagans invented these figures in order to make themselves the creators of everything in the human world. (This line was still being taken to account for the pagan data by Father Richard Simon and Bishop Stillingfleet more than a century later.) I doubt that Vives was a serious Christian in view of the persecution of his family by the Spanish Inquisition, and in view of his Jewish origins. His general views about human behavior were quite naturalistic.[17] But neither he nor other Renaissance scholars were ready to challenge the Biblical world-view in print, or maybe even in theory. However, by amassing the pagan historical data that conflicted with *Genesis*, and publicizing it, they made European intellectuals aware of the problem of reconciling, or explaining away the conflicts as Philippe de Mornay tried to do.[18] Besides dredging up the recorded claims of ancient writers about the length of human history, they also reported the Aztec claims about the age of the world.[19] In so doing

---

[16] Cf. Vives' commentary in St. Augustine, *Of the Citie of God*, Book XII, chap. 10, pp. 450-51. This text is discussed in Ernest A. Strathmann, *Sir Walter Ralegh, A Study in Elizabethan Skepticism* (New York, 1951), 200.

[17] On Vives' Jewish background and his naturalism, see the excellent new study on him, Carlos G. Noreña, *Juan Luis Vives* (The Hague, 1970).

[18] Cf. Strathmann, 200.

[19] Cf. Jean Jacquot, "Thomas Harriot's Reputation for Impiety," *Notes and Records of the Royal Society of London* 9 (1952), 170.

they provided some of the basic information that La Peyrère and his friend, Claude Saumaise, were to use to pose a fundamental question in the next century about the validity of Scriptural history.

The discovery of America was to become more upsetting for European thinkers. The recent study by Huddleston on theories about the origins of the American Indians from 1492-1729 shows that neither Columbus nor Vespucci saw a serious problem in integrating the Indian world into the Scriptural one.[20] Bendyshe, in one of the earliest histories of anthropology, written in 1865, mentions a declaration of 1512 that the Indians were descendants of Adam and Eve.[21] Various Spanish writers, starting with Pedro Martir de Angleria identified Hispaniola with Solomon's Ophir. However, Magellan's voyage and further exploration of America made it more difficult to explain how people from the Biblical world got to the New World. If everyone alive was a descendant of Noah and his family, then the ancestry of the Indians and the logistics of their travels required explanation. As Huddleston shows, most of the debate that raged over more than 200 years was over alternate theories of where the Indians came from, Phoencia, China, the Lost Tribes, Norway, etc.[22] However, starting with Paracelsus in 1520, a polygenetic explanation was proffered. The Indians had not come; they were created in the New World. They were *not* Adamites.

Around 1520 an English poet, John Rastell, had said, regarding the Indians,

> But howe the people furst began
> In that countrey or whens they cam
> For clerkes it is a questyon.[23]

Paracelsus is generally credited with the first answer that does not try to derive the Indians from the Adamic-Noachide world. His theory is not a pre-Adamite one, but rather offered the possibility that the Indians are descended from a second and different Adam. In the *Astronomia magna*, he wrote:

---

[20] Lee Eldridge Huddleston, *Origins of the American Indians, European Concepts, 1492-1729* (Austin and London, 1967), 3-6.

[21] T. Bendyshe, "The History of Anthropology," in *Memoirs read before the Anthropological Society of London*, 1863-64, I, 353.

[22] Cf. Huddleston. See also Don Cameron Allen, *The Legend of Noah* (Urbana, 1963).

[23] John Rastell, *A New Interlude and a mery, of the nature of the iiii Elements*, published London c. 1520, cited in Huddleston, p. 8.

> We are all descended from Adam. And I cannot refrain from making a brief mention of those who have been found in hidden islands and are still little known. To believe they have descended from Adam is difficult to conceive—that Adam's children have gone to the hidden islands. But one should well consider, that these people are from a different Adam. It will be difficult to maintain, that they are related on the basis of flesh and blood.[24]

However, Paracelsus added two further features to his theory which kept it from being automatically heretical. The first was that "it is credible that they (the Indians) were born there after the Deluge"; and the second that "perhaps they have no souls."[25] The first possibility would not make the double Adam theory necessarily contrary to Scripture, since no challenge is raised to the account in *Genesis*; just an addition is made to what is discussed in it. The second possibility eliminates theological difficulties. If the Indians have no souls, they are not involved in the human-Divine drama, as it works out in Providential history. Paracelsus' first point, of the independent creation of the Indians *after* the Flood, was held to as late as Lord Kames' account in the eighteenth century, as a way of explaining the racial differences without directly challenging Scripture.[26] Paracelsus' second point has been misunderstood by the historians of anthropology, who are anxious to make Paracelsus the modern originator of the polygenetic theory. Paracelsus, in raising the possibility that Indians do not have souls, immediately links this with the case of nymphs, sirens, sylphs, salamanders, etc. As the great expert on Paracelsus,

---

[24] Theophrast von Hohenheim, called Paracelsus, *Sämtliche Werke*, Abt. I, Bd. 12, ed. Karl Sudhoff (Munich and Berlin, 1929), 35 : "also seind wir alle von Adam hie. und so mag ich das nit underlassen, von denen ein kleine meldung zu tun, die in verborgenen insulen gefunden seind worden und noch verborgen sind, das sie von Adam zu sein geglaubt mögen werden, mag sichs nit befinden, das Adams kinder seind komen in die verborgenen insulen, sonder wol zu bedenken, das dieselbigen leut von einem anderen Adam seind; dan dahin wird es schwerlich komen, das sie fleisch und bluts halben uns gefreunt sein." The translation is that given by Slotkin (p. 42), who gives other similar texts from the *Astronomia Magna* and *Weiteres zum Astronomia magna*.

[25] These citations are given in Bendyshe (p. 354) to the 1605 edition, which I have not been able to consult. I have not yet found the passage he was quoting, but these views are like those found in the discussions in both the *Astronomia magna*, and *Weiteres zum Astronomia magna*, as well as in *De nymphis, sylphis, pygmaeis et salamandris et de caeteris spiritibus*, in *Sämtliche Werke*, Abt. I, Bd. 14, ed. Karl Sudhoff (Berlin, 1933), 115-151. The latter work is translated in *Four Treatises of Theophrastus von Hohenheim called Paracelsus*, trans. Henry Sigerist (Baltimore, 1941).

[26] Cf. Henry Home, Lord Kames, *Sketches of the History of Man* (Glasgow, 1819), II, 236-40, where the view is developed from a conjecture of Buffon's.

Dr. Walter Pagel, has pointed out to me in a discussion of the text, these entities are all involved in Paracelsus' theory of wild spirits that pervade the world. They are not other human species, but special kinds of sub-human beings.[27]

Paracelsus, in raising the possibility of an independent origin of the American Indians, set the stage for further daring speculation leading to the full pre-Adamite theory of La Peyrère. (In the major refutation of La Peyrère by Samuel Desmarets, the ancestors of the theory are seen as Maimonides, in the chapter cited, Paracelsus, and those who believe in the eternity of the world, Cesalpino and some of the Socinians of the time.)[28] Some people debated whether satyrs were Adamic.[29] Others pursued the polygenetic implications of Paracelsus' view, while almost all scholars were still trying to place all of the new information about the inhabitants of the globe within the Biblical context.

Giordano Bruno presented some indications of polygenetic and even pre-Adamite speculation, which may have directly influenced the crypto-pre-Adamite thinking in the circle of Sir Walter Ralegh. Pondering over the racial differences between the Ethiopians, the American Indians, various mythical beings, like those in the caves of Neptune, the Pygmies, Giants, etc., Bruno said that all these beings "cannot be traced to the same descent, nor are they sprung from the generative force of a single progenitor."[30] From Cabalistic literature,

---

[27] It is obvious in reading Paracelsus' discussions, he was not really concerned with the American Indian problem, but rather with developing his own cosmology and theology, and incorporating the Indians into it. The best studies on Paracelsus' theory are Walter Pagel, *Paracelsus : An Introduction to Philosophical Medicine in the Era of the Renaissance* (Basel and New York, 1958), and *Das medizinische Weltbild des Paracelsus, seine Zusammenhange mit Neuplatonismus und Gnosis* (Wiesbaden, 1962). I am most grateful to Dr. Pagel for his help in discussing with me Paracelsus' role in the development of the pre-Adamite theory.

[28] Samuel Desmarets, *Refutatio Fabulae Prae-Adamiticae* (Groningen, 1656). "Quaeritur primo, An Adam, Primus omnium hominum & totius generis humani Parens sit agnoscendus ?" Affirm., pp. 1-9. Maimonides, Crellius, Cesalpino, Paracelsus, and the Kabbala are discussed as offering negative answers. Regarding Paracelsus, Desmarets put his view in relation to the problem of nymphs, mermaids, sirens, Tritons, Pygmies, sylphs, gnomes and salamanders.

[29] See, for instance, F. Hédelin, *Des Satyres, brutes, monstres et demons* (Paris, 1627).

[30] Jordani Bruni Nolani, *Opera Latine Conscripta*, ed. F. Fiorentino et al. (Naples, 1879-91; repr. Stuttgart and Bad, 1962), I, pt. 2, p. 282 : "Quia multicolores sunt hominum species, nec enim generatio nigra Aethiopum, et qualem producit America fulva,

he had learned of a theory that mankind came from three protoplasts, one giving rise to the Jews, and the other two, created two days earlier, (hence pre-Adamitic) to the rest of mankind. Bruno had also heard of a similar Chinese theory deriving mankind from three differently named protoplasts, 20,000 years ago.[31]

Bruno, like Paracelsus, was partly concerned with accounting for the new data brought to light by voyages of discovery, and partly in placing it, and everything else into a speculative Renaissance cosmology, influenced by Hermetic and Cabalistic views. In his *Spaccio della Bestia trionfante* of 1584, Bruno has the gods discussing what they shall make men believe, counter to the evidence, and this includes making them not believe the pagan records that the world is over 20,000 years old, or the findings about "a new part of the world, where are found memorials of ten thousand years and more."[32] (Imerti, in his notes to his translation of this text of Bruno, suggests it was inspired by accounts of the Aztec Calendar Stone, which had been hidden after the Conquest. It came to light in 1551, was buried by the Spanish ecclesiastical authorities in 1558, and rediscovered again in 1790.)[33] It is also suggested that it might be better to affirm that the American Indians are not men, though they resemble them in shape and intelligence, and often are wiser about the gods. Bruno had also suggested in some passages that men as well as animals and plants might be generated from the womb of Nature where they were.[34]

Bruno was in London from 1583-85, where he wrote the *Spaccio*. He may have met or directly influenced those who, a few years later, were directly accused of holding the pre-Adamite theory, and developing an atheistical or naturalistic picture of the world. Sir Walter Ralegh was accused of running a school for atheists from 1592 onward.[35]

Udaque Neptuni vivens occulta sub antris, Pygmeique iugis ducentes saecula clausis, Cives venarum Telluris, quique minaerae Adstant custodes, atque Austri monstra Gigantes, Progeniem referunt similem, primique parentis Unius vires cunctorum progenitrices."

[31] Text given in Slotkin, 43.

[32] Giordano Bruno, *Spaccio della Bestia trionfante*, in *Dialoghi italiani : Dialoghi metafisici e dialoghi morali*, with notes by Giovanni Gentile, 3rd ed., ed. Giovanni Aquilecchia (Florence, 1958), 797-98.

[33] Giordano Bruno, *The Expulsion of the Triumphant Beast*, trans. and ed. Arthur D. Imerti (New Brunswick, 1964), 307, n. 52.

[34] Bruno, *Cabala del cavallo Pegaseo*, Dialogo Secundo, in *Dialoghi Italiani*, 882-91.

[35] On the accusations against Ralegh in this period, see Pierre Lefranc, *Sir Walter Ralegh, écrivain, l'œuvre et les idées* (Quebec, 1968), chap. xii.

Thomas Nashe declared in 1592 and 1593, "I heare say there be mathematicians abroad that will proove men before Adam" and, "Impudently they persist in it, that the late discovered Indians are able to shew antiquities thousands before Adam." [36] It has been assumed that Nashe was referring to Ralegh's friend, Thomas Harriot, as the mathematician, and probably to Harriot and Christopher Marlowe as the impudent ones. After Marlowe was killed reports were filed by a government undercover agent that "Marloe tolde him that hee hath read the Atheist lecture to Sir Walter Ralegh & others."[37] Another agent, Baines, whose report was sent to Queen Elizabeth, gave the details of Marlowe's supposed lecture in which he was alleged to have stressed the conflict between the Biblical account of the world as 6,000 years old, and the Indian and ancient pagan accounts which made the world about 16,000 years old.[38] After Marlowe's death, Ralegh was accused over the next decade of being irreligious, having irreligious cronies, and encouraging disbelief in Christianity, all of this leading up to his imprisonment.

Much scholarly ink has been spilled throughout the years over the question whether Harriot, Marlowe and Ralegh actually held the pre-Adamite theory, and were atheists. Nothing in the published or unpublished writings of these authors so far found indicates they ever stated such views. Ralegh and Harriot had been in the New World, and had first-hand knowledge of the facts in the case. Harriot's account, *A Briefe and True Report of the New Found Land of Virginia* (1588), shows he discussed Indian views of the creation of mankind with the natives. He later worked on Biblical chronology, and is supposed to have calculated the dating used by Ralegh in his *Historie of the World*. Harriot's papers show he was influenced by Bruno, but apparently after the 1592-93 charges.[39] The quantity and quality of the attacks on Harriot, Marlowe and Ralegh seem to indicate that something unorthodox was going on in their circle. I lean towards the evaluation of two French scholars, Jacquot and Lefranc, and Paul Kocher, about the evidence, namely, that in Harriot's case, he

---

[36] Thomas Nashe, *Pierce Pennilesse* and *Christs Teares over Jerusalem* in *Works*, ed. R.B. McKerrow (London, 1910), I, 172; II, 116.

[37] This is in the Cholmley report, published in F.-C. Danchin, "Etudes critiques sur Christopher Marlowe," *Revue germanique* 9 (1913), 576.

[38] The text appears in Kocher, *Christopher Marlowe*, 34-36. See also Lefranc, 375-77.

[39] On Harriot, see Jacquot's "Thomas Harriot's Reputation for Impiety," 164-87; and Lefranc, esp. 344-52.

was exploring all sorts of 'new' ideas (some recovered from antiquity), and was influenced by Bruno, and by the results of the explorations. Ralegh, as Lefranc shows, was also influenced by Italian ideas. When Ralegh wrote the *Historie of the World* in the Tower of London, no sign of the pre-Adamite theory appeared in it. The radical view, that Lefranc uncovered, attributed the reception of the fundamental Revelation to Hermes Trismegistus rather than Moses.[40] The attacks on Harriot, Marlowe and Ralegh, I think, cannot just be dismissed as attempts to blacken their characters. The attacks attribute to them a specific, detailed view about the Christian religion, and about the pre-Adamite theory. The form of the theory stated by Nashe and Baines is more precise than any preceding version, and concentrates more directly on the American Indian problem. This would seem to indicate that the Ralegh group, in the 1590's, in some manner had raised the pre-Adamite theory, especially with reference to the explorer data. Harriot and Ralegh had more direct and detailed information than speculative thinkers like Paracelsus and Bruno. However, the Ralegh group was evidently either too afraid or too tentative to commit even the most restrained version of the pre-Adamite theory to paper.

Elizabethan pre-Adamism, whether actual or in the minds of the beholders, was the most advanced form of the theory to be presented during the Renaissance. In the data we have, it consisted of a straight-forward presentation of the conflict between the explorer data and pagan historical claims, and the Biblical view. However, the only indications of any general counter-theory to the Biblical view are in vague charges that the Ralegh group did not believe in Christianity, and tended towards some form of naturalism. Unfortunately, we possess no statement *by* Harriot, Marlowe or Ralegh as to what their pre-Adamic views really were, or what they made of this theory. As far as the future development of the theory went, neither the rumors and attacks against the Ralegh group, or their possible covert views seem to have played any role whatsoever. When the theory became a major theme, with the dispersion of La Peyrère's views, even in England, no reference is made to an earlier English version.

In the course of the sixteenth century, the revival of pagan histor-

---

[40] Lefranc's chapter IX on Machiavelli's influence on Ralegh, and chapter XIII, placing Ralegh's religious views in the context of Italian ideas of the period are very interesting. However, I am somewhat sceptical that Ralegh was as immersed in Italian libertinism and Averroism as Lefranc interprets him.

ical accounts, and the puzzlement over the explorer data, led some avant-garde intellectuals to consider radical versions of the pre-Adamite theory. At least in England the opponents saw the dangerous implications for the Christian world-view. Theoreticians, such as Paracelsus and Bruno, were probably too speculative and deviant to be taken seriously as offering satisfactory explanations of the new data. The English pre-Adamite theorists, if such they were, enunciated no theory, but just the clash of an accepted cosmology with new information. Had the pre-Adamite theory not been raised anew in the seventeenth century (and not been accepted by the anthropologists of the nineteenth century), the few versions of it in the Renaissance would have been written off as bizarre reflections of some of the strange figures produced in those strange times. However, in terms of what was to happen, the Renaissance proved to be a period of transformation from odd speculations mainly intended to embellish and reinforce the Biblical picture of the world, to a jarring confrontation of an accepted world view of the nature and destiny of man with ancient and modern facts that simply did not fit it.

Huddleston shows quite clearly that all those who wrote at any length on the problem of the origin of the Indians in the sixteenth century held that the Indians were part of the Adamic world. Papal decrees asserted (in contrast to Paracelsus) that the Indians were truly men. The debate that went on among the experts was whether the Indians came from Carthage, Atlantis, China, Palestine, etc. They sought clues in ancient pagan and Judeo-Christian writings.[41] Late in the century, the great Spanish theorist, Joseph de Acosta still insisted : "The reason which forces me to say that the first men of these Indies came from Europe or Asia is so as not to contradict the Holy Scripture which clearly teaches that all men descended from Adam, and thus we can give no other origin to man in the Indies." [42] So Acosta tried to work out a land-bridge theory. In 1607, Gregorio García, in his *Origen de los indios*, contended that the first fundamental premise to considering the problem was that all "men and women had, and have, since the begining of the World, proceeded, and taken their beginning and origin from our first parents Adam and Eve; and sub-

---

[41] See Huddleston, chap. I.

[42] Quoted in Huddleston, p. 50, from Acosta's *Historia natural y moral de las Indias* (Mexico, 1940), 75-76. Huddleston also quotes Juan de Castellanos as writing a year before Acosta, in 1589, "Pues no son en estado de inocencia que hijos son de Adán y descendientes" (p. 46).

sequently from Noah and his sons, who were all who remained alive after the General Deluge."[43] The theorists might cling to a monogenetic explanation, but certain radical Renaissance speculation had already set the stage for a revolutionary reconsideration not only of the problem of the origins of the American Indians, but also of the authenticity of the Biblical account itself.

In the period from Bruno and the Ralegh group to La Peyrère, practically nothing seems to have developed to contribute to the theory. The only figure who may have played a further role was Vanini. In his *De admirandis naturae reginae deaque mortalium arcanis*, he offered the view that some "have dreamed" that the first man originated from mud, putrified by monkeys, swine and frogs. Other atheists, he reported, held that only the Ethiopians came from monkeys.[44]

Francis Bacon had commented that the people of the West Indies were probably younger than the inhabitants of the Old World.[45] And Campanella advanced the thesis of the plurality of worlds, in which the inhabitants of the other worlds were not Adamites.[46]

In spite of the evidence of the clash of ancient historical data and the findings of the explorers with the accepted Biblical view, the academic and theological establishment managed to remain quiescent about the problem, assisting only in burning or killing such of the worst offenders as Bruno, Vanini and Marlowe. The crisis of the pre-Adamite theory occurred when the Renaissance developments were formed into a new Biblical interpretation by Isaac La Peyrère, 1596-1676. La Peyrère, unlike his brave predecessors, put his theory not just in terms of the clash of data, but principally in terms of a new theology. His pre-Adamite theory was generated from the Bible itself, and then reinforced by the Renaissance developments. He was able to offer, within the Judeo-Christian world view, a theory that would encompass the new data, but at a tremendous price.

To appreciate La Peyrère, as the culmination of Renaissance speculations and ruminations, I think one has to take him at his word, his

---

[43] Quoted in Huddleston, 61.

[44] Lucilio Vanini, *De admirandis naturae reginae deaque mortalium arcanis* (Paris, 1616), 35. The passage was considered significant enough in the history of anthropology that it is quoted both in Bendyshe, 355, and Slotkin, 80.

[45] Francis Bacon, "Of vicissitude of things," *Essays* (London, 1958), 232. Bacon just said, without comment regarding the Biblical view, that "if you consider well, of the People of the *West Indies*, it it is very probable that they are a Newer, or a Younger People, than the People of the Old World."

[46] Citations from Tommaso Campanella given in Slotkin, 80-81.

printed word. He was not a scholar in the Renaissance sense, and gave few indications of his sources. He read or knew about the trivial pre-Adamism in Maimonides. His theory indicates that he knew about Guillaume Postel's Messianism and probably Judah Halevi's views. Other than that, his theory seems to have been self-generated out of his reading of the Bible in Latin and French. (His friend Richard Simon claimed he knew neither Greek nor Hebrew).[47] When La Peyrère became notorious, after his book on the Pre-Adamites was published in 1655, he offered several different origins of his theory. He attributed it to a dead brother, to his pastor, and to his reading of St. Paul's *Romans* 5:12-15. The latter seems most probable in view of the form of his argument.

To appreciate his theory, one first has to see it as a whole. La Peyrère was a Calvinist of Portuguese Jewish origins from Bordeaux. He arrived in Paris to work for the Prince of Condé in 1640. In Paris he was in the circle of Mersenne, Hobbes, Gassendi, La Mothe le Vayer, Grotius, etc.[48] In 1642-43 he wrote his masterpiece, a theological system based on the pre-Adamite theory, and proving the imminent coming of the Messiah, who would rule with "le roi universel," the King of France.[49] The first part of his work, the *Prae-Adamitae* was dedicated to Richelieu, and banned by him. The second part, the Messianic section, *Du Rappel des Juifs*, was published in 1643. The theoretical guts of his case only circulated sub-rosa until Queen Christina encouraged or paid for the publication of *Prae-Adamitae* in 1655.[50]

---

[47] Richard Simon wrote a brief biography of La Peyrère in a letter to Mr. Z.A., Paris 1688, *Lettres*, II, 23-28. He reported (p. 27) that La Peyrère "ne savoit ni grec ni hebreu."

[48] For biographical details see my introduction to the forthcoming Olms photo-reproduction ed. of La Peyrère's *Men before Adam* as well as the discussions of La Peyrère in René Pintard, *Le Libertinage érudit* (Paris, 1943); David Rice McKee, "Isaac de la Peyrère, a Precursor of the 18th Century Critical Deists," *PMLA* 59 (1944), 456-485; Leo Strauss, *Spinoza's Critique of Religion* (New York, 1965), chap. iii; Hans Joachim Schoeps, *Philosemitismus im Barock*, and *Barocke Juden, Christen Judenchristen* (Bern and Munich, 1965). Schoeps (*Philosemitismus*, pp. 16-18) had seen that La Peyrère's theory was that of a Marrano. La Peyrère's friends considered him a Jew, and he indicated that he *was* in St. Paul's sense. His epitaph begins :
"La Peyrère ici git, ce bon Israélite
Huguenot, Catholique, enfin Préadamite."

[49] Originally La Peyrère seems to have thought of Condé as "le roi universel"; later he gave the role to Pope Alexander VII, and finally to Louis XIV.

[50] On Queen Christina's role, see Sven Stolpe, *Christina of Sweden*, ed. Sir Alec Randall (New York, 1966), 130. La Peyrère was living next door to Christina when she was in Belgium in 1654-55.

The letters of the time indicated that his work was read in manuscript all over Europe, was refuted in 1643 by Grotius, was commented on by all the savants. The whole theory, the *Prae-Adamitae* plus *Du Rappel des Juifs*, is a Messianic vision of a Marrano, establishing the central role in the imminent Messianic age of the Jewish Christians. We lack the original version of the *Prae-Adamitae*. Apparently it consisted of the Biblical argument that *within* Scripture alone, it can be established that there were men before Adam, and that the Bible is *only* the history of the Jews, not the history of mankind. This case is made by analyzing St. Paul's views on the origins of sin through Adam (hence a sinless world must have pre-existed), and analyzing the evidence in *Genesis* that there must have been people prior to Adam. By critical examination of the creation stories in *Genesis*, the problem of Cain's wife, Lilith, etc., La Peyrère tried to show that non-Adamites are involved in the Biblical presentation. Then, as a result of Grotius' criticisms, of La Peyrère's involvement with Saumaise, who had gathered together the ancient chronological data in his *De Annis Climactericis* (1648), and of La Peyrère's studies on Greenland and Iceland, he was able to fortify his case with classical, explorer and anthropological data. Grotius had called La Peyrère's view a dream, and contended the Indians were of Norwegian origin, descendants from Leif Erikkson's expedition.[51] La Peyrère, during his stay in Copenhagen, 1644-47, gathered information on Iceland and Greenland, showing that the Eskimos were there before the Norse invasions, and that it was more likely that the Eskimos came from America than that the Indians came from the arctic.[52] Saumaise aided the building up of La Peyrère's case by putting together the ancient pagan claims about astronomy and astrology, showing that Chaldean, Egyptian, and other data went far back beyond the Biblical dating.[53] La Peyrère

---

[51] Hugo Grotius, *Dissertatio altera de Origine Gentium Americanarum adversus obtrectatorem* (n. p., 1643). The attack on La Peyrère is on pp. 13-14.

[52] Cf. Isaac La Peyrère, *Relation du Groenland* (Paris, 1647), and *Relation de l'Islande* (Paris, 1663). They were both written as letters to La Mothe le Vayer, the latter dated Dec. 18, 1644, the former June 18, 1646. In the *Relation du Groenland* (pp. 273-76), La Peyrère argued that it is more probable that the Eskimos come from the Indians. The long correspondence of La Peyrère with the Danish savant, Ole Worm, is also interesting on this matter. Cf. *Olai Wormii et ad eum Doctorum Vivorum Epistolae*, 2 vols. (Copenhagen, 1751), 916-957.

[53] Claude Saumaise, *De Annis Climactericis* (London, 1648), Praefatio.

wrote Saumaise thanking him for his scholarly efforts "on behalf of my pre-Adamites."[54]

The point in La Peyrère's theory, unlike any previous form of pre-Adamism, was to separate Jewish history from secular history. Jewish history, for La Peyrère, was providential; secular history just a pointless state of nature. After an indefinite period of sordid, brutal pre-Adamitic history, God created Adam, the first Jew, to commence the salvation history of all mankind. This history runs through three main stages, the election of the Jews starting with Adam, the rejection of the Jews at the time of Jesus, and the recall of the Jews to the central role in Providential history, which is to take place at any moment. This recall is to take place by (a) the conversion of the Jews to a minimal Christianity, (b) the converts (i.e., Marranos) joining with the King of France (a theory possibly borrowed from Guillaume Postel), (c) the converts rebuilding Jerusalem, and (d) the coming of the Jewish Messiah who will rule the world with the converts and the King of France.[55]

To make his theory more than just one more Messianic vision, La Peyrère adduced a powerful collection of evidence to show, as Judah Halevi had claimed, that Jewish history is the inner core of world history, and that the converts were the crucial actors in the seventeenth-century culmination of the Divine historical drama. La Peyrère called his view "a theological system" based on the news that there were men before Adam. Unlike his predecessors, he built up a system within Judeo-Christianity, and used the classical historical and new explorer and anthropological data to buttress his case. In so doing, he, of course, triggered off a most powerful criticism of the authenticity and value of the Bible. Once his internal evidence within the Bible was taken seriously, it then became exceedingly difficult to maintain Scripture as *the* account of the origins and destiny of mankind. Besides deriving pre-Adamism from the Biblical texts, La Peyrère also initiated the study of the Bible as a historical document by challenging whether Moses wrote the text we have, and whether the text we possess is authentic. He proposed a way of recon-

---

[54] Mentioned by La Peyrère in his letter to De La Mare, June 1660, BN. Coll. Moreau 846, f. 286^v.

[55] La Peyrère's theological history is analyzed in my introduction to *Men before Adam*, in my introduction to the forthcoming photoreproduction, edition Olms, of *Du Rappel des Juifs*, and in my "The Marrano Theology of Isaac La Peyrère," *Studi internazionali di filosofia* 5 (1973), 97-126.

ciling pagan history with the Bible, and a means of accepting the explorer data as independent of Biblical history. The currents that were developing in the sixteenth-century ruminations came to a climax in La Peyrère's work. All the new information could make sense if one were willing to isolate Jewish history from secular history. La Peyrère tried to do this so that Jewish history would remain in the center of the stage, while secular history recorded the milling around of the various kinds of pre-Adamites; the world, however, would be saved through the activities of the Jews. (It is interesting to note that in one way La Peyrère was more tolerant than anyone else of his time. In his theory everybody would be saved no matter what they believed or what group they belonged to. Jewish history was the way the salvation drama worked out, but both actors and audience would participate in the ultimate results.)[56]

La Peyrère combined the information gained through the rediscovery of the pagan historians, the explorer data, the pre-Adamite elements within the Bible, and the possibility of an eternal universe into a theory still centered in Judeo-Christianity. But he was, as he sadly reported, immediately rejected by all the Jewish and Christian theologians. He was refuted *ad nauseam* during the seventeenth century. He was arrested and forced to recant. But his accomplishment, in a form he probably did not anticipate, quickly opened the door to a non-religious interpretation of the nature and destiny of man. Spinoza, Richard Simon and Vico, each stressing different elements in his theory, developed the bases for a secular evaluation of human history.[57] Spinoza made the reduction of the Bible to a mere account of Jewish history a stepping-stone to a naturalistic interpretation of world affairs. Early Hebrew views could be interpreted as part of the history of human superstition. The course of human events could be understood in terms of psychology and sociology. Simon made the Bible an object of secular historical study, to be interpreted not as the basis of history, but in terms of the best available historical information. Vico accepted the isolation of Jewish history from world history. World history could be studied scientifically, while Jewish history remained absurd because it was directed by God. The further developments over the centuries of historical, anthropological, archeological and geological

---

[56] This appears in the final chapter of *Prae-Adamitae*.

[57] La Peyrère's influence on Spinoza, Simon and Vico is discussed in a paper of mine, "Biblical Criticism and Social Science," in the *Boston Studies on the Philosophy of Science* 14 (1974), 339-60, and in the introduction to *Men before Adam*.

information finally made a secularized form of La Peyrère's theory part of the commonsense of educated mankind. The Bible could be accepted as an historical document exhibiting the views of an early group from about 1200 B.C. to 100 A.D. The polygenetic origins of mankind could be seen as a plausible explanation of the varieties of the human species. In terms of this the Enlightenment and nineteenth-century thinkers could work out a naturalistic, evolutionary picture of human development.

This tremendous transformation of the general framework in which the nature and destiny of man was understood grew in part out of a few brave Renaissance attempts to advance a new form of the pre-Adamite theory. The humanistic information, the results of the Voyages of Discovery, the consideration of various naturalistic theories provided the base from which a revolutionary systematic form of the pre-Adamite theory could be launched. An alienated visionary, La Peyrère, caught in a world between Judaism and Christianity created by the Spanish forced conversion of the Jews, was then able to offer a Messianic version of pre-Adamism to justify the role of his Marrano group in the fate of the world. The rapid secularization of La Peyrère's reconciliation of ancient history, the explorer data, early anthropology and Biblical reconstruction provided one of the fundamental bases of the modern intellectual world.[58]

Washington University

---

[58] A recent study by Jean-Paul Oddos, *Recherches sur la vie et l'œuvre d'Isaac de La-peyrère, 1596 ?-1676*, Thèse de 3ᵉ Cycle, Université des sciences sociales, Grenoble II, 1971-74, holds, contrary to the view which I have defended, that La Peyrère was a genuine Protestant. His work came to my attention after the present article was completed and in press. I hope to discuss Oddos' work on another occasion.

THE FLY AGAINST THE ELEPHANT :
FLANDINUS AGAINST POMPONAZZI ON FATE

RICHARD LEMAY

> "At adversarii reverentia forte quidam protinus obturatis auribus reclamabunt : 'Episcopus, hoc est, musca, cum Pomponatio, hoc est, cum Elephanto congredi audet.' Sed ii nos minime turbant, nec nos ut lupi raucos reddunt..."
>
> Flandinus, *Apologia*, "Ad Pomponatii P. auditores Sermo," f. 2ᵛ.

According to a consensus of most historians, the works of Pietro Pomponazzi which date from the period 1516 to 1520 represent a watershed between the medieval Aristotelian tradition and Renaissance thought. The sequence of works that followed the publication of the *De immortalitate animae*, that is, Pomponazzi's own *Apologia* (1517) and *Defensorium* (1519) as well as the spate of mild or angry refutations directed against each and all of these works, established this controversy about the soul as a crucial stage in the coming of age of Western thought. Two works unprinted[1] in Pomponazzi's own lifetime appeared to put the seal on his determination to turn his back on medieval theology and philosophy, especially in their use of Aristotle as a support. These works, each of which was completed in 1520, are the *De incantationibus*, an attack on the notion of miracles, and the *De fato*, a repudiation of the Christian in favor of the Stoic doctrine of fate.[2]

---

[1] In that early age of the printing press, leaving a work unprinted was not tantamount to keeping it from public knowledge. This is shown by the large number of manuscript copies of Pomponazzi's *De incantationibus* and *De fato* which circulated before these works were printed two generations later. But the fate of an unprinted work was uncertain : manuscript copies of Flandinus' works never multiplied.

[2] The *De incantationibus* was printed for the first time in Basel in 1556 by G. Grataroli and again in the same city and by the same publisher in 1567 when it was accompanied by an edition of the *De fato*.

Among the opponents of Pomponazzi's doctrines was the suffragan bishop of his own native town of Mantua,[3] an Augustinian Hermit named Ambrosius Flandinus. Reacting violently to the publication and diffusion of Pomponazzi's ideas, he wrote two works with the intention of upholding orthodox tenets of Catholic theology in the areas treated by Pomponazzi, but he stretched his concern to include traditional philosophical views as well. His first work, which is on the immortality of the soul, was published in 1519 at Mantua[4] and has been duly noticed, though scarely studied by historians.[5] The second work, which is directed against Pomponazzi's doctrine of fate, has remained in manuscript until today; since its contents and tone are virtually unknown, we shall examine it here in this paper in honor of Professor Paul O. Kristeller, through whose inexhaustible love of learning and solicitude for its continuation and expansion we owe the privilege of being able to study it. A fuller and hence truer picture of the intellectual climate in the Italy of the early sixteenth century should emerge, we hope, from our examination of this work of Flandinus, whose scholarly merits and intellectual strength, however, are no match for those of a Pomponazzi.

Flandinus' Encounter with Pomponazzi

Born at Naples in 1462, the same year as Pomponazzi, Ambrosius Flandinus entered the Order of the Augustinian Hermits in his native city and there received his early education.[6] After 1503 he is to be

---

[3] The titular bishop of Mantua at that time was Cardinal Sigismondo Gonzaga. However, since he was also Papal Legate and member of the Roman Curia, he could not attend much to his pastoral duties in Mantua. Consequently, a suffragan bishop was needed to fill in for the titular bishop. Cardinal Sigismondo died in 1524 and his nephew Ercole, the son of Isabella d'Este, after much pressure on Clement VII, was made a cardinal and seems to have succeeded to all his dignities. In the colophon of his commentary on Plato's *Alcibiades*, completed in 1526, Flandinus indicates that Ercole is already by then the "bishop elect" of Mantua and his immediate superior : "Expliciunt commentaria ... elaborata sub umbra [alarum] illustrissimi et reverendissimi Herculis Gonzagae et electi Episcopi Mantuani ...." (P. O. Kristeller, *Iter Italicum*, I [London and Leiden, 1963], 275). On Isabella, see Julia Cartwright, *Isabella d'Este, Marchioness of Mantua, 1479-1539 : A Study of the Renaissance*, 2 vols. (New York, 1903).

[4] With the title *De animarum immortalitate contra Petrum Pomponatium* (Mantua, 1519).

[5] The first general description of this work is found in Giovanni Di Napoli, *L'immortalità dell'anima nel Rinascimento* (Turin, 1963), 300-301.

[6] A short biography of Ambrosius Flandinus can be found in Fr. Lauchert, *Die italienischen literarischen Gegner Luthers* (Freiburg, 1912), 239-240, who combines data

found in Northern Italy, first in Piacenza, and then in Bologna, where he was *regens* in 1508.[7] He appears to have been in Naples again some time between 1509 and 1514,[8] but he then appears once more in Mantua as a noted preacher.[9] After a short trip to Rome and Naples during the year 1517, he returned to Mantua with the title of bishop *in partibus* of Lamocensis and suffragan of Mantua.[10] During the latter trip, possibly undertaken in connection with his elevation to the episcopal rank, he met Agostino Nifo in Naples and discussed with him Pomponazzi's recent work *De immortalitate animae*. Flandinus seems to have spent the remainder of his life in Mantua where he died in 1531 at the age of 69. From the pulpit of the cathedral church at Mantua—a not insignificant post considering the enormous political and cultural influence of the Gonzagas—Flandinus exercised his undisputed talent as an orator and thereby gained notoriety among Italian intellectuals and churchmen.[11]

Flandinus' acquaintance with the powerful Gonzaga family introduced him into a society of which Pomponazzi himself was no obscure member. It is important to note, however, the significantly different level of support that each received from such patrons. The only members of the Gonzaga family with whom Flandinus seems to have had direct and friendly relations were Francesco, the Gonzaga ambassador to the papal court in late 1524, and Federico di Bozzolo, to whom he

---

from Ossinger, Tiraboschi and Hurter, adding however some minor errors. For example, the date of Flandinus' promotion to suffragan bishop of Mantua is given as 1519 in Lauchert, while all other evidence, particularly Pomponazzi's *Apologia* III, 1, shows the date to be 1517.

[7] Probably not at the university proper but in the Augustinian Convent of the town.

[8] Lauchert makes him a Provincial of his Order in 1514, which Perini states to be based at Naples. Perini further makes Flandinus a Provincial of the "provinciae coloniae" in 1505.

[9] Perini notes the esteem Pomponazzi expresses for Flandinus' fame as a preacher. Pomponazzi calls him "vir divinissimus ac per universum decantatus" (*Apologia* II, 1) and "praedicatorem celeberrimum" (*Apologia* III, 1). However, Pomponazzi's opinion of the man's learning and courage as found in the same passage must also be noted. The entire first chapter of *Apologia* III is in fact a debunking of Flandinus' learning and character; he is presented as the chief of the *cucullati* who had attacked Pomponazzi's *De immortalitate animae* and lacked sound arguments.

[10] In Pomponazzi's *Apologia*, written in November 1517, Flandinus is described as being merely a monk and preacher at Mantua during the Lent of 1517, but as now suffragan bishop of Mantua, i.e. in November of 1517.

[11] See pp. 76-78 below for the list of his works.

dedicated his *Commentary on the "Parmenides" of Plato*.[12] Both had a somewhat marginal importance in the sphere of the Gonzagas' political, ecclesiastical and cultural influence. And while Cardinal Sigismondo Gonzaga was the titular bishop of Mantua, his relations with his suffragan bishop, Flandinus, are nowhere recorded as intimate or even familiar. On the contrary, although a suffragan bishop in the city and diocese, Flandinus never appears at any of the brilliant gatherings of humanists, artists and politicians at the Mantuan court, nor anywhere in the vast network of correspondents and agents maintained throughout Italy by the Gonzagas.[13] On the other hand, the Marchioness Isabella d'Este and her court showed the highest esteem for Pomponazzi, a native of Mantua, who was then a celebrated professor at Bologna. Isabelle personally entrusted her son Ercole, the future cardinal, to the good care of Pomponazzi during the young man's studies at Bologna from the year 1523 on. Indeed this university had been selected over all others for the education of Ercole precisely because of Pomponazzi's presence there.[14] It is thus difficult to see how Flandinus could have hoped for much support from the court for his attack on Pomponazzi.

A well-known feature of the Renaissance in Italy was the competition among scholars and artists for the patronage of the grandees in Church and politics : one form of this was to dedicate one's work to

---

[12] Flandinus' Commentary on the *Parmenides* of Plato, signed "per Reverendissimum S.T. Doctorem ac Episcopum Lamocensem et Suffraganeum Mantuanum Ambrosium Parthenopeum" (Tiraboschi, VII, 1) was thus composed after 1517, the date of Flandinus' promotion to the episcopate.

[13] Some biographers (Lauchert, 279; Perini, II, 72; Tiraboschi, VII, 1, 246 [ed. Rome, 1784) mention a legation of Flandinus to Pope Clement VII on behalf of the Marquess of Mantua. The only evidence produced is a reference in the Dedication Letter to Pope Clement VII to be found in Flandinus' *Apologia* of 1524 : "Cum ipse mecum conciperem virtutem tuam ... et animi insuper tui spectrum *Francisci Gonzagae*, Illustrissimi Marchionis Mantuani ad tuam Beatitudinem *legati*, tuae quidem Sanctitatis perstudiosi, praeconio effulgeret nitidissimum ..." (f. 1). To read this passage to mean that there was a legation of Flandinus to Clement VII is to misconstrue the text. There is only one legate of the Marquess of Mantua to the Pope mentioned in this text, and he is Francesco Gonzaga. A kinsman of Marquess Federico, then reigning in Mantua, Francesco Gonzaga replaced Castiglione as the Gonzaga ambassador to the Vatican late in the year 1524. (See Cartwright, *Isabella*, II, 245.) Francesco later conspired against the Marquess, now Duke Federico, and was executed. Perini's error in reading Flandinus' letter becomes obvious when he makes Francesco the Marquess of Mantua and takes the legation to be one led by Flandinus.

[14] Cf. Cartwright, II, 212-213.

a powerful personage. While his *De immortalitate animae* of 1516 was dedicated to Marcantonio Contarini, a Venetian patrician, it is only with the *Apologia* of 1517/18, when Pomponazzi clearly feels on the defensive, that he begins to dedicate works to powerful people. The *Apologia* is dedicated to Sigismondo Gonzaga, Cardinal of Mantua and Apostolic Legate; the *De nutritione* of 1521 is again dedicated to a Cardinal, namely, Domenico Grimani, patriarch of Aquileia.[15] The increasing importance in the ecclesiastical dignity of the dedicatees of Pomponazzi's works would suggest that he had become conscious of a need for protection in high ecclesiastical circles. A famous former student of his, Pietro Bembo, now Cardinal and secretary to Pope Leo X, discreetly intervened in 1518 at the height of the attacks against Pomponazzi's *De immortalitate animae* to quash the inquisitorial procedure already initiated on the order of Leo. The result of Bembo's action was that Pomponazzi's teaching contract at Bologna could be renewed that year for a period of eight years and at a considerably increased salary.[16] Another high ecclesiastic, who was himself a former professor, namely, Cardinal Cajetan, was probably operating in favor of Pomponazzi in those troubled days, though with understandable discretion, as Gilson has suggested.[17] The reason for Cajetan's caution was that his fellow Dominican, Bartolomeo Spina, was at that time leading a one-man crusade against the Cardinal, making him directly responsible for Pomponazzi's doctrine of the mortality of the soul according to Aristotle.[18]

In his *Apologia* of 1517 Pomponazzi recounts the amusing story of his encounter with Flandinus, whom he lists as the principal of the "cucullati" who had attacked his doctrine of the soul without giving sound reasons.[19] He had reports to the effect that "a certain brother Ambrosius of Naples," while preaching in the Cathedral of

---

[15] See the 1525 edition of Pomponazzi's works, *Tractatus acutissimi, utillimi et mere peripatetici* ... (Venice, 1525), ff. 112^v-139^v. In the *De nutritione*, I, ch. 14, Pomponazzi argues at length against the *De Theologia Platonica* of Marsilio Ficino.

[16] Cf. Di Napoli, 267 and n. 55. The record of the negotiations conducted by the *Reformatores* on this occasion survives in the Archivio di Stato at Bologna. See Archivio del Reggimento, Ser. Libri Partitorum, vol. 15, f. 155^v.

[17] Etienne Gilson, "L'affaire de l'immortalité de l'âme à Venise au début du XVIe siècle," in *Umanesimo europeo e umanesimo veneziano*, ed. V. Branca (Florence, 1963), 44. Cf. also Di Napoli, 302-309.

[18] See Gilson, 41-50. Gilson (p. 41) singles out Spina as "le plus important [personnage] de la controverse en dehors de Pomponazzi lui-même."

[19] *Apologia*, III, 1 (Venice, 1525), f. 72^v.

Mantua during the Lent of the same year 1517, had delivered a long and subtle sermon in which he claimed to have proved the immortality of the soul. This Ambrosius then added these words : "A certain man from among your fellow citizens, struck with senility and acting with a raving mind, wrote a scribble (*scartabulum*) in which he asserted that souls are mortal." Aroused by the apparent challenge, Pomponazzi says he wrote several letters to brother Ambrosius and further sent messengers entreating him to state his interesting arguments proving the immortality of the soul, but brother Ambrosius never replied. Despairing of the monk's good faith, Pomponazzi ultimately demanded through a friend that he come forward and state his arguments within one month, failing which he would publicly denounce him as "a garrulous and windy talker, a chatterbox, a man of no weight whatsoever." But Pomponazzi then learned that Ambrosius, now bishop of Lamocensis and suffragan of Mantua, had returned from Rome and was staying at the Hermits' Convent in Bologna. He immediately went there in person to see Flandinus in order to hear his arguments. In the encounter, which took place before the assembled monks of the convent, Ambrosius heatedly denied ever having attacked Pomponazzi but claimed, on the contrary, that he always spoke well of him. However, he knew that Pomponazzi had a bad reputation in Mantua and that someone was laying a trap for him.[20] Finally, pressed by Pomponazzi to come to the problem of the immortality of the soul, Ambrosius

---

[20] If this threat was not deliberately contrived by Flandinus to upset Pompazzi, the situation in Mantua must have soon altered in favor of Pomponazzi. The solid support of the Marchioness and the influence of Bembo at the Papal court favored Pomponazzi. But perhaps Flandinus was alluding to the Inquisition and to his friend Spina, who intermittently filled the role of inquisitor in the region before 1523. In Flandinus' *Apologia*, Polixenus, who displays many features that tend to link him with Spina, notes that the Sophista-Pomponazzi's defense sounds at times like a recantation delivered through fear of the inquisitor : "Bonum est quod Palinodiam canit : forte inquisitoris formidat potestatem" (II, 4, f. 65).

Di Napoli (308) praises Spina's liberal attitude of begging Pope Leo X not to silence Pomponazzi so that it might be possible to argue with him. But in the prologue to his *Quaestio de strygibus* (1523), Spina clearly states that he occasionally played the role of inquisitor while teaching both theology and natural philosophy. Since the witch trial in Ferrara which occasioned the composition of the *Quaestio de strygibus* (1523) had taken place some time before, Spina's allusion to his function as inquisitor must include a certain period prior to 1523. For the *Quaestio de strygibus* we have used the Rome edition of 1576, but the colophon of the entire volume (p. 180) indicates that it was first published in 1525. The colophon of the *Quaestio de strygibus* proper (p. 90) gives 1523 as the date of its completion.

fell back on Nifo, whom he said he had just met in Naples and to whom he had shown Pomponazzi's *De immortalitate animae*. He adds that when he met Nifo again a few days later, he learned that Nifo had already written "39 quaterniones" against Pomponazzi's treatise. Given this state of affairs, Ambrosius declared to Pomponazzi that the dispute was now between him and Nifo.

Flandinus' Works

The encounter in Bologna is of capital importance for an understanding of the ensuing relations between Flandinus and Pomponazzi and of the later intellectual activities of Flandinus. Evidently chafing under the sarcasms which Pomponazzi later directed against him in his *Apologia*, Flandinus set about to write his refutation, which finally appeared at Mantua in 1519 under the title *De animarum immortalitate contra Petrum Pomponatium*. Flandinus was then 57 years of age and this was his first work to appear in print. It may thus be said that Pomponazzi's taunt led Flandinus to join the ranks of published authors,[21] but alongside avowed enemies of Pomponazzi, namely, Bartolomeo Spina, Girolamo Amidei [22] and others.

Flandinus' work is in the form of a series of Dialogues between four contestants, on one side, who argue in succession, and the *Sophista*, on the other side, who is obviously Pomponazzi. The four contestants are : Polixenus the Aristotelian, Philoplato the Platonist, Alchindo representing Arab philosophy,[23] and Celestino the theologian. At the conclusion, the four protagonists sit in judgment and condemn the

---

[21] Flandinus was keenly sensitive on this point of being known as a published author. In his *Apologia* (III, dialogus ultimus, f. 250) he makes Pomponazzi taunt him with his lack of notoriety : "[Sophista] Ego in re litteraria non postremas partes tenui. Tu quis sis et unde venias novit nemo."

[22] Cf. Di Napoli, 268.

[23] Di Napoli, 300-301. Flandinus' several commentaries on works of Plato qualified him for the surname of Philoplato in 1519. Although a Philoplato is also introduced in the *Apologia* of 1524, he never speaks and the brunt of the charge against Pomponazzi is carried by Philaletes, a name covering both philosophy and theology as truth. Alchindo is clearly derived from the name of Al-Kindi and stands for Arab philosophy, as Di Napoli has rightly seen. As for Polixenus, who was the Aristotelian in 1519, he stages a somewhat rearguard action in the *Apologia* in favor of natural philosophy, upholding some validity for the "science" of astrology and also for the natural laws by which dream-visions can be explained. Again, this complex of traits in the Polixenus of 1524 suits Spina's activities at that time, namely, as a teacher of natural science and theology.

doctrines of Pomponazzi. In his *Apologia* of 1524, which has almost the same structure and participants, Flandinus boasts that he had silenced Pomponazzi with his own *De animarum immortalitate*.[24] It must be noted, however, that in the same *Apologia*, the character named Polixenus makes a somewhat similar claim,[25] and we shall identify him below with another participant in the immortality controversy.

The only other work published by Flandinus was a collection of Sermons for Lent and the Advent, printed in Venice in 1523.[26] He thus remained known to posterity principally as a preacher of some reputation and a controversialist of slight importance, as Pomponazzi had predicted of him in 1517. Yet his ambition to be known as a scholar and a writer was evidently strong.[27] and he produced a number of other works which remain unprinted to this day, including the *De fato contra Petrum Pomponatium pro Alexandro Aphrodisio apologia* with which we shall be concerned.

The most complete and up-to-date list of Flandinus' works, both in print and in manuscript, has been given by Professor Kristeller.[28] There are but two printed works as enumerated above and confirmed by Kristeller's list. Of the manuscript works listed by earlier bibliographers, Kristeller has located copies of all but one of the three

---

[24] *Apologia*, III, 8 : "Haec omnia tu, ut mordicus teneas errorem de animae mortalitate materialitateve; in qua re confutatus reiectusque ab Episcopo Ambrosio numquam amplius os hoc tuum putre aperuisti" (f. 154v). The use of the indirect form by Philaletes-Flandinus to refer to his own works should not disturb the reader, for Philaletes also frequently uses the direct, first person form in describing his personal encounter with Pomponazzi. It may merely be a sign of haste in composition.

[25] *Apologia*, III, 3 : "[Polixenus] Hoc argumento [tutior pars sequenda] contra te usus sum in libro quarto *De immortalitate animorum* et nescivisti respondere" (f. 128v). Bartolomeo Spina published two works against Pomponazzi in 1519, the *Flagellum* against his *De immortalitate animae*, and the *Tutela veritatis* against his *Defensorium*. A third work entitled *Propugnaculum* was directed against Cajetan's interpretation of Aristotle. Cf. Gilson, 45; Di Napoli, 302 ff.

[26] *Conciones Quadragesimales* (Venice, 1523). Tiraboschi (VII, 1, 246) states that these *Conciones* also contain sermons for Advent.

[27] See note 20 above and also *Apologia*, III, 29, f. 240. Polixenus praises Philaletes' learning (III, 28, f. 232 ff) and his invincibility in debate (II, 30, f. 240v). Philaletes himself boasts of his own long association with letters and tends to depreciate Pomponazzi's reputation among men of letters (I, 4, f. 11v-13; I, 14 [13], f. 39v).

[28] P.O. Kristeller, "The Contribution of Religious Orders to Renaissance Thought and Learning," *The American Benedictine Review* 21 (1970), 40-41. See now Professor Kristeller's *Medieval Aspects of Renaissance Learning, Three Essays*, trans. and ed. Edward P. Mahoney (Durham, N.C., 1974), 138-39.

works against Luther, namely, the *Apologia adversus Lutherum*, which is dated by earlier bibliographers as of 1520. While this would seem a rather early, and therefore somewhat suspicious date, Flandinus may very well have had knowledge of the mission of Cardinal Cajetan to Luther in 1518. At any rate, in his *Apologia* of 1524 Flandinus repeatedly mentions the spreading and "nefarious" influence of Luther's doctrines which he assimilates with the Hussite heresy, and which he accuses Pomponazzi of having fostered as if in conspiracy with Luther.

To the list of the works of Flandinus presented by Kristeller may perhaps be added three titles mentioned in the *Apologia* which have never been traced : 1) a commentary on *De caelo*, Bk. III (f. 156^v);[29] 2) a commentary on *Physics*, Bk. II (f. 117^v); and 3) a *Refutation of the Prognostications for the Year 1524* in two books (f. 172^v). Flandinus himself notes that Agostino Nifo and many others have also written on the last topic.[30]

Flandinus' *Apologia* against the *De fato* of Pomponazzi

Despite the gloating by Philaletes and Polixenus that they had silenced Pomponazzi by their works on the immortality of the soul, the indomitable and somewhat aroused Peretto completed, but left in manuscript form, his last two major works, namely, the *De incantationibus* and the *De fato*. As Kristeller has rightly observed, these two works are by far the most elaborate and significant for Renaissance philosophy.[31] Flandinus, however, viewed these later works as an open defiance by Pomponazzi of the counsels of moderation enjoined on him by ecclesiastical authorities and also as a personal challenge.[32] How-

---

[29] This may be doubtful, however, owing to the wording of the passage : "Quod de forma elementi Averroes ut alias memini me dixisse in Commentario in 3um Aristotelis Librum De Caelo verum esse ostendit" (f. 156^v). The formulation may imply either Averroes' *Commentary* or a commentary by Philaletes on the same book of the *De Caelo*. The passage on f. 117^v concerning Philaletes' supposed commentary on *Physics*, II is also ambiguous.

[30] "Obmitto quod omnes hi nugivendi tam turpiter de futuro diluvio anno domini 1524 mentiti sunt; quos redarguerunt non modo Episcopus Ambrosius duobus libellis editis adversus eos, sed Augustinus Niphus, alii permulti" (II, 14 [13], f. 172^v).

[31] P.O. Kristeller, *Eight Philosophers of the Italian Renaissance* (Stanford, 1964), 76-78.

[32] Clearly retaliating for the humiliation he suffered from Pomponazzi's *Apologia* of 1517, Philaletes-Flandinus here addresses the Sophista in these terms : "Cum te audio

ever, he again took his time, just as he had done in the case of the *De immortalitate*, and issued only in 1524 his rejoinder entitled *De fato contra Petrum Pomponatium pro Alexandro Aphrodisio apologia*.

The only known copy of this text is Codex A VII 5 of the Biblioteca Universitaria at Genoa. It is probably the copy mentioned by earlier bibliographers as at Vintimiglia; the Mantuan copy has not been traced in modern times.[33] We have used a microfilm copy of the Genoese manuscript lent to us by Professor Kristeller, for which we wish to thank him most heartily on this festive occasion as we offer to him these first fruits of its study. The codex has 252 folios, which are approximately 30 × 20 centimeters (12 × 8 inches) in size, written 22 × 15 centimeters (9 × 6 inches), 29 long lines a page in a clear, elegant humanistic cursive for the text proper. In the three liminary pieces and for all titles of books and chapters the scribe uses a highly formal *libraria* which is easily mistaken for print. This may well indicate an original, even an autograph copy, if not the very dedication copy intended for Pope Clement VII.

The three liminary pieces consist of a dedication letter to Pope Clement VII (f. 1-1^v), an address to Pomponazzi's disciples (ff. 2-3) and a short *argumentum* summarizing the aim and occasion of the work (f. 3). The text proper follows (f. 3^v) and is entitled: "AMBROSII PARTHENOPEI EREMITAE Sacrarum Litterarum Professoris et Episcopi Lamocensis ac Suffraganei Mantuae De Fato contra Petrum Pomponatium pro Alexandro Aphrodisio Apologia." It is divided into three books of unequal length. The first book contains seventeen Dialogues (eighteen Dialogues numbered, but the ninth missing), ff. 3^v-52; the second book has eighteen Dialogues (seventeen numbered, but there are two numbered "7") and runs from f. 52 to f. 117^v; the third book, which is much longer, has thirty-two Dialogues (there is no Dialogue "7" but there are two Dialogues numbered "24"), ff. 118-251^v. There then follows a final judgment which is couched in legalistic form and pronounced by the *Convivae* sitting in tribunal: "Iudices pro Philalete in Sophisten," ff. 251^v-252. Again a certain haste in the composition is evident from the repeated errors in the numbering of the Dialogues. In addition, each book carries a varying form of the general title, which may indicate a modification of the

---

talia effutientem [in the *De fato*], hominis amentiam atque furorem obstupesco, qui neque in disceptationem preteritis annis descendere, neque causam dicere, neque publico ullo aut legitimo iure tecum agi volueris" (II, 12, f. 98).

[33] Cf. P.O. Kristeller, "The Contribution," 41; *Iter Italicum*, I, 243.

original plan and intention. While the first book bears the title given above for the whole work, it actually deals with the arguments of Alexander's chapters 1 to 6 and with Pomponazzi's discussion of them. The second book is entitled: "Liber secundus De Fato et Libero Arbitrio ab eodem Episcopo Ambrosio Eremita sacrae Theologiae magistro editus" and examines chapters 7 to 11 of Alexander's *De fato* together with Pomponazzi's refutation of them. Finally, the title of the third book confirms this procedure of following the order of Alexander's text: "Liber tertius De Fato editus ab eodem Episcopo Ambrosio et Mantuae Suffraganeo, ubi quae ab Alexandro Aphrodisio in capite 12 dicuntur et sequentibus (*sic*) defenduntur, explanantur, roborantur, Sophista reclamante et iustam rationem subeunte."

The original intention of Flandinus was to have covered all the portions of Pomponazzi's five books of the *De fato* against Alexander. He decided, however, that was not necessary.[34] As we have it, Flandinus' work limits itself to discussing one by one the nineteen chapters of Alexander's *De fato* and to upholding its doctrines against the attacks in Pompanazzi's own *De fato*, who is here labeled the Antialexander.[35] The entire work thus consists of sixty-seven Dialogues in which the doctrines of Alexander are repeated, the Sophista-Pomponazzi is made to break in frequently with the recital of his own *De fato* (read either by himself or by another member of the gathering), challenging the interlocutors to refute him, and finally bearing the onslaught of the charges raised by the two principal participants beside him, Philaletes and Polixenus.

Philaletes clearly dominates the discussion which he directs at all times and to which he contributes the sharpest, longest and most elaborate arguments. Polixenus, on the contrary, spends most of his efforts in supporting the views of Philaletes and in goading Philaletes and Sophista to expand or clarify some point. Only rarely does he propose arguments of his own. Although his opposition to Pomponazzi seems milder and more polite, reflecting even a trace of consideration for the latter's works and reputation, Polixenus is

---

[34] "Erat in animo sequentes libros errorum, ineptiarum et temeritatis refertissimos excurrere et confutare, sed quiescere statui; quoniam ea levitate causam omnem tuam certe constituis ut etiam sine ullo alio adversario, languentibus bonis omnibus ruitura sit. Quid enim ad eam subvertendam, et scripta omnia explodenda oppugnatione ulla opus est, quae et ipsa suis sese telis labefactare apertissime, et authorem suum habeant hostem omnium infestissimum?" *Apologia*, III, 32, f. 251ᵛ.

[35] *Apologia*, I, 3, f. 9ᵛ.

nevertheless in basic agreement, at least in the *Apologia*, with Flandinus and opposed to Pomponazzi. However, he may be described as seeking a middle ground between Philaletes and Sophista on certain specific points such as the validity of astrology and the reality of dream visions. The role filled by Philaletes in the *Apologia* makes it a certainty that he stands for the author, unless we are prepared to hold that the principal aim of the book, namely, to uphold Alexander's doctrines against the recent attacks of Pomponazzi, is not that of Flandinus himself. Other allusions in the work to the previous dealings between the "fictitious" Philaletes and Pomponazzi during the immortality controversy further confirm this identification of Philaletes with Flandinus.

As to the form of the *Apologia*, it should be noted that extensive portions of Alexander's work in the Barbaro translation are quoted at length along with lengthy extracts from Pomponazzi's *De Fato*. It is noteworthy that the quotations from Alexander are often more explicit and longer than those found in the work of Pomponazzi, who also relied on the Barbaro translation.[36] Flandinus' presentation of these passages from Pomponazzi's *De fato* establishes beyond any doubt that Flandinus had in fact a manuscript copy of this work at his disposal.

In two separate passages of the *Apologia*, Philaletes-Flandinus recapitulates his changes of attitude toward Pomponazzi since the publication of the latter's *De immortalitate animae*. For the light that they throw on the intellectual climate prevailing in traditionalist circles at this point in the evolution of Renaissance philosophy, it would seem worthwhile to give these passages in translation. In the first, Flandinus declares:

> What human being can be persuaded by this book of yours entitled *De fato* which you have recently completed? Of course you write: "I have taken the trouble to insert the pious and candid formula of caution against impiety which your doctors normally use, that whatever novelty is adduced may be considered acceptable, provided it receives the approval of the highest authorities (*collegio amplissimo*), especially of the Supreme Pontiff." This indeed

---

[36] Thus both Pomponazzi and Flandinus ignore the earlier medieval translation, if they ever knew of its existence. See Pierre Thillet, *Alexandre d'Aphrodise : De fato ad imperatores; version latine de Guillaume de Moerbeke* (Paris, 1963), p. 10, n. 2 and p. 27, n. 4. Cf. F. Edward Cranz, "Alexander of Aphrodisiensis," in *Catalogus Translationum et Commentariorum : Medieval Translations and Commentaries*, I, ed. P.O. Kristeller (Washington, 1960), 107-111.

I always do myself and wish to maintain for whatever work I have published in the past and shall publish in the future. But this attitude nowhere shows in all your vain writings. It is a wonder to me that there are people who think that you are not merely reproducing the condemned opinions of factious thinkers, with the criminal and insidious aim of giving them help and support, but, on the contrary, that in discussing these opinions in a manner befitting the learned you are aiming with the purest intention and with great ability simply to stimulate their minds. Who could believe it when you could be heard ever so often to state that the Stoic doctrine of fate is true, trying to prove your point like a beggar going from to door for approvals ? When you published that little book of yours *On the mortality of the soul* according to natural reason,[37] you were rebuked by Bishop Ambrosius[38] and many others. Moreover, you were ordered by the Supreme Pontiff Leo X to desist from muttering this kind of thing in the future. I had then hoped to see you desist from such follies and return to the way of truth. This hope was not to last, nor did you leave us long in the dark concerning your evil designs against the Christian Commonwealth. With your next book *De incantationibus* there was no one who did not finally suspect what you had in mind from the very beginning. Lastly, with this book *De fato et providentia* no one can remain so blind as not to see why you piled up all these pious statements with the aim of reinforcing the ungodly sect of the Hussites and the Lutherans. We confess, however, our gratitude that you have so quickly removed this delusion from our mind : discarding the mantle of the good man and good philosopher you made us perceive the true nature of your character and designs. Now at last you see the inescapable outcome, for neither could your wiles remain hidden, since you realize you fell into suspicion of heresy from the time of your very first disputations on the mortality of the soul, nor did your conspiracy turn out the way you had expected. You nevertheless returned to your habits as a dissembler and this time began to attack openly not only Alexander but the whole Christian Commonwealth which you had hitherto attempted to overthrow without success. (I, 14, f. 41-41ᵛ)

In the second passage, Flandinus' own strong feelings of revulsion at Pomponazzi's doctrines are manifested in an outburst which is characteristic of the attitude underlying the entire work :

Surely there was a time when I who am now so horrified at your behaviour, shared with the rest of your disciples a high opinion of your ability, steadfastness and godliness. Yet your own writings have shown beyond all preju-

---

[37] "Cum edidisses libellum illum *de animae mortalitate* secundum lumen naturale, fuissesque ab Ambriosio Episcopo reprehensus et a quampluribus aliis, quin immo a Pontifice Maximo Leone Xº (f. 41ᵛ) iussus ne talia de cetero mussitares..." This parody on the title of Pomponazzi's work was first contrived by Bartolomeo Spina in his work of 1519. Cf. Gilson, 45.

[38] This reference to Ambrosius the author in the third person is a sort of mannerism or affectation which in no way indicates that Philaletes is anyone other than Flandinus. See note 23 above.

dice what a stupid, worthless and vain man you are. Your ungodliness I personally suspected long ago, not through prejudice but after reading your books. The character you display in them was also deemed filthy, coarse and horrendous by many a reader. For my part, I still judged you neither unlearned, futile or despicable. But when your *Apologia* was published,[39] I realized that you were a sickly, shameless wrangler. After your *De incantationibus*, and finally your *De fato*, I must judge you to be a foul and cunning scoundrel. While one may concede that you are endowed with a strong, sharp and perceptive mind, still it is utterly ruined by your indecent depravity and by doctrines that are neither sound (*liberalis*) nor derived from Sacred Scripture, nor even suited to your mind. You picked them up from some seditious commentaries condemned long ago and subsequently removed from circulation to be left in [deserved] obscurity. (III, 8, f. 147)

This sort of abuse is repeated *ad nauseam* by Philaletes-Flandinus in the *Apologia* and it is frequently shared in by Polixenus, though in a somewhat more restrained manner. A similar tone can be noticed not only in Flandinus' earlier *De animarum immortalitate*, but also in Bartolomeo Spina's two works against Pomponazzi's *De immortalitate animae*, namely, the *Flagellum* and the *Tutela*.[40] Of all the adversaries of the Mantuan philosopher who wrote against his doctrine of the soul, Flandinus and Spina stand out as a unique pair who make themselves conspicuous by the abuses they heap on the person of Pomponazzi. Flandinus' declarations to the disciples of Pomponazzi in his liminary address, where he protests against any unfriendliness on his part toward the master and promises to avoid all insults, must therefore be taken with some reservation : they stand in clear contradiction with his actual performance. The address to the disciples contains the following declarations :

... If you will but consider that my endeavor is inspired by righteous motives (as indeed I think it should be deemed holy by anyone who claims the name of a true Christian), it is proper that I ask you to refrain from thinking that I hate your master when I seem to recoil from the opinions of the man. For I have never been engaged in war with him (*qui secum inimicias nullas unquam gesserim*) ;[41] on the contrary, I have always pitied his condition. Nor have I loathed him or called for more grievous sanctions against him. In truth, I know of no better way to succor your minds than to explain at some length my reasons for disagreeing strongly with him on the matter of fate : he holds

---

[39] This is the work in which Pomponazzi had labelled Flandinus the chief among the "cucullati." Philaletes-Flandinus is obviously still smarting from the attack.

[40] Cf. Di Napoli, 308.

[41] This candid admission merely repeats a similar one recounted by Pomponazzi in the *Apologia* of 1517. See above note 19.

the Stoic doctrine of fate to be not merely probable but true, while he considers the opinion of the upholders of free will in man to be false and unsubstantiated... In spite of all my efforts, there will be someone who, moved by respect for my adversary, will exclaim with closed ears : "The bishop, that is, a mere fly, dares to enter into dispute with the elephant, that is, Pomponazzi." These people do not deter us, nor will they, like wolves, make us hoarse.[42] For it is permissible, even salutary, to fight an enemy of truth whose aim is to inflict mortal wounds. We so much wish for truth to stand out in the light that we fear neither the conspiracy of detractors nor the onus of labor heavy on an old man. On the other hand, we beg all to consider that no man is ever to be placed so far above the condition of man that it would be an impertinence to cast doubt on the soundness of his doctrines.[43] We feel our demand to be all the more reasonable because in our dispute with him our purpose is to remain within the bounds of moderation and to aim solely at the truth... Finally, for fear that our Sophist or any of his followers might complain that we have distorted his words or have reported them in a tendentious or incompetent fashion, I promise that whenever the Sophist is made to speak in these Dialogues, he will utter no other expressions than those he has himself written with his uncouth grammar. It will thus be clear for all to see whether he belongs with those ignorant and fickle doctors mentioned in Peter [II Peter, ch. 3] who deface the Scriptures for their own undoing. Such people, once committed to a given opinion, will consider no other that may differ from it, but rather twist whatever can be found in the Scriptures to support their own opinion. Whether your man truly belongs with them, I pray you examine carefully. (ff. 2-3)

After this unconvincing *captatio benevolentiae*, Flandinus outlines the subject matter and the aim of his *De fato contra Petrum Pomponatium pro Alexandro Aphrodisio apologia* in the following *argumentum* :

Subject treated in the following work by Bishop Ambrosius : The Stoics held that all events occur by the law of fate, thereby mutilating the freedom of the human will. Later came Alexander of Aphrodisias who, detesting their doctrine as entirely false, composed a book in which he solved all their arguments, established truth by sound reasons and showed the Stoics' opinion

---

[42] A popular belief during the Middle Ages was that the sight of a wolf rendered a man hoarse. Cf. Maurice Giele, "Un Commentaire averroiste sur les Livres I et II du Traité de l'âme," in M. Giele, F. Van Steenbergen and B. Bazan, *Trois Commentaires anonymes sur le Traité de l'âme d'Aristote*, Philosophes Médiévaux, XI (Louvain and Paris, 1971), II, q. 11, p. 86 : "lupus, visu suo, reddit hominem raucum." Flandinus writes : "nec nos, ut lupi, raucos reddunt."

[43] This statement is reminiscent of a remark by Baptista Mantuanus, *Opus aureum in Thomistas*, edited by P.O. Kristeller in *Le Thomisme et la pensée italienne de la Renaissance* (Montreal and Paris, 1967), 137 : "... insolens sane dictum et imprudens, quasi velint eum [Thomas Aquinas] eximere de numero hominum." Flandinus knew the works of Baptista, whom he cites at f. 225ᵛ.

to be laughable. After the [enemies of freedom] had been decidedly put to rout, there arose this impostor of a Sophist who attacked Alexander, declared his arguments to be wrong, empty and of no value and proceeded to prove his charge against Alexander by analyzing and refuting his arguments. Seeing this, bishop Ambrosius was appalled (*egre tulit*) at the temerity and impudence of the man. Moved therefore to uphold the truth, he fights on the side of Alexander, holds fast with Thomas Aquinas, and reduces the Sophist to impotence, showing him to be totally devoid of competence in all the liberal arts. (f. 3-3^v)

The Date of Composition of the *Apologia*

From the Dedication Letter to Pope Clement VII, in which the *Apologia* is presented as just completed, it is obvious that the work must be dated as after November 1523, the date of Clement's election to the papacy. Further, since Francesco Gonzaga is mentioned in the same letter as the ambassador of the Marquis of Mantua to the papal court, we can take October 1524 as the *terminus a quo*, because at that time the previous ambassador, Baldassare Castiglione, still holds the post in Rome. The earliest letter of the new ambassador Francesco to Isabella d'Este in Mantua seems to date from early December 1524.[44]

Other passages in the *Apologia* also point to the year 1524 as the period in which the work was composed. For instance, Flandinus-Philaletes mentions a work of his in which he ridiculed the prognostications of almanac makers concerning floods which were to occur in the year 1524.[45] His refutation, which is based on the failure of these predictions, shows that most of the year, or at least a certain part of it, had already elapsed at the time the *Apologia* was being written. Also, in the earlier part of the work, the participants at the banquet, while enjoying the pleasantness of Philaletes' villa and garden, begin to feel the discomfort of the intense heat produced by the sun at the summer solstice (II, 3, f. 57^v). This allusion to the summer solstice would suggest a date later than the middle of June 1524 for the composition of the *Apologia*. Finally, brief allusions to the affairs of Italy at the time the bishop is writing likewise suggest the year 1524. Such are the imminent invasion of Italy by Francis I and the military

---

[44] Cf. Cartwright, II, 245.
[45] See note 29 above.

preparations of the Connétable de Bourbon as Captain General of the League[46] that was hastily organized to face this eventuality.

On the other hand, the *terminus ad quem* for the composition of the *Apologia* cannot be too late in 1525. In the work Pomponazzi is always spoken of as alive and as a continuing menace to good morals and the Christian Commonwealth by reason of his teaching and writing. Flandinus frequently demands he cease his pernicious activities. Since Pomponazzi fell seriously ill in April 1525 and died on 18 May following, completion of the *Apologia* must be dated as prior to April 1525. Furthermore, the dedicatory letter to Clement VII, while alluding to the Church's troubled times during the reign of this Pope, makes no mention of the disaster of Pavia in which Francis I was captured by the imperial army. An important prop of Clement's secret and devious diplomacy was thus removed in dismal failure. Since the disaster of Pavia took place on 24 February 1525 and no reference to it appears in Flandinus' expression of his wishes for the success of the Pope's reign, it would seem natural to date this letter as prior to February 1525.

The convergence of these factors inclines us to place the composition of the *Apologia* some time during the year 1524 and to date its completion and dedication to Clement VII late in November or December. As in the case of his *De animarum immortalitate*, a reply to Pomponazzi that took some three years to materialize, Flandinus' long *Apologia de fato* was composed more than four years after the work of the Mantuan that it attempts to refute.

Identification of the Characters in the *Apologia*

The form of the *Apologia* resembles that of Flandinus' earlier *De animarum immortalitate* but it also differs from it noticeably. The dialogue form is used in both. However, while in the earlier work each participant stands for a clearly identifiable philosophical

---

[46] *Apologia*, I, 17 [16], f. 48 : "Modo audio totam Italiam laborare seditionibus magnosque tum in ea tum in Gallia legi exercitus, quorum Capitaneus Generalis totiusque ligae magnus ille Dux ... [line and a half left blank] electus fertur ut impios Ecclesiae Romanae hostes castiget, trucidet, ac retaliet." The title Captain General could suggest Federico Marquess of Mantua, who indeed was active in these preparations. But the mention of the headship of the League (*totius ligae*), and of the fact that this Captain General is "reported" to have just been elected fit the Connétable de Bourbon much more aptly.

tradition (Platonism in Philoplato, Aristotelianism in Polixenus, Arabism in Alchindo and Theology in Celestino)[47] and argues in turn with the Sophista-Pomponazzi, in the *Apologia* the dialogue is a running encounter in which the protagonists play unequal roles. Philaletes dominates the scene, leaving but crumbs to the others except for Polixenus, who does manage to play a respectable role, based mainly, however, on the defence of a few points on which he disagrees but slightly with Philaletes. Secondly, while some participants bear similar names in both works, they do not appear to represent the same people in each. In 1519, the Philoplato of the *De animarum immortalitate* most likely stood for Flandinus himself, who had by then composed several commentaries on the works of Plato and not distinguished himself as a partisan of Aristotle. In the *Apologia* there is also a Philoplato, but he never speaks; indeed, he does not even appear in the seating arrangement for the banquet. On the other hand, Philaletes himself occupies the center position. Although he is assigned no particular place, Polixenus is treated with special respect because of his venerable age.[48] Like Philoplato, the Sophista is also not assigned any particular seat. The ensuing discussion is entirely between the Sophista, on the one hand, and Philaletes and Polixenus, on the other. The other guests, who hereafter are referred to simply as *Convivae*, eat and drink heartily, occasionally goading the protagonists to further dispute. At the conclusion they will sit as a jury passing judgment, pronouncing in favor of Philaletes' doctrines and condemning those of the Sophista.

Is the scene imagined for the dialogue of the *Apologia* purely fictitious, the product of Flandinus' literary imagination, or is there here some trace of actual discussions which were prompted by the realization that Pomponazzi's later works were gaining a wide audience ? The question deserves careful scrutiny. The identification of the Sophista with Pomponazzi himself is obvious. So too is that of Philaletes with Flandinus as the author : Philaletes carries the main and nearly exclusive argument of the *Apologia* against Pomponazzi's *De fato*. Granting the validity of this identification, we must note that from the *De immortalitate animarum* of 1519 to the *Apologia* of 1524, Flandinus has altered his description of himself from that

---

[47] See note 22 above.

[48] This is perhaps the only detail in the traits of Polixenus that could stand against his identification with Spina, who was but 47 years old in 1524.

of a follower of Plato to that of a lover of truth. In fact, Flandinus has shifted from the category of a philosopher to that of a theologian-philosopher and strict disciple of Thomas Aquinas.

Since Polixenus is sometimes mentioned in the *Apologia* as the author of two works against Pomponazzi which are different from those of Flandinus, there is a compelling reason to find a contemporary figure behind this character. Given the sustained hostility of the *Apologia* against Pomponazzi, which is likewise shared by Philaletes and Polixenus, we are left with a choice from only a few of the contemporaries who wrote a refutation of Pomponazzi's doctrines. Neither Javellus, nor Contarini, nor Nifo would have uttered the deliberately malicious charges set forth in the *Apologia* against Pomponazzi. Consequently, our choice is restricted to two figures among those who wrote against Pomponazzi's *De immortalitate*. If Polixenus stands for a real historical figure, he must be either Bartolomeo Spina, the Dominican friar who wrote two works against Pomponazzi's *De immortalitate* in 1519, or Girolamo Amidei of Lucca, a Servite who published an *Apologia pro animae immortalitate in Petrum Pomponatium* in 1518.[49] However, as Gilson has observed,[50] the most important adversary of Pomponazzi on the question of the immortality of the soul was Bartolomeo Spina. And indeed the cluster of historical data concerning his personality, activity and works can be shown to fit exactly the character traits and the ideas displayed by Polixenus in Flandinus' *Apologia*.

For one thing Spina, who stood in the front line among the adversaries, heaped abuses on the ideas and personality of Pomponazzi in his two works of 1519, the *Flagellum* and the *Tutela*. Furthermore, in a third work published that year, Spina established a direct link between Cajetan's interpretation of Aristotle's doctrine of the soul and Pomponazzi's thesis on its mortality. While the same theme does reappear in Flandinus' *Apologia* [51] through the mouthpiece of Philaletes, the censure of Cajetan is much toned down, and animosity toward him is in general absent—indeed, Cajetan is referred to with respect either as the "Archiflamen" or the "Cardinalis Glossator" (f. 163, f. 177 and f. 180). Nonetheless, a certain distrust of the Cardinal's

---

[49] Cf. Di Napoli, 268.

[50] See note 17 above.

[51] *Apologia*, III, 6, f. 142ᵛ: "Addo nunc Glossatorem illum Archiflaminem erudi[ti]s-simum in qu. 115 partis primae S[ancti] D[octoris], a quo tuum tibi modum sustinendi animae mortalitatem mutuasti."

thesis does show in that Philaletes prefers to dismiss the Cardinal's authority when he has another that is equally valuable.[52] Thus Polixenus-Spina is not allowed to repeat his charge directly against Cajetan, and Philaletes-Flandinus, in deference both to Cajetan and his own friend Spina, takes a middle position between attacking and ignoring the Dominican Cardinal. At any rate, the closeness of the relation between Flandinus and Spina is evident. The decisive clue for the identification of Polixenus with Spina remains the citation of the two works against Pomponazzi's doctrines of the soul ascribed to Polixenus and which surely must be the two works of Spina published in 1519.

Other passages in the *Apologia* reveal some divergence of opinion between Polixenus and Philaletes, thus requiring a separate identity for each of these characters. As is well known, one *locus* of the scholastic debate on human freedom was the question of the stars' influence upon man's activity, and this question is explicitly discussed in the present dialogues.[53] With the not infrequent inconsistency of theologians who pretend to recognize the validity of the laws of nature but explain them in a way that will safeguard dogma, Flandinus accepts as true a basic axiom of medieval physics that was also the principal foundation of astrological science, namely, the influence of the stars on material things of this world, including man's body and the vegetative and sensitive parts of his soul. While he is unable and unprepared to oppose the physical science of his times, Flandinus aims at making an arbitrary exception in favor of the intellectual soul on the grounds of man's ethical responsibility. His position thus does not advance one inch beyond the thesis expounded by Thomas Aquinas, who remains his principal authority throughout the *Apologia*. Reduced to its core, Flandinus' argument has a twofold hinge : first, astrology is patently false since it denies man's free will;[54] and secondly,

---

[52] *Apologia*, III, 15 [14], f. 180 : "Potest aliter responderi, ut respondet Reverendissimus Cardinalis Glossator Sancti Doctoris. Sed de hac hactenus."

[53] *Apologia*, II, 3 : "[Sophista] Omne agens praeter Deum movet et movetur. [Philaletes] Verum, non tamen omne movetur caelo, quoniam non agens caelo excellentius ut est mens nostra. Atqui de caelo controversia agitur praesens, quoniam de fati imperio" (f. 63). Cf. J. Stufler, "Der hl. Thomas und das Axiom : Omne, quod movetur, ab alio movetur," *Zeitschrift für Katholische Theologie* 47 (1923), 369-390; R. Effler, *John Duns Scotus and the Principle "Omne quod movetur ab alio movetur"* (St. Bonaventure, 1962); L. Leahy, *Dynamisme volontaire et jugement libre : Le sens du libre arbitre chez quelques commentateurs thomistes de la Renaissance* (Paris, 1963). Flandinus later attempts to explain what Aristotle really meant by this axiom (III, 29, f. 237ᵛ).

[54] The position is no different from that of either Thomas Aquinas, who is Flandinus'

astrology has been repeatedly condemned by Civil and Canon Law and by a majority of great thinkers whose names he lists.[55]

Polixenus objects to the stated position because it shows too much disrespect for an equally impressive number of eminent authors of old who favored astrology.[56] Moreover, on the precise point of divination, Polixenus shows an inclination to disagree with Philaletes' thesis, almost to the point of siding with the Sophista-Pomponazzi (II, 16 [17], f. 112; III, 10 [9], f. 158). Philaletes-Flandinus replies that the validity of some predictions which are realized must be ascribed to the work of demons and unclean spirits (III, 10 [9], ff. 150^v-161; I, 16 [15], f. 45; I, 15 [14], f. 42^v). This final explanation leaves Polixenus quite unsatisfied for he had wished to be convinced by arguments based on the laws of nature and long observation (III, 10 [9], f. 158).

Granted that Polixenus is Spina, his particular disagreement with Philaletes-Flandinus on these points can be easily traced to his situation during those years as a part-time inquisitor and lecturer in theology and natural science. On the occasion of an inquisitorial process against witches in Ferrara a short time before, Spina had been consulted as an expert by the judges and assessors and was requested to put his opinions in writing. The resulting work, which is entitled *Quaestio de strygibus*, was published in 1523,[57] the year before Flandinus' *Apologia* was composed. It shows Spina to be much more cautious

---

principal guide, or of Pico della Mirandola, whom Flandinus knows and cites at III, [13], f. 171^v. In the latter passage (f. 172^v), Flandinus mocks the astrological vagaries of Lucas Bellantius, who had tried to answer Pico.

[55] *Apologia*, II, 16 [17], f. 112 ff. contains a long recital of ancient and more recent condemnations of astrology by Church Fathers and medieval canonists respectively. The ancient condemnations are supplied through long quotations from Saints Jerome, Augustine and Ambrose.

[56] Although he seems at first to share Philaletes' views concerning the validity of astrology, Polixenus poses the questions which must have been on the mind of every believer in the "science" of astrology at that time : "The intellect receives from the senses ..., the senses in turn depend on the heaven 'per accidens' in as much as the body is totally subjected to the action of the heavens; therefore the act of intellection somehow is under the influence of the heaven" (*Apologia*, I, 14 [13], f. 39). Philaletes decides, quite gratuitously, that God's Providence placed the human mind above the order of physical nature. It is not even, properly speaking, moved by God; it is only inspired and attracted by Him through an "illumination," which is not a *motus*. In a later section (II, 16 [17], ff. 109^v-114), where the final assault on astrology is delivered, Polixenus warns Philaletes to distinguish carefully between "mathematical" and "judicial" astrology, so as not to condemn astrology indiscriminately.

[57] See above note 20.

regarding those actual instances of visions and predictions that occur among simple believers. Thus, while Flandinus shows himself to be enthused by Platonic philosophy, which he considers perfectly adapted to Christian times,[58] and while he is resolved to preserve those elements of Alexander's doctrine that are in agreement with Catholic dogma but to reject any suggestion that man's mind may be bound by the laws of the physical universe, the prudent and hedging Polixenus-Spina is probably a better representative of the Renaissance conception of natural science.

If then the Polixenus of the *Apologia* is Bartolomeo Spina, which seems to us to be a well confirmed hypothesis, some further details in the *Apologia* take on a more realistic color. Flandinus, who like Pomponazzi was 62 years of age in 1524, frequently complains of the inconveniences of old age[59] and mildly reproaches Polixenus-Spina for taking advantage of it (f. 185). Spina, who was born in 1477, was then 47 years old, an age that seems to correspond to the maturity he is given in the *Apologia*. The mention of his seniority at the moment of the seating arrangements does not necessarily imply advanced old age, but merely that he is older than the other participants, who are probably meant to be a group of younger disciples of Pomponazzi. The identification of Polixenus with Spina also has this further interesting significance : it reveals that discussions like the one here reported may have frequently taken place, perhaps in some pleasant villa maintained by Flandinus near Mantua. These two kindred spirits, Flandinus and Spina, may very well have shared their concern over the influence of the works of Pomponazzi, and have frequently devised imaginary situations in which they successfully confounded their common enemy.

---

[58] *Apologia*, I, 18 [17], f. 51^v : "Haec Plato de providentia et fato. Quibus quid ab ore hominis gentilis accipi possit ad nostram religionem accomodatius ? Quid, praesertim ea aetate, potuisset dici praestantius atque divinius ? Nam cum alii deos immortales sua dumtaxat curare, res vero humanas vi quadam naturae regi gubernarique existiment, Plato non aliter fere quam nostrae religionis doctores fecerint loqui de fato et providentia videtur ..." Such candid confessions of the "religion" of Plato illustrate vividly, in our opinion, why Plato became so much in vogue among the religion-minded humanists who, like Philaletes-Flandinus, tended to shun natural science.

[59] He suffers from gout (*podagra*) (f. 180), he is easily tired (f. 63) and frequently retires to rest, his hair is white (f. 13), and so forth.

Some Highlights from the *Apologia* of Flandinus

Flandinus' prejudices against Pomponazzi and his methods in the dispute have already been analyzed by Di Napoli.[60] His claim to be a disciple of Egidio da Viterbo would invite comparison with this substantial thinker : but Flandinus, who was unable to produce any significant or original thought to compare with his avowed master, suffers badly from such a comparison. In reality, the strength of his convictions, which are buttressed by an impressive apparatus of arguments, lies rather in the great confidence he appears to have both in his authorities and in his own talents and earnestness as a preacher. A perusal of his *Apologia* confirms this judgment. The main impression derived from reading the *Apologia* may be summed up in these two observations : first, its main thesis is a mere restatement of the views of Thomas Aquinas on the freedom of the human will and on God's Providence; and second, the tone is one of constant abuse and distrust of the Bolognese professor, who is further declared to be a heretic and, like Hus and Luther, inspired by the devil to overthrow the Christian Commonwealth (ff. 41^v, 48, 49^v, 54 and 250^v). Within this larger frame of intention and its realization, we may single out for consideration a few other characteristics and positions of the *Apologia*.

While restating Thomas' thesis, Flandinus shows himself to be acquainted with later developments of scholastic theology, mostly in the use of logical distinctions added in the period after Thomas to shore up the fortress of scholasticism under attack. Such are the distinction between *sensus compositus* and *sensus divisus*, rightly credited by Flandinus to Heytesbury and Sermoneta among others, and the distinction between *determinatio de inesse* and *determinatio de possibili* and other distinctions credited to Duns Scotus. The range of Flandinus' acquaintance with later scholasticism may be gauged by the relatively large number of later schoolmen whom he cites : at least twenty-seven authors are explicitly named, extending from Albertus Magnus to Cajetan. Older scholastics like Peter Lombard, Anselm and Hugh of St. Victor are also cited on more than one occasion.

Alongside these medieval writers, Flandinus cites more ancient authorities. We may recognize here the enlarged classical heritage claimed by the humanists : twenty-three Greek authors are included

---

[60] Di Napoli, 300.

in his list of citations, in addition to nine others specially identified as commentators on Plato and Aristotle.[61] Seldom, however, is any direct quotation adduced from these authors; they are merely used as a parade. Of ancient Greek, Latin, and Oriental writers on judicial astrology (no medievals, except a few Arabs, are included) Flandinus knows some sixteen names or groups (e.g. *Egyptii astrologi*)! Five Arab astrologers or philosophers mentioned are Almandal [?], Albumasar, Haly, Averroes and Avicenna. Finally, the list of ancient authorities includes some sixteen Latin poets and philosophers, among whom Cicero dominates, just as he had in Pomponazzi's own *De fato*, and about fourteen Greek and Latin Church Fathers. The procession further extends to numerous names included in extracts from Augustine and Jerome which Flandinus reproduces at length. Some Canonists and Glossators who condemned astrology are also mentioned.

For the most part, these authorities are merely names, since Flandinus in fact mainly utilizes three authorities: Aristotle, Thomas Aquinas and Averroes. Duns Scotus plays a much more modest role. Were it not for its dialogue form, the *Apologia* would thus resemble the most commonplace medieval *Summa* or *Quodlibet*. The main novelty of the work is that, inasmuch as the *Apologia* is a defense of Alexander against Pomponazzi, passages from both authors fill its pages and Pomponazzi's doctrines are systematically rejected in favor of those of Alexander. After all, was it not with the intention of upholding Alexander's thesis in what it had in common with "Catholic truth" that the work was undertaken in the first place?[62] Hence the paradoxical situation that the fountainhead of the "materialistic" Alexandrinist school of the philosophers of the Renaissance is suddenly promoted to the dignity of a model of Catholic theology. The advantage gained from the move is seen in regard to the crucial point of the reality of dream-visions, which Alexander openly supported and which are upheld with the necessary qualifications by Philaletes-Flandinus over the objections of Polixenus (III, 18 [17], ff. 189-194ᵛ). Pomponazzi, it is true, had not directly challenged the point in his *De fato*, but in the *De incantationibus* he had sought for "naturalistic" grounds to explain visions. By Christianizing Alexander, Flandinus

---

[61] The works of Plato mentioned are the *Laws, Epistles, Republic, Gorgias, Phaedrus, Protagoras, Theatetus* and *Euthydemus*.

[62] *Apologia*, III, 18 [17], f. 189 : "Decretum nobis est Alexandrum philosophum eminentissimum tueri, in his scilicet que ne latum quidem unguem a catholica veritate fuerint abiuncta."

is able to maintain in the *Apologia* that dream-visions can effectively announce the future. However, he is careful to distinguish between legitimate visions sent by God or his angels, such as the dream of Joseph intimating the flight to Egypt, and the evil dreams inspired by the devil and unclean spirits.

Some interesting observations may be made regarding the authority Flandinus accords to Aristotle and Averroes. While on the one hand their authority is frequently invoked to support a logical, physical and metaphysical element of proof, on the other hand the scars of the conflicts of late scholasticism show in the role they play in the *Apologia*. Although Averroes is still treated as a standard authority in the interpretation of Aristotle's *Physics* and *Metaphysics*, he is ranked below Alexander (f. 215^v) whenever he is in conflict with him. But it is regarding Aristotle that the *Apologia* shows the most curious alteration of confidence, for in Book III, dialogue 3, on the subject of Aristotle's denial of the existence of demons, Philaletes explodes into a violent attack against Aristotle :

> You think, perhaps, that no firm argument can be found against Aristotle when he strays so wide away from the truth ? As if he had not also erred in so many other instances ? ... Oh, what a crime to admit that Aristotle has erred ! (f. 129)

He adds for good measure that Aristotle is further to be blamed for inducing Alexander to believe the Universe to be God. On this, the Sophista exclaims : "This is hard to take !" Polixenus himself voices his astonishment :

> I am dumbfounded to hear you say these things against Aristotle, my friend; for it is the consensus of all nations that Aristotle must be considered the Prince of philosophers. His disciple, Alexander of Aphrodisias, conqueror of nations and terror of all Greece, is also held by all in the highest esteem.[63]

To which Philaletes retorts :

> And who made him a Prince [of philosophers] is not evident to me ! Still this did not exempt him from error : surely, all those who harassed [*vexaverunt*] him did not wish to consider him as the Prince of philosophers !

Philaletes then gives a long list of Aristotle's critics from antiquity

---

[63] How strange that Polixenus-Spina could confuse Alexander of Aphrodisias and Alexander the Great, and that Philaletes-Flandinus should raise no objection !

through the Middle Ages.[64] But on the point in question, Flandinus sets out to prove that Aristotle believed in demons (according to his biographer Philoponus) as well as in divination (according to Eusebius and Aristocles).

Flandinus' criticism of Aristotle, however, is by no means universal. In the present passage it is limited to two doctrines : first, the division of the soul into a corruptible part and an incorruptible part, and secondly, the description of God in *Metaphysics*, Bk. XII as an "eternal animal," from which Alexander is said to have derived his "raving" opinion that the Universe is God. Soon after, however, criticisms from ancient and medieval thinkers who derided or at least questioned Aristotle in some way are recounted by Philaletes-Flandinus. For example, Albertus Magnus questioned Aristotle's opinion on the number of celestial movers and Duns Scotus underscored Aristotle's vacillation on the question of the soul. However, Aristotle remains for Flandinus, as he had been for most medievals, the "master of those who know," while Averroes is still his most faithful commentator.

In view of the fact that Flandinus cites so many of the ancient authors favored by Renaissance philosophers, one might have anticipated a certain eclecticism in his thought, but there is nothing of the sort in the *Apologia*. None of these newly favored authors is used to supply an original thought or argument alongside those of Aristotle and Averroes—not Plato, nor the neo-Platonists, Proclus and Jamblichus, nor Hermes Trismegistus. The question then arises : how do we reconcile Flandinus' excessive reliance on Aristotle and Averroes with his savage attack on Aristotle's authority ? The answer might seem to lie in the dramatic change of attitude toward Aristotle's authority already evident in the works of Chrysostomus Javellus. Gilson has perceptively emphasized this remarkable moment in Renaissance and early modern philosophy.[65] We shall stress the basic agreement between Javellus and Pomponazzi in the latter's *De nutritione*, published in 1521, that is, two years after his *Defensorium*—to which Javellus' *Responsiones* were attached—and more than ten years before the complete development of Javellus' stand.

---

[64] Among the medieval thinkers included are Egidius Romanus, Albertus Magnus, Durandus, Henry of Ghent, Herveus Brito, Duns Scotus, Gregory of Rimini, John Baconthorp, Pierre d'Ailly, Johannes Canonicus, Francis of Meyronnes and Nicholas of Cusa.
[65] Gilson, 51.

In his *De nutritione,* Pomponazzi takes to task those of his contemporaries who hurl the accusation of heresy at whoever deems Aristotle to have maintained that every kind of soul in this world is mortal. All who recognized that Aristotle actually held this opinion have, in Pomponazzi's judgment, perceived Aristotle's doctrine correctly. Such are, among others, Alexander, Abubacer, Avempace, Gregory of Nyssa, Gregory Nazianzen, John Duns Scotus and Herveus Brito. And yet, Pomponazzi notes, some of them were eminent theologians, holy men and worthy soldiers of Christ, especially Duns Scotus and Herveus. Nobody would dream of calling them heretics or schismatics, and Pomponazzi concludes with the biting remark : "It seems to me that in our times there are some who would not consider you yourself to be a Christian, unless you agree to declare Aristotle a Christian."[66] If we compare this remark with Javellus' ultimate stand that the philosophy of Aristotle and philosophy as such are not convertible, it is easy to see that both Pomponazzi and Javellus were attempting to free "Christian" philosophy from the yoke of Aristotle.

Appearances notwithstanding, Flandinus' diatribe against Aristotle in the *Apologia* has a quite different tone. Once those doctrines that are incompatible with Christian truth have been explained away or ridiculed, Aristotle's philosophy is for Flandinus the most solid anchor of Christian philosophy and theology, all the more since Aquinas derived all his philosophy proper from Aristotle.[67] Some contemporaries saw precisely in this dependence on Aristotle the weakness of Thomistic and scholastic philosophy generally. In another passage of his *Apologia,* Flandinus puts this complaint in Pomponazzi's mouth : "[Sophista]... Contra eos scribo quorum ambitione vel inscitia fit ut Aristoteles religionis nostrae caput et vertex habeatur" (I, 15 [14], f. 43v). Far from taking up the quarrel in the spirit indicated by Pomponazzi, Javellus or Cajetan, Flandinus insinuates that Pomponazzi wishes to remove Aristotle from his towering position in philosophy only to take the place himself : "[Sophista]... Quid si me caput constituam ?"

The last characteristic of the *Apologia* which we shall examine concerns the endless abuses and insults leveled at Pomponazzi. Since this feature is also abundantly present in Flandinus' *De animarum*

---

[66] *De nutritione,* I, 11, in *Tractatus utilissimi* (Venice, 1525), f. 121.

[67] *Apologia,* I, 10 [9], f. 27v : "Neque aliud Thomae, opinor, aliud a dogmatibus Aristotelis persuasum in philosophia, qui omnem suae doctrinae rationem ex fontibus peripatheticis hausit."

immortalitate, it may be considered to be an idiosyncrasy of his. In Freudian terms, the pattern of this stream of insults may well be a reflection of the author's warped ambitions and frustrations. In spite of the sly assurances in his liminary *Address* not to resort to insults, Flandinus misses no opportunity to ridicule his opponent, belittling the philosopher whose fame is distasteful to him and threatening him constantly with ecclesiastical censures. Flandinus disparages Pomponazzi's learning, his mental fitness, his moral character, and his motives in writing and teaching. Pomponazzi is said to misunderstand or wilfully to misconstrue the meaning of Alexander's arguments; he is unable to unravel the true thought of Aristotle and yet he "sells" Aristotle and philosophy to the Italians (ff. 195 and 218^v). He discusses the opinions of the Stoics without having read their books (ff. 81, 118, 131, etc.). Pomponazzi is also charged with plagiarizing many authors for some of his most telling arguments : they include Seneca, Avicenna, Aquinas, Duns Scotus, Buridan, Cajetan, and John Canonicus.[68] His private life is not unblemished; he is hypocritical, greedy, lustful, gluttonous, slothful and untidy.[69] He is ignorant of correct grammatical usage, dialectic, and theology, and he seeks novelty for the sake of popularity.[70] By his writing and lectures he stirs up revolts against established authorities. He thus follows in the wake of all arch-heretics, hiding his true designs and lending a secret hand to the Hussite and Lutheran rebellions against the Church (ff. 41^v, 98, 250^v). He is conceited and arrogant, disrespectful of all authorities, deeming himself superior to all philosophers and thinkers, past and present.

Reduced to its core, the conflict between Flandinus and Pomponazzi as seen in the *Apologia* of Flandinus is the perennial one between conservative tradition and the inventive spirit of the innovators. A passage from the early portion of the *Apologia* well illustrates this opposition of the inveterate traditionalist who is frightened at the merest suggestion of change :

> [Philaletes] ... You may already perceive what is going to happen to you. Though a few among the ignorant mob, more interested in novelties than in showing their friendship, seem to praise these inventions of yours by which

---

[68] Seneca, f. 89; Avicenna, f. 115; Buridan, f. 155^v; Duns Scotus, f. 144, 177; Cajetan, 141^v; Aquinas, f. 45; and John Canonicus, f. 166.

[69] *Apologia*, II, 10 [11], f. 90^v and passim. His greediness is especially stressed in this passage.

[70] *Apologia*, f. 68; 36^v. On Pomponazzi's ignorance of dialectic, see ff. 172, 174, 183 and 229^v.

> you have perpetrated a crime against the authority of the wise, you are nevertheless pressed from all sides. All good men shun your doctrines, all resist your speeches. Christian Princes confer no honors on your followers, priests forcibly keep you away from their churches and the sacraments. If you persist in your obstinacy, I can tell you what will become of your cause : you shall no longer be called citizens, since you have abandoned the consensus of the Christian Community; nor Christians, since you fight against Christian religion and peace; nor philosophers, because you do not yield to the persuasion of truth... You will be detested by all good men when they discover that you stand against human freedom and despise truth. You will have against you not only good men everywhere but also all nations : for there is no place on earth where the notice of your serious error will not have reached... I shall not mention the fact that you so love and promote your cause, you are so proud of yourself that you consider all others to be ignorant or insane. How vainglorious, how alien this is to philosophical humility ! (I, 4, f. 11^v)

The Sophista-Pomponazzi retorts that perhaps his party has better reason for their position than all the rest.[71] To which Philaletes-Flandinus answers :

> How do you know that you alone are in the right so that you judge the entire community (*Rempublicam*) to be in the wrong ? You mean to say that all have been in error ? So many generations of ancestors, such universal agreement of all nations as exists to-day ? ... As for you, you are never deceived, you never err ? How can you think that ? Do you believe that God is gracious to you alone while He shows Himself angry and hostile toward those who worship Him, and this because they do not follow you in your error ?... Do not dare say that God favors you alone and keeps you alone in happiness for having revealed to you such a measure of truth that what seems evident to you remains unknown to all others ...

Conclusion

In conclusion, the *Apologia de fato contra Petrum Pomponatium pro Alexandro Aphrodisio* stands firmly for the uncompromising preservation of traditional faith and ecclesiastical authority, which are to be strengthened if necessary by the Inquisition. Flandinus' vast reading both in scholastic writers and in the authors newly in vogue during the Renaissance turns somewhat sterile from an eclecticism motivated solely by the pastoral worries of a monk and bishop. In the arguments and replies of his *Apologia* Flandinus puts forward nothing that had not been stated previously in medieval scholasticism. Pomponazzi's strenuous challenge to the basic tenets of scholastic theology and philosophy is thus met with a barricade constructed from the débris of that tradition.

---

[71] "Quid si nos caeteris rectius sentimus ?" (f. 11^v).

There may be cause for wonderment that the fear of novelty in intellectual debate which Flandinus displays in his *Apologia* could be contemporaneous with the mental excitement stirred up by the works of a Pomponazzi or a Copernicus. The difference in intellectual attitudes is rooted in two totally different sets of factors in the psychological and sociological spheres. Set against Flandinus' almost pathological craving for tradition, Pomponazzi's stubborn insistence on the need to face the ultimate consequences of Aristotelian axioms in physics and metaphysics appears refreshing in comparison. His position boils down to this : in the matter of the metaphysical basis of free will in man, if the uncontrovertibly Aristotelian principle that "all motion, save that of the prime mover, initiates from outside the thing moved" be true, then there is no valid reason to except man's will from this tight network of causation. Ethical and religious considerations cannot be allowed to interfere by arbitrarily carving out for the human soul an independent sphere of action and thereby contradicting the entire system. By carrying Aristotelianism to its ultimate consequences, Pomponazzi has uncovered the inescapable dilemma : either God is outside the Universe, and then the machinery of the Universe is absolutely determined in its operation and the human will loses its privileged condition; or, against this view, God is part of the Universe, and then the laws of nature are his providence and man's free will is but a particular case of the operation of nature. The latter view was the position of the Stoics, who emphasized the paramount role of the stars and heavens as the origin of all motion, and it was this position which Pomponazzi seems ultimately to have favored.

Another way out of the dilemma for traditional Christian doctrine was Javellus' suggestion that Christian theology and philosophy renounce their age old dependence on the Aristotelian system which had become paralyzing in its effect. The intent and effect of Javellus' distinction between Aristotelian philosophy and pure philosophy was to make room for a Christian ethics that is completely independent from science and natural laws. But the traditionalist Flandinus recoils in horror from any of these new directions and moves all powers on earth to prevent or check this abandonment of comfortable tradition.[72]

The City University of New York

---

[72] I wish to thank Professor Edward P. Mahoney for his deft condensation of a lengthy original draft of this article, and for his expert rewriting of many of its passages to make the present version as trim as it is.

PIETRO POMPONAZZI AND THE MEDIEVAL TRADITION OF GOD'S FOREKNOWLEDGE *

MARTIN PINE

The deep knowledge of Aristotle and his Greek and Arabic commentators possessed by the Renaissance Aristotelians is well known. Less well known, perhaps, but equally important is their extensive command of medieval theology and philosophy. Even when these Renaissance thinkers differed with their predecessors in the medieval tradition, the differences are often based on subtle distinctions evidencing a wide reading and deep understanding of medieval authors. For a full comprehension of many major conceptions of the Renaissance Aristotelians, we must examine the medieval sources they cite, and the particular treatment of them as found embodied in the Renaissance works. Such an examination will allow us to see when a Renaissance author simply follows medieval tradition and when he uses this tradition as a starting point for an original synthesis.

It is the purpose of this paper to examine Pietro Pomponazzi's conception of God's foreknowledge in relation to the medieval tradition on which he draws. The problem of God's foreknowledge is a major, though neglected, theme of Pomponazzi's *De fato*.[1] His own

---

* Research for this paper was begun on a National Foundation for the Humanities Summer Grant, 1968. It was completed during a sabbatical leave from Queens College in the Fall, 1969. The paper was read at the Renaissance Seminar of Columbia University on December 1, 1970. I want to thank my colleague, Professor Edward P. Mahoney of Duke University, for many valuable references and suggestions.

[1] Petri Pomponatii philosophi et theologi doctrina et ingenio praestantissimi, *De fato, libero arbitrio, praedestinatione, providentia Dei libri V* in *Opera* (Basel, 1567). All references are to Petri Pomponatii Mantuani, *Libri quinque de fato, de libero arbitrio, et de praedestinatione*, ed. Richard Lemay (Lugano, 1957). Hereafter, *De fato*.

The problem of foreknowledge has been largely neglected in the secondary literature on the *De fato*. Pomponazzi's position is stated without much analysis in Giovanni Sante Felici, "Piero [sic] Pomponazzi e la dottrina della predestinazione," *Giornale critico della filosofia italiana* 7 (1926), 31-32. Another outline of the position is found in E. Maier, *Die Willensfreiheit bei Laurentius Valla und Petrus Pomponatius*, Renaissance und Philosophie, VII (Bonn, 1914), 86-87. The importance of the doctrine is undervalued by G. Saitta, *Il pensiero italiano nell'Umanesimo e nel Rinascimento*, 2nd. ed., II (Florence,

solution, first stated in Book II, is later elaborated and deepened in the remaining books of the treatise (Pomponazzi, *De fato*, 184-185, 288-290, 338-340, 397-399). The problem may be stated as follows. God's omniscience includes in its eternity a determinate and infallible knowledge of all future events. But if God knows all future events, then these events can occur only in the way foreknown by Him. And if they are thus determined by God's knowledge, the contingency of future events, including those dependent on the human will, is destroyed. For no power of the will can produce something not foreknown by God. Always operating within the foreknown pattern, the will loses its freedom of choice. Because Christian thinkers took free will as a precondition for deliberation and moral responsibility, they sought to establish a doctrine of divine foreknowledge which preserved contingency. For they saw that the destruction of contingency and free will subverted the moral order which God Himself had established.

Pomponazzi's discussion begins with the basic distinctions developed by Boethius and St. Thomas. The development of his own position, however, soon involves a sharp critique and rejection of these earlier views. His final answer also involves consideration of the positions of Scotus and Ockham.

Let us begin where Pomponazzi does with the views of Boethius and St. Thomas. Boethius' discussion of divine foreknowledge unites two essentially opposed views, the Aristotelian view of definite and contingent knowledge as time-related and the Neoplatonic view of timeless divine knowledge.[2] Aristotle tried to save contingency, Boethius explains, by maintaining that all events—present, past, future—are determinate or indeterminate only at a given time (Aristotle, *De interpretatione*, c.9). At any given time X, something is determinate only if it is past or present in relation to X. For anything past or present in relation to X is settled and definite. On the view that truth

---

1961), 334-335. It is just barely mentioned by F. Fiorentino, *Pietro Pomponazzi* (Florence, 1868), 444. The importance as well as the neglect of the *De fato* has been properly emphasized by Paul O. Kristeller in *Eight Philosophers of the Italian Renaissance* (Stanford, 1964), 78.

[2] The following discussion of Boethius rests largely on the excellent work of Marilyn McCord Adams, "The Problem of God's Foreknowledge and Free Will in Boethius and William Ockham," (Ph. D. diss., Cornell University, 1967), 18-104. See also J. Isaac, *Le Peri Hermeneias en Occident de Boèce à Saint Thomas* (Paris, 1953), 13-34. For a discussion of the Neoplatonic view of eternity see A. H. Armstrong, *The Architecture of the Intelligible Universe in the Philosophy of Plotinus : an Analysis and Historical Study* (London, 1940).

corresponds with reality, Aristotle holds that propositions about these events are either determinately true or determinately false. Our knowledge of them is therefore determinate. But events which are future in relation to a given time X are determinate only if something in the past or present in relation to X necessitates them. In that case, they come to be of simple necessity. And the mind can grasp them as determinately true or determinately false. However, all and only all events which are future in relation to X and not necessitated by something past or present in relation to X are indefinite and contingent. On the Aristotelian correspondence theory of truth, we know them indefinitely because there is nothing yet definite with which our propositions could correspond or fail to correspond. They are therefore in principle and by definition unknowable (Adams, 28). Such events are future contingents whose existence guarantees deliberation and free will. It would appear then that for Aristotle no mind, not even a divine mind, can have prescience of future contingents. And so indeed was Aristotle interpreted by almost all medieval thinkers from Boethius to Ockham. This conclusion was clearly unacceptable to Christians who could allow no qualification of God's omniscience. But the moment they tried to establish God's omniscience in regard to future events within the Aristotelian categories, contingency seemed to disappear.

This is precisely the problem that disturbs Boethius at the beginning of Book V of the *Consolation of Philosophy*.[3] God's omniscience is not simply a knowledge of all things. It is a knowledge of all things at a definite time, before they come to be. If God knew at any past time X all events that will come to be and not come to be in the created world, then his foreknowledge of these events is determinately true or determinately false at that time. But on Aristotle's theory, any knowledge which is determinately true or determinately false corresponds to some determinate reality. Therefore the knowledge that these events are either determinately true or determinately false of itself implies that they are actually true or actually false at the time of cognition and at all times prior to their occurrence. Thus they will occur or fail to occur of simple necessity. This in turn eliminates contingency and with it deliberation and free will. A solution to this problem requires a theory of divine foreknowledge which unites contingency with infallibility.

---

[3] Boethius, *The Consolation of Philosophy*, trans. by "I. T." (1609), revised by H.F. Stewart (Cambridge, Mass., 1918), V, 373-381.

Boethius' most impressive solution—one taken up by St. Thomas Aquinas—rests on his assertion of the superior cognition of divine intelligence. The Aristotelian strictures about definite truth and falsity apply to the human mind, says Boethius, because all human thought is bound to the time process, to the unfolding of events within successive moments. But the divine intelligence operates in an entirely different way because God's cognition is eternal (Adams, 59). Flowing from the divine, eternal nature, God's cognition intuits everything at once. In this intuition there is no succession for the eternal possesses the whole of its interminable being at once, immutably, and forever. The eternal is not an endless succession of individual moments or endless time. It is rather the possession of all possible moments at once. In brief, the eternal is timeless (Adams, 60-73).

This view of eternity, derived from Plato and the Neoplatonists, provides Boethius with his solution.[4] In eternity, the divine intelligence grasps all particulars in one intuitive cognition. The cognition of any specific event, even a future event, is thus no longer dependent on its occurrence within the temporal sequence. Divine knowledge, Boethius now claims, is not dependent on the nature of the thing known but on the power of the divine cognizing faculty (Boethius, 389). Divine intelligence, existing within the eternal nature of God, rises above reason in its cognition of all future events outside the temporal sequence. This divine knowledge is not an adequation of reality within time for only the concepts of human reason must correspond to events within time.

This immediate, intuitive, and definite knowledge of future events, argues Boethius, is not really a foreknowledge, a knowledge of events before they come to be. It is simply a "seeing out," an eternal intuitive glance, encapsulating all events in a single instant (Boethius, 403, 405; Adams, 74-77). Thus the knowledge of any event within God's eternal intelligence is not the foreknowledge of the event but simply a knowledge of the event as it actually is, outside the temporal sequence. For this reason, the eternal glance of God imposes no necessity on the event. Boethius claims that this is analogous to human knowledge of a present event. Just as our mere knowledge of a present event imposes no necessity on it, so God's knowledge of a future event imposes no necessity on that event. The future contingent therefore

---

[4] On the sources of Boethius, see Adams, 69-72 and H. R. Patch, "Necessity in Boethius and the Neoplatonists," *Speculum* 10 (1935), 393-404.

preserves its contingency within the temporal sequence while it is at the same time definite for God. In sum, Boethius ends by claiming that the Aristotelian principles which prescribe the conditions for determination of definite knowledge are not applicable to the divine mode of cognition. The future contingent, unknowable to the human mind which is bound to the time process, is in fact knowable to the divine intelligence which in its eternal vision sees it as a present actuality (Adams, 76-77).

Boethius' solution played a major role in St. Thomas' formulation of the problem.[5] Like Boethius, Thomas claims that God knows the future contingent as a present actuality. The mode of this knowledge is the divine essence which through its eternity possesses all time as actually present in a "total simultaneity." Stressing that God's knowledge cannot be bound to the temporal sequence, Thomas holds that the future mode cannot exist for divine knowledge. For if God should know the future in a genuinely future mode, His knowledge would be uncertain and possibly false (Groblicki, 25). As either uncertainty or falsity would imply imperfection in the divine essence, God's infallibility would be impugned.

The present nature of all future events within God's eternity, says Thomas, does not destroy the contingency of the events within nature. The future event remains contingent within nature while it is certain and definite for God. God's definite knowledge does not impose necessity on the contingent event because the existence of a thing differs from its existence in the soul. A stone exists, for example, as a material thing yet the mind knows it through an immaterial category. The immaterial understanding of the stone within the mind does not make the stone immaterial in actuality; nor does the determinate knowledge of the future contingent within the divine mind make the future event determinate within nature. So God's knowledge of the future as a present determined fact does not impose determinacy on the contingent event.

---

[5] For a convenient collection of all the relevant texts of St. Thomas (with the exception of *Summa Theologiae*, I, q. 19, a. 8) see J. Groblicki, *De scientia Dei futurorum contingentium secundum S. Thomam ejusque sequaces* (Cracow, 1938). See also M. Benz, "Das göttliche Vorherwissen der freien Willensakte der Geschöpfe bei Thomas v. Aq. in I *Sent.*, d. 38, q. 1, a. 5," *Divus Thomas* (Freiburg) 14 (1936), 255-273; J. Stufler, "Die Lehre des h. Thomas von göttlichen Vorherwissen der freien Willensakte der Geschöpfe," *Zeitschrift für Katholische Theologie* 61 (1937), 323-340; A. E. Whitacre, "The Divine Concurrence and Free Will," *Blackfriars* 4 (1924), 1328-1341; 1388-1398.

In a second consideration of the problem, Thomas goes beyond Boethius. God's definite knowledge of future contingents also derives from the fact that His knowledge is the cause of all things. Clearly His knowledge of which He is the source must be certain and infallible. But how can this certain and infallible knowledge which causes all events allow for contingent occurrences? Although God's knowledge is absolute and invariable as a first cause, says Thomas, it produces its effects through secondary causes which are contingent. The contingent causes of future events assure their contingency because such causes are immediate. And events are directly caused by their immediate rather than their remote causes. The sun, Thomas explains, acts necessarily by producing light and heat for all plants. But all plants do not necessarily grow because their proximate causes, seeds, are at times defective and do not receive the beneficent energy of the sun. These defective contingencies of plant life in no way affect or diminish the necessary power of the sun. Similarly, God's knowledge, conceived of as the First Cause, necessarily causes all events. But His power operates through secondary contingent causes which as the immediate causes of events preserve their contingency (Groblicki, 22-23, 32).

Thomas finds, however, that he must further qualify this view when considering the divine essence in the aspect of pure will. From the second solution, it appears possible that something can occur other than the way in which the divine will decrees it. For assuming the omnipotence of the divine will, it is difficult to see how created defects can deflect its irresistible power. Moreover, if contingency refers only to secondary causes, it appears that contingent events are separable from and independent of divine intention. To meet this objection, Thomas notes that it is better to say that God wills some events necessarily and some contingently. The contingency of future events is thus preserved directly by the divine will which orders them contingently.[6] This view is stressed again when Thomas holds that the divine power, existing above the categories of necessity and contingency, can appropriate these categories to its will. In this appropriation, God orders some events in a contingent mode and some in a necessary mode (Groblicki, 36).

In Thomas' solution, the activity of the divine will as it produces

---

[6] St. Thomas Aquinas, *Summa theologiae* in *Opera Omnia*, IV (Leonine edition, Rome, 1888), I, q. 19, a. 8, p. 244.

necessary and contingent events is not very closely examined. It is not very clear how the activity of the will in this operation is related to the activity of the intellect. Perhaps this lack results from Thomas' view that intellect and will are united in God. In any event, it appears that the prime emphasis in the doctrine of foreknowledge is that all future events are known in their present actuality to God, and that the will produces what is foreknown by God as it directs divine foreknowledge to its completion. It is true that the will always acts in accord with the grades of created being so that it orders necessary causes for necessary events and contingent causes for contingent events. But it is apparently the case that the willing of future contingents involves producing what is present to God in an eternal vision of the actual moment of occurrence.

By insisting on the supremacy of the divine will, Duns Scotus reverses the Thomistic relationship of the divine will and intellect. This reversal is the basis for his rejection of Thomas. And he provides a new solution to the problem of foreknowledge based on the activity of the divine will.

Against Thomas, Scotus charges that the subordination of the divine will to the eternal vision of the divine intellect actually destroys the possibility of future contingencies. Nothing can be present to God in eternity, Scotus notes, which has not in fact been created. Thus if God sees a future event as present within his eternal vision, that event must have already been created in eternity. Then it will have to be created again in time for its actual moment of occurrence. This leads to the absurd conclusion that God would have to create a being or event twice, once in eternity and once in time.[7] Furthermore, God's knowledge is not free prior to some movement of the divine will. God's eternal knowledge consists of cognizing all possible things, and prior to any movement of the divine will, this cognition is involuntary. For God knows all possible things necessarily, just as vision necessarily sees all things present to it. Hence, if God knows all future events simply through His eternal knowledge, He knows them necessarily. This necessity in turn imposes a necessity on the events themselves, thereby destroying their contingency. Should the actual future

---

[7] Duns Scotus, *Lectura in librum sententiarum* in *Opera Omnia*, XVII (Vatican City, 1966) Lectura 1, dist. 39, q. 5, b, 487. For a discussion of this point see H. Schwamm, *Das göttliche Voherwissen bei Duns Scotus und seinen ersten Anhängern*, Philosophie und Grenzwissenschaften, V (Innsbruck, 1934), 10-12; E. Gilson, *Jean Duns Scot, Introduction à ses positions fondamentales* (Paris, 1952), 312.

event be among the possibilities present to God's mind, Scotus concludes, God could only know the actual outcome of a future contingent in a necessary way. And this would destroy the contingency of the event (Duns Scotus, 492; Schwamm, 9, 41, 53; Gilson, 318).

To avoid knowing future events necessarily, which in turn imposes necessity on them, God must be able to know them freely, outside the realm of all possible things. And since God's will is totally free, He can will any event into existence. The contingency of future events is preserved, says Scotus, because God contingently wills them into existence. But the will does not act blindly. It freely chooses future events from the possibilities presented to it by the divine intellect. After its choice is made, it communicates its decision to the divine intellect (Schwamm, 22-44). The free choice of the divine will preserves the contingency of the future event. For the divine intellect now knows the future event not from the necessary knowledge of all possible things but from the actual free choice of the divine will. Because this choice is itself contingent, the contingency of future events is preserved.

Scotus believes, then, that the contingency of future events is preserved because they occur within the unfolding temporal sequence by a free act of God's will. Still, difficulties arise which Scotus attempts to solve, not always with uniform success. How could a future event remain contingent, it was asked, if it occurred through a definite prior decision of the divine will? While the divine will might decide without any compulsion, the decision, once made, was irrevocable and unimpedible. Hence it would seem that the future event is determined by this decision and is no longer contingent. The position apparently establishes God's freedom but not the indeterminacy of events. Yet Scotus insists that the events are contingent because the act of the divine will is contingent : the contingency of the one preserves the contingency of the other. Why? The answer is that freedom in God's will, as in the human will, includes a capacity for willing opposites at the same instant of nature. Scotus means that although the divine will chooses X to exist at t-1, the will still possesses at the very moment of choice the capacity for not willing X at t-1. The argument, it should be noted, is not that the divine will actually wills X and not-X at t-1. Rather it is that the very ability to will the opposite of what is in fact willed provides for the contingency of the event (Schwamm, 22-24). In other words, the fact that an event can be other than what it is provides sufficient basis for establishing its contingency.

There is still another major objection which Scotus attempted to meet. If the divine will freely determined all future events, then the acts of the human will were included in that determination. The act of the divine will apparently predetermined the act of the human will. Even granting the divine capacity for willing opposites without succession, it would still be clear that God always wills one thing, not two contradictory things. Had the free act of God destroyed the free will of man? Of course, Scotus denies this. And it is important to note that he always maintained the freedom of the human will. It is not our task here to examine Scotus' doctrine of free will but we may simply note that he maintains the freedom of the human will despite its apparent predetermination by the divine will. His solution, to say the least, was paradoxical since he insisted that the human will could not be the total cause of its own action (Schwamm, 27-28). Such total independence, he admitted, would destroy omniscience by allowing that the human will could be determined by some power God is unaware of. God must foreknow the determinations of our will as part of his foreknowledge of future contingencies. Yet the only way that He can foreknow this is through the free determination of the divine will.

It was this central weakness of the Scotist solution which attracted critics in the fourteenth century. Much of the criticism of Thomas Anglicus (Thomas Wilton) and Petrus Aureoli was summed up by William of Ockham (Schwamm, 108-130). Ockham notes that faith assures us that God must have determinate knowledge of future contingents. But he finds that Scotus is unable to solve the paradox of an event which is at once determined by the divine will and still contingent within nature. Examining Scotus' definition of the contingent activity of the divine will, Ockham denies that this will can will opposites at the same instant of nature. Such a power, Ockham holds, rests on some non-evident capacity which can never be actualized. Indeed should this capacity ever be actualized, God would will contradictory events, which is clearly impossible. Now whatever cannot be actualized in any conceivable way, must never be posited.[8] However,

---

[8] William Ockham, *Predestination, God's Foreknowledge and Future Contingents*, trans. Marilyn McCord Adams and Norman Kretzmann (New York, 1969), 72-73, hereafter cited as *Predestination*. Cf. William Ockham, *Tractatus de praedestinatione et de praescientia Dei et de futuris contingentibus*, ed. Philotheus Boehner (St. Bonaventure, 1945), 33, hereafter cited as *Tractatus*. See also *Ordinatio*, Distinctions 38-39, translated in Ockham, *Predestination*, 85.

the conclusive objection to Scotus' doctrine is that the Subtle Doctor provides no way to preserve the freedom of the created will which was specifically mandated by God. In the Scotist explanation, either the created will must follow the determination of the divine will or we must end by admitting that the divine will is less than omnipotent. For, notes Ockham, "when the divine will exists as determined [to one of two opposites] a created will would coact, and consequently no act of the created will would be imputable to itself" (Ockham, *Predestination*, 49). On the other hand, if the created will does act freely in a manner not predetermined by God, then the divine will cannot possibly be the basis for the knowledge of the act of the created will. In that event, Scotus' doctrine of foreknowledge is completely eliminated (Ockham, *Ordinatio*, 88).

For these reasons Ockham decides that the Scotist view of foreknowledge does not represent an adequate rational theology. Ockham's attempt to reconcile future contingents with God's omniscience starts with God's knowledge. Unlike Boethius and Thomas, Ockham does not allow the possibility that God's eternal knowledge is timeless.[9] He rejects entirely the Neoplatonic intelligible universe in which the divine intelligence by a mere intuition of a simple form attains to a timeless knowledge of all particulars. Instead he argues that God, though eternal and immutable, exists when time exists without being in time. God is not therefore merely an outside witness to the temporal process but actually present during the duration of its temporal unfolding, though not within its continuous succession. To exist when time exists or with time means that God's acts occur at a specific time. Hence they are datable. It becomes literally true, for example, to say that God judged at some point T that A will be B at Tn (where Tn is later than T). This means that the Aristotelian notion of definite and indefinite knowledge as time-related appears to hold for God. For if God knows determinately at T that A will be B at Tn, then at all times after T up to Tn, it is settled and necessary that A will be B at Tn. When generalized, this argument eliminates contingency and free will. On the other hand, if it is indeterminate for God at T that A will be B at Tn, then it is indefinite and contingent after T up to Tn that A will be B at Tn. When generalized, this argument eliminates foreknowledge and omniscience. Within the Aristotelian

---

[9] The following discussion of God and time is based on Adams, "The Problem of God's Foreknowledge," 128-167.

categories, then, Ockham concludes that determinate foreknowledge cannot be squared with contingency and free will. To prove contingency, Aristotle would have to deny divine prescience.

To uphold the viewpoint of faith which declares for determinate divine foreknowledge and future contingency, Ockham re-defines Aristotle's notions of determinate and indeterminate truth. According to Aristotle, we recall, the determinate truth of a future event is something made definite in the past or present relative to that future time. But now Ockham maintains that the determinate truth of a future event is something that is yet to be settled by what will be real or actual in the future. An event can therefore be determinately true in the future and still not be settled by something past or present in relation to that future time. On the theory that knowledge corresponds with reality, determinate knowledge of such a future event will also depend on what is real or actual in the future.[10]

Applying this theory to God's foreknowledge, we may say that God determinately foreknows which part of a future contingent will be and which will not be. "Nevertheless," Ockham says, "He knows it contingently and He can not know it and He could never have known it" (Ockham, *Predestination*, 55). This means that because determinate knowledge is not determinate until the future time, it is logically possible at any and all times up to the future time for the event to be other than it will be at the future time. Corresponding to this logical possibility, God's determinate foreknowledge is contingent in the sense that He is able not to know the outcome of a future contingent because the outcome is indeterminate until the future time. If this is true at any point prior to the future point of determination, it is true for all points. So we may say that God was able never to know the outcome prior to the future determination because at all points prior to the determination it remains logically possible for it to be other than what it will be.

Ockham is aware that his solution is not entirely satisfactory. In noting that God has determinate foreknowledge of future events which He still knows contingently, Ockham concludes that it is difficult to determine the mode by which God knows this. A final answer to this difficult problem, Ockham concludes, can only be provided by faith (Ockham, *Predestination*, 49-50).

---

[10] Ockham, *Predestination*, 55; cf. Ockham, *Tractatus*, 19. See also *Ordinatio* in *Predestination*, 92. For a full discussion see Adams, "The Problem of God's Foreknowledge," 174-80, and Adams and Kretzmann in *Predestination*, Introduction, 14-16.

This historical sketch underlines some of the major aspects of this problem in medieval thought. By restricting myself to those sources which Pomponazzi himself cites or which have clearly influenced his discussion, I have tried to put his treatment into historical perspective and to make clear his own contribution to the subject.

Pomponazzi begins, as I have said, with the distinctions of Boethius and Thomas. The total simultaneity of God's eternal life gives divine cognition an immediate, intuitive knowledge of the whole temporal sequence. God's knowledge may be compared to a constant vision within one undifferentiated eternal instant of the whole temporal process. Therefore his knowledge is constant, definite, and infallible. But where Boethius and Thomas eliminate the future mode within God's eternal knowledge, Pomponazzi insists on it. Differences of time, Pomponazzi declares, are not totally dissolved in an eternal timeless cognition. Events are distinctly present, past, and future to eternity. And they are therefore known by God within these modes. When an event is present or past for eternity, God knows it as "outside its causes," reduced from potentiality to actuality. Such an event is occurring or has occurred within the temporal sequence so that it is determinate and definite (Pomponazzi, 290, 337-338). But God knows future events in two ways. When an event has not yet occurred within the temporal sequence, God knows that event as a genuine future contingent. Since that event is itself undetermined, is "within its causes," it is a genuine potentiality. And God knows it as such. He knows only that it can occur or not occur. But God also knows the moment at which the event will occur. In knowing that moment of determination, He knows the future event as determined. Both moments, present to God's eternity in a single undivided intuition, provide God with a double knowledge of the future. The future as future God foreknows as indefinite and contingent. The future as present God knows as definite and determined (Pomponazzi, 339). In God this knowledge is not divided sequentially but conceptually. In man, Pomponazzi notes, such differences require positing differences of time, but in God a difference of mode or concept suffices. In foreknowing the future in its full contingency, God is able to prescind from His knowledge of the future as determined (Pomponazzi, 341-343). It is this gap, so to speak, in divine foreknowledge which preserves contingency and free will.

Pomponazzi's view of divine foreknowledge leads him to strong criticisms of Boethius and St. Thomas. He rejects their Neoplatonic view that God's eternal mode of cognition permits a determinate knowledge of an event which remains contingent in nature. Instead, Pomponazzi appears to insist on Aristotle's view of knowledge as adequation and representation. Knowledge, he says, depends on the accurate conception of the thing known, so that the principle of the known object must be in the knower. If the object is contingent, then it cannot be known as determinate or necessary, for such knowledge would be false. Accepting the view that knowledge is time-related, Pomponazzi concludes that the future contingent can be known determinately only at the moment of its occurrence within the temporal order (Pomponazzi, 330-331). Moreover, there is the problem of the status of knowledge itself. The contingent and determinate, he says, contain inherently opposite principles. They are not convertible except by comparisons and likenesses which are not literally meant. What is by nature contingent cannot therefore be necessary when related to a different order of perception. If we could combine contradictories in this way, all certain knowledge would disappear. "One nature would be changed into another," says Pomponazzi, "and then man could become an ass" (Pomponazzi, 334).

Pomponazzi's position, then, rejects the Neoplatonic view that the eternal mode of cognition can produce a form of knowledge totally opposed to the knowledge produced within the temporal order. However and whatever God may know, He cannot possess a knowledge which is totally divorced from and contradictory to the principles of the temporal order. The basis of this criticism is the charge that Boethius and Thomas have attempted to combine mutually contradictory positions. They appear, on the one hand, to accept the Aristotelian view of the future contingent as in principle unknowable and, on the other, to assert that in the Neoplatonic universe the future contingent is indeed knowable. In rejecting this contradiction, Pomponazzi holds that the eternal mode of cognition cannot of itself produce a knowledge totally opposed to the definition of knowable objects. What is needed, he decides, is a qualification of the view of eternity which allows for a closer correspondence between the eternal and temporal orders. Hence he has provided God with a purely contingent mode of knowledge, the future as future. At the same time, he has not impugned God's infallibility because He has allowed for a simultaneous definite knowledge of the future—the future as determined, as a present or past occurrence within God's eternity. But the future as present or past is intuited within the divine essence only when the future event is beyond its causes, when it is actually definite within the temporal order.

While rejecting important aspects of the Thomistic doctrine of divine foreknowledge, Pomponazzi returns to Thomas when considering the nature of divine causation. With Thomas (and against Scotus), Pomponazzi holds that God's knowledge is the cause of things. And since it is God's eternal decision to will what He knows, it must be determined how God's omnipotent will can order events within the temporal sequence without predetermining them. Here Pomponazzi follows Thomas' position that God orders necessary causes for necessary events and contingent causes for contingent events. Therefore what God determines to occur contingently will have contingent causes and what He determines to occur necessarily will have necessary causes. Pomponazzi accepts this basic distinction because it seems impossible that God does not know that He has caused any future event. How can he be ignorant of what He Himself causes and which nothing can impede? Even if He can prescind from the knowledge of the future as determined, how can He prescind from the knowledge that He has caused the future? The answer that God knows that He has prepared contingent causes for contingent events and necessary causes for necessary events is not sufficient. So Pomponazzi again goes beyond Thomas in bringing this position into agreement with his own views of divine foreknowledge. If we ask how God determines the existence of Socrates for a future year, the answer is that Socrates' existence is determined contingently for that year. Just as God knows the future as future indeterminately, so He determines the future as future indeterminately. A future event which is determinate insofar as it is truly future is a contradiction in terms. Thus Pomponazzi concludes that a future event is truly contingent for God because it is both known and determined contingently (Pomponazzi, 397).

An immediate result of Pomponazzi's close examination of the willing of future events is that the activity of the divine will looms larger for him than for Thomas. In discussing the nature of God's contingent activity, Pomponazzi rejects the view of Scotus that the contingency of the divine will can be expressed as the capacity for willing opposites. If God, says Pomponazzi, is the sole determining agent for the existence of Socrates for moment A, then either He can determine that Socrates exist for moment A or not determine it. If He has in fact determined Socrates' existence for moment A, then He cannot produce the opposite without changing the determination because Socrates cannot exist and not exist at the same time. On the other hand, if God has not yet determined the existence of Socrates for moment A, then since Socrates will either exist or not exist for moment A, God must make a determination. Thus God would still be changing from indeterminacy to determinacy. However we phrase it, Pomponazzi insists that God's only mode of possessing a determination other than the one He makes is to change to that new determination. He possesses no non-evident capacity for willing opposites simultaneously (Pomponazzi, 394).

Here Pomponazzi's criticism of Scotus is remarkably similar to Ockham's. And there also appear to be other similarities between Pomponazzi and Ockham. So it is not surprising that Lemay, in his excellent critical edition of the *De fato*, says that Pomponazzi's view of divine foreknowledge appears to be the same as Ockham's (Pomponazzi, 148, n. 1). On first glance this view has much to recommend it. Both Pomponazzi and Ockham hold that God's intuitive cognition provides a foreknowledge which is simultaneously determinate and contingent. Both agree that the determinate aspect of God's foreknowledge does not eliminate contingency in nature. Both hold that the genuinely contingent mode of divine foreknowledge depends neither on the divine will nor on the purely present mode of all God's knowledge.

Nevertheless, there are significant differences in their positions. Pomponazzi's view of divine foreknowledge is based on his qualification of the Neoplatonic view of eternity. This is made absolutely clear by his constant reference to Boethius whenever he touches on divine cognition or makes the distinction between temporal and eternal knowledge. Moreover, Pomponazzi's view preserves God's infallibility because the eternal cognition includes both the determinate and contingent modes of knowledge.

Ockham's position, however, rests on the complete rejection of the Neoplatonic view of eternity. Its basis is the re-definition of Aristotle's notion of determinate and indeterminate truth. By Ockham's own admission, his position seems to create a problem for God's infallibility, a dilemma totally lacking in Pomponazzi. For if, as Ockham argues, God's judgment at T that A will be B at Tn (where Tn is later than T) may in fact be settled contingently, "it is yet possible that things will be settled in the future in such a way that it will not have been true to say that God knows A will be B at Tn" (Adams, 193). Thus, it is possible that if God so judges at T, He may be in error. And this of course raises a question about His infallibility.

In conclusion, two points should be stressed. In the first place, Pomponazzi's view of divine foreknowledge elaborates a natural theology. In view of his earlier assertions in the immortality treatises and the *De incantationibus* that a rational theology is a contradiction in terms, this is of itself quite remarkable.[11] By allowing Gods' foreknowledge and will to coincide partially with the temporal sequence, Pomponazzi clearly feels that he has saved contingency without impinging on divine omniscience and omnipotence : God both knows and wills these contingent events as determinate in the degree that their moment of occurrence is present to Him in eternity and in the degree that He has willed their definite outcome. But God is evidently able to prescind from this definite knowledge and determination when He knows and wills the future as future.

Secondly, I think it is possible to say that Pomponazzi was correct when he asserted the originality of his own view of divine foreknowledge. This view is not Boethian or Thomistic because it rejects their concept of eternity which eliminates the future mode in divine knowledge. It is not Scotist because it does not make God's foreknowledge dependent on the activity of the divine will. It is not Occamist because it does not make divine foreknowledge dependent on a re-definition of the Aristotelian notions of contingent and determinate truth. It is, I would like to suggest, simply Pomponazzian.

Queens College, The City University of New York.

---

[11] Pietro Pomponazzi, *De immortalitate animae* 15, f. 51^v a; *Apologia* III, 3, f. 73^v b; *Defensorium* 30, f. 104a. All references are to the Collected Edition: Petri Pomponatii Mantuani, *Tractatus acutissimi, utillimi, et mere peripatetici, De intensione et remissione formarum ac de parvitate e magnitudine, De reactione, De modo agendi primarum qualitatum, Tractatus de immortalitate animae, Apologiae libri tres, Contradictoris tractatus doctissimus, Defensorium autoris, Approbationes rationum defensorii per Fratrem Chrysostomum Theologum ordinis predicatorum divinum, De nutritione et augmentatione* (Venice, 1525); Petrus Pomponatius, *De naturalium effectuum causis sive de Incantationibus* (Basel, 1567), 312-324.

EDITIONS OF THE LATIN ARISTOTLE ACCOMPANIED BY THE COMMENTARIES OF AVERROES

F. EDWARD CRANZ

Recent scholarship has moved toward a better appreciation of the importance and vitality of the Aristotelian tradition during the Renaissance.[1] The following notes are an attempt to outline one special phase of the tradition, the publishing history of the 'Averroistic Aristotle' from the first separate editions of the early 1470's through the great *Opera omnia Aristotelis et Averrois* of 1550-52 and 1573-76.[2]

From the introduction of printing at least until the Basel *Opera* edition of 1538, collected editions of Aristotle's works regularly include not only 'the Philosopher' but also 'the Commentator.' It is true that Philippus Petri made a start toward a collected edition of the thirteenth-century vulgate translations by themselves, when he published the *Organon* in 1481 and the works 'de naturali philosophia' in 1482,[3] but he had no successors.

---

[1] As on many other occasions, Paul O. Kristeller both consolidated earlier research and pointed out the directions for future study. See his "Renaissance Aristotelianism," *Greek, Roman, and Byzantine Studies* 6 (1965), 157-74; the article is a revision of his *La tradizione aristotelica nel Rinascimento* (Padua, 1962).

[2] The main features of the story may be found in E. Renan, *Averroès et l'Averroïsme*, 3rd ed. (Paris, 1866). For a modern summary of the sixteenth-century 'revelation of Averroes' see H. A. Wolfson, "Revised plan for the Publication of a *Corpus commentariorum Averrois in Aristotelem*," *Speculum* 37 (1963), 88-104. Much information on the translators and on editions may be found in M. Steinschneider, *Die hebraeischen Übersetzungen des Mittelalters und die Juden als Dolmetscher* (Berlin, 1893). For early humanist editions, see L. Minio-Paluello, "Attività filosofico-editoriale aristotelica dell'umanesimo" in *Umanesimo europeo e umanesimo veneziano*, Civiltà europea e civiltà veneziana : Aspetti e problemi, II (Florence, 1964), 245-62.

[3] *Gesamtkatalog der Wiegendrucke* (henceforth GW) #2391 and #2336. On the thirteenth-century translations, see *Aristoteles Latinus*, ed. G. Lacombe, et al., 2 vols, with supplements (Rome, 1939; Bruges and Paris, 1961); A. Mansion, "Texte latin d'Aristote utilisé à la fin du Moyen Âge," *Bulletin de philosophie médiévale* 3 (1961-62), 169-76. The printed versions of the vulgate translations are usually based on what the *Aristoteles Latinus* calls the 'nova translatio,' but they were continually revised, generally in the direction of a 'better Latin.'

It is also true that the humanists had long proclaimed their intention to replace the 'scabby' Aristotle of the medieval, vulgate versions with one as elegant and eloquent in Latin as he had been in Greek.[4] But their program of translation was slow to be completed, and the only early 'humanist' edition of the collected works of Aristotle is that published by Benedictus Fontana at Venice in 1496. In the Preface we find the usual statement of the humanist mission. "Erat iam tot elapsis annorum curriculis apud Latinos tuos Aristoteles ipse decor et norma comitatis et elegantiae non solum barbarus et incomptus, verum adeo falsus, in tantum depravatus sive interpretis illius antiqui ignavia sive scriptorum inscitia ut non solum parum utilis sed et laboriosus nimium fastidiique plenus omnibus appareret." But now Johannes Argyropylus has devoted years to translation "ut Aristoteles ipse in suam pristinam et Graecam elegantiam comitatemque Latinus reversus fuisset."[5]

The edition is an impressive one but even at the end of the fifteenth century, Fontana, despite his humanist zeal, must still reprint many of the vulgate translations. And the edition of 1496 had no successor until the Basel edition of 1538.

Meanwhile, in the period from 1470 through 1542, there appeared ten complete, or nearly complete, editions of the Latin Aristotle accompanied by the commentaries of Averroes.

Laurentius Canozius of Padua was the first to print Aristotle together with Averroes, and during the years c. 1472-1475 he issued the *Physica, De anima, Metaphysica, De coelo et mundo, Parva naturalia* together with Averroes, *De substantia orbis, De generatione et corruptione*, and *Meteorologica*.[6] While the volumes were published separately, they may be said to constitute a first *Opera* edition of the works of natural philosophy central in the Italian universities. The format of these handsome editions is adapted from the manuscript tradition and sets the pattern which lasted a century. To take the *Physica* as typical, Canozius first printed a paragraph of the text in the vulgate translation and followed this by the same text in the translation

---

[4] On the humanist translations, see E. Garin, "Le traduzioni umanistiche di Aristotele nel secolo XV," *La Colombaria* 8 (1951), 57-104. On p. 57, Garin cites Petrarch's often repeated statement : "interpretum ruditate vel invidia ad nos durus scaberque pervenit [Aristoteles]."

[5] GW #2341, aa2. Here, as elsewhere, I have modernized the Latin of the quotations except for proper names.

[6] GW #2443, 2349, 2419, 2357, 2427, 2388 and 2423.

contained within Averroes' Commentary; finally, in smaller type, he prints the Commentary itself, in the medieval translation.[7]

The Canozius editions contain no prefaces or other preliminary material to throw light on their purpose. It is worth noting, however, that Laurentius Canozius was not merely a printer but also an artist in his own right, whom Lucas Pacioli called supreme in perspective for his time.[8] Even in these earliest editions, the Averroistic Aristotle has its connections not only with the university and with academic philosophy but also with the larger cultural movements of the time.

The Canozius editions were restricted to natural philosophy and lacked the *Organon, Ethica, Rhetorica,* and *Poetica,* on all of which the thirteenth century had possessed Latin versions of Averroes' commentaries. The Commentary on the *Poetica,* in the translation of Hermannus Alemannus, was printed at Venice in 1481, in an edition which also contained Aristotle's *Rhetorica* and Alfarabius' summary of it.[9] Perhaps the Alfarabius summary was intended as a substitute for Averroes; in any case there was no Renaissance edition of Averroes' Commentary on the *Rhetorica.*

The *Organon* and the *Ethica,* with commentary, were printed in 1483 in the first single edition of the collected works, and the fifteenth century thus had in print the whole medieval corpus of Averroes commentaries with the exception of the *Rhetorica.* The 1483 edition also included Aristotle's *Politica* and *Oeconomica* in the vulgate translation.[10]

Nicolettus Vernias served as editor of the 1483 edition, and he tells

---

[7] A reproduction of the first folio of the *Physica* may be found in Fig. #4 of *Manoscritti e stampe venete dell'aristotelismo e averroismo ... Catalogo di Mostra presso la Biblioteca Nazionale Marciana* (Venice, 1958), henceforth cited as *Mostra*; the copy photographed is of particular interest since it contains the remarkable miniatures of Ariostea di Ferrara. For a convenient summary of the corpus of Averroes commentaries available to the thirteenth century in Latin, see Ermanegildo Bertola, "Le traduzioni delle opere filosofiche arabo-giudaiche nei secoli XII e XIII," in *Studi di filosofia e di storia della filosofia in onore di Francesco Olgiati* (Milan, 1962), 256-65.

[8] On L. Canozius, see the article (s. v. Lendinara) by G. Fiocco in Thieme-Becker, *Künstlerlexikon* 23 (1929), 48-49. Some information on the publisher for Canozius, Johannes Philippus Aurelianus, may be found in G. Antonelli, *Sulle opere di Aristotele... impresse in Padova e dal Canozio* (Ferrara, 1842), 17 ff.

[9] GW #2478. It may be that the editor Lancillotus de Zerlis 'modernized' the translation; he speaks of the difficulty he had "propter penuriam exemplaris unius tantum et stilum veterem in modernum reductum" (al). The commentary on the *Poetica* was reprinted with different works in 1515; see BN, *Cat. gén.* IV, 96, #689 under Aristotle.

[10] GW #2337 (see also #2338).

us in his preface that the impulse for the work came from Marcus Sanutus while the latter was studying at Padua and while his father Franciscus Sanutus was serving as Prefect of Padua (vol. III, f.1ᵛ). Vernias repeats the usual complaints of editors about the corruption of previous texts, but he speaks in detail only about the *Metaphysica*. He suggests that readers may wish to turn to Thomas Aquinas or Albertus for those portions of the *Metaphysica* on which Averroes did not comment (*ibid.*). This should caution us against letting out-of-date assumptions about 'Paduan Averroism' falsify our understanding of the printing history with which we are concerned.[11] The primary concern in these editions is the knowledge of nature. Aristotle is the best interpreter of nature, and Averroes is 'the Commentator' on Aristotle. But Albertus Magnus and Thomas Aquinas are engaged in the same endeavor, and students can use them to supplement Averroes.

The *Opera* edition of 1483 represents the consolidation of the medieval tradition of Averroes commentaries, as far as it was to be made available in the Renaissance, and it provided the basic format of later editions through 1542. But in the years following 1483 we begin to find a gradual increase in the available translations of Averroes. In contrast to the thirteenth century, these translations are made from Hebrew versions of the original Arabic, and the Latin West profits from a long and independent tradition of Jewish philosophy. In the first stage, the two most important patrons are Domenico (later Cardinal) Grimani and Johannes Pico della Mirandola; Elias Cretensis Hebraeus or del Medigo is the most important translator.[12]

Evidence of this new activity is the publication in 1488 of Elias Cretensis' translation of the Middle Commentary on Books I-III of the *Meteorologica* and of the Preface to Book Lambda of the *Metaphysica*, dedicated to Cardinal Grimani.[13] In his Preface, Elias indicates that he had done the translation because Pico requested it; Elias

---

[11] On this problem, see the judicious remarks of P.O. Kristeller, "Paduan Averroism and Alexandrism in the Light of Recent Studies," in *Aristotelismo padovano e filosofia aristotelica*, Atti del XII Congresso Internazionale di Filosofia, IX (Florence, 1960), 147-55.

[12] On Grimani, see P. Paschini, *Domenico Grimani, Cardinale di S. Marco* (†1523). Storia e Letteratura, IV (Rome, 1943). On Elias Cretensis, see U. Cassuto, *Gli ebrei a Firenze nell'età del Rinascimento* (Florence, 1968), 282-99. On Pico and Elias, see Bohdan Kieszkowski, "Les rapports entre Elie del Medigo et Pic de la Mirandole...," *Rinascimento*, 2nd ser., 4 (1964), 41-91, especially 62-3, 78-9.

[13] GW #3108. The description in the GW and elsewhere falsifies the title. Me^{ce} should be read as *Metaphysicae* and not as *Medicinae*.

himself does not have a high regard for the work of a translator. He briefly defines for Pico the translator's function, and it is clear that he hopes to find a middle ground between the vulgate tradition of 'verbum e verbo' and the new humanist demand for elegance and eloquence : "... quia traducens non solum sententiam servare debet, imo et verba... Et ideo quanto magis potest eisdem vel consimilibus verbis est utendum, non tamen omnino ut verba iacent, nisi hoc commode fieri possit" (a2). The quarrel runs deeper than we might think, and perhaps deeper than the translators realized. The Latin West had seen an extraordinary philosophic development thought out in the language of the medieval Latin translations of Aristotle and of Averroes; it was by no means sure that the philosophic continuity could be preserved if the basic texts were to be shifted into Ciceronian Latin.

In 1489 Bernardinus Stagninus at Venice published another collected edition of Aristotle with Averroes, and for the first time it bears the title : *Omnia Aristotelis opera cum commento Averrois*.[14] It includes the new translation of the *Meteorologica* commentary by Elias Cretensis and adds the *Sex principia* of Gilbertus Porretanus, with the commentary of Albertus Magnus, and the *Physionomia*; further it replaces the vulgate versions of the *Ethica*, *Politica*, and *Oeconomica* with the humanist versions of Leonardo Bruni. But it still lacks not only many of the smaller Aristotelian or pseudo-Aristotelian works but also the *De animalibus* as well as the *Rhetorica* and *Poetica*.

Octavianus Scotus republished the 1489 edition without essential change in 1495-96.[15] In 1497 it was reissued in combination with Averroes' *Destructio destructionum* accompanied by the commentary of Augustinus Niphus.[16] In his prefaces Niphus suggests that he was responsible for the whole edition and not merely for the *Destructio destructionum*. He dedicates his work to Cardinal Domenico Grimani both because of his high office and because of his marvellous knowledge of the liberal disciplines; all men of letters (*omnes litterati*) seek out the Cardinal as their one patron.[17] Again it is to be noted that Averroes appears not so much as the exponent of a specific philosophic position but rather as part of the general learning of the times.

---

[14] GW #2339.
[15] GW #2340.
[16] See GW II, col. 574 and #3106.
[17] The verso of the title page, without signature, of GW #3106.

At about the same time other small additions to the available Averroes material were made in separate works. In 1497 Aldus Manutius published a translation by Elias Cretensis, made at the request of Pico, of several of Averroes' *Questions* on the *Analytica priora*.[18] The translation was printed along with some logical works of Laurentius Maiolus, and the volume contains an interesting exchange of letters between Aldus and Maiolus, an exchange which again illuminates the tensions between humanist and philosophic Latin. Aldus had originally refused to publish what Maiolus had sent him, since the Latin was not sufficiently elegant and needed polishing; Maiolus continued to urge their publication and argues that Aldus should not think it a disgrace "nudam ab eloquentia tradere sapientiam" (aii^v).

Toward 1497-1500 another volume appeared containing several short works of Averroes, including the *De concordia inter Aristotelem et Galenum*. Baptista de Avolio dedicated the volume to Cardinal Grimani. He praises the Cardinal for his devotion to the liberal arts, and he describes him as believing Averroes to be the most expert and most faithful interpreter of the divine mind of Aristotle.[19]

In 1501, Paganinus de Paganinis reissued the *Opera* edition of 1495-96 perhaps together with the *Destructio destructionum* of 1497.[20] It reappeared in 1507-1508 under the editorship of Marcus Antonius Zimara, who added marginal notes as well as his *Solutiones contradictionum in dictis Aristotelis et Averrois*.[21] Both the notes and the *Solutiones* were continually revised and appear regularly in later editions. Finally, the last folio edition patterned directly on that of 1495-96 appeared in 1516-19.[22]

---

[18] F. R. Goff, *Incunabula in American Libraries* (New York, 1964), M-83; the volume and its contents are discussed by J. Dukas, *Recherches sur l'histoire littéraire du quinzième siècle* (Paris, 1876). The Averroes Questions were reprinted, with works of Aegidius Romanus, in 1522; see BN, *Cat. gén.* I, 292b #5.

[19] GW #3109, ai^v.

[20] *Index Aureliensis, Catalogus librorum sedecimo saeculo impressorum* (Baden-Baden, 1962 - -), henceforth cited as I.A. *107.693. The description in I.A. is incomplete; the whole set is rarely found.

[21] *Deutscher Gesamtkatalog* (henceforth DK) 6.5956. On this edition, see Edward P. Mahoney, "The Date of Publication of an Edition of Aristotle by Marcantonio Zimara," *The Library* 26 (1971), 53-56. On M. A. Zimara, see *Enciclopedia filosofica*, 2nd ed., VI (Florence, 1967), 1212-13.

[22] DK 6.5957.

Meanwhile in 1511 a volume had been published at Milan containing Paulus Israelita's translation of Averroes' Middle Commentary on the *De coelo* as well as the prooemia to the *Physica* and to Book Lambda of the *Metaphysica*.[23] Paulus Israelita (Riccius or Ricius)[24] explains that he has taken the Hebrew corpus of learning as his special province, and he is specially concerned to use the Hebrew tradition to improve the Latin Averroes. "Nec solum eiuscemodi tria prooemia, sed universa in Averoi Latino editio, ut quandoque aliquibus ex conphilosophis nostris patefeci, crebris corruptelis erroribusque abundat. Haec admonuisse volui ne quando aliqua huius prooemii et aliorum subsequentium, quae de Hebraeorum bibliotheca excerpsi, a Latina editione discriminari conspexeris, in querulam et criminatoriam vocem prorumpas" (f. VII).

In 1520-21 Jacobus Paucidrapius at Pavia published an edition of the *Opera* which differed slightly both in format and in content from the tradition established by Octavianus Scotus from 1495-6 through 1516-19.[25] In the first place, the new edition is in octavo as against the earlier folio volumes, and the prefaces emphasize its character as an *Enchiridion* or *Enchiridiolon*. Secondly it takes further account of the improvements to be drawn from the Hebrew tradition; the editor tells us that a manuscript of Paulus Ricius has enabled him to correct two thousand errors in the first books of the *Organon*.[26] Finally, we are told that the volume represents a further modernizing and correcting of the Latin of the vulgate translations, "Demum Fabri Stapulensis auspicio freti Topica Elenchosque non modo expolivimus, verumetiam inepta quaeque limatioribus verbis illustriora reddidimus."[27]

Despite these changes, the edition of 1520-21 remains essentially the same as that of 1516-19. It does not include the new translation by Paulus Israelita of the Middle Commentary on the *De coelo* nor Aristotle's *De animalibus*, *Rhetorica*, or *Poetica*. It nevertheless long

---

[23] I.A. *109.804.

[24] On Paulus Riccius, see the note by Delius in *Religion in Geschichte und Gegenwart*, 2nd ed., IV (1930), 2028.

[25] The edition is very rare; I have used the copy in the Harvard College Library.

[26] In the volume containing the *Physica*, Ai^v. In the volume containing the *Organon* (Ai^v) we find the presumably less accurate statement that the errors had been corrected "collato Arabico codice."

[27] Volume containing the *Organon*, Ai^v.

remained standard and was reissued at Lyons by Scipio de Gabiano in 1529-30 and by the Giuncta in 1542.[28]

But while the old *Opera* editions continued largely unchanged, the early 1520's saw a number of important separate editions of new translations. In 1521 Jacob Mantinus translated from the Hebrew Averroes' Epitome of the *De partibus animalium* and of the *De generatione animalium*.[29] In his dedication to Pope Leo X, Mantinus notes that the Latin translations of Averroes had been attacked for much the same reasons as the earlier translations of Aristotle, and he offers much the same defense for Averroes as that earlier offered for Aristotle : "Sed quoniam multos et praesertim eruditos ab huius lectione interpretis [scil. Averrois] avertit inculta horridaque barbaries, quae non tam ipsius authoris est culpa quam illius qui primus ex Arabico in vestrum sermonem transtulit huius volumina, dedimus operam... ut si non multum ornate atque expolite, saltem non nimis barbare aut aspere loqueretur" (Ai^v).

A much more substantial addition to the corpus of available commentaries resulted from the publication in 1523 of the translation of a number of logical works by Abram de Balmes.[30] The translations are dedicated to Cardinal Grimani, whose patronage of Averroist publications thus extends from the versions of Paulus Israelita of 1488 through these translations of Abram de Balmes published in the year of the Cardinal's death.[31]

In a long and interesting preface, Balmes defends Averroes against several contemporary attacks. He begins with the argument that only the Greek text and the Greek commentators are a proper basis for the study of 'the Philosopher'; it would seem that the Graecists have

---

[28] I.A. *107.906 f. and *107.914 f.; *108.037 f.

[29] I.A. *109.808.

[30] I.A. *107.887. On Balmes, see J. Heller in *Encyclopaedia Judaica*, III (1929); 1008-09; G. Mazzuchelli, *Gli Scrittori d'Italia* (Brescia, 1753-63) II, 1, 191.

Balmes also dedicated to Cardinal Grimani a translation of the *Epistola expeditionis* of Avempace. In the letter, he speaks of his translation of a *Compendium* of Averroes (see M. Steinschneider, *Revue des études juives* 5 (1882), 113-7; Mazzuchelli, *loc. cit*, lists a Venetian publication of 1552 with a similar title, but I know of no copy. Finally, M. Cruz Hernández, *Filosofia hispano-musulmana*, II (Madrid, 1957), 49 mentions a Paraphrase of the *De anima*, translated by Balmes and said to have been published at Venice in 1532; no copy is known to me.

[31] Another translation dedicated to Grimani was that of Averroes' Middle Commentary on the *Physica* by Vitalis Dactylomelos; it was never published (Steinschneider, 114).

displaced the humanists as the main enemy of the Latin, Averroistic Aristotle. Balmes replies, *inter alia*, that the truth and fidelity to Aristotle are better found in Averroes than in the corrupt Greek manuscripts. Balmes must also face the older 'humanist' attack on the Latin of the Averroist tradition. In his reply he defends accuracy as more important than eloquence, and he brings his position into relation with his own Jewish education : "... quia mea prima ineunte aetate meis Hebraeis litteris meis Talmudisticis gymnasiis inmissus sum, quibus veritas praeponitur, spreta eloquentia... Romani enim dicacitatem, Hebraei vero veritatem semper praehonorandam censuerunt" (AAiii).

In 1524, Jacobus Mantinus published a translation, also from the Hebrew, of the Epitome of the *Metaphysica*, and he dedicated it to Cardinal Hercules Gonzaga.[32] The same year saw the publication of Averroes' Epitome and Middle Commentary on the *Analytica priora* in the translation of Johannes Franciscus Burana; the final editing had been done by Hieronymus Bagolinus after Burana's death.[33] Unlike the other translators we have noted, Burana was not a Jew; he began his philosophic studies in Greek and Latin, and it was only later that he turned to Hebrew and Arabic.

This burst of Averroes publication in the early 1520's was followed by a period in which little new appeared although, as already noted, there were reissues of the 1520-21 *Opera* in 1529-30 and in 1542. During the same period we find a simiar decline of general Aristotelian publication, and doubtless the storms of the Reformation were partly responsible in each case.

General Aristotelian publication resumes actively in the late 1530's, and the resumption is accompanied by a new orientation. The old vulgate translations of the Middle Ages have almost disappeared, and it is the new and humanist translations which now dominate. Thus the edition of the *Opera* in Latin, published at Basel in 1538, carries on and virtually completes the elimination of the 'scabby' Aristotle first attempted in the Fontana *Opera* of 1496. The editor Simon Grynaeus writes in his Preface : "Equidem scabricies illa linguae qua male doctus [Aristoteles] principio multis in operibus valde balbutiebat

---

[32] I.A. *109.809.

[33] BN Paris, *Cat. gén.* 21, 453-54; the volume was reprinted in 1539 at Paris (I.A. *107.988). On Burana, see Mazzuchelli II, 4, p. 2424; on Bagolinus, see C. Vasoli, *Dizionario biografico degli Italiani*, V (1963), 267.

adhuc, pro virili per doctos curatum est, ut paucis admodum exceptis castigeretur."³⁴

While the new modes did not immediately affect the *Opera* editions of Aristotle accompanied by Averroes, we soon see signs of change in other Averroistic publications. Thus in 1540 Hieronymus Scotus at Venice published an edition of the *Physica* which had only one translation of the Aristotelian text (a revised version of the vulgate) and which included only the "digressiones" of Averroes rather than his whole commentary.³⁵ In 1542 Scotus published a volume containing the *Metaphysica* in the translation of Cardinal Bessarion, and again it was accompanied only by the "digressiones" of Averroes.³⁶ Finally in 1542 Scotus published a collection of four Averroes commentaries, without Aristotelian texts, and he included for the tirst fime the epitome on the *De generatione et corruptione* of Vitalis Nissus.³⁷

The full response to the new situation is the magnificent new edition published by Junta at Venice in 1550-52.³⁸ Here, for the first time, we find an Aristotle-Averroes *Opera omnia* which fully deserves the title. It includes the works of Aristotle not commented by Averroes and also the works of Averroes which are not Aristotelian. Further, it goes a long way toward incorporating the new humanist translations of Aristotle as well as the new translations of Averroes from the Hebrew.

In his great Preface, Thomas Junta speaks with the proud assurance of one who had been "born and educated to publish books for the common service of all" (v. I, f. 3). He had recently issued a complete Galen, and now he adds to it a complete Aristotle with Averroes.

By publishing Aristotle and Averroes together, Thomas Junta hopes to serve a purpose of reconciliation and to end destructive faction. According to Junta's account of changes in scholarly judgment, during his grandfather's time and earlier, men had thought nothing useful in philosophy or medicine which did not come from the Arabs; now his own age is contemptuous of the same Arabs and values only the Greeks (v. I, f. 2 ff.). Junta himself maintains that one should learn and profit from both. The Greek commentators are to be specially praised for making clear Aristotle's meaning, but the Arabs made

---

³⁴ I.A. *107.968, aii.
³⁵ I.A. *108.001.
³⁶ I.A. *108.031. For other comparable editions, see I.A. * 107.999 and *108.030.
³⁷ For a description, see *Mostra* p. 110 #191.
³⁸ I.A. *108.193. For a description of the contents, see P. Camerini, *Annali dei Giunti* (Florence, 1962 - -), vol. I, 1 #559, pp. 382-86.

an important contribution in exploring the difficult questions which Aristotle left unanswered. Similarly, Junta steers a middle course in the old debate between vulgate and humanist translations, and he defends some use of a revised vulgate "...in quo propterea fuimus veteri translatione contenti, quod eam ab eruditis maxime desiderari videbamus quodque esse fideliorem judicabamus, cum praesertim nostra impensa et doctissimorum hominum laboribus eo deducta sit, ut in latino sermone colorem quendam Aristotelicae puritatis et eloquentiae possis agnoscere" (v. I, f. 3).

A second preface, by Marcus de Odis, tells of the editorial work involved in the edition ; it had been begun and almost completed by Johannes Franciscus Bagolinus, and after Bagolinus' death de Odis carried it through the last stages. Bagolinus had first sought out the best versions of Aristotle, and he made wide use of the humanist translators except for Argyropylus : "omisit autem Argyropilum, hoc solum nomine, quod eum paraphrasten potius quam interpretem crederet" (v. I, f. 6^v). For the *Organon*, however, and for the main works of natural philosophy, Bagolinus kept the old translations but further corrected them. He performed the same task in the case of Averroes, and for the Aristotle commentaries he used Paulus Israelita, Vitalis Nissus, Abram de Balmes, Johannes Franciscus Burana, and Jacobus Mantinus. Where he was compelled to use the old translations from the Arabic he devoted great effort to making them as correct as possible, "aliosque veteres ignotos nobis Averrois enarratores mendis refertos, quos Suessanus et Zimara dum Averroim corrigerent intactos reliquerunt, in melius reduxit : quas quidem castigationes ex clarissimorum solertissimorumque virorum Pomponatii, Hispani, Hieronymi Bagolini patris, Marci Antonii Passeris de Ianua, Vincentii Madii, atque aliorum complurium scriptis collegerat, neque nos quoque parum praestitimus in hac re, dum logicam Patavii publice et philosophiam profiteremur" (v. I, f. 7). The editorial work of Bagolinus and of de Odis was particularly extensive in the case of Averroes' Long Commentary on the *Analytica posteriora*. Three translations were available, by Burana, Abram de Balmes and Mantinus (incomplete). The editors chose Burana's text as basic but then supplemented and corrected it by the other two versions. It might also be noted that the 1550-52 edition is the first to include Hebrew super-commentaries on Averroes, and it adds Levi Gersonides on the *Organon* in the translation of Mantinus.

The *Opera omnia* of 1550-52 is a most impressive publication, and it consolidates the essentials of what Professor Wolfson has called "the second revelation" of Averroes, from the Hebrew.[39] A comparable edition by Cominus de Tridino appeared at Venice in 1560; it adds the version of Elias Cretensis of the Middle Commentary (Books I-VII) on the *Metaphysica*.[40] Finally, a somewhat modified and expanded edition was published by the Junta at Venice in 1562 and repeated in 1573-6.[41]

The edition of 1562 represents the high point of the development we have traced, and in some ways it goes beyond even the edition of 1550-52. Thus, for the *Analytica posteriora*, we find not only a revised version of the vulgate translation but also all three of the sixteenth century versions of Averroes' Long Commentary (and it will be remembered that in each case the Commentary contains the complete Aristotelian text).

But in some of the new material of the 1562 edition, one may perhaps see signs that the reconciliations attempted by Thomas Junta will not be permanently successful. Thus in the case of the *De anima*, Michael Sophianus had been asked to do one more 'modernization' of the vulgate version to bring it into better accord with the Greek text and with good Latin. Sophianus tells us in his dedicatory letter, to Cardinal Franciscus Gonzaga, that a revision of the vulgate in this manner was impossible : "Etenim tralationem illam adeo foedam ac ineptam esse repperi, ut nec Aristotelis verba fideliter exprimeret et pluribus in locis eius sententiam perverteret" (Supplement to v. VI, *ibid.*, † ii^v). Sophianus was therefore compelled to make a new version, printed in the 1562 edition as a third translation in addition to the vulgate and the translation from the Arabic. But even in his new translation Sophianus was not free to depart from the vocabulary of the vulgate version, since this vocabulary was essential to Aristotelian and Averroist philosophy : "... sed necesse habui, quoad eius facere possem, verba et genera loquendi, quae ab hoc eodem auctore [Aristotele] et Averrois elocutione iam inde ab initio in scholas irrepserant, quamvis horrida parumque Latina retinere" (*Ibid.*, † ii^v). It is clear that Sophianus is straining at the bit and that he would much prefer to present a good 'humanist' Aristotle; but such an

---

[39] H.A. Wolfson, "The Twice Revealed Averroes," *Speculum* 36 (1961), 373-92. The "first revelation" was that of the thirteenth century.

[40] I.A. *108.423.

[41] The 1562 edition is I.A. *108.456 (reprinted by Minerva, Frankfurt, 1962); for a description, see *Mostra* p. 114 f. #194. The 1573-6 edition is I.A. *108.599.

Aristotle would not speak the 'language of the schools,' and the philosophers would not understand him.

The edition of 1562 also adds as a supplement the notes of Bernardus Tomitanus on various Aristotelian and Averroist works, including Book I of the *Analytica posteriora*. Here we find, *inter alia*, a careful analysis of the Latin text (Supplement to v, I, f. 1 ff.). But for the first time in the editions whose history we have been following, the primary point of reference is the Greek original. In a curious way, such gifts from the Greeks threaten the very existence of the Latin Averroistic Aristotle. The Latin Aristotle, and even more the Latin Averroes, lose their status as separate and autonomous worlds of thought; they must more and more become ancillary to the *Graeca veritas* and to philology as queen of the sciences.

In any case, the great Aristotle-Averroes editions of 1550-52 through 1573-76 had no direct successors. One might note that roughly contemporary with them, the *Opera omnia* of Thomas Aquinas were published in 1570, and there is a sense in which we might call this an Aristotle-Thomas edition.[42] Of the eighteen volumes, the first five consist of commentaries on Aristotle; each commentary of Thomas is accompanied by two Latin translations, one the vulgate version of the Middle Ages and the other a new 'humanist' translation. And somewhat later, at the end of the sixteenth and the beginning of the seventeenth centuries, the Jesuit College at Coimbra issued an almost complete series of Aristotelian 'courses,' regularly combined with a Latin humanist translation and in many cases with the Greek text.[43] But as far as general publishing history is concerned, complete editions of Aristotle as 'the philosopher' and as 'the interpreter of nature' were becoming less important. More and more the complete editions begin to present Aristotle as first of all a 'Greek author'; such editions will contain the Greek text alone or, more commonly, accompanied by a translation into humanist Latin. The Graeco-Latin edition of Isaac Casaubon, published in 1590, sets the pattern for the next centuries.[44]

Connecticut College

---

[42] For a description of the edition, see Paris BN, *Cat. gén.* 187, 561, f. #1.

[43] For examples of these editions, see I.A. *108.717; *108.724-25; *108.731-35 etc.

[44] I.A. *108.708. On the important preface of Casaubon, see J. Glucker, "Casaubon's Aristotle," *Classica et Mediaevalia* 25 (1964), 274-96.

A FIFTEENTH-CENTURY HUMANISTIC BESTSELLER:
THE MANUSCRIPT DIFFUSION OF LEONARDO BRUNI'S ANNOTATED LATIN VERSION OF THE (PSEUDO-) ARISTOTELIAN *ECONOMICS*

JOSEF SOUDEK

In 1968 I submitted to the public a listing of the extant written copies, penned in the fifteenth and early sixteenth centuries of Leonardo Bruni's Latin version (1420-21) of the spurious Aristotelian *Economics*.[1] Though essentially of bibliographical character, this survey was intended to serve several other purposes too. The chief one among them was to determine how widely and where Bruni's version circulated as compared with the two earlier medieval Latin translations of this supposedly Aristotelian work on moral philosophy—the anonymous translation of all three books of it (*translatio vetus*), done about 1280, and the translation or revision of two of its three books (I and III) by Durand d'Auvergne completed in 1295 (*translatio* or *recensio Durandi*)—which were still copied and studied, while Bruni's version became gradually known to scholars and readers from various walks of life. The survey showed that Bruni's translation rapidly replaced the two older translations within the sixty years after its first publication (1420-1480) and that at the end of the fifteenth century there were four times as many handwritten copies of Bruni's work as of the two older translations combined. Equally impressive was the total number of the manuscripts of Bruni's version then in circulation. Though not all of them survived, my list comprised 223 extant copies and 6 copies either known to be lost or which I was unable to locate.

While preparing my list for publication I was of course fully aware that it was in no way exhaustive and that further research would divulge copies in known collections which I had failed to notice, or in

---

[1] "Leonardo Bruni and His Public : A Statistical and Interpretative Study of His Annotated Latin Version of the (Pseudo-) Aristotelian *Economics*," *Studies in Medieval and Renaissance History* 5 (Lincoln, 1968), 51-136, esp. 102-129 : "Appendix II. Survey of the Extant Manuscripts."

as yet unacatalogued collections.² My assumption, based on the experience of seasoned bibliographers, turned out to be correct. Since the publication of my list eight additional manuscripts were brought to my attention, four of them by Professor Kristeller alone whose generous aid had already enabled me to include in my first compilation a considerable number of items in catalogued as well as uncatalogued collections which otherwise would have escaped my searching eyes. These eight new copies to be discussed in the following pages are not merely numerical accretions to an impressive sum total; they are interesting individual items which, in some cases, have modified some of my earlier findings and in others have lent further support to conclusions drawn from the material available for the original survey.

Two of the eight copies are manuscripts which are, or were at one time, deposited in the libraries of Oxford colleges; the one, MS. New College 228, is still extant, while the other, the final portion of the MS. Balliol College 242 containing the *Economics*, disappeared at some time after 1540.³ The mere fact that these two manuscripts were acquired and located in England in the middle of the fifteenth century and in the first half of the sixteenth century respectively modifies my speculations about the spread of Bruni's Latin version of the *Economics* outside of Italy.⁴ Based on the items in my list of manuscripts I presumed that no handwritten copy of Bruni's work had reached England before the first half of the seventeenth century. The copies at present deposited in the British Museum (nos. 15a-19 in my list), in the libraries at Cambridge (nos. 10-12) and in the Bodleian Library at Oxford (nos. 21-27) were indeed acquired by their former English owners and the respective libraries between the seventeenth and twentieth centuries.⁵

---

² *Ibid.*, 102.

³ Both manuscripts which I overlooked while preparing my list of 1968 were brought to my attention by Professor George B. Parks. In addition, he furnished me with invaluable bibliographical references.

⁴ "Leonardo Bruni and His Public," 69-71; there I concluded "that Bruni's version of the *Economics* was received, from the early 1460's on, first in Spain, Belgium, and Switzerland, then in Germany and France, and finally in Poland" (71).

⁵ The earliest date of acquisition for those manuscripts in English collections which I had included in my list of 1968 was the one for the MS. Arundel of the British Museum (no. 16 in my list); it was most probably bought by Thomas, Earl of Arundel (1592-1646) in the early decades of the seventeenth century and it was presented by his heirs in 1681 to the College of Arms in London from where it was transferred in 1831 to the British

The older of the two new manuscripts, the now lost copy of Bruni's version of the *Economics* in MS. 242 of Balliol College (no. 218a in the list of additional manuscripts at the end of this paper) is particularly noteworthy for the original owner of the codex in which it was contained, for the channel through which the codex came into his possession, and finally for the intention which possibly motivated him to purchase it. The copy of the Latin version of the *Economics* by Bruni formed the third and last text, probably filling several leaves beginning with folio 192, of a volume consisting of copies of Bruni's Latin versions of the three main writings by Aristotle on moral philosophy, the *Nicomachean Ethics*, the *Politics* and the spurious *Economics*. When the antiquary John Leland (1506?-1552) visited Balliol College in or about 1540 he saw there this codex and made the following note of it : "Ethica et Politica Aristotelis, interprete Leonardo Aretino ad Martinum 5. — Oeconomica Aristotelis, eodem interprete ad Cosmum."[6] There is also still on the verso page of the fly-leaf in the beginning of the codex a note concerning the content of the volume and its donor to the college library. It reads as follows : "Ethica Aristotelis / Politica Ar. / Yconomica Ar. / ex traductione Leonardi // Liber domus de Balliolo in Oxon' ex / dono Reverendi in Christo patris et domini / Willelmi Gray Eliensis Episcopi."[7] Both entries

---

Museum. For the history of the Arundel collection and the near impossibility of ascertaining exact dates of acquisition of individual codices see the preface by J. Forshall to the *Catalogue of Manuscripts in the British Museum*, New Series, I (London, 1840), iv-v.

[6] *Joannis Lelandi antiquarii De rebus britannicis collectanea* (generally and simply referred to as *Collectanea*), ed. Thomas Hearn, 2nd. ed., IV (London, 1774), 65. The notes of Leland were just rapidly jotted down and frequently garbled records, and not carefully prepared catalogue entries. This fact one has to keep in mind when reading the above-cited notation which is somewhat erroneous. Bruni's Latin translation of the *Nicomachean Ethics* was indeed dedicated to Pope Martin V (the dedicatory epistle is copied in the Balliol MS. on fols. 3^v - 4) whereas his translation of the *Politics* was dedicated to Pope Eugene IV (the dedicatory epistle is copied on fol. 87-87^v) and his version of the *Economics* to Cosimo de' Medici. As to John Leland's visit to Oxford it may be recalled that Leland, then the official "antiquary" of King Henry VIII and the first person to hold such position in English history, was on a commissioned tour of the libraries of all cathedrals, abbeys, priories and colleges in search for records and writings on the history of England. On Leland's life and career as the first English antiquary cf. Sidney Lee's interesting account in *The Dictionary of National Biography* (*DNB*), XI (London, 1921-22), 892-896.

[7] R.A. Mynors, *Catalogue of the Manuscripts of Balliol College, Oxford* (Oxford, 1963), 265. Mynors's catalogue offers more detailed descriptions of the manuscripts at Balliol College than the older, yet still useful compilation by H.O. Coxe, *Catalogus codicum*

are sufficient evidence that the MS. 242 of Balliol College contained indeed a copy of Bruni's version of the *Economics* and the reference to the donor on the flyleaf makes it equally certain that the codex is one of the two hundred manuscripts which William Gray (ca.1414/16 - 1478), the bishop of Ely, gave before 1477 to Balliol College. Gray had received his early theological training at the College, and he had served for two years as its chancellor before embarking on further studies on the Continent—first at the University of Cologne and later in Florence, Padua and Ferrara—and on a notable ecclesiastical career which culminated in his bishopric of Ely. As a man of noble birth and of considerable means, derived mainly from prebends, he also devoted a part of his energy to building up a collection of handwritten books which was to form the nucleus of the library of his alma mater; wherever he resided, in England or abroad, he employed scribes for making copies of such books which he could not purchase, or he bought large quantities of books from university stationers and from the scholarly Florentine bookseller Vespasiano da Bisticci. While in Italy he became acquainted with humanistic studies through Guarino Veronese, through Niccolò Perotti who for some time was member of his resplendent household at Ferrara and finally, as 'the king's proctor' at the papal court in Rome (1446-1454), through Pope Nicholas V, the patron of the *studia humanitatis*. In Rome he also may have met some luminaries of this intellectual movement such as Lorenzo Valla and Flavio Biondo and he certainly made there the acquaintance of Poggio Bracciolini. The manuscript that was to become MS. 242 of Balliol College was among those which Vespasiano sent to him in England after Gray took permanent residence again in his native country. The texts were written in a neat Italian hand while Gray was still in Italy (some time between 1444 and 1454) and the beginnings of each book of the three Aristotelian works were adorned with headings in red capital letters and lavish initials.[8] Considering Gray's interest in works of the Italian

---

mss. qui in collegiis aulisque Oxoniensibus hodie adservantur, I (Oxford, 1852), Part II. Concerning MS. 242, however, Coxe (82) omitted any reference to the lost copy of the *Economics* version by Bruni.

[8] In my brief account of William Gray's life in the text I have followed to a large extent Mynors's narration—his impressive essay on "William Gray and His Books" on pp. xxiv-xlv of the lengthy introduction to his just mentioned catalogue (n. 7)—but also the much shorter and no less fascinating sketch of Gray's career by Reginald Lane Poole in *DNB*, VIII (London, 1921-22), 655-656. A discrepancy between the two authors' views concerning Gray's attitude towards the *studia humanitatis* will be pointed out in the next note (n. 9).

humanists at that time, it appears to be only natural that he should have selected Bruni's Latin versions of the three Aristotelian writings on moral philosophy as the most suitable ones for the library of Balliol College. But, as has been recently pointed out,[9] it would be too rash to infer from this selection that Gray took in this matter an uncompromisingly humanistic attitude towards the study of ancient authors and of Aristotle in particular. Among the books on Aristotelian moral philosophy we find in Gray's library, next to the humanistic Latin translations by Bruni, the scholastic commentaries on the Aristotelian writings by Francis de Mayronis and by St. Albert the Great, commentaries which at that time were still in vogue among academic teachers and with which Gray, a theologian trained in the traditional manner, was well familiar from his studies at Balliol College, at the University of Cologne, then famous for its scholastic teachings, and, most of all, at Padua, one of the three leading Italian centers of Aristotelianism. Gray's purchase of Bruni's Latin versions of the Aristotelian works on moral philosophy, including the *Economics*, also lends further support to my earlier observations[10] that it is difficult, if at all possible, to determine whether a person in the fifteenth century who used the humanistic version of the *Economics* did so because he was interested in the Latin garb of this translation or whether he was interested primarily in the contents and would have used either one of the two medieval versions or Bruni's humanistic translation if available.

The younger of the two manuscripts at Oxford, New College, MS. 228 (no. 27a in the list at the end of this paper) is notable for the place of its origin, for the scribe who copied Bruni's Latin version of the

---

[9] Mynors, xxxv. The acquisition of Latin translations of works by Aristotle and of scholastic commentaries on them, writes Mynors, "may remind us not to overestimate the importance of Gray's interest in 'humane' studies; he has never abandoned his original objective of collecting all the best works in theology and philosophy...." A similar note of caution regarding Gray's commitment to the humanistic movement is sounded again on p. xlv where Mynors evaluates Gray's intellectual orientation as expressed in the sort and quality of the handwritten books which he acquired for his collection. There Mynors states as follows : "Gray ... was no renaissance prelate-patron... Nor was he specially devoted to the new classical learning ...." Poole, on the other hand, on p. 655 in the above-cited article in *DNB* (n. 8) speaks emphatically of "Grey's [later corrected by Poole to Gray's] devotion to humanism and his patronage of learned men." Poole furthermore claims that it was this devotion that "found favour in the eyes of Pope Nicolas V" who, on the strength of it, procured for Gray the coveted bishopric of Ely. But Mynors asserts (p. xxxiv) that "there is no evidence ... that Gray knew the Pope through other than official contacts ..."

[10] "Leonardo Bruni and His Public," 52, 86.

Economics and also for the prior owner of the manuscript. Like the codex in Balliol College, the one of New College, now deposited in the Bodleian Library, contains Bruni's Latin versions of the *Nicomachean Ethics, Politics* and of the spurious *Economics*. The texts were written in England on parchment at the middle of the fifteen century, apparently by three different hands. The scribe of the first part of the codex containing the translation by Bruni of the *Ethics*, who signed at the end of the text (fol. 89^v): "Finit liber Ethicorum. Anno domini 1452. Per me Jo. R.," may be identical with John Russell, grammar master at Oxford in 1446-47. Whether the text in the third part containing the Latin version by Bruni of the *Economics* was penned by the same hand is dubious. At one time it was presumed that it too was written by John Russell but on expert re-examination it turned out to be another and slightly later hand. Whoever the scribe may have been, he attempted to follow John Russell's style in script and decoration so faithfully that, at first sight, one would believe it was Russell himself who had copied the text.[11] At any rate, the New College manuscript originated in England at the middle of the fifteenth century and it was decorated with initials in "an English humanistic style... a simplified version of the initials in... manuscripts written for Duke Humfrey."[12] Whether the codex once belonged to Duke Humfrey (or Humphrey) of Gloucester (1391-1447)

---

[11] The manuscript was first, though unsatisfactorily, described by H. O. Coxe, I, Part 7, (Oxford, 1852), 84. Yet he points expressly to the note at the end of Bruni's Latin translation of the *Ethics* (fol. 89^v) and to the abbreviation of the scribe's name, "Jo. R.," whom Emden has identified as John Russell. Cf. A. B. Emden, *A Bibliographical Register of the University of Oxford to A.D. 1500*, III (Oxford, 1959), 1608-09. The MS. 228 of New College was more accurately described in an exhibition catalogue issued by the Bodleian Library, titled *Duke Humfrey and English Humanism in the Fifteenth Century* (Oxford, 1970), 21-22, item no. 37. Dr. R. W. Hunt, the Keeper of Western MSS. at the Bodleian Library, helpful as so often before, generously examined the manuscript for me and detected that the supposed John Russell was not the scribe of the copy of Bruni's Latin version of the *Economics*. Dr. Hunt also made available to me a photocopy of the fols. 188^v - 193^v from which I was able to see that the scribe in copying the Bruni translation has used a manuscript which comprises the preface and both books of the pseudo-Aristotelian work as translated by Bruni but not the commentary (annotations) on the two books. The composition of the text was not recognizable in Coxe's description; Coxe, for reasons unknown to me, identified the Bruni version as "De rei domesticae administratione liber primus"—which sounds like a suprascription of Book I but which is not found in the manuscript.

[12] Cited from the just mentioned (n. 11) exhibition catalogue of the Bodleian Library (p. 22).

who, as is well known, was personally acquainted with Bruni, I would not know; nor do I have any explanation for how this volume came into the possession of William Warham (ca. 1456-1532), the last archbishop of Canterbury of the pre-Reformation Church of England, whose name appears in the volume as a former owner of it. Like Gray, Warham was a scholarly man, undoubtedly and enthusiastically dedicated to the cause of the "new learning"—he was the chief patron of Erasmus in England—and as much an avid reader of books as a zestful book collector. Educated at New College, he bequeathed to his school a considerable portion of his books, among them the manuscript under discussion.

The third manuscript, now in England—Additional MS. 27 491 of the British Museum (no. 18a in the list at the end of this paper)—is of Italian provenance and it was acquired by the British Museum about one century ago. Its present location would suggest taking it up here; but the fact that the first owner of this copy of Bruni's version of the *Economics* was an Italian and a person distinctly connected with the humanistic movement in his native country makes it seem advisable to review this manuscript together with others in my list that originated in Italy, the cradle of the 'new classical learning,' as did the overwhelming majority of the fifteenth-century copies of Bruni's annotated Latin translation. In conformity with the practice in my earlier study,[13] I shall deal with the six remaining manuscripts in my list, all of Italian provenance, in such a way that the four whose owners or scribes are definitely known will be treated in a sequence corresponding to the social standing of the former owners or scribes; while the two manuscripts, now in German collections, whose earlier owners or scribes cannot be traced will complete the descriptions of individual items.

Seen in this perspective, the most prominent manuscript is that from the Collection of the late Commodore Tammaro de Marinis at Florence (no. 95a in the list at the end of the paper).[14] It is a piece

---

[13] "Leonardo Bruni and His Public," 66-85 : III. The Circulation of Manuscripts Among Various Social Groups.

[14] I owe my knowledge of this copy to Professor Kristeller who noted it in the catalogue of the New York bookseller William H. Schab, *Catalogue No. 46* [New York, 1968 ?], 2-3 with two color plates. The codex was subsequently sold to the late Commodore Tammaro de Marinis, himself a wealthy bookseller and collector and the author of the renowned work on the library of the kings of Aragon, *La Biblioteca Napoletana dei Re d'Aragona*, 4 vols. (Milan, 1947). Since the extensive description of the codex in Schab's

of ostentatious splendor, a profusely illuminated parchment codex which most probably belonged at one time to the famous collection of the kings of Aragon at Naples. It was written and provided with impressive initials by the Spanish calligrapher and illustrator Gabriel Altadell (or, as he signed on fol. 160, "Altadellus" or, in the Spanish original form, "Ell Tadell"). He was in the pay of king Alfonso "the Magnanimous (1416-1458) for whom he worked from September 30, 1450 until November 19, 1451; therefore, the texts in this codex—Bruni's translations of the *Ethics* and *Economics*, followed by Bruni's *Isagogicon moralis disciplinae*—must have been penned at some time between these two dates. If I presume that Altadell copied Bruni's version of the *Economics* for Alfonso's library and not as a gift to be made by Alfonso, then this copy would be the fifth of Bruni's translation in the royal library at Naples.[15]

From a courtier in the entourage of the kings of Aragon in Naples, Marino Tomacello (or Tomacelli or Marinus Tomacellus who was born in 1419 or 1429 and died in 1515), comes another copy of the humanistic Latin version of the *Economics*, consisting of 25 parchment leaves which contain what I consider the original part of Bruni's work (preface and book I with the commentary on it). It is now MS. Patetta 303 at the Vatican Library (no. 212a in the list at the end of this paper).[16] Tomacello was a Neapolitan nobleman, related through his mother to Pope Innocent VIII. Because of his noble descent and his aptitude for handling political situations, he served the kings of Aragon as ambassador to Florence and in other diplomatic missions. Just as fervently interested in the arts and letters as in diplomacy, Tomacello moved in the literary circles of his native town, was married to the daughter of the famous humanist Panormita (Antonio Beccadelli) and was a friend of Giovanni Giovano Pontano (Joannes Jovianus

---

catalogue, though learned but oriented toward the bibliophilist aspects of this coveted item, was inadequate for my purposes, Professor Kristeller inspected the volume in Florence in the summer of 1969, shortly before the death of De Marinis. On Gabriel Altadell and his work for Alfonso, cf. De Marinis, I, pp. 15-16 and nn. 133 and 134 on pp. 35-36. It may be interesting to note here that Altadell, after having left the service of King Alfonso, was employed by Don Carlos, Prince of Viana, and wrote for him as a first piece of penmanship Don Carlos' Spanish translation (1462) of Bruni's Latin version of the *Ethics*, now Add. MS. 21 120 of the British Museum.

[15] "Leonardo Bruni and His Public," 72-73.

[16] Professor Kristeller came across this manuscript while scanning the yet uncatalogued collection of the late Prof. Patteta (Torino), whose heirs bequeathed it some thirty years ago to the Vatican Library.

Pontanus), a pupil of Panormita who dedicated one of his writings—"De aspiratione," 1469—to him. Considering Tomacello's background and inclinations, it should not surprise us to learn that he possessed a sizable collection of handwritten books, now dispersed among various major Italian libraries, and that King Ferrante of Aragon, the son of Alfonso, requested him to purchase in Florence manuscripts for the royal library at Naples.[17]

The third copy of Bruni's work in this group, now Add. MS. 27 491 of the British Museum, fols. 17v-24v (no. 18a in the list at the end of this paper),[18] is notable for its former owner, for the context in which this copy of Bruni's translation of the *Economics* appears, and finally for a strange parallelism between this and one other codex. The British Museum codex, comprising 54 paper leaves with eight different texts written in a humanistic cursive of the fifteenth century, belonged to Girolamo Aliotti (Hieronymus Aliottus, 1412-1480), the well known Benedictine author who, after a varied ecclesiastical career, became (1446) abbot of the monastery of SS. Flora and Lucilla in Arezzo. There he laid the foundation of a library, mainly of humanistic literature, from which the manuscript in the British Museum comes.[19] The codex consists mainly of writings and translations by Bruni.

---

[17] There exists no comprehensive study of the life of Tomacello; Mario Emilio Cosenza's *Dictionary of the Italian Humanists*, IV (Boston, 1962), 3422 lists a good number of widely scattered references in Italian publications on manuscript collections concerning the activities of Tomacello in the area that interests us here.

[18] The manuscript, acquired by the British Museum between 1854 and 1875, is unsatisfactorily described in the *Catalogue of Additions to the Manuscripts in the British Museum. 1854-75.*, II (London, 1877), 325-326. I had overlooked it when preparing my list of 1968 and Professor Kristeller therefore brought it to my attention. In addition, he inspected the text of the *Economics* version for me in the summer of 1969 and corrected some errors in the catalogue description which would have affected adversely my own labors.

[19] From the rich literature on Aliotti, whose biography can be found in every pertinent encyclopaedia—one of the more recent is the brief article by Francesco Tinello in the *Enciclopedia Cattolica*, I (Vatican City, 1948), 887-888—I want to select the quite detailed account of Aliotti's career and less than flattering evaluation of his professional and literary "accomplishments" in Voigt-Lehnerdt's *Die Wiederbelebung des Classischen Alterthums*, 3rd ed. of Voigt's work, II (Berlin, 1893), 222-229. Of the library of Aliotti (referred to by Voigt as "Agliotti") and of the collection of books in the abbey Voigt said (229) : "... Wie er seine behaebige Abtei in Arezzo hatte, war sein Ehrgeiz nur noch darauf gerichtet, die Bücher und kleineren Werke der berühmten Maenner seiner Zeit abschreiben zu lassen und so in seinem Kloster eine Bibliothek der Neueren zu errichten ... Aber auch dieser Plan stockte schon im Beginn ..."

The collection of works by Bruni begins with a copy of his version of the *Economics*. Following it are Bruni's treatise on *De re militari*, his *Vita Aristotelis*, and finally his Latin translation of one of Boccaccio's novellas (*Decamerone*, IV, 1), entitled *Fabula Tancredi*. Preceding the collection are Niccolò Perotti's Latin translation of St. Basil's oration *De invidia* and a Roman history of Ruffinus Sextus. Interspersed in the collection are two pieces by other authors, one from the pen of Petrarch and the other from the pen of an anonymous writer who in the middle ages was thought to be St. Bernard of Clairvaux. Only the latter is of interest here because it is a treatise on household management written in the form of a letter bearing the title *De cura rei familiari opusculum* in the copy of the codex under consideration while in most of the numerous fourteenth- and fifteenth-centuries copies the treatise is entitled an epistle.[20] The content of the MS. in the British Museum is to a large extent identical with that of the MS. 459 of the Biblioteca della Fraternità dei Laici at Arezzo.[21] Whether the latter, too, belonged at one time to Aliotti or to the library of his monastery could not be ascertained. Yet it is worthy to note, apart from the similarities, three significant differences between the two codices. In the Arezzo manuscript the aforementioned translation by Perotti and the writings by Bruni are preceded by a copy of a treatise by Aliotti titled *De optimo vivendi genere diligendo*; the pseudo-St. Bernard epistle is missing, and instead the collection of humanistic texts and translations is completed by an oration of Battista Guarini.

The MS. Vittorio Emanuele 1331 in the Biblioteca Nazionale Centrale at Rome (no. 133a in the list at the end of this paper),[22] the fourth in this group, is revealing in some respects and puzzling in

---

[20] That the pseudo-St. Bernard *Epistola* should have been copied immediately following the pseudo-Aristotelian *Economics* as translated by Bruni is interesting. As I pointed out in "Leonardo Bruni and His Public," 99, it was more common to combine the younger medieval translation of the *Economics* by Durand d'Auvergne than Bruni's version with the *Epistola* erroneously assigned to St. Bernard. In my paper I cited only one example, namely, in a codex which originated in the late fifteenth century in Germany. From the manuscript in the British Museum, which was first owned by Aliotti and then by his abbey and which was written in Italy between 1446 and 1480, we can see that the combination of these two texts was practiced in Italy, too.

[21] The Arezzo manuscript is briefly described by Kristeller in his *Iter*, I, p. 4.

[22] This and the later mentioned handwritten books in the *Fondo Vittorio Emanuele* of the Biblioteca Nazionale Centrale at Rome are not catalogued; Professor Kristeller saw them there and communicated to me the information given in the text.

others. It is a codex consisting of 65 parchment leaves of which the first fifty contain a copy of Bruni's annotated version of the *Economics* in an arrangement which, in my opinion, is the oldest one after Bruni in 1421 completed his work on the spurious Aristotelian treatise.[23] The *Economics* is followed by Bruni's *Isagogicon*, a sequence of the two Bruni works resembling the one in the manuscript written by Altadell. The puzzling aspect of the manuscript concerns the identity of its scribe and of its previous owners. The scribe signed at the end (fol. 65v): "... Ego Galeottus Petri filius... Fano ... hoc opus propria manu transcripsi." Prior to this note there is a reference to a family name "Matenotius"; if the latter can be interpreted as a slip by the writer who meant to sign "Martinotius," then the scribe would be identical with Galeottus Martinotius (i.e. Martinozzi) who penned in 1448 and 1450 respectively three more copies of works by Bruni—they are now MSS. 1332, 1333 and 1334 of the Biblioteca Nazionale Centrale—that were owned by members of this noble family which resided in Fano and Siena.[24]

The two copies of Bruni's translation of the *Economics* written in Italy in the fifteenth century and now in German collections—the one in Hanover and the other in Munich—are of interest mainly for the context in which they appear in the respective codices. In the MS. IV. 406ᵃ of the Niedersächsische Landesbibliothek at Hanover[25]

---

[23] I dealt with the history of Bruni's work on the *Economics* and its transmission in "The Genesis and Tradition of Leonardo Bruni's Annotated Version of the (Pseudo-) Aristotelian *Economics*," *Scriptorium* 12 (1958), 260-268 and in "Leonardo Bruni and His Public," 54-62. In both papers I showed that the above arrangement—Preface, Book I, Commentary on Book I, Book II, Commentary on Book II—can be traced back to the MS. Laur. 79 c. 19, which represents the most authoritative copy of Bruni's version written by Antonio de Mario. In the later paper I listed on p. 129 in group "*N*" one dozen copies, some fragmentary like the one in the Vittorio Emanuele manuscript, in which this pattern is observed. I should have added the MS. 154 of the Biblioteca della Fraternità dei Laici at Arezzo (no. 57 in my 1968 list) which I put erroneously into the second section of group "*O*". Together with the present item 133a and the earlier item 57, there are now 14 copies of this kind known.

[24] My statements as to the identity of the scribe and owners of the Rome manuscript (113a) are based on information given me by Professor Kristeller. M.E. Cosenza in his *Dictionary* (see n. 17), III, 2211 lists a Pietro Martinozzi da Fano (Petrus Fanestris) who owned a copy of Ovid's *Fasti*; this Pietro da Fano, however, lived in the sixteenth century (he made the entry of ownership of the said manuscript in 1549) and at best may be related to our scribe.

[25] The manuscript is listed in the catalogue of E. Bodemann, *Die Handschriften der kgl. öffentlichen Bibliothek zu Hannover* (Hanover, 1867), 70. The description of the

the *Economics* is followed by Guarino's Latin version of Plutarch's *De liberis educandis* and Vergerio's treatise *De ingenuis moribus*. The three texts copied next to one another represent, as in so many other codices, a sort of "humanistic anthology" of writings on family life and education.[26] These treatises, framed at the beginning and at the end by two other most probably unrelated ones, are now united in a codex of 83 paper leaves; they were written by different, well-trained but by no means outstanding Italian hands at the middle of the fifteenth century.[27] The room spared for the initials was never filled in and the suprascriptions in red ink are unpretentious. Unfortunately, nothing is known about the scribes or the contemporary owners of the manuscript.

The copy in the MS. Clm. 8482 of the Bayerische Staatsbibliothek[28] is veritably buried under a pile of groups of texts unrelated to one another. In this compendious volume of 290 incompletely counted paper leaves, which was owned by the Munich Augustinian monastery from the fifteenth century until the dissolution of the monastery, there are collected at random letters of kings, popes and prelates concerning an urgently advocated war against the Turks, decrees and directions by emperors and popes given to their chancelleries, and other historical documents from the middle of the fifteenth century (the latest being dated 1454). In between these copies of sam-

---

manuscript, based on a table of contents from the early eighteenth century on the flyleaf in front of the codex, is inadequate. I saw the codex in the autumn of 1970 and I was generously assisted in my work on it by Dr. Karl-Heinz Weimann, the director of the manuscript division of the Landesbibliothek, who also supplied me with a photostat of the copy of Bruni's version of the *Economics*.

[26] An analysis of the origin and character of such anthologies was given in "Leonardo Bruni and His Public," 95-98.

[27] The script used by these hands looked to me like the Gothic *rotunda* as employed in Bologna and in Florence at the time of Salutati; samples of it may be found in B.L. Ullman, *The Origin and Development of Humanistic Script* (Rome, 1960), figures 1, 3 and 5 and the comments on them on pp. 12-13.

[28] I became aware of this copy through a reference to it in the essay by Hermann Goldbrunner on "Durandus de Alvernia, Nikolaus von Oresme und Leonardo Bruni. Zu den Übersetzungen der pseudo-aristotelischen Ökonomik," *Archiv für Kulturgeschichte* 50 (1968), 200-239. In n. 125 (p. 230), Goldbrunner adds the Munich copy to my list of 1968. The codex containing this copy is very poorly described in the *Catalogus codicum manuscriptorum Bibliothecae Monacensis*, IV, Part 1 (Munich, 1874), 31-32. In fairness to the authors of this generally inadequate catalogue (C. Halm and his collaborators) it should be admitted that a half-way acceptable description of this codex would have taken up more space than was assigned to them and a command of minutiae that is hard to find even among learned cataloguers.

ples of diplomatic correspondence one finds excerpts from classical Roman literature (Terence and the historian, Sallust), and finally assorted letters, orations and prefaces by outstanding humanists (Bruni, Poggio and Guarino among them) and testimonial orations delivered at the University of Vienna on the occasion of the bestowal of academic degrees. Of interest here is a group of texts on fols. 152ᵛ-159 [29] consisting of a copy of Book I of the *Economics* in Bruni's translation with his dedicatory epistle to Cosimo de' Medici (no. 48a in the list at the end of this paper), an oration of unknown authorship upon the occasion of the wedding of an unidentified Duke of Milan, and an oration by Guarino at a similar occasion in the house of the Este, lords of Ferrara. Presuming that these three texts are parts of a unit, then we are confronted with three treatises on the subject of the science of *Economics* as understood by Bruni and his contemporaries, namely, the affairs of the family, including the relation of husband and wife as extensively treated in book III (Bruni's *liber secundus*) of the *Economics*. The orations delivered at weddings are dedicated to deliberations of the "art of matrimony," a science, Guarino points out towards the end of his oration, which is comparable to agricultural "husbandry" or the military craft of navigation. In other words, the two orations on matrimony belong to a literature on a more specialized subject matter, then known as the *res uxoria*,[30] within the larger field of economics. By taking the place of the genuine Book II of the Economics, which was probably deliberately omitted, they, together with book I, form that kind of humanistic anthology of writings concerning family life of which I have spoken. My speculations about the reasons for combining the three texts are further strengthened by the frequent references in the anonymous Milanese oration to tracts, primarily by ancient authors but sometimes from

---

[29] The texts on fols. 152ᵛ-159 were kindly inspected for me by Dr. Natalia Hochstein (Universitätsbibliothek, Munich) and a microfilm of these leaves was supplied by the Bayerische Staatsbibliothek. From both sources I learned that (a) the cataloguers counted the written leaves only—e.g. the five vacant leaves between the *Economics* and the Milanese oration were not counted—wherefore the numbering of the folios of the three texts here reviewed is incorrect (as probably the pagination of the entire codex), (b) the texts were penned by two different Italian hands about the middle of the fifteenth century and (c) the leaves with these texts were bound together with the others in the tome whose texts were written by German hands of the same period.

[30] On the *res uxoria* treatises in this connection see "Leonardo Bruni and His Public," 98.

the Renaissance, extolling the virtues and desirability of married life.

Important as such detailed information as here submitted from the Munich copy of Bruni's work may be and as gratifying as the confirming and modifying observations alike regarding the textual transmission, the copyists and the original owners of the handwritten copies may appear—the greatest value, in my eyes, of the additional items listed below remains in the expectation that the number of extant copies of Bruni's Latin version of the *Economics* from the fifteenth and early sixteenth centuries (if and when as completely assembled as is humanly possible) should turn out to be not very far from 250 items. Yet, while twenty copies would still have to be discovered to make this expectation come true, it can already be said without exaggeration that Bruni's endeavor to acquaint his readers with this piece of ancient Greek deliberation on the *res familiaris* ought to be counted among the bestsellers of humanistic literature.

APPENDIX

ADDITIONS TO THE 1968 SURVEY OF EXTANT MANUSCRIPTS

LONDON, British Museum
18a   Add. MS. 27 491, fols. 17^v-24^v : Preface, Books I and II
    Catalogue of Additions to the Manuscripts in the British Museum, 1854-75, vol. 2 (1877), 325-326.

OXFORD, New College
27a   MS. 228, fols. 188^v-193^v : Preface, Books I and II
    H. O. Coxe, *Catalogus codicum manuscriptorum qui in collegiis aulisque Oxoniensibus hodie adservantur*, vol. I, pt. 7 (Oxford, 1852), 84.

HANOVER, Niedersächsische Landesbibliothek
46a   IV. 406a, fols. 5-13^v : Preface, Books I and II
    E. Bodemann, *Die Handschriften der kgl. öffentlichen Bibliothek zu Hannover* (Hanover, 1867), 70.

MUNICH, Bayerische Staatsbibliothek
48a   Clm 8 482, fols. 152^v-155 : Preface, Book I
    Catalogus codicum latinorum Bibliothecae Regiae Monacensis, comp. C. Halm, G. Laubmann and others, IV, 1 (Munich, 1874), 31-32.

	FLORENCE, Collection of the late Commodore Tammaro de Marinis
95a	s.n., fols. 161-171 : Preface, Books I and II
	William H. Schab Gallery, *Catalogue Forty-Six* : *Incunabula, Renaissance Texts, etc.* (New York, 1968), 2-3.

	ROME, Biblioteca Nazionale Centrale Vittorio Emanuele II
133a	Vittorio Emanuele 1 331, fols. 2-32 : Book I (fragm. at the beginning), Commentary on Book I, Book II, Commentary on Book II
	P.O. Kristeller, *Iter Italicum* (London and Leiden, 1963 - -) III (forthcoming)

	VATICAN CITY, Biblioteca Apostolica Vaticana
212a	cod. Patetta 303, fols. 1-25^v : Preface, Book I, Commentary on Book I
	P.O. Kristeller, *Iter Italicum* (London and Leiden, 1963 - -) III (forthcoming)

SUPPLEMENT

LOST

	OXFORD, Balliol College
218a	MS. 242 [fols. 192 squ.] : ?
	H.O. Coxe, *Catalogus codicum manuscriptorum qui in collegiis aulisque Oxoniensibus hodie adservantur*, vol. I, pt. II (Oxford, 1852), 82.

Queens College, The City University of New York

NICOLETTO VERNIA ON THE SOUL AND IMMORTALITY

EDWARD P. MAHONEY

One of the topics that has most interested recent historians of Renaissance philosophy is the problem of the immortality of the soul, in particular the controversy that followed the publication of Pietro Pomponazzi's *De immortalitate animae* in 1516.[1] It has gradually become clear that the controversy did not arise without historical antecedents. Not only had there been a long history of discussions on the issue during the middle ages, but the topic continued to be of importance to philosophers of the fifteenth century.[2] I should like to examine here the views on immortality of one of Pomponazzi's own teachers, Nicoletto Vernia (d. 1499),[3] not in order to demonstrate any direct influence on Pomponazzi, but to delineate more fully the philosophical scene in Italy during the decades just prior to the so-called Immortality Controversy. We shall see that Vernia went from a rather literal Averroist position on the demonstrability of the immortality of the individual rational soul and from an openly Averroist reading of Aristotle on the matter to a position in which he uses the Greek commentators to attack Averroes and to effect a conciliation of Plato and Aristotle on the soul's preexistence. At the same time, he also identifies Aristotle as much as possible with orthodox Catholic belief and argues where necessary against Plato and the commentators.

---

[1] See for example Giovanni di Napoli, *L'immortalità dell'anima nel Rinascimento* (Turin, 1963); Paul O. Kristeller, *Eight Philosophers of the Italian Renaissance* (Stanford, 1964); Bruno Nardi, *Studi su Pietro Pomponazzi* (Florence, 1965).

[2] See Sofia Vanni Rovighi, *L'immortalità dell'anima nei maestri francescani del secolo XIII* (Milan, 1936); Paul O. Kristeller, "Pier Candido Decembrio and his Unpublished Treatise on the Immortality of the Soul," in *The Classical Tradition : Literary and Historical Studies in Honor of Harry Caplan* (Ithaca, 1966), 536-58; idem, *Renaissance Concepts of Man and Other Essays* (New York, 1972), 22-42; Eugenio Garin, *La cultura filosofica del Rinascimento italiano* (Florence, 1961), 93-126.

[3] Pietro Ragnisco, *Nicoletto Vernia : Studi storici sulla filosifia padovana nella 2a metà del secolo decimoquinto* (Venice, 1891); R. Persiani, "Nicoletto Vernia, Contributi biografici e bibliografici," *Rivista Abruzzese* 8 (1893), 199-212; Paolo Sambin, "Intorno a Nicoletto Vernia," *Rinascimento* 3 (1952), 261-268.

What is particularly interesting about this dramatic shift, which is paralleled by a similar shift in the position of another of Vernia's students, Agostino Nifo (1470-1538),[4] is the strong influence that the late ancient commentators, Themistius and Simplicius, had on the evolution of Vernia's psychological doctrines. This fact would seem to be further evidence that when, toward the end of the fifteenth century, as a result of the impact of humanism, more writings of the Greek commentators became available, these new philosophical materials had a direct and substantive effect on philosophical life at the University of Padua.[5]

The first work to be studied is a treatise, found in a Marciana manuscript, which has recently been identified as Vernia's.[6] It takes up the question whether the human soul is united in existence with the body as its true substantial form or whether it is eternal and one for all men. At the very beginning of the treatise, Vernia says that he had determined to do three things to resolve the problem, namely (1) to address himself to the doctrine of Plato, (2) then to set forth what Aristotle thought according to his most famous commentators, both Greek and Arab, and (3) finally to make clear the doctrine of the Latin commentators and the truth of the Catholic faith.[7] Vernia then states that poor health and the press of teaching made it impossible for him

---

[4] Edward P. Mahoney, "Agostino Nifo's Early Views on Immortality," *Journal of the History of Philosophy* 8 (1970), 451-60.

[5] See my articles, "Nicoletto Vernia and Agostino Nifo on Alexander of Aphrodisias : An Unnoticed Dispute," *Rivista critica di storia della filosofia* 23 (1968), 268-296; and "A Note on Agostino Nifo," *Philological Quarterly* 50 (1971), 125-132. Cf. Paul O. Kristeller, *Renaissance Thought* : *The Classic, Scholastic, and Humanist Strains* (New York, 1961), 40-42 and 114-117.

[6] See Giulio F. Pagallo, "Sull'autore (Nicoletto Vernia ?) di un'anonima e inedita quaestio sull'anima del secolo XV," in *La filosofia della natura nel medioevo* (Milan, 1966), 670-82. I examined the treatise at the Marciana in the Spring of 1963 and studied it on microfilm before seeing Pagallo's excellent article. I did notice the resemblance to Vernia's *Contra perversam opinionem*. However, Pagallo was the first actually to prove Vernia's authorship by his careful and thorough comparison of passages in the treatise to passages in various of Vernia's other writings.

[7] "Utrum anima intellectiva humano corpore unita tanquam vera forma substantialis dans ei esse specificum substantiale, eterna atque unica sit in omnibus hominibus," Biblioteca Nazionale Marciana (Venice), Cod. Lat. VI, 105, ff. 156, 1-160ᵛ, 1. Since I shall follow the folio numbers presently on the manuscript, my references will not always agree with those of Pagallo. Hereafter this work will be referred to as *UAIH*. I am presently preparing an edition of this treatise for publication. Subsequently, I hope to publish a longer study of the work.

to carry out this proposed arrangement, but perhaps he simply means
that he could not cover all the points fully, since the treatise is in fact
divided into three general parts dealing with these topics. However,
less than a column of the manuscript is given to (1), the doctrine of
Plato, and the only commentator discussed at length in (2) is Averroes.
Alexander of Aphrodisias is cited briefly, but his works are not quoted,[8]
and what is said both of Alexander and of John Philoponus (*Joannes
Grammaticus*) is derived from Averroes. On the other hand, neither
Themistius nor Simplicius, both of whom play a key role in the other
treatise that we shall examine, is ever cited. Indeed, the basic purpose
of the second part of the treatise is to present and defend from criticism Averroes' basic psychology, while the aim of the third part is to
demonstrate that Averroes' interpretation of Aristotle's views on the
intellective soul is the accurate one and that the interpretations of the
Latins, notably Albert, Thomas and Scotus, are to be rejected.

Vernia is very explicit in this treatise in declaring that he considers
the doctrine of Aristotle to be identical to that of Averroes, his Commentator (*suus commentator*). And the latter's position is that the
intellective soul is eternal and one for all men, joined to them not as
their substantial form but in the manner in which a sailor is joined
to his ship or an Intelligence to its orb.[9] After a long presentation of
objections to Averroes' position and replies to them, as well as exegesis
of technical points of his psychology, Vernia turns in the third part of
the treatise to a direct assault on the position of Albert and Thomas,
namely, that the intellective soul is the substantial form of the body,
united to it in existence and numbered according to the number of
bodies, while still being separable from the body after death. Some of
the eleven arguments which Vernia presents against this position were
standard in the Averroist tradition, as for example the second argument, namely, that intellective souls cannot be multiplied, since they
would be extended, and the fourth, that souls cannot be multiplied and
separable from the body, since there would now be an infinite number
of them, given the world is eternal for Aristotle (f. 159, 1-2). But the
most interesting discussions are to be found in the first argument,

---

[8] Vernia, *UAIH*, f. 156, 1 and f. 158, 1. Girolamo Donato's translation of Alexander's *De anima* was not published until 1495, though it had been completed sometime before January 21, 1491. See n. 22 below.

[9] *Ibid*, f. 156, 2. See also ff. 156^v, 2; 156bis^v, 2; and 159^v, 2. For the term *suus commentator*, see f. 159^v, 2 and f. 160, 2.

which Vernia develops at length and which attacks the notions of creation and individuation.

Vernia asks what could be the adequate cause of the multitude and distinction of intellective souls and he proposes three answers, namely, (1) God taken as creator, (2) the quiddity or essence of the soul itself, and (3) an individual property or *haecceitas*, as Scotus would call it. Then, in order to discredit these proposals, he presents three basic suppositions of Aristotle's thought, the last of which is that the intellective soul is eternal both *a parte ante* and also *a parte post*. He justifies this supposition by noting that the individual soul could come into existence only through generation or creation. The first alternative is quickly eliminated, since it would be a return to the already rejected position of Alexander, that the soul is generable and corruptible (ff. 157bis, 2-158, 1). However, the other alternative, creation, obviously concerned Vernia, since he takes pains to marshal six arguments against it. The following is a sampling of these arguments. First, it is a basic principle of Aristotle's teaching (one that is also demonstrated by Averroes) that nothing comes into being from nothing, that is, by creation. The third argument is that if the soul came from non-being into being, it would be corruptible according to Aristotle's dictum that whatever so comes into being must be corruptible (*De caelo*, I, ch. 3, 270a12-17). And the fifth argument is that since God does not, according to Aristotle, do or make anything outside himself, he does not create anything (f. 158, 1-158ᵛ, 1). Vernia now uses these six straightforward arguments and his three suppositions regarding Aristotle's thought to argue that the creation thesis entails both the *de facto* existence of an infinite number of intellective souls infused in an infinite number of bodies and also the existence of an infinite number of Intelligences of the same species. Since both consequences are clearly in contradiction to Aristotle, he concludes that Aristotle denied creation both in the sense intended by Christian believers (*fideles*) and also in the sense of the emanation doctrine taught by Avicenna and opposed by Averroes (f. 158ᵛ, 1-2).

Finally, turning to the remaining ways that souls could be multiplied, Vernia takes up the Scotist doctrine of *haecceitas* and the Thomist doctrine of individuation through the soul's relationship with the body. He first gives arguments against the *haecceitas* view to show that multiplicity of souls could result only from multiplicity of bodies and he then offers other arguments to show, in turn, that a relationship to the body, such as that proposed by Thomas, is insufficient to account for the individuation of an immaterial soul. This attack on Thomas and his conception of the manner in which the soul is individuated is later renewed in the second major argument of the third part of the treatise (ff. 158ᵛ, 2-159, 2).

The preceding summary of some highlights of Vernia's early treatise on the intellective soul[10] underlines its strikingly Averroist approach to the psychology of Aristotle and its clear rejection of key doctrines of the medieval Christian Aristotelians, especially Saint Thomas and Duns Scotus. This acceptance of Averroes, on the one hand, and rejection of the Latin commentators, on the other, is further underscored in the sixth argument against the plurality of the intellective soul. Vernia explains that while Thomas and Scotus, in accord with Catholic belief, would maintain that the human soul cannot know God and the other separate Intelligences while united with the body, but can do so only after death, this is false according to Aristotle. In saying this Vernia is simply upholding a characteristically Averroist position.[11] He proceeds to attack at length Thomas's reasons for denying the vision of God to man in this life and even points out serious difficulties with the notion of the gratuitous infusion of a light to the soul after death which enables it to see Him. Vernia argues that God could just as well refuse to give this light and the soul would then never reach its proper end, which is completely absurd according to natural philosophy. Indeed, if a man has lived virtuously for a long period of his mortal life, God ought, out of justice, grant him direct cognition of Himself and the Intelligences during this life. It would not suffice, Vernia adds, to object that God does not do this because of the original sin of man, since such a statement, though in accord with religion (*sanctissime dictum*), is completely foreign to Aristotle. If someone should say that Aristotle did think this, then Aristotle would be admitting that he was very Christian (*christianissimus*), which is ridiculous. Both Aristotle and

---

[10] Other interesting philosophical topics which are discussed include whether the separate intellect knows by an eternal intellection, whether intelligible species are necessary and that the agent intellect illuminates but does not abstract.

[11] Vernia, *UAIH*, f. 159ᵛ, 1. On the Averroist doctrine that man can know the separate substances in an intuitive fashion during this life and that this is the felicity proper to him, see Alfred L. Ivry, "Averroes on Intellection and Conjunction," *Journal of the American Oriental Society* 86 (1966), 76-85; Philip Merlan, *Monopsychism, Mysticism, Metaconsciousness : Problems of the Soul in the Neoaristotelian and Neoplatonic Tradition* (The Hague, 1963); Bruno Nardi, *Sigieri di Brabante nel pensiero del Rinascimento italiano* (Rome, 1945), 11-90; idem, *Saggi sull'aristotelismo padovano dal secolo XIV al XVI* (Florence, 1958).

his commentator, Averroes, erred greatly on the question because they could not attain to knowledge of such matters solely by the natural light of reason (f. 159ᵛ, 1-2). Vernia ends the third and last part of the treatise obviously confident that he has shown the Latin commentators' view of Aristotle, that the intellective soul is the true substantial form of the human body and yet separable from it, to be erroneous. Such a view stands in opposition both to Aristotle and his commentator, Averroes (f. 160, 2-160ᵛ, 1).

The early treatise on the intellective soul was undoubtedly written before 1489, the year that Pietro Barozzi, the bishop of Padua, issued a decree forbidding public discussion of the Averroist doctrine of the unity of the intellect.[12] There is no personal mention of Vernia in the decree, but a letter addressed to him from Barozzi in 1499 leaves little doubt that he was the object of the bishop's attack.[13] And if we are to believe Vernia himself, he had already finished a treatise against Averroes, namely, the *Contra perversam Averrois opinionem de unitate intellectus et de animae felicitate quaestiones divinae*, by September 18, 1492. However, it was only published for the first time in 1504, that is, after Vernia's death in 1499.[14] Vernia states in the dedicatory letter to Cardinal Domenico Grimani that he has been working night and day on his commentaries on Aristotle in order to prepare them for publication.[15] Nonetheless, he wanted first to publish his opusculum on the immortality and plurality of the soul, in which he has refuted Averroes, that treacherous and lying author of a wicked doctrine. Vernia admits

---

[12] For the text, see Francesco Scipione Dondi Dall'Orologio, *Dissertazioni sopra l'istoria ecclesiastica di Padova : Dissertazione nona* (Padua, 1817), 130-31; Pietro Ragnisco, *Documenti inediti e rari intorno alla vita ed agli scritti di Nicoletto Vernia e di Elia del Medigo* (Padua, 1891), 8-9. Cf. Pagallo, 671 and 678.

[13] Barozzi accuses Vernia of having spread the doctrine of the unity of the intellect throughout almost all Italy. For the text of the letter, see *Nicoleti Verniatis Theatini philosophi perspicacissimi contra perversam Averrois opinionem de unitate intellectus et de animae felicitate* (Venice, 1505), f. 2ᵛ. I shall use this edition and not the first edition of 1504 (cited in the following note). In the text I shall hereafter refer to it as the *Contra perversam opinionem* and in the notes as *CPAO*.

[14] See *Acutissimae quaestiones super libros de physica auscultatione ab Alberto de Saxonia editae* (Venice, 1504), which contains Vernia's treatise. It was again printed with Albert's work at Venice in 1516. Cf. Di Napoli, 185-188.

[15] The manuscripts of Vernia's commentaries are today lost, though we do have a "Prohemium" on the *De anima*. Cf. H. O. Coxe (ed.), *Catalogi Codicum Manuscriptorum Bibliothecae Bodleianae Pars Tertia Codices Graecos et Latinos Canonicianos Complectens* (Oxford, 1854), col. 819-21. I am presently editing this text for publication. There are references to Themistius and Simplicius in the "Prohemium."

that he had on occasion attempted to present arguments for Averroes' completely erroneous theory of the unity of the intellect to the university students, but he insists that he had done so only for the sake of disputation and the sharpening of their intellectual powers. He therefore attacks those petty philosophers who have spread the rumor that he actually followed the position of Averroes (f. 2). While it seems impossible for us to determine Vernia's sincerity in denying that he had ever held to the unity of the intellect as anything more than a philosophical position (and thus claiming that he did not necessarily believe it to be true), it is clear that he had undergone a radical change of heart regarding the rational demonstrability of personal immortality and the true interpretation of Aristotle's psychology.[16]

At the beginning of the *Contra perversam opinionem*, Vernia states that two of the most serious questions concerning the soul are whether the intellective soul is the substantial form of the human body and whether it can achieve happiness while united with the body—both questions were of key importance in the earlier treatise. Moreover, the three tasks which Vernia proposes in order to answer these questions are reminiscent of the division of the earlier work, namely, (1) to set forth the opinions and arguments of the philosophers who disagree with Aristotle, (2) to explain what Aristotle and his most renowned commentators hold, and (3) to clarify the pure truth of Christian faith by solving all the arguments of the philosophers which seem to oppose it (f. 3, 1; Pagallo, 680).

Vernia starts the first part of the treatise with a cluttered review of ancient philosophers, suggesting both that Parmenides, Melissus, Xenophanes, Anaxagoras and Thales all held God and the intellective soul to be identical, and also that the error of Averroes and other Aristotelians regarding the unity of the intellect sprang from that opinion (f. 3, 1-2). After some brief remarks on other pre-Socratic philosophers, Vernia states that Plato thought the world and our intellective souls were made by God from eternity. He uses texts from the commentaries on the *De caelo* of Simplicius and Averroes to argue that Plato and Aristotle agree on the eternity of the world, and then, in order to show that Plato did consider the intellective souls to have been created from eternity, he quotes Plato's *Timaeus* (41 A-D), but in

---

[16] Pagallo (p. 674) has argued correctly, in my opinion, that Vernia does not uphold the so-called "Double-truth" theory in the *UAIH*. Some doubts have been cast on Vernia's character by Nardi, *Saggi*, 95-126.

the translation of Marsilio Ficino.[17] However, the discussion on Plato's psychology which follows is not based on Ficino, but is culled from Albert the Great; the passage from the *Timaeus* was undoubtedly inspired by Vernia's reading of Albert.[18]

Vernia explains, following Albert, that according to Plato the intellective souls were created from eternity by God and placed in companion stars and that they possess in themselves the forms of all intelligible things. But when they are poured into bodies, the souls cannot exercise their proper operation and they forget these forms. However, after the body is purged through study, the soul is excited to reminiscence, since learning is recollection for Plato, as Boethius also says.[19] Furthermore, Plato thought that if souls lived well and happily while they are in bodies, they would, on their withdrawal from the body, return to their companion stars, as Macrobius also notes regarding Plato. On the other hand, those souls which have lived evilly must be purified before they can return to the dwelling of their star, and they can thus be sent to another human body, but not to the body of a brute as Pythagoras supposed.[20] Vernia ends the first part of the treatise with a brief statement of Avicenna's views on the soul, cognition and human felicity. Although he here quotes Averroes' statement that Avicenna always stood midway between the Aristotelians and the *loquentes* (which would entail that Avicenna is not a wholly accurate guide to Aristotle), he will later list him, along with Plato and Aristotle, as close to the truth, that is, the Christian faith, on many points.[21]

Vernia begins the second part of the treatise, which is devoted to

---

[17] Vernia, *CPAO*, f. 3, 2-4, 2. See Plato, *Opera*, trans. Marsilio Ficino (Venice, 1491), f. 225,2.

[18] For Albert's use of *Timaeus* 41, see *Liber de natura et origine animae*, ed. B. Geyer, *Opera omnia*, XII (Aschendorff, 1955), II, ch. 8, p. 31; *Summa de creaturis, II : De homine*, ed. A. Borgnet, *Opera omnia*, XXXV (Paris, 1896), q. 5, a. 3, p. 75, and q. 61, a. 2, p. 524. Cf. Leopold Gaul, *Alberts des Grossen Verhältnis zu Plato*, Beiträge zur Geschichte der Philosophie des Mittelalters, XII, 1 (Münster, 1913), 12-21.

[19] Vernia, *CPAO*, f. 4,2. See Albert, *De hom.*, q. 5, a. 3, p. 75; *De nat. et or. an.*, II, ch. 15, pp. 41-42; *De anima*, ed. A. Borgnet (*Opera*, V; Paris, 1890), III, tr. 1, ch. 10, p. 347. In the *UAIH*, Vernia gave a similar, though briefer account of Plato, including the same quotes from *Timaeus* and Boethius's *De consolatione*. This would seem to indicate dependence on Albert in that work also.

[20] Vernia, *CPAO*, f. 4, 2. See Albert, *De hom.*, q. 5, a. 3, pp. 73 and 75; *De nat. et or. an.*, II, ch. 7, p. 30. Almost all Vernia's other allusions, e.g. the reference to Macrobius, are borrowed from Albert.

[21] Vernia, *CPAO*, f. 4ᵛ, 1 and f. 9ᵛ, 2. See Averroes, *Commentaria in libros physicorum Aristotelis* (*Opera*, IV; Venice, 1562), II, comm. 22, f. 57, 1.

Aristotle and his commentators, with the startling thesis that Alexander of Aphrodisias did not deny the immortality of the intellective soul, since he considered both the agent and the potential intellects, which are parts of the soul, to be eternal. He uses passages from Girolamo Donato's translation of Alexander's *De anima*, which was published in 1495, as well as others from Donato's now lost translation of the *De intellectu*, and explains that Averroes mistakenly attributed to Alexander the thesis that the potential intellect is mortal because he did not have the former work.[22] In his argument here against the standard interpretation of Alexander's psychology he cites not only these new translations of Alexander but also Ermolao Barbaro's translation of Themistius' paraphrases on the *De anima* and now lost translations of Simplicius' commentaries on the *Physics* and *De anima*.[23] Vernia has of course dramatically altered his position on Alexander from his statement in the early treatise that Alexander considered the soul to be generable and corruptible—which is what in fact he did hold.

Averroes, the second Aristotelian commentator examined, is presented as having held that there is one intellective soul which reasons in all men and which has two powers, the agent and the possible intellects (f. 5,2). Vernia gives ten arguments for Averroes' doctrine of the unity of the intellect, several of which repeat material from his early treatise. The first argument, for example, uses the first and second suppositions of Aristotle's thought that Vernia had sketched in the earlier work, namely, that infinity is not repugnant to individual nature and that possibility and existence do not differ in eternal beings. In like fashion, the fifth, sixth, and seventh arguments, which are directed against the multiplicity of souls by way of creation, closely resemble remarks found in the earlier treatise's arguments against

---

[22] On Renaissance translations of Alexander, see F. Edward Cranz, "Alexander Aphrodisiensis," in *Catalogus Translationum et Commentariorum : Medieval and Renaissance Latin Translations and Commentaries*, I, ed. Paul O. Kristeller (Washington, 1960), 77-135, especially 85-86; idem, "Alexander Aphrodisiensis : Addenda et corrigenda," in *Catalogus ...*, II, ed. P.O. Kristeller and F. E. Cranz (Washington, 1971), 411-22. For a fine discussion of Greek learning at Venice in the late fifteenth century, see Deno J. Geanakoplos, *Greek Scholars in Venice ; Studies in the Dissemination of Greek Learning from Byzantium to Western Europe* (Cambridge, Mass., 1962).

[23] Vernia, *CPAO*, ff. 4ᵛ, 1-5, 2. I have examined the whole question in the first article cited in n. 5.

creation.²⁴ Vernia will answer these arguments only in the third part of the *Contra perversam opinionem*, but he does take up at this point the question of whether the intellective soul, contrary to Averroes, gives existence to the body. After setting forth a series of arguments to show the difficulties which arise from denying the multiplicity of intellective souls, he declares that he follows the best Aristotelians (*peripatetici*) and holds that according to Aristotle the intellective soul is a form which gives existence to the body and is multiplied according to the number of human bodies, just as Christian believers (*fideles*) hold.²⁵ Just previously Vernia had marshalled the authority of the Greek commentators against Averroes to claim that all of them, namely, Theophrastus, Alexander, Themistius and Simplicius (the last of whom reports in his *De anima* that any disagreement between Plato and Aristotle is only verbal), think that according to Plato and Aristotle the intellective soul is the substantial form of the human body, which formally gives it its existence and is thus multiplied in individual men, and that the soul was created by God from all eternity, is infused in bodies so that it perfects them in time and then, after it has been freed from the body, and if it has lived well and happily, it returns to the dwelling place of a star. Vernia concludes that all the Greek commentators therefore differ with Averroes on the unity of the intellective soul, just as do distinguished Arabs like Alfarabi, Avicenna and Algazel (f. 6ᵛ, 1). What is surprising, however, is that Vernia has simply attributed to the Greek commentators as a group views on the soul which he had previously attributed to Plato and which he had himself culled from Albert the Great.²⁶

Following this complete reversal of position on Aristotle and the unity of the intellect, Vernia takes up what he considers to be Jandun's best argument against the multiplicity of the rational soul, namely, that if the soul were united with the body as its substantial form, it

---

²⁴ Vernia, *CPAO*, f. 6, 1-2. Cf. *UAIH*, ff. 158, 1-2; 158ᵛ, 1; and also 157bis, 2. The citations from the *Physics* in the eighth and ninth arguments (f. 6ᵛ, 1) are also to be found in the *UAIH* (f. 158, 1).

²⁵ "Meliores ergo insequendo peripateticos et probatiores dico quod intellectiva anima est forma dans esse humano corpori secundum Aristotelem et multiplicata ad multiplicitatem eorum sicut fideles ponunt." Vernia, *CPAO*, f. 7ᵛ, 1.

²⁶ For Albert's views on Plato's doctrine of the soul, its origin and state after death, see Gaul, 100-106. And for Simplicius' remarks on the fundamental agreement of Plato and Aristotle, see his *In libros Aristotelis de anima commentaria*, ed. M. Hayduck, *Commentaria in Aristotelem graeca*, XI (Berlin, 1882), p. 245, line 12. See also 247, 14-15; 254, 28; and 263, 10.

would be extended. He had himself adopted the argument in his early treatise, but he now attempts to refute it, arguing that all souls are indivisible (f. 7ᵛ, 1-2). Moreover, while in the earlier work Vernia had considered Averroes to be the most accurate guide to Aristotle's psychology, referring to him as "his Commentator," he now concludes that Averroes stated a falsehood when he said that the intellect is one, since this would mean that it did not give us our existence (f. 9,1). Adapting a phrase from Saint Thomas, Vernia calls Averroes "the perverter of philosophical learning."[27]

Notwithstanding Vernia's rejection of Averroes' interpretation of Aristotle's psychology, there is no evidence in the *Contra perversam opinionem* that he simply embraced the position of any of the medieval Christian Aristotelians, particularly Thomas.[28] While he adopts some of their ideas, he presents an exegesis of Aristotle (namely, what he has ascribed to the Greek commentators) that flatly contradicts theirs' on some basic points, notably in the reconciliation of Plato and Aristotle on the nature of knowledge and in the attribution to Aristotle of Plato's doctrine of the preexistence of the human soul. Both issues are taken up during Vernia's lengthy discussion of the problem of whether knowledge takes place in men through a modification in the intellective soul caused by the acquisition of intelligible species. Vernia appears to reject, in openly declared opposition to Jandun, any need for such species[29] and he holds that when knowing takes place there is only a

---

[27] "philosophiae disciplinae depravator." Vernia, *CPAO*, f. 11ᵛ, 1. Cf. Thomas Aquinas, *Tractatus de unitate intellectus contra Averroistas*, ed. Leo W. Keeler (Rome, 1957), 38, par. 59 : "philosophiae peripateticae depravator." Vernia had already cited this work (f. 5, 2).

[28] Eugenio Garin appears to believe that Vernia became a Thomist in the *Contra perversam opinionem*, but he offers no evidence. See his *Storia della filosofia italiana*, I (Turin, 1966), 452. On Thomas's influence during the Renaissance, see Paul O. Kristeller *Le Thomisme et la pensée italienne de la Renaissance* (Montreal, 1967). For an English version, see P. O. Kristeller, *Medieval Aspects of Renaissance Learning, Three Essays*, ed. and trans. E. P. Mahoney, Duke Monographs in Medieval and Renaissance Studies, 1 (Durham, N.C., 1974), 27-91. See also my paper, "Saint Thomas and the School of Padua at the End of the Fifteenth Century," in *Proceedings of the American Catholic Philosophical Association : Thomas and Bonaventure, A Septicentenary Commemoration* 48 (1974), forthcoming. 277-85.

[29] See John of Jandun, *Super libros Aristotelis de Anima Subtilissimae Quaestiones* (Venice, 1552), III, q. 6, f. 61, 2; q. 7, ff. 54ᵛ, 2-65, 1; q. 10, f. 69, 1-69ᵛ, 1; q. 14, f. 72, 1-72ᵛ, 1. I shall analyze the views of Vernia on intelligible species on another occasion. For discussion of the topic at Padua during the last decade of the fifteenth century, see my article, "Antonio Trombetta and Agostino Nifo on Averroes and Intelligible

change in the senses, adding that all the Greek and most of the Arab commentators, as well as Albert among the Latins, would agree. But what is intriguing is that he then cites Themistius and Simplicius, as well as Averroes, to argue that Plato and Aristotle were in fundamental agreement regarding the nature of knowlege, despite the difference in their language. Moreover, he takes Aristotle's remark, that the intellect comes from without,[30] to mean that it existed prior to its union with the body. After explaining that it is the excessive flux of the matter in the body which causes the soul to forget what it knew previously, he attributes to Aristotle the same doctrine that he had earlier presented as Plato's, namely, that it is through study, learning and exercise that the soul is enabled to recall what it had known in its preexistent state.[31] Subsequently, after introducing six arguments from Plato to show that he held that the soul was produced from eternity, Vernia reconciles three of these arguments with passages from Aristotle's *Physics*, *De caelo* and *De anima*. He further claims that according to the Greek commentators Aristotle agreed with Plato on the soul's eternal existence, and he adds the argument that since Aristotle holds the soul to be immortal, he also holds that it is eternal and therefore caused by God's eternal production, just like the world itself.[32]

To justify his claim that Aristotle did in fact teach that the individual human soul is immortal, Vernia lists several passages in the *De anima* and *Metaphysics*. He immediately criticizes Duns Scotus for having taught that Aristotle wavered in doubt on whether the intellective soul is immortal, especially since this view does not square with the Greek commentators. Vernia replies to arguments for Scotus' position, stressing among other things that Aristotle explicitly states in the third book of the *De anima* (ch. 5, 430a20-25) that the intellective soul is immortal, remains after death and remembers nothing. What is highly significant is that Vernia adds that this is the position of all the best commentators, especially Themistius and Simplicius.[33] Vernia appears eager to show that the immortality of the soul is

---

Species : A Philosophical Dispute at the University of Padua," in *Storia e cultura nel Convento del Santo a Padova*, ed. Antonino Poppi (Vicenza, 1976), forthcoming.

[30] Vernia, *CPAO*, f. 7, 1. This is of course the νοῦς θύραθεν, *De generatione animalium*, II, ch. 3, 736b28-29.

[31] Vernia, *CPAO*, f. 5ᵛ, 1-2 and ff. 6ᵛ, 1-7, 2.

[32] Vernia, *CPAO*, f. 8, 1. Cf. Albert, *De nat. et or. an.*, II, ch. 1, pp. 18-20.

[33] Vernia, *CPAO*, f. 8, 2. Cf. Duns Scotus, *Quaestiones in Libr. IV Sententiarum*, *Opera omnia*, X (Lyons, 1639), dist. 43, q. 2, pp. 27-30.

demonstrable. He gives, first of all, nine arguments for immortality from Avicenna and others which are borrowed, without acknowledgment from Albert's *De homine*.[34] He also adds statements from Albert's *De natura et origine animae* regarding the soul's mode of knowledge after death,[35] but he rejects Albert's own position and adopts instead a conception of the soul's separation and felicity derived from Simplicius.[36]

Before concluding the second part of the *Contra perversam opinionem*, Vernia presents two theses already discussed but not defended in detail. The first is that both the intellective soul and the cogitative soul are multiplied. Taking his lead from Thomas, Vernia cites Themistius to show that both he and Theophrastus held that the intellect is multiplied; he then adds the authority of Simplicius, who considered the intellective soul to be both multiplied and incorruptible.[37] Vernia apparently takes the testimony of these commentators as sufficient to conclude that Averroes erred when he said that the intellect was one for all men and did not give man his existence. He rejects Averroes' doctrine that another soul, namely, the cogitative soul, gives man his existence, and he argues that the true interpretation of Aristotle is that there is only one soul in any living thing, namely, the intellective soul which gives man his existence. Consequently, on this latter issue Vernia sees Aristotle in agreement with the doctrine of religious faith and truth as set forth by Albert, Thomas and Scotus and in disagreement with the Greek commentators.[38]

---

[34] Vernia, *CPAO*, f. 8ᵛ, 1-2. Cf. Albert, *De hom.*, q. 61, pp. 518-9, 523-7 and 529.

[35] Vernia, *CPAO*, ff. 8ᵛ, 2-9, 1. Cf. Albert, *De anima*, III, tr. 3, ch. 9, p. 384; *De nat. et or. an.*, II, ch. 13-15, pp. 37-42.

[36] Vernia, *CPAO*, f. 9, 1. See Simplicius, *In Aristotelis physicorum libros quattuor posteriores*, ed. Herman Diels, *Commentaria in Aristotelem graeca*, X (Berlin, 1895), p. 965, lines 29-30. On the psychology of Simplicius, see A. Chaignet, *Histoire de la psychologie des grecs*, V (Paris, 1893), 357-375.

[37] Thomas Aquinas, *De un. int.*, 77, par. 120. See *Libri paraphraseos Themistii ... in libros de anima ... interprete Hermolao Barbaro* (Treviso, 1481), III, ch. 27, 28, 32 and 39, ff 1-1ᵛ, ff 2ᵛ, and ff 5. Cf. Themistius, *In libros Aristotelis de anima paraphrasis*, ed. R. Heinze, *Commentaria in Aristotelem graeca*, V (Berlin, 1890), 100-101, 103-104 and 107-108. See Simplicius, *In libros Aristotelis de anima commentaria*, 240-248 and 259-260. For a discussion of the influence of Themistius on late thirteenth-century philosophy, see my article, "Themistius and the Agent Intellect in James of Viterbo and Other Thirteenth Century Philosophers (Saint Thomas, Siger of Brabant and Henry Bate)," *Augustiniana* 23 (1973), 422-67.

[38] Vernia, *CPAO*, f. 1-2; cf. f. 6ᵛ, 1. See my article, "Nicoletto Vernia and Agostino Nifo," 275-6, n. 30.

The second thesis is that for Aristotle the soul will return to the dwelling place of a star if it has lived well in this life. Vernia argues for this position by a heavy use of passages from Macrobius and also by a rather forced attempt to find parallels in remarks of Aristotle.[39] He adds, perhaps to make his case for immortality more secure or simply as a humanistic flourish, a string of quotations from Cicero which favor personal immortality. He ends the second part of the work with a final jibe at Averroes, remarking that the felicity of the Arabs, especially that of Averroes, ought to be called misery rather than felicity and was never enjoyed by any man, or if it was, then only for a short time.[40]

At the beginning of the *Contra perversam opinionem*, Vernia had announced that in the third part of the treatise he would explicate the truth of the faith and solve all the arguments of the philosophers against it. He begins by announcing that while two of the theories examined, namely, that of Plato and Aristotle and that of Avicenna, are close to the truth, that is, the teachings of the Christian faith, each also states things in opposition to it. He does not propose simply to refute their positions, given that they agree in some points with the faith, but only to argue against those aspects of the doctrine attributed to Aristotle by the Greek commentators which run counter to the faith.[41] He holds with the Church and truth that the intellective soul is the substantial form of the human body, giving the body its existence formally and intrinsically, and that it is created by God not from all eternity but anew and infused in the body. The soul is multiplied and individuated in the body not by a relationship to the body (which is of course the Thomist position), but by what Avicenna and Scotus respectively call "property" and *haecceitas*, and which Vernia would call an "affection."[42] He then adds that there is only one soul in each living

---

[39] Vernia, *CPAO*, f. 9, 2-9v, 1. Cf. Macrobius, *In somnium Scipionis expositio* (Venice, 1492), f. 8v and f. 26v.

[40] Vernia, *CPAO*, f. 9v, 1-2. He quotes from the *De senectute*, *De amicitia* and *Tusculan Disputations*. The felicity of Averroes is of course the beatitude resulting from cognitive union with the separate substances. See *UAIH*, ff. 159v, 1-160, 1 and n. 10 above.

[41] Vernia actually maintains dialectical tension by replying to the first set of objections which he will give against the view he has attributed to the commentators. He appears to hold, furthermore, that not all that they say can be refuted.

[42] This represents a reversal of his position in the earlier treatise, since he there rejected the *haecceitas* doctrine of Scotus. See *UAIH*, f. 158v, 2. For a similar conciliation of views or terminology regarding individuation, see Agostino Nifo, *Liber de intellectu*

thing and that Albert, Thomas and Scotus all agree on this point. Vernia emphasizes not only that he believes all these things on faith but also that they can be proved by natural reason and that they can be shown to be in accord with Aristotle, since they do not, as many believers and holy men think, contradict his principles. Indeed, Vernia boldly defends the thesis that temporal creation is possible and in agreement with statements of Aristotle and he attempts to explicate texts from various works of Aristotle to justify the thesis. We have thus come full circle from his insistence in the early treatise that creation was contrary to the principles of Aristotle (ff. 9^v, 2-10, 2; *UAIH*, f. 158, 1-2).

When Vernia turns to consider the position of Plato and Aristotle as he finds it in the Greek commentators, he appears to believe that it cannot be easily refuted. He thus presents four arguments based on remarks of Albert,[43] as well as texts from *De anima*, I, ch. 3, against the preexistence and transmigration of the soul along with rather thoughtful replies to them. For example, to the second argument from Albert, namely, that inasmuch as the number of souls would always be equal to the number of bodies no one could be generated until someone else died, he retorts that according to the interpretation of Plato and Aristotle here at issue, God has produced from eternity a number of souls which will always be greater than the number of bodies existing at any moment. He adds that those who accept this interpretation of Plato and Aristotle could plausibly maintain an actual infinity of souls, holding as they do to the eternity of the world (f. 10-10^v, 2). Vernia makes a special effort to put the best possible interpretation on the passages in *De anima*, I, ch. 3, where Aristotle seems to oppose the notion of the soul in motion and also the possibility of transmigration or resurrection.[44] He argues that Aristotle had in mind those who thought Plato's position involved the dead rising, whereas Plato himself never held such a view. In like fashion, Vernia insists that Plato and his student, Aristotle, differ only in terminology and not in fact on the supposed motion of the soul, since Plato never meant by motion a physical motion but only an operation of the soul. It is no

---

(Venice, 1503), I, tr. 1, ch. 17, f. 10^v, 1; tr. 3, ch. 32, f. 37^v, 2. Cf. Nardi, *Sigieri*, 162-163. The term *affectio* may have been borrowed from Ficino, *Theologia platonica*, XV, ch. 12, *Opera omnia*, I (Basel, 1576), 351.

[43] See Albert, *De anima*, I, tr. 2, ch. 5, pp. 149-150, and III, tr. 1, ch. 10, p. 347.

[44] Cf. Albert, *De anima*, I, tr. 2, ch. 5, pp. 148-150.

surprise that Vernia again avails himself of Simplicius in arguing for this conciliation.[45]

At this point Vernia returns to the ten arguments for Averroes' doctrine of the unity of the intellect which were given in the second part of the *Contra perversam opinionem*. His replies further underscore his abandonment of key ideas of his early treatise and also reveal some of his disagreements, at least from the vantage point of religious truth, with the Greek commentators. For example, to the ninth and tenth arguments, which stress that the philosophers hold that nothing can be produced from nothing, he replies that this is true only of change or mutation in the philosophical sense (*philosophica transmutatio*), but not of what is brought about through creation. It is noteworthy that while Vernia had earlier used the Greek commentators' belief in a multiplicity of souls against Averroes' theory of the unity of the intellect, he shows here that their interpretation of Plato and Aristotle agrees with Averroes in holding to the impossiblility of a beginning of the intellective soul. Indeed, in his reply to the seventh argument, he again speaks of Plato and Aristotle maintaining the eternal production of souls (ff. 10ᵛ, 2-11, 1).

In the short part of the work that remains, Vernia takes up the manner in which the universal is received into the soul, contrasting the notion of innate species concreated with the soul, which he ascribes to Plato, with the position of Albert. He brings the *Contra perversam opinionem* to a conclusion not with any detailed recapitulation of what he has said about Aristotle, but rather with some final remarks on Plato and the Platonists. While divine Plato (*divus Plato*) came close to seeing the truth, he did not see it completely, since only Christian believers, who are illuminated by the light of the faith, can completely attain the truth and satisfy all that is asked in these difficult problems.[46] Vernia appears to mean here that only the philosopher who is a Christian could successfully refute Plato's doctrine of the soul's eternal existence from all eternity (which is also the doctrine of Aristotle according to the Greek commentators as Vernia understands them). He attacks this doctrine of Plato once again, but now judges that the reply which he had earlier given to the second argument, namely, that according to the commentators' view of Plato and

---

[45] Vernia, *CPAO*, f. 10ᵛ, 1-2. Cf. Simplicius, *In Aristo. phys. libros*, p. 965, lines 7-8. Vernia also uses Simplicius in his reply to the third argument, namely, that if the soul left and reentered bodies it would be *per se mobile* (964, 19-30).

[46] The phrase "divine Plato" is to be found in Plotinus, Themistius and Ficino.

Aristotle there could be more souls than bodies, to be inadequate. First of all, a number of bodies could be generated which would equal the excess number of souls. Secondly, since each form has its proper receiver, there must be different individual bodies, each of which will be distinctly suited to be the instrument of an individual intellective soul.[47] Vernia had also noted earlier that Plato's argument that souls are produced from all eternity fails since God acts contingently and freely, not necessarily, and he bids his reader look at Scotus on the question.[48] He concludes by accepting whatever the theologians hold concerning the felicity of the soul after death, by stating that the Platonists had some glimmering of the truth, and by insisting, somewhat surprisingly, that whatever the theologians say about the soul is in no way incompatible with the statements of Aristotle. He then submits himself to the correction of the Church and suggests that Trombetta's work against Averroes be read if a more detailed critique of Averroes be desired.[49]

There was a strong reaction of Vernia's ideas even before the actual printing of the *Contra perversam opinionem* in 1504. In his own *De intellectu* (1503), Agostino Nifo attacks those contemporaries who say that rational souls are eternal both *a parte ante* and *a parte post*. Nifo takes them to hold that there is a finite number of souls and that a soul goes from one body to another on the death of the former, and he also explains that they attribute the theory of recollection to Aristotle as well as to Plato.[50] Nifo gives arguments for the position, shows that it was held by various Platonists and states that Aristotle did not hold to the soul's preexistence. However, while Nifo argues that God creates the soul, he insists (perhaps impressed to some degree by Vernia's work) that he can himself give only persuasions, not demonstrations, to show that the soul does begin simultaneously with the body.[51] Some fifteen years later, in his *De immortalitate animae* (1518) against Pomponazzi, Nifo again refers to the theory of the preexistence

---

[47] Vernia, *CPAO*, f. 11, 2. Cf. Aristotle, *De anima*, I, ch. 3, 407b12-24; Albert, *De anima*, I, tr. 2, ch. 7, pp. 159-160.

[48] Vernia, *CPAO*, f. 11, 1. Cf. f. 10, 2. See Duns Scotus, *Quaestiones in Lib. I Sententiarum, Opera omnia*, V, 2 (Lyons, 1639), dist. 8, q. 5, pp. 810-822.

[49] Vernia, *CPAO*, f. 11, 2-11ᵛ, 2. See Antonio Trombetta, *Tractatus singularis contra Averroistas de humanarum animarum plurificatione ad catholice fidei obsequium Patavii editus* (Venice, 1498).

[50] Nifo, *De intellectu*, I, tr. 3, ch. 14, ff. 31ᵛ, 2-32, 1.

[51] *Ibid.*, I, tr. 1, ch. 14-20, ff. 9, 1-12, 1.

and transmigration of the soul. He goes on to cite Vernia's now printed work and presents as its central thesis that the soul immediately becomes the form of a new body on the death of its previous body, adding that Vernia could not believe that Aristotle wanted the soul to remain without a body. Nifo launches several arguments against Vernia's position and adds that he has himself proven many things against it in his own *De intellectu*.[52] And finally, in the commentary on the *De anima* which he finished at Pisa in 1520, Nifo again adverts to Vernia, including him among those who avoided an infinity of souls by holding that when one man ceases to exist another begins who is informed by the soul of the previous man. Nifo also explains that according to his teacher Aristotle does not disagree with Plato. He adds that Vernia allows of transmigration in order to avoid an infinite multitude of souls and the lack of any activity in disembodied souls. Nifo then gives objections and replies to Vernia's position and claims that Vernia completed his treatise many years after his own *De intellectu*.[53] He insists that Vernia's position is opposed to Aristotle and has similarities to the doctrine of the unity of the intellect. After citing passages in Aristotle which undermine Vernia's position, Nifo concludes that while it is Platonic, it does not seem Aristotelian. He holds himself that souls after death are completely without bodies.[54]

While it would appear at first glance that Nifo has misrepresented Vernia's philosophical position, since he attributes to Vernia the conception of Plato and Aristotle which he had taken from the Greek commentators and which he had criticized at the end of the *Contra perversam opinionem*, Vernia may be speaking in the last few columns of the work primarily in the name of the *faith* and *truth*. It seems quite likely that Vernia did take the commentators' view to be the true interpretation of the mind of Aristotle, for it is striking that he gives no point by point refutation of their reconciliation of Plato and Aristotle

---

[52] Agostino Nifo, *De immortalitate animae libellus* (Venice, 1518), ch. 58, f. 13ᵛ, 1, and ch. 66, f. 15, 1-2.

[53] As early as 1497, Nifo had announced in print that he had written a treatise against the unity of the intellect entitled *De intellectu*. See *Destructiones Destructionum Averrois cum Augustini Niphi de Suessa expositione* (Venice, 1497), I, dub. 23, f. 23, 2, and VI dub. 3, f. 76ᵛ, 1. For further discussion, see my *JHP* paper cited in n. 4. However, a difficulty remains since Vernia had claimed to have finished his *Contra perversam* in 1492, which is the same year that Nifo claims to have finished his own *De intellectu*.

[54] Agostino Nifo, *Collectanea ac commentaria in libros de anima* (Venice, 1522), III, comm. 5, f. 25, 1-2 (second pagination). For the date of completion, see f. 91ᵛ, 2.

on preexistence and transmigration. Nonetheless, it must be conceded that Nifo's presentation of Vernia is still not completely accurate, since he does not allude to some of Vernia's defences of the commentators' position, especially that there are more souls than bodies.

The noticeable shift in Nicoletto Vernia's views on the soul and immortality, which has been revealed by examining and comparing his early treatise and the later *Contra perversam opinionem*, is especially interesting since he explicitly attributes this change in outlook to his reading of the Greek commentators and Arabs other than Averroes, presumably Avicenna. Two months before his death, Vernia composed a testament in which he admits that for most of his thirty-three years as professor at Padua he had taught that Averroes' doctrine of the unity of the intellect was also the doctrine of Aristotle, but after many years, when he looked at learned Greeks and Arabs, he discovered that Averroes' doctrine was at variance with Aristotle as well as with the faith.[55] We can thus conclude that the newly available translations of Alexander, Themistius and Simplicius had impelled him to rethink his position, as did his study of Avicenna. These new translations, which were the result of the labors of scholars like Ermolao Barbaro, Girolamo Donato and others, were a major source of the great impact that the work of the humanists began to have on Aristotelian philosophers at the close of the fifteenth century. Vernia's late treatise, the *Contra perversam opinionem*, is one of the very first treatises to reveal the heavy use of the Greek commentators, a practise which was to become common among Italian Aristotelians of the sixteenth century and which is evident in the *De intellectu* (1503) and other writings of his student, Agostino Nifo.[56] The *Contra perversam opinionem* is also one of the first examples in the Renaissance of a deliberate attempt to conciliate Plato and Aristotle, especially on the nature of the soul and knowledge; by the middle of the sixteenth century there would develop an important tradition of such conciliations. The Greek commentators, Themistius and Simplicius, obviously inspired Vernia's adoption of a "conciliating" position.[57]

---

[55] For the text, see Ragnisco, *Documenti inediti*, 10-15, especially 10-11. Cf. Nardi, *Saggi*, 99.

[56] See my articles cited in notes 4 and 5. For an excellent study of the influence of Simplicius' commentary on the *De anima* during the Renaissance, see Nardi, *Saggi*, 365-442. However, Nardi never mentions Vernia.

[57] For an earlier attempt at conciliation, see Bessarion, *In calumniatorem Platonis*, III, ch. 28, in L. Mohler, *Kardinal Bessarion als Theologe, Humanist und Staatsmann*,

In conclusion, our analysis of the early treatise on the soul and of the *Contra perversam opinionem* has thrown new light on the philosophical scene at the University of Padua toward the close of the fifteenth century. It is quite clear that a good deal of attention was given to the question of the demonstrability of the soul's immortality by Vernia, who was the common teacher of Nifo and Pomponazzi, two of the central figures in the later Immortality Controversy. The roots of that controversy must be traced back to their days at Padua, as must Nifo's use of the Greek commentators. Vernia's dramatic shift from literal Averroism to opposition to Averroes resulted in great part from his later study of the commentators, particularly Themistius and Simplicius. Inasmuch as the availability of their works, as well as those of Alexander, was the outcome of the translating activities of the humanists, it seems appropriate to consider the evolution of Vernia's psychology another instance of the influence, albeit indirect, of humanism on philosophy during the Renaissance.[58]

Duke University

II (Paderborn, 1927), 411-13. Professor Frederick Purnell is presently preparing a monograph on this later Plato and Aristotle *comparatio* tradition, with special emphasis on Jacopo Mazzoni.

[58] See Paul O. Kristeller, *Studies in Renaissance Thought and Letters* (Rome, 1956), 13, 339-43 and 577-80.

TOMMASO CAMPANELLA:
THE AGONY OF POLITICAL THEORY
IN THE COUNTER-REFORMATION

JOAN KELLY-GADOL

This paper arises out of a study of the social and political thought of Fra Tommaso Campanella : Campanella the Utopian Socialist and spokesman of the Counter-Reformation.[1] It is a prologomenon to such a larger study, concerned not with an analysis of his political writings but with establishing a sound methodological position with respect to the problem of interpretation his political writings present.

This problem is basic to any study of Campanella's political theory. In the tortuous, politicized character of his writing, he contrasts sharply with the great social and political thinkers of the High Renaissance. The thought of a More and a Machiavelli, personal as it is, is always lucid and for the most part consistent, despite its complexities; and although it draws its vitality, insights, and interests from the social, political, and cultural life of the time, it sustains itself independently of circumstance. Once we have understood the key relations between the society and the culture into which such men were born, it is possible to study their thought in the abstract, to consider its purely intellectual content, because it is not broken into, not interrupted or deflected by forces outside itself. Campanella's social and political thought, utterly bound up with the circumstances of his life, is perennially at variance with itself. It pulls apart in opposing directions, for his life of thought became a life of personal and political struggle. Whereas Renaissance society fostered the cultural movements that arose in its midst and gave its thinkers intellectual scope, Cam-

---

[1] I am grateful to the Trinity College Historical Society and the Committee for Medieval and Renaissance Studies of Duke University, the Charles Andrews History Society of Yale University, the History Department of Wesleyan University, and the graduate History students at The Graduate Center of The City University of New York for affording me the opportunity to develop my ideas on this topic in papers addressed to them. A Junior Fellowship awarded by The National Foundation on the Arts and the Humanities enabled me to begin my research in the period of the late Renaissance.

panella's philosophical ideas were condemned as soon as they were formulated. His life was forced into patterns he would never have chosen; and as the powers that deprived him of personal freedom came to penetrate and permeate his thinking, his thought was forced into strange and constrained patterns as well. His political writings accordingly reveal not merely tension but duplicity, not merely inadvertent inconsistency but flat and unresolved contradictions.

It is my contention that Campanella—at least as a social and political thinker—will forever baffle or elude the historian who would ascertain what he "really" meant. The methodological procedures appropriate to the study of social and political thought before and after the Counter-Reformation must be abandoned or modified here, where the psycho-social modalities of such thought become paramount. Yet, as I hope to demonstrate, the resistance of Campanella's ideas to the usual methods of interpretation and systematization is itself historically significant. It tells us a great deal about the political climate of Italy in the late sixteenth and early seventeenth centuries and its devastating effects upon one of the bearers of Renaissance cultural traditions. It shows how political theory was transformed during the Counter-Reformation, not just in content but in its very character.

Were it not for the repressive atmosphere of late sixteenth century Italy, an Italy dominated by Spanish power and the Counter-Reformation Church, Campanella might never have turned to political issues. His early interests were purely philosophical. Born in Stilo, Calabria, in 1568, he belongs to that small group of South Italian thinkers who dominated the philosophy of Renaissance Italy in its

---

[2] For Campanella's philosophy, see Léon Blanchet, *Campanella* (Paris, 1920); Ernst Cassirer, *Das Erkenntnisproblem in der Philosophie und Wissenschaft der neueren Zeit* (Berlin, 1922), I, 240-57, II, 79-84; Bernardino M. Bonansea, *Tommaso Campanella : Renaissance Pioneer of Modern Thought* (Washington, D.C., 1969).

Campanella's express opposition to "Aristotelianism" can be found in almost all his writings. For his belief that he was criticized, calumniated, and persecuted chiefly because of the non-traditional, and specifically non-Aristotelian, character of his thought, see his correspondence, Tommaso Campanella, *Lettere*, ed. Vincenzo Spampanato (Bari, 1927), especially pp. 7, 133. In the latter, a letter of July 1607, comparing his persecuted life to that of Pico, he says, "Ma io in bassa fortuna nacqui e dalli ventitré anni di mia vita sin ad ora, che n'ho trentanove da finir e settembre, sempre fui perseguitato e calunniato, da che scrissi contra Aristotile di diciotto anni...."

For the place of Thomism in Renaissance thought, and in particular the development of Thomas' authority in the sixteenth century, see Paul Oskar Kristeller, *Le Thomisme*

final phase.² These so-called "natural philosophers"—Telesio, Bruno, and Campanella—all sought to approach the physical world without the mediation of Aristotle's categories and classificatory schemes, to wrest from sense experience itself the "real" forces and principles of nature. Campanella enthusiastically adopted this empirical program in his twentieth year, after reading Telesio. His first major work is a defense of Telesio's efforts to study nature directly, "according to its own principles." As a response to one of Telesio's (Aristotelian) critics, this *Philosophia sensibus demonstrata* of 1590 announced Campanella's philosophical opposition to Aristotelianism, but what was for him initially a philosophical conflict became political as well. For by the late sixteenth century, these Italian thinkers began to encounter opposition from determined efforts to shore up the Aristotelian tradition in philosophy, particularly in its Thomistic form. The Counter-Reformation, in this respect as in many others, proved to be a Counter-Renaissance as well.

Campanella's tragic life, which clearly testifies to this fact, also reflects the mounting pressure of the Counter-Reformation as that movement gained momentum. Telesio died a peaceful death in 1588, and the twenty-year old Campanella, who had never met him, was free to mourn at his obsequies in the Cathedral of Telesio's native Cosenza in Calabria. Giordano Bruno met a sorrier fate in the decade of the 90's. If Campanella, the young Dominican, ever met the older friar, it would have been while they were both prisoners of the Holy Office in Rome in 1594.³ Bruno was released from that confinement only by death. His intellectual and personal career was over: in 1600, at the age of fifty-two, he was burned alive in the Campo dei Fiori in Rome. Campanella, twenty years his junior, survived this first arrest by the Inquisition and a later, far more terrible one in which he was "put to the question" several times and sentenced to a life of incarceration. He was to carry out the greater part of his intellectual work in prison: at times in fairly comfortable quarters, at others in dungeons, often

---

et la pensée italienne de la Renaissance (Montreal and Paris, 1967). For an English version of this essay, see now P. O. Kristeller, *Medieval Aspects of Renaissance Learning, Three Essays,* ed. and trans. Edward P. Mahoney (Durham, N.C., 1974), 27-91.

³ There is one possible allusion to such a meeting in Campanella, and it is not favorable to Bruno : "Vidi Romae detineri in carceribus haereticum impudenter asserentem non magis credendum esse Scripturis quam Ariosto." However, it should be borne in mind that Campanella was again in prison when he wrote this. See Luigi Firpo, *Il processo di Giordano Bruno* (Naples, 1949), 105, n. 2.

suffering the confiscation of manuscripts during unexpected searches and seizures by emissaries of the Holy Office. Certain other manuscripts were lost by friends to whom he entrusted them for publication. All told, forty-eight works of his are known to be lost (although some are earlier versions of extant writings); still, fifty-two works have come down to us, the bulk of them designed to provide a new philosophical synthesis.[4]

In the spirit of Renaissance universality, he compiled a work on *Universal Philosophy or Metaphysics* in eighteen books and a *Theology* in thirty; his *Philosophia rationalis* contains books on Grammar, Rhetoric, Dialectics, Poetics, and Historiography; his *Philosophia realis* books on Physiology, Ethics, Politics, and Economics. Campanella's intellectual interests, as he confesses in one of his poems, were boundless and inexhaustible: "...che quanti libri tiene il mondo / non saziâr l'appetito mio profondo..."; and it was probably the conviction that his insatiability was the seal of Divinity that sustained his incredible labors: "...e quanto intendo più, tanto più ignoro. / Dunque immagin sono io del Padre immenso."[5] Despite misery, torture, imprisonment, and continuous apprehension for the fate of his manuscripts, he completed his *œuvre*, which stands as the final expression of Renaissance natural philosophy; and like Bacon and Leibniz (who was in many respects his successor), he hoped to provide by means of his philosophy a new system of universal knowledge, an *Instauratio scientiarum*. But Campanella's philosophical work also has a political dimension which reflects his relation to his period. From the conflicts of that period derive the tremendous tensions characteristic of his thought. Opposing ideas arise out of the claims of what he ultimately took to be the two manifestations of God, the "books" of Nature and Scripture. The demands of a radical sensism clash, for example, with those of an idealistic theory of illumination. And such tensions as mark his purely philosophical writings seem minor when compared with the contradictory positions his political writings contain. These writings account for more than a third of his works; but because he became not

---

[4] Professor Luigi Firpo of the University of Turin has worked steadily on the bibliography and biography of Campanella since the 1930's, providing critical editions of a number of his writings and placing each of his works in the context and circumstances of Campanella's life. I am here and throughout indebted to his *Bibliografia degli scritti di Tommaso Campanella* (Turin, 1940).

[5] "Anima Immortale," *Tutte le opere di Tommaso Campanella*, ed. Luigi Firpo (Milan, 1954), I, 17.

only a political, but also a politicized thinker, it is my contention that none of these treatises can be taken at face-value.

Campanella's independent, restless, combative personality was undoubtedly as responsible for initiating his life of persecution as was the unorthodox character of his philosophical thought. A year after publishing his first book defending Telesio, he was imprisoned and tried by a Tribunal of the Dominican Order in Naples. His sentence reveals that it was not his Telesian ideas alone that led to this brush with the authorities, but the fact that he had left his rural monastery of Altomonte for the more congenial intellectual atmosphere of a secular house in Naples.[6] From this point on, his life was never to be free of political danger, but he was to learn only slowly the political virtue of prudence. Released in 1592 after several months of confinement, he disobeyed the order to return to his Province, travelling instead to Rome, Florence, and Padua. He met Galileo in Padua and wrote a great deal (including another *Apologia pro Telesio*), but his efforts to secure a position which would afford him relative safety and independence came to nought. He failed to obtain from the Grand Duke Ferdinand II of Tuscany a Chair at Pisa or Siena, and renewed harassment was soon followed by a second incarceration.

Before he arrived in Padua, Campanella's manuscripts had been seized by agents of the Holy Office, and once in that city, he had been brought up on charges of sodomy. Then in the summer of 1593, the Holy Office in Padua arrested him on a number of charges, all of them adding up to heresy.[7] Although his defense, which he finally gave in 1595, was still obstinately entitled *Defensio Telesianorum* (indicating

---

[6] Firpo, *Bibliografia*, 23. Luigi Amabile, *Fra Tommaso Campanella. La sua congiura, i suoi processi e la sua pazzia*, 3 vols. (Naples, 1882), I, 25-35.

[7] Further charges were added to the initial ones during his imprisonment which explains the discrepancy between Firpo and Bonansea's account. Both agree that he was charged with discussing matters of faith with a Jewish sympathizer. To this, Bonansea adds (2) that he authored the book *De tribus impostoribus* on Moses, Jesus, and Mohammed, (3) that he espoused the philosophy of Democritus, (4) that he was critical of the constitution and doctrine of the Church (pp. 27-28). Firpo mentions (2) possession of a book on geomancy, (3) authorship of a trivial sonnet disrespectful of Christ, (4) holding that all positive religions are equivalent (*Tutte le opere*, p. xix). From Amabile (*Campanella. La sua congiura*, I, 67-75) it appears that Bonansea is referring to the first set of charges made in Padua and Firpo to the second set made in Rome. In addition to these charges, Campanella had to defend himself against the charge of heresy for a number of purely philosophical propositions taken from his *De sensu rerum*, the work that was seized before he arrived in Padua.

that his Telesian ideas were a chief concern of his prosecutors), the Campanella we meet from the end of 1593 on is acutely conscious of his need for political protection. It is from this time that the list of his political writings begins—almost all of them designed to gain that protection for him. It is a long list and a puzzling one. It contains several works advocating the establishment of a universal papal monarchy; it includes a Utopian proposal for social reform along the lines of a rational, socialistic society; it contains a number of pro-Spanish treatises and apologies for Spanish imperialism, and a number of pro-French works defending Richelieu's anti-Hapsburg policies. It ends only a year before his death in exile in France, closing with the politic, if not political *Horoscopus Serenissimi Delphini* which he drew up in 1638 for the future Louis XIV.

His earliest political writings are patent efforts to improve his standing before the Inquisition during his imprisonment in Padua in 1593-94. He had been accused among other things of disapproving of the doctrine and government of the Church. In the prison of the Holy Office, he composed two (lost) treatises on the desirability of a Papal-dominated ecclesiastical state and the means such a state should employ to extend its power over the nations of the world.[8] These works apparently did not help his case which was becoming rather grave as investigation led to more charges being added to the original ones. He was transferred to Rome in 1594, tortured twice and returned to prison. There he wrote two more treatises, the first of his pro-Spanish works. These were designed to gain favor with the Hapsburgs and have them intercede with the Holy Office for him, and in point of fact, the Archduchess Maria, widow of Karl of Styria, did write to Clement VIII on his behalf.

The first of these treatises, *Discorsi ai principi d'Italia*,[9] is a plea to the petty princes of Italy, urging them not to oppose the Spanish monarchy in Italy or in Europe but rather to unite in support of Hapsburg dominion. Arguments of the most diverse kinds are presented, apparently everything Campanella could think of. There is the pragmatic argument: that the days of Italian empire are over; that

---

[8] *De monarchia Christianorum* and *De regimine ecclesiae*; these works, which were lost in his arrest of 1599 in Calabria, were rewritten and developed later as *Monarchia Messiae* and *Discorsi universali del governo ecclesiastico* (Firpo, *Bibliografia*, 103-105, 139-142, 177-178).

[9] *Discorsi ai principi d'Italia ed altri scritti filo-ispanici*, ed. Luigi Firpo (Turin, 1945), 91-163.

Italy is divided into a number of principalities and republics which are all too weak to aspire to dominion, and that the Spanish Crown already controls the greatest number of these, the Kingdom of Naples, Sicily, Sardinia, the Duchy of Milan—as well as the Tyrrhenian Sea. There is the argument from fear: if the Hapsburgs do not attain world hegemony (*monarchia di tutto il mondo*), the Turks will. Under the Hapsburgs, because they are Catholic Christians, people and princes will at least remain lords of what they have, paying but little tribute. The Turks, on the other hand, will reduce everyone to the status of slaves and vassals and will be hostile to learning as well. Hence the Italians should unite behind Spain against the "foreign" Turkish threat. Finally, the inevitability of Spanish world empire is considered, the providential character of which Campanella clearly discerns in Scripture and the stars, and even in the "fatal order" of world history in which "monarchy marches from east to west." "I say it is impossible," he sums up, "to resist this monarchy, and those who oppose it will fall, and in particular republics are disfavored [by the stars], such as those [singling out, now, the opponents of the Hapsburgs] of the Low Countries, Switzerland, and Venice..."[10]

The second treatise aimed at winning Hapsburg favor was directly concerned with the Netherlands, a *Discorso sui Paesi Bassi*.[11] This is a completely pragmatic work, analyzing in Machiavellian fashion the mistakes in Spanish policy that led to revolt in the Netherlands and the obstacles to suppressing it. The remedies, given in the form of "inviolable rules" for the Spaniards to follow, are intelligent, generally humane, but they also display not a little astuteness and cynicism. Campanella would have the Spaniards lift all taxes that go beyond those traditionally due the Crown. And instead of draining the country of its wealth every year, he would have the Spaniards conscript the most bellicose youths and send them to the Indies to fight for the King. He would remove the Inquisition, permitting local bishops to attend to matters of heresy; and he advises the bishops to avoid the severity of the Spanish and Roman Inquisitions. He would have the Spaniards man the military garrisons but put the civil government in the hands of other peoples: Netherlanders, Germans, even Italians. Step by step, he responds to the grievances of the Netherlanders and advocates measures which indeed would have strengthened Spanish

---

[10] *Ibid.*, 133-135.
[11] *Ibid.*, 65-88.

hold on the land, including advice to play off one religious group against the other. He concludes that if the King succeeds in creating dissension among the Netherlanders by these means, he may be able to regain the Provinces without further bloodshed. Or, if the outcome seems uncertain, he may, after taking these measures and disarming the Netherlanders thereby, launch an unexpected military attack.

All the moves are presented here with the detachment befitting a game of chess, although the game is clearly called suppression of liberty, religious and political, by Campanella himself. He regards the Netherlanders (and northerners in general) as liberty-loving by nature: "I popoli oltramontani sono da natura loro nati alla libertà."[12] But their love of freedom, which he admires, enters his calculations only because those who would "reduce them to subjection to the King of Spain"[13] must reckon with it as an additional source of resistance. When we consider that Campanella set down these Machiavelli-like rules at a time when he was imprisoned for heresy, deprived of liberty, and fearful of his life, we cannot but wonder just how "Machiavellian" —how realistic, how prudent, and how cynical— his political writings may be. The overt message of these early writings stands in sharp contradiction to what we would imagine were his natural sympathies; and they are also beset by internal contradictions which reflect the different interests of the powers to whom he needed to appeal. He barely manages to reconcile the claims of a Papal and a Spanish world-monarchy on the international level by maintaining that the Spanish Empire at once serves and is supported by the spiritual authority of Christianity and the Pope. But he falters on the national level of Italy, where Spanish and Papal differences really count. In the same *Discourses to the Princes*, which justify Spanish rule in Italy, he outlines a plan for a federation of Italian states under Papal leadership. And he says expressly: "To aggrandize and exalt the Papacy is the true remedy to secure us from becoming the prey of the King of Spain and to support both the glory of Italy and Christianity..."[14] Conflicts such as these

---

[12] *Ibid.*, 67.

[13] The heading of the work reads: "Discorso di Fra Campanella circa il modo come i Paesi Bassi, volgarmente detti di Fiandra, si possano ridurre sotto l'obbedienza del Re di Spagna ..." (65).

[14] *Ibid.*, 152. Campanella advocates (151-156) the formation of a federated Europe under Papal leadership and, short of this, a federated Italy—neither of which would serve Spanish interests.

are not to be resolved in some higher "systematic" unity.[15] They have to be traced to the personal and political struggles from which they emerged.

Even Campanella's non-political writings from 1593 on need to be viewed, I believe, in the context of his threatened life. Consider, for example, his first work after his release from prison in 1595. He was still confined, awaiting sentence in the monastery of S. Sabina in Rome, when he wrote a *Dialogo contro Luterani, calvinisti ed altri eretici*. This was to be the first of a number of works on the problem of heresy. In a sense, these could be classified as political writings, for they ultimately form part of Campanella's scheme for a universal Christian monarchy. But they would appear to be political in another sense as well. Not until he had been charged with heresy did Campanella evince any interest in the problem; and it was while the charge was hanging over his head that he wrote and sent copies of this first work to the Commissario of the Inquisition, the Cardinal Protector of the Dominican Order, the Archduke Maximilian, and Maximilian's son, Rudolph II.[16] At the end of 1596, three years after he had been accused, Campanella was himself condemned to make a public abjuration "de vehementi" because of strong suspicion of heresy. Then, some years later, in prison again, the author of this dialogue against Lutherans and other heretics wrote the following sonnet, filled with Erasmian sentiment, which portrays the Lutheran as a good Samaritan:

> From Rome to Ostia a poor man went;
>   Thieves robbed and wounded him upon the way:
>   Some monks, great saints, observed him where he lay,
>   And left him, on their breviaries intent.
> A Bishop passed thereby, and careless bent
>   To sign the cross, a blessing brief to say...
> At last there came a German Lutheran,
>   Who builds on faith, merit of works withstands;
>   He raised and clothed and healed the dying man.
> Now which of these was worthiest, most humane?
>   The heart is better than the head, kind hands

---

[15] Bonansea imposes a systematic unity upon Campanella's political ideas by ordering them under the arbitrary headings of the real, ideal and theocratic state. See "The Political Thought of Tommaso Campanella," in *Studies in Philosophy and the History of Philosophy*, ed. John K. Ryan (Washington, D.C., 1963), II, 211-248. This essay is chapter 12 of his book, *Campanella*. This chapter in particular suffers from an ahistorical treatment of Campanella's thought, as does the book generally.

[16] Firpo, *Bibliografia*, 158-159. *Lettere*, 8-9.

Than cold lip-service; faith without works is vain...
But none can doubt the good he doth his brothers.[17]

The problem of where Campanella stands with respect to the great religious and political issues of his age is further obscured by the one political action in which he participated and the life of suffering and incarceration that was its consequence. He was free only a few months after his abjuration of 1596 when the Holy Office again arrested him, this time because one of its prisoners in Naples denounced him as a heretic. This was in March 1597. He was kept in prison until December of that year and then released, on condition that he return to his Province and be confined to a monastery there. He returned to Naples and withdrew to a monastery in his native town of Stilo in the summer of 1598. Campanella was now thirty years old. Perhaps he could have resumed his philosophical work quietly and in seclusion, but he did not. His philosophical output for 1598-99 is, for him, scanty, and in the course of 1599 he became increasingly involved in a strangely unrealistic plot to overthrow Spanish rule and the Catholic hierarchy in Calabria with the assistance of the Turks and to establish a kind of theocratic commune of which he himself would be the head.[18] This took place, let it be noted, after he had written two works advocating a Papal monarchy for Italy and the world and two works promoting the interests of the Spanish Empire also in Italy and throughout the world: works in which one consistent feature is that the interests of Christian Empire, be it Papal or Spanish, are persistently pitted against those of the Turks.

Denounced by two participants in the plot, the conspirators were captured and those who were not summarily executed were sent in chains to Naples. Campanella was imprisoned there, in the Castel Nuovo, one of the principal fortresses in which the Spaniards maintained a military garrison. He was arraigned before the civil tribunal for rebellion and before the ecclesiastical tribunal for heresy. His "examination" which began in January 1600 was gruesome. He claimed innocence in his first interrogation before the civil tribunal, was thrown into a dungeon, actually a cleft in the bedrock of the Castle, to remain there for seven days. Then followed torture. He "confessed," admitting that he preached about the coming political

---

[17] Sonetto 42, *Tutte le opere di T.C.*, I, 110. I have followed, with minor changes, the translation by John Addington Symonds, *The Sonnets of Michael Angelo and Tommaso Campanella* (London, 1878), 150.

[18] This entire episode is presented at length, with documents, in Amabile's three volumes, *Campanella. La sua congiura*. See n. 6 above.

upheaval but denying that he was part of a conspiracy to bring it about. He was told to draw up his defense and began to do so along prophetic lines, arguing for the imminent approach of the Millenium.

One section of Campanella's *Defense*[19] was an astronomical treatise, a fairly systematic work confuting the theories of Aristotle and Ptolemy—but also of Copernicus and Telesio—and setting forth his own view of an irregular but steady approach of the sun to the earth which will ultimately be consumed by the sun's great heat. Another section consisted of a collection of specific prophecies drawn from Scripture and celestial "signs"; they announce an impending cosmic social renewal, a reordering of the heavenly bodies and the kingdoms and laws on earth, an event to commence around 1600. Although these ideas recur in several of the works he wrote around this time, again the circumstances in which they were formulated cast some doubt on Campanella's convictions. Perhaps such prophetic notions do explain his participation in the futile Calabrian conspiracy; but certainly, as part of his defense, they were intended to demonstrate to his judges that he was in fact a prophet rather than a conspirator, a seer rather than a rebel. His desperation at this point can be gauged by the fact that by April of 1600 he began to feign madness. The ecclesiastical action against him began now, and he persisted in this attitude of insanity through three interrogations, including an hour of torture. Probably in the hope of sparing him further examinations of this sort, a Fra Pietro of Stilo presented to his judges the *Defense* which Campanella had drawn up, but to no avail. On the fourth and fifth of June 1601, he was subjected to the cruel torture of "the vigil" to test whether his insanity was genuine. This was the usual torture of the rope, suspending the body of the victim by his tied hands over a blade which cut into his flesh whenever he yielded to the strain of holding himself in the air; but the vigil refined this cruelty by continuing it for forty hours. Campanella endured the ordeal without breaking. Adjudged insane, he could not be executed, although he had to wait a year and a half, until January of 1603, to learn of the sentence from Rome condemning him to life imprisonment.

It was during this period of torment and waiting, while imprisoned in the tower of the Castel Nuovo, that Campanella wrote his two most renowned political treatises : *De monarchia Hispanica*, his vindication of Spanish hegemony and imperialism, and his Utopian *Civitas Solis*.

---

[19] Firpo, *Bibliografia*, 136-139.

The Spanish Monarchy[20] he composed between 1600 and 1601, while pretending to be mad, and it was submitted to his judges as part of his defense by Fra Pietro. Campanella's intention was simple enough: to make evident his desire to serve Spain and demonstrate how useful he would be as a counsellor. But the work is an extraordinarily complex, a truly Baroque structure incorporating realistic, useful advice on economic, social, and political matters[21] along with extravagant predictions of Spanish world-empire and the establishment of a universal Christian theocracy.

Among the practical considerations, Campanella notes the poverty of the Spanish Crown, the fact that the King is forced to borrow steadily and heavily despite the influx of silver from the New World. On this point, he correctly recommends a shift in economic policy from concern with bullion to cultivation of genuine wealth in agricultural and industrial production. He deplores the scarcity of corn, meat, wine, oil, and cloth that drives prices beyond the reach of the populace in Spain and in Italy; and he deplores the taxes that force people into "unproductive" lives as brigands, soldiers, and religious. If the Crown would set up State cloisters and seminaries where men and women could engage in useful labor—workhouses, in short—people would not need to join religious orders or turn to begging, thieving, and war out of sheer want. The population should be looked upon as the source of wealth throughout the Empire, and this holds for the Indians, too. Campanella would have them trained in mechanical occupations and even sent abroad as a mobile labor force. He pointed out that Spain was suffering from a population shortage, a problem made more acute by warfare and monasticism. The King could scarcely man the vast areas Spain had conquered; why not train the conquered Indians, then, to carry out the necessary work of Empire? Let them build great cities along the coasts of Africa and Asia; let them till the soil and cultivate the mechanical arts throughout the Spanish domains.

There are few scruples here about conquest, exploitation, and slavery. Spanish rule, Spanish imperialism Campanella regards in this and his other pro-Spanish works as providential. In *The Spanish*

---

[20] *Della Monarchia di Spagna*, ed. Alessandro d'Ancona in *Opere di Tommaso Campanella* (Turin, 1854), II, 77-229.

[21] Much of the general, practical advice—on counsel, military affairs, income of the state, industry and agriculture—Campanella lifted whole from Botero's *Ragion di stato* and *Grandezza della città*. The corresponding passages are given in Rodolfo De Mattei, *La politica di Campanella* (Rome, 1927), 18-69.

Monarchy, which is shot through with the millenarian prophecies that constituted his formal *Defense*, the Spanish Empire appears as the final phase of the Holy Roman Empire. It is destined to absorb all of Europe (including the Austrian Hapsburg domains), the New World, Africa; then just as Alexander had overpowered the Persians, so will the Spanish monarchy extend its sway over the Turks. Then will the end of the world be at hand. Philip (III) should, therefore,

> cause it to be publicly preached and proclaimed abroad, that the end of the world is at hand, and that the time is now come when there is to be one sheepfold under one shepherd, that is, the Pope; and that he himself is another Cyrus, whose office it is to see these things brought about, and to gather all the flock into that one sheepfold; and that whatever nation or kingdom shall refuse to yield him obedience shall be brought to destruction...[22]

Thus the accused rebel against Spanish rule in Calabria wrote in support of Spanish rule, and the accused heretic was just as obliging in condemning heresy, one of Spain's major obstacles to hegemony in Europe.

Several of Campanella's suggestions for combatting heresy are aimed at thought and learning. As befits his intellectual Italian nature, he advocates curriculum reform combined with a rather subtle manipulation of scholars. Greek and Hebrew schools should be closed north of the Alps and the study of Arabic cultivated instead, so that the disputatious Northerners may be led to quarrel with Moslems rather than Catholics. Theology should be banished from northern universities; and as for Philosophy, he argues for schools of thought more congenial to Christianity than Aristotelianism, such as Platonism, Stoicism, and—Telesianism. Most ingenious is his proposal for the encouragement of mathematical learning. Mathematics is innocuous on the one hand, serving to divert the mind from theological and political matters, and on the other hand, it can be of great practical value to the Crown. Indeed, if German scholars were rewarded for pursuing the mathematical sciences, particularly geography and astronomy; if they were subsidized and sent to the New World, the King would at one stroke acquire maps and surveys of the lands and heavens of the new regions of his Empire and would diminish the incidence of heresy in the old.

These stratagems, however, are supplements, not substitutes for the usual methods of suppressing heresy. Campanella expects the

---

[22] *Monarchia di Spagna*, 101.

Spanish King to maintain orthodoxy. His Empire rests upon and is justified by the unity of religion: the Spaniards "... hold the New World by religion, which gives unity to this hemisphere and to that one, and losing the [support of the] Papacy, they will immediately lose that hemisphere and their acquisitions in Europe which they hold more by religious zeal and the Inquisition than they do by arms and money..."[23] He therefore advises the King to promulgate a law binding upon all the princes subordinate to him: they are to extirpate heresy by war should any people or country abandon Catholicism; and unless individual heretics can prove by signs that God is on their side, "bring them to the stake and burn them if you can."[24]

All this detailed advice, which is generally very practical, is embedded in a context of political ideas which can only be termed fantastic. The leading theme of *monarchia*, of temporal government of the world, is clearly derived from Dante.[25] But Campanella's *De monarchia* has none of the abstractness that lends at least a formal kind of cogency to Dante's ideal of world-government. It is actual Spanish dominion over Europe and the world that Campanella is advocating, and he offers his treatise as a campaign-plan for a Spanish-Catholic Crusade. He incorporated in it his earlier work on subduing the Netherlands; he further advises the King of Spain to restore the Holy Roman Empire to his rule, either by controlling an election or, if need be, by marching into Germany and conquering it; and then, united with the other Catholic powers under the direction of the Pope(!), the Spanish King—now Emperor—is to set about making his Empire truly universal and thoroughly Catholic. In Counter-Reformation terms, the medieval ideal of theocratic empire and Joachite apocalyptic prophecies are here revived with all their ideological trappings: the passages from Scripture, the prophecy of the four World-Kingdoms from the *Book of Daniel*, and the idea of the continuity of the fourth and last of the Empires, the Roman, by *translatio imperii*, the transfer of authority from the ancient Caesars to the Franks, the Germans, and to Spain. In 1600, with the Church riven and Christendom resolving into several sovereign states, Campanella articulates a program of Empire willed by God, founded upon the true faith, and

---

[23] This theme, which runs through *The Spanish Monarchy*, is also to be found in the *Discorsi ai principi*, especially 142-143, 154-155, 158-159.
[24] *Monarchia di Spagna*, 157.
[25] Perhaps by way of Botero.

established under Papal guidance by the Spanish King acting as the "arm" of the Church.

Whatever his private thoughts about *The Spanish Monarchy* may have been—and saving his life by means of it was surely one of them—the work came to enjoy a sinister success. Although he was a prisoner of Spanish and Papal power for the greater part of his life, this "Italian friar and second Machiavel" (as he is called in the Preface to a 1659 English edition of *The Spanish Monarchy*)[26] was regarded abroad as a spokesman for Spanish and Papal designs. His pro-Spanish writings, which remained unpublished in Italy and virtually unknown in Spain, were translated, published, and avidly studied in France, England, Germany, and the Netherlands for insight into the plans of the Escorial and the Vatican[27]—an ironic fortune, matched only by that won by his second major work of these years, his *City of the Sun*. This work has given rise to exactly the opposite view of Campanella, endearing him to historians of Liberal persuasion as a victim of the Papal Church and Spanish State, and earning him a conspicuous place in the histories of Socialism as an early spokesman and martyr for the cause of a just, humane, and egalitarian society.[28]

---

[26] *A Discourse Touching the Spanish Monarchy*, trans. Edmund Chilmead (London : Philemon Stephens, n.d.). To the first English edition of 1654, William Prynne added for this 1659 edition the following frontispiece and "admonitorie Preface" : "Thomas Campanella. An Italian Friar and Second Machiavel. His *advice to the King of Spain for attaining the Universal Monarchy of the World*. Particularly concerning England, Scotland and Ireland, how to raise Division between King and Parliament, to alter the government from a Kingdome to a Commonwealth. Thereby embroiling England in Civil war to divert the English from disturbing the Spaniard in bringing the Indian Treasure into Spain. Also for reducing Holland by procuring war betweixt England, Holland and other Seafaring Countries, affirming as most certain, that if the King of Spain become master of England and the Low Countries, he will quickly be sole Monarch of all Europe, and the greatest part of the new world."

[27] See Firpo's introduction to *Discorsi ai principi*, 51-53.

[28] The first and still fundamental biographical and bibliographical study of Campanella by Luigi Amabile makes the *City of the Sun* the key to his thought and to the Calabrian uprising. The later writings which are not liberal and empirical in outlook he interprets as opportunistic. In addition to the three volumes cited above, see *Fra Tommaso Campanella nei cestelli di Napoli, in Roma ed in Parigi*, 2 vols. (Naples, 1887). John Addington Symonds creates the same impression of Campanella as anti-clerical, liberal, and democratic by his selection of Campanella's poems in *The Sonnets of Michael Angelo and Tommaso Campanella* (1878). Modern Socialism first acknowledged Campanella as a predecessor, albeit a Utopian one, in Engel's classic essay of 1880, *Socialism : Utopian and Scientific*, which was soon followed by Paul Lafargue's chapter on Campanella in vol. I of Eduard Bernstein, K. Kautsky, *et al.*, *Die Geschichte des*

There is a great deal in his life story to support the Liberal and Socialist interpretation of Campanella as a rebel against the State and Church of his time : the Calabrian conspiracy; the twenty-seven years passed in Neapolitan prisons until the Spaniards released him (thanks to the intervention of the Master Provincial of the Dominicans of Calabria); the two subsequent years in the prison of the Holy Office in Rome. Even when he regained his liberty in 1628, having won the favor of Urban VIII, the sixty-year old Campanella was still viewed with suspicion. He was prohibited from teaching or publishing his works; and after only five years of such "freedom" in Rome, he was forced to flee Italy altogether because of a fresh conspiracy against the Viceroy of Naples in which at least two of his friends were implicated. Was he all along, as the Spaniards suspected, an opponent of Spanish imperialism, at least in Italy ?

Despairing of Spanish aid for his cause by 1610, Campanella had stopped writing apologies for the Spanish Monarchy; and once he was freed in Rome in 1628, his political writings took on a pro-French coloration. Even in the early pro-Spanish writings, there are those inconsistencies which might indicate that his apologetic intent was occasionally blunted by a desire to see Italy united against the foreigner, against the Spaniards. But if we grant that Campanella's opposition to Spanish rule in Italy was genuine, does this entail that he supported the cause of the populace against it ? Was he a democrat and a social radical as well as a patriot and political rebel? Some of his poems seem to bear out this possibility;[29] but the major source supporting the notion of Campanella's social radicalism is the *City of*

Sozialismus in Einzeldarstellungen (Stuttgart, 1895), 469-506. From Lafargue on, Campanella has appeared in the various histories of social thought as a Utopian thinker (Lafargue being more attentive than his successors to Campanella's numerology and what he took to be his Cabalistic ideas) and as a participant in a popular rebellion for communal objectives.

Croce's "liberal" reading of Campanella departs from Amabile's, in part because of his greater intellectual sophistication, but also because he sought to refute the Marxist position of Lafargue by contending that Campanella's socialist ideas bear no vital relation to the social ills of his time. He continues to regard Campanella's theocratic, imperial writings as merely opportunistic; but unlike Amabile, he has no great esteem for the *City of the Sun* either. See Benedetto Croce, "Sulla storiografia socialistica : il communismo di Tomasso Campanella," in his *Materialismo storico ed economia marxistica* (Bari, 1961), 181-221.

[29] In particular, "Della plebe," *Tutte le opere*, 97 (also in Symonds, 143).

the Sun,[30] which is usually taken as expressing his aims in the Calabrian conspiracy.

The economic and social ideas of the book, like the genre of the work, are closely related to Sir Thomas More's *Utopia*.[31] The description of the utopian state is given by a Genovese sea-captain. On the island of Taprobane (Ceylon), he came across a people who had fled India during the Tartar invasions and who sought in their new land to lead "a philosophical life in common." There is no private ownership among these people who live according to natural law. All things are held in common, so the society is spared the vices of both the poor and the wealthy. Everyone is "rich" in the sense of having everything necessary for a good life; and all are "poor" in the sense of owning nothing. Even the family has disappeared from this society, for Campanella, in agreement with Plato's *Republic*, attributes to family feeling the desire for private property and the *amour propre* that follows from it.[32] Devoted to the public good, the entire community is a family in the City of the Sun, and everyone is called father, brother, son according to age.

Lacking private property, the Solarians are spared a division of classes based upon the ownership of wealth. Everyone is engaged in productive labor, and they deem "noble" (*tenuto di più gran nobilità*) those who have mastered most of the arts and are most skilled at

---

[30] *La Città del Sole* in *Scritti scelti di Giordano Bruno e di Tommaso Campanella*, ed. Luigi Firpo (Turin, 1949), 407-464. The work appears in English in several anthologies but there are only two translations, one by T.W. Halliday and one by W. J. Gilstrap. The Gilstrap is the better of the two but certain passages are omitted from it, and it is based upon only one seventeenth-century Latin edition.

[31] Campanella places the work in the tradition of Plato and More : "Se tu cerchi republica senza abuso di ministri, bisogna andare in Cielo, o fingerla come Platone e Tomaso Moro o come la *Città del sole* ..." *Monarchia Messiae con due discorsi della libertà e delle felice suggezione allo stato ecclesiastico*, ed. Luigi Firpo (Turin, 1960), 36. It was probably an Italian Utopian work that inspired him to write the *City of the Sun*, however. In 1601, the year before he composed it, he wrote a sonnet inspired by Anton Francesco Doni's *I mondi* : "Senno senza forza de'savi delle genti antiche," *Tutte le opere*, 28. Certain features of Campanella's work are closer to Doni's than to More's, e.g., the abolition of marriage and the family; although Doni, as all Utopian writers, is himself indebted to More.

[32] "... tutta la propreità nasce da far casa appartata, e figli e moglie propria, onde nasce l'amor proprio; chè, per sublimar a ricchezze o a dignità il figlio o lasciarlo erede, ognuno diventa o rapace publico, se non ha timore, sendo potente; o avaro e insidioso e ippocrita, si è impotente. Ma quando perdono l'amor proprio, resta il commune solo." *Città del Sole*, 416.

them: "Hence they laugh at us for calling craftsmen ignoble and calling noble those who learn no craft but are idle and maintain for their idleness and pleasures so many attendants to the ruin of the republic."[33] There are officials who regulate the affairs of the city and distribute its goods, seeing to it that each has what he needs and gets no more than he deserves. But the officials are popularly elected, in response to their merits alone; and although the government is headed by a single figure called Sol (meaning Metaphysics "in our language," says Campanella), the government is constituted by republican principles.

The question of Campanella's social radicalism cannot be explored here;[34] but what we can show is that his Utopia does not represent a departure from his ideas on theocratic monarchy.[35] Hence we cannot accept it, as some scholars have, as an expression of a "modern" (liberal, democratic, and socialistic)—and for that reason a sincerely held—body of thought, while rejecting his ideal of *monarchia* as "medieval" and a product of expediency. Read in the context of his life, the *City of the Sun* also reveals an essentially apologetic intent. And far from being "utopian" in the sense of abstract and removed from the real powers and forces of the time, it is addressed to them, just as much as *The Spanish Monarchy* is. Let us recall that the *City of the Sun* was written in 1602, while Campanella was awaiting his sentence from Rome. If any work was intended to clarify his role in the Calabrian conspiracy with respect to the Church, it was this one. In it we find in more moderate form the same Joachite prophecies, the same expectation of a great cosmic and social renewal which constitute the major part of his *Defense* and of his writings of the next two years, most of which are redactions and elaborations of his *Defense*. The Solarians also believe that the sun is approaching the earth. They prophesize the imminent "unification of the world" and the establishment of "a great new monarchy." There will be "... a reform of laws and arts, a coming of prophets, a renewal. And they say this will bring

---

[33] *Ibid.*, 417-18.

[34] This topic should be dealt with in relation to his views on popular movements and in connection with his other, very practical writings on economics.

[35] Firpo has done this in a somewhat different way, finding in the *City of the Sun* an idealized conception of priestly monarchy which Campanella was to transfer to actual politics in what Firpo regards as his second stage of thought (to be discussed below). See his Introduction, *Discorsi ai principi d'Italia*, 13-14, 44-51.

a great gain to the Christians; but first there will be an uprooting and a sifting, then a building and a planting." [36]

Now what kind of *monarchia* will this predicted world-government be? Although the City of the Sun is obviously intended as its pattern, it will bring "great gain to the Christians." The Solarians live according to the law of reason and nature, but this we know from Campanella's other writings is what will induce all peoples ultimately to adopt Christianity: "All men, being rational because of the First Reason which is Christ, are implicitly Christian..."[37] In the quasi-deistic City of the Sun, the religion of reason is already Trinitarian in character, and Campanella remarks that Christianity adds only the sacraments to the natural law. Moreover, he maintains that the combination of the Christian and the natural law—whether by the Solarians becoming Christian or the Christians adopting the Solarian (natural) way of life—this union of reason and religion will dominate the world.[38] Viewing the City of the Sun from this vantage-point, we can discern clearly enough in its features the institutions of the Church. The absence of private property and of the family finds its antecedents in the propertyless condition of "our priests and monks."[39] The Solarian system of elected officials resembles the constitution of the clergy, reformed as Campanella advises in his writings on the Church, so as to be a system of election according to merit alone.[40] Indeed the entire Solarian society *is* the Church in that broader use of the term familiar to Medieval Europe, the Church as Christian society, lay and clergy. United in one religion, bound by one set of laws, the Solarians are one flock led by one shepherd, Sol—who is a High Priest: "All the chief magistrates are priests, and Sol is the high priest, and their function

---

[36] *Città del Sole*, 459. Also, 462-63.

[37] *Discorsi universali del governo ecclesiastico* in *Scritti scelti di Giordano Bruno e Tommaso Campanella*, 476.

[38] "Se questi, che seguon solo la legge della natura, sono tanto vicini al cristianesmo, che nulla cosa aggiunge alla legge naturale si non i sacramenti, io cavo argumento da questa relazione che la vera legge è la cristiana, e che, tolti gli abusi, sarà signora del mondo." *Città del Sole*, 458.

[39] *Ibid.*, 416. Also in *Discorsi della libertà*, 38 : "Perché i principi ecclesiastici non han moglie né figli, l'amor de' quali disregolato suole apportare grandissimi danni nel governo..."

[40] "... in Roma non solo ogni persona virtuosa è partecipe del dominio, ma anche al papato e alla suprema monarchia del mondo, sendo notorio che non solo i baroni e nobili, ma l'infimi della plebe ancora si fan vescovi, cardinali e papi, quando abbondano di virtù ." *ibid.*, 27. Also pp. 28-29.

is to purge the conscience of the people."[41] The *City of the Sun*, in short, is a model of that destined universal state, at the head of which, even in his pro-Spanish writings, Campanella consistently but not surprisingly placed the Pope.

Thus this work, too, has the effect of a double exposure. An archaic vision of Christian Empire is superimposed upon the Utopian image of a socialist society in the Renaissance tradition of More, much as this same vision is imposed upon the pragmatic and astute Machiavellian outlook of *The Spanish Monarchy*. Different as they are in other respects, both works exhibit the same theocratic scheme: an ideal of Christian monarchy which Campanella was to continue to propose over the following years in works addressed to the reigning Popes. With regard to this ideal, the *City of the Sun* is consistent with his pro-Spanish writings and his pro-Papal ones (although these two sets of writings are incompatible with each other on several other points), and its democratic and socialistic institutions conform to it as well. They establish in society at large the natural and Christian way of life, mirroring the economic, social, and political institutions of (certain aspects of) the Church. Hence I find no justification for singling out Campanella's democratic and socialistic ideas, as his great nineteenth-century biographer Amabile has done, to regard them as representative of his thought while dismissing as mere camouflage his theocratic, imperial ones.

On this point, I find myself in complete agreement with the most authoritative of the recent Campanella scholars, Luigi Firpo. Although he can in no sense be likened to those Catholic historians who find neither heterodoxy nor opportunism in Campanella,[42] Firpo disputes the Liberal contention that all of Campanella's political writings except the *City of the Sun* are cynical expedients.[43] However, he continues to maintain that this work served no apologetic purpose,[44]

---

[41] *Città del Sole*, 447.

[42] Giovanni Di Napoli is the leading exponent of this orthodox view of Campanella, as the title of his work indicates: *Tommaso Campanella, filosofo della restaurazione cattolica* (Padua, 1947). Campanella's midnineteenth-century editor, Alessandro d'Ancona, *Opere di Tommaso Campanella*, also regarded him as a consistently orthodox figure, as does Bonansea, *Campanella*. Although Bonansea incorporates the more recent positions of Firpo and Amerio, his static, systematic treatment of Campanella's thought minimizes to the point of suppression its tensions and contradictions and disregards the possibility of hypocrisy and deception on Campanella's part.

[43] *Lo Stato ideale della Controriforma*: *Ludovico Agostino* (Bari, 1957), 307-329.

[44] *Ibid.*, 322-23.

and that its ideal of Christian monarchy was genuinely held. Expediency undoubtedly prompted Campanella's writings on behalf of Spanish imperialism, and even his pro-Papal writings, but in their theme of *monarchia*, Firpo believes there is a core of sincere conviction. Profoundly Roman and Catholic in inspiration, Campanella's conception of theocratic monarchy was the only kind of "reform" that fit the political realities of Counter-Reformation Italy; and having learned this through bitter experience, Campanella renounced his rebellious messianism to espouse the cause of the Universal Papal Church, henceforth earnestly seeking to promote its advance.[45]

Whereas the Calabrian conspiracy is central to the interpretations of Liberal historians such as Amabile and to the historians of Socialism, the sincerity of Campanella's "conversion" is critical to Firpo's interpretation of Campanella's ideas on ecclesiastical world-government.[46] After learning of his sentence, Campanella had sought but failed to escape from the tower of the Castel Nuovo. He was then transferred to a subterranean dungeon in the Castle of S. Elmo in 1604. Here he endured a truly Promethean punishment, bound to his "Caucasus," as he called it, for four inhuman years of solitude, darkness, and cold. It was during these years, with the aid of his confessor, that he is thought to have come to understand and accept his suffering in orthodox Catholic terms, to repent of his former efforts at independent reform, and to recognize his mission to be one of adherence and servitude to Holy Mother Church. His poems of this time express attitudes of self-abasement and renewed dedication;[47] the prophetic strain is dominant in his thought; and from this period stems his *Monarchia Messiae*, setting forth the plan of a Papal dominated world-government, and *Atheismus triumphatus*, an apology for the "true universal religion against Anti-Christianity and Machiavellianism." If the

---

[45] Firpo, Introduction to *Discorsi ai principi*, 7-20, 44-51.

[46] Firpo, *Tutte le opere*, xxvii-xxix. Also, *Lo stato*, 323-24. The basis of this view has been provided by Romano Amerio's several studies of Campanella's philosophical and theological works in which he finds a development from a naturalistic to a religious orientation stemming from the time of Campanella's conversion. See in particular: "Il problema esegetico fondamentale del pensiero campanelliano," *Rivista di filosofia neoscolastica* 31 (1939), 368-87; "Attualità di Tommaso Campanella," *Convivium* 13 (1941), 554-74; "Un'altra confessione dell'incredulità giovanile del Campanella," *Rivista di filosofia neoscolastica* 45 (1953), 75-77. Léon Blanchet also sees Campanella as developing from an early naturalistic orientation to a genuine reconciliation with the Church and the orthodox Thomistic tradition. See his *Campanella* (Paris, 1920).

[47] Edmund Gardner, *Tommaso Campanella and his Poetry* (Oxford, 1923), 19-20.

experience of conversion is taken as formative, as a spiritual crisis in which his ideas and feelings were reoriented along traditional lines, a portrait of Campanella emerges which is at variance with the earlier Liberal view but not wholly incompatible with it. The young Campanella *is* heterodox and rebellious, but the mature Campanella from c. 1605 on modifies and reshapes his earlier ideas with increasing orthodoxy and adheres to the cause of Papal Monarchy until his death some thirty-five years later in France.

The merit of this interpretation lies in its psychological plausibility. It can account for the tenacity with which Campanella clung to life and for his heroic labors through all the vicissitudes of his imprisonment. What sustained him if not a profound conviction that his suffering was the very sign of his mission to serve the Church and guide it toward its proper end? Is not his conversion a classic case of the victim identifying himself with his oppressors and accepting their punishment of him as deserved?

Yet I would argue that Campanella's "conversion," and the political writings subsequent to it, can be understood just as well as a dreadful mockery, as the only possible response, desperate and tragic as it was, to the powers that controlled his society and his life. How much irony is there in a man who writes in the Roman prison of the Inquisition an apology for ecclesiastical government which he entitles *Discourses on Liberty and on Happy Subjection to the Ecclesiastical State?* Liberty from sin, he tells us in this work of 1627, is more necessary than any other form of freedom; and "it is to liberate us from such servitude that we institute courts and judges, police and soldiers, executioners and prisons, exiles, and all the other instruments of government which we cannot live without."[48] Has black become white, as the Jesuits were ready to assert should the Church so command? Or is Campanella at once astute and sardonic in making it appear so?

I find no more reason to accept his "conversion" at face-value than I do his political writings. With regard to confessions and retractions made in prison, Campanella himself cautions us about their reliability: " The condemned do this every day in Naples, confessing then denying with vain hopes; the ultimate penalty suggests all kinds of thoughts... some even pretending madness to escape it..."[49] There is more than

---

[48] *Discorsi della libertà*, 19. Bonansea uses this work as confirmation of what he takes to be Campanella's lifelong theocratic position (*Campanella*, 244).

[49] *Discorso politico del Padre Fra Tomaso Campanella tra un Venetiano, Spagnolo e Francese, circa li rumori passati di Francia* in Amabile, *Castelli* II, 210-211.

enough in Campanella's activities and writings to warrant a healthy scepticism toward both his newly acquired orthodoxy and his advocacy of Christian empire. It is true that he continued to write on this theme after his first transfer from the dungeon of S. Elmo in 1608. Along with his prodigious philosophical and theological output, he developed the two main lines of the ecclesiastical writings begun in S. Elmo in apologies for, and works of practical advice on, the establishment of a Papal world-state and in *Quod reminiscentur*, his great work on reconciling heretics and infidels to the Church through missionary work and propaganda. However, he also continued his pro-Spanish writings after his "conversion," down to 1609 or 1610 when he apparently lost hope of gaining Spanish assistance. That is, he wrote both pro-Papal and pro-Spanish treatises at the same time, as he had during his first arrest by the Inquisition in Padua; and his pro-Papal *Monarchia Messiae* and *Del governo ecclesiastico* actually belong in inspiration to that Paduan period, not to the time of his "conversion," being redactions of the treatises written during that earlier imprisonment. Moreover, during the period of his "conversion" and the years subsequent to it, Campanella was actively seeking Papal support. His pro-Papal writings and works on heresy and missionary activity were dedicated and sent, then re-dedicated and sent, from his prison to Paul V, Gregory XV, and Urban VIII as they succeeded one another, the advent of each new Pope arousing vain expectations and feverish activity on his part to obtain his release.

Another and far more serious set of questions regarding his imperial theories is raised by his pro-French writings. As he regained his freedom after the last two years of imprisonment in Rome, Campanella steadily shifted his allegiance from the Spanish and Hapsburg cause to that of France, proposing in one instance a Papal-French alliance to reduce Spanish power and a plan to transfer the Imperial title from the Hapsburg to the French house.[50] But it is not as if he merely sought in these late works to make the French state the "arm" of the Church, to use French power to achieve the aim of Christian *monarchia*.[51] Rather, the old imperial ideal gives way to the policies of Richelieu, predicated as they were—and as Campanella acknowledges—upon a

---

[50] *Aphorismi politici pro saeculo praesenti* and *Comparsa Regia* in Amabile, *Castelli* II, 291-97, 299-347.

[51] This is the position common to those who find in Campanella a consistent aim of Christian unity and theocracy. See, for example, Francesco Grillo, *Tommaso Campanella in America. A Critical Bibliography and a Profile* (New York, 1954), 27-31.

clear-sighted acceptance of the emerging state-system of Europe with its demand for balance-of-power politics and the subordination of religion to the interests of the sovereign, secular state.

The theme of Christian empire does appear in the very beginning of a dialogue among a Frenchman, Spaniard, and Venetian which he wrote in Rome between 1632 and 1633. It is Louis XIII's turn, in this *Political Discourse on the Rumors circulating in France*,[52] to liberate Italy (from the Spaniards who are now "foreigners" while the French "right" to Milan and Naples is upheld), and to recapture Constantinople and seize the Holy Land from the Turks. But this is unmistakably a *pro forma* statement, as is the concluding passage in which the hitherto pragmatic Venetian of the dialogue ascribes to Satan the present opposition between the Hapsburgs and France and foresees the eventual return of France's Protestant allies to the faith. In the body of the work, the theme of Christian unity and empire is dropped, and taking its place is a brilliant defense of Richelieu's objectives: to frustrate the Spanish aim of universal monarchy, to set limits upon the power of Austria—and to combine with the Protestants of Sweden, Holland, and Germany in order to do so.

Although Campanella cites Biblical precedents for allying with heretics and infidels, there is a significant change in intellectual tone, as well as of theme, in this work. The tension between astute political judgments and the providential imperial ideas which is felt in most of his political writings is here personified in the spokesmen for the Spanish and the Venetian point of view. As if to mock the speciousness of his former speculative mode of political reasoning, Campanella has the Venetian listen with ill-disguised impatience as the Spaniard and the Frenchman rehearse his old astrological and Scriptural "arguments," each proving by means of them the destined preponderance of his own state. As spokesman for Richelieu, the Venetian sets the political discourse straight by placing it upon its proper Machiavellian basis: power.

> The Venetian responded: I have listened to you with indifference because I do not wish to talk about or listen to these principles of numerology and astrology, nor any such abstractions. The Venetian school teaches that those states will advance which have the most prudent advisers, the best military leaders, the greatest number of troops, the support of their people, and finally

---

[52] In Amabile, *Castelli* II, 185-214. For a slightly abridged English version based upon another manuscript (and not ascribed to Campanella) see Thos. Hodgkin, "Richelieu and his Policy: A Contemporary Dialogue," *English Historical Review* 17 (1902), 20-49.

money in abundance, with eloquent spokesmen who know how to persuade their own people not to rebel and foreigners to come over to their side. Now these things are to be found in France rather than Spain, as everyone knows.[53]

Prudence, political realism, and *raison d'état* have apparently triumphed —as befits a work written to win Richelieu's patronage, which Campanella gained, in fact, the following year when he fled to France.

It is true that the major changes in Campanella's political thought correspond to the course of events over the forty-five years of his "career" as a political writer: the shift from Hapsburg to French preponderance and the failure of the forces of the Counter-Reformation to restore the unity of Christendom. Looked at in this perspective, he may well appear as a theorist of the Counter-Reformation, providing an ideological reflection of political developments within the Catholic world of his time. But to my mind, there is another, more fundamental way in which his political thought represents the force of the Counter-Reformation, and this is by its essentially enigmatic character. For not even his Machiavellian apology for Richelieu can be taken as a *bona fide* political view, one that Campanella may have harbored all along beneath the veil of his theocratic ideas. His *Political Discourse* of 1633 is as ambiguous in this respect as his other political writings are with regard to the interests of the Pope and of Spain. The Venetian who rejects providential arguments makes his own prediction at the end that Richelieu's Protestant allies will return to the Church. And alluding to "invisible and opposing forces" that direct historical events, he points out that a great deal has been written on such matters by those who (referring to Campanella himself?) are "sentinels of the divine judgment."[54] In the light of the major section of the dialogue, the old theocratic conclusion seems bizarre, but why is it there at all? Is it because Campanella was too accustomed by now to the archaic framework of a united and providential Christian monarchy to abandon it altogether? Or did he feel constrained to embed his ideas within it, because a purely prudent justification of Richelieu's policy, which might please Richelieu, would arouse too much opposition in Rome and might lend support to Richelieu's opponents?

As Campanella admits in a letter of 1607 to Philip III: he had

---

[53] *Discorso politico*, 187. For Campanella's relation with and influence upon *raison d'état* literature, particularly in France by way of Gabriel Naudé, see L. Firpo, *Il pensiero politico del Rinascimento e della Controriforma* (Milan, 1966), 781-4.

[54] *Ibid.*, 214.

"only words and thought" by which to save himself;[55] and the clear message of his political writings is that he felt compelled to use word and thought to tell his would-be sponsors and saviors what they wanted to hear. If we could single out from the host of conflicting positions contained in his writings a set of ideas which express a theoretical, as opposed to an apologetic intent, we would classify Campanella as a genuine political theorist. But to my mind his writings do not support the privileged position of any one set of ideas, and he himself seems to thwart our efforts to make them do so. In the projected edition of his complete works which he prepared in the relative security of France, he included *all* his political writings, the pro-Spanish ones and the ones on Papal monarchy which are at variance with each other and which are both contradicted by the defense of Richelieu's statist policies in the pro-French ones. Despite their inconsistencies with each other as well as with the events of his life, he repudiated none of them, as if to say that the political thought of Fra Tommaso Campanella is to be grasped in all of them together—and none in particular.

The tragedy of social and political thought in the Counter-Reformation, as represented by Campanella at least, is that politicization deprives it of the status and significance of theory. It is only in a chronological sense that Campanella stands between Machiavelli and Hobbes, and between More and Winstanley. Dialectically, his thought could not and does not mediate between them. Campanella may differ with More and Machiavelli, but his thought does not advance beyond their views. It does not represent a distinct stage in theoretical reflection upon the development of the state and the socio-economic institutions of early modern European society. Yet his political writings are not, for that reason, to be neglected. They can be made to yield positive insights if they are studied, not for their theoretical content but for their practical advice and the reasons that led Campanella to suppose that his various proposals, practical and theoretical, would find a welcome in high places. In short, we can turn to advantage his "sensitivity" to the interests of his would-be patrons and learn from his responses to them, not so much about the history of ideas, but a great deal about the economic, social, and political realities of his time.

City College, The City University of New York

---

[55] Tommaso Campanella, *Lettere*, 82.

PROTAGORAS IN THE RENAISSANCE: AN EXPLORATION

CHARLES TRINKAUS

This study is an attempt to determine the way in which several Renaissance thinkers regarded the thought of Protagoras, probably the most important and possibly the greatest of the Greek sophists. Although knowledge of Protagoras was clearly not very widespread in the Renaissance among either humanists or philosophers, no attempt will be made to survey the extent of his familiarity. Rather discussion will concentrate on a few fairly well known mentions or discussions of this thinker. Because both Renaissance knowledge of Protagoras and contemporary knowledge and understanding of him rest on such slender foundations, the value of this study will be somewhat factitious. The topic acquires its importance not so much from any demonstrable strength of influence or depth of understanding of Protagoras in the Renaissance but rather from our contemporary historical sense of a similarity between the Greek sophist movement and the Italian Renaissance humanist and Platonist movements. It is the consensus of a number of both ancient and Renaissance historians that even if there was no connection between the two, there ought to have been.[1]

---

[1] The so-called "rehabilitation of the sophists" is an interesting chapter of recent intellectual history which cannot be surveyed here. Werner Jaeger's *Paideia : The Ideals of Greek Culture* (trans. Gilbert Highet, second English edition, New York, 1945, first German edition 1933, I, 286-331 : "The Sophists : Their position in the history of culture, The origins of educational theory and the ideal of culture, Education and the political crisis") has had perhaps the greatest influence in suggesting the ancestral "humanist" character of the sophists, and Jaeger stresses the role of Protagoras among them. Although Jaeger regarded Socrates and Plato as the culmination of Greek Paideia, his stress on the moral and educational role of Protagoras has suggested his similarity to the Italian humanists. Two books of 1948 continued to emphasize the continuity of an educational-rhetorical tradition from the sophists to, and through the Middle Ages : H. I. Marrou, *Histoire de l'éducation dans l'antiquité* (Paris, 1948) and E. R. Curtius, *Europäische Literatur und lateinisches Mittelalter* (Bern, 1948). It was P. O. Kristeller who in his Martin Classical Lectures, published in 1955 as *The Classics and Renaissance Thought* (Cambridge, Mass.; repr. New York, 1961 in *Renaissance Thought : The Classic, Scholastic and Humanist Strains*), led scholars to a more explicit interest in the possible

The men of the Renaissance, however, viewed their past in their own ways. Humanists viewed western intellectual history in keeping with their notions of the need for a revival of Roman moral, rhetorical and historical thought. Following Cicero, they recognized that there were Greek precedents for this which they thought to be Socrates, Plato and subsequently the Stoics and the fourth century rhetorical schools. They had a mixed attitude toward Aristotle due to his dominant

---

sophistic origins of Renaissance humanism, though the Roman rhetorical tradition was always seen as the immediate model. My essay of 1960 on Bartolommeo della Fonte's inaugural orations ended on this note : "A Humanist's Image of Humanism : the Inaugural Orations of Bartolommeo della Fonte," *Studies in the Renaissance* 7 (1960), 125. J. E. Seigel's *Rhetoric and Philosophy in Renaissance Humanism* (Princeton, 1968) attempts to follow Kristeller's conceptions closely and suggests Cicero as the model of Renaissance humanists combining rhetoric and philosophy, Gorgias and sophist rhetoric as a model for "anti-philosophical" humanists such as Lorenzo Valla. Protagoras receives no mention. Heinrich Gomperz, *Sophistik und Rhetorik* (Leipzig and Berlin, 1912), had stressed a similar dissidence between Greek sophists and philosophers, and characterized the former, including Protagoras, as strictly rhetorical in their positions. Meanwhile Mario Untersteiner's *I sofisti* (Turin, 1949, Eng. trans. by Kathleen Freeman, Oxford, 1954) attempted a major reassessment of the importance of the sophists, especially Protagoras and Gorgias whose philosophical importance he sought to vindicate. Antonio Capizzi devoted an entire volume to a markedly extended edition and translation of the testimonies and fragments of Protagoras, to a philological analysis of key terms critical of Untersteiner in some respects, and to his own interpretation of Protagoras' place in the history of philosophical thought : *Protagora. Le testimonianze e i frammenti. Edizione riveduta e ampliata con uno studio sulla vita, le opere, il pensiero e la fortuna* (Florence, 1955). Also Rodolfo Mondolfo in his *La comprensione del soggetto umano nell' antichità classica* (Florence, 1958, Ital. trans. from original Spanish edition of Buenos Aires, 1955) gives major play to the role of Protagoras and the sophists in the development of an ancient activistic and subjective concept of man that was revived in the Renaissance. Of predictable future significance is W. K. C. Guthrie's third volume of his *A History of Greek Philosophy : The Fifth Century Enlightenment* (Cambridge, 1969) which devotes the first three hundred and nineteen pages to the sophists and gives particular emphasis to the "humanist" character of Protagoras' thought. Nancy Struever in her *The Language of History in the Renaissance : Rhetoric and Historical Consciousness in Florentine Humanism* (Princeton, 1970) is very much influenced by Untersteiner and other recent studies of the sophists and constantly makes comparisons between the qualities of Italian humanist ideas and those of the Greek sophists. Her study makes essentially external comparisons between the two groups whereas I attempt an "internal" comparison in this article by looking at how Protagoras was interpreted in the Renaissance. The above account is very inadequate, particularly on recent studies of the sophists, and conveys little idea of the revisionistic character of these discussions. My allusions to Protagoras will inevitably reflect some of these new conceptions, but I gratefully avoid setting forth a synthesis of my own since my concern is with Renaissance views of him.

influence among contemporary scholastic theologians and natural philosophers. But all this could be very confused. Petrarch, for instance, did not distinguish between Socrates and Isocrates. A more accurate knowledge of antiquity grew only gradually.

We, meaning at least some twentieth-century historians, view their past differently and place great stress on the Greek sophists as the original founders of the type of intellectual movement with which we identify the Italian humanists, and we regard the sophists as having at least exercised an indirect influence on the humanists through Cicero and the Roman rhetorical tradition. As far as the Renaissance Platonists are concerned, they, following the tradition, reputation and direct statements concerning the sophists in the texts available to them, regarded them as diametrically opposed to Socrates and Plato and as the corrupt purveyors of a pseudo-knowledge or falsehood, or certainly no more than amoral orators. By and large the humanists also followed this tradition, occasionally acknowledging the ancestral importance of such rhetoricians as Tisias and Gorgias. We, on the other hand, are aware that this traditional view of the sophists has been subjected to significant revision in the modern study of Greek thought. It is now necessary to recognize that the sophists, still controversially, doubtfully, and variously interpreted, have been given a massive importance in the history of Greek and western thought by scholars such as Jaeger, Untersteiner, Guthrie and many others. Moreover, it is now generally acknowledged that many of the sophists were genuinely philosophical and not only opportunistically rhetorical as they were thought to be as recently as by Heinrich Gomperz (1912).[2]

Unquestionably Protagoras is now considered as the most formative and influential of these sophists, though the importance of Gorgias also must be recognized. Therefore the following question is raised in this paper: if Protagoras is thought by contemporary scholars to be in so many respects similar to the humanists and affiliated thinkers of the Renaissance in outlook and in the range of his intellectual and educational interests, what then did these thinkers of the Renaissance in fact know of Protagoras and how did they interpret his thought?

Although, as we have indicated, our study will be based on a few fairly well known references to Protagoras, it is not intended to claim that there were no others. We do not for instance look at the Aristotelian tradition where Aristotle's references to Protagoras in the *Meta-*

---

[2] In his *Sophistik und Rhetorik* (Leipzig and Berlin, 1912). See n. 1.

physics could have been an occasion for comment. We shall be concerned with discussions of Protagoras as illustrations of the process by which knowledge and understanding of Greek thought grew or failed to grow in the Renaissance, and we shall be even more concerned with the extent to which these Renaissance thinkers identified with or rejected the ideas of this Greek thinker whom we are inclined to regard as their ancestor and as a man whose ideas of education, ethics and the origins of human culture, as we have been able to identify them principally from Plato's *Protagoras*, were in many features similar to those of the humanists.

The early Italian humanists, strongly Christian in their religious and moral concerns, admired Socrates and Plato, whose works they knew only from the *Timaeus*, the *Meno* and the *Phaedo*. They thought of the Platonic and Stoic traditions as ones with which, though pagan, they might identify themselves in opposition to scholastic Aristotelianism. They also considered themselves specifically as Ciceronian, but Platonic and Stoic also through the eyes of Cicero, as it were. Sophist and sophism, on the other hand, were terms of opprobrium for them, and they frequently characterized the nominalist scholastics of the fourteenth century as purveyors of *ventosa sophistica*—"windy sophistic."[3] Their growing preoccupation with a humanly centered theology, philosophy and ethics led them to admire Socrates as the first Greek thinker to turn philosophy to the study of man and to consider him, not the sophists, as their principal Greek predecessor in accord with what Cicero so frequently asserted concerning his own intellectual antecedents.

Perhaps if they had also possessed Cicero's lost translation of Plato's *Protagoras*, they would have had a different notion of at least this sophist. Protagoras and other sophists were not completely unknown in the Middle Ages and early Renaissance, as they are mentioned and quoted in such Latin writings as those of Cicero, Seneca and Aulus Gellius, and in works of Aristotle that were translated early.[4] Nor were the humanists averse to utilizing ideas and topics drawn from them, as may be illustrated by Petrarch's repetition of the story of the Choice of Hercules told by Prodicus but known through Cicero's citation of

---

[3] E. g. Salutati, *De fato et fortuna*, Cod. Urb. Lat. 201, f. 21 and f. 23^v; cf. Trinkaus, *In Our Image and Likeness*, I (Chicago, 1970), 86-7, 357, n. 91.

[4] Capizzi's (431-4) much more extensive assemblage of ancient references to Protagoras are conveniently indexed.

Xenophon.⁵ But this knowledge was anecdotal, fragmentary and generally critical. Plato's *Protagoras* was first translated again by Marsilio Ficino as part of the *Opera platonis* ca. 1466-68 and began to circulate in printed editions beginning in the 1480's,⁶ so that its influence was necessarily a late one, long after the humanists' notions of their movement and its past had been variously formulated. Protagoras' myth,⁷ as attributed to him and related by Plato in the dialogue, strongly supports the notion of rhetoric and ethical education as critical in ensuring a civil order of "reverence and justice," and it corresponds to a fundamental conception of the humanists concerning their own moral and educational role in society. The humanists took over this conception from Cicero, particularly his declaration at the beginning of his *De inventione* that orators through their art of rhetoric brought civilization to mankind. But Cicero's view may be traced back through whatever number of intermediaries to Plato's *Protagoras*, which he had indeed also translated.

Moreover, another aspect of Protagoras' thought that might have been supposed to have had a sympathetic reception among the humanists was his dictum that "Man is the measure of all things." Surely an appealing statement for the Renaissance, a more comprehending discussion of its meaning might have occurred if Plato's *Theatetus* had been translated earlier than Ficino's version, also of 1466-68.⁸ However, as we shall see, the saying was known and not entirely ignored, though suprisingly infrequent in mention, because of the several references to it and to Protagoras' position concerning it in Aristotle's *Metaphysics*.⁹ Although Ambrogio Traversari translated Diogenes Laertius' *Lives of the Philosophers* in the 1430's, and this contained an important sketch of Protagoras' career and a number of anecdotes, it provides very scanty information concerning his ideas. Sextus Empiricus' more elaborate interpretation of Protagoras' dictum seems also not to have been of any influence, since, prior to Giovanni Francesco Pico della Mirandola, Sextus was apparently not studied, despite the existence of a few manuscripts of the Greek text and a Latin translation.¹⁰

---

⁵ T.E. Mommsen, "Petrarch and the story of the Choice of Hercules," in *Medieval and Renaissance Studies* (Ithaca, 1959), 175-96.

⁶ P. O. Kristeller, *Supplementum Ficinianum* (Florence, 1937), I, cil-cl, lx-lxi.

⁷ Plato, *Protagoras*, 320b-322b.

⁸ See n. 6.

⁹ *Metaph.* : 1007b18-23, 1009a6-13, 1009b1-6, 1047a4-7, 1053a35-36, 1062b12-13. Cf. Capizzi's index and passages.

¹⁰ R. H. Popkin, *The History of Scepticism from Erasmus to Descartes* (New York,

Another problem was that Protagoras was frequently confused with Pythagoras, an easy orthographical error, though some modern scholars do indeed relate his thinking to the Pythagorean school, and there remains the mystery of Protagoras' choice of the word *metron*—"measure"—whatever its and his authentic meaning, which could also serve to associate him with Pythagoras. Petrarch, for example, quotes a genuine fragment out of Seneca, that "you can dispute about everything with equally convincing arguments on both sides, even about the problem of whether everything is disputable on both sides," and attributes it to Pythagoras. However, the context is interesting as he also finds it appropriate to quote the Socratic dictum, "this one thing I know, that I know nothing," and Gorgias and Hippias in the same passage in support of his own skeptical stance of pious ignorance in his *De ignorantia*.[11] Petrarch was reflecting the influence of Cicero's probabilism and semi-skepticism of the *Academica* here, which have some genuine dependence on sophist as well as Socratic doubt. Thus without true historical awareness Petrarch was betraying the existence of certain common positions in sophists, Socratics, Ciceronians, and himself as humanist.

Leon Battista Alberti was one of the few thinkers of the Renaissance to use Protagoras' "Man the measure" dictum. Appropriately he employs it on one occasion in the midst of a discussion of the dignity of man which occurs in book two of the *Libri della famiglia*. The date is a little uncertain because Alberti made a first draft in 1433-34 but apparently inserted supporting classical quotations over the next few years.[12] It is also quite clear that Alberti attributed no special significance to the passage in this usage, nor for that matter to the other classical quotations included along with it. He wishes to stress the greatness of man's powers and his active employment of them, and chides Epicurus for conceiving of the gods as passive, for how can man who should imitate God imitate nothing? Rather, as Anaxagoras said,

---

1964, repr. 1968 ed. used here), 17, n. 3 citing mss. supplied by P. O. Kristeller : Marc. lat. X 267 (3460) and Vat. lat. 2990, ff. 266-381ᵛ; cf. Kristeller, *Iter Italicum*, II (London and Leiden, 1967), 252 and 358. C. B. Schmitt, *Gianfrancesco Pico della Mirandola* (The Hague, 1967), 49-54 and *passim*.

[11] L. M. Capelli, *Petrarque : Le traité De suis ipsius et multorum ignorantia* (Paris, 1906), 89; cf. Cassirer, Kristeller and Randall eds., *The Renaissance Philosophy of Man* (Chicago, 1948), 125-6.

[12] Cf. L. B. Alberti, *Opere volgari*, ed. Cecil Grayson, I (Bari, 1960), 379; L. B. Alberti, *The Family in Renaissance Florence, I libri della famiglia*, Eng. trans. by Renée N. Watkins (Columbia, S. C., 1969), 2.

God created man to contemplate the heavens and the works of God, which is confirmed by man's erect posture. Chrysippus and the Stoics attest that man was made to observe and manage things; everything was created to serve man, while man was intended to preserve human society. It is at this point that he states, "Protagoras, another ancient philosopher, seems to some interpreters to have said essentially the same when he declared that man is the mode and measure (*modo e misura*) of all things." Next he mentions Plato's letter to Archytas of Tarentum to the effect that men were born to serve their fellows. Finally, he draws a conclusion that is of great interest in revealing Alberti's own conception of man but which patently lacks precise relationship to the positions of the ancient thinkers he cited in support of it. "It would take a long time to pursue all the sayings of the ancient philosophers in this matter, and very much longer to add the many statements of our own theologians. For the moment these have occurred to me, according to which, as you see, all of them admire, not leisure and passivity in man, but operation and activity."[13] Nonetheless it is of more than passing interest that Protagoras' famous saying, whatever its original meaning, was drawn into use by Alberti in support or embellishment of his own discussion of man.

Alberti, in the same years, made another passing use of Protagoras' dictum in his *De pictura* (*Della pittura*), apparently composed in Latin in 1435 and translated into a volgare version in 1436.[14] There, in book one, Alberti is stressing the importance of the proportionality of the objects of a painting to each other and suggests that the human figures in it present the best criterion or scale of comparison.

> Comparison is made with things most immediately known. As man is the best known of all things to man, perhaps Protagoras, in saying that man is the scale and measure of all things, meant that accidents in all things are duly compared to and known by the accidents in man. All of which should persuade us that, however small you paint the objects in a painting, they will seem large or small according to the size of any man in the picture.[15]

---

[13] Grayson ed., 131-2; Watkins trans., 133-4. The translation is my own, slightly more literal than Watkins'.

[14] Cf. Leon Battista Alberti, *On Painting and Sculpture, The Latin Texts of 'De Pictura' and 'De Statua,'* edited with translations, introduction and notes by Cecil Grayson (London, 1972), 3.

[15] *Ibid.*, p. 53 Grayson's translation; pp. 52, 54 for Alberti's original Latin version. For Alberti's subsequent Italian version, cf. *Della Pittura*, ed. Luigi Mallé (Florence, 1950), 69-70.

Clearly this use of Protagoras also is shaped to fit Alberti's own conceptions, as scholars have indicated. But perhaps a little greater subtlety is in order. Alberti declares that man is the most noticed thing in the painting to us. Though obviously he is utilizing the externally depicted figure of a man as an objective measure in the painting, and is not asserting the subjective criterion of judging the "nature" of things which is most generally considered to have been Protagoras' meaning, nonetheless Alberti is alluding to the subjective experience that, for an individual viewing a painting, man will be the most noticed thing in it. The human figure is not just a convenient measuring rod for the painter to get his dimensions into accurate scale, but the space will be subjectively viewed and measured by the human observer in accord with the proportionality of all objects and relationships to the man in it with whose presence and artistically depicted situation the observer will subjectively identify. Not exactly Protagoras, but not as totally opposed to Protagoras' clearly anthropocentric conceptions as at first it might seem.

Moreover, another feature of Alberti's statement is curiously related to the thought of Protagoras insofar as we can know it. He speaks of "the accidents of things" being made known by comparison with "the accidents of man." Again, it is the observer who subjectively becomes acquainted with, not the reality or essence, but the imitated image of an object in its accidentality of size, shape, color etc. by comparison to the imitated image, not of the reality or essence, but of the "accidents" of the man in the painting. Alberti could not have known Plato's *Theatetus*, yet what is discussed in that dialogue is Protagoras' position that a man judges the accidental qualities of things by his sense perceptions, which in turn are determined by the accidentality of the condition of the particular individual—the sick man judging something as cold which the healthy man judges as warm. Although Protagoras, in Plato's exposition, is talking not about an imitative representation of this situation but of the actually mimetic or subjectively perceptual character of knowledge, it is still of interest that Alberti attributes to Protagoras a meaning that in some ways approaches the one he seems to have had, at least as Plato depicted it in his dialogue. But this interpretation, for which Alberti had no basis in any of the texts then available to him, can thus derive from no direct historical knowledge of Protagoras' thought. It may thus rather derive from Alberti's own insights in discussing the art of painting, particularly that an imitation of a reality can only be produced by a manipulation of an imitation of its accidents. In thinking about the artist and the viewer in a new way, Alberti, as certain scholars have pointed out,[16] resorted to the analogy of the rhetorical relationship between orator and audience, the conception of which in its Latin sources derived from the Greek rhetorical tradition in which Protagoras had an important formative role. But Alberti in his interest in visual perspective became involved, through his analogy of orator and painter, in some of the philosophical problems arising out of the situation of an orator using words to communicate meanings by manipulating the responses in the mind of the reader. Alberti related these problems more specifically to the perspectival and optical problems of the painter which could be solved only by arranging or manipulating the representations of the accidents of the things depicted through perspective, proportionality, light, shade and color in order to control the response of the viewer. Protagoras' apodictic statement, though isolated and truncated, was in fact a philosophical assertion, the relevance of which to his own problems Alberti grasped even to the extent of reading into it greater meaning than the language itself contains. Moreover, the anthropocentric character of Alberti's conception of the artistic act is also evident in the manner in which he utilized Protagoras.

A more strictly rhetorical usage of Protagoras occurred shortly after Alberti's two references of the late 1430's, and though less intrinsically interesting, it comes from the hand of a humanist who was deeply concerned with the theoretical aspects of rhetoric, namely Lorenzo Valla. Moreover it is to be found in the first version of his important philosophical and methodological work, his *Disputationes dialecticae* of 1438/9,[17] and it was repeated in all subsequent redactions without apparent modification. In book three, which in general attempts to demonstrate the rhetorical nature of the syllogism and other dialectical figures, Valla takes up the problem of the "conversion" or *antistrophon*, in which an opponent who has been impaled on the horns of a dilemma reverses the figure and re-impales the initial proponent. Valla presents his main example in a long direct quotation from Aulus Gellius which recounts an episode, also presented in more abbreviated

---

[16] Rensselaer W. Lee, "Ut pictura poesis; Humanistic Theory of Painting," *Art Bulletin* 22 (1940), 197-269, esp. 201, 219; J. R. Spencer, "Ut rhetorica pictura," *Journal of the Warburg and Courtauld Institutes* 20 (1957), 26-44; esp. 31-2, 36-44.

[17] Urb. lat. 1207, ff. 151v-158v; *Opera omnia* (Basel, 1540) 744-5, Lib. III, cap. xiii, "De dilemmate antistrephonteque sive conversione." Cf. Aulus Gellius, *Noctes Atticae*, V, 10.

form by Diogenes Laertius, in which Protagoras agrees to teach the young man Euathius the art of argumentation. It is agreed that as part of his fee Euathius will give Protagoras what he is owed when he wins his first court case. Euathius delays taking a case presumably to avoid the payment. Finally Protagoras brings suit charging willful refusal to pay. He declares that if Protagoras wins his case he will have to be paid, but if he loses the case, Euathius will have won and also must pay. Euathius replies that if Protagoras wins the case, Euathius will have lost and will not have to pay, and if Euathius wins he will not have to pay. The jurors, confronted with this do not know what to decide and delay the trial to avoid an impossible decision. Valla, after giving a further example from Lactantius, presents his own solution, addressing the court as though he were Protagoras and showing how he should win. Valla's actual concern was not with Protagoras but with Aulus Gellius' fallacious handling of the dialectical problem presented. However, the example does present another reminiscence of Protagoras within the context of a rhetorical-dialectical problem with which he apparently was authentically concerned in his career and writings, however little of his methodological treatises have survived. Valla, however, reveals no awareness of Protagoras' historical importance as the most theoretically oriented of the fifth-century sophists— in his systematization of rhetoric, his epistemology, and his theory of the origins of human culture.

Cardinal Nicholas of Cusa makes important references to Protagoras in his *De beryllo* of 1458 (some manuscripts and early editions confusing him with Pythagoras, as is also true with Alberti's texts).[18] These seem to have developed out of his earlier concern with numbering, measuring and weighing, activities in which the mind of man approached, by assimilation, the nature of the divine intellect. Toward the beginning of book one of his *De sapientia* (written in 1450), the Idiot says, "Since

---

[18] Nicholas of Cusa, *Opera omnia* (Heidelberg edition indicated below as H), vol. XI, *De beryllo*, ed. L. Baur (Leipzig, 1940), 6, 13ff.; 20, 5ff.; 48, 14ff.; 51, 6. *Opera omnia* (Strassbourg, 1488 edition, reissued, ed. Paul Wilpert, Berlin, 1967 indicated below as S r) II, p. 711, 6; pp. 717-8, 24; pp. 734-5, 65, 66; p. 736, 69. Giovanni Santinello, *Leon Battista Alberti, una visione estetica del mondo e della vita* (Florence, 1962), 287, n. 44 alludes to the mixture of usage of "Pythagoras" and "Protagoras" both by Alberti and Cusanus and shows that Cusanus at least understood it was properly "Protagoras." Cf. also Luis Martinez-Gomez, "El hombre 'Mensura rerum' en Nicolàs de Cusa,"*Pensamiento* (Madrid) 21 (1965), 41-63, of which there is a resumé in *Nicolò Cusano agli inizi del mondo moderno : Atti del Congresso internazionale in occasione del V centenario della morte di Nicolò Cusano, Bressanone, 6-10 settembre 1964* (Florence, 1970), 339-45.

I have said to you that wisdom shouts in the piazzas and its cry is to dwell in the highest places, I will try to show this to you; and first I would like you to say what you see going on here in the market." The Orator replies, "I see over here money being counted, in another corner wares being weighed, in the opposite one oil and other things being measured." To which the Idiot comments, "These are the works of that reason by which men surpass beasts, for the brutes cannot number, weigh and measure; now consider, Orator, and tell me through what, in what, and from what this is done."[19] This, of course, is to assert that counting, weighing and measuring is the measure of man rather than that man is the measure of all things. And the effort of the dialogue is to argue that all these human activities derive from the divine exemplar. "Thus infinite wisdom is simplicity gathering into itself all forms, and it is the most adequate measure of all."[20] Thus, as Plato in the *Laws*, Cusanus declares that "God is the measure of all things."[21] For Plato, it was important to assert this in opposition to Protagoras' dictum. For Cusanus, on the other hand, we know that God is the measure by the similitude of man being the measure of all things—a subtle and crucial difference.

Nicholas does not weaken his stress on measuring as the characteristic human activity. In the first chapter of *De mente* the Idiot says, "I think that no one is or was perfectly a man who did not form some concept of the mind; indeed, I hold and I conjecture that the mind is the measure and limit of all things; in truth, it is called *mens* from *mensurans*."[22] And in chapter nine he is asked, "why, since as you say, Idiot, that it is called mind from measure, is the mind carried so avidly to measuring things?" "So that it may attain the measure of itself...," he replies. In this pursuit of itself as a live measure in measuring other things the human mind also assimilates itself to their modes of being. "For it conforms itself to possibility as it measures all in their possible ways; thus [it conforms] to absolute necessity as it measures all in unity and simplicity as though God; to necessity in [created] complexity as it measures all in its characteristic mode of being; and to determinate possibility as it measures all things accordingly as they exist. It also

---

[19] *Idiota de sapientia* (Heidelburg edition, ed. L. Baur, Leipzig, 1937), V, p. 6, lines 5-13 (Strassbourg reprint), I, 217 : "Quoniam tibi dixi ... etc."

[20] H : V, p. 20, lines 16-18; S r : I, 224 : "Sic infinita sapientia est simplicitas omnes formas complicans et omnium adaequatissima mensura...."

[21] 716c-d.

[22] H : V, 48, lines 17-20; S r : I, 238 : "Puto neminem esse ... etc."

measures symbolically by means of comparison, as when it uses number and geometric figures, and it transforms itself according to the likeness of such things. Hence, to those subtly perceiving, the mind is the live and unrestricted likeness of the infinite Equality."[23] This means that by its characteristic mode of being, that of measuring, the human mind manifests its likeness to the divine mind, which is the second member of the Trinity, the Word, or, as Cusanus also calls it, Equality.

Needless to say that this is a far cry from what Protagoras is alleged to have meant by anybody, and so far he has not been mentioned. But it presents the necessary context of Cusanus' own thinking within which it can be understood why he became excited about the Protagorean saying and defended it in *De beryllo*. The *beryllus*, of course, is a lens and the dialogue is built around this metaphor of a measuring device. Near the beginning, in enumerating the premisses of his argument, he comes to the third: "In the third place, note the saying of Protagoras: man is the measure of all things." Then follows a statement which we shall quote, followed by the fourth premiss in which he refers to Hermes Trismegistus because the two statements together make so clear his own use of the metaphor of measuring.

> For with sense man measures sensible things, with intellect intelligible things, and he attains to what are beyond the intelligible in excess; and he does this according to our premisses, for while he knows that the cognoscitive soul is the end of knowable things, he knows from the sensitive power that sensible things ought thus to be just as they can be sensed, concerning intelligibles, thus as they can be understood, concerning those which exceed moreover, thus as they exceed. Hence man finds in himself as if in a measuring reason everything that has been created.

The next premiss adds an essential clarification of this assertion of the measuring mind as a microcosm of the created world:

> Hermes Trismegistus said man is a second god. For just as God is the creator of real entities and natural forms, so man is the creator of rational entities and artificial forms which are nothing but likenesses of his own intellect, just as creatures are the likenesses of the divine intellect. Therefore man has an intellect which is in the likeness of the divine intellect in creating.

It is therefore by creating images and likenesses in the image and likeness of the divine intellect that the human intellect gathers into itself the created world. The mind is simultaneously the image of God and the image of the world.

---

[23] H : V, 89, lines 8-11; S r : I, 262 : "Philosophus. Admiror, cum mens ... etc." H : V, 90, lines 3-10; S r : I, 262 : "Conformat enim se ... etc."

In this famous statement Cusanus is also saying that God creates realities but man creates works of art. Moreover the realities are images of the divine intellect, which is clearly conventional Neoplatonic doctrine. But Cusanus is extending this theory to assert that man both makes images of his own ideas when he creates things and acts, and that he learns to know the realities which God has created only as images and likenesses the knowledge of which man can gain by measuring them. Man can know God as well as sensible and intelligible realities only through measuring images. Hence, as we shall see, he is led to show a more sympathetic understanding of Protagoras' position in the disputes of both Plato and Aristotle against him—that man knows realities only as his own senses reveal them to him. But to make Cusanus' position clear, we must complete the quotation of this fourth premiss:

> Hence [man] creates likenesses of the likenesses of the divine intellect. Just as there are extrinsic likenesses, namely artificial figures, so there are intrinsic likenesses, namely natural forms. In this way man measures his own intellect through the power of his own works. And from this he measures the divine intellect, just as truth is measured through an image; and this is enigmatic knowledge.[24]

Man sees divinity through a glass, darkly, but he also sees earthly realities, which are likenesses of divinity, through the images of his own measuring.

Therefore at the end of *De beryllo*, which is the lens of man's mind which by measuring discovers the unseen truth of the divine glory, he says:

---

[24] H : XI, 6f.,; S r : II, 711, 6, 7 : "Tercio notabis dictum protagore: hominem esse rerum mensuram. Nam cum sensu mensurat sensibilia, cum intellectu intelligibilia, et quae sunt supra intelligibilia in excessu attingit, et hoc facit ex premissis, nam dum scit animam cognoscitivam esse finem cognoscibilium : scit ex potentia sensitiva sensibilia sic esse debere : sicut sentiri possunt, ita de intelligibilibus ut intelligi possunt, excedentia autem ita ut excedant. Unde in se homo repperit quasi in ratione mensurante omnia creata."

"Quarto adverte. Hermetem trismegistum dicere hominem esse secundum deum. Nam sicut deus est creator entium realium et naturalium formarum, ita homo rationalium entium et formalium artificialium quae non sunt nisi sui intellectus similitudines, sicut creaturae dei divini intellectus similitudines, ideo homo habet intellectum qui est similitudo divine intellectus in creando. Hinc creat similitudines similitudinum divini intellectus : sicut sunt extrinsecae artificiales figurae, similitudines intrinsecae naturales formae, unde mensurat suum intellectum per potentiam operum suorum, et ex hoc mensurat divinum intellectum, sicut veritas mensuratur per imaginem, et hec est enigmatica scientia."

One thing remains, that we see how man is the measure of things. Aristotle said that Protagoras had said nothing profound in this. Nevertheless it seems to me that he held to something of great soundness. And first I consider that Aristotle rightly said in the beginning of the *Metaphysics* how all men by nature desired to know, and he declared this [desire] to be in the sense of sight, which man does not have for the sake of actions only but because we delight in it because of knowledge as it manifests many different things to us. If therefore man has sense and reason that he may use them not only for conserving life in this life but so that he might know, then sensible things must exist in order to nourish man in a double way, namely, that he might live and that he might know. Moreover it is more important and more noble to know because it has a higher and incorruptible end.[25]

In this statement Cusanus stresses the value of a knowledge of objects which comes through the senses. And he dwells, like Alberti, whose conception of Protagoras so much resembles that of Nicholas, on this *più grassa Minerva*,[26] finding in the very variety, contradictoriness and changeability of the sensual world the manifestation of the divine Creator. By contrast, for Plato and Aristotle, not this subjective experience but the objective knowledge was what mattered (though Cusanus' idea is certainly Platonist). Obviously, however, Protagoras as we are able to know him did not, like Cusanus, have such a religious end in his outlook. Taking into account the controversially different ways he is interpreted, certainly one side of Protagoras' quarrel with both Plato and Aristotle (or rather their quarrel with him) was his emphasis that judgement takes place through the sensation of constantly changing appearance. Cusanus shows here a delight in the sensuous world for which he found support even in the meagre knowledge

---

[25] H : XI, 48f. ; S r : II, 734 : "Restat adhuc unum ut videamus quomodo homo est mensura rerum, aristoteles dicit prothagoram in hoc nihil profundi dixisse, mihi tamen magna valde dixisse videtur, et primo considero recte aristotelem in principio methaphisice dixisse : quomodo omnes homines natura scire desiderant, et declarat hoc in sensu visus quem homo non habet propter operari tantum, sed diligimus ipsum propter cognoscere, quia multas nobis differentias manifestat. Si igitur sensum et rationem habet homo non solum ut illis utatur pro hac vita conservanda : sed ut cognoscat tunc sensibilia ipsum hominem pascere habent dupliciter : scilicet ut vivat et cognoscat. Est autem principalius cognoscere et nobilius : quia habet altiorem et incorruptibilem finem."

[26] Alberti, *Della pittura* (op. cit.), 55. He wishes to be regarded not as a mathematician measuring abstract forms but as a painter placing things to be seen, and : "... per questo useremo quanto dicono più grassa Minerva...." Giovanni Santinello argues the interrelatedness of the thought of Alberti and Cusanus in his appendix, "Nicolò Cusano e Leon Battista Alberti : Pensieri sul bello e sull'arte," 265-96, reprinted from *Nicolò da Cusa, Relazioni tenute al convegno interuniversitario di Bressanone nel 1960* (Florence, 1960), 147-83.

he had of Protagoras and of Aristotle's criticism of the contradictoriness of his doctrine.

Indeed Cusanus embraces the very contradictoriness of the experience of the world as necessary to its cognition and to apprehension of divinity itself :

> For sensible things are the books of the senses in which the intention of the divine intellect is described in sensible figures, and the intention is the manifestation of God the Creator Himself. Wherefore, if you wonder concerning anything, why is it this way or that, or is constituted this way or that way, there is one reply : because the divine intellect wished to manifest itself to sensible cognition so that it might be known sensibly. For example, why is there so much contrariety in the sensible world ? You would say for this reason, because opposites placed next to each other illuminate more, and the one knowledge is of both. So small is sensory cognition that, without the presence of contrariety, it would not apprehend differences. For this reason every sense wants contrary objects that it might discern better; therefore what is required for this is in the objects. For thus it is you progress through touch, taste, smell, sight and hearing. And consider carefully how each sense has a power of knowing, and you will find every object in the sensible world ordered for the service of learning. So the contrariety of primary objects serves tactile learning, that of colors the eyes, and so for all. In all these so varied objects there is an admirable revelation of the divine intellect.[27]

We need not carry this discussion of Cusanus' use of Protagoras further, though he has more to say. What is important to observe is not only that he used Protagoras within the confines of his own intellectual and philosophical system, which was vastly alien to Protagoras, but that he was able to discern the one element in the extremely fragmentary bit of Protagoras' thought known to him that he could exploit and fit to these purposes, namely Protagoras' measuring of the sensible world through individual sensations. This served

---

[27] H : XI, 49, 8.; S r : 735, 66 : "Sensibilia enim sunt sensuum libri in quibus est intentio divini intellectus in sensibilibus figuris descripta, et est intentio : ipsius dei creatoris manifestatio. Si igitur dubitas de quacunque re cur hoc sic vel sic sit vel sic sic se habeat : est una responsio, quia sensitive cognitioni se divinus intellectus manifestare voluit ut sensitive cognoscetur, puta cur in sensibili mundo est tanta contrarietas, dices ideo quia opposita iuxta se posita magis elucescunt, et una est utrius que scientia : adeo parva est cognitio sensitiva quod sine contrarietate differentias non apprehenderet, quare omnis sensus vult obiecta contraria ut melius discernat, ideo que ad hoc requiruntur sunt in obiectis. Sic enim si pergis per tactum : gustum : olfactum : visum : et auditum. Et attente consideras quam quisque sensus habeat cognoscendi virtutem tu reperies omnia obiecta in mundo sensibili et ad servitium cognoscitive ordinata. Sic contrarietas primarum qualitatum servit tactive; colorum oculis : et ita de omnibus. In omnibus his adeo variis admirabilis est ostensio divini intellectus."

Cusanus' ambitious and paradoxical goal of showing man that he could even find God manifested in the world of sensible attributes by using his own senses as measuring devices. Although Cusanus' dialectic of otherness (derived from the Pseudo-Dionysius and Proclus) must seem undeniably appropriate to anyone versed in the Platonist and Neoplatonist traditions, it also leads him to a kind of sacred sensuousness to match his "learned ignorance." It is essential not to overlook the sincerity of his strategy of achieving theocentrism through anthropocentrism, nor, on the other hand, his truly late medieval delight in sensible objects.[28]

Another great Renaissance Platonist, who had better reason to know Protagoras since he had translated all of Plato's dialogues, including the *Protagoras* and the *Theatetus*, by 1468, namely Marsilio Ficino, found less reason to admire him. At least his casual comments are in a matter of course very negative. He refers, for instance, to thinkers who denied the existence of God, such as Diagoras, or who doubted whether one could prove the existence of God or not, such as Protagoras, but always in a glancing and hostile allusion.[29] He refers, of course, to the well-known fragment, also well-known in the Middle Ages and the Renaissance because it is cited several times in the writings of Cicero.

A more central and important mention of Protagoras has to do with the question of sense-knowledge. In book eleven, chapter six of his *Theologia platonica* Ficino set forth his proofs that the soul is immortal through its capacity to know eternal truths. Asserting that, "there is no truth in sensible things," he asks, "but why not in the soul?", and continues, "perhaps there is truth in the soul, but not, as Protagoras and Epicurus believed, in that part of the soul which is the sense, because it looks outside itself and is compelled to feel with a certain

---

[28] In this, despite the sparseness of the texts, Cusanus made a brilliant use of Protagoras as the dialectical counter-part of Parmenides, whom he knew of through Proclus' commentary on Plato's *Parmenides*, the latter, affirming being as unity and identity, the former speaking for the Parmenidean realm of Non-being with its multiplicity, contradiction and otherness. Some modern students, interestingly, also interpret Protagoras as deliberately affirming the opposite realm to Parmenides' Being and see his thought as formed in reaction to the Pythagorean-Parmenidean tradition rather than simply being an outgrowth of the Heraclitean one as Plato seems to have supposed. Cf. especially Untersteiner, pp. 45 ff. and p. 50, n. 18 where he discusses earlier literature. Cf. also Italo Lana, *Protagora* (Turin, 1950), 80-83.

[29] E. g. *Commentarium in Philebum*, cap. xxv, *Opera omnia* (Basel, 1572, repr. Turin, 1959), 1231; *In Convivium platonis*, Orat. III, cap. v, *Opera*, 1333.

passion and is deluded by the frequent clouds of sensible things."[30] His knowledge of the *Theatetus* is echoed here.

The problem of sense-knowledge, as we saw in Cusanus, was, of course, connected with the Protagorean dictum that man is the measure of all things. Ficino alludes to the saying more than once, usually to dismiss it in an offhand way, as, unlike Cusanus, he considered it totally opposed and alien to his own philosophy. However, Plato's *Theatetus* was constructed around Socrates' exposition and refutation of Protagoras' sensualistic epistemology. Ficino wrote a short commentary on this dialogue, probably in the 1460's.[31] He seems, however, to have made it more an epitome than a commentary, for he follows the argument very closely, introducing little of his own except historical allusions to other thinkers who espoused similar doctrines and references to other Platonic dialogues where similar sophist arguments are refuted, and he does not take any special notice of the section of the dialogue generally designated today as "The Apology of Protagoras." It would seem as if Ficino considered the Protagorean theory of knowledge so palpably false that he had no need to discuss it other than to bring out Socrates' arguments.[32] He also alludes to the Protagorean position, that the opinion of anyone, based on sensation, is as true as that of anyone else, in his commentary on the *Philebus* and also in his commentary on the *Cratylus*. In the latter instance and at the beginning of the commentary on the *Theatetus* he places Protagoras among thinkers such as Heraclitus who regarded all reality as a constantly changing flow. In his commentary on the *Laws*, when he comes to Plato's declaration that God, not man, is the measure of all things, Ficino says, "By these words Plato seems to confute Protagoras, saying man is the measure of things, whose error is subtly refuted in the book *De scientia* (i.e. the *Theatetus*)."[33]

---

[30] *Theologia platonica*, ed. R. Marcel (Paris, 1964), II, 140 : "Non est igitur in rebus sensibilibus ... etc."

[31] *Opera*, 1274-81. Cf. Kristeller, *Supplementum*, I, cxvi.

[32] It is of some interest, however, that Ficino [p. 1279 : "Hinc Theatetus, scientiam esse veram opinionem ... etc."] seems to assign Protagoras' position that knowledge is true opinion to the realm of the orator and of public affairs, rather than science.

[33] Cf. *Opera*, 1235 (*Philebus*), 1275 (*Theatatus*), 1311 (*Cratylus*), and 1499-1500 (*Laws*) : "Quippe quum Deus omnium sit mensura, praecipue nobis, qui videlicet eatenus vel prosequi, vel fugere debemus singula, quatenus divinae menti voluntatique vel consonare, vel dissonare censentur. Hinc illud in Platonis epistola : Sapienti quidem viro lex Deus est, insipienti vero libido. Ambiguus vero hic legitur textus : alibi enim legitur ut traduxi. Quibus verbis Plato videtur Protagoram confutare, dicentem rerum mensuram hominem esse. Cuius error in libro de Scientia (i.e. *Theatetus*) subtiliter confutatur."

One might expect that a philosopher as deeply influenced by a direct knowledge of Plato as Ficino was, the first Latin to be so since antiquity, would have at some point in the elaboration of his own thinking to reckon with the problems that Protagoras raised. As I have indicated elsewhere, it was important to him to refute the epistemologies of nominalism, which were in some ways a late medieval counterpart to that of Protagoras. Ficino, as a matter of fact, refers to the capacity of the human soul to count and measure in book six of the *Theologia platonica*. In general this was an aspect of Platonism which was not particularly important to Ficino in contrast to Nicholas of Cusa who, as we have seen, turned the measuring capacity of man both toward the world and toward man into a sign of man's similitude to God. Cusanus also stressed sense-knowledge as a part of measuring. Ficino, however, speaks of man's capacity to number and measure as a proof that the soul is not corporeal since number is an image of unity which is incorporeal while everything corporeal is multiple. Measuring and numbering, therefore, are non-sensory capacities and activities of the human soul and can for Ficino have little to do with Protagoras' sense-knowledge. Ficino introduces them as a contrast to the illusory knowledge of the boy who sees his image in a well and thinks it is himself.[34] Yet something of the dialectical interplay of sense-knowledge of a world in constant flux which is not knowledge but opinion, and the unchanging intellectual knowledge of eternity, which was so important to Plato and in his own way to Cusanus, and which kept Plato at least constantly presenting the ideas of Protagoras in his dialogues, penetrated also into Ficino here. But remarkably little of it was related by him to Protagoras. In this particular discussion he does not mention him once.

On the other hand, it seems characteristic of Ficino that he refers several times to man's innate knowledge of God as stated in the *Protagoras* and makes a more elaborate comment on it in his commentary on the same dialogue. Although the idea is presented by Protagoras as part of his myth depicting the condition of man, Ficino ordinarily refers to it as a statement made by Plato and wishes to refute what he alleges are Protagoras' arguments against it. As we shall see his whole treatment is very ambiguous. For instance in book fourteen, chapter ten of the *Theologia* he wishes to answer an objection of "the

---

[34] *Theologia platonica* (ed. Marcel), Lib. VI, cap. 2, vol. I, pp. 227-8. On Ficino's rejection of nominalism cf. *In Our Image and Likeness* (Chicago, 1970), 466-7.

followers of Lucretius" to his own claim that the knowledge of God, innate in man, was his most characteristic and distinguishing quality. It is objected that such knowledge was inculcated by early political leaders for political purposes. "Not at all," said Ficino :

> It is impossible to say how rapidly human discoveries are changed, even true ones, let alone the false and simulated ones. All human customs change in a short time into opposite customs. Also the laws are opposite in different peoples at the same time, and what some consider wicked others think virtuous. Moreover, what is more ancient than religion? And what more glorious? But the founders of the laws certainly did not invent religion for the sake of coercing the people. For religion flourished in the world before there were cities and homes, and the scattered primitive men worshipped God, and those lawgivers themselves feared the divinities. Indeed Plato confirms this in his *Protagoras*, saying that men, even before they assembled or spoke or practiced any arts, from their beginning out of a natural knowledge worshipped God and erected altars and shrines. Moreover, at some point men would have rejected the yoke of religion, so hard it is and contrary to so many goods of life, had it been false and not founded on the stability of truth.

Of course, it was Protagoras who put forth the idea in his speech in the dialogue. But Ficino turns immediately to argue against Protagoras, as though he had said the opposite.

> But perchance Protagoras might say religion is not natural but seems so because we drink it in at a tender age. We reply as follows to Protagoras: he learned from infancy to speak and drink, still speech and drink are natural. Everywhere and always men speak and drink because it is natural. But in some times and places they speak and drink in a different manner because the order of action is established by opinion rather than by nature. Similarly God is worshipped among all peoples in all ages because it is natural, although not by the same sacraments and rites. Speech because it is natural attains its end, which is the wish to communicate one to another. Drink also attains its end, which is to restore the body. I do not see why religion is not possessed from birth for its end. Its end is to enjoy God, its wish to enjoy Him forever.[35]

Possibly Ficino makes Protagoras the opponent of the position he took in the dialogue, because he questions his sincerity. Modern scholars have also questioned his sincerity because the notion of both an innate knowledge of God and of virtues seems to contradict other positions Protagoras seems to maintain.[36] Ficino may be considered then the first scholar to resolve the Protagoras question this way.

---

[35] *Theologia*, II, 289-90 : "Dici enim non potest... etc." to " ... suum votum perpetuo frui."

[36] For discussions of this controversy cf. Capizzi (255-62), who rejects Protagorean authorship, and Guthrie (III, 63-5, 265-6, 268-9), who accepts Protagoras as author

A little earlier in the *Theologia platonica*, book fourteen, chapter eight, Ficino refers to the same passage of the *Protagoras* in discussing man's similarity to God in that he worships himself. In doing so he actually also worships God because he heeds the voice of conscience which is the face of God in his soul.

> They also think it wicked to dishonor the august majesty of their own mind by vile thoughts and sordid earthly cares, as though it were a divine statue. Indeed this natural notion generates shame and modesty in mankind so that we venerate not only the presence of other men as though they were divine but also the conscience of our own mind, as Pythagoras teaches, as though it were the face of God, which eagerly stimulates repentance of misdeeds in us even if we do not fear the punishment, and delights us with the memory of good deeds, as if the celestial soul would always shrink from the earthly blemish of sins. ... Plato in his *Protagoras* especially considers it to be a sign of our divinity that we alone, as if participants in the divine lot on account of a certain kinship with God, know God and desire Him as our Creator, invoke and love Him as our Father, venerate Him as a King, fear Him as a Lord.[37]

Ficino repeats this passage word for word in chapter two of his *De Christiana religione*.[38] It obviously was a central idea to him. Yet it is specifically this notion of the innate sense of reverence and justice that Plato attributes to Protagoras in his dialogue.

Ficino, it would seem, was of two minds about Protagoras. He found it difficult to grant to him an insight of which he approved. Yet despite attributing it to Plato instead of Protagoras, he really knew that it was not Plato but Protagoras who had spoken both of man's primeval worship of God and his innate moral sense. Ficino's commentary on the *Protagoras*,[39] written presumably in the 1460's, but possibly later, shows that he continues to be ambivalent. Yet at a certain point he feels compelled to give Protagoras some credit, which he later weakens. It occurs at the point where Protagoras agrees to present his ideas

---

and points to the statement on innate knowledge of divinity as the sticking-point of the controversy.

[37] *Theologia*, II, 274 : "Augustam quoque suae mentis maiestatem ... etc." to "... timemus ut dominum."

[38] *Opera*, 2.

[39] *Opera*, 1196-1200. It is possible and likely that this epitome was written before 1469 along with his translations, in accord with Kristeller, *Supplementum*, I, cxvi. The content, however, particularly the references to *prisca theologia*, suggests it could have been written after 1474, the date of the completion of the *Theologia platonica* and the composition of *De Christiana religione*. It was obviously written before 1484 when it was first published with the *Opera platonis*.

in a myth, which Ficino immediately takes to be a reference to what he called the *prisca theologia*, the prehistoric (as it were) possession of religious insights by poet-prophets who present their thoughts in the form of poetic myths. Protagoras' narrative of the gifts of Epimetheus, Prometheus and Zeus obviously appealed to Ficino. He says :

> At this point Protagoras by long circumlocutions proves that virtue can be taught. In these narrations it should be noted that he refers to certain mysteries of the ancients (*priscorum*). It is quite legitimate, although he may be a sophist, to read some good in him, and though he speaks prolixly in Plato, to derive something useful.[40]

Ficino then proceeds, not so much to paraphrase as to interpret the passage allegorically, relating it to his own conception of the creation and development of human civilization. He makes it quite clear that he knows it was Protagoras who attributed the knowledge of divinity and worship to man before he possessed the arts or civil justice.

> Indeed, because that divine gift revealed itself immediately on account of that very kinship with the higher beings, man worshipped God before he spoke or practiced any of the arts; certainly on account of its miraculous power he first lifted the divine gift into something divine before he extended it through human beings.

Ficino even finds a similarity to Christ and to the Genesis account of creation.

> Prometheus, afflicted with pain on account of that gift, signifies that our demonic overseer [Christ], in whom also there can be passions, was moved by a certain mercy toward us, considering us on account of that gift of reason itself, given, or rather excited by him to lead a so much more miserable life on earth than the beasts as it is more care-ridden and deplorable. Protagoras, having observed this, put Epimetheus so far as it concerned this condition ahead of Prometheus. This, moreover, seems to be in a certain way similar to that saying, "It repenteth me to have made man (Gen. 6:6)." Also it may be recalled that man, just as it is held here as well as in Moses, was created last and out of earth. Also here the world had its beginning as if in a Mosaic way. But we speak of these things in other places.[41]

---

[40] *Opera*, 1297-8 : "Ad haec Protagoras longis probat ambagibus doceri posse virtutem. In quibus notanda quaedam priscorum refert mysteria. Decet quamvis Sophista sit, nonnulla etiam legisse bona, et cum prolixe loquatur apud Platonem, utilia quaedam adducere."

[41] *Opera*, 1298 : "Quoniam vero divinum ... etc." to "... mundum initium habuisse." Ficino goes on to develop his interpretation of the myth of Prometheus in a significant way, as has been noted by Olga Raggio, "The Myth of Prometheus, Its Survival and Metamorphoses up to the Eighteenth Century," *Journal of the Warburg and Courtauld*

Ficino continued to interpret Protagoras' speech, developing his ideas on the gifts of *aidos* and *dikê* (*pudor et iustitia* as he translates them), showing how the former is really *temperantia* and that Plato would add *prudentia* and, in time of war, *fortitudo*, thus getting the four cardinal virtues. Ficino shows a high esteem for this account of the ethical basis of *civilitas* which one must assume reflects his close association with the humanist tradition and humanist moralists.[42] Yet it is the Platonist translator of Plato who is first able to appreciate this account of the origins of civilization.

> We, moreover, hold concerning all which has hitherto been disputed that it reposes in the depths of the mind in that golden saying of the ancients. First of all God Himself provides and counsels in all ways everywhere for our life and safety. Then civil virtue is a divine gift by which the commonwealth will be rightly and happily governed, lest anyone should perchance trust in himself without divine grace. ... Finally we may remember how necessary it is that inviolate justice be sent from heaven, if those voices of the ancients sound eagerly in our ears. At one time miserable mortals, before civility was delivered from heaven, could not live separately lest they be continually attacked by wild beasts, nor again in communities lest they mutually destroy each other. Thus safety, which all the arts at once could not grant to us, at last was granted by justice alone.

Ficino's interest in this vision of divinely given virtues out of which civilized society originated but which needed to be sustained by education in the humanities and by the very processes of society itself was obviously strong, however grudging his willingness to recognize Protagoras' authorship of it. He continues summarizing Protagoras' description of the role of the arts, but he clearly believes that the original gift of the aptitude for justice, as a gift of grace, was more

---

Institutes 21 (1958), 54, n. 56. Perhaps insufficient attention has been given to Protagoras' role, as depicted by Plato, in providing here a basic western myth of civilization. Ficino, though citing also Plato's *Philebus* and his *Timaeus*, basically follows Protagoras' version that Prometheus could give the intellect and technical arts but not *civilis virtus* which had to come from Zeus through Hermes. "Iuppiter igitur per Mercurium, id est, per angelum divinae voluntatis interpretem, civilis scientiae leges, id est, voluntatis suae decreta ad humanae societatis generisque salutem spectantia mentibus nostris inscribit ... Unde intimus in nobis praesidet iudex inextinguibile rationis lumen, rectum veri falsique et boni malique examen, inevitabilis conscientiae stimulus."

[42] *Opera*, 1298. Cf. also for Ficino's sense of the civic role of humanism the passage on same page beginning : "Cum vero ostenderit hactenus civilem virtutem ... etc." to "... sed arbitrio, et exercitatione proveniant."

important than Protagoras' argument that virtues can be taught. He concludes by saying:

> After this Socrates, lest the sophist might be admired by the audience on account of certain good things he narrated, having taken them from others, by a certain ironic, urbane and artful method of argument rendered him ridiculous to those who were present.[43]

Thus Ficino, as many scholars after him, saw a basic contradiction between the two positions of Protagoras presented in Plato's dialogue, namely that reverence and justice are divine gifts innate in mankind, and that they may be and need to be taught. He either attributed the first idea to Plato, toned down Protagoras' meaning, or interpreted him as having borrowed it from others. Protagoras' use of myth excited him because he could relate it to his own notion of *prisca theologia*, and Protagoras' concern with the moral basis of civilization received his approval however much he doubted his authorship. He was little interested in the man-the-measure question, accepting Plato's refutation of its sensualism of the *Theatetus*, whereas it was just this question that attracted Alberti and Cusanus.

Other references to and discussions of Protagoras in the Renaissance may well be turned up by further study. Within the frame of those we have examined there emerges an interesting but tentative conclusion. Interest in Protagoras on the part of the humanists and rhetorical theorists was small or anecdotal. Alberti, who was led to cite him because of his mathematical and artistic concerns, also did see the possible relationship of his man-the-measure dictum for discussing the nature and nobility of man. Protagoras does not seem to have interested other writers on the nature and dignity of man, though this must be subject to further study. Nor did he attract those concerned with the role of the humanities as the basis of civilization. It was the Platonists, Nicholas of Cusa and Marsilio Ficino, who dealt most centrally with his ideas, Ficino having the best knowledge of him and interpreting him negatively. Perhaps this is not surprising, since Protagoras' thought has come down to us from antiquity primarily in philosophical sources and it was the ancient philosophers who seem to have discussed him more than the rhetoricians. As a Greek "humanist" Protagoras seems to have made more of a stir within the confines of philosophy. What-

---

[43] *Opera*, 1299 : "Nos autem omnibus ... etc." to "... feliciter gubernaturum." and "Denique quam necessaria ... etc." to "... illum praesentibus deridendum."

ever his thought may have been, he was honored by having Democritus, Plato and Aristotle as his critics.

Protagoras in the Renaissance seems to have been understood in the context of each commentator's own thought and concerns, rather than with true understanding and precision. But this too is not surprising in view of the fragmentary knowledge possessed of him. Nor did the Renaissance disagree concerning Protagoras more than modern scholarship does, nor did it misunderstand him any more inadequately. In fact, in certain ways what is even more surprising is how many of the modern issues concerning the meaning of Protagoras' thought are already recognizable in Renaissance discussions. What is very certain, however, is that the Renaissance did not discern in him its predecessor, however much we today are inclined to see a resemblance.

The University of Michigan

VOLUPTAS,
MOLLE QUODDAM ET NON INVIDIOSUM NOMEN:
LORENZO VALLA'S DEFENSE OF *VOLUPTAS*
IN THE PREFACE TO HIS *DE VOLUPTATE*

MARISTELLA DE PANIZZA LORCH

In 1431 Valla published his first extant work, the *De voluptate* from Pavia. The treatise began with a paragraph-long defense of the title and specifically of *voluptas*. Valla eliminates this passage completely in the following versions of the dialogue : [1]

---

[1] The dialogue was conceived in Rome where it is said to have taken place at the Curia of Pope Martin V. The main interlocutors are Leonardo Bruni, Antonio Beccadelli (Panormita), and Niccolò Niccoli, respectively in the role of 'Stoic,' 'Epicurean' and 'Christian.' It was later revised and amplified in three subsequent stages. The second version (Milan, 1433) presents us with a radical re-elaboration as far as the external elements are concerned (interlocutors and scene) and with some amplifications and excisions. The third version (Naples, 1440-49) offers a minor change in interlocutors but a substantial number of additions, especially to Book III which is reserved to *christiana voluptas*. The fourth version adds to version III only a few passages and introduces a few stylistic changes. For the whole issue see the Introduction to my edition, *Lorenzo Valla, "De vero falsoque bono"* (Bari, 1970) and also my articles, "Le tre redazioni del *De voluptate* del Valla," *Giornale storico della letteratura italiana* 121 (1943), 1-22, and "Le tre redazioni del *De vero bono* del Valla," *Rinascimento* 6 (1955), 349-64. Passages from the dialogue will be from the above critical edition, cited as *ed.*, page and line or page and paragraph.

The literature on Valla's dialogue on pleasure is quite abundant. We have gone beyond the point of view of Timmermans, Pastor, and Voigt which, roughly speaking, identifies Valla's thought with the one of the Epicurean in the dialogue. Already in 1885, Fiorentino seemed to be aware that Valla seriously intended to allow for the presence of Epicureanism within the Christian framework. Valla's biographer Mancini insists in seeing the author's thought in Book II as in perfect harmony with the two previous books. As far back as 1940, Corsano ("Note sul *De voluptate* del Valla," *Giornale critico della filosofia italiana* 21 [1940], 166-84), underlined Valla's preoccupation with a realistic morality, thus setting the direction for further interpretations. G. Saitta (*L'Umanesimo* [Bologna, 1949], 193-262) seems to be obsessed by the idea of a rationalist Valla, an anti-religious freethinker who idealizes and divinizes nature. F. Gaeta (*Lorenzo Valla, Filologia e storia nell'umanesimo italiano* [Naples, 1955]), perceptively interprets the dialogue as more than an attempt of conciliation between Christianity and Epicureanism. The dialogue for him is a proof of a new dimension of the world. Radetti (see particularly

If one of my serious and severe friends, astonished at such a title (*De voluptate*), contests from the very beginning my firmness of character and silently asks me what strange desire came over me to write about pleasure, towards which we have never been completely inclined or certainly never wanted to seem completely so; if, I say, a friend asks me justly and friendly the reason for this choice of title, I will and must answer him immediately. He should know that I have never deflected from that original behavior of mine (and I can prove it). In spite of this, however, I preferred to entitle these books *De voluptate*, that is, to use a word, *voluptas*, which is gentle and pleasing, instead of *De vero bono*, which I could have done. This whole work in fact deals with the highest good which we decreed to be *voluptas*.

At this point this friend of mine might object: do you really mean to say that *voluptas* is the highest good? Yes, I say it and I affirm it and I affirm it to the exclusion of any other good except *voluptas*. Such is the thesis that I have decided to prove. If I shall succeed, as I hope and pray, it will not seem absurd that I have taken up this subject matter, or that I have so entitled

---

"La religione di L. Valla," in *Medioevo e Rinascimento, Studi in onore di B. Nardi*, II [Florence, 1955]) stresses Valla's morality of action and optimism. Most recently Trinkaus, Fois and Di Napoli have contributed exhaustive studies. See Charles Trinkaus, *In Our Image and Likeness*, I (Chicago, 1970), 103-170; M. Fois, *Il pensiero cristiano di L. Valla nel quadro storico culturale del suo ambiente* (Rome, 1969); G. Di Napoli, *Lorenzo Valla. Filosofia e religione nell'umanesimo italiano* (Rome, 1971). For Trinkaus Epicureanism is a ploy, "a paradoxical, ironical way of saying something" (110). Part of Valla's rhetorical method is the disregarding of the historical doctrine of the two sects. Most interesting is Trinkaus' study of the relation of Valla to Saint Augustine. We recently had the privilege of reading a still unpublished book by B. Polka. In his study Polka remarks on the static quality of traditional Epicureanism, the inability or unwillingness of fifteenth-century humanists to read Epicurus in a different light from what their predecessor Zabarella had done, that is, as *philosophus*, in order to help reason, not to enhance faith. Valla was the first to understand the "novelty" of the Bible, to grasp its dynamic implications. The *De vero bono* is unique in content and religious fervor, a work without a classical model.

On Valla's concept of rhetoric, see J. E. Seigel, *Rhetoric and Philosophy in Renaissance Humanism* (Princeton, 1968) and C. Vasoli, *La dialettica e la retorica dell'Umanesimo* (Milan, 1968), 28-77. In order to see the present analysis in proper perspective one should also consult the works of E. Garin, especially *L'Umanesimo italiano*, 2nd ed. (Bari, 1958) and *La Filosofia*, I (Milan, 1947), 241-42; G. Radetti, "L'epicureismo nel pensiero Umanestico del Quattrocento," in *Grande antologia filosofica*, VI (Milan, 1964), 839-961; V. Santangelo, "Retorica e letteratura nel *De vero bono* di Lorenzo Valla," *Giornale italiano di filologia* 16 (1963), 30-45; and F. Montanari, "Lorenzo Valla," *Studium* 4 (1961), 270-82.

I shall examine the problems and issues raised in this paper at greater length in a monograph which I am preparing for publication entitled *A Reading of Lorenzo Valla's "De vero falsoque bono" in the Light of its Variants*. Together with Prof. Kent Hieatt, I have already completed for publication a translation of the dialogue, which will be published by Abaris Books, New York, with the title *On Pleasure*.

my work. Thus this good which I present which is the true good, the only good and it consists in *voluptas* is twofold... (*ed.* p. 151, appar. I 3-5).[2]

In versions II-III-IV the preface is in a matter-of-fact tone. No further mention to the *insolens cupido*. The "strange desire" to use the word *voluptas* has become through the years a deeply felt and rationally justified conviction. Along with the word *cupido*, the word *voluptas* disappears from the opening of the dialogue, where it had stood originally like a provocative challenge, the symbol of freedom from every *auctoritas* on ethical matters :

> When I undertook the discussion of the cause of the true and the false good, which is dealt with in the three following books, it seemed best to me to follow a logical division of the subject according to which we are to believe that only two goods exist, one in this life, the other in the future life (*ed.* p. 1, 3-6).[3]

The rest of the preface, as we shall see, remains unaltered through the versions. In the *De voluptate*, just as in the dialogues entitled *De vero bono*, Valla presents himself as a *miles christianus* who intends to use the acquired freedom in the service of the Christian cause.

The closing sentence of the quoted preface of the *De voluptate* and

---

[2] Cf. Introd. to ed., XLIII. We follow Valla's graphic habits and therefore omit diphthongs :

"Si quis forte ex amicis gravibus ac severis, hunc admiratus titulum, statim in principio constantiam meam requirat, tacitusque a me postulet quenam insolens mihi cupido incesserit scribendi de voluptate, cui nunquam penitus dediti fuimus aut certe nunquam penitus dediti videri voluimus, huic ego iuste et amice requirenti quamprimum satisfactum esse et volo et debeo. Itaque sic accipiat me a vetere quidem illo instituto non deflexisse permanereque in priore et probata mihi diu sententia, sed hosce tamen libros maluisse *De voluptate* inscribere, molli quodam et non invidioso nomine, quam *De vero bono* quod poteram ; siquidem de vero bono, quam eandem voluptatem esse placet, in omni hoc opere disputamus.

Quid tu, ille inquiet, aisne voluptatem esse verum bonum ? Ego vero aio atque affirmo, et ita affirmo ut nihil aliud preter hanc bonum esse contendam. Cuius causam suscipiendam mihi ac probandam putavi. Quod si obtinuero, ut spero et opto, non absurdum erit me vel hanc materiam sumpsisse vel hoc nomen nostro operi tribuisse. Enimvero hoc de quo dico bonum, quod verum, quod solum, quod voluptatem esse volumus, duplex est."

The translation of this passage which appears in the text is my own. The translations in the text from the *De vero falsoque bono* are by A. Kent Hieatt and myself. When in my opinion the Latin itself is necessary to my argument, the quotation in Latin appears in the text itself.

[3] "Instituenti mihi de causa veri falsique boni dicere, de qua tribus hisce libris explicatur, placuit hanc potissimum sequi partitionem ut duo tantum bona esse credamus, alterum in hac vita, alterum in futura."

the above-quoted opening sentence of the dialogues *De vero bono* seem to include a contradictory statement. Originally, in the *De voluptate*, Valla stated clearly that the *bonum* was one and only one and that it was *voluptas*. The author intended to examine it in its twofold form (*duplex*). Later, in the following versions of the dialogue, he decided (*mihi placuit*), for some reason that he does not specify, to follow another division of the subject, that is, to speak from the very beginning of two goods (*duo bona*). Did Valla change his mind about *voluptas* being the only good ? Certainly not. The statement which follows, identical in all versions, proves the contrary :

> Necessarily we shall have to deal with both of them, but in such a way as it will appear that we have gradually moved from the first to the second (*ed.* p. 1, 3-7).

We can thus infer that even considering two goods instead of one, the first is a *gradus* towards the second and one is not substantially different from the other. Since the first good leads to the highest *voluptas*, they should both be *voluptates*. It is also interesting to observe that when, further on in the dialogue, namely in Book III, the issue is restated by the "Christian" interlocutor who is defining *christiana voluptas*, Valla uses the same adjective *duplex* as in the *De voluptate* and expresses essentially the same idea :

> From all of which it is to be understood that not the honorable (*honestas*) but pleasure must be desired for itself by those who wish to experience joy, both in this life and in the life to come. This experience is twofold (*duplex*) : one pleasure now on earth, the other hereafter in the heavens (*ed.* p. 110, 28-33).

Let us anticipate the conclusion which we reach not only at the end of the present analysis but after the analysis of the whole dialogue carried out in the light of its variants : the statement that Valla makes in an audacious and challenging tone at the beginning of the *De voluptate* is the key idea of the work. This statement holds true up to the very end : the highest good is one in substance, although it takes a twofold form and it is *voluptas*.

A further confirmation resulted from the defense of the word *voluptas* in the *Defensio* and in the *Apologia*.[4] Valla was right when he sensed from the very beginning the controversial quality of the word *voluptas* as it was commonly used. As early as 1431, when he was in

---

[4] See Introduction to my edition, LI-LII. The *Defensio* differs from the *Apologia* only in stylistical and technical aspects. On the word *voluptas* in particular see L.Valla *Opera Omnia* (Basel, 1540), 799-800.

his twenties, he wanted the reader of his treatise to understand that his *voluptas* carried a special message. He was not understood. Indeed the word became the target of attacks, as witnessed by Poggio's and Facio's *Invectives* (and by Valla's defense in the *Antidotum* and the *Recriminationes*), by letters, but mostly by the defense at the time of his trial in 1444.

In the *Apologia* he defends himself against enemies, *calumniatores imperiti*, by first listing the *questiones* and then answering them one by one. He assumes an aggressive tone and makes ample use of that vocabulary which is also strongly present in the preface (the part of it the versions have in common) and in polemic instances of the dialogue in every version : "de philosophia certamen proposui," "nonne preter legem certaminis est aggredi me Theologie armis idque a tergo non a fronte ?" (*Opera Omnia*, 797). He explains the meaning of *voluptas* in Greek and Latin authors, but mainly insists on the use made of it in the Bible, illustrating his point by citing many examples from Scripture. Finally with indignation he exclaims : "Cur vero verba Dei contempsimus ?" (*Op. Omn.*, 798).

It is, he implies, the essence of his *voluptas* which counts, not the word. That the essence is Christian is confirmed by many references and quotations. Moreover, everybody knows Epicurus was *parcus, continens, modestus*. Valla also claims immunity from attack in this respect. (It is interesting to observe that he relates himself to Epicurus in a most natural manner.) Indeed, he continues in his defense, not even his enemies have been able to attack him on the ground of his personal morality (*Op. Omn.*, 798b). His conclusion reflects the anger and frustration of a man who has been forced too many times to defend a point of view which was to him so clear and orthodox :

> As for myself, most Holy Father, as I have indicated in that very work [*our dialogue*], I do not make it a question of words. Let each one call it as he likes : *voluptas* or *fruitio* or *delectatio* or *gaudium* or *felicitas* and *beatitudo*, provided it remain perfectly clear that no true *virtus* can exist besides the one of serving God, as I have attempted to prove. Thus we shall avoid the insult of those lovers of antiquity who declare that these men possessed true *virtutes*...[5]

---

[5] "Ego vero, Sanctissime Pater, ut in opere ipso testatus sum de nomine non laboro. Appellet quisque ut volet sive voluptas sive fruitio sive delectatio sive gaudium sive felicitas sive beatitudo, dum res ipsa manifesta sit appareatque id quod probare statueram nullam esse veram virtutem nisi Deo servire; ne insultare nobis amatores gentilium possint, qui volunt in his hominibus veras fuisse virtutes." *Opera Omnia*, 798b. (My own translation).

Valla opens the horizon for an ample interpretation of the word *voluptas* while directing his defense at the *amatores gentilium* who had refused to recognize him as a *miles christianus*:

> Where are those who accuse me of not being loyal to my faith? Indeed I have fought continually for it and truly am still fighting at this very moment. Whereas those very people who accuse me are attacking our faith, it is I who defend it...[6]

In short, the defense of the word *voluptas* in the *Apologia* is carried out in a strong polemic tone and conveys Valla's conviction that it has profound Christian and Biblical implications. This is also, as we shall see, clearly stated in the part of the preface of our dialogue which all the versions have in common.

We may add parenthetically that when we meet military vocabulary or metaphors in the dialogue on pleasure, it is Valla the *miles christianus* who speaks. He echoes Paul in particular, but this echo has become an intimate part of Valla's personality. It seems to appear most naturally when the author wants to define his position against the *amatores gentilium*, the *oppugnatores fidei*.

A reading of the *Defensio* and the *Apologia* side by side with *De vero bono*, version III (1444-49) confirms that several topics defended at the time of the trial were modified, others amplified in *De vero bono*, version III, in relation to *De vero falsoque bono*, version II (1433). Since the passages are listed in the Introduction to my edition (p. LII), I shall limit myself here to a few remarks. Two very significant new elements of version III of the dialogue are related to the *questiones* of the *Defensio-Apologia*. The long passage on the nature of *voluptas* as *amor* ("Voluptas ipsa amor est... Amatio ipsa delectatio est...") with the implication that God should be loved not as *causa finalis* but as *causa efficiens*, appears for the first time in version III (*ed.* pp. 114, 10-115, 15) and finds its correspondence in the *Dialectica* (*Op. Omn.* 665 ff.) The thesis of the *Defensio-Apologia* "De auctoritate sanctarum scripturarum de voluptate" must be seen in relation to the modifications of Book III, ch. IX in version III, beginning with the new title. The two added quotations in version III (*Ezech.* XXI : 9 and Psalm XXXV : 9) also appear in Valla's defense. Thus is seems clear that in his successive exploitations of the concept of *voluptas* Valla

---

[6] "Ubi sunt qui me sentire dicunt male de fide? Qui assidue pro illa pugnavi et hoc tempore, si vera loqui licet, pugno, ut ipsi criminatores mei dicendi sint fidei oppugnatores, ego propugnator.' *Ibid.* (My translation).

does not intend to contradict basically the Ciceronian definition of it by the 'Epicurean':

> Pleasure, then, is a good, from whatever source, located in a sense of delight felt by the soul and the body. This is approximately what Epicurus meant, and what the Greeks called ἡδονή. As Cicero says : "No better word can be found than 'pleasure' (*voluptas*) to express in Latin what the Greeks meant by ἡδονή. All people everywhere include two things under this word : joy within the soul through pleasurable emotion, and cheerfulness in the body." (*ed.* p. 21, 26-31).

The emphasis of the successive additions, which are mostly in Book III, is on its Christian origin and content. Here is an example :

> Honorable behavior, as we Christians understand it, however, is the same as I have said the principle of the honorable was in the first place, before the other conceptions of it : honor (*honestas*) is not to be desired for itself, as something severe, harsh, and arduous, nor is it to be desired for the sake of earthly profit; it is to be desired as a step towards the perfect happiness which the spirit or soul, freed from its mortal portion, will enjoy with the Father of all things, from whom it came.
>
> [3] Who would hesitate to call this happiness "pleasure," or who could give it a better name ? I find it called by this name, as in Genesis, "paradise of pleasure" and in Ezekiel, "fruit and tree of pleasure", and the like, when the goods associated with the divine are spoken of. We find in Psalms : "thou shall make them drink of the torrent of pleasure," although in Greek the meaning is rather "of joy," or "of delights" than "of pleasure." For it does not read : "From the torrent χειμάρρουν," but : τὸν χειμάρρουν τῆς τρυφῆς σου ποτιεῖς αὐτούς," which properly is "joy" or "delights," not connected with "delecto" ["I give pleasure"] but with "delector" ["I am given pleasure"] or "delectat" ["it gives pleasure"]. In one sense action is being signified, as in the word "exhortation" or "exhorting"; in another sense a quality is meant, as in the word "exultation," or "state of being uplifted." I do not see that there is any difference between "pleasure" (*voluptas*) and "delight." Those who wrote in Latin, wishing to express (as I think) what they understood as a "great experiencing of delight," chose "pleasure" (*voluptas*) as a translation, as in this passage : Μεθυσθήσονται ἀπὸ πιότητος οἴκου σου καὶ τὸν χειμάρρουν τῆς τρυφῆς σου ποτιεῖς αὐτούς, "they shall be inebriated with the plenty of the house; and thou shall make them drink of the torrent of pleasure (*voluptas*)." From all of which it is to be understood that not the honorable but pleasure must be desired for itself by those who wish to experience joy, both in this life and in the life to come (*ed.* p. 110, 8-31).
>
> Love itself is pleasure...The act of love itself is delight or pleasure or beatitude or happiness or charity, which is the last end ... (*ed* p. 114, 13-15).

There can be no doubt that *voluptas* is not only the *summum* but also the *unicum bonum*. There is no substantial difference between earthly and divine *voluptas*.

Why then did Valla eliminate the original statement of the *De voluptate*? I often asked myself this question in connection with long or brief but significant passages which the author eliminated from the text of the original dialogue, the *De voluptate*. The answer which I offer now in the form of a hypothesis is confirmed by the results which I have obtained in other cases, in fact in the majority of cases of excisions from the original text. This excision like most of the following ones is prompted by reasons of style and logic. While working on his text from about 1433 to 1449, Valla seems on occasion to be inspired principally by the need to reach the maximum of clarity, cohesion and conciseness. He seems to eliminate what could be considered superfluous in the argument, what risks to slow down the reading, or what from a logical point of view he judged superfluous or damaging. In my opinion this is the reason for which already in 1433 (that is, at the time of his sojourn in Pavia, during the first re-elaboration of the dialogue involving a change of scene, characters and title) he renounced a passage which must have been dear to him because it was so typically his own in content and style and which reflected with admirable intuition the meaning, the scope and mostly the audacious novelty of his work.

Let us read the initial paragraph of the *De voluptate* vis-à-vis the defense of the word *voluptas* in the *Apologia* which we have analyzed above. The difference in tone is an index of a completely different milieu and circumstance. At the opening of the *De voluptate* (1431) Valla speaks to friends, *graves et severi*, still however *amici*. It seems that none of them had criticized or even seen the work,[7] for Valla's tone is quite relaxed, not that of a man defending himself against attacks but rather that of a writer attempting to foresee objections. One of the objections might involve his consistency of behavior and his firmess of character. He had always been known as a man completely free of *voluptas*. How then could such a man reveal himself as a defender of *voluptas*? The iteration of the *penitus* is an index that the easiest misunderstanding could come from being taken for a vulgar *voluptuarius*, as it had been for centuries customary in the case of Epicurus. This attack had become a fact by 1444, as we can see from the *Apologia* where Valla defends both Epicurus and himself from such accusation. In the *De voluptate*, however, it is still a vague fear, and Valla does not seem to resent such insinuations from a friend. Indeed it sounds like

---

[7] Apparently Panormita was very desirous of seeing the first copy of it (Introd. to my edition, XXXI-XXXII).

an innocent question, posed without malice, not even expressed verbally (*tacitus*). Valla seems to be most desirous to respond (*quamprimum satisfactum esse et volo et debeo*) to such a reasonable and friendly question (*iuste et amice requirenti*). There is no inconsistency of character. The work should be read without autobiographic implications. The reason for the choice of the word *voluptas* in the title should be looked for in the nature of the word itself: the word is tender, flexible, supple (*molle*), and pleasing (*non invidiosum*), a *nomen* which is engaging at first sight and which Valla could bend and mold to his heart's content. The most obvious title would have been *De vero bono* since the book deals from beginning to end with *voluptas* as the true good.

Here, answering the congenial friend who seems to be astonished by such a topic, Valla changes tone. Assuming the defiant and polemic attitude we know so well, with full awareness of its novelty and its audacity, he proclaims as his credo the theory that *voluptas* is the only and highest good: "Ego vero *aio* atque *affirmo* et ita *affirmo ut nihil aliud preter hanc bonum esse contendam.*" If I succeed—he concludes—"ut spero et opto," nobody will see any absurdity either in the title or in the topic. Finally with a stubborn insistence he underlines the audacious issue: "Enimvero hoc de quo dico *bonum,* quod *verum,* quod *solum,* quod *voluptatem* esse volumus duplex est: alterum in hac vita, alterum in futura" (*ed.* p. 151).

In conclusion: this passionate beginning suggests that what induced the young Valla to write on pleasure was indeed an intuition of new implications of the concept of *voluptas,* intuition which expressed itself in a first moment with a singular attraction for the *nomen, molle et non invidiosum.* He began, so to speak, by falling in love with the *nomen* which he felt could become the carrier of a new message. His philological instinct did not deceive him. In 1444, hardened by a long fight and more conscious of the revolutionary implications of the word in a biblical or generally Christian sense, he changes tone. With the sharpening of his historico-philological method he had been able to develop fully his thesis in a direction which was compatible with his first work. The changes (in particular, the additions) introduced in the dialogue throughout the years are a proof that Valla remained a passionate defender of Christian *voluptas* as he was in his twenties. In 1444 he was more than ever a *miles christianus* fighting for Christ with the arms of the new *dialectica.*

In the preface of the *De voluptate* which follows the opening statement (a part which all versions of the dialogue have in common), we find a young *miles christianus* who intends to guide us towards the second *bonum* (the heavenly good) which can be reached *religione et virtute*. He immediately dismisses *religio* as sufficiently dealt with by Augustine and Lactantius. He plans to limit his field to the *verae virtutes*, that is, he is concerned with ethical not with theological problems. Also in this field he acknowledges the two Christian authors as predecessors. In fact, he echoes from the very beginning *De civitate Dei*, *De opificio* and *Divinae Institutiones*. The truth is one but the proofs must vary. Valla's originality, we conclude, will be in method, a method fitting with the needs of his time. Different patients, according to the well-known simile, need different medicines (*ed.* p. 1, par. 1-2).

Valla's patients are mostly *docti*, as he states here and often throughout the work. Evidently he intends not Boethius alone (whose four Books of the *Consolatio*, as we read in the *De libero arbitrio*, are here confuted). These *docti* include, among the ancients, Aristotle and also Plato and even Cicero, when he acted as an authority in *philosophia*, that is, when he discussed the *summum bonum*. It is for them and against them that Valla employs his new arms. When in Book III, dealing with the joys of Paradise, he intends to guide the *voluptuarii*, that is, the common men inclined towards pleasure, he will express himself in a completely different very sympathetic tone. His theory of *voluptas* is intended especially for unmasking intellectual hypocrisy. The *docti* whom Valla attacks more directly are a whole group of humanists more or less contemporary: at the Roman Curia in the early fifteenth century Francesco da Fiano, who requested the admission of the great pagans into Paradise in his *Contra ridiculos oblocutores et fellitos detractores poetarum*; Traversari, who proposed the lives of the great pagan philosophers as a model to the lives of Christians in the prologue to his translation of Diogenes Laertius' *Lives*; Alberti and Palmieri, who both exalted those Roman heroes whom Valla here reduces to common human proportions; and especially Bruni, not so much the translator of Aristotle's *Ethica*, which Valla praises and admires, as the eloquent *philosophus* on the subject of the *summum bonum* in Aristotelian terms.[8] The *aegri-docti* belong to Valla's own world, and his anger as much as his enthusiasm in defending the Christian cause is real and sincere (*ed.* p. 2, par. 4). The old exemplary figure of the Stoic *sapiens* of Boethius' *Consolatio*, revived by Boethius

---

[8] Cf. Fois, 111-20.

of Dacia in his *De summo bono*, had again become the admired model of Valla's contemporaries. Valla cannot tolerate such admiration and thus his indignation is genuine. Moving in the footsteps of the Fathers, oblivious of his weakness, carried away by the ardor of defending his *respublica*, young Valla has not weighed, he says, "quantum onus *a se* susciperetur," because the success of his enterprise is not in his hands but in the hands of God (*ed.* p. 2, par. 5). He is an *adolescens necdum tiro*, a newly levied soldier—a statement which was never changed not even in 1444—but what an *adolescens!* The relation between Valla and the Bible is immediately and clearly established (*ed.* p. 2, par. 5-6). Valla is David, the defender of faith killing Goliath.

Valla's use of the David figure is a particularly effective index of Valla's position in relation to most contemporary humanists, Bruni in particular, whom he introduces as the Stoic interlocutor in the *De voluptate*. Donatello's first David of 1408 was transferred from the storerooms of the Cathedral to the Palazzo Vecchio in 1416 to take on the new role of civic-patriotic symbol. The inscription attached to the statue reads : "To those who bravely fight for the fatherland, the gods will lend aid even against the most terrible foes." The fatherland in this case is a city republic, the helpers the pagan gods and the inspirer of such symbolism is Leonardo Bruni in his *Laudatio Florentinae Urbis*.[9] Whereas therefore Donatello's David, reflecting the civic feelings of the Florentine Bruni, becomes the symbol of the freedom and the strength of the Florentine republic which the gods are ready to help, and thus expresses a pagan-Christian synthesis, the young Valla, the humanist without city, fights for the *christiana respublica*, like the biblical David, against the admirers of paganity. Thus the function of Leonardo Bruni as Stoic interlocutor in the *De voluptate* is enriched with a new meaning. He is faced by the young Valla appearing as a new David and a new Jonathan (*ed.* p. 2, 24-27).

At this point of the preface the metaphors taken from the military world build up to a crescendo which carries the young soldier to victory : "*scuto... armis... victoria...* Si mihi in hunc *campum descensuro* et in Christi honorem *pugnaturo* ipse Jesus *scutum* fidei dederit et *gladium* illum porrexerit, quid nisi *de reportanda victoria* cogitemus?" With victory comes the refrain : "Hec omnia fide nostra... efficiente et Dei verbo." (*ed.* p. 2, par. 6).

---

[9] Cf. H. W. Janson, "The Image of Man in Renaissance Art from Donatello to Michelangelo," in *The Renaissance Image of Man and the World*, ed. Bernard O'Kelly (Columbus, 1966), 77-100.

It is only after Valla has proclaimed himself the soldier of Christ sure of his victory against the past and contemporary infidels that he introduces us to the *nova ratio*, the new method hinted at before (p. 2, 9), which he intends to use in order to "coercere sive curare homines." Since *honestas*, the ethical ideal of the intellectuals, is defended more rabidly by the Stoics, "satis nobis videtur hosce adversarios contra nos statuere, assumpto patrocinio epicureorum" (*ed.* p. 2, 38-40). We notice that Valla has dedicated six paragraphs, a whole page and a half, to his *aegri-docti*, that is, to defining his position against his adversaries, before mentioning Stoics and Epicureans. Whence we suspect that it is not his intention to resuscitate in a historical sense the two sects (which the Christian in Book III defines as the noblest sects of antiquity), but only to exploit them as symbols of two opposite conceptions of life. At this point the word *voluptas* appears for the first time in versions II, III, IV of the dialogue, since these versions do not present, as we have seen, the defense of the word *voluptas* at the opening of the treatise. It appears in connection with a mild apology for the tone of the first two books vis-à-vis the third, which is dignified by virtue of the subject itself. Invoking the well-known rhetorical law of the correspondence of style to subject-matter, Valla states that it is only appropriate to the *causa voluptatis* to mix in "quedam hilariora et prope dixerim licentiosa": "... it was necessary for me to exchange that rude, strong and excited manner which I often use in favor of this more relaxed and agreeable way of speaking" (*ed.* p. 3, par. 8). Thus, if we interpret Valla literally, we are made to believe that we owe the free and joyful tone of the first two books to rhetorical reasons : a sad style is inappropriate to the *causa voluptatis* (*ed.* p. 3, 6-8). In my opinion this is not completely true. On the other hand we cannot deny that Valla the *rhetor* regards these first two books as a pièce de force, as far as style is concerned, the exercise of a particular style which is not his usual one. Besides, the above statement reiterates the rhetorical use he makes of the Stoics and the Epicureans, while the word *voluptas* appears in a most unobtrusive manner in the expression *causa voluptatis*.

As for the style of the preface we can say without hesitation that it is *acre, vehemens, incitatum* from beginning to end. The preface closes with a violent blow to the *sapientie sectatores* which makes us visualize them in their reality of contemporaries of the author rather than in the proposed symbolic entity as 'Stoics' :

> Non modo enim anteferimus epicureos, abiectos homines et contemptos,

> honesti cultoribus, *sed etiam probamus* hos ipsos sapientie sectatores non virtutem sed umbram virtutis, non officium sed vitium, non sapientiam sed dementiam fuisse sectatos (*ed.* p. 3, 13-16).

The irony emphasizes the bitterness of the attack:

> meliusque fuisse facturos si voluptati operam nisi dederunt dedissent... (*ibid*. 16-17).

The author's insistence on the second part of the sentence ("sed etiam probamus") attracts the attention of the reader to the hypocrisy and the arrogance of the disciples of *sapientia*, whereas the 'Epicureans' appear praised in a Christian manner, since they are generally scorned, like the Pharisees of the Gospel. Because of their humility they are the proper means for Valla's challenge to the *sapientie sectatores*.

Finally we arrive at what is for us the key question. What role does the word *voluptas* play in the war of the adolescent Laurentius-David-Jonathan against the enemies of Christ? The *nomen* is mentioned twice towards the end of the preface (*causa voluptatis* at p. 3, 7 and *si voluptati operam... dedissent* at p. 3, 18). The reader is so overcome by the ardor of a Valla *propugnator fidei* that he loses connection with the bold opening statement on *voluptas*. Thus the long opening paragraph of the *De voluptate* remains in suspense, detached from the rest of the preface, more a kind of subtitle than an integral part of the preface itself. One has to read the whole dialogue in order to become aware of what is the function of *voluptas*. That is why, we conjecture, Valla decided to eliminate it. By so doing he obeyed more an intrinsic reason of logic and style than an extrinsic cause. He acted only partially in response to objections.

The eliminated passage is in any case most enlightening because from the very first lines of the work it allows us now to grasp the originality of the means and of the approach. Through this first page of the *De voluptate* we have an intuition that Valla's position is different not only from that of Bruni but also from that of Raimondi and Filelfo, that is, from the defenders of Epicurus. We have clearly the impression that looking for a word, a *nomen* to represent views so different from those of his contemporaries, almost instinctively he chose *voluptas*:

> hosce tamen libros maluisse *De voluptate* inscribere molli quodam et non invidioso nomine...

Thus we should not be surprised if this *voluptas*, Valla's own very special *nomen*, has only an incidental connection with the word as it appears in Cicero, Seneca, Aristotle or even Augustine or Lactantius.

In the original intentions of the author *voluptas* was meant to be the key to his very own conception of life. In the rest of the preface, however, which, as we said, remained untouched from version I to IV, the meaning of *voluptas* is implied, not explained. One has to read the three Books of the treatise in order to understand how Valla molded the *molle nomen* to fit a world antithetic in many ways not only to the one of some contemporary humanists but to the one of Epicurus as well.

Obviously it was the new interest in Epicurus which inspired Valla to use Epicureanism in such an original manner. Zabarella, Raimondi, Filelfo and also Bruni are in the background. But these humanists, even when defending Epicurus, kept on reading him as a *philosophus*, as a source of ethical wisdom.[10] The *orator* Valla instead celebrates Epicurus as the *antiphilosophus*, the prototype of the common man who lives well because he trusts an infallible instinctive drive. Valla's originality reveals itself most clearly in the development from this *voluptas* as instinctive drive to a *voluptas amor Dei* and *charitas*. The additions and the modifications of the dialogue point in this direction.

On the other hand it would be an error and a distortion of Books I-II to assert that the *hilariora et prope dixerim licentiosa*, the joy of Books I and II, are toned down from version I to IV. The freedom which our young Laurentius-David professes again and again in Book III against every form of established human rationalistic authority in the name of the *veritas* which comes to us through faith, begins, almost unconsciously, as a freedom of the senses, freedom to enjoy every sensual experience guaranteed as good by a nature which is God (*ed.* p. 18, 15-16). The identification of nature with God, which has troubled many interpreters, indeed does not imply any sort of immanentism. Valla conceives of nature as good because created by an infinitely good God, a great anthropomorphic God who comes to us *placidus, mitis, propitius* (*ed.* p. 120, 1), who is splendor, beauty and power but mostly love, and therefore gives to the soul, as supreme enjoyment in Paradise, his fatherly embrace (*ed.* p. 135, par. 23). Given such a premise, most sincerely felt by the author, we must also admit that his ebullient *voluptas* is also joy of life, a natural *voluptas*.

This trait strikes the reader at a first reading in both the content and style of the dialogue, which moves from the deep overaccentuated cosmic pessimism of the Stoic to the open, loosely connected, witty,

---

[10] B. Polka takes up this point quite convincingly in his unpublished essay.

often paradoxical Epicurean oration, culminating in the eulogies of *voluptas* towards which Books I and II seem to flow. The much more extended eulogy of Book III, the prefiguration of Paradise, is the natural culmination of the previous ones, as the author had suggested in the opening statement of the *De voluptate*.

Barnard College, Columbia University

RICHARD DE BURY AND THE
"QUIRES OF YESTERDAY'S SOPHISMS"

NEAL W. GILBERT

When historians deal with obscure, difficult, or relatively unexplored periods in the history of philosophy, they are apt to fall back upon anecdotes and testimonials to fill out their pages. The history of late mediaeval and Renaissance nominalism certainly qualifies as such a period, for nominalism has "not yet been illuminated by writers on the history of philosophy with the light that it deserves."[1] This reproach by an eighteenth-century writer still stands today, in spite of all the scholarly work that has gone into the editing and interpretation of mediaeval sources. There still is not a general consensus as to the motivation behind nominalism, to say nothing of the way in which it tried to resolve its central issues, whatever they were. A conscientious French scholar, assigning himself the task of describing "l'université de Paris et la doctrine occamiste," has to admit that "we do not have precise information concerning Ockhamist agitation at Oxford, and hardly much more on the moment when Ockham's doctrine penetrated into the University of Paris."[2] He continues nevertheless with a statement of what may be taken as the received doctrine on the reception of Ockhamism at Paris: "It was among the young logicians in the faculty of arts that *the subtle dialectic of the bachelor of Oxford* had the most chance of a favorable reception. Eighty years earlier it was in the Street of Straw that they were impassioned for arguments stirred up by doctrines of Averroes: it was now around *the subtleties of Ockhamist logic* that they battled. The young bachelors, in the course of these disputes, easily lost the sense of respect that they should have shown toward the masters."[3] As evidence for these statements about Ockhamist logic, an edict of the Paris Faculty of Arts from the year 1339 is

---

[1] This was the judgment of Jacob Brucker, *Historia Critica Philosophiae*, III (Leipzig, 1746), 904.

[2] E. Amann, article "Occam," *Dictionnaire de théologie catholique*, XI (Paris, 1931), cols. 895-96.

[3] *Ibid.*

cited : in it the Faculty explicitly say that the doctrines of 'William called Ockham' were being discussed publicly and privately at Paris, even though they had not been authorized as official texts and had not been examined as to their suitableness "either by us or others."[4]

This edict of 1339, together with one from the following year, about which there had been considerable scholarly controversy,[5] constitute a skeleton which has been fleshed out into the imposing story that we might call "The Storming of Paris by the Ockhamist Logic." There may be a core of truth to this story, as there is to many legends. But the legend needs to be reexamined continually, as research produces new evidence and new vistas open up. Fresh insights are being provided in abundance by historians of mediaeval logic, long a neglected field. We are finding that what has come to be called "Terminist" logic was part of a tradition that was much older and broader than had been suspected. Many aspects of this logic have yet to be explored thoroughly; in particular, the connections between this logic and that of Ockham and of the movement that came to be called, in the late fourteenth and early fifteenth century, the *"via moderna"* are by no means as clear as secondary works have been assuming. One assumption commonly made must be scrapped : namely, the assumption that Ockham was the initiator of Terminist logic or the only thinker to apply its techniques. There were many other writers on logic before and during Ockham's lifetime who can be called "Terminist," perhaps with better credentials than his.[6] We must recognize that there was a host of candidates for the honor, if such it be, of promoting "Anglican subtlety" : we need not continue to assume that Ockham alone supplied the logical sophistication for which British thinkers in the late Middle Ages were famous. Nor need we assume that the "doctrines of William of Ockham"

---

[4] "... istis temporibus nonnulli doctrinam Guillermi dicti Ockham (quamvis per ipsos ordinantes admissa non fuerit vel alias consueta, neque per nos seu alios ad quos pertineat examinata, propter quod non videtur suspicione carere), dogmatizare presumpserint publice et occulte super hoc in locis privatis conventicula faciendo..." *Chartularium Universitatis Parisiensis*, II (Paris, 1891), 485.

[5] See Ernest A. Moody, "Ockham, Buridan, and Nicholas of Autrecourt : The Parisian Statutes of 1339 and 1340," *Franciscan Studies* 7 (1947), 113-46; also Ruprecht Paqué, *Das Pariser Nominalistenstatut* (Berlin, 1970).

[6] "When Ockham's logical works are compared with the treatises on logic produced by his contemporaries and by many who were his predecessors, he is seen to have been less of an innovator and fabricator of verbal distinctions, than a critic of the innovations and verbalism of his times." Ernest A. Moody, *The Logic of William of Ockham* (London, 1935), 26.

discussed at Paris were exclusively logical. For at the early stages of Ockham's career the doctrines that gave most offense to ecclesiastical dignitaries (e.g., the investigating commission at Avignon in 1326) were theological doctrines: if other propositions of Ockham were condemned, it was because churchmen suspected that they would lead to theological errors if applied to theological subject matter. Ockham himself thought that logic was neutral with respect to metaphysical or theological issues, although he did recognize its usefulness in helping the student of theology to avoid "*sophismata.*" To be sure, there has always been a contrary tendency in the Christian tradition, a tendency to regard logic or dialectic as the "seedbed of heresy"; some pious minds have never been convinced that logic could be anything but dangerous. The uncritical taking over of this hostile point of view has seriously distorted our picture of fourteenth-century thought, blinding us to the possibility that other, perhaps equally pious minds of that period may have seen logic not as a threat but as an ally to religious devotion. A re-assessment of the whole *via moderna* seems urgently needed, both in its mature stage and in the preliminary stage, before the battle lines between it and the *via antiqua* began to be so sharply and institutionally drawn.

Beside the Paris edicts of 1339 and 1340, there are two other sources of information about intellectual developments at the University of Paris that have been extensively used. They are observations made by distant observers, one, Pope Clement VI, at Avignon, and the other, Richard de Bury, in England. These observations belong to a period roughly five years after the Paris edicts, and hence have been presumed to reflect the climate of opinion at Paris in the 1340's. Richard de Bury (1287-1345) was an English bishop and man of affairs, the author of a well-known treatise on book-collecting entitled *Philobiblon*. In the ninth chapter of this work, Richard had complained about the scandalous way in which youthful students were hurried through their university training in order to "qualify" for papal preferments. He singles out the University of Paris as a particular offender in this respect: "Alas! by the same disease which we are deploring, we see that the Palladium of Paris has been carried off in these sad times of ours, wherein the zeal of that noble university; whose rays once shed light into every corner of the world, has grown lukewarm, nay, is all but frozen. There the pen of every scribe is now at rest, generations of books no longer succeed each other, and there is none who begins to take place as a new author. *They wrap up their doctrines in unskilled discourse, and are losing all propriety of logic except that Anglican subtleties, which they denounce in public, are the subject of their furtive vigils."*[7] This passage, which has been much cited as testimony concerning the reception of nominalism at Paris, should be compared with a section of the previous chapter, in which Richard speaks of the help he has received in his book-collecting from mendicant friars: "What small rabbit could escape so many keen-sighted hunters? What little fish could evade in turn hooks and nets and snares? Was some devout discourse uttered at the fountain-head of Christian faith, the holy Roman Curia, or was some strange question ventilated with novel arguments; did the solidity of Paris, which is now more zealous in the study of antiquity than in the subtle investigation of truth, did Anglican perspicacity, which, illuminated by the lights of former times, is always sending forth fresh rays of truth, produce anything to the advancement of science or the declaration of the faith, this was instantly poured still fresh into our ears, ungarbled by any babbler, unmutilated by any trifler, but passing straight from the purest of wine-presses into the vats of our memory to be clarified."[8]

---

[7] As translated by Ernest C. Thomas in his edition of Richard de Bury, *Philobiblon* (London, 1888), with a few slight changes and with my italics. The italicized passage reads as follows in the Latin: "Involvunt sententias sermonibus imperitis, et omnis logicae proprietates privantur; nisi quod Anglicanas subtilitates, quibus palam detrahunt, vigiliis furtivis addiscunt" (p. 89, Thomas ed.). The passage should be compared with Roger Bacon's lament in 1292, in which he complains that the *moderni saeculares* have neglected the ways of the ancient wise men, including (be it noted) master William Sherwood, the Terminist logician. Roger Bacon, "Compendium studii philosophiae," in *Opera Quaedam Hactenus Inedita*, ed. Brewer (London, 1859), 428-29.

I should mention that I regard the *Philobiblon* as Richard's own work, although I recognize that Robert Holcot has some claim to be considered at least a collaborator: see Beryl Smalley, *English Friars and Antiquity in the Early Fourteenth Century* (Oxford, 1960), 67. For Richard as the sole author, see Noel Denholm-Young, "Richard de Bury (1287-1345)," in *Collected Papers on Mediaeval Subjects* (Oxford, 1946), 17; also Ernest Thomas in the preface to his edition of the *Philobiblon*, xliii-xliv. Denholm-Young bases his view to a certain extent upon Richard's use of the *cursus* of the Roman Curia.

[8] "Quis inter tot argutissimos venatores lepusculus delitesceret? Quis pisciculus istorum nunc hamos, nunc retia, nunc sagenas evaderet? A corpore sacrae legis divinae usque ad quaternum sophismatum hesternorum, nihil istos praeterire potuit scrutatores. Si in fonte fidei Christianae, curia sacrosancta Romana, sermo devotus insonuit, vel si pro novis causis quaestio ventilabatur extranea, si Parisiensis soliditas, quae plus antiquitati discendae quam veritati subtiliter producendae iam studet, si Anglicana perspicacitas, quae antiquis perfusa luminaribus novos semper radios emittit veritatis, quicquam ad augmentum scientiae vel declarationem fidei promulgabat, hoc statim nostris recens infundebatur auditibus nullo denigratum seminiverbio nulloque nugace

Concerning this passage, the distinguished Jesuit scholar Franz Ehrle wrote : "For the position of nominalism at Paris, it seems to me, the remark of the *Philobiblon* is definitive, and even for the decisive time toward the middle of the fourteenth century. Ockhamism was officially forbidden and banned also in the faculty of arts, yet was nevertheless in general zealously cultivated and diffused. From 1340 to 1474, we find no official declaration regarding it other than the doctrinal judgments of 1346-1352, which show that the theologians guarded their domain carefully."[9] Such being the case, one might ask, why do we not turn to the *un*-official pronouncements, that is, to records of actual disputations and lectures held at Paris during the first part of the fourteenth century ? This would seem to be the obvious move, but it has no doubt been discouraged by the belief that Ockhamist discussions were carried on in secret and hence have left no residue in the manuscripts. This convenient belief could have been promoted by the reference in Richard's letter to men who "denounce in public" the "Anglican subtleties" that they discuss in their "furtive vigils." The assumption would be that Richard de Bury knew of the edict of 1339, which he may well have, and that he knew the "facts" to which it alluded, which he need not have (could he not have gotten his information from the edict alone ?). Moreover, even if it were indeed the case that Richard knew the edict of 1339, there remains something puzzling about his reference to "Anglican subtleties." For that document made no bones about mentioning Ockham by name : why should Richard not have followed suit ? What motivation could Richard de Bury have had for omitting the name of Ockham ? The answer to this question will already, I hope, have been suggested : namely, there were many Anglican logicians who could have contributed to what little subtlety Paris could claim—some of them, as I shall show, right in Richard's own circle of protegés.

Let us examine the passage from the *Philobiblon* for clues as to Richard's attitude toward school logic and his familiarity with its

---

corruptum, sed de praelo purissimi torcularis in nostrae memoriae defaecandum transibat." *Philobiblon*, 74-75. Thomas in his notes shrewdly spots the word *seminiverbius* as a translation of the Greek *spermologos*, 'babbler,' which the Athenians accused the apostle Paul of being (Acts, XVII, 18).

[9] Franz Ehrle, *Die Sentenzenkommentar Peters von Candia, des Pisaner Papstes Alexanders V*, Franzikanische Studien, Beiheft IX (1925), 244. Richard de Bury's remarks about the University of Paris have also received prominence by being cited in a footnote in the *Chartularium Universitatis Parisiensis*, II, 588.

subtle Anglican expositors. Richard lists three localities from which his mendicants procured books for him : (1) the "Roman Curia" (meaning, no doubt, Avignon, where the Papal curia was then located), (2) Paris, and (3) England. From Avignon the friars brought Richard a *sermo devotus* or a *quaestio extranea*. From Paris, probably from the university and its surrounding book sellers or conventual libraries, "whatever was published toward the augmenting of science or the clarification of the Faith." From England, the same, although there is a very definite contrast expressed between "Parisian solidity" and "Anglican perspicacity." The main point Richard is trying to make is that he gets his information directly from written accounts, not through unreliable and frivolous oral gossip. As a bibliophile, he stresses the variation in size of his acquisitions : from huge tomes of canon law down to the slender quire [10] of yesterday's sophisms. Richard does not say that the quires of sophisms came only from England, nor does he specifically identify them as products of "Anglican perspicacity." By a process of elimination, however, we may conclude that they came from England rather than from the other source of supply, Paris, which had a tendency to work with established authors and did not add new increments of knowledge. In this sense the British have more vigor and more perspicacity, and in this sense they are closer to the Ancients, whose superiority Richard lauds in the opening section of Chapter 9.[11] There is, in the same chapter, a suggestion that Richard's own preference is not for these new additions currently being made to knowledge by the British, but for the books of the Ancients. Nevertheless, he collects both. This is not to say that he does not recognize the superiority of the treatises of the Ancients when it comes to academic training. Richard was an admirer of Aristotle and a supporter of the educational methods that formerly prevailed in the universities. He complains about "youthful and beardless" students who "echo back the *Categories* and *De interpretatione* with infantile babbling." It is not the treatises of Aristotle, "into which he poured his lifeblood," that Richard objects

---

[10] '*Quaternus*' in the original : for the meaning of this term in the mediaeval book trade, see A. G. Little and F. Pelster, *Oxford Theology and Theologians c. A. D. 1282-1302* (Oxford, 1934), 57-61.

[11] In a passage which takes its place among the almost endless series of adaptations of a line from Priscian. See Hubert Silvestre, " 'Quanto iuniores, tanto perspicaciores' : Antécédents à la Querelle des anciens et des modernes," *Recueil commémoratif du Xe anniversaire de la Faculté de Philosophie et Lettres, L'Université de Kinshasa* (Louvain and Paris, 1968), 231-55. Silvestre deals with Richard de Bury briefly on pp. 246-47.

to, but rather their maltreatment or neglect by immature boys who are dedicated to ecclesiastical advancement rather than to genuine learning.[12] Hence to be "deprived of logical propriety" was, in Richard's view, a serious failing and, far from blaming the students at Paris for cultivating "Anglican subtleties" in their off hours, he is praising them for picking up what logical rigor they could.

Since Richard de Bury's entire literary output consists of this work and some official letters, we must take seriously the indications given in the *Philobiblon* of his interests. Valuable clues may be found in Richard's list of the topics discussed by the learned and perspicacious clerks at his table. These consisted of (1) ostensive investigations of arguments; (2) recitals of physical processes and treatises of Catholic doctors; and (3) edifying "moralities."[13] This is more or less what we would expect from the make-up of the group of scholars who participated in these household discussions. For if we look at the members of the Bishop of Durham's inner circle of clerks,[14] we find that, far from being a collection of proto-humanists averse to all logic whatsoever, this group of university men was in fact a nest of dialecticians or former sophisters. Let us take them in order.

(1) Thomas Bradwardine (died 1349) is given as the author of a collection of *insolubilia* in manuscripts.[15] He is, of course, better known

---

[12] "... Categorias, Perihermenias, in cuius scriptura summus Aristoteles calamum in corde tinxisse confingitur, infantili babutie resonant impuberes et imberbes." *Philobiblon*, 86. On the practice of sending rolls of graduates and scholars to the pope periodically, asking for benefices, see W. A. Pantin, *The English Church in the Fourteenth Century* (Cambridge, 1955), 50.

[13] *Philobiblon*, 72-73.

[14] The standard list of members of Bury's inner circle comes from Wiliam de Chambre, as reported to a chronicler : "Willielmi de Chambre Continuatio Historiae Dunelmensis," in *The Publications of the Surtees Society*, IX (1839), 127-56.

[15] Recently edited by M. L. Roure, "La problématique des propositions insolubles au XIIe siècle et au début du XIVe, suivie de l'édition des traités de W. Shyreswood, W. Burleigh, et Th. Bradwardine," *Archives d'histoire doctrinale et littéraire du Moyen Age* 37 (1970), 205-326. Roure bases his text on an Erfurt mss., Ampl. 0 76, and uses a Venetian codex as a corrective. While he acknowledged the existence of a third mss. at Bruges, Roure seems to have been unaware of the existence of two more: one at the Vatican (Vat. Lat. 2154), another at the Bodleian (Canon. Misc. MS 219). For the former, see A. Maier, *Codices Vaticani Latini : codices 2118-2192* (Vatican City, 1961), 90-92; for the latter, see James A. Weisheipl, "Ockham and Some Mertonians," *Mediaeval Studies* 30 (1968), 190. Emden, *A Bibliographical Register of the University of Oxford to A. D. 1500* (Oxford, 1957), I, 245, reports that a Spanish mss. shows that Bradwardine wrote this treatise on insolubles during his regency in arts at Oxford.

as the writer of important works on physics and mathematics (he no doubt furnished the "recitals of physical processes" mentioned by Richard) as well as the vast and imposing *De causa Dei contra Pelagium*.

(2) Richard Fitzralph (died 1360) may be listed as a defector from the ranks of Anglican logicians. Long after his association with Bury and hence after the writing of the *Philobiblon*, Fitzralph underwent a "conversion" away from the dialectical "Aristotelian dogmas and argumentations" of his Oxford days.[16]

(3) Walter Burley (died after 1344) was the major "sophister" of the group, by far. Aside from some lesser works ("quires"?) of sophisms, there is his major work, *De puritate artis logicae*, which is full of *sophismata*.[17]

(4) John Maudith (floruit 1309-1343), a fellow of Merton College, seems to have been a mathematician and astronomer rather than a

---

[16] J. A. Robson, *Wyclif and the Oxford Schools* (Cambridge, 1961), 89. Robson believes that this 'conversion' was more 'protested than real,' and suggests (88) that it was closely connected with Fitzralph's extended stay at Avignon (most of the decade from 1334 to 1344). Robson quotes (91) a prayer in which Fitzralph thanks God for his deliverance from the Aristotelian dogmas and argumentations of the schools. It includes a reference to 'frogs and toads croaking in the swamps.' The comparison of dialecticians with frogs and toads was derived from the Church Fathers and could be found in a section of Gratian's *Decretals* dealing with profane letters. 'Froglike *garrulitas*' became a standard label for the vice of undue commitment to dialectical argumentation. Cf. J. de Ghellinck, "Un aspect de l'opposition entre Hellénisme et Christianisme : l'attitude vis-à-vis de la dialectique dans les débats trinitaires," *Patristique et Moyen Age*, III (Gembloux, 1948).

[17] Walter Burleigh, *De puritate artis logicae tractatus longior*, ed. P. Boehner (St. Bonaventure, 1955). Roure (article cited in n. 11 above) has edited Burley's *Insolubilia* from a Paris mss. (B. N. lat. 16, 130) and one in the British Museum (Royal 12 F. XIX). Roure mentions two "other mss." of *insolubilia* attributed to Burley (Erfurt, Ampl. Q 276 and O 76), but notes that the text is very different from the one given in the Paris and British museum mss. In fact, the work on insolubles in Ampl. Q 276 is by another member of Richard de Bury's circle, Walter Segrave (see n. 21 below). The confusion that surrounds the writings of Walter Burley illustrates the situation with respect to logical textbooks emanating from Oxford during this period : they circulated as 'quires,' convenient for student use. Perhaps longer texts suffered dismemberment in this way. The Erfurt mss. Q 276 also contains *sophismata* by Burley (Incipit : "Circa signa universalia iiii proponimus inquirere ..."): see Jan Pinborg, *Die Entwicklung der Sprachtheorie im Mittelalter*, Beiträge zur Geschichte der Philosophie und Theologie des Mittelalters, XLII² (Münster, 1967), 153. Burley also wrote a treatise *De consequentiis* : see L. M. De Rijk, *Logica Modernorum*, II (Assen, 1967). Thus we have separate works by Burley on *Insolubilia*, *Sophismata*, and *Consequentia*—all were no doubt connected with the practical exercises in logic required in the schools.

logician : at any rate I have not been able to locate any *sophismata*, *consequentia*, or *insolubilia* by him.

(5) Robert Holcot (died c. 1349) was a Dominican, and hence could conceivably have been one of the mendicants whom Bury relied upon to supply him with books. In the past Holcot has been regarded as a sceptic or fideist, mainly because he proposed to distinguish the *logica fidei* from ordinary logic. This view must now be revised, on the basis of Hoffmann's thorough analysis of Holcot's theological method. From this study it emerges that Holcot was characteristic of his period in attempting to apply to theological expressions the linguistic and philosophical sophistication gained from a "long tradition of development and refinement of logical techniques" going all the way back, in mediaeval times, to Adam of Balsham in the twelfth century.[18] Holcot left no strictly logical writings of his own, and sometimes expressed concern over the tendency of theological students to become heavily involved in dialectic. Yet his own writings are permeated with the logical doctrines of the day, for example, his debates with Bradwardine (also, as we have seen, a member of Richard de Bury's circle) over future contingents. No doubt Richard regarded both Bradwardine and Holcot as prime examples of "Anglican perspicacity," showing the benefits of their Oxford training in logic.

(6) Richard Kilvington (died by 1362) could have supplied no end of *sophismata*, or at least forty-nine of them. A fellow of Oriel College, Kilvington had primary interests in logic and science.[19]

---

[18] Fritz Hoffmann, *Die theologische Methode des Oxforder Dominikanerlehrers Robert Holcot*, Beiträge zur Geschichte der Philosophie und Theologie des Mittelalters, n.s., V (Münster, 1972), 385. Holcot quotes with approval passages from an Archbishop of Canterbury, Simon of Mephan (died 1333), warning scholars against undue 'subtlety of questions.' At the table of Richard de Bury, Friar Robert must have contributed little to the 'investigations of arguments' or to the 'recitals of physical processes' : his forte was clearly 'edifying moralities.'

[19] The name Richard de Kilvington is one of those that gave great trouble to scribes (Emden, II, 1050, lists over thirty variants). His *Sophismata* have been published in part by Curtis Wilson, *William Heytesbury : Medieval Logic and the Rise of Mathematical Physics* (Madison, 1956), 163-68. Wilson (170) lists six mss. of Kilvington's *sophismata*, at the Vatican, the Bodleian, and the Biblioteca Universitaria, Padua. To these should be added two Erfurt mss (Ampl. 0 76, no. 7, and F 313, no. 6) with the same incipit, "Ad utrumque dubitare potentis facile speculemur, ut dicit..." This incipit is also close to that of Bruges de la Ville 497, ff. 64-73ᵛ. Duhem discusses briefly and with distaste Kilvington's questions on the Sentences of Peter Lombard, in *Études sur Léonard de Vinci* (Paris, 1913), 446-48.

(7) Richard Bentworth (died 1339) was sufficiently interested in Aristotelian philosophy to have Walter Burley dedicate to him a commentary on the *Politics* (Bentworth, who was Bishop of London, died before it was completed),[20] but he has left no record of any interest in logic. Bentworth held a degree in civil law, which may explain this fact, for logic did not play as large a role in the training of mediaeval lawyers as it did in that of theologians.

(8) Walter Segrave (died before 1349) wrote some *insolubilia* : in fact, this seems to have been all that he wrote.[21]

Thus we see that at least five of Richard de Bury's close friends and members of his "family" have left works on logic, works that seem to reflect the logical exercises required of them as undergraduate "sophisters." Of the other members of the group, Holcot assuredly was no stranger to the logical tradition. Since these were the men whose disputations and discussions gave Richard so much pleasure, we are entitled to assume that he valued logical training highly, and considered it to be the factor that gave Oxford its advantage over other universities, including Paris. This impression is reinforced by the report that Richard collected quires of yesterday's sophisms, the by-product of that logical training to which every Oxford undergraduate was subjected, and which caused foreign students so much distress. "Logical propriety" was the hallmark of Oxford talk, if we are to believe Richard de Bury, presumably even when it concerned theological matters. And it was by no means the exclusive property of William of Ockham, although Ockham was obviously a major influence among British logicians. Considering Oxford's reputation for subtlety in logic, it is not surprising that this group of alumni should have exhibited an interest in logic. We need not suppose that they inflicted strictly logical debates upon their bookish patron, but there is at least a possibility that the "ostensive investigations of arguments" engaged in by the diners at Richard's table reflected their early exposure to dialectical exercises and their familiarity with *sophismata*, *consequentia*, and other logical devices. At any rate it is clear that Richard de Bury had ample opportunity to gain

---

[20] See Anneliese Maier, "Zu Walter Burley's Politik-Kommentar," *Ausgehendes Mittelalter*, I (Rome, 1964), 93.

[21] Incipit "Sicut vult philosophus 2° metaphysice, non solum debemus..." These insolubilia of Walter Segrave are found in two Erfurt codices, Ampl. O 76 and Q 276. See Pinborg, 157. Emden (III, 1664) lists another mss., at the Bodleian (Libr. Canonici Ms. latin 219); this is the mss. that also contains Bradwardine's *Insolubilia* (see n. 11 above).

a first-hand impression of the lasting effects of British logical training. (The same, by the way, cannot be said for Richard's friend and correspondent, Petrarch, whose exposure to Oxford logic must have been distant at best.) And considering this direct exposure, it is all the more striking that Richard does not mention William of Ockham by name. If "Ockham's logic" completely dominated the scene at Oxford during the first half of the fourteenth century, why would Richard de Bury have been so reticent?

My contention is that the school logic that gave to his countrymen their "logical propriety," in Richard's eyes, was in large part the practise of responding *de sophismatibus*, an exercise that gave to students who had weathered two years of this ordeal a precision of thought that was the despair of their counterparts across the Channel, as well as the scandal of humanistic critics such as Petrarch. Ockham's logic was closer to Aristotle's *Organon* than it was to this school tradition,[22] although there are of course traces of Terminist logic in Ockham's works on logic as well as in his theological writings. Such traces are inevitable in the fourteenth century: what university instructor could have escaped the doctrine of supposition, for example? As we shall see, the tradition of responding *de sophismatibus* was not foreign to Paris either, but it had apparently been neglected, at least in comparison with its vigorous pursuit at Oxford. When Richard de Bury acknowledged that Paris was "more zealous in the study of antiquity," he means that the established authors were more in the center of scholarly attention than they were at Oxford. This gave Paris its "solidity," but at the same time limited its intellectual adventurousness. The resentment of non-Anglican masters at the University of Paris reflects, I suspect, an underlying respect, however grudging, for this logical tradition.

Let us turn now to the other testimony frequently cited for the inroads of Ockhamist logic at Paris, the letter of rebuke addressed by Pope Clement VI to the masters of Paris in 1346: "Some masters and scholars of arts and philosophy, laboring away there in the sciences, having disregarded and despised the texts of the Philosopher and of other masters and ancient expositors, whom they ought to follow, to the extent that they do not stand in the way of the Catholic faith, and the true expositions and writings by which science itself is supported, are turning to other varied and extraneous sophistical doctrines, which

---

[22] See Moody, *Logic of William of Ockham*, 25-26.

are said to be taught in certain other *studia*, and to opinions that are useless and superficial rather than genuine options, from which no fruit can be gained."[23]

The man who wrote these words had himself been a master at Paris. As a Benedictine monk, Pierre Roger (c. 1290-1352), the future Pope Clement VI, had been active for sixteen years at the University of Paris. He was better known as an orator than as a thinker; it was in the former capacity that he pronounced three eulogies on Thomas Aquinas. From the Paris days of Pierre Roger, we have the record of a dispute that he engaged in over a period of time with a Scotist opponent, Franciscus Mayronis.[24] The future pope thus knew at first hand the complexities of Scotist theology, and it may be surmised that he did not particularly enjoy them. His own doctrinal position is not too clear: it has been argued by his recent editor[25] that Pierre Roger implicitly accepted the doctrine of Thomas as the base from which he argued. Hence although Pierre never mentions Aquinas by name, he would presumably invoke him as one of the dependable "ancient doctors" named by his opponent, namely, "Alexander of Hales, Thomas Aquinas, Bonaventure, and Egidius of Rome."[26] There is nothing whatever in the exchange between the two men to suggest that either of them was familiar at this date (1320-21) with Ockhamist logic or Ockhamist theology. Pope Clement's notebooks, recently investigated, show him to be a man of wide-ranging interests, no stranger to physics, for example. More importantly for our topic, Clement had copied down some *sophismata*, presumably while still a student.[27] This fact may be interpreted in two ways: either as indicating a youthful interest in logic, or (since there were no later notes on the subject) a mature disinterest in logic. I am inclined to interpret them in the latter fashion, for this reason: all that we know of the mind of Clement VI suggests that his forte was rhetoric rather than logic. Although his arguments against Fransciscus Mayronis evince

---

[23] *Chartularium Universitatis Parisiensis*, II, 588.

[24] *François de Meyronnes, Pierre Roger, Disputatio (1320-1321)*, ed. Jeanne Barbet, Textes Philosophiques du Moyen Age, IX (Paris, 1961).

[25] *Ibid.*, 32.

[26] *Ibid.*, 108-9.

[27] These were found by Anneliese Maier among the Borghesi mss. in the Vatican Library. Cod. Borgh. 247, f. 219 contains a juristic question and some *sophismata*: "Hic sunt sex probanda et solvenda: 1º quod omnis propositio est vera ... 2º quod omnis propositio est falsa..." A. Maier, "Der literarische Nachlass des Petrus Rogerii (Clemens VI) in der Borghesiana," *Ausgehendes Mittelalter*, II (Rome, 1967), 255-315, at 308.

some familiarity with school logic, they rather suggest that the *"syllogismus expositorius"* and allied logical devices did not comprise a medium in which Pierre Roger felt at ease. Moreover, if his basic allegiance was to Thomas Aquinas, then it would be quite consistent for him to feel that *sophismata* were not particularly beneficial to a student bent upon acquiring theological depth. For Thomas was more concerned with the logic of Aristotle than with the mediaeval accretions to that logic.

In order to grasp this attitude and to see in what respects it differed from the attitude of the Oxford thinkers, it will be helpful to review briefly the relationship of Christian thought to logic or dialectic, and particularly to the logical exercises most cherished in the Stoic schools of antiquity, the practice that came to be known as "sophistry." But first, lest we be led astray by modern connotations of the word, or its relatives, let us make precise the meaning of the term "sophistry." English-speaking readers of philosophy, who have grown accustomed to thinking, with Hume, that "sophistry" should be cast into the flames along with illusion,[28] must make a conscious effort to re-adjust their vision and their vocabulary when dealing with the earlier, Latin-speaking academic world in England.[29] They must recognize that "sophistry," far from being considered a vicious practice, was enjoined upon all candidates for the Bachelor's degree,[30] and thus even upon seekers of theological degrees, who had to fulfill these requirements for the arts degree before they could be admitted to theological study.

---

[28] David Hume, *An Enquiry Concerning Human Understanding*, ed. Selby-Bigge (Oxford, 1902), 165. Hume was not very sympathetic with our "scholastic headpieces and logicians" : *A Treatise of Human Nature*, ed. Selby-Bigge (Oxford, 1888), 175.

[29] The same remark holds, I suspect, for Italian-speaking students of philosophy. When Italian humanists picked up a volume of English 'sophistry,' they seem to have connected it, not with respectable undergraduate studies, but with the Sophists disparaged by Plato.

[30] "After about two years of attending ordinary lectures and disputations, the undergraduate had to take an active part in the public disputations *de sophismatibus*, for which reason they were known as *sophistae*; at Oxford they were called *sophistae in parviso*, from the locality of the disputations in arts." James A. Weisheipl, "Curriculum of the Faculty of Arts at Oxford in the Early Fourteenth Century," *Mediaeval Studies* 26 (1964), 154-85 at 154. Weisheipl adds in a footnote that "The term *sophista*, however, was frequently extended to signify any undergraduate in arts." For 'sophists' at Oxford, see Hastings Rashdall, *The Universities of Europe in the Middle Ages*, ed. Powicke and Emden (Oxford, 1936), III, 153; and Henry Anstey's introduction to *Munimenta Academica* (London, 1868), lxxviii-lxxix.

The word "sophistry" in English reflects the terminology of the mediaeval schools : it is not a Greek word,[31] but is derived from the term "sophister," which in its turn reflects the logic requirements set, for example, at Oxford. In fact, *all* Oxford undergraduates became "sophisters," whether they liked it or not, and the distinction between logicans and anti-logicans cannot be drawn according to exposure or non-exposure to sophisms, but must be drawn according to how long in their academic careers such men continued to be interested in the philosophical problems raised by *sophismata*. We have seen that a highly-placed theologian such as Pope Clement VI had, at one time in his career, copied down some of the standard *sophismata*.[32] Even friars destined for a preaching career had to endure the resolution of sophisms. The resolving of sophisms was considered to be the basis for that "wonderful subtlety of logical science" by which Oxford was distinguished among all the universities of the world.[33] It was not just an Oxford requirement, however. The statutes of the Anglican nation at Paris in 1252 specifically required the bachelor of arts to swear that he had spent at least two years responding *de sophismatibus*.[34] The drive to achieve subtlety had made itself felt very early in Paris : already in the twelfth century, *sophismata logicalia* were discussed with great

---

[31] There is, indeed, a Greek word *'sophisteia,'* which is said by Liddell-Scott to be the equivalent of "sophistry," but still the letter "r" in the English word betrays the school origin of the term.

[32] Unfortunately, Miss Maier only gives two of the six *sophismata* listed by Clement. The second sophism she does give, however, is a standard insoluble, to be found in many collections, e.g., that of John Buridan : see Theodore K. Scott's translation of his *Sophisms on Meaning and Truth* (New York, 1966), 191.

[33] An Oxford statute of 1408 presumably reflects earlier logic requirements : "Quia per solemnes determinationes Bachillariorum in facultate artium nostra mater Oxoniae Universitas, et praecipue ipsa artium facultas, multipliciter honoratur, ac mira scientiae logicalis subtilitas, qua praefata mater nostra supra caetera mundi studia dignoscitur hactenus claruisse, per fructuosum exercitium in eisdem potissimum suscipit incrementum ..." See "Forma secundum quam Magistri determinaturos admittere debent," in the "Libri Cancellarii et Procuratorum," *Munimenta Academica, or Documents illustrative of Academical Life and Studies at Oxford*, ed. Anstey (London, 1868), 241. The statute spells out the necessity for the candidates to swear that they have frequented the *Parvise* for at least a year, 'disputing, arguing, and responding *doctrinaliter*' (242). It should be noted that these logical exercises were separate and distinct from the hearing of lectures on 'the four logical books' (including the *Sophistical Elenchies*), which were also required.

[34] *Chartularium Universitatis Parisiensis*, I (Paris, 1889), 228.

interest by the school of the Parvipontani.[35] Nor was the practise of responding *de sophismatibus* restricted to just the Anglican nation at Paris, although it happens that we have the statutes of that nation which explicitly spell out the requirement.[36] It may well be, however, that it was members of the Anglican nation at Paris who especially excelled at these logical exercises : this would not be incompatible with their being also highly cultivated at Oxford, for there was considerable traffic between the two *studia*.[37] It was in the context of the consideration of *sophismata* that the distinction between *reales* and *nominales* made itself felt in the thirteenth century ; the men designated by these

---

[35] Martin Grabmann, *Die Geschichte der scholastischen Methode*, II (Berlin, 1956), 112-13. This 'logical hair-splitting' (the term is Grabmann's) provoked an indignant reaction on the part of Alexander Neckham, a defender of Aristotelian natural science (Grabmann, 115). See also L. M. De Rijk, *Logica Modernorum*, I (Assen, 1962), 64-65.

[36] Two scholars of the Gallican nation at Paris who had determined *de sophismate* in that nation are mentioned in the papal legate's resolution of the troubles of 1266 (*Chartularium*, I, 451). Siger of Brabant, who was a member of the Picard nation, dealt with some notorious *sophismata* (such as "God does not exist") at Paris, at about the 1260's or perhaps earlier : See the "Sigeri de Brabantia *Impossibilia*," edited by Pierre Mandonnet in *Siger de Brabant et l'Averroïsme Latin au XIIIe siècle, II*me *Partie, Textes inédits* (Louvain, 1908), 73-94. (The last sophism, dealing with future contingents and tomorrow's sea battle, sounds very much like any one of dozens of recent articles in *Mind* or the *Philosophical Review*.) Mandonnet is undoubtedly correct in stressing that Siger did not uphold the propositions contained in the *sophismata* himself but only used them as springboards for discussion. This point must be kept in mind if we are to do justice to the entire tradition of *sophismata*.

[37] When we find the term "Anglicana" in mediaeval documents concerning logic, we should consider whether the reference might not be to the nation at the University of Paris as well as, or even rather than, the country of England. The Anglican nation was composed of a heterogenous group of masters "from the British Isles, Holland and part of Flanders, from the Germanies, Sweden, Denmark, Norway, and Finland, also from Hungary and Slavic lands." Pearl Kibre, *The Nations in the Mediaeval Universities* (Cambridge, Mass., 1948), 19. The Anglican nation was one of the three smaller nations who faced the largest and most powerful, the Gallican nation. During the Hundred Years War so few strictly British masters were left in the Anglican nation that attempts were made to change the name to the *natio Alemannica* : see Franz Ehrle, *Der Sentenzenkommentar Peters von Candia*, 245 (which, incidentally, is still the richest source of official documentation for the external history of the nominalist movement). The grouping at the University of Paris explains, to a great extent, the ease with which British ideas and techniques were exported to German countries during the mid-fourteenth century, and also, perhaps, why they encountered such resistance in Italy, and were only received there after Italians brought them back with them from their direct studies at Oxford. In general, the intellectual life of the fourteenth century is a complex tangle of rivalries : between 'nations' in the universities, between nations in the modern sense, between religious orders, between religious and seculars, between faculties, and so on.

labels had different views as to what, if anything, "follows from the impossible," for example.[38] From the twelfth century on we hear a steady stream of complaints against the resolving of *sophismata*, mostly from scholars strongly attached to grammar or rhetoric (dialectic's rivals in the curriculum of the liberal arts).[39]

---

[38] This emerges from the consideration of a collection of *sophismata* discussed at Paris in the 1280's or 1290's, found by Franz Pelster in a Vatican manuscript, which begins, "*Hic incipunt sophismata determinata Parisius a maioribus magistris tam gallicis quam anglicis,*" [Note that *sophismata* were debated in the Gallican as well as the Anglican nations : but it may be significant that the reporter feels the need to state the fact], Vat. lat. 7678, as cited by Franz Pelster, "Nominales und reales im 13. Jahrhundert," *Sophia* (Naples and Palermo) 14 (1946), 154-161. The writer describes his opponent as holding to the opinion of certain persons, namely, *nominales*, that 'from the impossible anything follows,' while according to the truth and the view of the *reales*, 'from the impossible nothing follows.' Notice that the nominalists are not characterized as *moderni* by this thirteenth century writer : this label for the nominalists only becomes fixed in the fifteenth century, after the claims of Wyclif and the Realists had been officially refuted by the Council of Constance. There are anticipations in the fourteenth century, but, in my opinion, it is futile to try to find a fixed meaning for the term *moderni* (or its counterpart, *antiqui*) until after that Council. As we have just seen, the contemporary terms for a certain important opposition were not *moderni / antiqui*, but *nominales / reales*. I realize that this hypothesis is not the prevailing one, but this is not the place to present evidence for it.

The *sophismata* found by Pelster date, in his judgment, from the late thirteenth century, as we have seen. References to *nominales* from the thirteenth century are rare, at least in modern secondary literature. It may well be that this scarceness is due to our neglect of the *sophismata* tradition rather than to an abrupt discontinuity in the nominalist trend itself. For a reference to a nominalist in the same sort of context from the twelfth century, see the "Munich dialectic" edited by L. M. De Rijk in *Logica Modernorum*, II² (Assen, 1967), 558, line 6.The 'nominalist' opponent is thought of as denying that anything grows, contrary to Aristotle and common sense. This sounds like an outrageous proposition (*sophisma*) designed to test the student's grasp of Aristotle. (For the twelfth century, this may be anachronistic, but certainly by the time of the Paris *sophismata* cited by Pelster it would not be; cf. p. 158 of his article : "Tercio dissentimus Aristoteli proponenti in libro de generatione aliquid augmentari.")

[39] About 1160, for example, Pierre de Blois deplored the 'subtlety' of one of two boys committed to his charge : he would have preferred boys who were ready to be instructed in the foundations of grammar and the knowledge of the 'authors' rather than boys who were (like the older of the two nephews) eager to fly to the tricks of the logicians, which they learned not in the customary books but in 'leaflets and quires.' (See Letter of Petrus Blesensis from Paris, c. 1160, *Chartularium*, I, 28). Pierre complains bitterly about the uselessness of 'summaries and trickinesses of the *sophismata*' : boys who are accustomed to them come to scorn the writings of the Ancients and to condemn anything that is not found in the notebooks of their masters (*Chartularium*, I, 29).

John of Salisbury's correspondent and successor at Chartres, Petrus Cellensis, a Benedictine abbot, likewise deplored the logic instruction at Paris and envisaged a

The name "*sophista*" and the cultivation (or rather weeding-out) of *sophismata* go back to very early times in Oxford,[40] where a collection of them was made by a Dominican friar in the early thirteenth century. We may conclude that these subtleties were not the exclusive property of the Franciscans, nor were they first introduced into England or Paris by William of Ockham.[41] Albert the Great attributed the

---

Christian school where would be no "entanglement of *sophismata*." (See Petrus Cellensis, Ep. 73 [to John of Salisbury], Migne, PL, Vol. 202, col. 520A.)

The complaint seems to have been perennial : Stephen of Tournai, writing to the Pope about the year 1200, deplored the confusion into which the study of sacred letters had fallen as a result of the "new and recent summaries and commentaries" which the masters impose upon their students. (See Letter of Stephen of Tournai to the Pope, *Chartularium*, I, 47-48.) According to Stephen, blasphemous doctrines are bandied about by teachers of arts, so that there are as many errors as doctors, as many scandals as auditoria, as many blasphemies as streets, in Paris (I, 48). The indictment specifically takes in dialecticians : "... facultates quas liberales appellant amissa libertate pristina in tantam servitutem devocantur, ut comatuli adolescentes earum magisteria impudentes usurpent, et in cathedra seniorum sedeant imberbes, et qui nondum norunt esse discipuli laborant ut nominentur magistri. Conscribunt et ipsi summulas suas pluribus salivis effluentes et madidas philosophorum sale nec conditas. Omissis regulis artium abjectisque libris autenticis artificum muscas inanium verbulorum sophismatibus suis tanquam aranearum tendiculis includunt" (I, 48). It is hard to believe that it is Paris logic, rather than Oxford logic, that is being castigated, and that the date is "between 1192 and 1203" (Denifle and Chatelain).

[40] A Bodleian manuscript lists over two hundred titles, some explicitly called *sophismata*, compiled by a certain 'Richard the Sophist,' who has been identified by De Rijk as Richard Fishacre (died 1248). This Richard, if indeed it is he, was a Dominican who is said to have influenced Robert Kilwardby at Oxford and St. Bonaventure at Paris : D. A. Callus, "Introduction of Aristotelian Learning to Oxford," *Proceedings of the British Academy*, XXXIX (1943), 229-81, at 258-59.

[41] This observation would hardly seem necessary but for the fact that many writers still apparently have the impression that William of Ockham was singlehandedly responsible for the popularity of 'Terminist logic' and for introducing 'the logic of Peter of Spain' into the mainstream of British speculation. The resolving of sophisms long antedates Peter of Spain on the Continent; Terminist logic was developed by William of Sherwood at about the same time as Lambert of Auxerre and Peter of Spain. The relation between these three writers has not been satisfactorily settled. Critical editions are now under way : of Peter of Spain by De Rijk and of Lambert of Auxerre by Alessio. William of Sherwood's treatise on logic has been edited by Grabmann, although my colleague John Malcolm has found, on the basis of a re-examination of the Paris manuscript (Bib. Nat. Lat. 16,617), that Grabmann's text contains many errors, some of importance. When these critical editions are available to scholars, it may be possible to determine more precisely the priorities between the three writers, and hence the details of this phase of Terminist logic. De Rijk's work has already made it abundantly clear that the initial stages of the movement reach far back to the time of Abelard.

That Duns Scotus made use of 'Byzantine' (i.e., Terminist) logic was quite clearly

ignorance of Paris teachers in the thirteenth century to the fact that they followed *sophismata* rather than philosophy.[42] But at Oxford, Albert's fellow Dominican, Robert Kilwardby (died 1279), was not so antagonistic to the *sophismata*, and thereon hangs my tale, for Kilwardby, as a regent master at Oxford and as Archbishop of Canterbury, had much to do with setting the tone of British philosophy and theology. He had taught at Paris before entering the Order of Preachers, and had established a reputation for knowledge, "especially in grammar and logic."[43] Kilwardby himself wrote *sophismata*, both logical and grammatical.[44] It was Kilwardby who, "with the consent of all the masters, regent and non-regent, of Oxford," condemned Thomas Aquinas' doctrine of the unity of substantial forms in 1277 : along with this and other errors in natural philosophy were condemned four grammatical and ten logical errors.[45] The Oxford condemnations are

pointed out by Carl Prantl in the 19th century, so that there is really no excuse for secondary sources to continue to associate Ockham with Terminist logic in such a way as to suggest that he had no British predecessors in this tendency. For Prantl's evidence, see his *Geschichte der Logik im Abendlande*, III (Leipzig, 1867), pp. 202-32. Prantl's summation of the influence of Terminist logic (233) is still worth consulting. To say that nominalism could not have arisen *without* Terminist logic is by no means the same as saying that they are equivalent.

The *sophismata* exercises in Oxford were being carried on from as early a time as we have any scholastic results at all : Fishacre's questions are the first such documents to have survived from the early days of scholastic teaching in England : see A. G. Little and F. Pelster, *Oxford Theology and Theologians* (Oxford, 1934), 30. Pierre Duhem, while conceding that the practice was common to Paris and Oxford, thought that Oxford placed an exaggerated importance upon the solution of sophisms. See Duhem, *Etudes sur Léonard de Vinci, Troisième Serie* : *Les précurseurs Parisiens de Galilée* (Paris, 1913), 441. Later (444) Duhem speaks of "l'esprit de subtile chicane que développe aisément la continuelle analyse des sophismes." Clearly the rivalry between Paris and Oxford had not yet subsided by Duhem's time.

[42] "Non ergo tantum secundum theologos falsum est quod dicunt, sed etiam secundum philosophiam ; cuius causa dicti est ignorantia, quia multi Parisienses non philosophiam, sed sophismata sunt secuti." Albertus Magnus, "De quindecim problematibus," ed. Mandonnet in *Siger de Brabant, IIme Partie*, 29-52, at 35.

[43] Nicolaus Trivetus, *Annales*, ed. Hog (London, 1845), 278.

[44] "Die sophismata logicalia et grammaticalia des Robert Kilwardby," in Martin Grabmann, *Die Sophismataliteratur des 12. und 13. Jahrhunderts mit Textausgabe eines Sophisma des Boetius von Dacein*, Beiträge zur Geschichte der Philosophie und Theologie des Mittelalters, XXXVI¹ (Münster, 1940), 41-50.

[45] *Chartularium Universitatis Parisiensis*, I, 558-59. It should be stressed that these items do not condemn the study of logic or the consideration of *sophismata* but rather the abuse of logic, which presupposes a commitment of a serious kind to the study of logic (masters persisting in these abuses are to be expelled from Oxford).

generally taken to be the reaction of "conservative Augustinians" to the Aristotelianism of Albert and Thomas, and of course this is true. But it is important to recognize that these British "Augustinians," who held to the "more solid and healthy doctrine" of Alexander of Hales, Bonaventure, and their like,[46] did not necessarily reject logic or the consideration of *sophismata*. In point of fact, the Augustinian tradition, as we shall see, was from the start more receptive to the resolving of *sophismata* than the Aristotelian. And this, I believe, goes a long way to explain why "subtleties" were more cultivated at Oxford than at Paris in the late thirteenth and early fourteenth centuries.

In order to understand the complexity of the mediaeval tradition of *sophismata*, it will be useful to begin by examining the usage of the term in philosophical Greek. In Greek there are various verbs and nouns derived from *sophos*, "wise," including the denominative verb *sophidzo*, "to make wise" or "to become wise." From this verb Plato seems to have concocted the playful noun *sophisma* for the product of intercourse between unworthy men and philosophy (*Republic*, 496A). In Aristotle the term *sophisma* does not occur in the *Sophistical Elenchies*, to our surprise and to the confusion of the tradition of school logic in the West. For the resolving of *sophismata* derived in the main from the Stoics, as we shall see. Later dialecticians in the Latin West, as they moved from an earlier period in which they learned the liberal arts in the Roman framework transmitted chiefly by Augustine to a period in which all the works of the *Organon* became available for study, were forced to effect a merger between Aristotelian and Stoic logic. The obvious place to deal with *sophismata* would be in connection with the *Sophistical Elenchies*. But Aristotle introduces the term *sophisma*, in the *Organon*, only in the *Topics* (162a16) to describe a "contentious syllogism" (*syllogismos eristikos*), something that appears to be an *apodeixis* but is not.[47] The other uses of *sophisma* in Aristotle occur,

---

[46] The phrase is that of John Peckham, Kilwardby's Franciscan successor as Archbishop of Canterbury, who renewed the condemnations of his predecessor. See Decima L. Douie, *Archbishop Peckham* (Oxford, 1952), 296, n. 1. Peckham insists that he is not opposed to philosophy, but to 'certain profane novelties of words [*prophanas vocum novitates*] introduced into the heights of theological speculation over twenty years ago' [i.e., c. 1265]. *Registrum Epistolarum Fratris Johannis Peckham*, ed. Martin, III (London, 1885), 901.

[47] Cf. the wording of Pope Clement's letter of 1346 : "oppiniones apparentes non existentes" (n. 23 above). In Boethius' translation of the Topics, the Greek term is

interestingly enough, in a political context (as in Plato). The devices by which democrats exclude the wealthy from participation in politics are characterized by Aristotle as *sophismata*.[48]

The Stoics, on the other hand, gave a central place to the resolving of *sophismata* in their logical training. Diogenes Laertius (VII, 43) tells us that Stoic dialectic considered *sophismata*, "whether due to words or to things"; they specifically included "insolubles" (*apora*). Chrysippus wrote an entire book "*On Sophismata*," of which we have only the title.[49] But we know something of his manner of treating *sophismata* from the unsympathetic account given by the sceptic Sextus Empiricus, who regards Chrysippus' "solutions" of *sophismata* as ineffectual.[50] Stoic influence is very much in evidence in Galen's remarks on *sophismata*: he holds that their resolution presupposes a grasp of the principles of sound argument, such as is to be found in geometry. Galen maintained that the ability to solve *sophismata* shows that one has scientific knowledge rather than unfounded opinion based upon authority.[51]

The practical Roman mind was not as receptive to the merits of resolving sophisms as the Greek. Cicero speaks with obvious dislike of the "contorted and prickly *sophismata*" of Stilpo, Diodorus, and Alexinus, "for thus fallacious little conclusions are called."[52] Presum-

---

taken over into Latin: "[Est] sophisma vero syllogismus litigatorius," *Aristoteles Latinus*, V¹, ed. Minio-Paluello (Brussels and Paris, 1969), 173.

[48] H. Bonitz gives the entries for *sophisma* on p. 689 of his *Index Aristotelicus* (Berlin, 1870). Aside from the rather casual 'definition' in the *Topics*, there are only four occurrences, all in the *Politics*: 1297a36, 1307b40, 1308al, and 1322a21. These would be better translated as 'stratagem,' 'device,' 'artifice,' or 'dodge' than as 'specious argument.' In close proximity to two of the above passages in the *Politics*, there occurs a section in which Aristotle speaks of the mind's being led astray (*paralogidzetai*), as in the puzzle, "If each is little, then all are a little." Aristotle does not call this puzzle a *sophisma* but a 'sophistical argument' (*sophistikos logos*) (1307b37).

[49] H. von Arnim, *Stoicorum Veterum Fragmenta* (Leipzig, 1903), II, 8. He also wrote on *apora*.

[50] Sextus Empiricus, *Outlines of Pyrrhonism*, II, xxii, "*Peri sophismatōn*." The work did not become widely known again until the Renaissance, so that this more detailed description of the practice of resolving sophismata did not have any influence upon mediaeval theory or practice.

[51] Galen, "On the Passions of the Soul and its Errors," *Opera omnia*, ed. Kühn (Leipzig, 1823), Vol. V, p. 73 *et seq*. Galen is scornful of men who have never learned to distinguish between true and false arguments: they should have acquired this ability by logical exercises. The passage is given in part by Von Arnim, II, 90.

[52] The passage merits careful attention. Cicero has been examining various sceptical arguments from previous thinkers who anticipated the position of the New Academy

ably Cicero is saying that these Megaric philosophers called their arguments *sophismata*, although possibly he could mean that people in general call the arguments of the Megarics *sophismata* : one cannot decide from this passage alone. More important for our purposes is what follows : Chrysippus was concerned to refute or "dissolve" *sophismata* (the term "dissolve" is Cicero's version of one of the cluster of Greek verbs used to express the process of "loosening" sophisms : it anticipates the mediaeval "*solvere*"). Cicero, as a confirmed Academic sceptic, finds Chrysippus' resolutions unconvincing. But in any event Cicero considered the whole subject unrewarding. The same attitude is taken by the Roman Stoic, Seneca, whose moral letters furnished mediaeval anti-dialecticians with an arsenal of quotations against *sophismata*. No standard Latin translation had been arrived at by Seneca's time for the Greek term *sophismata*, which in itself shows what little use Roman Stoics had for the practice of refuting them. "You have asked me," Seneca remarks to Lucilius, "to give you a Latin word for the Greek *sophismata*. Many have tried to impose a name on these, but none of them has stuck. Obviously since the thing itself has not been received by us, nor is it in use, the name has also been resisted. However Cicero's usage seems most appropriate to me : he calls them *cavillationes*. If anyone has surrendered himself to them, he weaves clever little questions, but he does not make any progress in life, nor does he himself become stronger or more temperate or loftier."[53] Seneca speaks for

---

to which he himself inclines. He lists some of the lesser thinkers to whom he might have appealed : "Atque habebam molestos vobis, sed minutos Stilponem, Diodorum, Alexinum, quorum sunt contorta et aculeata quaedam sophismata (sic enim appellantur fallaces conclusiunculae); sed quid eos colligam, cum habeam Chrysippum, qui fulcire putatur porticum Stoicorum ? Quam multa ille contra sensus, quam multa contra omnia quae in consuetudine probantur ! At dissolvit idem. Mihi quidem non videtur : sed dissolverit sane : certe tam multa non collegisset quae nos fallerent probabilitate magna nisi videret iis resisti non facile posse." Cicero, *Academica*, II, 75. Here we have, *in nuce*, the rationale behind the Stoic use of *sophismata*. Unlike the Megarics, who were trying to discredit dogmatic assertions, Chrysippus and the other Stoics were Dogmatists : for them, *sophismata* were an embarrassment unless they could be solved. *Sophismata* were a challenge to other Dogmatists too, of course, including the Peripatetics, but the Stoics seem to have given greater emphasis in their philosophical training to these dialectical exercises. Cicero would rather not bother with them.

[53] Seneca, *Ad Lucilium epistulae morales*, *Ep. 111*. Seneca's claim that Cicero translated *sophismata* by *cavillationes* is puzzling : the term does not appear in H. Merguet's *Lexikon zu der philosophischen Schriften Cicero's* (Jena, 1887). The word *cavillatio* does appear in the *De Oratore*, but as a rhetorical term. The Middle Ages did not know the *De oratore*, which is too bad : mediaeval anti-dialecticians would have relished Cicero's dismissal of *disserendi subtilitatem* in I, 68.

a whole strand of mediaeval thought when he warns Lucilius not to spend much time on sophisms: he admits that they have a way of holding one's attention by a "show of subtlety," but as a Roman Stoic, Seneca prefers to keep his attention upon his main task, that of "condemning life."[54]

Seneca's contemporary, the Apostle Paul, had an opportunity to argue personally with the Stoics and Epicureans at Athens: these discussions came out, in the Vulgate used by mediaeval philosophers, as disputations.[55] The Athenians, with their readiness to say or hear some new thing,[56] became for mediaeval moralists the prototype of pagan philosophers eager for "news." This seems a little ungracious, since in this particular case the "news" consisted of "Jesus and the resurrection." Be that as it may, the condemnation of "novelties" and the disparagement of "new" doctrines hovered over the mediaeval faculties of arts, and particularly over the dialecticians, who often were accused of being eager, like the Athenians, to tell or to hear

---

[54] "Hoc tamen habent in se pessimum : dulcedinem quandam sui faciunt et animum specie subtilitatis inductum tenent ac morantur, cum tanta rerum moles vocet, cum vix tota vita sufficiat, ut hoc unum discas, vitam contemnere." Seneca, *Ep. 111*. This passage would not have been available to most mediaeval anti-dialecticians, since it belongs to the section of Seneca's letters (89 to 124) known only to a few people during the early Middle Ages (Pierre of Blois knew them). See L. D. Reynolds, *The Medieval Tradition of Seneca's Letters* (Oxford, 1965), 120. However, the letters that were known contain ample ammunition for the anti-dialectician (as well as, unwittingly, for the dialectician). *Ep. 48* contains the following choice sophism : "Mus syllaba est; mus autem caseum rodit; syllaba ergo caseum rodit," which clearly calls for the distinction between material supposition and other kinds. Seneca, the stern moralist, can hardly contain his indignation over this sophism : "O pueriles ineptias! in hoc supercilia subduximus ? in hoc barbam demisimus ? hoc est quod tristes docemus et pallidi ? Vis scire quid philosophia promittat generi humano ? consilium." etc. Seneca wants philosophy to teach him what his obligations to a friend are, not to make subtle distinctions between the meanings of *amicus*, nor to solve riddles such as this one of the syllable devouring the cheese. "What difference does it make if I can't solve this?" The sophism is mentioned by Robert Holcot, *In librum Sapientiae*, Lectio XC A, with enthusiastic endorsement of Seneca's view of it. The last letter in the first grouping (*Ep. 88*) was a veritable treasure-trove of slogans against undue subtlety and the cultivation of useless knowledge : e.g., "plus scire velle quam sit satis, intemperantiae genus est," or again, "Audi, quantum mali faciat nimia subtilitas et quam infesta veritati sit." Robert Holcot quotes, from 'Petrus Ravenensis,' a passage that I have not been able to locate : "Odibilius nihil est subtilitate ubi sola est subtilitas."

[55] "Disputabat igitur in synagoga cum Iudaeis et colentibus, et in foro per omnes dies, ad eos aderant." (Acts XVIII, 17).

[56] "Athenienses ... ad nihil vacabant nisi aut dicere aut audire aliquid novi." (Acts XVII, 21).

something new, strange, and paradoxical. In his letter to the Colossians, Paul warns them against being misled by "specious arguments" or "through philosophy and vain deceit."[57] Several of the Greek Church Fathers shared the Apostle's antipathy for dialectic : they supplied mediaeval anti-dialecticians with many of their favorite comparisons : of dialecticians with spiders weaving webs for the unwary, or with bramble bushes waiting to trap the Christian or serving as hiding places for heretics.[58] St. Jerome continued this tradition for the Latin Church Fathers, asserting that the heresies of Eunomius, the Manicheans, and Novatus had the dialectic of Aristotle and Chrysippus as their source.[59]

Augustine's attitude was quite different, however, and this is of the utmost importance for our topic. Augustine conceded that Christians could profit from the rules of pagan dialectic : "the discipline of disputation is of very great benefit for penetrating and resolving all sorts of questions that occur in the Scriptures, although one must beware of quarrelsomeness and a certain puerile show of deceiving one's

---

[57] In the Vulgate : "... ut nemo uos decipiat in subtilitate sermonum" (Wordsworth and White) Col. II, 4. Merk, following other codices, has "in sublimitate sermonum." They agree on Col. II, 8 : "Uidete ne quis uos decipiat per philosophiam et inanem fallaciam, secundum traditionem hominum, secundum elementa mundi, et non secundum Christum." The *"pithanologia"* that has divided the codices in Col. II, 4 is a rather unusual Greek word : it appears once in Plato (*Theaetetus*, 162E), where Socrates contrasts a 'merely plausible sort of argument' with 'proof' (*apodeixis*). The same contrast appears in the well-known passage at the start of the *Nicomachean Ethics* (1094b26) : "it is as unreasonable to expect merely probable reasonings (*pithanologountos*) from a mathematician as *apodeixeis* from an orator." In any event, this chapter of Colossians provided opponents of *sophismata* with Scriptural ammunition. For example, Pope John XXII used Paul's letter when he complained in 1317, from Avignon, about certain theologians at Paris, who, "having postponed or neglected the necessary useful canonical writings and edifying doctrines, busy themselves with curious, useless and empty superfluous questions of philosophy, by which the discipline of study is itself dissolved, the splendor of its light is offended and consequently its utility for students is very much impeded," and added that "some others, desiring to know more than they ought ... are deceived by philosophy and inane fallacy according to the traditions of men." (See Letter of Pope John XXII to the masters and scholars of Paris from Avignon, May 8, 1317, *Chartularium Universitatis Parisiensis*, II, 200-201.) If there were any 'Anglican subtleties' on the Paris scene in 1317, they must have been Scotist subtleties (Ockam's logical and physical works were presumably not composed until after 1320). But Pope John XXII does not characterize them as 'Anglican' at all.

[58] See de Ghellinck, in the work cited in n. 12 above.

[59] Jerome, Commentary on Nahum, *Commentarii in prophetas minores*, Corpus Christianorum, LXXVI A (Turnhout, 1970), pp. 573-74 (PL, XXV, 1269).

adversaries. For there are many false conclusions of reasonings (called *sophismata*) that imitate true ones in such a way that they deceive not only the slow-witted but even clever persons who are not attentive."[60] The way to guard against such deception is to learn the rules of dialectic, which give us "the truth of connections." The truth of the propositions joined by these "true connections" is to be sought in Scripture. "Since therefore there may be true connections not just of true but even of false propositions, it is easy to learn the truth of connections even in those schools that are outside the Church."[61] "This art which they (the Stoics) call dialectic, which just teaches us to demonstrate consequences (*consequentia*), whether of true from true propositions, or false from false, need never be feared by Christian doctrine, just as the Apostle Paul was not afraid among the Stoics and did not refuse them when they wished to exchange ideas. For this art itself admits (and it is true) that in disputing no one is driven to a false conclusion by logic (*consequenter*) unless he has previously accepted something false, since the same conclusion is brought about whether he wishes it or not..."[62]

We are now in a position to understand why the mediaeval traditions influenced strongly by Augustine (which is to say, almost all of them except those that stressed Aristotle heavily) were willing to countenance the resolution of *sophismata* as a useful and indeed necessary

---

[60] "... disputationis disciplina ad omnia genera quaestionum, quae in litteris sanctis sunt, penetranda et dissoluenda, plurimum valet; tantum ibi cavenda est libido rixandi et puerilis quaedam ostentatio decipiendi adversarium. Sunt enim multa, quae appellantur sophismata, falsae conclusiones rationum et plerumque ita veras imitantes, ut non solum tardos, sed ingeniosos etiam minus diligenter attentos decipiant. Proposuit enim quidam dicens ei, cum quo loquebatur 'quod ego sum, tu non es.' At ille consensit; verum enim erat parte vel eo ipso, quod iste insidiosus, ille simplex erat. Tum iste addidit 'ego autem homo sum.' Hoc quoque cum ab illo accepisset, conclusit dicens 'tu igitur non es homo.' Quod genus captiosarum conclusionum scriptura, quantum existimo, detestatur illo loco, ubi dictum est : *Qui sophistice loquitur, odibilis est.*"Augustine, *De doctrina christiana*, II, xxxi (48).

[61] "Cum ergo sint verae conexiones non solum verarum, sed etiam falsarum sententiarum, facile est veritatem conexionum etiam in scholis illis discere, quae praeter ecclesiam sunt. Sententiarum autem veritas in sanctis libris ecclesiasticis investiganda est." *Ibid.*, II, xxxi (49). Prantl takes no notice of this passage. Henri-Irénée Marrou, *Saint Augustin et la fin de la culture antique* (Paris, 1958), 245, characterizes Augustine as deficient in the technique of dialectic, but he does recognise that Stoic dialectic was important for him : "Ailleurs Augustin insiste volontiers sur l'importance de la dialectique stoïcienne" (242), citing *Contra Cresconium* and *Ep. 118*.

[62] Augustine, *Contra Cresconium grammaticum*, I, 20 (Migne, PL, Vol. 43, col. 459). Notice that it is Stoic dialectic that gives us rules for *consequentiae*.

preliminary to the study of the Bible and the *Sentences*. Only those making a most strenuous attempt to accommodate themselves to the scientific approach of Aristotle could afford to dismiss the practice; and even for them it was extremely difficult, if not impossible, to disentangle it from the *Sophistical Elenchies*. Nevertheless, when a mediaeval scholar was commenting very faithfully on the text of the *Organon*, he generally avoided introducing into the analysis of the *Sophistical Elenchies* the term "*sophisma*"—even when, as in the case of Robert Kilwardby, he composed *sophismata* himself.[63] Thomas Aquinas uses the term *sophisma* only in his commentary on the *Physics*.[64] Needless to say, those who followed "the texts of the Philosopher and of his ancient commentators" in logic would not be tolerant of those who pursued "other varied and extraneous sophistical doctrines," to return to the language of Pope Clement VI's letter. In logic, this would mean that the masters at Paris should stick to the *Organon* and to "Porphyry's book,"[65] and not spend their time on notebooks containing the latest intriguing *sophismata* from Oxford.

After this excursion, we may now review the state of the question : were Richard de Bury in 1344 and Pope Clement in 1346 referring to the same doctrines as being taught at Paris ? In particular, were these the logical doctrines of Ockham ?

Richard refers to the Anglican subtleties which "they" (the Masters ?) "denounce in public" but make the subject of their furtive vigils. His wording rather suggests that he had in mind the edict of 1339. On the other hand, it is not absolutely certain that Richard was

---

[63] "... illa vero ratiocinatio deceptiva quae fit juxta syllogismum dialecticum in communibus omnibus facultatibus, litigiosus syllogismus vocatur in *Topicis* et in *Elenchis* ..." Robert Kilwardby, "De nomine logicae et ortu, sufficientia, subjecto et fine et diffinitione," ed. Bernard Hauréau in *Notices et Extraits de quelques manuscrits latins de la Bibliothèque Nationale*, V (Paris, 1892), 119-30 at 125-26.

[64] Where it only occurs twice, according to Roy Deferrari, *A Lexicon of St. Thomas Aquinas* (Washington, D. C., 1948), 1039. When Thomas writes on *Sophistical Elenchies* (if indeed he did compose the "De fallaciis ad quosdam nobiles artistas" given in *Opuscula Philosophica*, ed. Spiazzi [Turin and Rome, 1954], 225-40), he sticks very closely to the Aristotelian terminology, and uses such terms as *fallacia, argumentum sophisticum, sophistica disputativa*, and *paralogismus*, just as Kilwardby does.

[65] "*Veterem logicam*, videlicet *librum Porfirii, predicamentorum, periarmenias, divisionum et thopicorum Boecii*, excepto quarto ... *topica et elenchos, priora et posteriora* ..." Statute of the Faculty of Arts at Paris, on the manner of teaching in Arts, and of the books that ought to be lectured upon, March 19, 1255 (*Chartularium*, I, 278). Porphyry and Boethius would qualify as *expositores antiqui*. In grammar, ethics, and natural philosophy, there would be similar authorized texts acceptable to Pope Clement VI.

thinking of this official denunciation when he spoke of the "open disapproval" of "Anglican subtleties" : condemnations of British logic were widespread on the Continent, as readers of humanist literature from the fourteenth century know. Moreover, there is the plain fact that Richard himself is praising these Anglican subtleties, not deploring or denouncing them. Richard compiled his *Philobiblon* in order to promote the cause of the Christian faith : he hoped to encourage the building up of an arsenal of books for its defense.[66] Among such books, quires of sophisms held a place of honor : they were to help form the intellectual sharpness needed to strengthen the faith. Although there is no particular reason to believe that Richard de Bury would have excluded the logical writings of William of Ockham from this arsenal, there is no reason to assume that Ockham was the only British logician worthy, in his view, of study by the serious Christian student. The sophisms that Richard collected were more likely to come from day-to-day practitioners of the arts of sophistry than from the more extended logical works of Ockham, which remained closer to the text of Aristotle and had as their chief aim the facilitating of scientific demonstrations. Ockham's logical writings seldom descended to the consideration of those scandalous and outrageous theological propositions that gave such offense to pious ears. All things considered, it seems probable that Richard de Bury, if he had been asked to enumerate the writers on Anglican subtleties to which he had referred in the *Philobiblon*, could have listed dozens of English logicians who were well known in their day both in England and on the Continent, but have since disappeared from view. A few of them, such as Burley and Kilvington, have been recovered, but others remain unedited and lacking proper attribution. The basic feature of Richard's attitude, however, and the one that I wish to stress, is his general approval of the subtleties of Anglican logic.

With Pope Clement VI, the case is quite different. However vague his reference to "varied and extraneous sophistical doctrines," it is inescapably clear that he frowns on them and has no wish to encourage them. They contribute nothing whatever to the strengthening of the faith; at best, they distract students from their study of the basic works, the texts "which they ought to follow to the extent that they do not depart from Catholic faith." What were these basic works ?

---

[66] Joseph de Ghellinck, "Un évêque bibliophile au XIVe siècle. Richard Aungerville de Bury (1345)," *Revue d'histoire ecclésiastique* 19 (1923), 196.

"The texts of the Philosopher and of other masters and ancient commentators." By "ancient commentators," I take it that the Pope is referring to such writers as Porphyry and Boethius, whose books had been officially approved long since by the Paris faculty. While "responding *de sophismatibus*" could conceivably have fallen under the range of permissible activities envisaged by the Pope, it seems more likely that he would think of these logical exercises as leading students away from orthodox theology to the consideration of frivolous or even heretical opinions, i.e., to "sophistical doctrines." These doctrines are said to be taught in "certain other *studia*," and this description would certainly fit the Oxford *sophismata* we have noticed. Moreover, British logic was studied, it would seem, at conventual houses on the Continent. Irreverent theses are apt to appeal to youthful minds, especially those of young men who have been pressed into the religious life for economic reasons rather than from an inner call.

When Clement deplored the fact that "many" theologians had become involved in "philosophical questions and other curious disputations and suspect opinions of a foreign and varied sort," the most natural interpretation is that he was thinking of men such as Nicholas of Autrecourt, whose unseemly doctrines had been soundly reproved only the day before the Pope sent off his letter to the masters at Paris. The Pope distinguishes clearly, in his accusation, between the misdoings of masters of arts and theologians. In no case would masters of arts have been allowed to advance theological propositions and debate them as such : this would have immediately called down upon them the wrath of the superior faculty. The only way in which theological propositions could have been smuggled into the curriculum of arts was through their introduction as *sophismata*. That this indeed was done at Paris is known to us from the example of Siger de Brabant in the previous century. In his letter of 1346, the Pope is complaining about doctrines that are not found in the writings of Aristotle and his ancient expositors but are taught in other *studia*. What more likely candidates than the little leaflets that incorporated the mediaeval accretions of Terminist logic, now fallen into disuse at Paris but kept strenuously alive at Oxford through undergraduate sophistry ? To Clement's ears, the audacious propositions of Nicholas of Autrecourt might have seemed as "ill-sounding" as the *sophismata* that Oxford students were required to refute or distinguish. Why not, then, ban the whole lot of these "varied and sophistical doctrines" ? Then proper attention could be given to the "many true expositors and sayings of

saints and philosophers from which true theology can be drawn."
In his letter, Clement does not insist that the works of one theologian
alone contained all that was needed for the "true theology" that leads
to "true beatitude." Yet if Clement did lean toward Thomas Aquinas
personally, this would help explain why he had so little use for the
linguistic philosophy that had developed so strongly in England under
the encouragement of Kilwardby and others of like Augustinian
persuasion. Possibly Clement seized upon the obviously extreme and
unacceptable doctrine of Nicholas of Autrecourt as a pretext for
discouraging the whole tendency toward linguistic sophistication that
emanated steadily from Oxford. In this sense, the Pope's letter could be
said to be "anti-Nominalist" in intent, provided we take the term
"nominalist" in a very broad sense, to mean any careful linguistic
approach to philosophical and theological concerns. The continuity
of this tradition of *Sprachtheorie* is steadily coming more into view as
scholars explore its origins and development.[67] Clement VI had some
slight acquaintance with the *sophismata* tradition, as we have seen.
Very likely he was more aware of the extent of the trend we call
"Terminist" logic than were modern scholars until recent times. This
might explain why Clement did not wish to single out any particular
writer by name, preferring instead to indicate a general practice that
prevailed at other *studia*. A panel of theologians appointed by a
previous Pope had condemned many propositions found in Ockham's
commentary on the *Sentences*. But these could hardly be called "extraneous" to theological study: they were squarely in the domain of
theology, no matter how "heretical" they might have seemed to the
six theologians at Avignon in 1326. The same argument could be
applied to the views of Duns Scotus, with which Clement VI had
struggled in 1320-21 at Paris. If he had regarded Scotist doctrines as
being "extraneous" to theology, surely he would have called this to the
attention of his theological opponent, but he did nothing of the sort.
He recognized, apparently, that Scotus' doctrines were unquestionably
theological.

So far as pure logic goes, Pope Clement and Richard de Bury would
have agreed, it seems, that the best texts for university students were
those of Aristotle and his ancient commentators. The two men might
also have agreed upon the identity of the Anglican subtleties being

---

[67] Including Grabmann, Minio-Paluello, De Rijk, Pinborg, and many other scholars. For a recent survey, see Jan Pinborg, *Die Entwicklung der Sprachtheorie im Mittelalter*, cited in n. 17 above.

taught in clandestine fashion at Paris. But they would not have agreed in their evaluation of the usefulness of these British "innovations," for Richard regarded them as indispensable training for pious minds, while Clement considered them a subversive snare. This basic difference of attitude could be expressed, if you like, by saying that the Pope was opposed to "nominalism." But this disapproval extended to other writers than William of Ockham who practised Anglican subtleties. "The influence of the Avignon Popes on the University of Oxford, the birthplace of Scotism and Ockhamism, appears to have been slight in the fourteenth century, probably as a result of the Hundred Year's War and the great schism," observed Ehrle, "Nevertheless the general trend of the teaching of the Oxford masters does not seem to have escaped them. In his important letter of May 20, 1346 against the Nominalism that had also gained a foothold in Paris, Clement VI discussed, without giving names, 'other universities.' Must he not have been thinking in the first place of Oxford, of the native city of the 'Anglican Subtleties' which Richard de Bury discussed in his *Philobiblon?*"[68] The answer to that question is undoubtedly 'yes.' But this answer is badly misleading if we take it, as so many have done to mean that Richard de Bury attributed the *decline* of the University of Paris to the influence of 'nominalism.' Quite the contrary, for whatever propriety of logic the Parisians retained was due, in Richard's opinion, to their training in British-style sophistry. If Richard had been elected Pope, he might well have addressed a letter of rebuke to the masters of Paris, blaming them for failures of various sorts. But he certainly would not have blamed them for cultivating Anglican subtleties.[69]

University of California at Davis

---

[68] Ehrle, *Der Sentenzenkommentar Peters von Candia*, 102-3.

[69] Some further comments on fourteenth-century logic may be found in Neal W. Gilbert, "Ockham, Wyclif, and the 'Via Moderna'," in *Antiqui und Moderni*, Miscellanea Mediaevalia, IX (Berlin and New York, 1974), 85-125.

A PRE-ARISTOTELIAN MATHEMATICIAN ON DEDUCTIVE ORDER*

MALCOLM BROWN

(*Met.* B,1) λύειν δ'οὐκ ἔστιν ἀγνοοῦντας τὸν δεσμόν

The Academy of Plato's own time is a puzzle to us. Nor will we make much progress in solving it, so long as we remain ignorant of the researches and debates going on there. Instead of getting at the late Plato or the Academic Aristotle via the Academy, we will only be about the futile project of "untying the knot we do not know about." Clearly if we are not to deny ourselves this access to Plato and Aristotle,[1] we must sort out those evidences we have all the more carefully because they are so scanty. Proclus Diadochus preserves for us[2] an important collection of evidences of one part of the intellectual activity at the Academy in Plato's day: mathematical research. A methodical effort with this evidence would be repaid if it opened up, even to a slight extent, a new access route to Plato and the Early Academy. This would mean a patient application to these evidences of the methods of research set forth by Professor Kristeller, especially those relating to

---

* I am grateful to the National Endowment for the Humanities and to the Center for Hellenic Studies for their fellowships during 1969-70, which gave me time for the research of which this is part of the result. The late Glenn R. Morrow gave me the benefit of his helpful criticisms of an earlier draft of the paper.

[1] Harold Cherniss, in *The Riddle of the Early Academy* (Berkeley, 1945; repr. New York, 1962), is skeptical of approaching Plato this way : mathematics was no part of the "formal curriculum" of the Early Academy (65-68). Compare his review article "Plato as Mathematician," *Review of Metaphysics* 4 (1951), 395-425, which concludes that he was not a mathematician. But clearly one need not be a mathematician to discuss its foundations intelligently, and the concept of "formal curriculum" at the early Academy fits poorly onto our evidence about the research there. Much of the dialectic going on adjacent to the late Plato and the early Aristotle will have been the kind Aristotle called *peirastic* (cf. *Met. Γ*, 2, 1004b25 f.).

[2] *Proclus : A Commentary on the First Book of Euclid's Elements*, translated, with Introduction and Notes by Glenn R. Morrow (Princeton, 1970). Hereafter references will be to the numbers in the Friedlein text, which appear also in Morrow's margins, and will appear in the body of the article rather than in notes.

preserving and interpreting original sources.³ But what "news" could possibly be found out about Plato at this late date? It is only because many generations of scholars since Plato's time, scholars who built libraries, wrote commentaries, stocked their own minds with learning, and most of all who transmitted the love of such collection and study to their successors, that finding out anything new about Plato is even thinkable these days.

The evidence to be reviewed below supports the following reconstruction. Menaechmus, an able mathematician and companion of Plato's at the Academy when he was writing his late dialogues, put forward a problematic definition of mathematical "element," and drew important consequences for deductive reasoning from it. There is a clear bearing of this position on the dilemma set by Plato in the 'Dream' passage of the *Theaetetus*; there it is asked whether, if knowledge involves an order of composition-resolution,⁴ whereby the 'elements' in the known thing are identified as the simple starting points of the composition (thus the end points of the resolution), these ultimates themselves can be known. For they are by hypothesis incapable of further resolution. What Menaechmus suggested was that, anyhow in an important class of cases, one *cannot* identify uniquely these "ultimates," since it is equally possible, given some preliminaries, to compose B from A and, given the same, A from B. That is, since reciprocal demonstration is possible in mathematics, in cases where it is actually accomplished the order of prior-posterior is not absolute, but rather relative to one's argumentative context and purpose. Thus Plato's mathematical colleague takes the *Theaetetus* dilemma by the horns, saying in effect: "it is a quite harmless consequence you draw from your (and our) definition of knowledge in terms of elements.⁵ It does us no injury to accept the consequences that these end points of the steps of resolution will be only as knowable or as unknowable as the complex we began with. For on our account, nothing prevents one's resolving an alleged element into what, in another argument,

---

³ "History of Philosophy and History of Ideas," *Journal of the History of Philosophy* 2 (1964), 1-14. He emphasizes independent interpreting of primary sources on p. 8. As any of his students will testify, this is a prominent part of Kristeller's unwritten teachings as well.

⁴ The latinized "resolution-composition" is intended to recall the terminology under which the Renaissance authors knew the method.

⁵ Glenn R. Morrow has clarified the meaning of the "dream" by reference to this same group of "elementizing" mathematicians at the Academy, in "Plato and the Mathematicians," *Philosophical Review* 79 (1970), 303-33.

appears as a compound." It is just as clear that Menaechmus' problematic assertion about deductive order was repugnant to Aristotle, who rejects heatedly the claim of reciprocal demonstration and its consequence, that it is in principle possible to prove all things.[6] A variety of related problems about fixing the order of prior-posterior in reasoning were also under discussion among the group of Academic mathematicians associated with Menaechmus, problems such as when a predication is essential and universal, when a proposition is convertible, and various issues centered on the method of analysis and synthesis. It will help in the understanding of our fragment to connect it with some of these related issues.

I

Generally speaking, Kliem was quite right to say of Plato's mathematical companion Menaechmus that none of his writings is preserved.[7] But there is an important fragment that stands as an exception: Proclus quotes a statement of his at some length, without giving the title of the work, about defining a geometrical "element":

> The term "element" can be used in two senses, as Menaechmus says. For what proves is called an element of what is proved by it [thus in Euclid the first theorem is an element of the second, and the fourth of the fifth]. In this sense many propositions can be called elements of one another, for they are proved from each other. From the proposition that the exterior angles of a

---

[6] *Posterior Analytics* I, 3; cf. I, 23 and *Met.* A, 10 : 992b26-33. One result of this paper will be to suggest that the main sponsor of the doctrine that "all things can be proved," combatted in *Post. Anal.* I, 3 and again in the series of four chapters leading to I, 23, was Menaechmus (contrast Ross's comment to 72b5-6). References to *Post. Anal.* given hereafter in text, after "*A. Pst.*" The language of the rejection in I, 3 is harsh : reciprocal demonstration is "frivolous and impossible" (κενόν τε καὶ ἀδύνατον : 73a18-19); it corresponds in tone to the harsh remark in I, 22 about the effort to defend reciprocal predication by claiming that predicates, as Forms, may have other things said of them : such a deployment of Forms makes them "sound without sense" (τερετίσματα : 83a33). Aristotle and Menaechmus are likely to have had close contact at the Academy : Eudoxus taught them both, and if Stobaeus (*Ecl.* ii, 31, 115) has the right attribution of the remark about "no royal road to geometry," they both were teachers of Alexander.

[7] F. Kliem, "Menaichmos," Pauly-Wissowa *RE*, XV, 700. Much of the interpretation offered here stands independently of the case made for this material's being a fragment rather than just a testimonium. But the connections to Philip (section III) are loosened somewhat unless one accepts (as Morrow does not) my conclusion that the bulk of the report gives a genuine fragment. See below, n. 9.

rectilinear figure are equal to four right angles we can prove the number of right angles to which the interior angles are equal, and vice versa. This sort of element is like a lemma. But in another sense, "element" means a simpler property into which a compound can be analyzed. In this sense not everything can be called an element of anything, but only the more primary members of an argument leading to a conclusion, as postulates are elements of theorems. (Proclus, Morrow trans., p. 60, edited.)[8]

In the course of giving the quotation, Proclus intrudes at least one piece of illustrative material, which I have left in brackets, but the bulk of it is clearly signalled in the text (by the ὡς φησὶν formula) as deserving quotation marks. Proclus might be quoting Menaechmus' own words even in the example, the first being element of second, fourth of fifth, but it would not have been Euclid's work, since Euclid flourished a long generation later than Menaechmus. It will be argued below that the example about the exterior-interior angles of figures is likely to be integral to the fragment. Whether the remarks that bring in the technical terms "lemma" and "postulate" are original can be left an open question here; it is a question of some interest for the history of those particular technical terms, which are otherwise not attested so early, but it need not be settled for the purposes of the present argument.

Several things about the fragment show its connection with topics of the day at the Academy. The λέγεται διχῶς τὸ X formula, whose importance for interpreting the mid-fourth century Academy has been developed by G. E. L. Owen, and recently christened "the technical instrument of *Many Senses*" by Gilbert Ryle, strikes the eye at once.[9]

---

[8] I have inserted the square brackets, taken out a bracketed phrase Morrow inserted, and translated the γάρ in the sentence immediately following my brackets more literally. The Greek is as follows : τὸ στοιχεῖον λέγεται διχῶς, ὡς φησὶν ὁ Μέναιχμος. καὶ γὰρ τὸ κατασκευάζον ἐστὶ τοῦ κατασκευαζομένου στοιχεῖον, ὡς τὸ πρῶτον παρ' Εὐκλείδῃ τοῦ δευτέρου, καὶ τοῦ πέμπτου τὸ τέταρτον. οὕτω δὲ καὶ ἀλλήλων εἶναι πολλὰ στοιχεῖα ῥηθήσεται. κατασκευάζεται γὰρ ἐξ ἀλλήλων. δείκνυται γὰρ καὶ ἐκ τοῦ τέτρασιν ὀρθαῖς εἶναι ἴσας τὰς ἔξω τῶν εὐθυγράμμων γωνίας τὸ πλῆθος τῶν ἐντὸς ὀρθαῖς ἴσων καὶ ἀνάπαλιν ἐκ τούτου ἐκεῖνο. καὶ ἔοικεν λήμματι τὸ τοιοῦτο στοιχεῖον. ἄλλως δὲ λέγεται στοιχεῖον, εἰς ὃ ἁπλούστερον ὑπάρχον διαιρεῖται τὸ σύνθετον. οὕτως δὲ οὐ πᾶν ἔτι ῥηθήσεται παντὸς στοιχεῖον, ἀλλὰ τὰ ἀρχοειδέστερα τῶν ἐν ἀποτελέσματος λόγῳ τεταγμένων, ὥσπερ τὰ αἰτήματα στοιχεῖα τῶν θεωρημάτων.

[9] Even if it be questioned (see above, n. 7) *how much* of Proclus' report gives us uncontaminated material from Menaechmus, it is fair to insist on the opening line anyway, since the wording "element is said in two ways, as Menaechmus says" is the standard way of putting the material, at least that immediately adjacent to the "as So-and-So says," in quotation-marks. G. E. L. Owen has explored the move in argument involved

The particular X in question here is also a crucial one, "element," or "letter" and the complexes constructed out of them. The bearing is clear: Menaechmus is taking a position on the Academic topic of "simples and complexes," or "letters and syllables" in Plato's later theory of knowable things, of knowledge, and of language.[10] Aristotle is willing to concede some variety in the meanings of "element," as for example in the "lexicon" book of the *Metaphysics* (Delta, 3), where the geometer's meaning is laid out alongside the grammarian's and the physicist's. Within the geometer's sense (proof-parts), however, he makes no allowance for a further refinement of the sort Menaechmus is calling for. Indeed, in another context where he is disputing with some Anaxagoreans about physical elements, he pronounces dogmatically that elements *must invariably* be taken to be indivisible and finite in number: "this is the kind of thing that everyone in every context means by 'element'" (*De Caelo* 302a18-19).[11] What our fragment says of geometrical "element," namely that there is a sense in which it is permissive of divisibility into others of the same form, at once opposes Aristotle's assertion here[12] and appears comfortable about the (seemingly awkward) consequences of the "dream" in Plato's *Theaetetus*.

in saying διχῶς (or πολλαχῶς) λέγεται in "Logic and Metaphysics in Some Earlier Works of Aristotle," in *Aristotle and Plato in the Mid-Fourth Century*, ed. I. Düring and G. E. L. Owen (Göteborg, 1960), 163-190, and also in his "Aristotle on the Snares of Ontology," in *New Essays on Plato and Aristotle*, ed. R. Bambrough (New York, 1965), 69-95. See further G. Ryle, "Dialectic in the Academy," in *Aristotle on Dialectic : The "Topics,"* ed. G. E. L. Owen (Oxford, 1968), especially 74. It will be seen below that I hesitate between "many senses" and "many meanings" to render this tricky phrase. Aristotle may well have hesitated too. See now J. Barnes, "Homonymy in Aristotle and Speusippus," *Classical Quarterly*, n. s., 21 (1971), 65-80.

[10] Ryle called attention to this topic in his pair of essays in *Mind* (1939), "Plato's *Parmenides*," now reprinted in *Studies in Plato's Metaphysics*, ed. R. E. Allen (New York, 1965), 97-147. See further Ryle, "Letters and Syllables in Plato," *Philosophical Review* 69 (1960), 431-451; D. Gallop, "Plato and the Alphabet," *ibid*. 72 (1963), 364-376; Morrow (above, n. 5); and Myles Burnyeat, "The Simple and the Complex in the *Theaetetus*," an unpublished paper read to the Princeton Colloquium in Ancient Philosophy, December, 1970.

[11] τοιοῦτον γὰρ τι τὸ στοιχεῖον ἅπαντες καὶ ἐν ἅπασι βούλονται λέγειν. The neo-Anaxagoreans, who would have infinitely many of the same form (elements within elements) "don't know what 'element' means" (*De Caelo* 302b 14-15).

[12] The speculation comes readily to mind that Menaechmus was among those Anaxagoreans under lively attack here: his teacher Eudoxus is regularly connected with Anaxagoras and in particular with speculations about 'homoiomeries' in Aristotle's reports (cf. Alexander on *Met*. A, 8 : 989a19ff. and Syrianus on M, 5 : 1079b15).

The impasse which Plato puts the dream theory into can be sketched thus : it is futile to define the key factor in knowledge as "account" (logos) in the sense of something providing a "resolution into simples (elements)," since what are we then to say of the elements themselves ? Either they are further resolvable, in which case they have lost their privileged status as "firsts"; or they are not, in which case one cannot say strictly that they are themselves *known*. Aristotle pretty clearly wanted to take the dilemma by the nearer horn : granted, simples (indemonstrables) will not be known in the same way as compounds, yet there is a sense in which they can be said to be known. Aristotle distinguishes demonstrative from intuitive knowing to arrive at his own answer to the dilemma.[13] Menaechmus just as clearly answers the other way : there exist demonstrations which resolve *to and fro* between statements A and B.[14] Therefore, in these cases at least, we have reciprocal demonstration, and "all are elements of all";[15] thus no propositions in this group need be held indemonstrable, nor indeed will it even make sense to look for indemonstrables there. Neither demonstration nor the knowledge defined by it will need, or have, absolute firsts (*pace* Aristotle) when dealing with this kind of element.

These two answers to Plato's dilemma present a certain surface similarity : it looks as if conceding two senses (or meanings) to "element," as Menaechmus does, may not differ essentially from conceding two senses (or meanings) to "knowing." For the definition under debate says essentially : to give an argument (*logos*) is just to demonstrate from simples. And the two refinements may be put in a parallel. Aristotle's variation says : to give an argument (anyhow where this is possible) is just to demonstrate from simples. And Menaechmus' :

---

[13] Prof. Michael Rohr has called my attention to the possibility that Aristotle does not intend to allow two senses of "know" in *A. Pst.* but rather one, recursively defined.

[14] Two important signs of logical sophistication show up in this passage in *A. Pst.* (1) letters are used to stand for whole statements, not for terms, and (2) the argument proceeds by *substituting* one statement letter for another. Thus, by both (1) and (2) Aristotle shows himself in some respects up with the Stoics. I owe this observation also to Michael Rohr.

[15] The second part of the fragment, which says of the asymmetrical case that "no longer" is everything an element of any other, implies that in the first case the "all-in-all" *was* the case. Quite possibly all that is meant by the provability of "all things" is all the members of a given series, deductively arranged (thus the τῶν ἐν ἀποτελέσματος λόγῳ τεταγμένων will be taken to modify both consequences, not just that from the second sense of element). But even where Menaechmus concedes an asymmetrical arrangement, the *relative* form of his expressions suggests that he will not concede the necessity of any element in this sense's being indemonstrable. See below, n. 20.

to give an argument (anyhow relative to a given context) is just to demonstrate from other elements. Further, when he is combatting the doctrine of reciprocal proof, Aristotle is willing to consider the plan of allowing a double meaning to demonstration, to allow for the difference between items prior *to us* and those prior *simply*. Could we not then eliminate the difference between the two views entirely by reformulating Aristotle's this way : what is primary (or an element) relatively to us is not an element absolutely, so that in one sense (neglecting this relativity) we may say that an argument may be said to proceed *from* simple or *toward* simple indifferently, while in another sense (recalling the relativity), the order of prior and posterior must be fixed ? But we must recall how Aristotle understands priority "relatively to us." This order is fixed by reference to sense-familiarity. But clearly this will be no help in arranging the series of statements which *the geometer*, in his purely mathematical capacity anyway, is working with. Nor is the case improved if one resorts to the standard of *Met.* Z, 1035b4ff, which makes those things prior geometrically which are parts of the definition of another. Even if this applied neatly to the case of whole statements, the crucial question would be left open : What besides the requirements of the elementizer determines the order of simplicity in definition ? Aristotle calls some attention to this very embarrassment when he is setting up a specimen demonstration that B belongs to C because of A. A and B must not be convertible with each other, or what will entitle us to say that B belongs to C because of A any more than A to C because of B ? (*A. Pst.* II, 17 : 99a36-37). The quite different view of Menaechmus is that, in some interesting mathematical cases (and conceivably in all) it is the *symmetrical* pattern, not the asymmetrical one with its fixed prior-posterior order, that turns up. Given, as we often are in mathematics, this and that convertible properties of something, it is as reasonable to call for a demonstration of *that*'s inherence in it from *this* as *vice versa*. Nor will any amount of conjuring with orders such as "simpler/more complex," "essential/accidental," "causal/symptomatic" help to make one proof look more basic than the other. These asymmetries will only be "induced" upon the mathematical series from some independent asymmetrically ordered series, and the mathematician will rightly be able to insist that, independently of those (say epistemological or metaphysical) orders, the native *mathematical* order he is handling is symmetrical. Thus neither proof will have the advantage over the other from the point of view of "giving the mathematical account," or clinching a bit of knowledge.

An asymmetrical order, fixed in an absolute beginning, or absolute element, may have a certain appeal to pure reason and to the philosopher; but symmetrical deductive orders are what practitioners of the elementizing art often meet up with. And in the case of analysis-synthesis arguments, very important to the problem-solving technique in mathematics, these reasoners even *search out* such orders. This latter will be discussed further in section III below.

II

It is time now to get down to cases, such as triangles and polygons, and their properties. The example of the interior angle sum of a triangle, a perennial favorite among philosophers, was already shopworn at the Academy: is the "two right angles" property essential just to triangles among rectilinear figures? Aristotle takes it as a paradigm case of an essential property (*A. Pst.* I, 4), the property belonging to the triangle *as triangle*. The Menaechmus fragment uses a theorem which is a generalization of this to make the opposite point: since interior-angle properties can be proved from exterior-angle properties and *vice-versa*, there is no way of telling which belongs to the figure because of which.

Nothing forces us to treat the mathematical example, about the exterior and interior angles of a rectilinear figure, as an intrusion into our fragment rather than an integral part of it; to the contrary, several things argue for attributing it to our early Academic mathematician himself. No anachronism is involved in supposing Menaechmus familiar with it, since Aristotle is familiar with the proposition also. He refers to it twice in *A. Pst.* (I,24 : 85b37-86a3, and II, 17 : 99a18-21) and to its special cases dealing with the square and the triangle (*ibid.*; *cf.* I,4 : 73b33-74a3). Moreover Aristotle regularly connects the example with the same philosophical issues: those of essential (convertible) predication, and of proving that a property belongs to a certain subject "first" in the order of universality. Having an exterior angle sum equal to four right angles is *not* essential to triangles, still less to isosceles triangles, although it is necessarily true of both. The point is that the property belongs to triangles only *inter alia*, and it can be shown to be true of triangles because it is true of rectilinear figures in general. Thus the whole genus, rectilinear figure, is the first in the series triangle, square ...to which the property belongs *convertibly*. Thus neither the theorem itself nor the issue it raised about proof is of more recent vintage than the *Posterior Analytics*.

But could Proclus be grafting onto Menaechmus' remark an illustration which he got from Aristotle? Is the example otherwise attested at the Academy? Yes, the case of the triangle is indeed attested, and from a mathematician listed in that special set of early Academicians around Plato : Philip (of Opus).[16] Proclus relays a remark of his via Heron the engineer (Proclus 305f) about a theorem concerning interior angles of a triangle. Philip said that it was inappropriate to speak of a triangle's interior angles as if they were a function of its exterior angle, without adding that, strictly speaking, a triangle has no exterior angle. Quite possibly Proclus is reformulating Philip's objection when he here, and later at 384.9, uses the language of essential predication which is to become canonized in *A. Pst.* : one ought not argue in terms of the inessential feature of exterior angles when proving properties that belong to this figure *universally and* qua *triangle*. Philip's words, as relayed by Proclus, are πάντως, ᾗ τρίγωνόν ἐστιν. (Proc. 305.25).[17] Does Proclus, in relaying this, reformulate it? The possibility cannot be excluded. But again the issues themselves, with or without the canonical formulation, can be shown to have been already alive at the Academy, and among the very mathematicians associated with Menaechmus. In an independent report, Proclus speaks of mathematicians including "those around Menaechmus" giving their attention to conversion ἀντιστροφή, and to primary and essential predication τὸ πρώτως ὑπάρχον καὶ τὸ ᾗ αὐτὸ λαμβάνεται : Proc. 254.2-3). Thus we have a reliable report that, in whatever language they expressed it, mathematicians contemporary with and before Aristotle raised the question about properties belonging primarily, universally and essentially to figures, notably the triangle.[18] And they had also drawn con-

---

[16] As often happens (see K. R. Popper, "The Nature of Philosophical Problems and their Roots in Science," now reprinted in my *Plato's Meno* [New York, 1971]), the philosophical problem of ultimate elements in deduction has roots in some actual scientific work.

[17] Proclus elaborates Philip's objection (Proc. 378) and takes issue with Euclid's own version of the whole series of theorems, including the famous one about the interior-angle sum, following from this theorem. Some further discussion of these technical points appears in my review of the Morrow translation (*Archiv für Geschichte der Philosophie* 55 [1973], 82-86). It suffices for the present study to show that a special form of the theorem Menaechmus cites was argued about at the early Academy, and by mathematicians themselves as well as by Aristotle.

[18] Aristotle rehearses an actual proof of the "interior-angle sum" property in *Met.* Θ, 9 : 1051a24-26 which is very likely not the same form of argument as is now in Euclid. Ross, following Cook Wilson, only gets conformity between Aristotle and Euclid at the cost of taking the expression "dividing the figure" to refer to dividing the plane

clusions (not necessarily the same conclusions) from these considerations for proof and deductive order. Since the theorem appearing in Proclus' report is closely related to the one objected to by Philip, and the point Menaechmus makes about it amounts to exactly the denial of Philip's objection, we may make the likely inference that his example comes from Proclus' source, that is, from Menaechmus himself.

Menaechmus' non-essentialist view then comes to this: since one can prove the interior-angle property from the exterior-angle property just as well as *vice versa*, and both properties attach to the rectilinear figure as such (and with commensurate universality, or "first"), one may conclude that neither property is more "essential" than the other. So far as we permit the reciprocal demonstration to be the test, the two properties are levelled: neither turns out to be "simpler" or "more principiform" [$ἀρχοειδέστερον$ (see above, n. 8)] than the other, thus neither is the letter to the other's syllable. Nor do those Academicians who try to impose strict ("essentialist") order do a service to essences. For what certifies the essentiality of a property in a figure except that it be convertible with it, i.e. convertible with its definition? Yet it is this very convertibility which opens the way to the allegedly "frivolous and impossible" thing, reciprocal demonstration.

Since Menaechmus' suggestions about deduction are formed around the concept "element," as were Plato's related ones about knowing in the "dream" passage of *Theaetetus*, we might look for "element" in *A. Pst.*, anticipating that it would lead back to this same debate. The term occurs in exactly one passage (84b21,22,26), in exactly the right sense (proof-part), and making just the anticipated polemical point, aimed at (cf. 84a30-33) just the opponents we have independently identified with Menaechmus. Aristotle is returning, late in Book I, to score some more hits against "those who" hold that *all* things are capable of proof. This time, however, he is able first to block reciprocal proof by some polemical assumptions,[19] and then to reason from his

---

outside the figure into two infinite halves. See his comment *ad loc*. But there is no mention of extending a side of the triangle to produce an exterior angle, and if "dividing the figure" is given its most natural sense, we have a proof which conforms exactly to the *alternate* Proclus supplies to Euclid's, so as to meet Philip's objection (Proc. 378). Thus Proclus is taking sides with Philip and Aristotle against proofs which proceed via non-necessary features. Euclid seems not to have thought it made any difference; and in Menaechmus' discussion of deductive order a rationale for Euclid's position is provided: when properties are *reciprocally* provable, there is no basis for calling one more essential than the other.

[19] Ross's efforts to sort out the arguments of I, 22, an "excessively difficult" chapter,

own theory of proof and its "elements," "principles" or "simples."[20] All ultimate premises in a deductive argument are *stoicheia*, Aristotle says, but this means only those premises which are universal and "immediate." Thus if, in inserting middles between A and B to prove that one belongs to the other, one finds that he does *not* arrive at middle steps which are themselves incapable of further resolution, this is "no longer a proof, but rather the road up to the principles" (84b22-24). This is to say that, unless the "elements" on which one's proof is built are themselves incapable of division or resolution into things yet simpler, one's argument is not in strictness a proof, but rather a regress *toward* primary things. This remark, however, only asserts the thing at issue; it says that, on Aristotle's theory of proof, no argument will count as strictly a proof unless its premises are wholly exempt from further demonstration, whether in the form of reciprocal demonstration or of reducing the "more nearly a principle" to the "*still* more nearly a principle." To take the example of inserting a series of middles: given the effort to mediate A's belonging to B, and success so far as some C,D,E, unless one grants Aristotle his theory of intuitive propositions (simple and unmiddled), he is free to leave room in his theory of demonstration either for finding still further steps between, say, All A is E and All A is B, or for reducing one so-called element to another. The fact that, at a given stage of research, the "elements" look to the noetic eye like absolute unities ("atoms": 84b15) ought not prejudice further inquiry. Menaechmus might well concede that, before any reasoner sets down a proposition amongst

---

require him to interpret in what sense the arguments at the beginning are λογικῶς ("dialectical"). It seems a weak explanation he offers (573) that the principles Aristotle draws on cover too much ground (all reasoning, not just demonstrative science). Perhaps better is to understand Aristotle as making assumptions he knows are forced, in that they do not convince the opponents he is combatting (thus he says "if we must legislate, let this kind [reciprocal] of speaking ... not be proper predication" : cf. 83a14-17, and compare the "let it be hypothesized" of a18). The main object of this "fiat" form of establishing his premises would be a kind of forceable overturning of those Menaechmian opponents who appear to call forth harsh measures in argument (the angry language about Forms occurs nearby : they are "empty talk," 83a33).

[20] The terms of Aristotle's rejoinder show up the fundamental disagreement : they systematically eliminate the inflections on the key terms of our fragment. "Simpler" and "more primary" are answered by "simple" and "primary." Menaechmus' diairesis into the ἁπλούστερον is answered by Aristotle's divisions into the ἁπλοῦν (b35,37); and as against Menaechmus' relative term ἀρχοειδέστερον Aristotle answers with ἀρχή (I, 23, *passim*). Whether these "elements" are just relatively first or first without qualification is exactly the point at issue.

the "archai" of his book of *Elements* he should have cast about for ways of demonstrating it; but, so far from insisting that one of the "archoeidestera" at or near the beginning of his own series of arguments is intrinsically and in the nature of things indemonstrable (or, equivalently, appealing to the Nous of 84a1), Menaechmus' theory of demonstrative "elements" invites others to resolve *any* given reasoner's archai further.[21]

III

Quite independently of this fragment, we have evidence from a commentary on Archimedes[22] that Menaechmus discovered an ingenious solution to the problem of doubling the cube, using sections of the cone. The method of proof he employs is exactly the one for which the present fragment gives a theoretical justification: the combined method of analysis and synthesis. He begins by supposing the problem about the cube solved, i.e. by taking as elemental and known just what he will later compound out of other elements. Thus he starts with the assumption that certain equations (or proportions) are satisfied; this is in turn analyzed into a form soluble as a "solid locus" problem. What is "solid" about this stage of the argument is not the fact that cones are involved but rather the fact that the problem all began with the

---

[21] Apollonius is scolded by Proclus for trying to prove Euclid's first Axiom, about equals to the same thing being equal (Proclus, 194 f.). Proclus calls down the joint authority of Aristotle, the Stoics and "the geometers" on him; they all rightly saw that indemonstrables differ from demonstrables "in their nature" ($\tau\hat{\eta}$ $\phi\acute{\upsilon}\sigma\epsilon\iota$). Clearly Menaechmus must be left out of "the geometers," since his authority works in the opposite direction. Moreover Apollonius need not have been attempting anything foolish when he argued for that 'element'; he can have wanted to resolve equality into some kind of sameness, a very general sort of congruence. Thus his argument shows that first and third equal things are equal to each other by showing that they "occupy the same place" as the second. If he were wanting only to show the corollary for line segments (cf. Morrow 153, n. 27), he would have used the feminine gender of the articles, which he does not. Possibly, then, the emphasis in his phrase "same place" should fall not (where Proclus in his refutation puts it) on the "place," but on the "same."

[22] *Archimedis Opera cum commentariis Eutocii*, ed. I. Heiberg (Leipzig, 1881), III, 92-98. Thomas L. Heath's overenthusiastic interpretation is given in his *A History of Greek Mathematics* (Oxford, 1921), I, 251-255, II, 110-116. Kliem's cautious statement goes just far enough: "Accordingly Menaechmus must have known those of the properties of these two conic sections expressed in the above [2 quadratic] equations," *RE*, "Menaichmos."

cube.[23] Finally then he turns the deductive series around : beginning from conic sections, he synthesizes the answer to the cube problem. The fact that it is some portion of a cone which provides the solution is in a sense incidental to his result. Thus it may have been overenthusiastic of Heath to herald this work as the "discovery of conic sections"; since by itself it tells little about the essences of such sections, even while it makes ingenious use of their properties ("symptoms" as Apollonius was to call them). Menaechmus' solution, then, as we have it, only puts to work certain metrical *properties* of the conics in answering the difficult question of how to insert two mean proportionals, and this is still rather remote from the essence of the cone, or even of all its characteristic sections.

These latter essences were put into elegant order some three generations after Menaechmus, by Apollonius, who studied the cone as essentially the figure determining certain sections, these sections in turn as having properties, both primary (archika) and derivative (symbainonta). Apollonius, in his Preface, distinguishes primary properties (τὰ ἀρχικὰ συμπτώματα) from those connected with diameters, axes and asymptotes, the latter being derivative (τὰ συμβαίνοντα); he treats of the former in Book I, the latter in Book II. Tangent properties are in between : they are proved from other primary (causal) properties, but in Book I. Since he classifies these properties with other *Archika*, however, it is natural to suppose that he saw (what is true) that (a) the definitions of the sections, (b) their metrical (or "locus") properties and (c) their tangent properties, are *all* convertible with one another, thus reciprocally demonstrable.[24]

But Apollonius is later than Menaechmus, and not in communication with the Academy immediately around Plato. Can we find traces of his kind of skill with analysis-synthesis in a mathematician early enough to have influenced Plato and Menaechmus ? A fragment of Archytas, fr. 2, concerning *the three means*, can be interpreted, with some help from Iamblichus, to imply that he too, friend of Plato and teacher of Eudoxus, knew and used this powerful instrument. Without going

---

[23] See Heath, *History*, II, 116 : the title of a pre-Euclidean work on conics preserves just the symmetrical feature here under discussion : "Solid loci, continuous with Conics" (*ibid.*, 117-118).

[24] Cf. *A. Pst.* II, 17 : 99a16-23, where it is allowed that sometimes the subject, its causal features and the things caused by them all "follow" one another. An essential predicate is as much a subject as it is anything else; an archikon symptoma is as much an archē as it is anything else.

into details,[25] the following summary interpretation may be offered here. In fr. 2 Archytas gives definitions of each of the three standard means, and calls attention to the fact that the third mean, which used to be called "subcontrary," is now called "harmonic" on account of its usefulness in music theory. Iamblichus is reviewing the same stretch of early Pythagorean history, that from Hippasus to Archytas, when he brings up the view of "some" that what is "subcontrary" about the third mean is its relation to *both* of the other means (arithmetic, geometric), *taken jointly*. Just who the τινες are whose view Iamblichus is presenting, and refuting, is not at once clear; but from the context it appears that he is ascribing it to some of those elder Pythagoreans. In any case, there *is* a way of defining the third mean as the subcontrary to both of the others, in particular by constructing it according to an argument which Pappus reviews in detail.[26] The importance of all this for the present discussion is this: the two definitions of the third mean can be—and by very easy steps in accordance with early Pythagorean number theory—*reciprocally demonstrated*. Thus if one takes its subcontrariety to the other two as the third mean's definition or essence, the harmonic feature can be demonstrated as its property; and conversely, beginning with a definition in terms of harmonic theory, one can deduce its subcontrariety as a property. Thus, if this interpretation of fr. 2 can be made out, Archytas will be calling attention, a generation before Menaechmus, to a case of a pair of essences with just the right relation to found an analysis-synthesis upon. The matter of deciding which is the more "elementary" essence, which has demonstrative priority over the other, will be seen to depend upon which application one was then making of the thing, on which sort of problem

---

[25] See now my article, "Pappus, Plato and the Harmonic Mean," *Phronesis* 20 (1975), 173-184. See also notes 26-27 for the general outlines of the argument.

[26] Pappus also leaves it in doubt whose construction he is rehearsing (*Collectio*, ed. F. Hultsch, III [Berlin, 1878], p. 68, line 17-p. 70, line 8; cf. I. Thomas, ed., *Greek Mathematics*, II [Cambridge, Mass. and London : Loeb Library, 1941], 568-571). But a particular point in the construction is left entirely unexplainable, and in fact Pappus complains about this, unless the "archaic," pre-Archytan, definition (the one Archytas' own fragment calls older) of the third mean is appealed to. Thus the mistake which Pappus' argument calls attention to is removed by, and only by, supposing that is the "subcontrary," not the "harmonic" form of the third mean at issue. "Subcontrariety" as a relation of one magnitude (line) to two others taken jointly can be fully explained from the technical meaning of it in Apollonius' *Conics*, I, 5, which makes exactly the right sense of it to conform to the discussion in Iamblichus.

one was intending to solve with it. The "harmonic" application is certainly a serious one, and influential on Plato, as his scale-building in *Timaeus* confirms. But its "subcontrary" feature is of great usefulness in number theory, especially in producing a numerical algorithm for generating values approximately equal to pure quadratic surds.[27] The general point about the nature of this mean is that either property, its harmonic or its subcontrary one, is "essential" enough to serve as its definition. Putting the point in terms of Menaechmus' idea of "element," the definitions of this third mean, in music theory and in number theory, are *elements of each other*.

The more general point about method is this : a mathematician may begin with a locus problem and end in properties of certain conic sections, or begin with conics and end with loci; similarly he may begin with a scale-building problem and end in properties of certain infinite series, or carry out his deduction in the reverse direction. If he expresses indifference on the question, which is the *truly* primary or elementary end of his deductive series, this will be because he allows this question to be decided by his current research interests : at which end do I find the *problem* I am currently interested in *solving*?[28] To the onlooker (an Aristotle or a Plato, say) who is trying to keep track of at least the method involved, if not the details of the result, it may present a confusing appearance. Aristotle's complaint that, to look for analyses of one's "elements" is to substitute a "way up to principles" for a proof *from* principles is after all only a repetition of the complaint he used to hear Plato make when "he used to put this puzzle and inquire, are you proceeding *from* or *toward* the principles ?"[29] It will have been

---

[27] Various scholars, notably O. Toeplitz, have argued that this aspect of Archytas' work is reflected in the mathematical passage of *Epinomis*. This work is reviewed, and extended to the *Theaetetus*, esp. 154-155, in my article in *Journal of the History of Philosophy* 7 (1969), 359-379.

[28] A separate report in Proclus' same commentary (Proc. 77.15-78.13) goes into a controversy at the Early Academy between "those around" Menaechmus and "those around" Speusippus over exactly this matter : Menaechmus held the controversial position that the mathematician is *only* a problem solver, never a mere contemplative knower. Thus *all* his proofs are strictly speaking problems, none are *theorems*. In a separate paper read at the Institute for Greek Philosophy and Science, Colorado Springs, July 1970, I interpreted that other report, and connected it to Eudoxus' "exhaustions" and reactions to these at the Early Academy.

[29] *Nicomachean Ethics* I, 4 : 1095a32; Ross, in his note to *A. Pst.* 84b23-24, argues from the language in which the *Ethics* passage is put, that this fussing by Plato, endorsed by Aristotle, must have been part of the "oral teaching." Not remote, if so, from the

an unsettling reply, but not surprising from what we know of the practice and the theory of deduction of Menaechmus, if he returned "what I take as principles, or elements, varies from argument to argument, and, in the case of the method of analysis/synthesis, even within the same argument. Thus in these cases the direction you speak of becomes a matter of indifference."[30]

The disturbing consequences of this doctrine are clearly not local to mathematics, for it is acknowledged on all hands that mathematical proof is in some sense a model for all proof, and that, leaving aside the details, knowing and proving have a good deal to do with each other. But proving, and also setting up standards of strictness in proof, seem to have been occupying Academics around Plato, including mathematicians. And this mathematical doctrine, according to which all things are in principle provable, even the so-called elements themselves, would have seemed all the more powerful in that important pieces of mathematical practice harmonized so nicely with it. It is not likely to be merely coincidental, then, that the Academy at which Aristotle levels his complaints in *Metaphysics* A, 9, that "mathematics has become philosophy" (992a32f.) and that some are dreaming unrealistically about the existence of a science of Elements of All Things—no coincidence that this is the same Academy where Menaechmus and his fellow researchers in mathematics were at work. In any case, the doctrine of proof expressed in Menaechmus' statement about the two meanings of "element" would be full of consequences for Aristotle's own opposing doctrine of proof, whose ultimate *stoicheia* are *archai* in the strictest sense, entirely incapable of any proof, including proof *inter se*. The perversity of Menaechmus' position, from Aristotle's point of view, is well signalled by the way Aristotle joins it to that of extreme skepticism; while the latter ends by denying the possibility of know-

---

Academic environment in which Menaechmus will have been doing his analyses-syntheses. Plato and Eudoxus are independently reported to have done such things together (Proclus : 67.6-8).

[30] Bertrand Russell, at a time in his career when he was not yet committed to logicism or its indemonstrable "elements," said something strongly reminiscent of Menaechmus' remark (*Principia Mathematica*, "Preface," V) : "In mathematics, the greatest degree of self-evidence is usually not to be found quite at the beginning, but at some later point; hence the early deductions, until they reach this point, give reasons rather for believing the premises because true consequences follow from them, than for believing the consequences because they follow from the premises." Menaechmus and Apollonius have their modern counterparts, then, in Leibniz and Russell.

ledge, the former only saves the possibility of knowledge at the cost of making it trivial. Either way, the result is flatly inconsistent with the claims Aristotle is making for intuitively revealed indemonstrables. One strand, then, of the Academic debate over this fundamental issue about deduction leads us back to the pre-Aristotelian mathematician Menaechmus, who was in direct contact with Plato and Eudoxus at the Early Academy.

Brooklyn College, The City University of New York

PADUAN ARISTOTELIANISM RECONSIDERED

JOHN H. RANDALL, JR.

The tradition of Aristotelian philosophizing in the universities of Northern Italy, with its major seats at Padua and Bologna, which in the sixteenth century flowered in so impressive a contribution to the Renaissance thinking of the Italians, has been carefully examined by able scholars for over a century. Since the days of Francesco Fiorentino, and in the next generation Pietro Ragnisco, down to, in our century, Erminio Troilo and Bruno Nardi, to say nothing of Ernst Cassirer and Paul Kristeller,[1] there has never been lacking a small band anxious to study the sustained and cumulative thinking that could lead to a Pomponazzi and a Zabarella. This scholarship has itself been cumulative. At times, as with Nardi and Kristeller, it has added new documents to our knowledge. At times, as with Cassirer, it has found new relations between Paduan Aristotelianism and the diverse other currents of Renaissance thought, especially between its strong methodological interest and the various strands that were converging to form the complex of ideas we know as modern science. Given this growing

---

[1] Cf. F. Fiorentino, *Pietro Pomponazzi : studi storici su la scuola bolognese e padovana del secolo XVI* ... (Florence, 1869); P. Ragnisco, "La polemica tra Francesco Piccolomini e Giacomo Zabarella nella Università di Padova," *Atti del Reale Istituto Veneto di Scienze, Lettere et Arti*, 6th ser., IV (Venice, 1886), 1217-52; idem, "Una polemica di logica nell' Università di Padova nelle scuole di B. Petrella e di G. Zabarella," *ibid.*, 463-502; idem, "Pietro Pomponazzi e Giacomo Zabarella nella questione dell'anima," *ibid.*, V (Venice, 1887), 949-96; idem, "Da Giacomo Zabarella a Claudio Berigardo ossia prima e dopo Galileo nell'Università di Padova," *ibid.*, 7th ser., V (Venice, 1894), 474-518; E. Troilo, *Averroismo e aristotelismo padovano* (Padua, 1939); B. Nardi, *Saggi sull'aristotelismo padovano dal secolo XIV al XVI* (Florence, 1958); E. Cassirer, *Das Erkenntnisproblem in der Philosophie und Wissenschaft der neueren Zeit* (Berlin, 1906-20), vol. I, bk. I, ch. 2; P. O. Kristeller, "Paduan Averroism and Alexandrism in the Light of Recent Studies," in *Aristotelismo padovano e filosofia aristotelica*, Atti del XII Congresso Internazionale di Filosofia, IX (Florence, 1960), 147-55; idem, *La tradizione aristotelica nel Rinascimento* (Padua, 1962); idem, "Renaissance Aristotelianism," *Greek, Roman and Byzantine Studies* 6 (1965), 157-74; idem, "Two Unpublished Questions on the Soul of Pietro Pomponazzi," *Medievalia et Humanistica* 8 (1955), 76-101.

body of understanding, it seems appropriate today to undertake a reconsideration of Paduan Aristotelianism.

In this cumulative and exanding enterprise I have myself played a modest part. At Columbia University there has been since 1904 an Aristotelian tradition. My own teacher, Frederick J. E. Woodbridge, made central his interest in Aristotle and in Aristotelian thought. Hence when I found opportunity to spend a year in Italy in 1933-34, I naturally decided to do some work on the Italian Aristotelians. I was already thinking of writing about the career of philosophy in modern times, and here was a gap that needed filling in. I had also grown dissatisfied with the labors of Pierre Duhem on the medieval background of modern thought and science. Duhem was a Frenchman, and he liked the Masters of Paris of the fourteenth century. He was also a good Catholic: he disliked the predominant anticlericalism of the Italian universities of the late Middle Ages and Renaissance. So I suspected that modern science even before Galileo owed more to the Italians than he was willing to grant. I therefore set about attempting to explore that strand of thinking that runs through the Italian universities from Pietro d'Abano to Galileo, when it unites with many other strands of thought to create our modern physical science.

After much thought, study, and writing over the years, I found myself called on twenty-five years later to formulate briefly some preliminary conclusions about what I had been learning. At the Twelfth International Congress of Philosophy, held in Venice and Padua in 1958, I was privileged to read, in the Sala dei Giganti, a short paper on "Padua Aristotelianism : An Appraisal,"[2] in which I tried to indicate the place, as I then saw it, of the Paduan tradition of Aristotelianism among the other intellectual currents of sixteenth-century Italy, philosophical and scientific. Three major themes stand out. There is, first, the Paduan achievement in philosophical anthropology, in the doctrine of man, in which the Aristotelians achieved a naturalistic humanism that led on to Spinoza, in contrast to the supernaturalistic humanism of the Florentine Platonists. There is, secondly, the Paduan background of the sixteenth-century nature philosophies of Telesio and Campanella, so much more critical and responsible than those of the extravagant "nature enthusiasts" north of the Alps. And there is, thirdly, the fact that it was in the Italian universities that there

---

[2] *Aristotelismo padovano e filosofia aristotelica*, Atti del XII Congresso Internazionale di Filosofia, IX (Florence, 1960), 199-206.

came together the several intellectual strands that led up to the genius of Galileo at the end of the century. Galileo himself taught at Padua from 1592 to 1610, when the Grand Duke of Tuscany stole him away from the protection of Venice. In his thinking Galileo incorporated the results of the generations of Paduan discussions of scientific method, stretching back to Pietro d'Abano at the start of the fourteenth century, in his combination of *il metodo risolutivo* with *il metodo compositivo*.

In the philosophical anthropology of the Paduan Aristotelians, in their doctrine of human nature, after careful reconsideration, I should like to emphasize strongly once more the fundamental continuity of their thinking. There is still the prevalent myth that with Pomponazzi the followers of another Greek commentator, Alexander of Aphrodisias, revolted against the older followers of The Commentator, Averroes. But the essence of the Paduan doctrine of man was its combination of a secular and this-wordly conception of the conditions of human existence with an insistence that in its functioning human nature transcends these limitations. Man is a "mean" between the mortal and the eternal. The Paduans were not merely secularists, they believed in a rational science attainable by the human mind. In the act of knowing, man seemed to them to lift himself above the limitations of an animal body and to see What Is with a transparency and a clarity that no merely biological creature has any right to possess.

In the light of this persisting vision of man, both the older Averroistic notion of man and the newer view of Pomponazzi were attempts to explain how a natural being subject to the conditions of mortality could nevertheless rise to a Platonic vision of truth. This fundamental notion of man united the two views far more closely than superficial differences separated them. Thereafter down to Zabarella it is hard to assign thinkers to one or the other position, precisely because it was scarcely necessary to choose between two versions of the same basic conception of human powers. The earlier effort to assign the sixteenth-century thinkers to one or the other position now appears, in the light of what we have found out, to have been misguided.

What runs through all the Paduans is an appreciation of what man can do, of the power of the human mind. Pomponazzi's achievement is to have shown how to state man's uniqueness in purely functional terms, without entanglement in the earlier dubious language of different "substances." In so doing he made it possible for the sixteenth-century Paduans to come close to the functionalism of the Greek Aristotle, and of much present-day philosophizing. After Pomponazzi we encounter a functional Aristotle as the setting for the Aristotelian logical distinctions. We find the *operations* of things given more importance than the statement of their *essences*. This functional emphasis, powerfully supported by the use of Greek texts, marks the end of the older literal-minded "Averroism." It reaches its clearest formulation in Zabarella.

The third theme,[3] the role of Paduan Aristotelianism in the very complicated story of the emergence of modern science, has in the generation since Duhem assumed increasing importance. Much has been done, much suggested, and much criticized.[4] What is the present state of scholarly opinion? I have myself tried my hand elsewhere at this story from time to time.[5]

If the Paduans form a connecting link in the long chain of criticism of Aristotle's physics, the methodology actually taken over by Galileo and his successors is even more clearly the result of their fruitful reconstruction of the Aristotelian logic, fertilized by the discussions on method of the commentators on the medical writers, notably Jacopo da Forli (d. 1413) and Ugo Benzi of Siena (d. 1448). It is possible to trace step by step the gradual elaboration of scientific method from its first beginnings in Pietro d'Abano (d. 1315) to its completed statement in the great logical controversies of Jacopo Zabarella (1533-89), in which it reached the form analogous to that familiar in Galileo.

---

[3] Treatment of the second theme is omitted here because I have treated it fully elsewhere.

[4] Cf. A. Crescini, *Le origine del metodo analitico : il cinquecento* (Udine, 1965); M.A. Del Torre, *Studi su Cesare Cremonini. Cosmologia e logica nel tardo aristotelismo padovano* (Padua, 1968); N. W. Gilbert, *Renaissance Concepts of Method* (New York, 1960), especially chapter 7, "The Italian Aristotelians," 164-79; G. Papuli, *Girolamo Balduino. Ricerche sulla logica della scuola di Padova nel Rinascimento* (Manduria, 1967); A. Poppi, *La dottrina della scienza in Giacomo Zabarella* (Padua, 1972); idem, "P. Pomponazzi tra averroismo e galenismo sul problema del *regressus*,"*Rivista critica di storia della filosofia* 24 (1969), 243-66; W. Risse, *Die Logik der Neuzeit, I : 1500-1640* (Stuttgart and Bad Cannstatt, 1964); idem, "Averroismo e alessandrinismo nella logica del Rinascimento," *Filosofia* 15 (1964), 15-30; C. B. Schmitt, "Experience and Experiment : A Comparison of Zabarella's View with Galileo's in *De Motu*," *Studies in the Renaissance* 16 (1969), 80-138; C. Vasoli, "Problemi e discussioni logiche nel cinquecento italiano," *Annali delle Facoltà di Lettere, Filosofia e Magistero dell' Università di Cagliari* 29 (1961-5), 301-88.

[5] Cf. my *The School of Padua and the Emergence of Modern Science* (Padua, 1961); and my *The Career of Philosophy*, Vol. I, book I, chapters 10-13.

Part of this story I have myself tried to trace; the later sixteenth-century portion is being worked out in detail by one of my former colleagues, Professor William F. Edwards, of Emory University.

My attention was first called to the similarity between the outcome of this long Paduan discussion of method in Zabarella, and Galileo's statements on method, by Ernst Cassirer, who, after outlining Zabarella's conception of method, says: "Alle diese Ausführungen sind von Galileis Methodenlehre, in der wir sie völlig gleichlaufend wiederfinden werden, nur durch einen einzigen Zug getrennt, der allerdings entscheidend ist. Die Rolle, die der Mathematik in der 'beweisenden Induktion' zukommt, wird von Zabarella nirgends begriffen."[6] My own investigations convinced me that Zabarella and the Italians had indeed worked out the fundamental logical concepts of Galileo's method; the crucial step of making the principles and causes exclusively mathematical was taken by Galileo himself. Hence I tried to elaborate on Cassirer's statement of what seemed to me ascertained fact.

In an article of 1944,[7] Cassirer set off Galileo much more sharply from the Paduan tradition, accepting the "results" of my research, but not my "conclusions." Cassirer here argued that Galileo "found the first clear and sharp distinction between 'analysis' and 'synthesis' " in Euclid; that he gave to "the Greek classical method of 'problematical analysis' a new breadth and a new depth" by applying it to a subject to which it had never before been applied, namely, physical thought; and that he borrowed only his terminology—"resolutive" for "analytic" and "compositive" for "synthetic" method—from the Paduans.

More recently, Professor Neal W. Gilbert, one of the very best students of sixteenth-century discussions of methodology, in a note in the *Journal of the History of Philosophy*,[8] carried Cassirer's argument even further, and suggested not only that Galileo's conception of method can be derived completely from the Greek mathematicians, but also that there does not seem to be any reason to suppose that he borrowed even his terminology from the Paduans. This could just as

---

[6] E. Cassirer, *Das Erkenntnisproblem in der Philosophie und Wissenschaft der neueren Zeit*, I (Berlin, 1922), 139.

[7] E. Cassirer, "Galileo's Platonism," in *Studies and Essays in the History of Science and Learning Offered in Homage to George Sarton*, ed. M. F. Ashley Montagu (New York, 1944), 277-297.

[8] N. W. Gilbert, "Galileo and the School of Padua," *Journal of the History of Philosophy* 1 (1963), 223-231.

well have come from "the Greek mathematical works so recently made available to him by Federigo Commandino." Gilbert holds that "The methodology of the Aristotelians relied exclusively on the syllogism," which was for Zabarella, "a loyal Aristotelian," the single instrument of science (a statement that needs some qualification). He adds, "there is no mention of Zabarella in the whole mass of Galileo's writings"; and "no evidence that Galileo ever owned a copy of Zabarella's logic." Much of Gilbert's argument is based on Galileo's well-known dislike of "Aristotelians" and his opposition to Aristotelian thinking.

How do these criticisms stand up today? What is left of Cassirer's original thesis? Cassirer himself was convinced that Galileo was philosophically a Platonist, and that the shift to an exclusively mathematical language was the turning-point in the emergence of modern science from the sixteenth-century discussions. To me, on the other hand, it seems probable that as compared with Kepler or Descartes, Galileo is philosophically an Aristotelian;[9] and important as is the new language of mathematics, it is but one of the several strands that were united to form the new science. Cassirer and I had several most interesting discussions of Galileo's philosophical background during his brief stay at Columbia. Gilbert's position is obviously rather extreme. Both shared in what seems to Edwards and myself an unduly narrow and partisan view of the development of scientific method that does not appear to be justified by the complexity of the historical situation in sixteenth-century Italy.

Here I should like to add on this vexed question that Edwards has been working in just this field; that he has discovered much evidence to support Cassirer's original contention; and, most important of all, that his work bids fair to shed much light on the methodological developments of later sixteenth-century Italian thought. The coming of mathematics was indeed important; but it was not with Galileo, as Gilbert supposes, that it first entered into the Italian discussions of method. I should like to close by reporting some of Edwards' findings.

Edwards holds that both the Cassirer of 1944 and Gilbert seem to have fallen into the same dubious judgment, "that of *separating* the medico-philosophical (or Aristotelian) and the mathematical traditions too completely, and of supposing that what is found in the one must necessarily be absent from the other, or—if not that—at least that the

---

[9] See my *The Career of Philosophy*, Vol. I, book II, ch. 13.

inspiration for Galileo's thought must be found exclusively in the one or the other."[10]

In fact, the earliest of the commentators on the *Ars Parva* of Galen were already debating the question whether the "analysis" of which Galen speaks is the same as the "analysis of the geometers." The concept of "regressive demonstration" developed by the Paduan Aristotelian commentators on the *Ars Medica* and the *Posterior Analytics* was itself at bottom nothing but an attempt to provide the natural sciences with a method that would be equivalent in degree of certitude to the kind of demonstration *simpliciter* Averroes saw in mathematics.[11]

Edwards argues that at least twice before Galileo the mathematical and the philosophical traditions met and merged. In Galileo we have the third and final stage of a merging process that actually began over five centuries earlier, with 'Ali ibn Ridwan (d. 1061), the "Haly" of the Latins. Edwards makes this clear by analyzing in detail first Haly, then Averroes himself, in their methodological thought. He shows how Pietro d'Abano carried this concern with mathematical models to the Italian universities, and how Torrigiano dei Torrigiani (d. 1350) held that geometrical analysis, *doctrina resolutiva*, and demonstration *propter quid* (rather than *quia*) are all equivalent. The problem of the nature of analysis remained a central one in the Paduan tradition of commentary, so that contact with the mathematical sources was never lost, and did not need Galileo to reestablish it.[12]

Edwards concludes: "There was a continuous and ever more sophisticated and penetrating analysis of the problems first posed by Haly, Averroes and the early Latin commentators throughout the fourteenth, fifteenth and sixteenth centuries—problems which had their origin in the attempt to conciliate mathematical, medical (Galenian), and philosophical (Aristotelian) theories of method... The glory of successfully completing it belongs to Galileo..."[13]

"How, then—or *why*—shall we maintain that this whole tradition was unknown to—or despised by—Galileo ? Why must we suppose that he bypassed this rich heritage, and went directly to the Greek

---

[10] W. F. Edwards, "Randall on the Development of Scientific Method in the School of Padua...," in *Naturalism and Historical Understanding : Essays on the Philosophy of John Herman Randall, Jr.*, ed. J. P. Anton (Albany, 1967), 55.

[11] *Ibid.*

[12] *Ibid.*, 56.

[13] *Ibid.*, 65.

mathematicians for his concepts of *metodo risolutivo* and *metodo compositivo*? That a fresh study of these ancient sources enabled him to take the final and most rewarding step in the adaptation of the analysis of the geometers to the subject-matter of the natural sciences need not be denied, but that he did not profit by five centuries of labor by others in the same vineyard seems—in the light both of the record and of what we know of Galileo's wide-ranging and acquisitive mind—too much to be asked to believe."[14]

I judge that the forthcoming study of Edwards will reassure us that Galileo in a very real sense, however much he added to and perfected it, still belonged to the Aristotelian tradition of the Italian universities.

Columbia University

[14] *Ibid.*, 65-66.

NICCOLÒ LEONICENO AND THE ORIGINS OF HUMANIST DISCUSSION OF METHOD

WILLIAM F. EDWARDS

1. Introduction

Niccolò Leoniceno (1428-1524) is one of those Renaissance figures, now largely forgotten, who are interesting for a variety of smallish reasons. He is, for example, one of the foremost of the humanist professors of medicine in Italy in the fifteenth and sixteenth centuries (I am inclined to call them "medical humanists," to distinguish them both from the Aristotelian professors of logic and natural philosophy who exhibited the same tendencies, and also from the humanists themselves). A close study of his activities as a teacher, writer, and translator should therefore give us a clearer notion of the sort of changes wrought in the medical tradition by humanism, and enable us to form a better judgment of whether they were beneficial or harmful. I do not in this essay propose to investigate either the whole extent of Leoniceno's humanism, or the whole range of his activities as a writer and translator,[1] but only the most central of his interests as a student of Galen, namely, the interpretation of the so-called prologue[2] of the *Ars medica*. The *Ars medica* was the work of Galen on which Leoniceno lavished the greater part of his intellectual energy and love, offering not only the first modern (Latin) translation of it, but accompanying the translation with a careful explication of its highly controversial prologue on method. He entitled his work on the prologue of the *Ars* the *De tribus doctrinis ordinatis*, the first edition of which appeared in

---

[1] On Leoniceno, see Neal W. Gilbert, *Renaissance Concepts of Method* (New York, 1960), 102-4; L. Premuda, introduction to the re-edition of Leoniceno's *De Plinii in medicina erroribus* (Milan, 1958); Lynn Thorndike, *A History of Magic and Experimental Science*, IV (New York, 1934), 593-610; Cesare Vasoli, "Problemi e discussioni logiche nel cinquecento italiano," *Annali delle Facoltà di Lettere Filosofia e Magistero dell' Università di Cagliari* 29 (1961-5), 342-6; D. Vitaliani, *Della vita e delle opere di Niccolò Leoniceno vicentino* (Verona, 1892).

[2] That is, the first chapter of the first book of Galen's *Ars medica*, or *Ars parva*.

Venice in 1508,[3] and it is on this work, I think, that Leoniceno's principal claim to be remembered must be based. What he has to say there about method, or about what Galen meant by method (*doctrina ordinata, didaskaliai taxeos echomenai*), had an immediate and profound effect on the tradition of commentary on the *Ars*—a tradition that stretched back in time to 'Ali ibn Ridwan in the eleventh, and 'Ali ibn al-Abbas in the tenth century, and formed one of the chief streams of methodological thought throughout the Middle Ages and the Renaissance. Relying on his excellent knowledge of Greek and his acquaintance with various Greek sources on logic and method unknown to the earlier commentators on the *Ars*, Leoniceno wrenched the prologue of the *Ars* out of the hands of the Averroist-Aristotelians (whose prototype was Pietro d'Abano) and converted it (so to speak) into a platform on method for the medical humanists who followed him. After Leoniceno, the methodological *ménage à trois* of Galen, Aristotle and Averroes, first set up by 'Ali ibn Ridwan, and then sanctified in the Latin tradition by Pietro d'Abano, disintegrated, and henceforward commentators on the prologue of the *Ars* spurned any light they might receive from sources other than the purely Greek ones to which Leoniceno had pointed. More than this: Leoniceno focussed attention on a concept of method which though not unknown to the earlier tradition had certainly not been its primary object of attention, namely, on method as a logical instrument for the *organizing or structuring of a science as a whole*, rather than for the solution of particular problems within a science. It is method in the latter sense we tend to hink of when we use the phrase "scientific method," yet it is a startling fact that neither the humanists nor figures as important in our intellectual history as Galileo, Descartes and Newton seem to have used it always, or even primarily, in this sense. The humanists, particularly north of the Alps, certainly did not. Ramus did not. The primary sense of "method" for them is the one Leoniceno defines in his *De tribus doctrinis ordinatis*, so that if—as I think— he is the modern author of that concept of method he ought to receive a somewhat more important place in the history of philosophy and science than he has so far. In the remainder of this paper I shall attempt to give some substance to this suggestion.

---

[3] *Nicolai Leoniceni in libros Galeni e greca in latinam linguam a se translatos prefatio communis ... Galeni Ars Medicinalis Nicolao Leoniceno interprete que et Ars Parva dicitur ... Eiusdem de tribus doctrinis ordinatis secundum Galeni sententiam opus ...* (Venice, 1508).

2. The Immediate Background of the *De tribus doctrinis ordinatis*

What is *doctrina*? What is *doctrina ordinata*? Above all, what is *doctrina resolutiva*? These are the principal questions which had been asked by the commentators on Galen's *Ars medica* from the beginning of the tradition with 'Ali ibn al-Abbas in the tenth century, and they are the questions asked by Leoniceno in the early sixteenth century in his *De tribus doctrinis ordinatis*. In the first chapter of the first book of the *Ars medica* (the *Ars parva*, as it was generally called by the commentators), Galen says that there are three *doctrinae* which have order, adhere to order, or are ordered.[4] The first of these begins from the idea of an aim, and proceeds by way of resolution. The second proceeds by way of composition, i.e., composition of the things discovered by resolution. The third proceeds by way of dissolution of a definition.[5] These came to be called by the commentators (1) *doctrina resolutiva* (2) *doctrina compositiva* and (3) *doctrina definitiva*. There is no satisfactory English equivalent for the Latin word *doctrina* (Greek: *didaskalia*), because its meaning shifts somewhat in Latin according to the context. The meaning assigned to it by the dictionary is "teaching," "instruction," "science," etc., but none of these meanings, taken by themselves, is satisfactory. The one that comes closest to being satisfactory is "science"—the adjective *doctrinalis*, for example, often has exactly the meaning of our word "scientific"—so that when a commentator speaks of *doctrina ordinata* he means what we should mean if we spoke of a body of knowledge organized or structured according to a scientific principle or method. In fact, one would come very close to the meaning of *doctrina ordinata* by translating it simply as "scientific knowledge" (as opposed to knowledge which has not been cast into what we should recognize as a scientific form).

After the publication of Leoniceno's *De tribus doctrinis ordinatis* in 1508, commentaries on the *Ars medica* proliferated, so that in the sixteenth century we have more than in the preceding three centuries.[6] There were only eight important commentaries before the

---

[4] *Treis eisin hai pasai didaskaliai taxeos echomenai.* Leoniceno translates this as: *Tres sunt omnes doctrinae quae ordini inhaerunt.*

[5] "Prima quidem ex finis notione, quae per resolutionem fit; secunda ex compositione eorum, quae per resolutionem fuerunt inventa; tertia ex definitionis dissolutione, quam nunc instituimus." *Claudii Galeni opera omnia*, ed. C. G. Kühn, I (Leipzig, 1821; repr. Hildesheim, 1964), 305.

[6] Among the sixteenth-century commentaries on the *Ars* I have seen are those by Antonio Cittadino (Faenza, 1523); Giov. Manardi (Rome, 1525); Martinus Acakia (Paris,

appearance of Leoniceno's work. Of these, the commentary of 'Ali ibn al-Abbas—the earliest known in the Latin world—has already been mentioned. It was secondary in importance to that of 'Ali ibn Ridwan (d. 1061), on whose commentary the first of the great Latin commentators, Pietro d'Abano (d. 1315), relied heavily. Pietro, of course, did not write a commentary on the *Ars*, but a larger and more comprehensive work called the *Conciliator differentiarum philosophorum et praecipue medicorum*,[7] in which the problem of the nature of the Galenian *doctrinae ordinatae* as well as many other medical and natural philosophical problems are discussed. Contemporary with Pietro was a second great commentator, Taddeo degli Alderotti (d. 1303),[8] of whose theory of *doctrina ordinata* Pietro takes account, though he does not mention Taddeo by name. Whether Taddeo's commentary was known to Leoniceno, I am not certain. Leoniceno does not cite it, but perhaps his reason is that it does not take any positions significantly different from those already taken by Pietro and 'Ali ibn Ridwan on what Leoniceno considers to be the main questions about *doctrina ordinata*.

Torrigiano dei Torrigiani (d. circa 1350), the first great fourteenth-century commentator on the *Ars*, does take positions significantly different from those of Pietro, and receives a good deal of attention from Leoniceno in the *De tribus doctrinis ordinatis*. Torrigiano is cited by so many different names that there is a tendency to be confused about who he is, or even whether he is one person.[9] He is most often called *Plusquam Commentator*, this designation presumably having been attached to him because he overstepped the boundaries a mere commentator should observe. He is also known as *Monacus* (or *Monachus*), *Drusianus*, *Trusianus*, *Turisanus*, etc. Torrigiano takes Pietro d'Abano's interpretation of the prologue of the *Ars* as his chief object of criticism, disagreeing with him mainly on how *doctrina resolutiva* is to be understood. Pietro had identified *doctrina resolutiva*

1543); Jérémie de Dryvere (Lyons, 1547); Giov. Batt. Montano (Venice, 1554); Giulio Delphini (Venice, 1557); Nicolas Biese (Antwerp, 1560); Theodor Zwinger (Basel, 1561); Franc. de Valles (Alcala de Henares. 1567); Oddo degli Oddi (Venice, 1574); Ioh. Phil. Ingrassia (Venice, 1574); and Salvo Sclano (Venice, 1597).

[7] *Conciliator differentiarum philosophorum et precipue medicorum clarissimi viri Petri de Abano patavini* ... (Mantua, 1472). Hain *1; Goff P-431.

[8] *Thaddei Florentini ... in C. Galeni Micratechnen commentarii* ... (Naples, 1522).

[9] Angelo Crescini, *Le origine del metodo analitico* (Udine, 1965), 140, mistakenly identifies *Plusquam Commentator* with Averroes.

with the Aristotelian *demonstratio quia* (*a posteriori* demonstration, from effect to cause), whereas Torrigiano identifies it with the Aristotelian *demonstratio propter quid* (*a priori* demonstration, from cause to effect), his reason being that *doctrina resolutiva* is used in the science which is most truly *doctrinalis*, namely, mathematics (or geometry); and mathematicians do not use *a posteriori* demonstration.[10] But in order to defend this position, Torrigiano was forced to work out what can only be described as an odd theory of *resolutio*, or *doctrina resolutiva*, and none of the later commentators followed him in it. Leoniceno, as we shall see, believed Torrigiano was right in relating the Galenian *doctrina resolutiva* to mathematical or geometrical resolution, but wrong in holding (with Pietro and 'Ali) that it is a form of demonstration.

There are only three other fourteenth- and fifteenth-century commentators whose commentaries on the *Ars* were known and generally cited in the sixteenth century: Gentile da Foligno (d. 1348), Jacopo da Forli (d. 1413), and Ugo Benzi (d. 1439), each of whom wrote formal commentaries on the *Ars*. One of them—Gentile—added a series of *quaestiones* to his commentary, and treats the most controversial issues there rather than in the body of his commentary.

We have, then, eight important commentaries on the *Ars* before Leoniceno's own interpretation appeared, of which two—those of Pietro and Torrigiano— are crucial from the point of view of meaning of the Galenian *doctrina ordinata* (especially the meaning of the kind of *doctrina ordinata* called *resolutiva*). 'Ali ibn Ridwan's commentary is important as having set the general lines for interpretation of the prologue among the Latin commentators, and—in Leoniceno's view— the commentary of Ugo Benzi is also of considerable interest, because Ugo alone among the Latin commentators experienced doubts about whether the accepted interpretation of the Galenian *doctrina ordinata* was the correct one.[11] The accepted interpretation (beginning with

---

[10] I have discussed the differing interpretations of *doctrina resolutiva* offered by Pietro and Torrigiano in an essay entitled "Randall on the Development of Scientific Method in the School of Padua—a Continuing Re-appraisal," in *Naturalism and Historical Understanding—Essays on the Philosophy of John Herman Randall, Jr.*, ed. J. P. Anton (Albany, 1967), 53-68.

[11] *Expositio Ugonis Senensis super libros Tegni Galieni* (Venice : O. Scotus, 1498; H C (Add) 9015; Goff H-543), f. 2v, col. 1. For Leoniceno's discussion of Ugo's doubts, see the *De tribus doctrinis ordinatis*, ed. cit., f. 18v, col. 1.

'Ali ibn Ridwan, and rejected only by Torrigiano) was that Galen's *doctrina resolutiva* is to be identified with *a posteriori* demonstration as defined in the tradition of commentary on the *Posterior Analytics*, and his *doctrina compositiva* with the *a priori* demonstration defined in the same tradition. This leaves the Galenian *doctrina definitiva* without a correspondent in the Aristotelian theory of demonstration, and most of the commentators before Leoniceno had solved this problem by according it a less central place in their methodological theories. The central place goes to *doctrina resolutiva*, to which *doctrina compositiva* can be nicely related if it is identified with demonstration *propter quid*. That is to say, it can be fitted neatly into the Aristotelian theory of the demonstrative regress presented by all the commentators on the *Ars* before Leoniceno, the first phase of which was held to consist of the discovery (from sensible effects) of the causes of an effect (demonstration *quia*), and the second phase of a demonstration of the effect through its causes (demonstration *propter quid*).[12]

But while the earlier commentators all agreed on this initial step in the interpretation of the prologue of the *Ars*, namely, on the necessity of relating the Galenian *doctrina ordinata* to the Aristotelian forms of demonstration, finding it unsatisfactory only to the extent that it offered no means of interpreting the kind of *doctrina ordinata* Galen called definitional, problems arose at what might be called the next step, namely, how to relate the Galenian *doctrinae ordinatae* interpreted thus in Aristotelian terms to the resolution and composition (analysis and synthesis) of the "geometers." It was around this problem that the most intense controversy centered among the early commentators. I do not think any of them achieved a satisfactory solution to it. 'Ali ibn Ridwan, having first equated the Galenian *doctrina resolutiva* to the Aristotelian *demonstration quia* (from effect to cause), goes on to say that it is the same as the resolution of "the geometers and the founders of the sciences."[13] But other than giving a general description of reso-

---

[12] The concept of a demonstrative regress in the method of the natural sciences did not develop independently in the commentary on the prologue of the *Ars medica*. The initial suggestions (and suggestions only) for it are in Averroes' commentary on the *Posterior Analytics*, and Walter Burleigh's commentary on the *Physics*. In Pietro d'Abano's *Conciliator*, on the other hand, it appears in a rather rudimentary form.

[13] "Et geometrae quidem et authores scientiarum sciunt hunc modum doctrinae; et Aristoteles quidem iam posuit ipsum in *Analyticis*, id est, in libro *Posteriorum*." *Hali filii Rodbon in Parvam Galeni Artem commentatio* (Venice, 1557), f. 175^v.

lution that does in fact resemble the geometrical (or mathematical) resolution described by Euclid, 'Ali does not elaborate, and we are left in doubt as to what exactly constitutes *doctrina resolutiva* for Galen. When he gets around to giving a more concrete example (drawn from medicine), the resemblance to mathematical resolution remains, but the resemblance to the Aristotelian demonstration *quia* is considerably reduced. The reason for this is that the example he gives relates to the organization or constitution of the whole art (or science) of medicine, not to the establishment of one of its theorems or propositions by what is ordinarily called scientific proof. But the Aristotelian demonstration *quia* can hardly be held to relate to a task such as this, since according to the Aristotelians, demonstration *quia* is useful only for the discovery of the principles on which demonstration *propter quid*, that is, genuinely scientific demonstration, can be based. It would not, and could not, be used exclusively throughout a whole science. Even if it were, there would be no assurance that the science would have the kind of *overall* order that Galen, and even 'Ali himself, seem to be discussing. Furthermore, the resulting science could not even be called "science" in the proper sense of the term, since none of its theorems would have been established by truly scientific proofs.

Though 'Ali seems unconscious of these difficulties, Pietro d'Abano recognizes and faces them, however weak his solution to them may be. Pietro criticizes 'Ali for identifying the Galenian *doctrina resolutiva* with the analysis of the geometers. If the Galenian *doctrina resolutiva* is to be identified with the Aristotelian demonstration *quia*, Pietro argues, then it cannot also be identified with the analysis of the geometers, because mathematicians do not use demonstration *quia*, but only demonstration *propter quid*. *Doctrina resolutiva* is known to the mathematicians, Pietro admits, since it is connected with demonstration *propter quid* (which according to both 'Ali and Pietro is the same as the Galenian *doctrina compositiva*), but they do not make any use of it.[14] Pietro thus, in effect, retains the Aristotelian theory of demonstration in its integrity, but loses the possibility of connecting either it or the Galenian theory of *doctrina ordinata* with the mathematical concepts of analysis and synthesis. Or perhaps what I should say is that he can retain the connection between the Aristotelian and the mathematical theory of demonstration only if the latter is interpreted in a certain way, namely, as relating to what we should consider to be

---

[14] *Conciliator* (Mantua, 1472), f. 16-16ᵛ.

scientific proofs of individual theorems and propositions, rather than to the structuring of a whole science. But he does not choose to do this, and prefers instead simply to sever the connection with mathematics.

Torrigiano dei Torrigiani, faced with the facts that (1) mathematicians do not use demonstration *quia*, only demonstration *propter quid*, but (2) do use *doctrina resolutiva*, reached a conclusion exactly opposite to Pietro's: *doctrina resolutiva* and demonstration *propter quid* must be identical.[15] Torrigiano, as noted earlier, agreed with Pietro only in taking *doctrina resolutiva* to be a form of demonstration. If it is the same as demonstration *propter quid*, then it must be a movement from cause to effect, and it is not easy to find a way of saying that such a movement is "resolutive." In resolution, or analysis, one ordinarily assumes that some complex whole is reduced to its elements, or principles. But in what sense can a movement from a cause to an effect be conceived to be such an analytic process? A movement from an effect to its cause or causes can easily be conceived to be such a process, since one is, in a sense, breaking a complex whole (an effect) down into its elements or principles (causes). But certainly a *cause* is not complex in relation to its *effect*, and this would seem to be what Torrigiano's interpretation of *doctrina resolutiva* demands. He rises to the challenge (rather unsuccessfully, I think) by claiming that the resolution which takes place in *doctrina resolutiva* or demonstration *propter quid* is from the *remote* to the *immediate* cause. Formally, this is perhaps a satisfactory solution, since the remote cause of an effect may possibly be considered a complex whole in relation to its immediate cause, or causes. But would such a process really bear any resemblance to the procedure of the geometer, who assumes what he wishes to prove, and then reasons back from this until he reaches something already known (some self-evident truth, some proposition already proved)? It would not seem to. The most that can be said for Torrigiano, probably, is that he refocussed the attention of the Latin commentators on the possibility of a connection between mathematical analysis and the analysis that might be employed in medicine or natural philosophy, even though he did not successfully elucidate it. When Leoniceno did finally succeed in tying the two together, the connection was not made in the way 'Ali and Torrigiano thought it could be—that is, neither demonstration *quia* nor demonstration *propter quid* turned out to be reducible to mathematical analysis. Rather, there is an identity between

---

[15] *Plus quam commentum in Parvam Galeni Artem Turisani...* (Venice, 1557), f. 3.

doctrina resolutiva and mathematical analysis only if the former is understood to relate to the constitution and organization of a whole science. The end (*finis*) of the science being constituted by "resolutive" method will then function in the same way that the *assumptum* does in the analysis of the geometers.

3. Leoniceno's Argument

The preceding discussion, brief though it is, of the main directions and results of the earlier tradition of commentary on the prologue of the *Ars*, will give some notion of the situation that existed when Leoniceno published his *De tribus doctrinis ordinatis* in 1508. It cannot be said that the earlier commentators had to any significant extent explicated the Galenian *doctrina resolutiva*. They had merely reduced it—rather crudely—to one of the Aristotelian forms of demonstration. Nor can it be said that they had in any way illuminated the concept of mathematical resolution, or brought it into significant relation with either the Aristotelian theory of demonstration or the Galenian theory of *doctrina ordinata*. They had indeed—in conjunction with the commentators on the *Posterior Analytics* and the *Physics*—perfected the Aristotelian theory of demonstration, chiefly by working out the concept of a demonstrative regress in the method of medicine and the natural sciences, but, as Leoniceno saw, this was not at all relevant to what Galen had to say in the prologue of the *Ars*.

The advantage that Leoniceno enjoyed over the earlier commentators was his superlative command of the Greek language, and— perhaps even more important—his wide knowledge of the whole body of Greek literature on logic and method. Contrary to Leoniceno's repeated assurances, it may well be that Galen was not a "Platonist."[16] Believing that he was, Leoniceno argued that it is not permissible to interpret his thought by means of concepts drawn from Aristotle and the Aristotelians. Yet even this exaggerated view of Leoniceno may be excused if it helped him to free Galen from the grip of a by then somewhat stagnant tradition of methodological thought, and to turn what he (Galen) had to say on method to a new and creative use. There would be Aristotelians, like Zabarella, capable of benefitting from

---

[16] Galen is variously described by Leoniceno in the *De tribus doctrinis ordinatis* as "Platonicus" (*ed. cit.*, f. 19), "summus imitator" of Plato (f. 23ᵛ), and "homo Platonicus" (*ibid.*).

Leoniceno's new reading of Galen, without at the same time discarding what was of value in the tradition Leoniceno himself rather completely rejected. And let us make no mistake about this: Leoniceno's thought is not a more elegant and competent continuation of the medical tradition of commentary on the prologue of the *Ars medica* (hence of the medical tradition of speculation on method), but a radical break with it. After him, the *medici* were all Leonicenans. No longer would they deign to employ concepts drawn from traditions so "impure" and "barbarous" as either the pre-Leonicenan commentary on the *Ars*, or the commentaries on Aristotle's *Posterior Analytics* and *Physics*.

The argument of the *De tribus doctrinis ordinatis* is basically twofold. In the first part, Leoniceno combs the writings of those whom he calls the "ancient philosophers" for anything they had to say on the subject of the *doctrinae principales*—we should probably say, on the "principal methods"—and especially for what they had to say on the subject of resolution. In the second part, he presents a new concept of *doctrina resolutiva*, which he asserts to be Galen's; defends it against the concept presented by the earlier commentators; and in general works out his theory of *doctrina ordinata*, including the notions of *doctrina compositiva* and *doctrina definitiva*, the special functions or uses of each, and where they are employed by Galen and other writers. Much of the second part of the work is devoted to a highly effective polemic against 'Ali, Pietro d'Abano, Averroes (the commentator by whom Pietro was most influenced), and Torrigiano dei Torrigiani. The result of the argument taken as a whole is a clear distinction between what Leoniceno designates as *modus doctrinalis* (or *modus doctrinae*), and *ordo doctrinae* (or *ordo docendi*). The former, as we shall see, is the kind of method one uses to solve a particular problem or to answer a particular question within a science, and the latter is the kind of method one uses to organize or constitute a *whole* science. Leoniceno finds, or at least mentions, no earlier source for this distinction, probably because it would have been necessary to draw it from a "contaminated" source, namely, from Averroes and the Averroist commentators on Aristotle, all of whom make a clear distinction between *via* and *ordo doctrinae*. Their distinction is exactly the same as Leoniceno's, and it seems probable that it was in them that he first encountered it. However, the Averroist commentators—at least until after Leoniceno's work—seldom did more than mention *ordo doctrinae* at the beginning of their commentaries, where they explained what "order" the work they were about to interpret follows, and what method of demonstration (*via doctrinae*) it employs. In their logical thought, too, while they developed the theory of demonstration (*via doctrinae*) to a high degree, they neglected to develop the theory of order (*ordo doctrinae*) to the same degree. Leoniceno remedies this deficiency.

There was also in the earlier commentators on the *Ars* a customary distinction between "universal" and "particular" order,[17] which seems to be the same as the distinction Leoniceno labors to establish and clarify in the *De tribus doctrinis ordinatis*. But, having explained it, the earlier commentators do not make anything of it, or seem to forget about it, and immediately revert to their notion that the Galenian *doctrinae ordinatae* are forms of demonstration (hence, one supposes, of "particular" order). In any case, Leoniceno is certainly right when he charges the earlier commentators with not having distinguished clearly enough between *modus* and *ordo doctrinae*. Perhaps the truth is that they distinguished them, but held that Galen in the prologue of the *Ars* was talking about the former, not the latter.

Leoniceno, relying principally on Ammonius, Philoponus, John of Damascus, Alcinous, and Proclus, distinguishes four *modi doctrinales*: definition, demonstration, division, and resolution, stressing the fact that Platonists and Aristotelians alike agree in defining these four, and in holding that the fourth—resolution—is opposed to the other three. The "Platonists" are Alcinous and Proclus, Alcinous being described as a *philosophus Platonicus*, and Proclus as "a distinguished philosopher who especially cultivated the doctrines of Plato." The "Aristotelians" are Ammonius, Philoponus, John of Damascus, and Alexander of Aphrodisias, the last being examined not for what he has to say on the four *modi doctrinales*—as the most authentic among the "Aristotelians" Leoniceno names, Alexander does not of course recognize all four as *doctrinales*—but for what he has to say on the subject of resolution in general. Ammonius, Philoponus, John of Damascus, and Alcinous are also consulted on this latter point, that is, for what they have to say on the subject of resolution in general, as well as for what they have to say about it as a *modus doctrinalis* included among the customary four. Geminus is cited for his position that geometrical resolution is a means of discovering the principles of demonstration (*demonstrationis inventio*). The conclusion of this

---

[17] This distinction appears from Pietro d'Abano on, and is found in one of its clearest expressions in Iacopo da Forli's *Quaestiones ... super libros Techni Galeni* (Venice, 1546), f. 83ᵛ.

discussion, which it is unnecessary to report in detail, is that both Platonists and Aristotelians have almost exactly the same things to say on what the *modi doctrinales* and on what resolution are—Leoniceno seems to feel that such unanimity among philosophers of opposing loyalties strengthens his case greatly—and that all of them oppose *doctrina resolutiva* to *doctrina demonstrativa* (as well as to the other two methods, definitional and divisional). The earlier commentators on the *Ars* therefore cannot be correct in holding that *doctrina resolutiva* is a kind of demonstration.[18]

It might be noted that in denying that resolution is a form of demonstration, Leoniceno automatically precludes the possibility of a demonstrative regress in the method of the natural sciences, which was one of the most valuable notions developed in the Aristotelian tradition of commentary on the *Posterior Analytics* and *Physics*, and which was incorporated by the earlier commentators on the *Ars* in their interpretation of the Galenian resolutive and compositive methods. Just as the *Aristotelian* commentators combined demonstration *quia* and *propter quid* to obtain a complete method for use in areas like natural science, in which the *principia* of demonstration are not naturally known to us, so the earlier commentators on the *Ars* combined resolutive and compositive methods, as they understood them, to obtain a similar method for medicine. Medicine, too, deals with effects the causes of which are not naturally known to us (because they are hidden and insensible, like the causes of natural effects). Leoniceno retains the notion of resolution as a means of discovering the *principia* of demonstration, and it seems odd that he balked at the idea that—as a *modus doctrinalis*—it could be identical with the Aristotelian demonstration *quia*. Such an admission would not have damaged his case, so long as he was able to prevent the identification of the *Galenian* resolutive method with demonstration *quia* (or demonstration *propter quid*, as Torrigiano wished to maintain). The truth seems to be, however, that he was not particularly concerned with method as *modus doctrinalis*—that is, as the kind of method by which particular propositions are scientifically proved—and that he went to the trouble of carefully investigating the "ancient philosophers" on this aspect of method only for the purpose of showing how wrong the earlier commentators had been about the prologue, and to clear the way for his own interpretation. He may not have intended to substitute the four *modi doctri-*

---

[18] For this discussion, see the *De tribus doctrinis ordinatis*, ff. 13-16ᵛ.

nales of the Greeks for the theory of demonstration already fully worked out in the Aristotelian tradition. But the commentators on the *Ars* who followed him understood that to have been his intention, and themselves replaced the older Aristotelian theory with the one offered by Leoniceno. After Leoniceno's *De tribus doctrinis ordinatis*, we hear nothing more from the commentators on the *Ars* about the complementary use of resolutive and compositive methods to solve problems in the science of medicine, that is, about a "regress" in the method of medical science.

Nor is it clear the four *modi doctrinales* Leoniceno draws from the Greek writers on method are really all, in his mind, what we should call scientific methods for solution of particular problems in the sciences. That they are all methods a scientist will wish to use is clear, since it is often necessary to define, to divide, to demonstrate, and to "resolve" (in the sense Leoniceno wishes to assign to that term). But only one of them is demonstration or scientific proof, so that what we have from Leoniceno is perhaps better described as a general methodology for handling the particular tasks or problems a scientist confronts—a methodology which incorporates a theory of scientific proof, but which cannot as a whole be described as such a theory. Zabarella, to whom Leoniceno's thought was well known, and who in effect was its most important continuator in the late sixteenth century, rejected both definition and division as *modi doctrinales*, retaining only the two Leoniceno called resolution and demonstration.[19] But in Zabarella, the distinction Leoniceno sought to establish in the *De tribus doctrinis ordinatis* between (1) method as a way of handling special or partial aspects of a science, and (2) method as a way of constituting or organizing an entire science, is much clearer and more precise, and perhaps also slightly altered. As far as method in the second sense is concerned, Zabarella understands it in the same way Leoniceno does, even though the Galenian (Leonicenan) *doctrina definitiva* is rejected as a method for ordering an entire science, and new criteria are introduced for *doctrina resolutiva* (*ordo resolutivus*, as Zabarella calls it).[20] But method in the first sense is again brought

---

[19] See Zabarella's *De methodis*, in the *Opera logica* (Venice, 1578), book III, especially chs. 7, 9, and 11.

[20] See the *De methodis*, book II, ch. 4, for Zabarella's arguments against the concept of a definitional order; and the *De doctrinae ordine apologia* (Padua, 1584) for his criteria for order. *Ordo doctrinae*, according to Zabarella, is determined by either (1) the way in which we learn more easily (*facilius*), or (2) the way in which we acquire a more perfect knowledge (*melius*).

back to the meaning the earlier commentators on the *Ars*, like Pietro and Torrigiano, wished it to have, that is, it is treated as a theory of scientific demonstration.

4. The Galenian *doctrina resolutiva* according to Leoniceno's Interpretation

Turning now to the second part of Leoniceno's argument, it may be noted that the chief task here is to explicate the meaning of Galen's statement that *doctrina resolutiva* begins from an idea of an end (*a notione finis*), and proceeds by way of resolution. What did Galen mean by *notio finis*, or (more simply) *finis*? Pietro d'Abano had said that by *finis* Galen meant *effectus*, so that *doctrina resolutiva* (as we have seen) would be the resolution of an effect into its causes, or what was commonly called by the Aristotelians *demonstratio quia*. The other reading of *finis* to which Leoniceno strongly objected was that of Torrigiano dei Torrigiani. Torrigiano read it as *causa ultima*, that is, as the last cause to which we come in the process of resolving the remote cause (or causes) into the immediate one.[21] This is a very strained and improbable reading. Pietro's reading, on the other hand, is a more plausible one, and in addition had the backing of several centuries of commentary on the *Ars medica*.

The argument Leoniceno develops against Pietro's reading of Galen's *finis* serves also to invalidate Torrigiano's reading. Briefly, it is this. The *finis* from which Galen says resolutive method begins is not something that has already come about (like Pietro's "effect," or Torrigiano's "ultimate cause," both of which are conceived to be already existent), but something which is only intellectually conceived—a *finis mente conceptus*, as Leoniceno puts it—which we propose to realize, but have not yet actually realized.[22] He draws much support from Aristotle on this point, citing him in the *Ethics*, III, 3, the *Metaphysics*, VII, 7, and the *Physics*, II, 9.[23] In these passages, Aristotle describes the analytic process of thought followed by the physician and the carpenter in the discovery of the means to their ends (health for the

---

[21] I admit that I am a little doubtful that this is really what Torrigiano means, though it is the interpretation given by Iacopo da Forli in his *Quaestiones*, f. 84, col. 1. For Torrigiano's own presentation of his position, see his commentary on the *Ars*, f. 3-3ᵛ.

[22] *De tribus doctrinis ordinatis*, f. 17, col. 1.

[23] 1112b15-25; 1032b5-15; 200a15-25.

physician, a house for the carpenter), and in two of them compares it to geometrical or mathematical analysis. What is described, in other words, is an analysis or resolution beginning from an idea of an end, and Leoniceno takes this to be the kind of resolution Galen was talking about in the prologue of the *Ars*. The passage from the *Metaphysics* had been interpreted by Averroes in the past tense, so to speak—as explaining not how health is produced (*fiat*), but how it was produced (*facta sit*).[24] Averroes thus treats the end (health) as something already in existence—as an effect of causes, which are discovered by the analytic process of thought Aristotle describes there—not as something to be brought about. Leoniceno believes that if it had not been for this misinterpretation by Averroes, Pietro could not have read Galen's *finis* as *effectus*, and then gone on to explain the Galenian resolution which begins from an idea of an end as being demonstration *quia*.

What Leoniceno is saying, then, is that the earlier commentators like Pietro took the wrong *kind* of analysis (or resolution) from Aristotle to explain the Galenian *doctrina resolutiva*. Rather than taking the Aristotelian demonstration *quia* (which Leoniceno does not deny is a kind of analysis of an effect into its causes), they ought to have taken the analysis described in the above-mentioned passages from the *Ethics*, *Metaphysics*, and *Physics*. Further, when the Galenian analysis is so understood, there is no problem about relating it to geometrical or mathematical analysis. The two are the same, since the *assumptum* of the geometer functions in his analytic process of thought in exactly the same way that the *finis* of the physician functions in his—with this difference, of course, that the geometer reasons back till he comes to something known, while the physician reasons back till he comes to something he can produce himself. Neither begins his analytic process of thought from something already in existence, which makes their analysis quite different from that of the natural philosopher, who begins with existing effects. Leoniceno seems to have no reason for stressing the similarity of the Galenian *doctrina resolutiva* to mathematical resolution other than a desire to show that the earlier commentators did not understand the latter (nor the former, either, for that matter). Or, if he has a reason, he does not mention it. I think we must assume that he had none, even though—in the light of later developments—this particular way of connecting the resolutive method of the

---

[24] *De tribus doctrinis ordinatis*, f. 16, col. 1. For Averroes' interpretation, see *Aristotelis opera cum Averrois commentariis* (Frankfurt am Main, 1962), VIII, ff. 173-174.

medico-philosophical tradition with mathematical analysis is highly interesting. It seems, for example, that the *metodo risolutivo* of which Galileo speaks in one place, as well as the method he says in another place was taught to him by "my mathematicians," are the same as the resolutive method Leoniceno works out in the *De tribus doctrinis ordinatis*. I shall return to this point later.

It is necessary for Leoniceno to carry his argument one step further if the concept of resolutive method he is striving towards is to emerge clearly. Galen makes several other statements about *doctrina resolutiva* which cannot be understood by the interpretation offered by Pietro and the earlier commentators. Galen says, for example, that no one before him (among writers on medicine) has employed the kind of method which begins from a notion of an end—i.e., resolutive method—and that it is the method by which *all* the arts are constituted.[25] The first part of this statement—that none of the *medici* before him have employed resolutive method—would be silly (and false) if we understand his *doctrina resolutiva* to be demonstration *quia*, since that kind of demonstration is known to, and used by, everyone. Besides, it is plain that demonstration *quia* was used by medical writers preceding Galen, along with all the other *modi doctrinales* which Leoniceno investigated and defined in the first part of his work. So it is easy to show that by the interpretation of *doctrina resolutiva* given by the earlier commentators, this statement of Galen's would be foolish.[26] The second part of Galen's statement also would not make sense, namely, the assertion that all the arts are constituted by *doctrina resolutiva*, or (more accurately) by that kind of *doctrina* which arises from a notion of an end. One reason for this has already been given: demonstration *quia* cannot be, and in fact never has been, *exclusively* used throughout a science. But it is also evident, Leoniceno thinks, that the end from which Galen holds resolutive method begins is a particular *kind* of end only, not just *any* end. It is the end of a *whole* science or art—as e.g. health is the end of the science of medicine—so that when Galen says all the arts are constituted by the method which arises *a notione finis*, we can understand him to be talking about nothing except a method by which an entire art or science is constituted or organized, and the

---

[25] Galen, *Ars medica*, book I, ch. 1; Kühn edition, vol. I, p. 305.

[26] For this discussion, see the *De tribus doctrinis ordinatis*, f. 20^v, col. 2; and f. 22^v, col. 1.

end from which this kind of method begins can be none other than that for the sake of which the art or science is constituted.[27]

Leoniceno's term for method in this sense, as distinguished from method in the sense of *modus doctrinalis*, is *ordo doctrinae*. *Doctrina* is not ordered—i.e., we do not have *a* science—unless the resolutive or one of the other two methods of ordering a science (compositive and definitional) are followed in the teaching or writing of it. So long as we are not talking about the original constitution or organization of a science, it does not matter which order is followed. If we are, then only resolutive order can be followed, because it is the only one by which an art or a science can be constituted.[28] This is the unique merit of resolutive order in relation to the other two. *All* the arts are originally constituted by the use of resolutive method. Leoniceno adds that even after everything that must go into a science has been discovered (by resolutive method), resolutive method is still better for the teaching or writing of the *practical* sciences,[29] but does not suggest any reason why this should be so. One imagines it is because the aim of these sciences is action or production, and the most intelligible way to teach them is to begin by proposing their ends, and then to show what are the means to those ends. In the speculative sciences, on the other hand, the aim is knowledge merely, and we have knowledge of something only when we understand it through its causes. This would suggest the use of compositive (or perhaps definitional) method. Zabarella later made this use of resolutive method (in the sense of order) in the practical sciences, and compositive method in the speculative sciences, almost canonical.[30] He dropped the concept of a definitional method, and Leoniceno—if he were not such an ardent Galenist—might have done so too. Leoniceno himself does not find that the definitional order has any peculiar merit of its own—not even the one claimed for it by the earlier commentators, namely, that it is an especially compendious way, more conducive to memory, for teaching an art or a science. The resolutive way is equally compendious, he argues.[31] He retains definitional order apparently largely because Galen mentions it.

---

[27] *Ibid.*, f. 17-17ᵛ.
[28] *Ibid.*, f. 21, col. 2.
[29] *Ibid.*, f. 20, col. 1.
[30] *De methodis*, book II, ch. 9. He has already argued (ch. 7) that the speculative sciences cannot be treated in any order other than the compositive.
[31] *De tribus doctrinis ordinatis*, f. 20ᵛ, col. 1.

5. Impact of the *De tribus doctrinis ordinatis*

It is evident from what has been said that Leoniceno's principal contribution to the intellectual tradition in which he stood is the notion of method as a means of casting an entire body of knowledge into a scientific form. When this task was conceived as a purely pedagogical one—i.e., when *ordo doctrinae* was taken to be primarily the concern of the professor in his lecture hall, or of the same professor as he prepared to present an already completed science in written form—it could (and did) become a rather shallow concept (even though pedagogy—or at least good pedagogy—is not an undertaking lacking in importance). But it is obvious that Leoniceno's new concept of method offered the possibility of much more important and creative application. Understood in its full implications, it offered a plan for the reconstruction of any science, or even the construction of a new one. It does not seem surprising, therefore, that before much time had elapsed, the manner of the presentation of a science ceased to be the *commentary* on an appropriate work of Galen, of Aristotle, etc., and became instead the independent treatise. These independent works were at first unoriginal, and amounted to little more than a recasting of the materials contained in works that had been university texts for centuries. But the opportunity to reconceive and reconstruct a science (such as natural philosophy) *de novo* was there, and began to be exploited towards the end of the sixteenth century. Peter Ramus' complaint that the works of Aristotle were—not, as is so often supposed, false—but badly structured,[32] described a problem to which Leoniceno had already provided a solution. There is a method—or rather, there are methods—by means of which any body of knowledge may be reduced to a rational, easily intelligible, and scientific form. And there is one method—the "resolutive," soon to be called the "analytic"—by means of which any desired body of knowledge may be first constituted and organized in a scientific form.

It is hard to resist the temptation to see the foreshadowing not only of Ramus but also of Descartes in the theory of method presented by Leoniceno in the *De tribus doctrinis ordinatis*, but too much research into later developments in the tradition of commentary on the *Ars medica* (especially in Northern Europe) remains to be done to make it

---

[32] See the excellent discussion of this point by Walter J. Ong in his *Ramus : Method and the Decay of the Dialogue* (Cambridge, Mass., 1958), 45-7.

anything but wise to resist the temptation. What can be taken for certain here is the considerable influence of this medical humanist in the tradition of methodological speculation centered around the prologue of the *Ars medica*. He altered the direction and import of over 200 years of interpretation of the prologue, severing it from the logical and methodological thought of Aristotle (more directly, from that of Averroes), and turning it into what almost amounted to a manifesto on method for the humanist *medici* who followed him. To a large degree, of course, it had ever since Pietro d'Abano functioned as that kind of manifesto for the *medici*, but (as we have seen) they did not treat it independently of the highly developed tradition of commentary on the *Posterior Analytics*. They used it rather as another very important supporting text, and—in Leoniceno's view—misused it. After the *De tribus doctrinis ordinatis*, the position presented by Leoniceno in the *De tribus doctrinis ordinatis* that there are four "methods," (*modi doctrinales*) and three "orders" (*ordines doctrinae*), became almost credal with the commentators on the *Ars*, of whom Giovanni Battista Montano is perhaps the most important in the sixteenth century.[33] Also, and unlike the commentators preceding Leoniceno, their attention is now directed *primarily* to the concept of *order*, rather than to method of demonstration. It is medical writers like Montano, Manardi,[34] Oddo degli Oddi,[35] etc., about whom Zabarella so bitterly complains in his own *De methodis*. He suggests that the *medici* have usurped a field of thought—logic—belonging properly to the *philosophi*.

Not only did Leoniceno's work result in the separation of the medical and philosophical (or Aristotelian) traditions of commentary on the *Ars medica*, it also exerted what may be described, I think, as a generally salubrious effect within the Aristotelian tradition itself. Following the tradition of commentary on the *Ars* from (let us say) Pietro d'Abano to the last of the great pre-Leonicenan commentators (Ugo Benzi), one notes small refinements and modifications of the ideas making up the theory of scientific method for which the prologue of the *Ars* functioned as a platform. But it is hard to convince oneself that these ideas had not become somewhat set and conventional—that

---

[33] *Io. Baptistae Montani medici veronensis in Artem Parvam Galeni explanationes* (Venice, 1554).

[34] *Galeni ars medicinalis per J. Manardum versa, divinisque commentariolis ... docte illustrata ...* (Rome, 1525).

[35] *Oddi de Oddis patavini physici ac medici celeberrimi ... expositio in librum Artis Medicinalis Galeni* (Venice, 1574).

is, that they had not lost their vitality, and reached a point beyond which further development was unlikely. This conclusion presses itself on one even more insistently, if the tradition of commentary on the prologue of the *Ars* is viewed as an integral part (which it is) of the older and broader tradition of commentary on the *Posterior Analytics* and the *Physics*. The most important idea developed in this tradition —that of the demonstrative regress—had appeared in the earliest Latin commentators on the *Posterior Analytics* and *Physics*, been incorporated very soon in the tradition of commentary on the prologue of the *Ars*, and thenceforward remained more or less stable down to the beginning of the sixteenth century. Without some new factor like Leoniceno's attempt to reclaim Galen for what he considered to be a more purely Greek and Platonic tradition of methodological thought, it seems improbable that the rapid developments we see ensuing in the mid and late sixteenth century would have occurred. The *medici*, it is true, were left with nothing but the methodology Leoniceno proposes in the *De tribus doctrinis ordinatis*—four *modi doctrinales*, and three *ordines doctrinae*—and it seems doubtful to me that this was an overall gain for medical methodology. But this was their own choice; and by following Leoniceno so closely in his interpretation of the prologue of the *Ars*, and imitating him so ardently in his rejection of any ideas smacking of an Averroist-Aristotelian origin, they at least continued to present an annoying challenge to the Aristotelians.

Girolamo Capivaccio (†1589) was one of the first to rise to this challenge in a systematic way. But the *De differentiis doctrinarum* which he published in 1562—an attempt to combine or re-integrate the Galenian and Aristotelian theories of method—was a rather weak and eclectic work, and did not have much influence.[36] It is not till the appearance of the *De methodis* of Zabarella in 1578 that we have a really impressive and (in my judgment) successful attempt to reintegrate the newer (Leonicenan) and older traditions of commentary on the *Ars*, taking what seemed to be of most value from each of them, and recombining it into a complete and systematic theory of method. Capivaccio's error lay in trying to take everything from both traditions, with the result that his methodology has the appearance of being only patched and glued together. Zabarella, on the other hand, adopts Leoniceno's concept of method as the means by which a whole

---

[36] *Hieronymi Capivacii philosophi, atque medici ... opusculum de differentiis doctrinarum logicis, philosophis, atque medicis pernecessarium* (Padua, 1562).

science may be constituted or organized, finds that it after all has a source in the Aristotelian tradition, and trims away what seems to be redundant or useless in it, namely, the concept of a definitional order, leaving only a resolutive method (for the practical sciences) and a compositive method (for the speculative or theoretical sciences).[37] At the same time, he reinvigorates the concept of method as *modus doctrinalis* (Zabarella prefers to call this simply "method," and the other kind "order"), which Leoniceno had relegated to a rather secondary and dubious position, by cutting away the Leonicenan methods that seem to him incapable of producing knowledge (the divisional and definitional), and retaining only the resolutive and demonstrative.[38] These latter two he finds identical with the Aristotelian demonstration *quia* and *propter quid*, respectively, so that he is able to retain and further develop the old idea of a demonstrative regress in the method of the natural sciences.

From Zabarella, the Leonicenan theory of method passed over the Alps and into the by then vigorous stream of methodological speculation in Northern Europe. But this was not until 1587 (the Lyons edition of the *Opera logica*),[39] and it must be noted that there had been a much earlier transmission of Leoniceno's thought across the Alps. It seems to me that this is a crucial factor in the explanation of the origin of the methodological thought of Peter Ramus, though I am not yet prepared to do more than call attention to the presence of Leoniceno's ideas north of the Alps at a time when they might have been a factor in the development of Ramus' own theory of method. The first commentary by a Northerner (i.e., a non-Italian) on the *Ars medica* in which Leoniceno's methodology appears in a recognizable form is that of Martinus Acakia (1497-1551), professor of medicine at the University of Paris and physician to Francis I.[40] Acakia does not cite Leoniceno by name, but he does clearly distinguish between *ordo* and *methodus* (*modus doctrinalis*), in Leoniceno's terminology, like Leoniceno defining three kinds of order (resolution, composition, and

---

[37] *De methodis*, book II.

[38] *Ibid.*, book III.

[39] In addition to the nine works contained in the *Opera logica*, of which the *De methodis* was probably the most influential, the Lyons edition included the *Apologia de doctrinae ordine*, the *Tabulae logicae*, the commentary on the *Posterior Analytics*, and the *De naturalis scientiae constitutione*.

[40] *Cl. Galeni pergameni Ars Medica, quae et Ars Parva dicitur, Martino Acakia catalaunensi doctore medico interprete, et enarratore* (Lyons, 1561). This is the edition I have used. The first edition appears to have been published at Paris in 1543.

definition), and four kinds of method (division, definition, demonstration, and resolution).[41] In the commentary of Jérémie de Dryvere (1504-1554), on the other hand, which appeared in Lyons in 1547,[42] the Leonicenan theory of method is not only adopted, but explicitly attributed to Leoniceno. Leoniceno's first influential disciple, Giovanni Manardi, is also mentioned by Dryvere, which is further evidence of the impact Leoniceno's thought was beginning to have north of the Alps. It must be recalled, when we are speculating on the possibility of a connection between the thought of Leoniceno and Ramus, that Ramus' theory of method did not reach its final form until about 1557, and that in its first version (1546) it was rather rudimentary.[43] Further, it seems clear to me that when Johann Sturm added a third book to his *Structure of Dialectic* in 1543, entitling it *De triplici methodo*, he has come under the influence of Leoniceno's ideas.[44] In any case, if (1) the theory of method worked out in the tradition of commentary on the *Ars Medica* played any part in the shaping of Ramus' thought, and if (2) Leoniceno was, as I have argued, responsible for an abrupt renovation or reconstruction in that tradition, then it seems evident that his *De tribus doctrinis ordinatis* must be taken into account in any investigation of the origins of Ramus' theory of method. Leoniceno, it is true, would be only one of the sources (direct or indirect) on which Ramus drew, but he would be an important one.

Finally, we must not exclude the possibility that what Leoniceno had to say on method in his *De tribus doctrinis ordinatis* in 1508 influenced Galileo on the same subject, either directly or indirectly. Certainly, when in the *De Motu* in 1590 he speaks of the method taught to him by his teachers of mathematics, he is using the term "method" in the sense which Leoniceno gave to it, namely, a way of organizing a *whole* science, rather than a way of solving particular problems within a science. This method, he says, is "always to make what is said depend on what was said before, and, if possible, never to assume as true that which requires proof." He complains that this method is "not adhered to sufficiently by certain philosophers, who frequently, when they expound the elements of physics, make assumptions that are the same as those handed down in Aristotle's book *On the Soul* or those *On the*

---

[41] *Ed. cit.*, pp. 2-3.
[42] *Hieremiae Thriveri brachelii in Technen Galeni clarissimi commentarii* (Lyons, 1547), pp. 14-15.
[43] See Ong, 245-52, for an account of the evolution of Ramus' concept of method.
[44] Ong, 232-6.

Heaven, and even in the *Metaphysics*... even in expounding logic itself they continually repeat things that were expounded in the last books of Aristotle. That is, in teaching their pupils the very first subjects, they assume that the pupils know everything, and they pass on to them their teaching, not on the basis of things that the pupils know, but on the basis of what is completely unknown and unheard of."[45] Galileo is evidently not here talking about method in its traditional modern sense, but in the sense in which Leoniceno meant it when he defined a concept of *ordo doctrinae*. His emphasis on the need to begin with what is known to the student is not Leonicenan, but comes probably from Zabarella, who in adopting and reconstructing the Leonicenan concept of *ordo doctrinae* insisted that the only criterion for order is the way in which we learn better, or more easily.[46] Galileo's later remarks on method—e.g., in the *Dialogue on the Two Great Systems*,[47] can, I think, be construed as applying either to method in the sense of order, or to method in the sense in which we are now accustomed to use it ("scientific method"). Which concept he has in mind, or whether he even clearly distinguished them, is not clear from what he says.

Emory University

---

[45] Galileo Galilei, *On Motion*, translated with an introduction and notes by I. E. Drabkin (Madison, 1960), 50.

[46] See above, note 20.

[47] *Dialogo*, First Day, *Opere*, vol. VII, p. 75.

A POEM ON THE OCCASION OF THE NOVA OF 1572[1]

† C. DORIS HELLMAN

De Stella Nova, Quae Ante Bis Octo Annos, Sub Novembris Initium Fulgere Coepit Anno 1572. D. Rodolphi Gualtheri p.m.[2] Carmen.
  Quae prope Cassiopen nova stella sub aethere fulget
    Magnum aliquid terris insolitumque dabit.
  Aut nova lux mundo post tristia nubila surget,
    Attigit aut finem machina tota suum.
  At lucem sperare vetat quae regnat ubique
    Impietas, poenas iam luitura brevi.
  Ergo tui adventus stella haec nuntia, Christe,
    Afferre optatam qui potes unus opem.
  Vasta tua Andromeden circumstant undique caete,
    Undique in expositam monstra feraeque ruunt.
  Monstra mari surgunt, nec terris tutior illa est
    Praesentemque videt tristis ubique necem.
  Ergo veni, propera, festina dulcis Jesu;
    Ni venias actum est : ah bone Christe veni.[3]

The above poem is by Rudolph Gualter or Gualterus or Walther or Gwalter (1518-1586) who was not an astronomer but a sixteenth-century Swiss theologian, a former student of Bullinger, married to Zwingli's daughter, and acquainted with the leaders of the reform movement.[4] He was fifty-four years old when he saw the star.

It is fitting to call attention to this poem in a volume honoring Paul Oskar Kristeller because it appears in two sixteenth-century Swiss

---

[1] I have expanded abbreviations and followed modern typographic conventions regarding the letters i/j and u/v.

[2] It seems likely that "p.m." is here used as the abbreviation for "piae memoriae."

[3] Johann Wilhelm Stucki, *Prognosticon, sive praedictio certissima de anno Christi millesimo, quingentesimo octogesimo octavo, et iis qui sequentur usque ad magnum illum annum atque diem, quo magnus ille Deus, et Servator generis humani, ad magnum et universale vivorum ac mortuorum judicium exercendum veniet* (Zurich : Froschauer, 1588). 4º, 4 sign. + 2 leaves. The poem by Gualter is on the recto of the last leaf, the verso of which is blank. The copy used is in my personal library. See n. 7 below.

[4] See Zedler, XI, 1180-1181; *Dictionnaire historique et biographique de la Suisse*, III (1926), 717.

manuscripts known to him. To one of these[5] he drew my attention. To the other[6] I drew his. The poem also appears at the end of a little known 1588 printed prognostication by another Swiss theologian, Johann Wilhelm Stucki or Stuckius (1542-1607), from which I transcribe it.[7] To date I have not succeeded in finding other manuscript copies or any other printed edition of the poem.

To an astronomer the poem is valueless. Reference to the general position of the new star or supernova, in Cassiopaea, and the poem's date, 8 February 1573,[8] while the star was still visible, furnish no new nor useful knowledge. Moreover, the star is described as "sub aethere," that is, in the terrestrial region to which Aristotelian believers in the immutability of the heavens assigned unusual phenomena. Yet several of the observers of the 1572 nova had quickly realized its great distance. The nova of 1572 as an omen, a warning, a hope—there are many other instances of this both in prose and in poetry.

---

[5] Stadtbibliothek, Schaffhausen, Cod. Min 127 III, p. 523, where the poem's caption reads "De stella Nova, quae sub initium Novembris Anno 1572. lucere coepit." Other variations from the printed version are : line 2, the last word is "ferret"; line 9 begins "Vasta tuam Andromedem"; line 10 ends "monstra marina ruunt"; and the last line begins "Ni properes, actum est ...." It is signed and dated 8 February 1573. Gualter's poem is followed immediately, pp. 523-524, by Theodore Beza's poem on the nova, which became better known and was frequently copied in manuscript and print.

[6] Zentralbibliothek, Zurich, Handschrift F 22, p. 210, where the poem's caption reads "1573. De nova stella. Domini Rudolffi Gualtheri Carmen quae sub initium Novembris 1572 lucere coepit." Other variations from the printed version are : line 2, the last word is "ferret"; line 9 begins "Vasta tuam Andromadem"; line 10 ends "monstra marina ruunt"; and the last line begins "Ni properes, actum est..." Gualter's name is not repeated at the end but the poem is dated 8 February 1573. The manuscript is apparently tightly bound obscuring the inner margin. Therefore, in the available photocopy, the last word of line 7 is not completely legible, although it begins "Chr." Similarly, the end of the last word on line 9 is illegible. The last word on line 12, after "illa," is missing. In the two manuscripts, which are in very different hands, the poems are word for word the same.

[7] See n. 3 above. I have transcribed the printed rather than the earlier manuscript version to allow for any changes the author or Stucki might have made but have altered the punctuation to conform to modern usage and in partial conformity with the Schaffhausen manuscript. If there is any punctuation of the poem in the Zurich manuscript it is lost in the xerox copy because of the manuscript's tight binding. Stucki studied in Switzerland and abroad, was Chamberlain in Paris, professor at the Carolinum in Zurich, professor of theology and Canon at the Grossmünster, and director of schools. See Zedler, XL, 1183-1184; *Dictionnaire historique et biographique de la Suisse*, VI (1932), 392.

[8] This is the date given in both manuscript versions.

What is of genuine interest is that this particular poem was written by a prominent Swiss reformer and is extant in the same version in two manuscript copies in Switzerland, both presumably dating from the time of the nova, as well as in a book by an equally prominent contemporary, although younger, theologian, printed sixteen years after the star first shone forth. Both manuscripts contain numerous other items dealing with the 1572 star, and several of these are also duplications. Since the version published with Stucki's prognostication is not identical with the manuscript copies, one suspects that there once existed, at the very least, a third manuscript copy of the poem.

The star caused widespread comment throughout Europe and must have greatly impressed the people of Zurich, the scene of Gualter's activities. An unusual celestial phenomenon was useful for the Protestant reformers. They referred to it from the pulpit, wrote to each about it and disseminated the news for anyone who could read. They were not viewing the star as a threat to the Aristotelian scientific tradition but rather as a work of God and an omen, here announcing the coming of Christ. As such it appealed to a great many people who cared nothing about its distance from the earth or its precise position relative to the background of the known fixed stars.

The circumpolar constellations Cassiopea, in which the nova appeared, Cepheus, Andromeda and Perseus represent figures from mythology. The story of Perseus' rescue of Andromeda, daughter of Cassiopea and Cepheus, has often been told. She was chained to the rocks and exposed to the monster through no fault of her own but because of her mother's vanity. After the Edict of January, 1562 which had gained some recognition for Calvinism in France there had been ten restless years culminating in the Massacre of St. Bartholomew, August 23, 1572 to which Gualter may have been specifically referring in line 12. Therefore the nova first seen in October or early November of 1572 and whose appearance Gualter called "tui adventus... nuntia, Christe," could be interpreted as heralding a rescuer. Perseus as Andromeda's rescuer, although not mentioned by name in the poem, might be construed as Christ, the rescuer of humanity.[9]

---

[9] One probably cannot select a particular source for Gualter's reference to the tale of Andromeda. Among those who told that story and were probably read by him were Ovid, *Metam.* VI, 667 ff.; Apollodorus, *Bibliotheca*, II; Hyginus, *Poeticon Astronomicon* and *Fables*; Manilius, *Astronomicon*, I and V, 538 ff. Apollodorus and Hyginus used the word "cetus." (Reference to Apollodorus is to the Latin translations.) In the seventeenth century when the Jesuit astronomer Riccioli (*Almagestum Novum*, 1651, I, 406-408) describing the constellations referred to the tale he also used the word "cetus."

If one studies only those writings on the nova of 1572 that added to scientific knowledge, one has a lopsided picture of its impact. Its interest to the general public must be emphasized. Letters and poems about it, circulating in manuscript form, played the role of the newspapers of today. The star brought people together with a common topic of conversation although with even less basic information than the acquaintances who stood on the street corners discussing the latest Apollo trip to the moon.

But why was the poem added to a book printed long after the star could no longer be seen and after several bright comets had awakened similar amazement and furnished additional arguments against the Aristotelian tradition—in fact, in the same year that saw the publication of the first edition of Tycho Brahe's massive tome on the comet of 1577 ?

There had long been prophecies that dire events—even the end of the world—would occur in 1588.[10] Stucki, a scholar, must have been well informed about these.[11] Therefore, it is not surprising that he himself should issue one in that very year, moreover one heralding the "Servator generis humani" as indicated in the title. The numerous phenomena of the 1570's and 1580's, including the nova of 1572, several bright comets, and the great conjunction of 1583, had built up a feeling of anxiety. What was more natural than to tack on a short, versified prediction based on the new star, especially one written by a recently deceased theologian well known to Stucki's anticipated audience ? Indeed, the line above the place of printing on the title page of Stucki's *Prognosticon*, "Veni, Domine Jesu, veni, vide, vince" echoes the last two lines of Gualter's poem.

Queens College, The City University of New York

---

[10] See Carroll Camden, "The Wonderful Yeere," *Studies in Honor of Dewitt T. Starnes* (Austin, Texas, 1967), 163-179 and Margaret E. Aston, "The Fiery Trigon Conjunction : An Elizabethan Astrological Prediction," *Isis* 61 (1970), 159-187, and the references cited therein.

[11] For example see Stucki, A4ᵛ for the same prediction in verse as is cited by Cyprian Leowitz, *De Conjunctionibus Magnis Insignioribus Superiorum planetarum, Solis defectionibus*, ... (London, 1573), L4, where it is followed by a version of Beza's poem (see n. 5 above.) In Stucki's *Prognosticon* special attention is given to the positions of the sun and moon.

KEPLER'S MASTERY OF GREEK

EDWARD ROSEN

This year the civilized world commemorates the birth, exactly four centuries ago, of the eminent scientist Johannes Kepler (1571-1630). A recent book about him tells us that when he was a student at Tübingen University,

> Learning to read Greek was among Kepler's academic requirements in any event. To facilitate the process, he bought a copy of a then-current German translation of an old Greek account of a voyage to the moon : Lucian's *A True Story*. The translator was a son of the noted satirist George Rollenhagen. By reading the German alongside Lucian's original Greek text, Kepler mastered Greek.[1]

Kepler's academic record at Tübingen shows that he earned the grade "A" in Greek four times in the year 1590, on 20 January, 23 April, 22 July, and 18 October.[2] On 13 March 1594,[3] before completing his course of studies, he left the university to accept a teaching position which had just become vacant through the incumbent's death. While Kepler was still a student at Tübingen, did he buy a copy of Rollenhagen's translation of Lucian?

This translation was the third book in the *Vier Bücher wunderbarlicher... Reysen* by Gabriel Rollenhagen, who published these "Four Books about Wonderful Journeys" for the first time in 1603.[4] Therefore a copy could not have been bought by Kepler while he was still a student, since he ceased to be a student and became a teacher nearly a decade earlier, as we just saw. After Kepler ceased to be a student, when did he acquire a copy of Rollenhagen's translation of Lucian, which first became available in 1603 ? "In the year 1604... there was for sale in Prague [where Kepler then occupied the post of Imperial

---

[1] John Lear, *Kepler's Dream* (Berkeley and Los Angeles, 1965), 42.

[2] Edmund Reitlinger, C. W. Neumann, and C. Gruner, *Johannes Kepler* (Stuttgart, 1868), 210.

[3] Johannes Kepler, *Gesammelte Werke*, cited hereafter as "GW" (Munich : Beck, 1937 - -), XIV, 276:511.

[4] Karl Theodor Gaedertz, *Gabriel Rollenhagen* (Leipzig, 1881), 103.

Mathematician] Lucian's book about the trip to the moon, as translated into the German language by Rollenhagen's son," we are told by Kepler himself.[5] Hence our recent author is guilty of a gross anachronism when he says that Kepler bought Rollenhagen [in 1604] to facilitate the process of meeting the academic requirement of learning to read Greek in or before 1594.

Another anachronism is involved in our recent author's statement that "the student Kepler mastered Greek so thoroughly that his language professor at Tübingen, the famous Hellenist, Martin Crusius, tried to obtain his collaboration in a commentary on Homer."[6] Before examining this second anachronism, however, let us note the impropriety of calling Crusius "his language professor at Tübingen," as though Greek were the only language studied at that institution by Kepler. Having enrolled in the theological course with the intention of becoming a Lutheran minister, Kepler studied not only Greek but also Hebrew. The latter language was taught, not by Crusius (1526-1607), but by his younger friend Georg Weigenmaier (1555-1599).[7] In 1590 Kepler's grades in Hebrew were slightly lower than his unbroken record of "A" in Greek, but on 18 October 1593 he made the highest score in Hebrew again.[8]

Let us now return to the anachronism concerning Crusius, who began his Homer commentary on 15 July 1594.[9] More than four months earlier, on 13 March, Kepler had ceased to be a student, as we saw above. Therefore "the student Kepler" could not have collaborated on a Homer commentary which was started when he was no longer a student.

Crusius' commentary on Homer had reached Book VI of the *Iliad*[10]

---

[5] Edward Rosen, *Kepler's Somnium* (Madison, 1967; awarded the Charles Pfizer Prize by the History of Science Society, 1968), 33-34; *Joannis Keppleri Somnium* (Osnabrück, 1969; facsimile reprint of the 1634 edition, with an appendix by Martha List and Walter Gerlach), 30.

[6] Lear, p. 42. For a 1596 woodcut portrait of Crusius, whose surname was Kraus before it was latinized, see Erhard Cellius, *Imagines professorum tubingensium* (Tübingen, 1596), 12.

[7] Christian Friedrich Schnurrer, *Biographische und litterarische Nachrichten von ehmaligen Lehrern der hebräischen Litteratur in Tübingen* (Ulm, 1792), 136-149; Reitlinger, 86.

[8] Reitlinger, 210.

[9] *Diarium Martini Crusii*, cited hereafter as "D," 4 vols. (Tübingen, 1927-1961), I, 416, note, lines 1-2; the frontispiece reproduces a 1590 Crusius portrait in oil.

[10] D, I, 35: 32, 54:4.

when Kepler, having received a leave of absence from his teaching post, returned to Tübingen for a brief visit. On 12 March 1596 Crusius' diary relates: "In our faculty house we received at dinner Professor Johannes Kepler, who teaches mathematics at Graz. He has made certain new discoveries in astronomy. A handsome young man."[11] With the commentary on Homer already nearly a quarter of the way through the *Iliad*, Crusius and Kepler met at dinner on 12 March 1596. Yet Crusius' diary reports no effort on the commentator's part to obtain Kepler's collaboration.

Two weeks later Crusius sent the 128 handwritten sheets of his commentary on the first six books of the *Iliad* to a publisher. While waiting to find out whether his work was deemed to be a marketable commodity, Crusius did not propose to remain idle. "Meanwhile I shall write also on the other books of the *Iliad*, but much more briefly, I believe, than I did on the first two" (56 sheets), he noted in his diary on 26 March 1596.[12] Two days later Kepler was a dinner guest once more.[13] Again Crusius' diary records no attempt to enlist Kepler as a collaborator on the commentary.

While Kepler was still on leave and living in Stuttgart, he was shown an unsealed copy of a letter which had been dispatched to a third person by Crusius on 20 May 1596. The perusal of this document prompted Kepler to communicate with Crusius, thereby initiating their correspondence. This first Kepler-Crusius letter, sent from Stuttgart, was received by Crusius in Tübingen on 7 June.[14] Although it has not survived, its contents are to some extent known from Crusius' point by point reply of 9 June.[15] Like Kepler's first letter (of 5 June?), Crusius' reply of 9 June dealt with certain aspects of his recently published *Annales suevici* (Frankfurt am Main, 1595-1596) and related matters. Although he had just begun to work on Book IX of the *Iliad*,[16] he did not mention his commentary on Homer nor did he try to obtain Kepler's collaboration on it.

To Crusius' letter of 9 June, Kepler replied at once on 11 June.[17]

---

[11] D, I, 51:3-5.

[12] D, I, 59:27-29, 35-37.

[13] D, I, 62, note, line 2.

[14] D, I, 106:33-35; GW, XIII, 88:2; Kepler may have written his first letter to Crusius on 5 June, since their later letters regularly required two days to reach the recipient.

[15] GW, XIII, no. 46.

[16] D, I, 106:31.

[17] D, I, 101, note, lines 3-4.

Like his first message to Crusius, this too has not survived. It was received on 13 June by Crusius, whose summary of its contents shows that it treated much the same topics as its predecessor.[18] Two days later Crusius received from Kepler a coin which was relevant to a subject they had been discussing in their correspondence.[19] If Crusius had any notion of trying to secure Kepler's collaboration in the commentary on Homer, these two additional communications from Kepler in June 1596 would have provided him with suitable opportunities to do so. His silence is eloquent. More than two years had elapsed since Kepler had ceased to be a student at Tübingen. During all those twenty-seven months, both in his personal contacts with Kepler and in his correspondence with him, Crusius did not try "to obtain his collaboration in a commentary on Homer."

Kepler's first major work was printed in Tübingen after he had returned on 30 August 1596[20] to Graz, where he was too far away from the printer's shop to see his *Cosmographic Mystery* through the press personally. This editorial task was performed for the absent author by Michael Maestlin (1550-1631), his former professor of astronomy at Tübingen. Writing to Kepler on 10 January 1597, Maestlin sent the most affectionate greetings of the entire faculty, including Crusius.[21] But about the latter's commentary on Homer not a word was said, although by that time it had reached Book XVIII of the *Iliad*.[22]

About two months later Maestlin wrote to Kepler in part as follows:

> In your letter you leave it to me to decide to whom and how to distribute copies [of the *Cosmographic Mystery*] in your name. But I would have liked you to designate the persons for me more specifically. For in my judgment it is quite difficult for me to act in this matter... I really don't know to what others [besides three VIPs] you want copies to be given, nor do I think that these should be presented to all the professors. But to which? I certainly would have preferred to have their names listed for me. I likewise don't know which of your friends in the university should be honored, nor do I doubt that when the copies are being handed out, many will enroll themselves in that category. If I could hope for the favor of your reply in the near future, however, I would judge that this matter could wait.[23]

In the case of Crusius, however, Maestlin did not wait. Less than a

---

[18] D, I, 110:11-25.
[19] D, I, 112:6-8.
[20] GW, XIII, 94:11.
[21] GW, XIII, 103:61-63.
[22] D, I, 268:14, 25.
[23] GW, XIII, 112:158-171.

week after Maestlin wrote the above letter to Kepler on 9 March 1597, Crusius recorded in his diary that "in the name of the author, Professor Johannes Kepler, mathematician of the Estates of Styria, his [*Cosmographic Mystery*,] *Forerunner of Cosmographic Dissertations* was presented to me" on 15 March 1597.[24] Just the day before, Crusius had begun his commentary on Book I of the *Odyssey*, having sent off his remarks on the last twelve books of the *Iliad* four days earlier to be examined by a publisher.[25] The end of the *Iliad* and the start of the *Odyssey* might well be a turning point where a commentator on Homer would think about the advisability of a collaborator. Such an offer might naturally accompany a message of thanks acknowledging the receipt of a presentation copy of a newly printed work. But Crusius did not try to obtain Kepler's collaboration in the commentary on Homer on 15 March 1597.

Two days earlier Kepler addressed his third (lost) letter to Crusius. In it he sent drawings of two ancient coins, concerning which he sought Crusius' opinion. The latter replied at once, on 3 April 1597, according to the Julian calendar, which he followed in his diary.[26] But in his answer to Kepler, which he wrote with his own hand and which is still preserved in the Austrian National Library in Vienna, he used both the Julian date 3 April and the corresponding Gregorian date 13 April.[27] Only the latter date was mentioned by Kepler in his annotation at the end of Crusius' letter.[28] Hence Kepler's indication that Crusius' reply of 13 April (Gregorian) was an answer to his own letter of 23 March marks the latter as a Gregorian date. The editor of the letter in the new edition of Kepler's collected works erred, therefore, when he assigned Kepler's letter about the coins to 23 March, while at the same time dating Crusius' reply 3 April.[29] These two dates do not belong together. Kepler wrote his third letter to Crusius on 13 March, Julian (23 March, Gregorian); Crusius' instant reply was composed on 3 April, Julian (13 April, Gregorian).

Having rectified this chronological blunder, let us now look at Crusius' letter of 3/13 April. In it he told Kepler about his lengthy

---

[24] D, I, 298:15-16.
[25] D, I, 292:4; 298:7.
[26] D, I, 319:18-21.
[27] GW, XIII, no. 66:3.
[28] GW, XIII, 121:28.
[29] GW, XIII, 389.

theological writings,[30] but he said not a word about his commentary on Homer, now at Book I of the *Odyssey*, to which he had devoted the whole of the preceding day.[31] Once again, on 3/13 April 1597, had he been so minded, Crusius would have had an excellent opportunity to try to obtain Kepler's collaboration on the commentary. Once again Crusius' silence shows that he had no such idea. Instead he extended best wishes for a happy outcome of Kepler's impending marriage,[32] which was to take place within two weeks and to which the entire faculty of Tübingen University had been invited.[33]

Nearly a year later Crusius finished his commentary on Homer at noon on 4 March 1598, and then added a supplement by 8 A.M. before breakfast on 15 March.[34] Throughout this entire period of three and two-thirds years, from 15 July 1594 to 15 March 1598, while Crusius worked steadily at his commentary on Homer, he did not once try to obtain Kepler's collaboration.

Then, more than a year later, on 12 April 1599, Maestlin informed Kepler:

> Crusius is writing, or has nearly finished writing, a commentary on Homer. He recently asked me to examine the assemblies and meetings as well as the councils of the gods in Homer. For he is thoroughly convinced that in those passages the poet indicates favorable or unfavorable positions of the stars. If I found any such positions, he would be willing to include them too in that book. I replied that I am no astrologer, but wanted to consult you about the matter. My answer pleased him. Hence he asks you, if you could find anything, to write to him, with the promise that he would consent to give you honorable mention in this connection in his commentary.[35]

If we now compare what Maestlin told Kepler with what our recent author tells us, we can see how far wide of the mark our contemporary is. In the first place, when Kepler's help was sought in 1599 for the commentary on Homer, he was no longer a student, having left the university more than five years before. Secondly, his help was sought, not because he had "mastered Greek so thoroughly," but because his

---

[30] GW, XIII, 121:7-13.
[31] D, I, 319:9.
[32] GW, XIII, 121:18-20.
[33] D, I, 319:22-23. Kepler was engaged on 9 February and married on 27 April (GW, XIV, 276:522). The date of his engagement was erroneously given as the date of his wedding by Carola Baumgardt, *Johannes Kepler: Life and Letters* (New York, 1951), 29.
[34] D, II, 19:31-32; 22:30-35.
[35] GW, XIII, 330:210-218.

Cosmographic Mystery had demonstrated his knowledge of the heavens. Thirdly, Crusius did not approach Kepler directly. The commentator on Homer first asked Maestlin for help. It was Maestlin who wished to consult Kepler. Only then did Crusius appeal to Kepler, indirectly and through Maestlin as intermediary. Fourthly, it is not true that "Crusius tried to obtain his [Kepler's] collaboration in a commentary on Homer." The author of an extensive commentary who is willing to acknowledge a specialist's help in interpreting selected passages would regard him, not as a full-fledged collaborator, but rather as an incidental contributor.

Had Kepler accepted Crusius' indirect invitation, not to collaborate in the commentary on Homer, but to contribute astrological interpretations of selected passages, how much would he have added to Crusius' commentary? This massive product comprised 668 handwritten sheets, or only 92 fewer than his *Annales suevici*.[36] The latter work in its printed form contained 1889 numbered pages plus 65 unnumbered pages of prefaces and indexes, and its two folio volumes standing alongside each other measured 4 1/4 inches in thickness.[37] To this mountain of a commentary, Kepler's astrological contribution, had he made it, would have added a tiny pebble or two, and thus he would not have been a collaborator therein.

Lest it be thought that, apart from quantity, Crusius felt that the quality of his commentary on Homer might be improved by a collaborator, let us see how he delineated the scope of his own work and rated its achievement in comparison with previous Homer commentaries:

> (1) Expounding the text, fables, and myths, it inserts the true stories; (2) it analyzes all the speeches, over a thousand, by means of a rhetorical scheme; (3) and it sets forth everywhere the teachings about ethics, economics, politics, physics etc. The work is almost as long as my *Annales suevici*. It still lacks a printer[38] and a financial backer, although it has been elaborated as none

---

[36] D, II, 23:1-5.

[37] D, I, 70:1-5; 92:16-17.

[38] Crusius' commentary on Book III of the *Iliad* had been printed separately (Tübingen, 1595; D, IV, 60-61). The only other part of his commentary to be printed was a posthumous publication (Heidelberg, 1612) of his remarks on Book I of the *Iliad* (D, IV, 60-61). The commentary on Homer in 668 sheets was listed with the (probably) unpublished writings of Crusius by his biographer, Johann Jacob Moser, who translated Crusius' *Annales suevici* into German as the *Schwäbische Chronick* (Frankfurt am Main, 1733, 2 vols.), I, c2v.

of its predecessors has been at any time. From this commentary it would finally be understood how great a poet Homer is and how great his wisdom.[39]

Would a famous Hellenist, who regarded his commentary on Homer as surpassing all its predecessors, try to obtain the collaboration of a student, even if that student was Kepler?

What was the reaction of Kepler (not while he was a student, but when he was a teacher of mathematics and author of the *Cosmographic Mystery*) to Crusius' indirect invitation, as transmitted by Maestlin on 12 April 1599? More than four months later, on 19 August, Kepler replied to Maestlin:

> With regard to the councils of the gods... you neatly sloughed off onto me Crusius' most enormous, very troublesome, and utterly useless project, with the respectable pretext [that you are not informed] about astrology. Why aren't you rather the one to scrutinize all of Homer, assign his story to a definite place in chronology, since he is still not pinned down, allocate every one of his speeches to its own day, furnish the computation, and establish the timetable of his twenty years [ten for the *Iliad* and ten more for the *Odyssey*]? For in your plan I was to undertake the role of an astrologer, who studies a separate subject, whereas the aforementioned questions are examined by an astronomer. Yet if you do your part, I promise to work out such a book of timetables, and write down my opinion about each of the [astrological] aspects. If Crusius mentions anything of this sort in his commentary, the reference can't be welcome to me. For in Munich there is ... Herwart [von Hohenburg (1553-1622)] who is in the habit of studying such problems minutely. He would surely torment me with gigantic tasks, urging me to carry out everything which Crusius would have recommended. For two whole years now he has been bothering me to investigate that disposition [of the planets] which Lucan describes as presaging civil war in accordance with the prophecy of P. Nigidius Figulus.[40]

As is clear from the foregoing excerpt from his letter to Maestlin, Kepler declined Crusius' indirect invitation (not to collaborate in the commentary on Homer, but rather) to contribute an astrological section to it.

Let it not be thought, however, that Kepler had a low opinion of Crusius' intellectual accomplishments. On the contrary, when Kepler was a boy, "he tried to memorize all the examples in Crusius' (Greek) *Grammar*."[41] In later years he regarded himself as "equal to Crusius in

---

[39] D, II, 202:1-7.
[40] GW, XIV, no. 132:110-126.
[41] *Joannis Kepleri astronomi opera omnia*, 8 vols., ed. Christian Frisch, cited hereafter as "F" (Frankfurt am Main and Erlangen, 1858-1871), V, 476: line 4 up. Crusius' eminence

meticulous attention (to detail), far inferior (to him) in industriousness, superior (to him) in understanding. Crusius worked by synthesizing, Kepler by analyzing; the former was a rake, the latter a wedge."[42] This startlingly candid evaluation of himself in comparison with his former teacher Crusius was written by Kepler in 1597,[43] about two years before he received and declined Crusius' indirect invitation to contribute to the commentary on Homer.

That invitation came to Kepler, the teacher and author of the *Cosmographic Mystery*, not to "the student Kepler," who "mastered Greek so thoroughly." Although Kepler's record as a student of Greek at Tübingen was straight "A," he believed that the "French language should be learned in preference to Greek."[44] Nevertheless, he tells us, "later I came across the two books of Lucian's *True Story*, written in Greek, which I chose as my means of mastering the language."[45] By saying "addiscerem" he meant "mastering," not merely "learning,"[46] since he had already learned Greek at Tübingen and its preparatory schools. Moreover, he mastered Greek by reading Lucian, not by "reading the German (translation by Gabriel Rollenhagen) alongside Lucian's original Greek text," as we were recently told.[47] For Kepler came across the Greek text of Lucian a decade before he bought Rollenhagen's translation in 1604.

Having mastered Greek, Kepler translated some of Aristotle into German about 1613,[48] and some of Plutarch into Latin a decade later.[49] But these demonstrations of Kepler's mastery of Greek were performed long after his student days were over. Thus we see how little

---

as a Greek scholar was studied by B. A. Mystakidès, "Notes sur Martin Crusius," *Revue des études grecques* 11 (1898), 279-306. Crusius' Greek *Grammar* was published at Basel in 1562-1563.

[42] F, V, 477 : lines 21-20 up; Edward Rosen, "Kepler's Rake Was Not a Hoe," *Classical Outlook* 44 (1966-1967), 6-7, where the reference to F, VIII should be corrected to F, V.

[43] F, V, 479:5.

[44] F, V, 477:4-5.

[45] Rosen, *Kepler's Somnium*, 32; *Keppleri Somnium*, 30.

[46] Patricia Frueh Kirkwood's translation in Lear, 88.

[47] Lear, 42.

[48] Fritz Rossmann, *Nikolaus Kopernikus, Erster Entwurf seines Weltsystems sowie eine Auseinandersetzung Johannes Keplers mit Aristoteles* (Munich, 1948; repr. Darmstadt, 1966), 56-77; reviewed by Edward Rosen, *Archives internationales d'histoire des sciences* 3 (1950), 700-703.

[49] *Keppleri Somnium*, 97-184.

truth there is in the recent statement that "the student Kepler mastered Greek so thoroughly that his language professor at Tübingen, the famous Hellenist, Martin Crusius, tried to obtain his collaboration in a commentary on Homer."

City College, The City University of New York

THE POLITICS OF A POET:
THE ARCHIPOETA AS REVEALED BY HIS IMAGERY

W. T. H. JACKSON

Most of the poets of the High Middle Ages are anonymous in the sense that of their lives we know nothing. But of the Archipoeta we know less than nothing, for even his name is a mocking travesty of a title, probably a play on that of his patron, the Archicancellarius, Reinald von Dassel, Archbishop of Cologne. Only ten poems can be ascribed with any certainty to a poet whose sense of form and whose verbal agility equal or exceed those of any medieval poet. These ten short poems appear to be intensely personal and to reflect the idiosyncrasies of their author and his reactions to the events and personages of his time. There is no independent evidence about this remarkable man, no documents exist to which he was a witness; there are no records of his relations with other poets or with his patrons. He is thus to an even greater degree than most contemporary writers in Latin or the vernacular a *persona*, a poet who appears only in his works. Since many of these works present the poet in the first person, it is a natural assumption that the statements made there are those of the poet himself, that he is telling of his own feelings and views and using the vehicle of his verse to make known to the world his personal reactions to patrons, to emperors, to courtiers and to bishops.

Such a view might be described as a pathetic fallacy, although not in the way in which the expression is usually used. The ideas he expresses are, of course, his own but they are conditioned by the genre in which he writes and the effects which he wishes to produce. When a poet undertakes to write an epic, he knows that he must take an elevated subject and treat it in a noble style, that he must assume the *persona* of an objective narrator who nevertheless is aware of the deep significance of the events he records and who therefore tells them with the gravity and dignity they deserve. He sets himself to deal with the subject in a form which his readers will recognize as suitable for the subject. If he does not do this, he runs a grave risk of being misunderstood. His epic may be regarded as a mock epic, as a parody, as a satire, even as a piece of light verse. In other words, the poet must subordinate his personality to the demands of the genre in which he writes and he may assume only the *persona* which is appropriate to that genre.

The Archipoeta wrote only short poems. At first sight they may appear to suffer from a certain monotony of subject, for all contain an element of complaint. Usually it is a lament on the poet's poverty which leads to a plea for more aid and more frequent aid from his patron, Reinald von Dassel. There is no need to imagine that the poet did not need the support he asked for. He says himself that he was of a knightly family and that he was not prepared to perform any of the more menial jobs that might support him. But no poet was likely to secure the support of a prince of the church merely by writing versified complaint, and we must look for other explanations of the poet's apparent ability to move in the highest circles of the empire and address with freedom, almost with impertinence, the most important subject in the land.

The *persona* of the poverty-stricken artist is only one of several which the poet assumes. Its frequency is due to the fact that the great majority of his poems are written from the point of view of the humble commentator—or, more accurately, from the pose of the humble commentator. Since they are short poems of social comment, the author cannot assume the stance of the epic narrator nor the personal involvement of the elegist. He has chosen the "I" form to comment on contemporary events and must therefore assume one of two stances. He can present himself as superior to the events he describes and on which he comments, or he can speak as a seer, as one whose judgment of events was to be valued because of superior knowledge or even divine inspiration. There was plenty of precedent for such a stance—the political odes of Horace and the satires of Juvenal come to mind—but such an attitude would have committed the Archipoeta to a position which would have deprived him of all possibility of the use of irony, and it would have been inconsistent with his constant reiteration of his utter dependence on his patron. He prefers rather to portray himself as *poeta humilis*. Such an attitude offered several advantages. The poet could ask in the most brazen fashion for material assistance, since he was "poeta humilis et pauper." But, perhaps more important, it deprived his often waspish comments of any sting. Since he proclaimed himself as a poor poet who was singing for his supper, there was no need for his betters to take seriously the almost insolent comments which he made about them, particularly since such comments were often veiled by the stylistic methods which he employed.

In adopting his pose of "poeta humilis," the Archipoeta was careful to use the appropriate imagery. He describes himself in terms such as:

> sic et ego dignus morte
> prave vivens et distorte[1]   II, 39f.

or

> asperitas brume necat horriferumque gelu me
> continuam tussim pacior, tamquam tisicus sim.   III, 17

or

> Iam febre vexatus nimioque dolore gravatus   VI, 8

or

> Nudus et incultus cunctis appareo stultus;
> pro vili panno sum vilis parque trutanno.
> nec me nudavit ludus neque fur spoliavit :
> pro solo victu sic sum spoliatus amictu,
> pro victu vestes consumpsi, dii mihi testes.   VI, 18ff.

The poet is sick, poor, hungry and ill-clothed. He is the very prototype of the neglected artist, but still he struggles on to write poetry. The stance of sickness, weakness, and humility gives him the opportunity to poke fun at the great ones of the earth by comparing his own sad state to that of wealth and power. The apostrophe of his audience is often made through images and descriptive epithets which contrast forcibly with the poet's description of himself:

> Lingua balbus, hebes ingenio
> viris doctis sermonem facio.   I, 1f.

or

> stultus ego qui penes te
> nummis equis victu veste
> dies omnes duxi feste
> nunc insanus plus Oreste,
> male vivens et moleste …

compared with

> Pacis auctor, ultor litis
> esto vati tuo mitis …   II, 78ff.

---

[1] All quotations are taken from : Heinrich Krefeld, *Die Gedichte des Archipoeta*, ed. Heinrich Watenphul (Heidelberg, 1958). I have followed the numbering of the poems in this edition.

The Archipoeta spends a whole poem in extravagant praise of Reinald von Dassel, showering upon him every figure from the rhetorical textbooks— "Ulixe facundior Tulliane loqueris/columba simplicior... serpente callidior... Alexandro forcior... David mansuetior... Martinoque largior" only to conclude with a sharp contrast with his own position :

> Dum sanctorum omnium colitur celebritas
> singuli colentium gerunt vestes inclitas,
> archicancellarium vatis pulsat nuditas.
> Poeta composuit racionem rithmicam
> satyrus imposuit melodiam musicam
> unde bene meruit mantellum et tunicam. II, x, xi

The great/small topos was never better illustrated—the Archbishop and his companions in glittering robes, the poet in rags. But it is this tattered poet who is telling us of these great ones, and without him their fame would be nothing. It is he who provides them with the appropriate descriptive epithets and with their one claim to fame among posterity. The question of who is in fact *humilis* and who is *magnus* is thus left to the audience.

The poet helps the audience by the assumption of other stances. For, as a poet, he is also a seer. The appropriate imagery for the poet as prophet and seer is well enough illustrated by Horace :

> Quem virum aut heroa lyra vel acri
> tibia sumis celebrare, Clio ?

or in the great political odes such as III, 2, III, 3, IV, 4, and IV, 5. Even more appropriate for the Archipoeta is the calm statement of superiority made by Horace in Odes III, 1 "Odi profanum vulgus et arceo," which sets him above the common herd and makes his pronouncements infinitely more significant to those of a mere mortal. When the Archipoeta adopts the stance of a poet-seer, he does not use this kind of imagery. He refuses to set himself apart from the herd but rather claims that his powers, such as they are, are mere accidentals of his personality, traits which will be intensified by the liberal provision of good wine. The result is an ironical opposition of the statements of the Archipoeta on matters of grave concern—public policy, charity, the prowess of the emperor, and even the ultimate destiny of a man's soul—which are delivered in all seriousness and often with an air of authority, and the *persona* of the poet who is allegedly making these pronouncements : a man beset by poverty, ragged, sick, hungry, and apparently unable to write unless reinforced by wine and the generosity of his patron. The only justification for the Archipoeta's existence is his ability to exercise the poet's craft in the service of Reinald von Dassel and over and over again he emphasizes that without him the world would little note nor long remember what the Archbishop of Cologne did or even who he was. Here lies his ultimate strength, the reason why he is able to talk to his patron as he does, to beg without shame and even to be insolent if the spirit moves him, for without his poetic gift and the fame he spreads, Reinald would be a cypher.

The opposition between the various *personae* assumed by the Archipoeta and the ironic interplay between them is best seen in the two poems most intimately connected with political matters, Numbers IV and IX in Krefeld's edition.[2] Both are concerned with the successes enjoyed by Friedrich Barbarossa in his campaigns in Italy and each, from a different point of view, examines the problems of a man who, whether he likes it or not, finds himself in the position of a poet-laureate. There can be no doubt that in each of these two poems an actual historical situation is being described—Reinald von Dessel did ask his court poet to celebrate the deeds of Friedrich Barbarossa in epic fashion, and the Archipoeta was talking about actual achievements of the Emperor in his later poem. The poem which disclaims any ability to write an epic on the imperial achievement has thirty-three strophes (if the gap at strophe 21 is only two lines long), the poem on the *gesta Friderici* has thirty-four. The similarity—perhaps even identity—of length is surely not accidental. For what he had refused to do when requested by the Archbishop, he performs spontaneously—in his own fashion. Thus both poems are a testimony to his personal attitudes. One demonstrates his independence, his determination to write only when he wants and what he wants; the second demonstrates that if he wishes to do so he can celebrate the Emperor's achievements at least as well as an epic poet-laureate, even if not in a formal epic poem.

The two poems are a personal declaration of independence but

---

[2] The exact dates of the two poems are difficult to determine. Milan was captured on March 1, 1162, so that IX must have been written after that date. It seems probable, as Krefeld suggests, that the poem would be particularly suited for presentation in Novara, and that the most likely date would therefore be September/October, 1163. A date very close to this seems indicated for IV, although the evidence is much less clear. See Krefeld, 104 ff. and 131.

they are not necessarily conveyed in a true first person. In reading them we must distinguish between various types of utterance. The poet may actually speak as himself. This kind of declaration is much rarer than might appear at first sight. He may adopt various *personae*, all of them variations on *poeta*, through whom he expresses views which may coincide with his own, which purport to be his own, but which may be and frequently are poses to make a point with which, as a person, he does not agree. To all this should be added another and far more subtle method of indicating the views of the poet, not of the *persona*. The imagery and rhetorical techniques employed by the poet may be in obvious opposition to those demanded by the theme he is pursuing and thus may show more clearly than a personal statement could reveal what the poet really thought. A detailed examination of the poems will demonstrate the interaction of the two methods.

What we may call the "epic disclaimer" presents an opposition between the Archbishop, apostrophized in each of the first seven strophes of poem IV, and a poetical statement by a person who claims to be his humble, indeed abject slave, who yet happens to write poetry. Reinald is carefully described as a man of a clear judgment ("discrete mentis") but also as a person who would never go beyond the bounds of a wise man. Such a description means that he is capable of being convinced by logical argument ("probare potero multis argumentis"). In fact, however, no such logical arguments are produced. The Archipoeta prefers to pervert the whole situation and make it farcical. He quickly adopts the stance of the "poeta servus," ready for anything and prepared to go through fire and water ("ibo, si preceperis, eciam trans freta") for his master—but not prepared to do what he is asked. His excuse is that he is expected to do in a week what Vergil or Homer could not have done in five years. The implications are that the deeds of Friedrich would take these poets five years or more to write—if they undertook them. Is Friedrich then the equivalent of Aeneas and Achilles ? The Archbishop must think that he is, if he wants his tame poet to write an epic about his achievements.

The Archipoeta does not linger on this thought, for he has something else in mind. If a wretched poet is to write on such a magnificent subject, he must surely be inspired—and how is he to come by the inspiration which will make him the equivalent of Vergil and Lucan ? Even the little poetic fire and power of prophecy he possesses deserts him on occasion :

prophecie spiritus fugit ab Helya,

> Helyseum deserit saepe prophecia,
> nec me semper sequitur mea poetria.   IV, vii

The words are a sharp rebuke to the Archbishop—poetical inspiration cannot be turned on to order—made by the poet in his own person, a defense, one may say, of the poet against the Philistine, but made in the *persona* of the poet-slave which he has adopted. This assertion of independence is not allowed to become offensive. The Archipoeta quickly reverts to his favorite protective covering, that of the poet who cannot work in solitude or in a state of abstinence from food and wine. By adopting this stance he can evade the request to write a Barbarossa epic by demonstrating his unsuitability rather than his inability. Epic poetry belongs to the elevated style. It is a lofty genre, not to be attempted by flighty poets but by those who take their craft seriously. Such are the poets who are described in strophes x and xi. But the Archipoeta does not belong to this group. He does not abstain. His poetry is directly dependent on the quality and quantity of the wine he consumes:

> Tales versus facio quale vinum bibo   IV, xiv

and on the provision of food:

> nihil possum facere nisi sumpto cibo ...   IV, xiv

The situation is summed up in these lines:

> scribere non valeo pauper et mendicus
> que gessit in Latio Cesar Friedericus...   IV, xvi

This is not a mere request for financial support. It is a statement that great themes cannot be attempted by poor poets, a contrast made perfectly clear:

> unde sepe lugeo quando vos ridetis   IV, xvii

The poet then explains at considerable length why action should be taken to bring the poet of Barbarossa up to the standard required for an epic poet. He is too noble to beg—or to dig—and it would not be consistent with the dignity of Reinald to do other than support him, still less would it be right for a German as opposed to an Italian prelate. Suddenly the poem ceases to be a matter of whether the Archipoeta should write about the deeds of Barbarossa. The question to be discussed is the relation between poet and patron. After demonstrating that the poet whom Reinald von Dassel has been supporting, or failing to support, is incapable of handling an epic theme, because such a theme demands a man not dependent on occasional gifts of food and wine, the Archipoeta assumes the mantle of the seer (which he had previously discarded) and talks of the need for true patronage. Not only is generosity characteristic of any true Christian, it is also politically wise :

> In regni negociis potens et peritus
> a regni negocio nomen est sortitus;
> precepti dominici memor, non oblitus
> tribuit hilariter, non velud invitus.
>
> IV, xxvii

A clear connection is made between Reinald's position as chief minister and the necessity to give generously. The Archbishop owes his high position to political skill, but it is only the poet who can advertise his worthiness for that position.

To view this poem as a somewhat crude effort by the Archipoeta to obtain material benefits by saying that he cannot write an epic poem about the deeds of Barbarossa unless he is well paid for it is an oversimplification. The poet rarely speaks in his own person. He is stating that a "poeta humilis" cannot be expected to write the "sermo sublimior." If Reinald wishes his poet to speak of grave matters of state, then he must behave like a generous lord. His style must be appropriate to the epic style. The poet, while adopting for most of the poem the *persona* of the "poeta servus," speaks in the tone of the "poeta vates" and at times comes very close to lecturing his patron on his duties. Thus there is throughout the ironical contrast between the *persona* of the poverty-stricken, dependent, almost servile poet-laureate and the independent, superior, and quite unrepentant poet who is well aware of his value to his patron.

It is the second *persona* who is in evidence in the poem on the deeds of Friedrich Barbarossa, Number IX in Krefeld's edition. Although he does not fail to mention his patron, the Archbishop, the poem is not written from the stance of the "poeta humilis." Here the poet assumes the stance of *vates* and goes even further. He purports to be able to determine what is good for the world and to see the course of history. From the very beginning there is assumed identification between the panegyrist of Barbarossa and the poet-prophet who surveys the world and lays down the principles of imperial rule.

The poem is dominated by one image derived from a statement of Jesus himself: Render unto Caesar the things which are Caesar's. Cities and magnates who do so are praised, those who fail to do so are damned. But to this statement there is a corollary : Render to God the things which are God's. There is no explicit opposition between these two commandments, but the tension between them is implicit throughout the poem, as it was in contemporary politics, and it is indicated by a different and perhaps more subtle variation of the poetical stance.

The poem opens with what is apparently the standard apostrophe of the ruler. The poet does not appear as an individual *persona* but (in the second strophe) as a spokesman for Barbarossa's loyal subjects. It is not until strophe vii that a verb appears in the first person singular, unless we count "me pudet" in strophe iv. The poet has deliberately avoided the impression of offering a personal opinion. He is creating the illusion of being the spokesman of many and of setting down in verse what everyone in the empire believes. If he had actually done this, the poem would hardly be worth a comment. The imagery appropriate to imperial panegyric had developed, so far as the Christian West was concerned, at the court of Charlemagne, and subsequent poets had improved on it. There is ample evidence that Barbarossa himself was well aware of the importance of such poetic propaganda.[3] It would therefore seem reasonable that a poem in praise of the Emperor's deeds in Italy, whether written in response to a direct request or not, would employ the imagery appropriate to such an occasion, which would be familiar to the Emperor and to his chief advisor, Reinald von Dassel. But in fact the appropriate imagery is not used. Quite the contrary. In the first three strophes the poet uses only those images which would be appropriate to God, not to his secular regent. For convenience we may set side by side the attributes of Barbarossa, as the poem gives them, and the biblical passages with which they are connected.

mundi domine	Verbo Domini caeli firmati sunt; et spiritu oris eius omnis virtus eorum Ps. xxxiii.6
Cesar noster	Pater noster qui est in celis, sanctificetur nomen tuum Matt. vi.9
ave	Ave, Rabbi, et osculatus est eum. [The reference is to Judas] Matt. xxvi.49
	Ave Maria, gratia plena; Dominus tecum benedicta tu in mulieribus Luke i.28

---

[3] The subject is treated in the following works : Paul Lehmann, *Das literarische Bild Karls des Grossen* (Munich, 1934, repr. 1959); N. Rubinstein, "Political Rhetoric in the Imperial Chancery during the Twelfth and Thirteenth Centuries," *Medium Aevum* 14 (1945), 22ff.; Anette Georgi, *Das lateinische und deutsche Preisgedicht des Mittelalters*, Philologische Studien und Quellen, XLVIII (Berlin, 1969).

cuius iugum est suave	Tollite iugum meum super vos, et discite a me quia mitis sum et humilis corde; et invenietis quietum animabus vestris.
	Iugum enim meum suave est et onus meum leve.
	Matt. XI. 28, 29
Quisquis contra calcitrat	Saule, Saule quid me persequeris? Qui dixit : Quis es, Domine? Et ille : Ego sum Jesus quem tu persequeris; durum est tibi contra stimulum calcitrare.
	Acts IX. 4, 5
obstinati cordis est et cervicis prave	Caelum mihi sedes est, terra autem scabellum pedum meorum; quam domum aedificabitis mihi? dicit Dominus; aut quis locus requietionis meae est?
	Nonne manus mea fecit haec omnia?
	Dura cervice et incircumcisis cordibus et auribus vos semper Spiritui Sancto resistitis; sicut patres vestri, ita et vos. Acts VII.49-51
Princeps terrae principum	Et post regnum eorum, cum creverint iniquitates, consurget rex impudens facie, intelligens propositiones. Et roborabitur fortitudo eius; et non in viribus suis; et supra quam credi potest, universa vastabit, et prosperabitur, et faciet. Et interficiet robustos et populum sanctorum. Secundum voluntatem suam et dirigetur dolus in manu eius; et cor suum magnificabit et in copia rerum omnium occidet plurimos; et contra principem principum consurget, et sine manu conteretur.
	Dan. VIII. 23-25
	Haec dicit Dominus Deus : Ecce ego suscitabo omnes amatores tuos contra te, de quibus satiata est anima tua, et congregabo eos adversum te in circuitu : Filios Babylonis et universos Chaldaeos, nobiles, tyrannosque et principes, omnes filios Assyriorum, iuvenes forma egregia duces et magistratus universos, principes principum ... Ezech. XXIII.22,23
cuius tuba titubant arces inimice	Et septem angeli qui habebant septem tubas, praeparaverunt se ut tuba canerent Rev. VIII.6
tibi colla subdimus	Porro gens quae subiecerit cervicem suam sub iugo regis Babylonis et servierit ei, dimittam eam in terra sua, dicit Dominus, et colet eam et habitabit in ea.
	Et ad Sedeciam, regem Juda, locutus sum secundum omnia verba haec, dicens : Subiicite colla vestra sub iugo regis Babylonis, et servite ei, et populo eius et vivetis. Jer. XXVII.11, 12
tibi colla subdimus tygres et formice et cum cedris Libani vepres et mirice.	Domine, Dominus noster, quam admirabile est nomen tuum in universa terra!
	Omnia subiecisti sub pedibus eius oves et boves universas insuper et pecora campi,
	Volucres caeli et pisces maris qui perambulant semitas maris. Ps. VIII.2,8,9

Nemo prudens ambigit
te per dei nutum
super reges alios
regem constitutum

Quare fremuerunt gentes, et populi meditati sunt inania? Astiterunt reges terrae, et principes convenerunt in unum adversus Dominum, et adversus Christum eius.

Dirumpamus vincula eorum et proiciamus a nobis iugum ipsorum. Qui habitat in caelis irridebit eos et Dominus subsannabit eos. Tunc loquetur ad eos in ira sua, et in furore suo conturbabit eos. Ego autem constitutus sum rex ab eo super Sion, montem sanctum eius praedicans praeceptum eius. Dominus dixit ad me : Filius meus es tu; ego hodie genui te.   Ps.II.1-7
Ego constitui te hodie super gentes et super regna ut evellas et destruas et disperdas et dissipes et aedifices et plantes.   Jer.I.10
Subiecti igitur estote omni humanae creaturae propter Deum, sive regi quasi praecellenti, sive ducibus, tamquam ab eo missis ad vindictam malefactorum, laudem vero bonorum;
quia sic est voluntas Dei ut benefacientes obmutescere faciatis imprudentium hominum ignorantiam ...
                                                                                      1 Pet. II.13-15

The first general point to be noted about all the images used of Barbarossa in the first three strophes is that they are directly connected with God in their biblical context. The biblical passages show God as the ruler of the universe, and in a few cases there is clear reference to what happens to those who try to usurp his power, as may be seen in the quoted passages from Daniel and Ezechiel. Here, as frequently in the "Confession,"[4] the context surrounding a biblical reference often gives more of the poet's true opinion than the actual words which appear in the poem. The use of images and attributes which are used in Holy Writ of God himself must inevitably have caused the audience to think that the Archipoeta was concerned to show his Emperor as the only power on earth, a union of spiritual and temporal function. There is good evidence that Barbarossa himself was much of that opinion. He created two antipopes, Victor IV and Pascal III, and caused the latter to canonize his predecessor, Charlemagne, the earliest of those who had sought the union of spiritual and temporal powers. There can be little doubt that Barbarossa would be gratified to be described in divine imagery. But on closer examination the use of such imagery is not quite so flattering as might appear.

---

[4] No. X in Krefeld's edition. The frequent biblical allusions, when read in context, provide a brilliant satirical commentary on the relations between the poet and Reinald von Dassel.

We have already noted that in the passages in which several of the images appear, there are references to upstart kings whose aspirations were crushed. Other modifications are less obvious. The Archipoeta says: "cuius bonis omnibus iugum est suave." The passage from Matthew already quoted occurs in the following context: "Venite ad me omnes qui laboratis et onerati estis et ego reficiam vos." The whole point of the biblical passages is the relief given by Jesus to all those who come to Him, particularly the weak and oppressed, whereas Barbarossa's yoke is light "for all good men." Presumably the Emperor is the judge of who is good and who is not and the greater part of the poem seems to indicate that the imperial yoke was by no means light on those who did not conform to his plans. Nor is the allusion to Acts ix. 5 more encouraging. Anyone who thinks that the yoke is too hard is warned that it is difficult to kick against the pricks. The text shows that Paul is resisting the commands of God and that he cannot be allowed to do so for very long. Does Barbarossa think that resistance to him is tantamount to resistance to God? Apparently so, for in the very next strophe we are reminded of the fate of those who resist, and the biblical passages are concerned with the ruthless suppression of disobedience to the supreme ruler. The selection of images in these strophes presents Barbarossa as the supreme arbiter of all matters both temporal and spiritual, as something very close to God himself. It is clearly the duty of each member of the audience to decide for himself whether the images presented here are to be taken seriously. There can be little doubt that Barbarossa himself was prepared to accept them at face value because he believed he merited such attributes. We must examine the rest of the poem to find out whether he was right.

The third strophe gives a hint about the method of interpretation we should follow. (The poet is still speaking in the *persona* of the all-wise seer.)

> Nemo prudens ambigit te per dei nutum
> super reges alios regem constitutum
> et in dei populo digne consecutum
> tam vindicte gladium quam tutele scutum.   IX, III

The important word here is "prudens." Does it mean "wise" in the sense of "sensible," "aware of the arguments," wise in the sense of the man who builds his foundation on a rock[5]—such an interpretation

---

[5] "Omnis ergo qui audit verba mea haec et facit ea assimilabitur viro sapienti qui aedificavit domum supra petram" (Matt. vii.24).

would be complimentary to Barbarossa—or does it perhaps mean "anyone who knows what is good for him." Certainly the latter interpretation would be true for the Archipoeta, for he is in many respects a court poet, but it would also be true of the generality of the empire, if they wish to avoid the fate of Milan. Both power and protection are in the hands of the Emperor. Indeed it would appear that the spiritual arm, the papacy is totally without influence.

Another hint is given in the next strophe:

> Unde diu cogitans quod non esset tutum
> Cesari non reddere censum vel tributum.   IX, IV

The reference is clear: "Licet censum dare Caesari an non? Cognita autem Jesus enquitia eorum ait: Quid me tentatis, hypocritae? Ostendite mihi numisma census. At obtulerunt ei denarium. Et ait illis Jesus: Cuius est imago haec et superscriptio? Dicunt ei: Caesaris. Tunc ait illis: Reddite ergo quae sunt Caesaris Caesari et quae sunt Dei, Deo." But the poem seems to call for more than the biblical reference. The distinction between what is due to God and what is due to Caesar has been deliberately blurred by the imagery. And furthermore, a person who does not recognize the elevation of the Emperor's status is not only not "prudens"—he is not safe. What contribution is the Archipoeta to make? Since it is apparently dangerous not to pay "censum et tributum" to Caesar, he, poorer than the widow in the biblical story, will give his mite. And what is this mite? It is the use of his talent to praise Barbarossa. The poem written in praise of Barbarossa thus proves to be something which is performed because it is not safe to do anything else. Yet, if we read the passage in the Bible, his contribution is greater than that of anyone else: "Et sedens Jesus contra gazophylacium, aspiciebat quomodo turba iactaret aes in gazophylacium et multi divites iactabant multa. Cum venisset autem vidua una, misit duo minuta, quod est quadrans. Et convocans discipulos suos ait illis: Amen dico vobis quoniam vidua haec pauper plus omnibus misit, qui miserunt in gazophylacium."[6] Thus in the first three strophes we have imagery which implies that the Emperor is laying claim to the divine as well as the secular role, and a statement by his panegyrist that he is functioning as an official poet because he must pay his tribute to Caesar.

What follows is an *amplificatio* of the theme of the poet rendering service to his master—the picture of *potestas larga*, of the Emperor

---

[6] Mark xii.41 ff.

using his power for the benefit of his people. It is the function of a professional poet and of a formal panegyrist to call attention to these virtues—especially if he needs the money ("nos poetae pauperes"). The poet affirms strongly that he is writing from the Christian, not the classical point of view, as a son of the church, not a follower of Cicero or the Muses. It is from the Christian point of view that he will write of a man who has restored the image of Rome by undertaking its secular burdens. But the poet's statement actually goes further, for it plays on several possible meanings:

> Christi sensus imbuat mentem Christianam
> ut de christo domini digna laude canam,
> qui potenter sustinens sarcinam mundanam
> relevat in pristinum gradum rem Romanam. IX, VIII

The poet's task is to sing the praises of the Lord's anointed—anything from Saul to Barbarossa—but the presence of the word "christo" inevitably recalls "Christ," particularly since it is associated with "Christi" in the first line. The implication that Christ has inspired the poet to sing of things worthy of HIM is inescapable, as is the confusion between Christ and the Lord's anointed. The confusion between the secular and the spiritual is continued in the next strophe, where the decline of Rome and the consequent impudence of the barbaric tribes are described in language reminiscent of the spiritual life—"ortas in imperio spinas impiorum."

Yet the following strophes are clearly secular in intent. The Lombards are compared with the rebels against Jupiter, not those who rebelled against God. It is the tribute due to Caesar that they have refused to give; and the city of Ambrose, one of the greatest of the Christian fathers, is compared to Troy, which had resisted the will of the pagan gods. Yet the biblical imagery is always present:

> omnes erant caesares, nemo censum dabat
> ... ...
> ut quod erat Caesaris daret ei gratis. IX, XIII

The citizens of Milan should obey Barbarossa because of the biblical injunction to render to Caesar the things which are Caesar's. The reputation of the Emperor needs no further clarification—according to the poet, who has been building it for fifteen strophes—but it is a combination of the religious and the secular. The first half of the poem concludes with this reference:

> qui rebelles lancea fodiens ultrici
> representat Karolum dextera victrici. IX, XVI

Barbarossa is the heir of Charlemagne, whom he had canonized, at once the Emperor and the saint. It is clear that the imperial mandate to the Archipoeta, conveyed through Reinald von Dassel, had been to the effect that Barbarossa was to be celebrated as the combination of the secular and the spiritual powers of the empire. Yet the imagery which the poet, the independent seer, uses makes only too clear the incongruity between the Emperor's desires and what was really due to him as the tribute due to Caesar. In asking for more than this tribute from the poet, he has to suffer the consequences in veiled but nevertheless sharp sarcasm.

The second half of the poem moves to epic recital, but epic recital with a difference. It is clearly impossible in a short poem like this to use the full epic style, but there are ways of imitating it. The poet himself gives a hint of what he is going to do:

>Primo suo domino paruit Papia
>urbs bona, flos urbium, clara, potens, pia;
>digna foret laudibus et topographia,
>nisi quod nunc utimur brevitatis via. IX, xviii

In other words, rhetoric would call for a full treatment of Barbarossa's first triumph, Pavia—if this were not a short poem. Nevertheless, the roll-call of victories continues, complete with figures—hyperbole: "donec desunt Alpibus frigora vel nives"; apostrophe: "letare, Novaria, numquam vetus fies"; and many others. There are the appropriate references to Constantine and the denigration of the Byzantine empire, the almost inevitable comparison with the deeds of the Greeks, the assertion that an account of his exploits would be another *Aeneid*. All this is narrative, flattering, factual, inflated. Neither Barbarossa nor Reinald can object, even if they perceive the irony and even if they perceive that the high-sounding conflicts promised in strophe xxvii in words reminiscent of "arma virumque cano" prove to be punitive expeditions against highwaymen. To have removed these malefactors is one of the great "gesta Friderici," and there is no doubt that he has brought peace to Italy, but it is peace at the price of great cruelty and destruction. This certainly is not the peace which is brought to mind by the words "Iterum describitur orbis ab Augusto."[7] This is not the coming of the Prince of Peace. The whole strophe is a nicely ambiguous play on Christian and classical figures.

>Iterum describitur orbis ab Augusto

---

[7] "Factum est autem in diebus illis exiit edictum Caesaris Augusti, ut describeretur universus orbis" (Luke ii.1).

redditur respublica statui vetusto
pax terras ingreditur habitu venusto
et iam non opprimitur iustus ab iniusto.   IX, xxx

There is no harm in describing Barbarossa as Augustus—indeed that was one of his titles—but the first Augustus was parceling out the world for taxation purposes, as an absolute ruler with no regard for the babe who was born in Bethlehem of Judaea. Order is being restored but what is the "statui vetusto" to which it is returning? Is it that of Italy before the revolt or that of Augustus Caesar, Emperor of pagan Rome? The use of "respublica" and "vetusto" seems to imply the latter. The return of peace to the earth is a theme pursued by Ovid and particularly by Vergil in the Messianic eclogue (even though the actual word "pax" does not appear there), and it should not be forgotten that *pax Romana* implied the absolute control of the Emperor. It is naturally desirable that the just should not be persecuted by the unjust, provided we know which are which. Watenphul is no doubt correct in saying that the "hominibus bonae voluntatis" of Luke ii. 14 are the same as the "iusti," but this does not solve the problem. They may very well correspond also to the "prudens" of strophe iii. In the end it is the friends of the new Augustus who will triumph.

It is the same conception of Barbarossa as the heir to the secular principate which motivates the anti-Byzantine feeling of the next strophe. The "volat fama" is reminiscent of Vergil, while the scorn for the Greek emperor is more in accord with Roman scorn for the Greeks than with the official attitude towards the successors of Constantine, although it must be remembered that there was a long tradition of anti-Byzantine feeling in the West. The obvious intention of the poet is to show Barbarossa as a Western, legitimate successor of Augustus. The Christian element is deliberately played down. These are matters of general principle but, as the next strophe shows, there were actual historical events of great importance which colored the attitude of the poet. Barbarossa was at this time supporting an antipope against Alexander who, after a struggle with William I of Sicily, had endorsed his rule. This same Alexander had even cooperated with the Byzantines in his opposition to Barbarossa. It is thus incumbent upon the Archipoeta to describe William of Sicily as "tyrannus" or "rex iniustus" and to condemn the Byzantines who had dared to oppose Frederick. The Emperor, in this poem, has restored peace in Italy, but, as everyone knew, it was a peace of devastation, imposed in defiance of a duly elected pope by an Emperor who abrogated to himself both secular and divine powers. Thus the poet's statement in strophe vii becomes the grimmest of irony:

> Filius ecclesie fidem sequor sanam
> contempno gentilium falsitatem vanam.   IX, vii

In fact he is celebrating Barbarossa for the rest of the poem not as a Christian Emperor but rather as the restorer of the old Roman principate of Augustus, the pre-Christian, pagan rule in which the church could have no part. The images and the allusions make this clear. It is the *pax Romana*, not the *pax Christiana* which is being restored.

The last two strophes thus become of great importance, strophes 33 and 34, the years of the life of Christ and a final prayer. Reinald von Dassel, the Archbishop who alone supported the uncanonical election of the new antipope, Paschal III, the Archbishop who was chancellor first and bishop very much second, is described in language drawn from the Gospels. He is John the Baptist making straight the way of the Lord,[8] but the verbs used of his activities convey not peace but a sword—*preparavit, extirpavit, subiugavit*. Only the last verb is one of peace, *liberavit*, but this applies only to the poet himself. The poem he has just written has freed him from the constant pressure of the Archbishop to write about the deeds of Barbarossa and had perhaps brought in a little money as an incidental. The poet has celebrated the new *princeps principum* and his John the Baptist and has thus earned his pay. Nor does he spare the Emperor a highly ambiguous final strophe. Barbarossa is described as "nobilis," surely a reference more to his deeds than to his birth, and there is therefore an assumption that the ruthless deeds just described are noble. "Age sicut agis," "Go on acting in the way you are," continues the same idea.[9] Possibly such a statement constitutes poetic approval but it could equally well mean "This is the way to continue your policy of secular imperialism." Certainly the next line implies that this is the way to gain fame: "sicut exaltatus es, exaltare magis." Again the words are biblical and are almost always used in connection with God, not a secular ruler. The impression of Godlike power is continued in the last two lines,

---

[8] "Vox clamantis in deserto parate viam Domini; rectas facite semitas eius" (Luke ii.4).

[9] "Interrogabant autem eum et milites dicentes 'Quid faciemus et nos ?' Et ait illis: neminem concutiatis neque calumniam faciatis et contenti estote stipendiis vestris" (Luke iii.14).

which have a deliberately Old Testament quality,[10] the Lord of Hosts striking down His enemies :

> fove tuos subditos hostes cede plagis
> super eos irruens ultione stragis!

Vengeance is mine, saith the Lord, but Barbarossa is taking his own revenge, as if he were God himself.

The poem closes as it opened, with images reserved for God used of a secular ruler. The poet has fulfilled the command of his patron, Reinald von Dassel, and has glorified the Italian policies of his Emperor in words which could without difficulty be interpreted as a sincere endorsement of those policies. But this endorsement is made by the *persona* of the poet, the one who has been commanded to perform, the "prudens" of strophe iii, the "vidua pauperior" of strophe iv, the "filius ecclesie" of strophe vii. All these are masks and furthermore they are poses which carry ironical possibilities. The real views of the poet are to be sought not in the statements made by the various *personae* but in the imagery used by the poet himself. In applying to a secular ruler images which were, in the mind of the audience, associated exclusively with God, the poet strongly criticizes Barbarossa's usurpation of spiritual functions; by using the classical, imperial image and the epic form, albeit in mocking fashion, he associates Barbarossa not with the Holy Roman Empire but with secular Roman rule. His patron Reinald von Dassel becomes a secularized John the Baptist proclaiming the legitimacy of the new imperialism. The distinction so clearly proclaimed by the *persona* between the things which are Caesar's and the things which are God's is utterly denied by the poet's use or abuse of the imagery conventions of the two genres, the panegyric and the epic.

It is hard to escape the feeling that the two poems of the Archipoeta concerned with the deeds of Barbarossa are closely connected. His refusal to write an epic because he was not the man for such a task is nullified by his poem praising the very deeds which would have been the stuff of the epic and ostensibly showing his Emperor as the personification of imperial justice. Yet the imagery shows that he regards

---

[10] "Iudica illos, Deus, decidant a cognitionibus suis; secundum multitudinem impietatum eorum expelle eos, quoniam irritaverunt te, Domine" (Ps. v. 11); "Exsurgat Deus et dissipentur inimici eius et fugiant qui oderunt eum a facie eius. Sicut deficit fumus, deficiant. Sicut fluit cera a facie ignis, sic pereant peccatores a facie Dei et iusti epulentur et exultent" (Ps. lxvii.1).

these deeds as the subject for a mock-epic, not an epic, and his biblical imagery makes it clear that the tribute due to Caesar has been vastly exceeded by the powers which Barbarossa has abrogated to himself. The Archipoeta demonstrates that it is not the *persona* of the poet who tells the truth but the poet who juggles the imagery and conventions of a genre to produce effects which are often totally different from the apparent intention of the poem.

Columbia University

LOVE AND SEX IN THE *DECAMERON*

JOHN CHARLES NELSON

Although the *Decameron* is universally acknowledged as Boccaccio's masterpiece, the reading of it alone gives an inadequate picture of the author's narrative skills.[1] The genre of the novella, imposing a hundred times on the author the burden of telling a story which is *novus*[2]—extraordinary and unheard of—overturns the reality and complexities of the human psyche which Boccaccio knew so well and represented ably in the *Fiammetta* and in many passages of other so-called "minor" works. (The *Fiammetta*, noted Francesco De Sanctis, is the beginning of modern literature.)[3] It is principally the genre itself that accounts for Boccaccio's remarkable economy of words, his exclusion of almost everything that is not action, the reiteration of marvels, and the stylization and oversimplification of erotic behavior. Viewed anachronistically by the criteria of more modern fiction, these aspects appear as flaws; seen historically, they simply characterize Boccacio's narrative. Only an overview of his entire fictional work can "correct" the "limitations" which our twentieth-century reading of the *Decameron* tends to discover. In the *Fiammetta* we will find precisely what is missing in the love stories of the *Decameron*, whose enamorments are instantaneous—a finely drawn portrayal of the intimate workings of the human psyche as it runs the gamut of love emotions—coupled with a meticulously conceived (and historically important) first-person narrator's point of view.

According to our notion of romantic love, which derives much of its origin from Provençal literature some eight centuries ago and which Boccaccio in good measure shared, a distinction between love and sexuality is valid. I find it awkward to discuss love in the *Decameron* without also talking about sex. For Boccaccio, a naturalist, the latter

---

[1] This paper in an earlier form was given as a Da Ponte lecture at the Casa Italiana of Columbia University on February 12, 1968.

[2] See Enrico de' Negri, "The Legendary Style of the *Decameron*," *The Romanic Review* 43 (1952), 166-189.

[3] Francesco De Sanctis, *Storia della letteratura italiana* (Turin, 1966), 345.

was a large and essential part of the former. And it is particularly in his treatment of the role and value of sexual attraction and satisfaction that Boccaccio breaks with pre-existing Italian literary tradition in a striking fashion.

In the fourth story of the first day of the *Decameron* Boccaccio writes that there lived in a monastery "crammed with monks and holiness" a young monk whose youthful vigor neither fasting nor vigils could subdue. One day about noontime when all the other monks were asleep, he was walking near his church when he saw a very beautiful young girl, perhaps the daughter of some neighboring laborer, gathering herbs in a field. After striking up a conversation with her, he was able to lead her unseen into his cell. And while he was sporting with her less cautiously than he should have, they were overheard by his abbot. Thinking that he heard the shuffling of feet outside his door, the young monk peered through a little crack in the door and saw clearly that the abbot was standing there. But he saved himself from punishment by a clever stratagem. After a short while he went to the abbot and told him that he was going out to finish gathering some wood he had cut. During his absence the old abbot went to the monk's cell to take a look for himself at the girl who was there. A short while later the young monk was able to reverse their former roles as he spied the two of them through an opening, the old abbot lying on his back and the young girl on top of him. Later when the abbot scolded him and ordered him imprisoned the young blade of a monk promptly retorted, "Sir, forgive me! I have not been a member of St. Benedict's order for long enough to know every detail of it. Besides, you had not yet shown me that women should lie as heavily on men as fasts and vigils. But now that you have shown me, forgive me, and I promise never to sin that way again. Indeed, I will always do as I have seen you do!"[4] Stung by these words, the abbot pardoned the monk and they quietly put the girl out of the monastery—but then, Boccaccio adds mischieviously in concluding his tale, "you may be sure they let her in again, many a time thereafter."

Boccaccio's critics have been remarkably squeamish in discussing —or more frequently in not discussing—such tales in the *Decameron*.

---

[4] *Decameron* IV, 1. Here and elsewhere extended translations are those of Frances Winwar in Giovanni Boccaccio, *The Decameron* (New York, 1955). Some of the short translations are my own, some are Miss Winwar's.

The two most discerning commentators, Attilio Momigliano and Luigi Russo, simply skip all the erotic stories.[5]

First of all, let us observe that the word *amore* does not occur in this novella. Even in Boccaccio's vocabulary, this is not a story of love, but of carnality. There are a few details omitted from this brief resumé which we should fill in in order to illustrate one facet of Boccaccio's attitude toward sexuality : reaction to the opposite sex is powerful and instantaneous.

Of the young monk Boccaccio says that when he saw the young girl gathering herbs, "no sooner had he seen her than he was fiercely assailed by carnal concupiscence." Later, the abbot at first thought to open the monk's cell in the presence of all the other monks, in order to shame him and to avoid any possibility that the others would blame the abbot for punishing the monk. But on second thought he decided that the girl might be the wife or daughter of someone whom he would regret having offended. When he took the opportunity of seeing the girl for himself, she became frightened and began to cry.

But our abbot, casting his eyes upon her and finding her fresh and luscious, *old though he was*, suddenly began to feel the urge of the flesh no less violently than his young monk before him. And he began debating in his mind : "Truly, why shouldn't I take my pleasure when I can ? Sorrow and annoyance for that matter are always ready, whether I want them or not. Here's a fine wench, right at hand, and nobody knows a thing about it. Now if I can get her to do my pleasure, why shouldn't I have it ? Who will be any the wiser ? No one ! And a sin that is hidden is half shriven. This opportunity may not come to me again, and it is the best sort of wisdom to take advantage of a bounty when the Lord God sees fit to send it."

The old abbot's reaction to temptation is the same as that of the young monk : he cannot resist it. But he assuages his conscience with the spurious reasoning that clergymen use in several other stories of the *Decameron* in order to seduce credulous women.

---

[5] Giovanni Boccaccio, *Il Decameron : quarantanove novelle commentate da A. Momigliano* (Turin, 1966); Giovanni Boccaccio, *Il Decameron. Venticinque novelle scelte e ventisette postille critiche a cura di Luigi Russo* (Florence, 1939). As Aldo Scaglione has recently demonstrated in his *Nature and Love in the Middle Ages* (Berkeley and Los Angeles, 1963), the failure of De Sanctis and many later critics including Momigliano to discern the positive naturalistic ethic consciously proposed in the *Decameron* has tended to obscure the historical importance of Boccaccio's masterpiece.

And what is the young girl's response to the advances of the old abbot ? "The girl, who was neither of iron nor adamant, very obligingly lent herself to the abbot's pleasures."

In short, in Boccaccio's world, the sex drive operates as an irresistible force to which all alike succumb—men and women, young and old, clerical and lay.

I shall not attempt to draw any sociological conclusions from the *Decameron* as it relates historically to the mores of Boccaccio's times. However, one is easily reminded of Carlo Levi's observation in *Christ Stopped at Eboli* about the severe strictures which segregate the sexes and shelter nubile women from the company of men in the small Southern villages to which he was exiled by the Fascist regime : the reason for such a severe social code, he wrote, is the universally held belief in that region that sexual desire is so overwheming a force that any two people of the opposite sex who chance to be alone together will *of course* have sexual intercourse.

Now let us recall the story of Ricciardo and Caterina (V, 4)—a story of hot-blooded pre-marital love with a comic leitmotiv running through it. A young girl who ardently desires to enjoy the embraces of her sweetheart complains to her mother that she is very hot at night and must be allowed to sleep on the cool terrace in the open air where the nightingale sings. Her wish reluctantly granted, she receives a nocturnal visit from her lover : not only does she succeed in making the nightingale sing, several times, but the young couple, having fallen asleep in each other's arms, are discovered in broad daylight the next morning, she still clutching the "nightingale" in her hand. The young man's fright is turned to good use by Caterina's shrewd, indulgent father, who seizes the opportunity to conclude an advantageous marriage for his daughter.

Though it's quite a jump from *Giovanni* Boccaccio to *John* Crowe Ransom, I cannot read this story without being reminded of Ransom's humorous poem, "Philomela," based on the curious zoological fact that only the European species of the nightingale is gifted with marvelous melodic song; the American species—alas!—does not sing... Again, I refrain from any sociological comment.

The stories of adultery are too numerous to allow summarizing. You may call to mind the novella of monna Sismonda, who ties one end of a string to her big toe and lets the other dangle out of the window for her lover to pull as a signal; or of Bartolomea, who prefers Paganino, the young pirate who kidnaps her, to the weak-hammed old husband, a judge, who devised a saint-filled calendar with an incredible number of days of obligatory abstinence to explain to his wife the infrequency of their conjugal relations.

Before turning to one of Boccaccio's better known love stories, I would like to discuss perhaps his most popular sex story—one that has had such fortune, or misfortune, as to become a sort of off-color cocktail-party story.

An innocent 14-year old girl named Alibech, who lived in Gafsa, in Tunisia and who was not a Christian, had heard from the Christians in her city that their faith and service of God were a highly commendable thing. In response to her questions about how one best could serve God, she was directed to the hermits of the Theban desert. After a hard journey of several days she reached the humble dwelling of a holy man living in solitude, who marvelled to see her. Remarking her youth and beauty, however, he did not trust himself to take her in, but sent her further into the desert to another holy man. The second hermit also sent her on her way, until she came to the cell of a young, devout hermit named Rustico, who welcomed the opportunity to test the firmness of his devotion. However, the very first night temptation overwhelms him and he resolves to seduce his naive guest under the guise of serving God. He persuades Alibech to do as she sees him do, and they both take off their clothes. A moment later, Alibech exclaims, "Rustico, what is that thing that you have there, sticking out like that, which I don't have?"

"Ah, daughter," says Rustico, "this is the devil that I told you about."

As their conversation continues it develops that Alibech instead of a devil possesses hell; and that the greatest pleasure and service to God is to put the devil in hell—which they proceed to do, six times. In the remainder of the story Alibech eventually becomes so enthusiastic in the service of God that Rustico, who was living on roots and water, sees that his efforts to satisfy her are "like throwing a bean into a lion's mouth." Both are rescued when she is fetched home for marriage.

Here as generally in the *Decameron* the sexual drive is depicted as an elemental, irresistible force of nature—and with great possibilities as a subject for humor.

Among the many translators of the *Decameron*, some censored this story; others deleted it entirely. One editor substituted a tale of exemplary chastity—not, however, written by Boccaccio. Another translator left the spiciest passage in the original Italian; and even Frances Winwar, who in her preface contrasts her own forthrightness with the euphemisms and omissions of earlier translators, flinches at one point in this story.

Where she says of Rustico, "his flesh grew stiff," Boccaccio had written, in keeping with the parody of religion that runs throughout this novella, *venne la resurrezion della carne*, literally, there occurred the resurrection of the flesh—a metaphor which he borrowed from Apuleius. Simply an irreverent joke, one might say. A little boy who wants to shock his parents by appearing without his clothes thinks he will succeed all the better if he waits until the preacher is visiting them. But even jokes may have interesting implications. In this metaphor we have a confrontation between sex and religion, between naturalism and transcendentalism. In this novella, comic though it be, we see a champion of sexuality defying the theological-ecclesiastical complex which sought to limit sexuality severely.

In the famous first story of the *Decameron*, Ser Ciappelletto, a notary who delights in counterfeiting deeds and swearing false oaths, in creating ill-will and stirring up scandal; who is a murderer, a blasphemer, a frequenter of taverns, a homosexual, a glutton, a guzzler, and a caster of loaded dice—in short, says Boccaccio, *il piggiore uomo forse che mai nascesse*—by a blasphemous confession on his deathbed to a holy friar, comes to be revered as Saint Ciappelletto. In the *Decameron* we find not only the parody of sainthood, but parodies as well of relics, of miraculous cures, of Hell, Purgatory and Heaven, and even of dogma. Yet modern critics—Momigliano, Russo, and a great many others—are unanimous in denying to Boccaccio any serious criticism or questioning of the Christian religion. While I am not ready to proclaim that they are wrong, I do wish to submit that the question is not really settled. It can scarcely be fortuitous that the *Decameron* begins with not one, but three stories in which traditional assumptions about Christianity are given a surprising twist. It cannot be denied that the sexual morality of the *Decameron* reverses Christian teaching about sex.

From the stories just discussed and a number of others we may draw the following four conclusions concerning sex and sexual morality in the *Decameron* :

(1) Sexual desire and gratification are natural, universal and irresistible.

(2) Religious restraints on sex are ineffectual and hypocritical.

(3) Parental authority over people of marriageable age is deadly when based upon the conventions of class; it is best tempered by indulgent humanity and shrewdness.

(4) Adultery and fornication, typically, are rapturously enjoyable. Furthermore, adulterous wives are usually justified by the jealousy or stupidity of their husbands.

Before turning from the theme of sex to that of love, let us examine Boccaccio's own defense against the earliest critics of the *Decameron*. In the introduction to the fourth day, shortly following the story of Alibech, Boccaccio enumerates five charges which they have leveled against him : (1) that he likes women too much "and that it is not an honest thing for him to take so much delight in pleasing and consoling" them and even worse in commending them in his tales; (2) that at his age (though he was only about 40) "it is not proper ... to talk about women or to entertain them"; (3) that he would be far wiser to spend his time with the Muses on Parnassus than with these trifles, his novelle; (4) that he should think about earning a living; and (5) that the events in his stories didn't actually happen in the ways that he narrates them.

Boccaccio says that before answering them he would like to tell just half a story. He then proceeds to tell what we might call the 101st story of the *Decameron*.

Filippo Balducci is left a widower with a single young son, whom he brings up in the mountains in a life devoted to the service of God, in isolation from the world and its temptations. When Balducci grows older and his trips to Florence for supplies become a burden, he reluctantly agrees to take his son along with him into the city. The son is wide-eyed with wonder at the magnificent palaces and churches, until by chance "they came across a party of lovely young girls dressed in their Sunday best, on their way home from a wedding.

"And what may those be ?" asked the boy.

"Hush ! Lower your eyes and don't look at them," cried his father. "They're wickedness itself (*elle son mala cosa*) !"

To the lad's query concerning their name, the trapped father chooses to reply, "*Elle si chiamano papere* (they are called geese)," prompting the retort, "Father! Father! please see to it that I get one of those geese."

To the scores of legends and sermons that he had heard and read about the desirability of ascetic renunciation, Boccaccio answers with a story about the impossibility of such renunciation. The story concludes with this sentence: "[Il padre] sentì incontanente più aver di forza la natura che il suo ingegno (The father at once saw that nature was much stronger than his wisdom)."

Boccaccio then proceeds to answer the charges one by one:

(1) He openly confesses that he has tried *troppo* to please women and that women please him *troppo*. As he commends his audience of sweetest women (*dolcissime donne*) for their charming ways, their beauty and loveliness, it is evident that for Boccaccio women are symbols of the civilization and refinement which he idolized almost from the moment of his humble and illegitimate birth. He adds that he cares little for his critics' carping at the response of his God-created body to the *virtù* of the light in women's eyes.

(2) As for being a lover at his age, he answers that he is content to follow the example of Guido Cavalcanti, Dante Alighieri and Cino da Pistoia.

(3) Regarding his alleged neglect of the Muses, his somewhat obscure answer is quite revealing once its sense is perceived:

That I should remain with the muses on Parnassus, is good enough advice, I must admit. Nevertheless, since we can neither stay with the muses, nor they with us, can a man be blamed for taking leave of them, if he delights in the sight of creatures who resemble them? The muses are members of the fair sex, and although women cannot justly be ranked with them, still, they look like them, at first glance. Therefore, even if I liked women for no other reason, that should be sufficient. There's something else besides: women have been the reason for my writing a thousand verses, where the muses never gave me occasion for writing a single one. They were of great assistance to me, it's true, and showed me how to compose those thousand verses. Perhaps even in the writing of these stories, humble though they be, they may have come, sometimes, to keep me company for the sake of the women, or in appreciation of the resemblance they bear them. It is for that reason that I don't wander as far from Mount Parnassus or the muses, in the stories I weave, as some would have it.

From this passage we can draw at least these two conclusions: first, in saying that he has not wandered so far from the Muses as his critics think, Boccaccio is confidently asserting the poetic worth of the *Decameron*—a book that stands apart in its richness, its warmth, its humanity and its bourgeois vitality from Boccaccio's earlier works and those of all his contemporaries and predecessors, to give us a magnificent panorama of medieval society which is unparalleled, exception being made, if at all, only for Dante's *Comedy*.[6] Second, in equating women with the Muses, he gives striking affirmation of the poetic value of the real, of every-day persons and events.[7] With this attitude, small wonder that the *Decameron's* chief immediate success was achieved among the new Florentine burgher class, for and about whom it was chiefly written.

(4) In his reply to those who are ostensibly solicitous about the penury threatening him, Boccaccio retorts with fierce humanistic pride that many men who have pursued "fables" have caused their age to flourish, whereas many, on the contrary, who sought more bread than they needed, have perished in bitterness.

(5) As for the authenticity of his tales, he facetiously challenges his detractors to compare the *novelle* with their originals—that is, with the allegedly historical events which they describe.

And for good measure he adds a final challenge to his moralizing detractors: he will stand his ground in the knowledge that he and others like him follow nature; his *morditori* can become angry if they like—he will leave them alone with their corrupt appetites if they in turn will only leave him in peace.

The famous novella which immediately follows this passage is obviously a continuation of Boccaccio's naturalistic argument. Indeed, the polemical element in it is almost so strong as to damage the story esthetically.

The two chief characters of this story are a father and his daughter—Tancredi, prince of Salerno and the daughter, Ghismonda, whom he loved "as tenderly as any daughter was ever loved by a father." One character is striking by her absence : the mother—a fact which introduces a hint of incestual attraction. Generally in this novella, the father, at first affectionate and doting, then jealous and cruelly vindictive—plays the role given elsewhere to the jealous husband. But Boccaccio only hints at an affection that is more than paternal. Because of his tender love, Tancredi neglected to provide for Ghismonda's marriage until she had passed the normal age of marriage by several years. And when soon afterward she was left a widow, he

---

[6] For recent imaginative explorations of the rich world of the *Decameron* see Vittore Branca, *Boccaccio medievale* (Florence, 1956) and Giovanni Getto, *Vita di forme e forme di vita nel Decameron* (Turin, 1958).

[7] My interpretation of this passage and of the following novella of Ghismonda owes much to the analyses of Luigi Russo.

neglected to remarry her until, out of desperation, she decided to take a lover—one Guiscardo, "uom di nazione assai umile, ma per virtù e per costumi nobile più che altro (a man of very humble birth, but by virtue and habits nobler then any other)." Helped by Ghismonda's ingenuity born of love, the couple manage to rendezvous many times in her bedroom, Guiscardo arriving there by an old, forgotten stairway. But one afternoon, Tancredi, having fallen asleep in a hidden corner of his daughter's bedroom, awakens to see with his own eyes what he gladly would never have witnessed. As a result Guiscardo later is taken prisoner. Confronted by Tancredi, he replies with only one sentence: "Amor può troppo più che nè voi nè io possiamo (Love is far more powerful than either you or I)." We may take this statement as one important basis of Boccaccio's ethic.

When Tancredi scolds his daughter for lewdness, but especially for the dishonor involved in choosing "a youth of the lowest station," she replies with a long and defiant speech of self-justification, whose salient points are (1) that far from renouncing her love for Guiscardo, she will even continue to love him after they die, if that is possible; (2) being himself a man of flesh, Tancredi should have been aware that he had fathered a daughter of flesh, and not of stone or iron, who, having already been married, was all the less able to resist the pleasures that beckoned; and (3) that she chose Guiscardo not by accident but after deliberation, because his character alone rendered him the noblest man at court.

After this confrontation Tancredi nevertheless orders Guiscardo to be strangled. Then he cuts out Guiscardo's heart and sends it to Ghismonda in a golden cup. Very likely, Boccaccio is consciously making use of the phallic symbolism. Ghismonda kisses and praises Guiscardo's heart: "Ahi, dolcissimo albergo di tutti i miei piaceri (Ah, sweetest abode of all my pleasures)!..." She vows eternal fidelity, waters the heart with her tears and then pours upon it the poisons which she has prepared the day before. Drinking them, she prepares to die, but not before a final dialogue with Tancredi in which he at last takes pity—but too late to do aught but promise common burial for the lovers.

In the initial confrontation between father and daughter there is a curious reversal of roles. Tancredi, upon making his fatal discovery, weeps like a child. To his complaints Ghismonda answers with the confidence and forthrightness of mature adulthood. The effect is heightened by her singular address of her father, whom she calls simply "Tancredi"—his given name. She will not admit to being at fault; she refers to her love affair as *peccato naturale* and *peccato, se peccato è*. By implication, the real sin that one might commit in this life is abstinence, a sin against nature. And in her apotheosis of her lover's heart, she calls it her surest companion for the journey *a' luoghi non conosciuti* (to places unknown), not to the traditional Hell or Purgatory or Heaven.

In such a story as this lies the magic by which Boccaccio, who is so medieval, can seem so modern—indeed, so contemporary. Boccaccio through Ghismonda is a spokesman for flaming youth, for sexual freedom, iconoclasm, amorous selection according to individual merit and desire rather than by the dictates of lineage, for eager, sensual yet idealistic love; for youth in rebellion against stern parental authority that dotes but does not understand, that upholds conventional morality, chastity, class privilege and property rights.

Practically all civilized societies have seen love as a disruptive force whose thrust must be controlled in order to preserve kinship lines, property ownership and the family itself as the basic social unit. Some have sought to channel it, some to suppress it, some even to ridicule it. Plato called love a "divine madness"; the classical world generally saw it as an irrational force.

It is only a slight exaggeration to say that love in the romantic sense is an invention of the twelfth century. Much that is typical in the *Decameron* is found in the theory and narratives of courtly love. Some of the most amusing pages, to us, in Andreas Capellanus' code-book of courtly love, *De amore*, are those detailing the impossibility of love in marriage (a tenet contradicted, however, by Boccaccio and several earlier authors). Marriage entails a legal contract which guarantees basic sexual and other rights to the husband. Hence it is impossible for a wife to give herself to her husband; he already owns her. The possibility of bestowing such a gift—hence the possibility of love—is reserved to the noble lady at court, who being, ideally, of higher social station than her suitor and having no obligations to him since she is married to another, can freely bestow her favors upon him. This love, by definition adulterous, is rejected by Dante, as it is also by theologians. Traditionally among the troubadours, and later in Petrarca, it requires a recantation. Boccaccio, though retaining its characteristics entirely in some of his stories, is most interested in those in which he can carry love to an exalted level of heroism. The story of Ghismonda is only one of these. In his early work, the *Filocolo*, Florio and Biancofiore exemplify a perfect love and one which ends happily, in marriage; in the *Filostrato*, the chief source of Chaucer's *Troylus and Creseyde*, a noble, perfect knight is betrayed by a faithless woman; and in the

Fiammetta a woman faithful to her lover is betrayed by him, leaving her sullen and unhappy. Standing above both Fiammetta and Creseida in Boccaccio's scale of values is the exalted heroism of several women in the *Decameron*—Ghismonda; Lisabetta, whose brothers kill her lover, but cannot destroy her love; and Guiglielmo Rossiglione's wife who is deceitfully fed her lover's heart. All three of these women die heroically without breaking faith with their respective lovers.

Boccaccio's attitude toward women, however, is not without its ambiguities and inconsistencies. Condescending and even misogynistic in a few passages, he somewhat anticipates the scurrilous *Corbaccio* in the tale of the vengeful scholar (VIII, 7). The novella of Rinaldo d'Esti (II, 2), on the other hand, is pervaded by an appealing, mythic aura as Rinaldo is rescued from shivering cold by a kind widow who gives him a warm bath, clothing, food, and sex. Boccaccio's indulgent humanity finds easy expression in such a story. But when the male's desires are thwarted, Boccaccio is capable, as in the *Corbaccio*, of throwing a prolonged tantrum. Such episodes, in which the author's personal feeling damages the esthetic quality of the narrative, are indicative of a less than total maturity in Boccaccio the man. One also feels that in his righteous zeal for the "rights of the flesh" he tends to ignore too completely rival claims, such as for example those of the doting husband whose sexual prowess is surpassed by that of the dashing lover.

There is, furthermore, a basic contradiction between the permissive, naturalistic sexual ethic of the *novelle* and the unfailingly "correct" and abstinent behavior of the seven young ladies and three young men who narrate the novelle. The latter, indeed, provide an esthetically successful, ideal element of contrast to the "realistic" stories which they frame; yet the implied moral choice offered the reader by the presentation of two contradictory modes of sexual behavior is never resolved.

In conclusion, I would like to submit that Boccaccio's naturalism is not at all a bad thing. It is well known that the Church Fathers had eagerly taken up a long classical tradition of misogyny. Woman was fickle, untrustworthy and corrupt. Passionate or excessive love even of one's mate was interpreted as adultery. St. Jerome expressed contempt for marriage, in accordance with his ideal of complete separation from worldly contacts. In one of his epistles he compares remarriage to a dog *revertens ad vomitum*. Clement of Alexandria enjoined all women to be ashamed at the very thought that they were women. Many medieval writers argued that woman has only one real virtue, that of chastity. To throw it off as Ghismonda did was an act of great presumption.

Of course in the late Middle Ages the Provençal poets had established, in literature, an opposite polarity: the courtly lady of the exalted nobility, adored and served almost in reverence, who might grant her lover a guerdon ranging from a smile or a token to complete physical union. Dante dramatically rejected that tradition in the episode of Paolo and Francesca, teaching that such love leads to perdition. Careful consideration of the many women of the *Commedia* will reveal that Dante's view of earthly women was conventional when not reactionary.[8] Francesco Petrarca also rejected, ultimately, the celebrated, lifelong love which inspired his *Canzoniere*, for in its last poem he identifies Laura with the perilous Medusa. Against this background, Boccaccio marks a milestone in the acceptance and humanization of woman in Italian literature.

Love in the *Decameron* is a phenomenon which is basically sexual and which in many novelle is a beautiful and ennobling experience. Its characteristic note is precisely the additional element beyond satisfaction of the senses. Boccaccio is particularly interested in showing how sexual love itself is the basis for exaltation, ennoblement, heroism. In order for love to be something rare and sublime, it is not necessary for it to be spiritualized and transcendentalized as was done variously by *stilnuovo* poets and Dante and Petrarca.

Boccaccio was devoted to literature as very few writers have been. And like the greatest of these, he knew that literature has most meaning when it is involved with life's central themes. Love, for him, is closely associated with sex; yet it is far more important than sex. He sought to demonstrate in many of his stories that love can be both sensual and inspired. His treatment of love is unique among Italians of the late Middle Ages and the early Renaissance. It is not until Ariosto that we again find an author with a Boccaccesque approach to love. Boccaccio embraced and represented in his stories a late medieval ideal which Dante and Petrarca and other writers seriously concerned with Christianity were ultimately forced to abandon. He modified and rationally defended that ideal in a new and striking fashion. And he did so with a verve that unmistakably springs from his own life experience and his own warmly human character.

Columbia University

---

[8] See Marianne Goldner Shapiro, "Woman, Earthly and Divine, in the *Comedy* of Dante" (Ph. D. diss., Columbia University, 1968).

PICO DELLA MIRANDOLA IN TUDOR TRANSLATION

GEORGE B. PARKS

The preliminary survey ("primo sondaggio") by the late Professor Weiss[1] of the earlier English interest in Pico includes mention of the translations by Thomas More and Thomas Elyot. There were in fact other Tudor translators, and I give the list here.

Pico's works of learning needed no translation from his Latin and were quoted at once by John Colet; they continued to be read in England for a century and a half, as Professor Weiss indicates. These works make up the bulk of the *Opera Omnia* which Pico's nephew published in 1496, two years after their author's death. The *Opera* were at once reprinted: Venice, 1498; "Bologna, 1498," which has been shown to be in fact Lyons, 1498-1500;[2] Strassburg, 1504; [Reggio, 1506]; Paris, 1517; Basel (expanded to two volumes), 1572.

The works of learning were the *Heptaplus*, the *Apologia*, the *Tractatus de ente et uno*, the *Oratio de hominis dignitate*, and the giant *Adversus astrologos*. The stout folio, which an early owner who numbered the pages by hand found to contain 531 pages, included also more personal matter. An initial ten pages were taken up by the "Vita" written by Pico's nephew. The verse prayer "Deprecatoria ad Deum" of one and one-half pages was inserted after the *Heptaplus*. A brief middle section of sixty-seven pages was labeled "Epistolae plures" but included other things. It was from these scattered personal items on fewer than one hundred pages that the Tudor translators made selections. Thomas More's book, the longest of the versions, numbered eighty pages in English.

The "Epistolae" section included some fifty letters, three of which attracted one translator. The most noted writings in it were three duodecalogues: "the XII Regulae dirigentes homines in spirituali pugna," which A. W. Reed called apophthegms on the struggle with sin; the "XII arma spiritualis pugnae," the named protections against

---

[1] Roberto Weiss, "Pico e l'Inghilterra," in *L'Opera e il pensiero di Giovanni Pico della Mirandola*, I (Florence, 1965), 143-58.

[2] Polain (Belgique) 3145; Proctor 8663-4.

sin, which begin "Voluptas brevis et exigua" and end "Crux christi," and add "Testimonia martyrum et exempla sanctorum"; and the "XII conditiones amantis," beginning "Amare unum tantum et contemnere omnia pro eo," and adding a succinct paragraph to transfer them "ad amorem dei." The duodecalogues were followed by a commentary on the psalm "Conserva me Domine," again a study of the relation of man to God.

In these four brief works Pico presented in half a dozen pages the moral life of man in its simplest terms as a war against sin, for which the continuing help of a just but loving God is essential. Here is no dogma; no intermediary stands between God and man except as Christ has been God's agent; man's devotion to God has no mystic overtones but is that of a child's simple dependence on a parent, however exacting. The theme is stated in a military metaphor of the war against sin, which Erasmus' *Handbook of the Christian Soldier* was soon to present with much greater range and complexity; but beyond the war, the "XII conditiones" and the "Expositio in Psalmum 16" moved on to the love of God itself. The pithy statements of the essence of the moral-religious life were in a sense the heart of the book.

Pico's *Opera* seems to have reached England at once, since Colet was reading the *Heptaplus* in May 1498.[3] A copy of the *Opera* was listed at Canterbury College, Oxford, by 1508;[4] a copy was owned by Bryan Rowe, Vice-Provost of King's College, Cambridge, before his death in 1521;[5] a copy was listed at Syon Monastery in Isleworth before 1526;[6] a copy was owned by John Claymond of Corpus Christi College, Oxford, before his death in 1537.[7] Though Thomas Cranmer does not seem to have owned the book, and it was not mentioned by John Leland or John Bale, it was in the Lumley library, probably acquired by the Earl of Arundel. In sum, it was known in the academic world for which its treatises were written, and it was known to at least one of the great collectors.

---

[3] Sears Jayne, *John Colet and Marsilio Ficino* (Oxford, 1963), 37. It is true that the *Heptaplus* had been printed separately (Hain-Copinger 13001*) about 1490, and Colet may not yet have had the *Opera*.

[4] Oxford Historical Society *Publications*, n.s., VI (1941), 86.

[5] Cambridge Bibliographical Society *Transactions*, II (1958), 346.

[6] *Catalogue of the Library of Syon Monastery*, ed. Mary Bateson (Cambridge, 1898), 145.

[7] *The Library*, 4th ser., 18 (1938), 405.

It was also known at once at court. Perhaps within little more than a decade after publication, three translations of the brief religious works were done in French and were presented to the King of England. One was done by a student of Bernard André, the French Poet Laureate of England, and we may suspect André of inspiring the other two. A much larger translation was done in English by Thomas More, and was published probably by 1510. Two other versions in English of the religious works were made in the course of the century.

Before describing these translations, we should note the breaking of one supposed link between Pico and England. A Latin poem in praise of Skelton as the first English poet was once ascribed to Pico by an editor of Skelton's works; the poem was, in fact, written by Erasmus.[8]

I list the Tudor translations of Pico.[9]

1. Dedicated to King Henry VII : a French version of the "Expositio in Psalmum 16," entitled "lexposicion du XVe pseaulme." (It is preceded by a prayer to the Virgin, "Ceste oroison de la vierge excellente," which is not in Pico.) No name is signed to the dedication or to the work itself. It is British Museum MS Royal 16.E.XXIV, fols. 3-10 of the total ten folios : parchment, a presentation copy. The Pico translation begins : "Se aucun parfaict veult recognoistre son estat ung peril a en luy, cest quil ne senorgueillisse de sa vertu." It ends "...nostre felicite est accomplie en la vision & fruicion de lhumanite de Jhesucrist... lequel nous doint paradis. AMEN."

Professor C. A. J. Armstrong dates this and the next item c. 1499, but he gives no evidence.

2. Dedicated to King Henry VII : "xii Reigles en partie excitantes et en partie adressantes lhomme en la bataille espirituelle"; followed by "xii armeures de la bataille espirituelle"; and then by the "xii condicions de lamoureux." These are translations without expansion of the three Latin duodecalogues. The text proper begins "Se le

---

[8] As demonstrated by William Nelson (*John Skelton, Humanist* [New York, 1939], 57); he gives the English verse translation by Preserved Smith of the panegyric. The ascription to Pico was made by Alexander Dyce, *Poetical Works of John Skelton*, I (Boston, 1871), lxvii.

[9] I learned of Items 1 and 2 from Professor Nelson, p. 22, and again from the article by C. A. J. Armstrong on William Parron in *Italian Renaissance Studies : A Tribute to Cecilia M. Ady*, ed. E. F. Jacob (London, 1960), 440.

chemyn de vertu semble a lhomme estre difficille" and ends "il nous a rachetez denfer par le precieux sang de son filz, lequel par sa grace nous doint paradis. AMEN."

This is British Museum MS Royal 16.E.XXV : parchment, a presentation copy in the same hand and design as 1, fols. 1-7. The MS was listed in the Royal Library inventory of 1542 (BM MS Additional 25469, fol. 23).

3. Dedicated to the King of England : four "petites œuvres contemplatives," including as one item the same works in a different French version : "Aucunes reigles de Picus Miran. adressantes les hommes en la bataille spirituelle"; "Douze armures de la bataille spirituelle"; and "Douze conditions de laymant." This item accompanies three translations of short works by Erasmus into French.

The manuscript is BM Royal 16.E.XIV, 31 folios; the Pico items are on fols. 4v-8.

The dedication is written by Gervasius Amoenus, who writes that he had completed the translations made for the King by another student, his roommate Henry Hault. The latter is identified elsewhere by Bernard André, Poet Laureate, as his former student, who died in January, 1508.[10] The king for whom he wrote was then Henry VII; the presentation to him was made for a *nouuel an*, and therefore 1509, the last that Henry VII would see. Amoenus is identified elsewhere as a French pupil-assistant of Erasmus, Amoenus Drocensis (that is, of Dreux).[11] He may have come to England with Erasmus in 1505, staying on when Erasmus left for Italy in 1506; in 1509, as he says in the dedication, he was enjoying the patronage of Mountjoy, patron also of Erasmus; the latter had not yet returned from Italy.

Hault's translation was thus made before 1508, and we conjecture that both Hault and the translator of Item 2 were inspired by André to emulate his use of French at the English court. The text proper begins (fol. 4v) : "La premiere reigle est que si la voye de vertus te semble estre dure pource quil y fault continuellement batailler a lencontre la chair, le diable, et le monde..." It ends (fol. 8) : "il nous a crees dung riens et quant par le saing de son filz il nous a rachetez des peines denfer."

---

[10] As noted by Nelson, 23. The reference in André's *Annales Henrici VII* (Rolls Series X, 108) reads : "Henricus Hawte sacerdos utraque lingua peritus olimque nostri ludi primarius discipulus correptus interiit."

[11] *Erasmi Epistolae*, ed. P. S. Allen, I (Oxford, 1906), 442, note.

4. Thomas More, translator of *The lyfe of Johan Picus Erle of Myrandula... with dyvers epistles & other werkis*. Published by Johan Rastell, [1510?], 40 leaves (STC 19898a).

Reprinted by Wynkyn de Worde, [1510?], (STC 19898). This edition was reprinted, edited by J. M. Rigg, London, 1890, xl, 77 pp.

The Rastell edition was reprinted in *The* [English] *Workes of Sir Thomas More*, edited by William Rastell, 1557 (STC 18076), pp. 1-34. *The Workes* was in part re-edited in facsimile by W. E. Campbell, Vol. I, 1931, with introduction and notes by A. W. Reed. I quote from the first edition.

Before the religious works More presented an abridged translation of the *Life* of Pico by his nephew Gianfrancesco Pico, which opened the *Opera Omnia*, and then translated three of Pico's letters, two to his nephew and one to "Andrewe Corneus," all on the conduct of life. Then followed a translation of "The interpretation upon this psalme Conserva me Domine"; the "xii rulys... partely exciting, partely directing a man in spirituall batail," paraphrased in twenty-three stanzas of rhyme royal; the "xii wepenis of spiritual bataile," the brief topics first translated into English prose, then severally expanded into twelve stanzas of rhyme royal; "The xii propretees or conditions of alover," likewise translated first into prose, then expanded into twenty-six stanzas of rhyme royal, each topic paraphrased in one stanza and followed by a second stanza (or by a second and third stanza at the end) which draws the parallel between the obligations of the earthly lover and those of the lover of God; finally "A praiour unto god," translating the sixty-six elegiac lines of Pico into twelve stanzas (eighty-four lines) of rhyme royal.

More's translations thus fall into two parts. The first, in prose, concerns the life of the scholar. The abridged *Life* emphasizes the shift from the life of ambitious learning to the devotion to God and man which would have led Pico into the monastic life if he had lived. The translated letters relate to the scholar in the world. The two to his nephew counsel him on meeting disappointment and on confronting calumny with a lofty resignation. In the letter to Corneus, Pico rejects the advice to lend his learning to the service of a secular prince, preferring instead the private life.

The second part expands into verse paraphrases the terse prose *regulae* describing the moral and religious conduct of the virtuous life. Two of the paraphrases, those on the "wepenis" and on the "conditions of alover," are not mere elaborations but are developed original compositions. It should be remarked that the two parts, the prose and the verse, deal with quite different topics : one with the life of the private scholar, the other with the achievement by every man of virtue and the love of God. The two parts have no organic connection and might well have been done at quite separate times.

When did More translate Pico ? His book was printed without date by More's brother-in-law John Rastell, then "dwellyng at the flete brydge at the Abbot of Wynchcombe his place." The late A. W. Reed noted that this was the only Rastell book published at that location and, arguing the book was therefore an early venture in the career of the printer, assigned it to the year 1510.[12] He also reasoned that the de Worde edition was a piracy of the same year, basing his judgment on the crowding of some lines at the bottom of some of the de Worde pages and on the omission of a blank in the sentence "In the city of   lived a woman called Circe," which de Worde ran together to read "In the city of lived a woman..." The 1557 edition of *The Workes* restored the blank.

The editor of *The Workes*, More's nephew William Rastell, supposed that More "translated [the Pico items] out of Latin... about the yeare... 1510.'"[13] William was born in 1508, however, and his father John, the first printer, had died long before 1557. This was a guess, in other words, and Professor Reed supposed that the younger Rastell remembered the date of publication rather than the date of composition.

More dedicated his book as a New Year gift, and Reed conjectured that the year was 1505. His reasoning seems to have been somewhat as follows, though it is not stated explicitly. The biography of More by his great-grandson Cresacre More (1626) remarks that "when More determined to marry, he propounded to himselfe, as a patterne of life, a singular lay-man John Picus Earl of Mirandula... [whose] life he translated and set out."[14] More married at the end of 1504 or the beginning of 1505, and Reed found 1504 a most likely year for the translation. More had incurred the king's wrath by speaking out in Parliament in January or February of that year against the full subsidy which the king required. He therefore withdrew to the Charterhouse, Reed thought, and presumably did his best to lie low until his father

---

[12] A. W. Reed, *Early Tudor Drama* (London, 1926), 8, n. 1 ; and again in *The English Works of Sir Thomas More*, ed. W. E. Campbell, I (London, 1931), Introduction, 18.

[13] *The Workes of Sir Thomas More* (London, 1557), ℭ iii.

[14] Pp. 18-19, cited by Reed, *Early Tudor Drama*, 73. The same idea had already been expressed by Thomas Stapleton in his biography in *Tres Thomae* (Douai, 1588).

had suffered a penalty in his stead. In his seclusion he did the translation, and though he was free enough later in 1504 to woo and marry Jane Colt, he carried through the preparing of the lengthy manuscript for the New Year's gift.

I believe I give the sense of the Reed argument. We know as a fact from the life of More by his son-in-law Roper that for about four years More practised "devotion and prayer" at the Charterhouse, living in the monastery "religiously," if "without vowe."[15] These four years would lie between 1499, when More came of age, and 1503 or 1504, when his father required him, according to Erasmus, to take his profession seriously, and when he therefore stood for Parliament at the start of 1504 and married at its end. We understand that More did not generally seclude himself in the monastery during this time, since he continued his law studies until his admission to the bar, perhaps in 1501, and lectured thereafter at Furnivall's Inn; and during the same years he worked vigorously at Greek, especially from 1501, even giving up Latin studies for a time ("sepostis Latinis litteris").[16]

It was presumably in these experimental four years or so that More was inspired to adopt Pico's pattern of life. For the biography of Pico which he translated emphasized Pico's life of scholarship unimpeded by family or by official ties, and it ended with the intent to turn away even further from the life of the world by taking on the monastic habit. This Pico pattern More in fact abandoned in 1504, except—and the exception is large—for the profound private piety which governed both their lives. This was the essential subject of the Pico duodecalogues, and I depart from Reed's idea here to note that it is much more likely that More translated them early on than that he waited until he had put the Pico ideal aside. He may have done the verses as early as 1497 or as late as 1504, and I do not see that we can choose any time between them, except as we might prefer dates closer to 1499.[17] We may bar the dates between 1505 and 1509, when More was sufficiently busy with his rapidly growing family, his extending professional life,

---

[15] William Roper, *The lyfe of Sir Thomas Moore*, ed. Elsie Vaughan Hitchcock, Early English Text Society, Original Series 197 (London, 1935), 6.

[16] *The Correspondence of Sir Thomas More*, ed. Elizabeth F. Rogers (Princeton, 1947), p. 46 : the letter (no. 2) to John Holt, 1501.

[17] I am glad to find the conjecture of an early date in the recent biography by Bernard Basset, S.J., *Born for Friendship : The Spirit of Sir Thomas More* (London, 1965), 55-57. Father Basset goes further in supposing that it may well have been the reading of the *Life* of Pico which moved More to the Charterhouse retreat.

his translations with Erasmus of Lucian in 1505-6, and the new activities consequent on the accession of Henry VIII in the spring of 1509.

I speak particularly of the verses, since the prose was presumably added to identify the author of the moral-religious writings, which we suppose were the basic source of More's interest. We cannot say if the verses were run off, in whatever year between 1497 and 1504, in one heat or from time to time. We know that More was writing Latin verses with William Lily in and after 1501, and we have evidence that More could write easily in formal English verse, that is in rhyme royal, in which he wrote the twelve stanzas of the elegy of Queen Elizabeth in 1503, the verse labels for eight of the nine tapestries in his father's house at much the same time, and the thirty-seven stanzas on Fortune for Lily's translation of Spiriti's *Libro delle sorti*. The Pico verse paraphrases number seventy-three stanzas and would have taken an appreciable time to do, or so we suppose in considering the difficulties of translation as well as versification. The prose translations would pose no special difficulties, except that they are fairly lengthy. I conjecture several months for the verse and less time for the prose, but I repeat that I see no need to suppose that the verse and the prose were done at the same time. The verse was important, as carrying the momentum of a piety which inspired More, whereas the prose, though it may once have impressed him as a picture of the life of a free spirit, needed no translation except as information to one who could not read Latin. The verse called for emulation as poetry, that is to say, while the prose gave only information.

To whom? We come at length to the dedication, which should tell us much, but does not. The Pico translations were dedicated "Unto his right entierly beloved sister in crist Joyeuce Leigh." Professor Reed identified her (p. 14) as the "Dame Joisse" to whom her mother Joysse Lee, in her will of 1507 (P.C.C. 22 Adeane), left a small legacy "by the licence of my Lady Abbesse of the said Minoresses"; the legacy was to be kept in a chest in the convent, and payments were to be made from it annually to the daughter. Dame Joisse was then a Franciscan nun, or Poor Clare as the English called those of the order, of the London convent which has left its name in the street still called the Minories. Her mother, a widow, was living in the convent, and desired burial in its church.

Since the nun has been confused in local histories with another Joyce Leigh,[18] I identify her further. In her will, Joysse Lee, widow of

---

[18] Owen Manning and William Bray, *The History and Antiquities of the County of*

Ricardus Lee, listed her children as Richard, Master Edward, Geoffrey, John, and Agnes Conyngton, Kateryn Hyllyngworth, and Dame Joisse. Her executors were her sons Richard and Edward and an unidentified Rauff Legh. The will was drawn in April 1507 and probated in the same month by the first two executors.

One of the sons can be further identified. Master Edward was Edward Lee, M.A. Cambridge, 1504, who was to become Archbishop of York. He was an early intimate of Thomas More, who wrote in 1519 in a controversy with Lee, of their "common home [that is, London], and the daily friendly intimacy of our parents, which led to my kissing you once, a most attractive small boy, when I was ten years older than you."[19] Actually Edward Lee was only four years younger, being born about 1482 as we count back from his death in 1544 at age sixty-two (see *D.N.B.*).

It would be interesting to know the age of Sister Joyce: that is, if the Pico translations were dedicated to, and perhaps the prose especially made for, a respected older family friend, or for a contemporary, or for a much younger person. We look to her father's will for more light. Richard Lee drew up his will in 1494 (P. C.C. 27 Horne); it was probated in 1498 by his son Richard and "Joice Relicte." Richard did not name or even number his children other than the eldest Richard, but he left them each one hundred marks "to be payed when they shall come to their lawfull age or ells be maryed." That is, all six were under the age of twenty-one in 1494, and one or more of the three daughters was under the age of twelve, the age of marriageability. We deduce that Sister Joyce could not have been born before 1474, and she may have been born after 1481. As a professed nun, she must have been at least sixteen in 1507 and thus could not have been born later than 1491. She could not then have been older than More or Richard Lee and may have been a decade younger. We go back to her grandfather's will. Sir Richard Lee, twice Mayor of London, drew his will in 1471 (P. C. C. 5 Watts), and it was probated in the same year by his widow and a son-in-law. His heir Richard, father of Sister Joyce,

---

Surrey, III (London, 1814), 497-8; John Tanswell, *The History and Antiquities of Lambeth* (London, 1858), 40-42 : both cited in *The Correspondence of Sir Thomas More*, 9, in a note on the dedication to Sister Joyce, which is there reprinted.

[19] Letter 75, *The Correspondence of Sir Thomas More*, 141 : "vel ipsius ut reliquam omittam, patriae communis gratia, vel parentum inter se nostrorum, tam amica, tam diuturna coniunctio, quae res effecerunt, ut ego te olim, puerulum certe scitissimum annis ipse decem provectior exosculatus."

was recipient of the largest single bequest, but he was not made executor as one would expect, and no mention was made in the will of his wife or children. Presumably he was not yet of age in 1471 and was unmarried. The conjecture is perhaps borne out by the will of Richard's mother Dame Leticia Lee, which was drawn in 1477 :[20] it mentions her son Richard, but says nothing of his having wife or child. I deduce that Richard was not married before 1477 and that Sister Joyce was indeed born at some time between 1478 and 1491.

A further contact of More with the Lee family has been noted by R. W. Chambers.[21] The wills of Sir Richard Lee and his son Richard both note their interest in their parish church of St. Stephen Walbrook, where each in turn was buried. Chambers notes that after his marriage Thomas More moved to Bucklersbury, which is in that parish. So More was a neighbor, as well as otherwise an intimate of the Lee family, before the publication of his Pico in 1510. Sister Joyce was of course already in the convent when More married in 1504-5, perhaps in her two-year novitiate; her father was dead, her mother was soon to move to the convent; Master Edward, who had gone up to Oxford in 1496, was pursuing his priestly career elsewhere; and the nun's eldest brother Richard was now or later to move to his Kent manor of Great Delee or Lee Magna (his will is P. C. C. 27 Horne). In effect, the Lees had left St. Stephen before Thomas More arrived there, and we must look for the earlier intimacies elsewhere.

The wills of the other Leigh family in Lambeth add no further information, and all our searches in Somerset House have thus provided us with little that is relevant to the Pico dedication. A look at its wording indicates More's affection for "myne hertly beloved syster," and his "tendre love and zele to the happy contynuance and gracyouse encreace of vertue in your soule." It names, however, no previous common interest in Pico, such as might have arisen if More had shown off his verses to his friends the Lees. Indeed we may well guess that they had been shown to, or for that matter written for, the women of his own family: his stepmother, his two sisters, his new wife. We cannot guess, in sum, the history of the poems, as we cannot do more than guess that the occasion of the New Year dedication was Sister Joyce's profession as a nun in or before 1507.

---

[20] R. R. Sharpe, ed., *Calendar of Wills in the Court of Husting, London*, II (London, 1889), 589-90.
[21] *Thomas More* (London, 1935), 93.

We can say with certainty that the New Year gift was much larger than was customary, as we see by comparing it with our Items 1 and 2 above, or with the later practise of the veteran in such matters, Henry Parker, Lord Morley, who made sixteen such manuscript gifts in the 1530s. More's verses alone would have been a sufficient gift, and the dedication notes only that he was adding the biography to the verses; evidently his enthusiasm for Pico accounted for his adding the three letters. But the main purpose of the translation was to convey the message of the duodecalogues, than which no work was "more profitable, neyther to thachyvynge of temperaunce in prosperite, nor to the purchasynge of pacience in adversite, nor to the dyspysynge of worldly vanyte, nor to the desyrynge of hevenly felycyte."

For the translation itself, we may take the prose versions as adequate, if somewhat awkward. The original title-page, for which to be sure More may not have been responsible, reads: "Johan Picus Erle of Myra[n]dula a grete lord of Italy an excellent conning man in all sciences & verteous of lyvinge. With dyvers epistles & other warkis of the seyd Johan Picus full of grete science vertew and wysedome. whos lyfe & warkys bene worthy & digne to be redde & oftyn to be had in memorye."

Two studies have noted the modifications which More made in the text of the Pico *Life* and letters. Professor Stanford E. Lehmberg has observed certain omissions or changes which suggest More's doctrinal interests, for example, an apparent willingness to approve appeal from the pope to a general council, or again a reflection of More's own moral code in his insertion of an original passage on honor as a concomitant of virtue rather than an antecedent of it.[22] Professor Myron P. Gilmore has noted, as did Lehmberg, the omission of much of the account of Pico's scholarly interests, which would not be of great interest to a nun; he has also observed the omission from the letter to "Andrewe" of a discussion of marriage, obviously for a similar reason. He observed that More omitted about one-sixth of the *Life* (some 1500 out of some 9000 words).[23]

We are more interested in More's verse. Its quality may be judged by comparing his version of the first of the twelve "Regulae" with the

---

[22] *Studies in the Renaissance* 3 (1956), 61-74.

[23] "More's Translation of Gianfrancesco Pico's Biography," in *L'Opera e il pensiero di Giovanni Pico della Mirandola*, II (Florence, 1965), 301-4.

later prose versions. He enlarged the original statements in one or two sentences each to rhyme-royal stanzas.

> Prima regula : si homini videtur dura via virtutis : quia continue oportet nos pugnare adversus carnem & diabolum & mundum : Recordetur quod quamcunque elegerit vitam etiam secundum mundum : multa illi adversa : tristia : incommoda : laboriosa patienda sunt.

> Who so to vertue estemith the waye/
> Bi cause we must have warre coutinuall
> Against the worlde/ the flessh/ the devill/ that aye
> Enforce them selfe to make us bond & thrall/
> Let him remember that chese what wey he shal
> Evin aftir the worlde/ yet must he nede susteyn
> Sorow/ adversite/ labour/ greife/ and payne.[24]

Elyot (Item 5 below) was to translate very awkwardly (in 1534) :

> First if to man or woman the way of vertue dothe seme harde or paynefull, bycause we muste nedes fyght agaynste the flesh, the divell, & the worlde, lette him or her calle to remembraunce, that what so ever lyfe they wyll chose accordynge to the world, many adversities incommodities, moche hevynes and labour are to be sufred.

The prose of W. H. (our Item 6 below) was better (in 1589) :

> If the way of vertue seeme hard unto men because we must continually fight against the flesh, the devill, and the world, let him remember that what way so-ever hee shall choose, (yea if it be according to the world) hee must suffer much adversitie, sorow, discommoditie and travaile.

Elyot and W. H. are generally accurate, though Elyot does not quite render the force of the "etiam"; it is also interesting that he added "or woman" because like More he dedicated his book to a woman. Elyot's prose is of course rugged, whereas W. H. is much smoother. More must expand, adding content and also strength in line four; his last line also, though not quite accurate, was expanded to add the final strength of "payne," and so revealed his firm command of the stanza form. The same quality is maintained through the later stanzas.

More's command of the medium in his translation of Latin verse may be seen in his "A praiour of Picus Mirandula unto god," which comes at the end of his book. I italicize in the Latin the words which More left untranslated, and I note in the same way the words which he added in the English.

---

[24] I modernize typographical conventions involving i and j, u and v, and expand abbreviations and contractions.

>   Alma deus *summa* qui maiestate verendus
>   Vere unum in triplici *numine numen* habes,
>   Cui *super excelsi flammantia moenia mundi*
>   Angelici servit *turba beata chori*:
>   Cuius & *immensum hoc oculis spectabile nostris*
>   *Omnipotens quondam dextra* creavit opus :
>   *Aethera* qui *torques qui nutu* dirigis orbem
>   *Cuius ab imperio fulmine missa cadunt* :
>   Parce precor miseris nostras precor ablue sordes
>   Ne nos iusta tui poena furoris agat.

>   O holy god of dredeful magestee
>   Verely one in iii and thre in one
>   Whom aungells serve whose wark all *creaturis* be
>   Which heven and erth directest *all alone*
>   We the beseche good lorde *with wofull mone*
>   Spare us wretchis & wassh away oure gilt
>   That we be not by thy just angre spilt.

This is much condensed; if More had not read Lucretius, he might well have been daunted by "flammantia moenia mundi." The end of the poem is, on the other hand, much expanded.

>   Ut cum mortalis perfunctus munere vitae
>   Ductus erit dominum spiritus ante suum
>   *Promissi regni faelicii sorte potitus*
>   Non dominum sed te sentiat esse patrem.
>   That when the *jornay of this* dedly life
>   My syly gost hath fynysshed, and *thense*
>   Departen must : *with out his flesshly wife*
>   *Alone* in to his lordis *high presence*
>   He may the fynde : o well of indulgence.
>   *In thi lordeship* not as a lorde : but rathir
>   As a *very tendre loving* fathir

Here, omitting the third line, the translation expands three Latin lines to seven English, adding a more dramatic sense and again an effective final couplet.

The most original part of More's work is the expansion of the "xii propretees or conditions of alover" into two stanzas each on earthly and on heavenly love. I take as example no. 11 (actually no. 10 in the original list).

>   Flere cum eo saepe : vel si absens ex dolore : vel si praesens ex laeticia.
>   To wepe often with his love : in presence for joye, in absence for sorowe.

> Diversly passioned is the lovers hert
> Now pleasaunt hope now drede and grevous fere
> Now parfite blis now bittir sorow smart
> And whither his love be with hym or ellis where
> Oft from his iyen there fallith many a tere
> For very Joy when they to gethir be
> Whan they be sondred : for adversite.
> Like affectiones felith eke the brest
> Of goddis lover in praier and meditation
> Whan that his love liketh in him rest
> With inward gladnes of pleasaunt contemplation
> Out breke the teris for Joy and delectation
> And when his love list eft to parte him fro
> Out breke the teris a gaine for paine & woo.

Presumably this was written without benefit of Petrarch, since it is doubtful that More knew Italian.

These samples may show Thomas More as more than competent in English verse, and particularly in the rhyme royal with its emphatic final couplet. To the modern reader his verse is usually more regular and therefore smoother than that of his most accomplished contemporary Stephen Hawes, whose hypermetrical lines, on the one hand, and somewhat prosy writing, on the other, are something of a stumbling-block today. We must add to More's early experiments in living his trial of writing in English verse, in which he proved a promising competence.

5. The second translator of Pico into English was Sir Thomas Elyot. Seeking a companion piece to his version of Cyprian's "Sermon of the Mortality of Man," he made a plain prose translation of the first of the Pico sayings, the "Rules of a Christian lyfe." He wrote the preface on 1 July 1534, calling Pico's work "a litel treatise, but wonderful fruitful, made by the vertuose & noble prince John Picus Erle of Mirandula, who in abundance of learning & grace incomparably excelled all other in his time & sens." We have said that the prose of his translation is heavy and without grace, though not without strength.

The translation was published in 1534 by Berthelet (STC 6157) and dedicated to Elyot's sister; the "Rules" occupied some ten pages in the small volume. It was reprinted by Berthelet in 1539 with the Cyprian (STC 6158). It was reprinted in a new context in Thomas Lupset's *Workes* in 1546 (STC 16932) and again in 1560 (STC 16933), which added the Elyot translations of Cyprian and Pico, together with Elyot's original dedication of 1534, to the four short treatises of the scholar Lupset who had died young. No sign is given of the reason for the addition of the Elyot translations, but we may guess that the printer Berthelet, who had brought out the Lupset works separately and now collected them, wished to piece out the book to a full four hundred pages. The Pico filled only nine pages.

In still another context, the Elyot Pico was added in 1585 to the edition published in Rouen of Richard Whitford's translation of the *Imitatio Christi* which he entitled *The Following of Christ* (STC 23960a). *The Following* had been originally published in 1531 (STC 23961) as one of the many works of the chaplain of Syon Monastery.[25] In adding "The Rules of a Christian lyfe" and also the "Golden Epistle of Saint Bernard" translated by Whitford, the publisher supplied no comment on the Pico or on its relation to the other devotional works in the volume. The same matter was reprinted in a later edition of *The Following* in 1615 in London (STC 23988).

Finally the "Rules" in the Elyot version was reprinted by J. M. Rigg in his reprint of the More *Pico* (London, 1890), 89-93.

6. A third English version of the *Twelve Rules and Weapons Concerning the Spirituall Battel* was made in prose by W. H. and published by Windet in 1589 (entered in the Stationers' Register 23 June 1589: STC 19898+, a copy in the Huntington Library). This ran to thirty-nine pages, including twelve pages of preface, and included almost the same Pico material as that which More used: "Twelve Rules"; "Twelve Weapons"; "Twelve conditions of a lover"; "The Commentarie upon the sixteene Psalme"; "To his nephew John Franciscus" (two letters). The translation is sober and skillful and without expansion, and one may say that Pico has here received a suitable and faithful English version.

The translator signs himself W. H. in the dedication of his book to his uncle Sir Nicholas Bagnoll, Knight Marshal of Ireland. Though the Bagnoll family tree[26] does not include a W. H., the State Papers Ireland reveal a relative by marriage, Henry Heron, who is described

---

[25] See Edward J. Klein, "The Life and Works of Richard Whitford" (Ph. D. diss., Yale University, 1937). The A. F. Allison and D. M. Rogers *Catalogue of Catholic Books in English Printed Abroad or Secretly in England* (Bognor Regis, 1956) ascribes the Pico translation in this edition (its no. 814) to Whitford. Actually the translation is verbatim Elyot.

[26] P. H. D. Bagenal, *Vicissitudes of an Anglo-Irish Family* (London, 1925).

as brother-in-law of the Knight Marshal's second son Dudley : presumably Dudley Bagnoll had married a sister of Henry Heron, or Henry Heron had married a sister of Dudley. In either case the two men were brothers-in law. Henry Heron was the son of Sir Nicholas Heron; another son of Sir Nicholas, we learn elsewhere, was William Heron. Both Henry and William Heron were thus, as brothers-in-law of Dudley Bagnoll, related by marriage to Dudley's father Sir Nicholas Bagnoll in a fashion which permitted them to address him as their uncle.

Both Bagnolls and Herons were English gentry, and the two Sir Nicholases had long careers as soldiers and administrators in Ireland from the time of Henry VIII. Sir Nicholas Bagnoll settled at Newry in County Down; his younger son Dudley moved on to Dunleckney in County Carlow. Sir Nicholas Heron was Sheriff of Carlow among his many dignities. Their respective sons were involved in fatal violence. A report noted that in November, 1586 Dudley Bagenall, with his brother-in-law Henry Heron, son of Sir Nicholas, and a party of twenty, took and killed Mortagh Oge (Kavanagh); in March, 1587 Bagenall was lured into ambush and killed, while the others escaped.[27] In October 1588 Henry Heron petitioned for relief because of the burning and plunder of his property by Art and Murlough Kavanagh.[28]

We do not know if William Heron was engaged in this feud. In 1588, on December 10, he signed the dedication of his Pico versions from Castle of the Island, that is Castleisland in County Kerry. In the course of 1589 he petitioned the Queen for "a lease in reversion," that is for a grant of land, as recompense for his service and that of his late father Sir Nicholas.[29] His own service is summarized in the petition as "his repair into Ireland in the late general rebellion of the Irish, and invasion of the Spaniard." We infer that his station at Castleisland near the southwest coast placed him among the forces assembled to prevent the landing of troops from the ships of the Spanish Armada.

This is all that I have been able to learn of the translator W. H., who seems to me unmistakably identified as William Heron. Since his petition speaks of his "repair into Ireland," he may have been in England during his brother's feuding; indeed he may have been serving in the Low Countries, where more than one Heron served. I do not

---

[27] *Calendar of the State Papers Relating to Ireland 1509-1603*, III (1586-1588, July) : document cxxviii, 111.

[28] *Ibid.*, IV (1588, August-1594) : document cxxxvii, 24.

[29] *Ibid.*, document cxlix, 71.

find any record of him at a university, and he disappears from my view after 1589. I do not find a Heron or Herne in the ensuing English campaigns in Ireland, and when the Ulster colony was organized, it was a John Heron, gent., who was among the "undertakers" recommended from London, and who settled in County Armagh, where the family long remained.

William Heron was then a soldier. His translation, he wrote, was "the fruytes of mine idle houres, which being not many, their labour can be neither great nor exquisite." Possibly the military language of the "Twelve Rules" and the "Twelve Weapons" may have seemed to him to justify the dedication of his book to Sir Nicholas Bagnoll. For his readers today a considerable irony inheres in the thought that the hard-bitten soldier, close to eighty years of age and refusing to give up his command, would look kindly on a sermon on the war with the world, the flesh, and the devil, especially at a time when the English command in Ireland was fighting for its life, and when in panic the English massacred the unfortunate shipwrecked Spaniards. For the dedication is nothing less than a sermon exhorting the Christian soldier to continue an unceasing war on sin. In our judgment, the preacher of the sermon must have been either very young or very naive or both. Our judgment may be wrong, and Sir Nicholas may have been a pietist and a willing listener to sermons. The translator makes no attempt to explain the fame of Pico, and we cannot tell how or why he came upon the volume.

We may judge the concision of W. H.'s translation by the following examples.

Pico. Sexta regula : recordare cum unam vicisti tentationem semper aliam esse expectandam : quia diabolus semper circuit quem devoret : quare oportet semper servire in timore & dicere cum propheta super custodiam meam stabo.

More. One synne vainquisshed loke thou not tarye
But lie in await for an other every howre
For as a wood lyon the fende oure adversarye
Rynneth a bout seking whom he may devoure
Wherefore continually uppon thy towre
Lest he the unperveied and unredy catche
Thou must with the prophite stonde & kepe watche.

Elyot. Remembre also, that as soone as thou hast vanquished one temtation, alway an other is to be loked for : The divell goeth alwaye aboute and seketh for hym whom he wolde devoure. Wherfore we ought to serve dylygently and be ever in feare, and to say with the prophete : I will stande alwaye at my defence.

Heron. Remember that when thou hast overcome one temptation, then another is always to be expected, for that the devill alwayes goeth about seeking whom he may devoure : Wherefore it behooveth us alwayes to be readie and regardfull, and to say with the Prophet : I will alwayes stand upon my watch.

The "Twelve Conditions of a Lover" might have found more expert statement in English after Petrarchism had reached so far, but we do not so conclude. I quote the last three.

Pico. Flere cum eo saepe : vel si absens ex dolore : vel si praesens ex laeticia.
Semper languere semper ardere eius desiderio.
Servire illi nihil cogitando de praemio aut mercede.

More. To wepe often with his love : in presence for Joy in absence for sorowe
To langwyssh evir and evir to burne in the desyre of his love.
To serve his love no thing thinkyng of ony rewarde or profite.

Heron. To shed teares with him often, either for griefe if he be absent, or for joy if he be present.
To languish often, and often to be enflamed with his love.
To obey him, thinking nothing of reward or recompence.

Heron's version of the "Commentary" on the sixteenth Psalm and of the two letters to Pico's nephew, which try less for epigrammatic effect, again seems smoother than More's. One sample, the opening of the first letter, shows a considerably greater freedom.

Pico. Discedenti tibi a me plurimas statim ad malum oblatas occasiones quae te perturbent/ & arrepto bene vivendi proposito adversentur : non est fili quod admireris : sed nequam quod doleas aut expavescas.

More. That thou hast had many evill occasions after thy departing which trouble thee and stonde agaynst the vertuouse purpose that thou hast takin : ther is no cause my son why thou sholdest eyther mervail therof be sory therfor or drede hyt.

Heron. Marvaile not my Sonne, neither take any griefe, or dismaye, that upon thys departure from me, there are so many occasions of evill ministred unto thee, which may disquiet thee, and withstande thy desired purpose of a good life.

Here we may praise Heron's shift of emphasis to the beginning of the sentence, at the same time that we note in More an often more forceful vocabulary. From force to smoothness may well be the theme of our history of translation.

Queens College, The City University of New York

INVENTION IN TUDOR LITERATURE : HISTORICAL PERSPECTIVES

RICHARD HARRIER

The literature of the English Renaissance was profoundly rhetorical. The most general pattern of educated speech—written or spoken—was the oration. Verse and prose were conceived primarily as instruments of persuasion or proof. Thus any piece of writing began as an argument, didactic in purpose, using the arts of language in various degrees of gorgeous display or subtle indirection.

The historian of literature must therefore study the English capacity for rhetorical invention from decade to decade, from writer to writer, in one genre and another. In this essay we shall focus our attention on some of the most significant evidence of rhetorical achievement. Our aim will be two-fold : first, to consider the inability and reluctance of literary historians to meet the challenge presented by a rhetorical literature; and second, to outline some evidence of qualitative change within the unbroken continuity of Tudor rhetorical practice.

The traditional view of English Renaissance literature is represented by the volumes of Thomas Warton, W. J. Courthope, and C. S. Lewis.[1] Despite the wide-ranging erudition of the last, its habits

---

[1] In *English Literature in the Sixteenth Century Excluding Drama* (Oxford, 1954), 104-105, C. S. Lewis remarked that Thomas Warton is "still our most reliable critic on much later medieval poetry." But Lewis' debt was larger than that. Warton initiated the idea that English poets who imitated the more conceited Italian sonnets were somehow un-English. See the excerpt on Wyatt's poetry in *Collected Poems of Sir Thomas Wyatt*, ed. Kenneth Muir (Cambridge, Mass., 1963), xxxvii. For Warton's formerly unpublished comments on Elizabethan sonnets, see Rodney M. Baine, ed., *A History of English Poetry : An Unpublished Continuation*, Augustan Reprint Society No. 39 (Los Angeles, 1953). Warton's three volumes covering English literature down to the age of Elizabeth I were originally published in 1774, 1778, 1781. These with the additional posthumous volume of 1790 were revised by W. C. Hazlitt in 1871. Their critical assumptions were influential upon W. J. Courthope's *A History of English Poetry*, Vol. II : The Renaissance and the Reformation (London, 1897). For a discussion of the interrelations of literary criticism and history see Hallett Smith, "An Apologie for Elizabethan Poetry," *New Literary History* 1 (1969), 35-43, and Sears Jayne, "Hallett Smith's Analysis of the Historical Assumptions behind his *Elizabethan Poetry*," 45-51.

of observation and ideas about development remain much the same as its predecessors'. Two primary assumptions of these histories are that style, conceived as a pervasive register of taste and sensibility, is the historian's central concern and that poetry, being more easily subject to stylistic analysis, may be used to define the major categories of each period. The prose of each period has therefore been thought of as background for poetry, a matrix of philosophical ideas which occasionally take specific form in theology or science. Lewis, for example, opens his history of English non-dramatic literature of the sixteenth century with a survey of "New Learning and New Ignorance."[2] His major chronological divisions are stylistic: "Late Medieval," "Drab," and "Golden"; and there is a systematic application of these categories to verse and prose, although the reader is frequently warned that they are generally inaccurate for prose. While Lewis was under no obligation to solve the theoretical problems of English prose style, he should not have tried to impose upon its phenomena descriptive categories which only obscure the issues. Further, Lewis, like other historians of prose, borrows from prose of the eighteenth and nineteenth centuries some broader conceptions of style which he uses to explain the difference between late medieval writing and that of the early modern period. Probably the best place to see this method in operation is in the essay on Lord Berners, in which he contrasts the "effortless and unflagging" prose of Berners' Froissart with the "workaday quality" of Defoe's pamphlets and novels (p. 153). The implications of this contrast are so important that we must examine them a bit further.

Probably the most widely used conception of English literary form has been the distinction between the "plain style" and the "ornate or eloquent style." This distinction has been employed for the discussion of both prose and verse; and it has been referred backward in time to Chaucer and Alfred, on one hand, and to Petrarch and the

---

[2] Although Lewis's essay may be challenged at numerous points, two especially must be noted. On p. 10 he argues that the "ruthless" thought of Plato is essentially antihuman. On p. 37 he asserts that the theological differences which led to the Reformation were essentially trivial, leading up to this dismissal of the Reformation in Germany : "Thus in Germany the new theology led into a quarrel about indulgences and thence into a quarrel about the nature of the Church. Whether it need have done so if Leo X had not wanted money, or if Tetzel (backed by the great house of Fugger) had not applied to the indulgences grotesquely profane and vulgar methods of salesmanship, may be doubted."

writers of classical antiquity on the other.[3] Our awareness of these polarities was given definition, however, by a more recent literary phenomenon, English prose of the later seventeenth century. That was a plain discursive prose which took as its ideal the communication of one "thing" for every word used.[4] Specifically associated with the Royal Society, this kind of language has become identified with rationalistic skepticism. One variety of it is exemplified by the "workaday" pamphlets and narratives of Defoe. By now it is virtually impossible to avoid the imposition of this stylistic key upon sixteenth-century and earlier writing, whether or not one is concerned to trace the origins of modern rationalism. But perhaps a restatement of some conventional lines of argument will make future discussions more flexible.

Generally speaking, the growth of inductive rationalism in English Renaissance culture has been associated with the anti-Ciceronian movement in prose composition. In the inevitable link between Latin and English writing this meant first of all a preference for Seneca and Tacitus as models. Translated into terms of English style it meant short syntactical members, sparing use of tropes and schemes, paratactic arrangement of short clausal units, and avoidance of that sweet music that gives shape to the Ciceronian period.[5] In the words of Hamlet's mother to Polonius it meant the attempt to deliver "more matter with less art." (*Hamlet*, II.ii.95).

Parallel with this anti-Ciceronian movement but also preceding it were two lines of native English plain style. One, in verse, is exem-

---

[3] The argument of R. W. Chambers on the early development of English prose has never been seriously challenged. See his "On the Continuity of English Prose from Alfred to More and his School," which is part of the Introduction to *Nicholas Harpsfield's Life of Sir Thomas More*, ed. E. V. Hitchcock and R. W. Chambers, Early English Text Society No. 186 (London, 1931, 1963). See also the notes below.

[4] This ideal was expressed by Bishop Sprat in his *History of the Royal Society* (1667). Its historical significance was stressed by George Sherburn in *A Literary History of England*, ed. A. C. Baugh, 2nd ed. (New York, 1967), 701-702.

[5] See particularly the "Preface to Anti-Ciceronianism" in George Williamson, *The Senecan Amble* (Chicago, 1951). "*Attic*" *and Baroque Prose Style : The Anti-Ciceronian Movement Essays by Morris W. Croll*, ed. J. Max Patrick and Robert O. Evans, with John M. Wallace (Princeton, 1969). Earl Miner attempted to challenge these works in "Patterns of Stoicism in Thought and Prose Styles, 1530-1700," *PMLA* 85 (1970), 1023-1034, using as evidence the relative numbers of editions of classical authors published. I can see no reason, however, why those statistics should be a key to education or to how the most important writers formed their styles.

plified by Chaucer's moral ballade "Flee from the prese" as it was reprinted in Tottel's *Miscellany* of 1557 (ed. Hyder Rollins, No. 238). In this kind of verse a broadly moral theme is given expression in simple language tending towards the proverbial and sententious. Although such moral verse stands in sharp contrast to the more "conceited" style of the English Petrarchists, it is clear that most poets wrote both kinds from Sir Thomas Wyatt and the Earl of Surrey on.[6] Whether they were as conscious of the opposition as we is hard to say, for it is difficult to make out what was implied by the English fondness for calling Chaucer their Virgil. Surely such a comparison did not imply that they thought Chaucer an artless writer. Rather, it would suggest that they found Chaucer's styles compatible with a sense of gravity and piety.

The native English line of prose has been traced from Sir Thomas More's writing back through the religious books of meditation and instruction to the *Ancren Riwle* and the sermons of Aelfric.[7] This tradition of prose is primarily a plain style, unevenly aggregate in sentence pattern, and only occasionally heightened by the insertion of double epithets where a single adjective would do. In describing these two lines of "native" plain style, one uses the term "native" advisedly, since there was always an interaction between English and the learned or courtly tongues, Latin and French. The humanist movement exemplified by the refounding of St. Paul's School in the early sixteenth century was simply a vigorous recurrence of an age-old process.

From our point of view, then, there appear to have been present in English Renaissance literature two broad streams of plain and ornate writing : with the ornate having its ultimate sources in Petrarch and Cicero and the plain having its characters defined by English religious works, Chaucer, and the Senecan revival. No doubt these lines of development have some kind of historical validity, but they have only an indirect connection with the theories of education and composition employed by Renaissance writers. It is important to state where the connection lies. "Style" in the modern sense I have been using above did not occur in the literary vocabulary of George

---

[6] In quotations, abbreviations and contractions have been expanded and modern typographical conventions followed in respect to i/j, u/v, and w.

For a systematic application of these distinctions see Douglas L. Peterson, *The English Lyric from Wyatt to Donne : A History of the Plain and Eloquent Style* (Princeton, 1967). Like most historians Peterson prefers the plain style of English.

[7] See n. 3.

Puttenham or Sir Philip Sidney. For them "style" was "ornament," and kinds of "ornament" were available in analyzed collections of tropes and "schemes." Further, the matter to be ornamented could be generated by reference to given "topics" or "places," also available in vast collections of "commonplaces." If there is a connection between the existence of plain and ornate styles of writing and rhetorical theory, it lies in the term "decorum." What was decorous depended upon several factors: the genre being used, the audience and occasion, and therefore the *persona* adopted for the delivery. The manipulation of plain and ornate patterns of speech was adjusted to this context, but it was the most subtle aspect of the rhetorical art and hardly subject to analysis, given their notion of "style." The fundamental changes in English writing between Skelton and Shakespeare are largely due to the development of new genres and larger linguistic potentialities enabling more subtle variations in decorum. In the second half of this essay we shall outline some of the developments in the new and more spacious concept of decorum.

First, however, we must eliminate from consideration an even more troublesome stylistic category, which has been forced back into Renaissance literature from the romantic age. I refer to "realism." At no time did the mimetic theory of Renaissance art share any primary assumptions with the fictional realism of later prose narrative.[8] In Renaissance representations there is an attempt to select the normative ideal from the flux of experience and *natura naturans*. In later romantic art there is a stress upon local and immediate contingencies as they strike the senses and an interest in recording the random episodes of a psyche as it reacts to sensation. The latter concept of realism is especially useless in dealing with English fiction of the sixteenth century. In that genre the limitations of the concept are inescapably clear.[9] In lyric and dramatic verse the problem is more subtle and complicated, for there is a notable increase in the skill with which Renaissance writers render their *personae*. This greater effectiveness of vocal tonality and expression should not be confused, however, with autobiographical sincerity, an idea which may be inseparable from romantic realism. Nor do the *personae* of Elizabethan drama, however convincing they may be, imply a narrative structure

---

[8] The best survey of mimetic theory is Rensselaer W. Lee's *Ut Pictura Poesis: The Humanistic Theory of Painting* (New York, 1967).

[9] On this problem see Walter R. Davis, *Idea and Act in Elizabethan Fiction* (Princeton, 1969).

of motivations or a causal chain of events like those we seem to find in the novels of Henry Fielding, Jane Austen, and George Eliot. To describe the transition from the late morality plays to the high Elizabethan drama of Marlowe and Shakespeare as a gain in "realism" is simply to beg the question. Instead, one should focus upon the persistent similarities between non-dramatic and dramatic forms throughout the age, between sonnets, stanzaic narratives, allegorical romance, and the stage plays.

The popular response to the stage plays of the 1590's like the response to the sonnet sequences, was proof that the rhetorical training of the educated could be communicated to the unschooled many. That Shakespeare never attended a university only shows that a university training was unnecessary to the development of a writer, especially one of genius. The unity of literary arts, popular and learned, is of course inseparable from an implied unity of educational institutions. When Lewis took the position that the program of the humanist educators was essentially hostile to the literature that developed, he logically excluded rhetorical principles as the basis of his history.

The crucial passage in his opening chapter is this one :

> It is not unusual to make a distinction that is almost a contrast between humanism and the 'neo-classical' school ... There are, no doubt, modifications as we pass from the fifteenth- and sixteenth-century humanists to critics like Rymer and Boileau : but the neo-classics are the humanists' lawful heirs. The worst of all neo-classical errors, that which turned Aristotle's observations on Greek tragedy into arbitrary 'rules' and even foisted on him 'rules' for which his text furnishes no pretext at all, began not with Richelieu nor Chapelain but in 1570 with Castelvetro (*Poetica d'Aristotele*, IV, II). Scaliger's critique of Homer (*Poetices*, V. II,III) is very like Rymer's of Shakespeare. Swift's contempt for natural science in *Laputa*, Johnson's in his critique of Milton's educational theory, Chesterfield's request that Stanhope should stick to useful books and avoid 'jimcrack natural history of fossils, minerals, plants, &c.' are all in the spirit of Vives and Erasmus. If Dryden departs from Aristotle to make 'admiration' the 'delight of serious plays', Minturno had led the way (*De Poeta*, II). The *Poetica* of Vida (1490-1566) is still a central book for Johnson and Pope. The differences between the humanists and the neo-classics have to be sought for by minute study : the similarities leap to the eye. We have no warrant for regarding our Elizabethan literature as the progeny of the one and our 'Augustan' as the progeny of the other. I shall notice in a later chapter the one point at which humanism, in the person of Scaliger, here following Plotinus, may have given to the Elizabethans something they could really use. Apart from that, all the facts seem consistent with the view that the great literature of the fifteen-eighties and nineties was something which

> humanism, with its unities and *Gorboducs* and English hexameters, would have prevented if it could, but failed to prevent because the high tide of native talent was then too strong for it. Later, when we were weaker, it had its way and our pseudo-classical period set in. (pp. 19-20).

The answer to this must be that it stresses theoretical issues which did not disturb the basic education shared by all Tudor writers. Practically speaking, there was not much difference between Shakespeare's schooling at Stratford, Spenser's at the Merchant Taylors' School, or Sidney's and Fulke Greville's at Shrewsbury. It was at that level that the conflict between "native talent" and the regimen of Cicero and Terence operated. Sidney's commendation of *Gorboduc* in *An Apology for Poetry* did not prevent him from saluting folk baladry. Nor did his critical orthodoxy prevent his writing *Astrophil and Stella* and the very popular *Arcadia*. Thomas Campion, who argued for quantitative meter, produced elegant accentual verses; and Samuel Daniel, who argued for English accentual meter and rhyme, produced comparable ones by the hundreds.

Lewis's attack upon the humanist program proceeds to stress their misreading of the classics, their disruption of the natural evolution of the Latin tongue, and finally the cultivation of a distorted ideal, a magnanimous man more Stoic and Cynical than Aristotelian. "This unmoved, unconquerable, 'mortal god' (as Henry More calls him), if modified in one direction gives us Milton's Christ : if in another, his Satan" (p. 54). According to Lewis, this ambivalent *persona* sums up what unity there was in Elizabethan culture. In his best apparel he is the hero of Spenser and Sidney who acts in the "secret assurance of his own worthiness." At his worst he is the new villain of the drama or the tearless and scornful hero, Shakespeare's Coriolanus, Chapman's Clermont, Dryden's Almanzor, Addison's Cato, Wycherley's Manly, Pope's self-portrait in the *Epilogue to the Satires* (pp. 53-54). Against these perverse tendencies, so argues Lewis, the native, essentially medieval sensibility of Malory's romances and Berners' Froissart, of Gavin Douglas' *Aeneid*, struggled with only partial success.

If we follow Lewis's argument to the point where he allows humanism a contribution to the greatness of Renaissance poetry we meet a familiar paradox. For it was precisely the elevation of the artist to godlike status that, according to Lewis, made possible poetic greatness. His explanation is briefly this : the Aristotelian tradition tended to subordinate art to nature; while the Neo-Platonic gradually affirmed the superiority of the artist :

> In the third century Plotinus completes the theory. 'If anyone disparages the arts on the ground that they imitate Nature', he writes, 'we must remind him that natural objects are themselves only imitations, and that the arts do not simply imitate what they see but re-ascend to those principles (λόγους) from which Nature herself is derived... Pheidias used no visible model for his Zeus' (*Ennead*, V.VIII). Art and Nature thus become rival copies of the same supersensuous original, and there is no reason why Art should not sometimes be the better of the two. Such a theory leaves the artist free to exceed the limits of Nature. Of these two conceptions it is the neo-Platonic, not the Aristotelian, which is really demanded by most Golden poetry; by the *Furioso*, the *Liberata*, the *Arcadia*, the *Faerie Queene*, and by many elements in Shakespearian 'comedy'. It is also directly asserted by some of the critics. 'The poet', says Scaliger (*Poet.* I.I), 'maketh a new Nature and so maketh himself as it were a new God'. It will be remembered how closely Sidney follows him. The poet, unlike the historian, is not 'captiued to the trueth of a foolish world' but can 'deliuer a golden'. (p. 320).

Sidney should not be cited, however, as one who turned Plato or the Neo-Platonists against Aristotle and Cicero. In fact he attempted to reconcile the apparently conflicting conceptions of nature and art he inherited. The central aim and strategy of his *Apology* is to preserve the uniqueness of the poet's art while maintaining its essential connection with oratory through their common basis in reason and the use of words to "figure forth." It may be outlined here briefly by selecting passages in the reverse order of their occurrence in his essay-oration, since his oratorical strategy is to establish his major point by indirection.

In the peroration he "conjures" the reader to believe with him "that there are many mysteries contained in poetry, which of purpose were written darkly, lest by profane wits it should be abused"; and "to believe with Landino that [poets] are so beloved of the gods, that whatsoever they write proceeds of a divine fury."[10] These appropriately heightened phrases contain the basic position that "poesy" as an art has its origin in and operates upon man's divine essence. At the end of his digression on the failures of English poets he cites as models two Latin orators and some unnamed amateur poets, after which he remarks: "But what? methinks I deserve to be pounded for straying from poetry to oratory: but both have such an affinity in this wordish consideration, that I think this digression will make

---

[10] Sir Philip Sidney, *An Apology for Poetry*, ed. Forrest G. Robinson, (Indianapolis, 1970), 87-88. This annotated text takes into account the recently discovered Norwich MS.

my meaning receive the fuller understanding ..." (pp. 84-85). "This wordish consideration" has included a critique on the use of similitudes for decorous and effective expression, thus climaxing an argument he introduced earlier in support of versifying: "For if *oratio* next to *ratio*, speech next to reason, be the greatest gift bestowed upon mortality, that cannot be praiseless which doth most polish that blessing of speech ..." (p. 53). Throughout, therefore, Sidney is paralleling each assertion of poetry's supernatural basis with a conscious attention to its necessary manifestation in words.

The distinction between oratory and poetry is not lost, however; and the climactic statement comes appropriately enough in the confutation, where Sidney deals with the objection that Plato banished the poets. There Sidney refers to the *Ion* to recall that Plato honored poetry even beyond what he himself would allow it: "sith he attributeth unto poesy more than myself do, namely, to be a very inspiring of a divine force, far above man's wit, as in the afore-named dialogue is apparent" (p. 67). The crucial emphasis here is the contrast between "a very inspiring" by a god or God and "man's wit." This distinction may have been a doctrinal caution, but it leaves "poesy" available to the normal capacity of man's wit. Sidney does preserve the classical similitude of "poesy" as "figuring forth" a truth, however; for he remarks in the digression that "poesy must not be drawn by the ears; it must be gently led, or rather it must lead; which was partly the cause that made the ancient-learned affirm it was a divine gift and no human skill; ... and therefore is it an old proverb, *orator fit, poeta nascitur*" (p. 72).

Both the distinction between poetry and oratory, and their connection, underlie the main division of the whole essay and its thematic emphasis. This main division comes between the exordium and the partition, when Sidney says that what he has just stated "will by few be understood, and by fewer granted" (p. 17). What the few will understand is that "the skill of the artificer standeth in that *Idea* or fore-conceit of the work, and not in the work itself" (p. 16). This understanding between the poet and reader or hearer accounts for the poet's unique relation to nature; for "the poet, disdaining to be tied by any such subjection, lifted up with the vigor of his own invention, doth grow in effect another nature," and "freely ranging within the zodiac of his own wit" delivers not a brazen world but a golden (pp. 14-15). Then returning to the relation between poetry and divinity, Sidney adds that our ability to perceive the golden world of "poesy" is "no small argument to the incredulous of that first accursed fall of Adam : sith our erected wit maketh us know what perfection is, yet our infected will keepeth us from reaching unto it" (p. 17).

After the opening context of the *Apology*, a fore-conceit which will satisfy only the few, the same argument is put into persuasive language beginning with the definition of "poesy" in Aristotelian terms as a *mimesis* or speaking picture. The body of the oration makes the same point as the fore-conceit but with one additional emphasis, that success in poetry depends upon "wordish" instrumentality and a solution to the problem of how to "figure forth" the irresistible image of virtue. Thus the "grounds of wisdom" urged by the philosopher "will lie dark before the imaginative and judging power if they be not illuminated or figured forth by the speaking picture of poesy" (p. 28). And the amorous poets must prove that they actually feel their passions by "that same forcibleness or *energeia* (as the Greeks call it) …" (p. 81). The thematic emphasis throughout is on poetry as a means to more than *gnosis*, to *praxis*, with virtue as its means and end. The importance of the digression is that it argues the sufficiency of English to fulfill all the aims of "poesy."

Briefly put, the significance of Sidney's *Apology* is this : it argues the essential unity of *ratio*, *oratio*, and "poesy." In the opening section just following the anecdote about horsemanship, Sidney states his argument in concise metaphorical form. Then the body of the oration elaborates the same position while illustrating in its very operation that this *oratio* is an embodiment of *ratio*: thus the whole prose piece gradually takes on the forcibleness of genuine "poesy." One cannot imagine a more convincing demonstration of an adequate poetic. But the importance of Sidney's *Apology* goes beyond its inherent perfection of design. The *Apology* summed up the working theory of the whole sixteenth century in England. Although no other writer of the age could have put it with Sidney's artfulness—his power of invention—most would have assented to its central premise that poetry, oratory, and reason worked through participation in man's divine essence, his erected wit. A central line of development may therefore be found in those Tudor genres which enabled the realization of this faith as the English language grew in power and range.

Of course it is not possible for the literary historian to discuss all printed and manuscript literature of the age under this guiding principle. For one thing, all the surviving documents do not constitute poetry or *ratio*, and therefore they may be *oratio* only in appearance.

But it is fundamental that the historian acknowledge this central literary faith. For the result of that conviction was a far greater range of expression than came to be allowed under the canons of refined sensibility which grew out of the neo-classic age and the romantic reaction. That is why modern conceptions of style are entirely misleading when reading the great works of the 1580's and 1590's. We are entirely unprepared for the freedom of invention in Elizabethan and earlier literature, because the writers then worked within the nearly infinite possibilities of *ratio*. They did not primarily express feelings, they found truth in words. We shall now survey some central examples of this marriage between poetry and oratory.[11]

The ease with which Sidney surveyed all the genres of prose and poetry, religious and secular, was not a demonstration of his skill at glossing over differences. Although—as I have said—no one else in the century could have written the *Apology*, all writers beyond the Puritans who distrusted the arts as devilish instruments would have subscribed to its central principles. Sidney's argument for an essential connection between *ratio*, *oratio*, and poetry gave "wordish" form to an operative faith which sustained the practical habit of deriving speech from set rhetorical topics and of analyzing language into figures of thought and sound. Thus stated, the relation of theory to practice must seem to the modern mind entirely paradoxical. On the one hand there was no need to depend upon what we might now term originality; on the other, there was a new world of literature to be mastered.

---

[11] In discussing George Gascoigne's stress upon invention in *Certain Notes of Instruction*, Lewis (271) made the correct observation that "Drab poetry, Golden poetry, and metaphysical poetry alike are dominated by an impulse which is the direct opposite of Wordsworthianism, naturalism, or expressionism." But in continuing to argue that Elizabethan poets were "usually more concerned—to fabricate a novel, attractive, intricate object, a dainty device," he fell into the error of equating Renaissance artifice with the most superficial result of rhetorical theory. Surely Gascoigne as well as Sidney could tell a dainty device from an invention of power and depth. In reading Elizabethan rhetoric books it is essential to understand that the term "artificial" could imply more than novel, intricate, and dainty. The term "artificial" should be thought of in the following context concerning the topics : "These *loci* or topics provided 'artificial' arguments, that is, arguments intrinsic to the subject and thus available through 'art'." (Walter J. Ong, S.J., "Tudor Writings on Rhetoric," *Studies in the Renaissance* 15 [1968], 48.) An Elizabethan poem or work (like More's *Utopia*) was manifestly "artificial" to the extent that it developed the inherent possibilities of the invention, which could of course be trivial or epic. The tenor of my argument here is that the greatness of Elizabethan poetry depended upon the discovery of a central subject which tended to eliminate triviality.

We must therefore face the question of just where the problem of invention lay.

The greatest challenge to the poet was the epic; and though very few epics were actually written, one must keep in mind that any poet who began to take himself seriously could hardly avoid thinking of each poem as preparation for that great task. Songs and sonnets were presented to the public as toys of vainer hours, but that very protest reveals the inescapable atmosphere of *gravitas* in which all writers lived. Perhaps it was the completeness of theory and overabundance of example that inhibited most poets from attempting the epic form. The epic was conceived as essentially a structure of praises, so the traditional topics of praise (epideictic oratory) had to be worked into a narrative.[12] As for the narrative itself, essential novelty of conception was not necessary. The English poet of the sixteenth century was expected to treat his readers to a new arrangement of the vast accumulations of heroic romance and classical epic. Both the local episodes and the general form of the epic were inescapably commonplaces to be given new dress or to be turned into hidden allusions to commonplaces. Thus the notes to editions of Spenser and Milton remind us of possible echoes set up in their readers' minds whether or not they are clues to actual sources employed by those poets. To borrow the sub-title of a recent book on the last great writer of classical epic in English, all Renaissance poetry—and especially epic poetry—was *The Poetry of Allusion*.[13]

The value of such a tradition lies of course in the conviction that it has identified the central areas of human experience and has given them apprehensible form. The challenge it presented, however, was necessarily inhibiting. For who dared to review what the greatest minds and voices of the past had said more forcefully, more elegantly, more enchantingly? No Renaissance poet would have thought it sufficient to offer the mere expression of his personal experience as a substitute for this feast of truth and reality. For the English poet in particular there was the almost insuperable task of sustaining a narrative voice equal to the demands of so exalted, extensive, and varied a form. What had to be acquired was the command of a poetic idiom of sufficient elegance, gravity, and musical variety. To that

---

[12] O. B. Hardison, Jr., *The Enduring Monument : A Study of the Idea of Praise in Renaissance Literary Theory and Practice* (Chapel Hill, 1962).

[13] Reuben Brower, *Alexander Pope : The Poetry of Allusion* (Oxford, 1959).

end all exercises in the lower forms—sonnet and pastoral, complaint, psalm, oration or epistle—were links in a chain of linguistic resources. By the 1580's the cumulative effect was sufficient to the task. Lewis observed that in the age of "Golden" poetry even minor poets sometimes composed like poets of the first rank. (See pp. 479-480.)

Much of the needed practice in adapting line-by-line syntax to a *concetto* or structural idea was carried on in the sonnet. The difference between Chaucer's translation of Petrarch's "S' amor non è" and Wyatt's of the same poem is fundamental. Chaucer turned Petrarch's fourteen lines into twenty-one lines of rhyme royal (three stanzas : *Troilus and Criseyde*, I. 400-420). Wyatt kept the sonnet form so far as he was able. The ruling principle of Chaucer's composition was amplification, and that principle links his poems with those of Wyatt's older contemporary, John Skelton. Skelton could assume that his audience was not primarily concerned with dramatic speed or narrative flow. The kind of expansion given any particular episode within a narrative scheme depended more on its inherent potentiality for expansion than upon its logical weight within the *concetto* of the whole work.

Skelton's lengthy *Garland of Laurel* illustrates this manner of composition. Once we are off on the allegorical journey we must be ready for anything and willing to pause when the poet lingers over his *topos*. But even Skelton's shorter and more dramatic poems illustrate the same principle at work. Thus the series of courtiers who frighten Dred in the *Bowge of Court* is limited only by Skelton's ability or desire to vary the familiar vices of court life. By design, however, Skelton usually chose as his discoursing *persona* one whose mind could be expected to wander associatively. In *Philip Sparrow* he invoked the naiveté of a very young girl attending a mass for her slain bird. In *Colin Clout* he exploited the freedom of unlearned forthrightness. The narrator of *The Tunning of Elinor Rumming* describes a scene which mirrors the riotous spirit of the drunken actors. Here local amplification becomes emblematic of chaos, as is shown in the extended catalogue of things the customers bring to pawn for ale at Elinor's tavern. The poems of Skelton, laureate in rhetoric, are historical proof that the most idiosyncratic of temperaments could work effectively within the assumptions of medieval rhetoric.

With the prose and verse of Sir Thomas Wyatt a different set of aims for the employment of rhetoric begins to affect English literature. One place this can be seen is in the prefatory material to his translation of Plutarch's *Quiete of Minde*. There Wyatt explains how he began to translate Petrarch's "of the remedy of ill fortune," and how he had found it tedious after having "made a prose" of nine or ten dialogues. This tediousness, however, Wyatt attributed not to Petrarch or his language, but to the limitations of the English language, which lacks the "plentuous diversite of the speking of" Latin.[14] He therefore sought out a treatise on the same theme which could be adapted to a concise and pithy style of English. The result was a translation so compact in manner as to deserve the term obscure; but it is deliberately so, and in a brief address "To the reder" he warns of his "shorte maner of speche" (ai^v). Although none of Wyatt's poems is intentionally tightened to the point of obscurity, there is a frequent tendency in his language towards complication of thought and metaphor. It may be that he considered the English language more suitable to this kind of rhetorical play than to the opposite one of extending thought over a longer pattern of elegant sound. Both effects had to be mastered before English poetic idiom could be used with complete ease and confidence.

Most of Wyatt's poems are short, but even the longer ones show a sense of internal proportions new to English literature. He preferred to write sonnets, *strambotti*, or lyrics which avoid elaboration. However, his most remarkable accomplishment is the rather lengthy verse epistles in *terza rima*. One is struck by the subtle variations in tonality Wyatt works into these three poems, depending upon how personal or public a manner he feels is right for each matter. One epistle is a heavily ironic dialogue; one contains a fable followed by a didactic peroration; and the third combines personal anecdote with satirical vignettes of court life. Wyatt's work as a whole introduces the new rhetorical skills which were to culminate in much greater poetry later on : a sense of proportioned variety within a fixed form or one logically designed for the matter, dramatic projection of different *personae* in discourse, and an attempt to combine resonance or elegance with verbal wit.

The influence of the sonnet went well beyond its demand for interior design, and beyond the challenge of matching wits with Italian and French writers. For even small groups of sonnets haphazardly produced led the poet into the crucial act of exploring his own choice between the active life of virtue and the secret worship of Cupid. The *Amoretti*

---

[14] C. R. Baskervill, ed., *Plutarch's Quyete of Mynde Translated by Thomas Wyat* (Cambridge, Mass., 1931), aij.

and *Astrophil and Stella* are semi-dramatic discourses about this dilemma. Spenser celebrates marriage as the solution to ethical and political necessities, but his view of the lady's psyche is traditionally Petrarchan. Sidney has to find a sophisticated escape from the trap of sensuality without embarrassing himself or the lady in question. Though less unified, Thomas Watson's earlier sequence, *Hekatompathia or Passionate Centurie of Love* (1582),[15] reveals through its commentaries the moral earnestness inseparable from sonnet writing.

Both the pastoral and the Ovidian epyllion served as complementary forms in the literary pre-occupation with the heroic choice.[16] In the eclogue the courtly man found an escape from his problems, sometimes by enjoying the adventures of a hero disguised as a shepherd. The pastoral also implied the portrayal of physical nature, landscape, and cosmos as the moral emblem of all human life, continuing the ancient analogy of the micro- and the macrocosmos. Logically, the *personae* of pastoral scenes became satirists of the courtly world, with its perversion of the simple virtues and uninhibited passions rooted in the Golden Age. When one considers how widely the connections of the pastoral could be made to reach, it is not surprising that we have no successful large-scale pastorals before Spenser's *Shepherd's Calendar*. Alexander Barclay's eclogues, written in the first decade of the century, are tiresome though occasionally vivid with observation. Barnabe Googe's *Eglogs, Epytaphes, and Sonettes* (1563) are smoothly unambitious. English poets could not compose great pastorals until they were also able to complete first-rate sonnet sequences, dramas, and approach the epic in verse or prose.

While the pastoral offered a complete context for the natural re-inforcement or test of the virtuous life, the erotic epyllion focused upon the conflict of sensory experience with spiritual integrity. That Ovid could be moralized was made clear to those limited to English by Arthur Golding's version of the *Metamorphoses* (1565, 1567). The first impressive imitation of the Ovidian technique was Thomas Lodge's *Scillaes Metamorphosis* of 1589. The more famous *Hero and Leander* by Marlowe was not published until 1598, by which time Chapman had completed the fable. The overwrought descriptions and

---

[15] Ed. S. K. Heninger, Jr., Scholars' Facsimiles and Reprints (Gainesville, 1964); and also ed. Cesare G. Cecioni (Catania, 1964).

[16] Hallet Smith, *Elizabethan Poetry : A Study in Conventions, Meaning, and Expression* (Cambridge, Mass., 1952), Chapters II and II, and pp. 293 ff. on the figure of Hercules. See also Elizabeth Story Donno, ed., *Elizabethan Minor Epics* (London, 1963).

conceits of the Ovidian genre were intended to suggest the sensory impact of physical nature upon the intellect. Nature tempts, conquers, or punishes the resistant spirit. The ultimate refinement of this genre is seen in George Chapman's *Ovids Banquet of Sence* (1595), in which Ovid's apprehension of Julia's (Corynna's) beauty is recorded through a separate treatment of each of the five senses, down to the lowest, where the poem must necessarily stop.[17] Especially in Chapman's case, we must attempt to appreciate the seriousness of an encounter with sensuality. For Chapman, like Shakespeare, Sidney, and Spenser, conceived of his heroic figures as more than normally vulnerable to the trials of sensation. In that way the inner greatness of heroic man could be measured against the vastness and power of the cosmos.

The erotic epyllion has a religious parallel in the allegorical interpretations of Solomon's *Song of Songs*. The spiritualizing of this paeon to physical love was of course a doctrinal necessity once the text had been taken into the holy canon. But doctrinal logic was supported by the traditions of epic and romance which assumed that spiritual greatness could be "figured forth" in physical dimensions. There was no finally unresolvable conflict between the rhetorical tradition of classical heroism and the Christian idea of the incarnation. For the principle of decorum did not imply the exclusion of any aspect of human nature; instead, it demanded that certain kinds of human experience be subordinated to others. Thus Spenser's conception of Arthur and of his marriage to the Faerie Queene fulfills the pattern of complete humanity also represented by Solomon and his queen or Christ and the Church. David's sinful love for Bathsheba and his regeneration under divine grace made the Penitential Psalms another religious complement to the literature of heroism. The recitation of the Penitential Psalms was a common penance; and their translation sometimes had autobiographical implications, as may be seen in the dramatic additions Wyatt gave to his version.

Between the publication of Tottel's *Miscellany* in 1557 and the *annus mirabilis* of 1579-1580 (North's *Plutarch*, Spenser's *Shepherd's Calendar*, and Lyly's *Euphues and His England*), it is difficult to observe any notable increase in English rhetorical powers. The very popular *Mirror for Magistrates*, in stanzaic verse, only attests to the public appetite for political rumination. Except for some gains in

---

[17] Rhoda M. Ribner, "The Compasse of This Curious Frame : Chapman's *Ovids Banquet of Sence* and the Emblematic Tradition," *Studies in the Renaissance* 17 (1970), 233-258.

metrical variety the *Mirror* was entirely a backward looking work, as indeed it takes up its theme where John Lydgate left off. The rhetorical complaint which the *Mirror* employed had better success later when Daniel and Shakespeare applied it to distinctly amorous themes.

Surrey's experiments with blank verse were virtually ignored throughout mid-century, while poets carried on a tireless production of fourteener couplets and the similar Poulter's Measure. The authoritative version of the *Aeneid* by Phaer and Twyne (all thirteen books) was in rhymed fourteeners. Seneca's tragedies and Ovid's *Metamorphoses* were rendered into much the same form. The efforts at blank verse by George Gascoigne (*The Steel Glass* and *Jocasta*) do not show as much inventive talent as his rhymed autobiographical poems or his profane *Discourse of the Adventures Passed by Master F. J.* (1573). Not in fact until the late 1580's and the wide adoption of blank verse for the drama is there any convincing evidence that the English Renaissance had been established as a literary movement equal to its ideals. The mastery of one genre made possible the mastery of all, and it is difficult to say which one was the key.

If only the records of the dramatic literature had survived we would find the efflorescence of Marlowe, Kyd, Greene, and Shakespeare inexplicable. It was in fact the non-dramatic genres which gave strength to the drama. Even Shakespeare in his line-by-line procedure is a rhetorician composing lyrics, complaints and orations. But the drama gradually induced a modulation between oratory and dialogue and brought in a greater variety of social types. Shakespeare gradually mixed and fused all the available genres into new unities: Plautine comedy, Ovidian melodrama, morality play and the wheel of Fortune narrative, English history, classical and domestic tragedy, pastoral and romance. The acquirement of verbal skills by all the social orders is saluted by Hamlet in this remark to Horatio on the language of the First Gravedigger:

> How absolute the knave is! We must speak by the card, or equivocation will undo us. By the Lord, Horatio, these three years I have taken note of it; the age is grown so picked that the toe of the peasant comes so near the heels of our courtier, he galls his kibe. (*Hamlet*, V.i.)

But while Shakespeare introduced regional and social dialects into his plays, he never abandoned the epic hero. In delaying his revenge upon Claudius Hamlet managed to put into English just about all one could hope to hear about the human condition.

New York University

JACOB BURCKHARDT (1818-1897) AND
VESPASIANO DA BISTICCI (1422-1498)

HELENE WIERUSZOWSKI

In his introduction to the English edition of Vespasiano da Bisticci's *Vite di Uomini Illustri*,[1] Professor Myron P. Gilmore underscores the great significance that this Quattrocento collection of biographies had in the genesis of Jacob Burckhardt's own masterpiece *The Civilization of the Renaissance in Italy*.[2] During a conversation that took place between Burckhardt and Ludwig von Pastor, the historian of the Papacy, during the latter's visit to Basel in 1895, Pastor asked Burckhardt discreetly whether he had published nothing besides the *Cicerone* about the impressions he gained from his Italian travels. According to Gilmore, Burckhardt brushed aside this suggestion that the inspiration for the *Kultur* "had been due to his travels in Italy and also to his earlier description of Italian works of art," and he recalled "that the first idea for his great book had come to him in Rome in 1847 on reading a copy loaned to him of Vespasiano da Bisticci's *Lives of Illustrious Men*."[3] Gilmore then adds: "Thus is established by the most direct testimony the place of the Florentine bookseller's biographies in the genesis of the most famous of modern works on the Renaissance" (p. xi). Later in his short preface Gilmore goes on to say: "Even without Burckhardt's avowal of the importance of Vespasiano, it would be possible to suggest a relationship between the biographies of the Florentine bookseller and the synthesis of the Swiss historian." The *Lives*, he explains, are marked by characteristics which are not only representative of the age but create the impression that the men they describe were different from those of other ages. Such men could

---

[1] *Vespasiano. Renaissance Princes, Popes and Prelates : The Vespasiano Memoirs. Lives of Illustrious Men of the XVth Century*, trans. W.G. and E. Waters. Introduction to the Torchbook edition by M.P. Gilmore (New York, 1963), pp. xi-xvi. English quotations used in the text will be taken from this translation, hereafter cited as *Memoirs*.

[2] Jacob Burckhardt, *Die Kultur der Renaissance in Italien*, 16th edition, ed. Walter Goetz (Leipzig, 1925).

[3] On the edition or manuscript he may have seen, see n. 11 below.

serve therefore as prototypes whom Burckhardt, from the perspective of a much later age, was able to see and describe as the Man of the Renaissance. Furthermore, the categories used as topics for the Six Sections that constitute Burckhardt's book were at least inspired by, if not borrowed from, the many-colored picture of Vespasiano's *Lives* when seen and analyzed in its cultural totality and uniqueness.[4]

For the report on Pastor's conversation with the Swiss historian in 1895 Gilmore gives credit to Werner Kaegi, who had discovered it in Pastor's diaries and had published its substance in his biography of Burckhardt. Gilmore welcomes Kaegi's find as the first unequivocal statement of the historian himself on the origin of his *Kultur*. However, reading Pastor's report in the original German, one cannot help noticing that in his English translation Gilmore has shifted the emphasis somewhat and changed the wording so that the statement sounds as if Burckhardt gave credit to Vespasiano alone. Although he disclaimed his Italian travels as a source of inspiration, Burckhardt stressed the importance of his occupation with Italian works of art as the root of his Italian books. This is what he said : "... ich hielt mich hauptsächlich an die Kunstwerke; zu tieferem geschichtlichem Studium kam ich damals noch nicht." Then follows the passage on his reading the *Lives* in Rome in 1847 and the impression they left on his imagination.[5]

Burckhardt's own testimony that he was mainly engaged in problems of art history at the time is borne out by the biographical facts.[6] From all we know, cultural problems had not as yet presented

---

[4] *Vespasiano. Memoirs*, Introduction, xiv ff.

[5] Werner Kaegi, *Jacob Burckhardt: Eine Biographie*, III (Basel and Stuttgart, 1956), ch. 8 : "Der Geschichtschreiber der Renaissance," 647-769, hereafter cited as 'Kaegi.' On Burckhardt's conversation with Pastor, see 647ff. Kaegi quotes the sentence correctly, editing only its beginning. The following is the passage as it appears in Pastor himself : "Auf die Frage, ob er nichts über seine italienischen Reiseeindrücke veröffentlicht habe ausser dem 'Cicerone,' bemerkte er : 'Sentiments de voyageur über Italien gibt es so viele, dass ich sie nicht vermehren möchte. Meine Eindrücke sind niedergelegt in den Briefen an meinen Vater; ich hielt mich hauptsächlich an die Kunstwerke; zu tieferem geschichtlichem Studium kam ich damals noch nicht. Aber unendlich bedeutungsvoll wurde es für mich, dass mir in Rom 1847 für einen Tag die Biographien des Vespasiano da Bisticci geliehen wurden. Damals entstand bei mir der erste Gedanke zur Kultur der Renaissance in Italien." Ludwig von Pastor, *Tagebücher, Briefe, Erinnerungen*, ed. W. Wühr (Heidelberg, 1950), 275.

[6] Kaegi, 647. Kaegi reacts to this statement with the ironic exclamation : "of all things (*ausgerechnet*) the biographies of Vespasiano ... strange indeed." On his explanation, see n. 18 below.

themselves to him, although his stay in Rome in 1847-48 was in all respects the most fruitful and creative year of his classical period. His first three books were rooted in the experiences, meditations and studies of this year, a year described by the historian in his later life in glowing colors and as the time of real meditation.[7]

Another argument against the assertion that *Die Kultur der Renaissance* was planned at this early period is the fact that the age of the Renaissance as such had not yet received a place of its own in Burckhardt's chronological scheme and in his concept of world history. As we know from a *Werkplan* drawn up in the winter of 1847-48, only a few weeks after his "encounter with Vespasiano," Burckhardt planned to write or to compose—perhaps in collaboration with others—a "library of the History of Culture" from antiquity to the end of the Middle Ages with the Gothic period as a climax and the last century as the "Schlussbild" of the Middle Ages under the heading "The Age of Raphael."[8] The same world-historical concept prevails in a lecture course on the History of the Middle Ages delivered at Basel in the academic year 1849-50. The Gothic period is again presented as the flowering period of European art and culture and the fifteenth century is described as the "Spätzeit," although here and there in the scheme Burckhardt allows the Quattrocento a kind of "Sonderleben."[9] Still then, and for some time to come, not Renaissance man but Renaissance art remains the axis around which the historian's thought revolved.[10]

---

[7] For the historical and biographical background, as well as Burckhardt's experiences on his Italian journeys, see Kaegi, 169 ff. and also the same author's introduction to his edition of the *Kultur der Renaissance in Italien* in vol. 5 of the *Jacob Burckhardt : Gesamtausgabe* (Basel, 1930), henceforth cited as *B.G.A.* See also F. Kaphahn's introduction to a selection of Burckhardt's letters : *Jacob Burckhardt : Briefe zur Erkenntnis seiner geistigen Gestalt* (Leipzig, 1935). On the period 1846-1860, see the relevant letters (152-254) and Kaphahn's comments (48-73). The enormous literature on Burckhardt is listed in *Deutsches Literatur-Lexicon*, II (1969), 355-363.

[8] Kaegi, 168 ff. and 648 ff. The *Werkplan* is known from a letter written to Andreas Heusler dated January 19, 1848 and from a later letter to F. von Preen dated May 31, 1874 (see *Briefe*, 360 ff.). Since Burckhardt's *Schlussbild* of the Middle Ages had by then been transformed into the actual *Kultur der Renaissance in Italien*, Burckhardt refers to it in the letter of 1874 under this title. See Kaegi, 648 ff.

[9] Kaegi, 650.

[10] Burckhardt had studied with Ranke among other great teachers. He specialized in the history of the Middle Ages, gaining a doctorate in 1847 with a thesis on Charles Martel. He turned to the history of art when his teacher and friend, Franz Kugler, invited him to Berlin to assist in the revising and reediting of his two handbooks of art. On Burckhardt's extensive contributions to both volumes, see Kaegi, 47-150.

To return to the statement of 1895 and the appreciation of Vespasiano's *Lives* as the root of Burckhardt's great book, it must be assumed that he considerably antedated not so much his encounter with as the influence of the *Lives* on his later work.[11] The remark made to Pastor obviously is that of an old man who, reminiscing on the past, sees every intellectual event he could recall reflected in the book which was later to be his pride and the source of his fame. What the reading might have awakened in him was the consciousness that in the *Lives* and similar works there was a treasure mine of information on human beings from different walks of life who were engaged in intellectual pursuits typical of that age. This was a mine to be explored and exploited once his mind and 'dreams' had widened sufficiently so as to envision clearly the mutual relations between culture—in the widest sense of the term—and art.[12]

As suggested above, Burckhardt's Italian experience did not immediately transform his historical and aesthetic outlook. His courses continued to center on the Gothic period as the first climax in the process of expressing an ideal of beauty in artistic forms in Christian Europe. Burckhardt described Gothic art, in its "complete spiritualization of form," as a counterpart to the art of the Greeks. On the other hand, there was stirring in Burckhardt's meditations that unforgettable experience of the perfect form realized in Italian art. An inner conflict between two contrasting ideals and the cultural values they implied was inevitable.[13] It is well known that the Italian classical ideal of harmony and proportion gradually won out. Slowly it succeeded in absorbing his interest and influencing his aesthetic judgments and artistic taste.[14] As a new historical perspective gained ground, urging him to find an outlet in creative writing, his mind turned definitely to the South, to the late Roman Empire and its decline in the age of Constantine the Great.

---

[11] Vespasiano's *Vite di uomini illustri* were first published from the *Codex Vaticanus* 3224 by Cardinal Angelo Mai in *Spicilegium Romanum*, I (Rome, 1839). Burckhardt had probably known this edition earlier. If he mentions in his conversation with Pastor that the *Vite* were loaned to him "for one day," it was perhaps the *Codex Vaticanus* itself to which he refers. The edition made by Cardinal Mai would certainly have been loaned to him for more than one day. See Kaegi, 170, n. 34.

[12] Kaegi, 647ff.

[13] This conflict is most dramatically described by Kaegi in his introduction to vol. 5 of the *B.G.A.* (see n. 7), xxiv ff.

[14] See Kaphahn in *Jacob Burckhardt : Briefe*, 63-65.

A new trip to Italy in the winter of 1853-54 was in the main dedicated to visiting, exploring and cataloguing works of art wherever they could be found or traced. While concentrating on this work in preparation for the *Cicerone*, Burckhardt discovered the cultural conditions for the changes in Italian art that he noted, and from this twin-outlook the development of medieval art appeared in an entirely new light. Signs of "the beautiful style" were apparent at least in some regions of Italy, especially in Tuscany, as early as the eleventh century. Later, local traditions as well as foreign influences acted on and partly transformed the basic elements of an essentially Christian culture.[15] But in contrast to the North the Italians never lost contact with a past that had left its traces on their soil. In the centuries that followed this first 'revival,' new trends grew, expanded and matured until a climax was reached in the first quarter of the sixteenth century when the ideal of a "perfect classical style" was finally fulfilled.[16] Although Burckhardt emphasized a continuity into the sixteenth century of the process of "reviving ancient civilization" he still insisted on the early Quattrocento as witnessing the decisive breakthrough of a new sense of style along with a tendency to rationalize by scientific methods the basic principles of the new ideal. The Quattrocento thus became for Burckhardt the Renaissance par excellence.[17] This sketch of the new cultural periodization that became the *Leitmotive* of the *Cicerone* (1854) was necessary to show how Burckhardt's interest in Quattrocento culture grew in close connection with his studies on Italian art. As is well known, Burckhardt's image of the Renaissance contains more than a description of the revival of *studia*

---

[15] Burckhardt, *Der Cicerone*, II, 10th ed. (Leipzig, 1910). See the short introduction to architecture, sculpture, painting (62ff.; 386ff.; 634ff.). On the survival of ornamental work such as that done by the Cosmates "in spite of general barbarization," see 22 ff.

[16] See Kaegi, 651 ff. where the process is summarized : "Im 'Cicerone' selbst ist ein umfassender kulturgeschichtlicher Grundbegriff ... nicht zu verkennen. Die Kunst des 15. und 16. Jahrhunderts, das Quattrocento und die klassische Kunst im engeren Sinn, erscheinen innerhalb dieses primären Grundbegriffs nur als die letzten Blüten der umfassenden Hauptepoche, die vom 11. bis ins 16. Jahrhundert reicht." See also ch. 6 : "Cicerone im klassischen Land" (425-528). Within this program it was rather difficult for Burckhardt to find the right, that is, organic places for the integration of Romanesque and Gothic art.

[17] In contrast to his *Cicerone*, Burckhardt decided on a more or less concentrated description of the Quattrocento and its sixteenth century "climax" for his *Kultur*. His reason was that the book had to have limits in terms of size. See Kaegi, 690, and also W. K. Ferguson, *The Renaissance in Historical Thought* (Boston, 1949), 188-194.

humanitatis. Werner Kaegi has rightly pointed out that the *Kultur* did not grow in the Scriptorium of Vespasiano despite the tribute which Burckhardt paid him.[18]

It was during his work on Italian art that Burckhardt began to accumulate the materials for his great book. After his return to Basel, and for a long time thereafter, he continued planning to fuse the two great topics into a comprehensive work of several volumes. But the plan became a child of sorrows, a *Schmerzenskind* or *Bresten*, in Burckhardt's life. Hard pressed by adverse circumstances, Burckhardt kept cutting it down to the material needed for a cultural image of the Renaisance. Several times during this process of reduction Burckhardt promised his friends and himself to merge the history of art with that of culture. He even repeated the promise publicly in the preface to the first edition that came out in 1860 in the form we know it now.[19] It was never to be, at least not in the form promised by the author.[20] Whether for better or worse, the famous "Essay" remained as it was.

When Burckhardt had decided to cut the umbilical cord that tied culture to art in his old plan, he had to perform a major operation on the enormous bulk of material collected during the ten years that had passed from the time of his Italian experience until the new book saw the light. In an earlier phase, he laid aside the thousand or so excerpts on art from Vasari and other authors with the intention of reintegrating them with the book on culture at a later date. The

---

[18] "Für ihn war die Renaissance [that is, *Die Kultur der Renaissance in Italien*] nicht im Scriptorium des Vespasiano da Bisticci gewachsen, bei aller Verehrung, die er dem Florentiner Buchhändler und seiner Werkstatt von Abschreibern antiker Texte zollte." Kaegi, 701. Kaegi makes this remark in the context of his discussion of the famous Six Sections. He denies that the Third Section, "Die Wiedererweckung des Altertums," holds the central position of the book. Burckhardt himself insists on this, but perhaps too much, since there are so many other aspects to be considered. See Kaegi, 701ff. and Ferguson, chs. 6 and 7.

[19] We can follow this process with the help of Burckhardt's letters. See *Briefe*, 118-121 and 219-221; Kaegi, 663-695; and *Briefe*, 243-44 (1858 to Maximilian II of Bavaria), and 246ff. (1858, August). It still seemed possible to Burckhardt in 1858, two years before the book appeared, to bring together the history of art with that of culture "in einer würdigen Parallele" (*Briefe*, 244). A magnificent description of the process is found in Kaegi, 653-59; 666ff.—see also 649.

[20] In 1867, again under pressure, Burckhardt published his material on art in a separate volume entitled *Die Kunst der Renaissance in Italien*. See the edition of H. Wölfflin in *B.G.A.*, vol. 6 (1932). However, it is no match to the *Kultur*, and it remains a fragment since it does not include painting and sculpture.

'rest' was organized according to topics which were to appear in the finished book as titles of sections and chapters respectively.[21] Among the staggering number of sources, Vespasiano's *Vite* certainly kept their place, especially for Section III, "The Revival of Antiquity." But Vespasiano was not among Burckhardt's favored authors who, like L.B. Alberti, Matteo Bandello, Dante and Enea Silvio Piccolomini (Pius II), were chosen to provide him with the actors on his Renaissance stage. In the light of a much broader range of topics than he had envisioned at the time he first planned the book, Vespasiano's contribution had truly to appear as less important. On the other hand, his esteem for Vespasiano as an author and as a source for the life of the age was not diminished. In addition to the biographical material Burckhardt resorted to Vespasiano for the colors and traits to paint the background and for the whole atmosphere that surrounded and affected the life of the personalities depicted in the one hundred and thirteen *Vite*.[22] To repeat Burckhardt's appreciative words : "For further information as to the learned citizens of Florence at this period the reader must all the more be referred to Vespasiano who knew them all personally, because the tone and atmosphere in which he writes, and the terms and conditions on which he mixed in their society are of even more importance than the facts which he records. Without being a great writer, he was thoroughly familiar with the subject he wrote on, and had a deep sense of its intellectual significance."[23]

Vespasiano da Bisticci, the famous Florentine bookseller, was not a learned man. In the eyes of his erudite countrymen, the humanists of the Quattrocento, he lacked the main equipment of a true literary man, namely, the knowledge of Latin for writing purposes. (He knew enough to read texts and to quote from them.) Besides his many weaknesses as a biographer, his modern critics point to his poor

---

[21] See the letter of August 1858 (to Paul Heyse) quoted in n. 19.

[22] They are quoted here from the magnificent illustrated edition of the Casa Hoepli in Milan, *Vespasiano da Bisticci, Vite di Uomini illustri del secolo XV*, ed. P. D'Ancona and Erhard Aeschlimann (1951). The text is that prepared by L. Frati (Bologna, 1892-93), excluding however Frati's abundant comments and Vespasiano's other works. The work is cited here as *Vite*. Giuseppe Cagni (below, note 26) calls attention to a new edition now in the course of printing by A. Greco, *Le Vite*, I (Florence, 1970), which, however, does not seem to fulfill the promise held out when it was announced. See Cagni in *Italia medioevale e umanistica* 14 (1971), 293, n. 2.

[23] *Kultur der Renaissance*, 16th ed. (Kröner), 199. The significance of the last sentence is rather lessened in the English rendering, *Vespasiano, Memoirs*, Intro., p. xvi. Compare with the German : "... er kennt das ganze Treiben."

grammatical constructions, the absence of stylistic refinement, the many colloquialisms, and the frequent chronological confusions and repetitions. Some treat him with a kind of benevolent condescension, styling him "buon cartolaio," "dabbene" or "onest'uomo." The final word has not been said since he has not yet found a modern biographer, who should be not only a historian but also a linguist able to pass judgment on his *volgare*.[24] However, even his critics would agree that had be been a skilled and trained rhetorician anxious to imitate ancient biographies, his value as a source would have been considerably diminished and his *Vite* would never have become what they are now, namely, a 'Reader' for the knowledge of the men and movements of his age—*das ganze Treiben*, in Burckhardt's words. To be sure he keeps excusing himself for writing at all, feeling in all honesty that he was not qualified; his excuse is that he was only gathering material for a literary man to use in a Latin biography.[25]

We are all the more appreciative of the bookseller's literary efforts because only the practical circumstances of his youth prevented him from getting an academic education and forced him to learn a trade instead. Furthermore, we must admire the man who, in the midst of an extremely busy life and often under difficult circumstances—the procuring or producing of manuscript books for a very demanding clientele being no easy matter—tried very hard to fill the gaps in his education. This we now know from the publication of Vespasiano's correspondence, or what remains of it, by Father Giuseppe M. Cagni.[26] In an Introduction to the bookseller's *Letters and Proems* which, if not a biography as such, contains everything necessary for one, Cagni

---

[24] The work usually quoted as a biography is the study of Enrico Frizzi, "Di Vespasiano da Bisticci e delle sue biografie," *Annali della Scuola Normale Superiore di Pisa* 3 (1886), 1-116. Only some thirty pages (83-116) contain biographical data. The rest is a view of the politico-literary world around Vespasiano mainly taken from his own *Vite*. Among these Frizzi distinguishes between biographies in the proper sense and memoirs just as Vespasiano happened to recall them.

[25] Among the critics who have remarked on his deficiencies but also on his great merits as a lively narrator and reporter have been E. Fueter, *Geschichte der neueren Historiographie* (Munich and Berlin, 1936), 99ff.; W. K. Ferguson, *The Renaissance in Historical Thought*, 18ff. : "Humanist Views of the Renaissance"; Vittorio Rossi, *Il Quattrocento* (Milan, 1949), 191 ff. For articles, see C. Neidhart, "Vespasiano da Bisticci und seine Papstleben," *Schweizerische Rundschau* 26 (1927), 897 ff. and 982 ff.; G. Caprin, "Il libraio fiorentino degli Umanisti Vespasiano da Bisticci" in *Il Quattrocento* (Florence, 1954).

[26] *Vespasiano da Bisticci e il suo Epistolario* (Rome, 1969), cited as "Cagni" for the Introduction, and Cagni, *Lettere*, and *Proemi*.

tells the story of how in 1449 Vespasiano engaged in "some easy studies of eloquence" (Cagni, 83ff.); how he was praised by his friend Gianozzo Manetti for this effort in self-education, since he considered it more commendable to get it "by artifice than by nature" (*Lettere* no. 6, p. 122); how a few years later he attended a course on Aristotle's *De anima*[27] and some of the symposia on the philosophical doctrines of Plato and Aristotle (*nell' una filosofia e nell' altra*) that took place in the house of Francesco Sacchetti (*Vite*, 432); and how he finally joined the Florentine Academy, at first in 1454 in the house of the Rinuccini and later, in 1462, when it had been transferred to the house of Giovanni Argyropoulos (Cagni, 85). Although Cagni's sources bear evidence of Vespasiano's membership in still another Academy, the *Pitagorici*, founded it seems even earlier, Vespasiano was especially proud that his name could be associated with the famous "Platonic Academy" that gathered somewhat later around the great Platonist, Marsilio Ficino.[28] Related to these activities was his attendance at lectures given by Argyropoulos on Platonic philosophy which seemed to have dealt with some essential questions of Platonism in relation to Christianity.[29]

---

[27] Cagni, 41, n. 1 : the lectures on Aristotle's *De anima* seemed to have been delivered in form of an "*Achademia*" (letter of A. Rinuccini to D. Cocchi, Florence, 1461). See n. 28 below.

[28] This is a confusing problem. Cagni tries to contribute to its solution by supplementing the information found in A. Della Torre's *Storia dell'Accademia Platonica* (1902) from letters of this group (84 ff.). See also his article, "Agnolo Manetti and Vespasiano da Bisticci," *Italia medioevale e umanistica* 14 (1971), 293-312. It seems that there was an *Accademia* in Florence before 1450 centering on Vespasiano himself (*ibid.*, 297). On the *Pitagorici*, see p. 297, n. 1. See also n. 31 below. I should like to thank Professor Giuseppe Billanovich of the Università Cattolica of Milan for this and other bibliographical references.

[29] Vespasiano speaks of a fight against paganism regarding the immortality of the soul in the *Vita* of Nicolò Nicoli (*Vite*, 437 ff.). On the other hand, he had before him an outstanding example of how Christian faith can be brought into harmony with pagan learning, and even with Hebrew scholarship and theology, in his friend Gianozzo Manetti. He confesses to be indebted to him for many years of instruction (Cagni, *Proemi* no. 9, p. 213). Also Manetti writes long letters to questions on ancient chronology and Christian doctrine (*Lettere*, no. 6 and 7). Gianozzo was certainly not only a Christian Platonist imbued with the metaphysical and ethical concept of love but he also practiced it; see the letter to Vespasiano (no. 6, p. 123) where he reassures his friend that his "inferiority in erudition" is completely compensated by their equality in the friendship that unites them. See the list of Manetti's *Opere* at the end of his *Vita*, p. 290; on his scholarship, *ibid.*, 259 ff.

Because of his close association with Argyropoulos as a student and member of learned societies, Vespasiano was so well informed about the activities of this Byzantine scholar that we can only regret that he did not write his *Vita* as he did for the Cardinal Bessarion (Cardinale Niceno) and for George of Trebisond (Giorgio di Trebisonda). It would be a very important contribution to our knowledge of Greek "letters" if all the notices spread over Vespasiano's several *Vite* were gathered and those relating to his lectures and disputations were identified as to the schools of thought they reflect. Burckhardt provides only a very summary and superficial sketch.[30] The same should also be done for the notices found in Vespasiano and others concerning the humanist societies or Academies of the time and the result compared with the research done by Kristeller on this topic.[31] The writer of this essay is by no means qualified to do this, especially not in a volume dedicated to a scholar who is universally recognized as "the master of those who know" in the field of Renaissance humanism. But to add just one item of correction aimed at Vespasiano's censors: the "da ben" bookseller knew Marsilio Ficino not only as the recipient of Cosimo's bounty but also as the author of some treaties in Tuscan *volgare* on aspects of his *Theologia platonica* (*Della christiana religione*) which the bookseller had procured and sent to a client.[32]

Among the fields in the program of *studia humanitatis* which Vespasiano attempted to master, history probably came easier to him than both eloquence and moral philosophy. Innumerable were

---

[30] See *Kultur*, 200, note. For the latest research on Byzantine learning in the Renaissance, see Paul O. Kristeller, *Renaissance Concepts of Man* (New York, 1972), 64-85.

[31] See above n. 28. Kristeller deals with the academies in his *Studies in Renaissance Thought and Letters* (Rome, 1956), 111 ff. He maintains that because of their informality, their lack of regulations, and their liberality in admitting as members interested people from all walks of life, these academies at first resembled the lay fraternities of an earlier time. As to the Platonic Academy in Florence, Kristeller is inclined to date its beginning in 1462, when Cosimo de' Medici gave Ficino a villa in Careggi and "placed several Greek manuscripts at his disposal." See also Paul O. Kristeller, *Eight Philosophers of the Italian Renaissance* (Stanford, 1964), 40. On Ficino's doctrines, see all of chapter 3 (37-53).

[32] Cagni, *Proemi* no. 9, p. 213. Cagni (213, n. 2) identifies the *alcune opere di Messer Marsilio* sent to Bernardo del Nero along with the *Commentario della Vita di Messer Gianozzo Manetti* as works listed and described in Paul O. Kristeller's *Supplementum Ficinianum*, I (Florence, 1937), 10-12, 71 and 89-90; II, 184-185 (*Dantis de Monarchia liber in linguam vulgarem translatus*). See also Paul O. Kristeller, *Il pensiero filosofico di Marsilio Ficino* (Florence, 1953), 17-18, n. 6; idem, *Die Philosophie des Marsilio Ficino* (Frankfurt, 1972), 14, n. 25.

the historians, biographers and political writers, both in Greek and Latin, whose manuscripts passed through his *bottega* to the desks of his copyists, translators and craftsmen until they landed on the shelves of his employers and clients. For more detailed historical information he could always refer to his learned friends, whose houses he frequented and whose conversation centered on "weighty subjects of the present or the past, or of the rule of popes, cardinals, kings or emperors; or of the wonderful men of the Roman Republic, compared with those of to-day" (*Proem* to the life of Alessandra de' Bardi, *Memoirs*, 439). Since no hero, whether past or present, could earn his fame with posterity unless he found a 'man of letters' who recorded his life, it was the historian who set the standard with the help of the authors he had consulted. Thus, in the proem to the *Vita* of Federigo di Montefeltro, first Lord and then Duke of Urbino, Vespasiano points to Fabius Maximus and his war against Hannibal to demonstrate the lesson that a general can make "intellect augment the force of battalions" (*Memoirs*, 83). In the *Vita* of the Duke, Vespasiano stresses the importance of history as a source of instruction : "it is difficult for a leader to excel in arms unless he be, like the Duke, a man of letters, seeing that the past is the mirror of the present" (*Memoirs*, 99). Here as well as in many other instances it becomes quite clear that the intermediate in the strange marriage between arms and letters, for which the Renaissance provides such magnificent examples, was history. The Duke's method of "winning the battle more by science than by force" (*Memoirs*, 92) was only one aspect of his studies and of the historical instructions that he received from the humanists. The other was the "faculty of wisely governing States and Lordships" (*Memoirs*, 105), a faculty which Vespasiano also recognizes and praises in Pope Nicholas V—whom he describes as "supremely gifted as a politician, as if he had...been brought up in the administration of important matters of state" (*Memoirs*, 38)—in Cosimo de' Medici, King Alfonso of Naples, Alessandro Sforza, Lord of Pesaro, and in some Florentine statesmen. It is indeed possible, as has been suggested by Vespasiano's translators, that Burckhardt borrowed many characteristics from Vespasiano's *Lives* for the portraits of the rulers he painted in the first Section of his book : "The State as a Work of Art."

The approach to the history of the past as a storehouse of examples and models for politics of the present is based on the opinion that the same causes, be they immediate or remote, will produce the same or similar effects. Applied to the relationship between politics and letters—or culture as a whole—the humanists formulated the famous law that the flourishing of the former, that is, Good Government, generates and supports the flourishing of the latter. As long as a republic is ruled by virtuous, patriotic and unselfish men, who care only for the glory, honor and fame of their commonwealth and the prosperity and happiness of its citizens and who practice justice, the *uomini singulari* in politics will always find their counterparts in the *uomini da lettere*, ready to commemorate their deeds: at the least they will support the arts and letters to benefit the state. On the other hand, when the state is ruled by citizens "not united for the common good" and when the sense and the practice of justice collapse (*la giustitia in tutto cadde per terra*), corruption, party rule and civil wars prevail, the *uomini illustri* will no longer take over or they will even cease to exist and along with them the writers who will lack heroes and deeds worthy of recording (Cagni, *Proemi*, 197, 210; *Vite*, 1, 385, 544ff). In this way, a whole civilization will be 'obscured' if not entirely blotted out.

The examples cited time and again and commented upon in lengthy surveys or even in short formulas by Vespasiano are of course Athens before the Thirty Tyrants took over, the Roman Republic as long as it was ruled by her best citizens and before it was destroyed by mob rule and the civil wars that ushered in the age of the dictators and emperors, and finally the city state of Florence, when the illustrious men, paragons of virtues and experts in managing a government, reappeared "in our own age." The short formula that Vespasiano uses dwells on the revival of letters in the person of the exponents of humanistic studies rather than on the statesmen and rulers who prepared the ground for them. Thus after the Golden Ages of Greece and Rome were over, fortunately saved for posterity in their "letters" and their art, there was a long period "of more than a millennium" during which the Latin language was 'obscured' and letters and arts, ruined by the barbarians, lay dormant. Come "this Golden Age of revival," *uomini singulari* in the Seven Liberal Arts and other faculties again saw and spread the light along with the rebirth of the Fine Arts, painting, sculpture and architecture.[33] The Studium of Florence, now

---

[33] See the Proem in *Vite*, 2. This is just a formula. Much more suggestive is the description of the Golden Age in a letter of Marsilio Ficino to Paul von Middleburg as quoted by Kristeller, *Il pensiero filosofico di Marsilio Ficino*, 13 : "Hoc enim saeculum... tanquam aureum liberales disciplinas ferme iam extinctas reduxit in lucem, grammaticam,

enriched by the program of *studia humanitatis* (grammar, oratory, "composition of letters," history) also contributed to this revival of letters. Vespasiano found its first beginning in the Latin writings of the literati of the fourteenth century, namely, Dante, Petrarch, Boccaccio, Coluccio Salutati and Luigi Marsili. The real *rinascita*, as the humanists saw it, was due to men steeped in both Greek and Latin letters, the great humanists and historians, namely Leonardo Bruni, Poggio Bracciolini, Nicolò Nicoli, Flavio Biondo da Forlì, whose lives Vespasiano wrote and whose historical ideas he adopted and adapted to the circumstances and conditions of the personalities to whom they were dedicated (*Vite*, 254ff, 295, 313ff, 440).[34] Thus he matches Biondo's description of the magnificence of ancient Rome and "the numerous remarkable men whom the Roman Empire produced" before its "overthrow by the Gauls, the Goths and other barbarous nations" (*Memoirs*, 415) by his own observation that in the city of Florence only a few traces of its former flourishing existence as a Roman colony were still to be found (*Vite*, 1 Proemio). At the other end of the millennium of darkness Vespasiano has noted the efforts of Pope Nicholas V to rebuild ancient Rome (below, p. 401)[35] and those of the valiant citizens of Florence to erect beautiful houses and public palaces "so that its beauty and decor is being daily increased" (Cagni, *Lettere* no. 24, p. 151).

Vespasiano, so it seems, is not too much concerned about an even loose chronology nor about what happened during the dark ages. They began with the disappearance of the Latin tongue (meaning literature) as last used by the Four Doctors of the Church, to whom he sometimes adds Bede! They end either with the Golden Age of the humanists or with the emergence of the three or four 'Latinists' of the Trecento from Dante to Luigi Marsili—in the latter case a hundred and fifty

---

poësim, oratoriam, picturam, sculpturam, architecturam, musicam, antiquum ad Orphicam lyram carminum cantum, idque Florentiae ... Fluentiae quinetiam Platonicam disciplinam in lucem e tenebris revocavit."

[34] See W. K. Ferguson, *The Renaissance* (18 ff.) on humanistic views of the Renaissance. On the topic of the connection between the civic spirit of the Florentines and their appeal to the *uomini illustri* of the Roman Republic, Cicero among others, as models, see the outstanding studies of Hans Baron on Leonardo Bruni and related aspects of the Renaissance. Here I mention only his "Cicero and the Roman Civic Spirit in the Middle Ages and Early Renaissance," *Bulletin of the John Rylands Library* 22 (1938), 72-97.

[35] Vespasiano received information on the invasion of Italy by the barbarians from the '*universale notizia*' of Pope Nicholas V (*Vite*, 23 ff.).

years have to be subtracted from the 'Millennium.' There is no niche in his chronology for the theological writers of the twelfth and the thirteenth centuries, whose works he purchased for his clients and sponsors, nor for the University of Paris, which he mentions as the place where a member of the Bardi house received his education (*Vite*, 542).[36] He completely ignores the existence of the Italian city-states and their role in the transmission of letters and the arts, a role later discovered and traced by Burckhardt. As regards the history of Florence, Vespasiano knew the chronicles of Giovanni and Filippo Villani, so highly esteemed by Burckhardt, and he should have read them for more information. He probably refused to consult them because they were written in *volgare* (*Vite*, 296). Burckhardt, on the other hand, and contrary to general opinion, never lost sight of the Middle Ages and its great art, once the object of his highest admiration, which had anticipated so many cultural elements of the later Renaissance and which had prepared and witnessed the work of Dante, intermediate between the two ages.[37] Although certain parallels between Vespasiano's and Burckhardt's concept of Quattrocento *rinascita* can be drawn—the role of Italy in spreading the *studia humanitatis* to the rest of Europe is one[38]—Vespasiano's account of cultural

---

[36] Vespasiano speaks of a Ruberto dei Bardi being at Paris at the time of Thomas Aquinas and Albertus Magnus. I find only one Roberto de' Bardi in the fourteenth century (1326) who studied at the Sorbonne. See R. Davidsohn, *Geschichte von Florenz* (Berlin, 1927), IV, 3, 139.

[37] See Kaegi, 689 f.

[38] Nowhere does Vespasiano express such remarkable patriotism as in his *Vite* of three high Hungarian prelates who, in his description, brought light to their hitherto obscure country by calling in scholars to teach at the new Studium at Buda, buying all the books they could in Italy and elsewhere and by sending for painters, sculptors and carpenters, etc. See *Vita* of Vitez Janos, Arcivescovo di Strigonia (Esztergom), *Vite*, 169 ff. Vespasiano among others was himself instrumental in procuring books on Platonism and Neoplatonism. It was he who introduced the young Bishop of Cinque Chiese (Pecs) into the circle of Cosimo and Argyropoulos and saw him go home to Hungary as an expert in *Plotinus platonicus* whom he had the intention to translate (*ibid.*, 176 ff.). The bishop who had the nickname Janus Pannonius had been sent by his uncle, the Archbishop of Strigonia, to Ferrara to study with Guarino. The third of these Hungarian prelates was the Bishop of Colocza, Hasnoz Giorgia (*ibid.*, 178-182). Vespasiano's clientele also included high English nobles as well as Portuguese and Spanish aristocrats. See Cagni, 71-75 and 109 ff. on Vespasiano's patriotic treatises. See also the articles of A. Reumont in *Archivio Storico Italiano*, 3rd ser., 20 (1874), 295, and T. Kardos in *La Rinascita* 3 (1940), 803-841; 4 (1941), 69-83. On the expansion of humanism, see Paul O. Kristeller, *Renaissance Thought*, II (New York, 1965), 69-101.

periodization could not possibly have served Burckhardt as the source or model for a history of Italian culture after the downfall of the Roman Empire.

Vespasiano's approach to art is still that of a medieval 'monk,' a chronicler or author of a *Vita*, who among other merits and virtues praises a bishop or abbot for having built or rebuilt the church and other buildings under his administration for the convenience and benefit of his monks, canons, parishioners or whoever happened to benefit by them. His name was then forever linked to the church. With few exceptions, as when the patron was also the master-builder under whose direction the *fabrica* carried out its work, credit was given to the patron rather than to the master-builder and his masons. Vespasiano observed for instance the bulding activities in and around the Church of St. Peter (and other Roman churches) and above all the Vatican palace under Pope Nicholas V, whose passion for building equalled that for the collecting of books. If he had money to spend, he used to say, there were two things he would do : buy books and build houses (*Memoirs*, 37, *Vite*, 27). Vespasiano, of course, praising the new palace as an abode worthy of "those Roman emperors who ruled the world" (*ibid*.), has no words to spend on the role played by L.B. Alberti in this achievement. An old friend of Nicholas V from their University days, Alberti was the architect and *spiritus rector* of the new structures, anxious to apply the rules he expounded theoretically in his *De re aedificatoria*. He also included the Borgo Leonino, the region surrrounding Church and Palace, in a great plan of reconstruction. Among the books on architecture which Vespasiano acquired for such libraries as the one assembled by Federigo di Montefeltro in Urbino must have been Alberti's famous work (*Vite*, 211).[39]

It is in Urbino, in the surroundings of the Lord, later Duke, Federigo that Vespasiano could have observed the activities of some great artists. However, for the building of the palace as well as for the decoration of some of the rooms, the studio and the library, credit is given only to the Duke himself. Although surrounded by architects, whose advice he sought, he was the one who decided on the style of the palaces to be built for him in Urbino and elsewhere. Vespasiano describes the Duke as so well versed in architecture that his knowledge in this

---

[39] See Joan Gadol, *Leon Battista Alberti, Universal Man of the Early Renaissance* (Chicago, 1969), 93 ff. and nn. 1 and 2 for literature on the building programs of Alberti and the Pope.

field matched that of any professional. It is thus to him that Vespasiano ascribes the guiding principles of the structure he began to erect : "We may see in the buildings he [the Duke] constructed the grand style and the due measurements and proportion [as he applied them], especially in his palace" (*Memoirs*, 100) : *l'ordine grande e le misure d'ogni cosa* (*Vite*, 208).[40] This is an appropriate way of mentioning the qualities which a "modern" bulding, according to Alberti, was supposed to have if it was to satisfy the contemporary sense of beauty. In the words of Alberti : If a palace or church was so constructed that the proportions of the parts to each other and to the whole are of the same ratio (*finitio*), then congruity or beauty (*concinnitas*) is achieved since it is ruled by the same law that controls the things created by nature.[41] Vespasiano emphasizes Federigo's interest in all branches of mathematics : they are also richly represented in his famous library which was in part stocked by Vespasiano (*Vite*, 211ff). It is known that the Duke befriended Alberti (Gadol, 9). We know that the master-architect who built one wing of the palace of Urbino and the beautiful cortile with its well proportioned arcades was the Dalmatian Luciano da Laurana (a place near Zara).[42] Burckhardt says of him that his work breathed the same spirit which permeated the works of Brunelleschi and Alberti although nothing is known about the relationship of Laurana with the Florentine artists (*Cicerone*, v. 2, 131).

According to Vespasiano, it was Federigo who took the initiative in calling to Italy a Flemish master especially skilled in oil painting, the mastery of which was not found to a great extent among the Italian masters he knew. Having arrived in Urbino, this master (Justus or Josse of Ghent) was soon engaged in several projects, among which was the decoration of the Duke's studio. He was soon

---

[40] Vespasiano uses similar terms when mentioning Cosimo's 'ordine' in his Badia of Fiesole in the *Vita* of the bishop of Ragusa (*Vite*, 152).

[41] The three elements that have to be present in a structure if beauty or harmony is to be achieved are *numerus, finitio, collocatio* (symmetry) as shown by Gadol (108 ff.) with examples drawn from the Pythagorean theory of music. I am also indebted to the author of this splendid book on Alberti for personal explanations.

[42] On this architect and his work in Urbino see Burckhardt, *Cicerone*, II, 131 ff.; W. Bombe, "Die Kunst am Hofe Federicos von Urbino," *Monatshefte für Kunstwissenschaft* 5 (1912), 456-474. For more literature see *Vite*, 108 ff., n. 2. Laurana was also the architect of the Palazzo Prefettizio in Pesaro built by Alessandro Sforza (Burckhardt, *ibid.*). It is probably the *Rocca* mentioned in the *Vita* of his son, Costanzo Sforza (*Vite*, 232).

joined and assisted by two great Italian painters, Piero della Francesca and Melozzo da Forlì. Vespasiano, to be sure, mentions none of the artists by name. It is typical of his approach, however, that he was able to describe in detail the picture program of this decoration : *fece dipingere*, so he says, *i filosofi e poeti e tutti i dottori della chiesa* (*Vite*, *ibid*.). He must have been pleased with the "portraits" of some of the great writers and thinkers whose books filled the shelves of the Duke's studio and library, among them Plato, Aristotle and Ptolemy, and with the allegories of the Seven Liberal Arts, to the cultivation of which he was proud to have contributed.[43] His is, incidentally, the only contemporary description of this pictural program that has come down to us (Bombe, 459). The association of the Flemish with the Italian masters resulted in an interchange of methods and techniques, so much so that art historians have a hard time in assigning these paintings to one or the other master (Bombe, *ibid*.). Vespasiano again would have given the Duke the credit for this fruitful exchange.

The same can be said about the works of architecture which Vespasiano saw arise and grow "almost daily" in and outside Florence (Cagni, *Lettere* no. 24, p. 151). For those who enjoyed the special protection of the Medici family, Cosimo was by far the most generous and liberal among the citizens who embellished the city at their own cost. In addition to his palaces, villas and gardens, the churches rebuilt or newly built were the most admired examples of his patronage and civic spirit (*Vite*, 413). Vespasiano reports the work done on both convent and church of the Badia of Fiesole and on the church and the Old Sacristy of San Lorenzo without even suggesting the name of Brunelleschi as the master-architect of the two latter structures. An exception is made with Donatello : in his case a commission from Cosimo—the pulpits of the church of San Lorenzo and the bronze doors and other ornaments for the Old Sacristy—is explained as a charitable work on the part of his patron (*Vite*, 418).[44]

To be sure, Vespasiano did not lack good taste and an eye for things beautiful, witness still to-day in many manuscript collections the

---

[43] See Bombe, 462 ff. and Burckhardt, II, 724f. The portrait of the Duke, the likeness of which Vespasiano emphasizes (*Vite*, 209), is probably the one carved in wood (intarsia) still found in the Duke's studiolo in the palace of Urbino. See the illustration in the Hoepli edition of the *Vite*, p. 200.

[44] Vespasiano makes it appear that it was Cosimo's sympathy with Donatello who was at this time 'unemployed' and his concern that sculpture in general was not very much in demand that led him to order these works from Donatello.

splendid books turned out by his *bottega*. He was able to describe scenery like that at his country house in Antella in the lyrical language of a poet (*Lettere* no. 41, p. 179).[45] He utterly enjoyed his occasional visits in the house of Nicolò Nicoli because it was filled with beautiful antique objects sent to the great scholar from all parts of the world and above all with the beautiful "antique" presence of the patron.[46] It seems no accident that it is here, in this *ambiente* created by an admirer of antiquity, that Vespasiano sees and mentions four great Florentine artists as friends and companions of the humanist rather than as recipients of his favors. They are Brunelleschi, Donatello, Luca della Robbia and Lorenzo Ghiberti (*Vite*, 441). An exceptional friendship indeed. As a rule, Vespasiano would have hesitated to weigh the merits of an artist (or artisan) on the same scale with those of a humanist. He is still moving on the borderline between the old medieval concept of the "artist" as the member of a craft, an artisan turned out by a workshop, and that of a student or scholar of his field who is learned in the sciences that are indispensable for producing modern works of art modelled "after nature." Vespasiano correctly described the role of science and a scientific ideal in the architecture of Federigo di Montefeltro. But he is completely confused as to the position of "Fine Arts" as a class by itself in a system of human activities.[47]

Vespasiano was not born to be a Vasari. Even his literary portraits lack color, shading and a firm design.[48] The reading of his *Vite* informs, entertains and often amuses us, but it does not in any way stir our sensitive and imaginative powers. Rather than creating images they read as somewhat conventionalized comments. Burckhardt, on the other hand, was not only a great scholar but also a man of visions and

---

[45] Attention should also be paid to his fine observation of face and hand on the tomb of the Cardinal Jacopo of Portugal in the chapel built for him in San Miniato in Florence (*Vite*, 106). See *Vite*, 105, n. 2; Burckhardt, *Cicerone*, II, 193ff. and 478. The tomb is the work of Antonio Rossellino (Ill. in *Vite*, 103).

[46] Burckhardt, *Kultur*, Section 3, ch. 6.

[47] There is no consistent classification of 'arts and sciences' in the *Vite*. In the Proemio to the whole book (*Vite*, 2), Vespasiano distinguishes between the Liberal Arts (all Seven) and the three "Fine Arts." There is no system whatsoever in the listing of the books in the sort of Catalogue to be found in his *Vita* of Federigo di Montefeltro (*Vite*, 211). Only once are artisans (carpenters) mentioned along with painters and sculptors. See above n. 38. But workshops generally transmit only technical skills; the cognitive or rational principles must be learned and studied like all the Liberal Arts and the Faculties. See Gadol, *L. B. Alberti*, 128 ff. on this point and also the literature cited on the question.

[48] See V. Rossi, *Il Quattrocento*, 191 ff.

dreams. Art and not books is what he loved best in the Renaissance, and while at a certain point he banishes the discussion of art-works from his book, it is absent only in the concrete sense of the word.[49] Like a distant projector it throws its rays on his pages, visible to all those who are willing to follow him deep down to the realm of poetry and meditation in which his book was rooted.

City College, The City University of New York

---

[49] See W. Kaegi, 649 : "Der ideelle Blickpunkt des Werkes lag ursprünglich auf der Kunst und ist im Grunde immer dort haften geblieben."

GREGOR HEIMBURG AND EARLY HUMANISM IN GERMANY

MORIMICHI WATANABE

Gregor Heimburg (c. 1400-1472) is best known as a jurist and politician who strongly criticized the Church in the fifteenth century.[1] But in order to understand the full range of his religious, intellectual, and political ideas it is important to recognize the influence of humanism on the growth of this controversialist and the role which he played in the development of early humanism in Germany. It is sometimes said that German humanism originated in the universities at Erfurt, Heidelberg, Leipzig, and Vienna.[2] But we must note that many lawyers who worked as advisors to secular or ecclesiastical princes in the fifteenth and sixteenth centuries were educated in Italy and contributed a great deal to the growth of humanism after returning to their own country.[3] Heimburg was one of the fifteenth-century German lawyers whose career and thought deserve a close study for our understanding of the diffusion of humanism in general and of its early manifestation in Germany in particular. Joachimsohn's impressive work on Heimburg, which appeared in 1891,[4] must be

---

[1] C. Ullmann, *Reformers Before the Reformation*, trans. R. Menzies, I (Edinburgh, 1855), 195-208; Kamil Krofta, "Bohemia in the Fifteenth Century," *Cambridge Medieval History*, VIII (New York, 1936), 99; Frederick G. Heymann, *George of Bohemia : King of Heretics* (Princeton, 1965).

[2] See, for example, Roberto Weiss, *The Spread of Italian Humanism* (London, 1964), 94.

[3] See Paul Lehmann, "Grundzüge des Humanismus deutscher Lande zumal im Spiegel deutscher Bibliotheken des 15. und 16. Jahrhunderts," *Aevum* 31 (1957), 253-268; reprinted in his *Erforschung des Mittelalters*, V (Stuttgart, 1962), 481-496; Hans Lieberich, "Die gelehrten Räte : Stadt und Juristen in Bayern in der Frühzeit der Rezeption," *Zeitschrift für bayerische Landes-Geschichte* 27 (1964), 120-189; Franz Wieacker, "Einflüsse des Humanismus auf die Rezeption," *Zeitschrift für die gesamte Staatswissenschaft* 100 (1940), 423-456; Lewis W. Spitz, "German Humanism," *Renaissance Quarterly* 21 (1968), 125-131.

[4] Paul Joachimsohn, *Gregor Heimburg*, Historische Abhandlungen aus dem Münchener Seminar, I (Bamberg, 1891). The other main biographies of Heimburg are

corrected and brought up to date on some aspects of Heimburg's life.

It is not within the scope of this paper to deal in detail with the complex history of early humanism in the German Empire and to discuss how humanism grew in Bohemia, the Netherlands, Austria, Swabia, the Palatinate, and Franconia.[5] We note in reviewing these developments that early humanism in Germany was fostered in the first instance by Italian humanists who came to the North, secondly by German students who after studying in Italian universities became advisors to princes and prelates, doctors for towns or cities, or teachers in universities, and finally by those Germans who contributed to its growth although, or precisely because, they did not visit Italy. The most famous of the first group was, no doubt, Aeneas Sylvius Piccolomini (1405-1464), whom Joachimsohn called "the apostle of humanism in Germany."[6] Pier Paolo Vergerio, Benedetto da Piglio, Jacopo Publicio, and Poggio Bracciolini may also be mentioned in this connection. The second group includes a large number of Germans who were influenced by humanism, such as Gregor Heimburg, Heinrich Steinhöwel (1412-1482), Thomas Pirckheimer (d. 1473), Laurentius Blumenau (c. 1415-1484), Niklas von Wyle (d. 1478), Sigismund

---

Joannes A. Ballenstadius, *Vitae Gregorii de Heimburg ... brevis narratio* (Helmstedt, 1737); Clemens Brockhaus, *Gregor von Heimburg : Ein Beitrag zur deutschen Geschichte des 15. Jahrhunderts* (Leipzig, 1861, repr. Wiesbaden, 1969).

[5] To mention some of the important works on this topic : Franz W. Kampschulte, *Die Universität Erfurt in ihrem Verhältnisse zu dem Humanismus und der Reformation*, 2 vols. (Trier, 1858-1860, repr. Aalen, 1970); Ludwig Geiger, *Renaissance und Humanismus in Italien und Deutschland* (Berlin, 1882); Georg Voigt, *Die Wiederbelebung des classischen Alterthums oder das erste Jahrhundert des Humanismus*, 2nd ed., 2 vols. (Berlin, 1880-1881); Paul Joachimsohn, "Frühhumanismus in Schwaben," *Württembergische Vierteljahrshefte für Landesgeschichte*, n.s. 5 (1896), 63-126, 257-291; Max Herrmann, *Die Reception des Humanismus in Nürnberg* (Berlin, 1898); Gustav Bauch, *Die Reception des Humanismus in Wien* (Breslau, 1903); Gustav Bauch, *Die Universität Erfurt im Zeitalter des Frühhumanismus* (Breslau, 1904); Karl Grossmann, "Die Frühzeit des Humanismus in Wien bis zu Celtis Berufung 1497," *Jahrbuch für Landeskunde von Niederösterreich* 22 (1929), 150-325; Hans Rupprich, *Die Frühzeit des Humanismus und die Renaissance in Deutschland* (Lepzig, 1938, repr. Darmstadt, 1964); Eduard Winter, *Frühhumanismus : Seine Entwicklung in Böhmen und deren europäische Bedeutung für die Kirchenreformbestrebungen im 14. Jahrhundert* (Berlin, 1964). See also Paul O. Kristeller, "The European Diffusion of Italian Humanism," *Italica* 39 (1962), 1-12; reprinted in his *Renaissance Thought II : Papers on Humanism and the Arts* (New York, 1965), 69-88.

[6] Joachimsohn, *Heimburg*, 103.

Gossembrot (1417-1493), Albrecht von Eyb (1420-1475),Peter Luder
(d. 1474), Hermann Schedel (1410-1485), Samuel Karoch, Rudolf
Agricola (1444-1484), and Sigismund Meisterlin (d. after 1491). The
significance of the last group as a whole is not to be neglected, but with
the exception of such famous ones as Martin Mair (Mayr, Mayer,
Meyer) (c. 1420-1480), most of them remain unknown or forgotten.

What then was the educational, intellectual, and political background of Gregor Heimburg ? How did he contribute to the spread
of humanism in Germany ? Born in the Franconian city of Schweinfurt
near Würzburg around 1400 as the son of the burgher Hans Heimburg,
mayor of Schweinfurt four times, Gregor was, as we shall see in more
detail, educated in local schools and studied at German universities.
Crossing the Alps like many aspiring youths of his time, he went to Italy
to study at the University of Padua and received the degree of Doctor
of Laws from the university in 1430.[7] In Nuremberg, to which he came
after graduation, Heimburg met Konrad III of Daun, Archbishop
of Mainz, who appointed him on June 21, 1430, his general
vicar in ecclesiastical affairs despite the fact that Heimburg was a
layman. In this capacity he went to the Council of Basel in 1432 which
had begun the previous year. After serving as representative of the
Emperor Sigismund in 1434 at the council, he became legal advisor
to the city of Nuremberg next year and continued to serve almost
continuously till 1461, in spite of the fact that there were occasional
frictions between the city council and Heimburg.[8] During this time his
services were not confined to Nuremberg. His legal counsel was sought
by many prelates and princes, such as the Duke of Saxony, the
Margrave of Brandenburg, the Archduke of Austria, the Kings of
Hungary and Bohemia, the Archbishops of Mainz and of Trier, and
the Bishops of Würzburg. He was also involved in the famous struggle
between Cardinal Nicolaus Cusanus, Bishop of Brixen, and Sigismund,
Duke of Austria and Count of the Tyrol (1446-1490). In 1459 he appeared
at the Congress of Mantua as Sigismund's representative not only to
defend Sigismund's cause, but also to oppose Pope Pius II's crusade

---

[7] See below, n. 26.

[8] On legal advisors in Nuremberg, see Georg Freiherr von Kress, *Gelehrte Bildung im alten Nürnberg und das Studium der Nürnberger an italienischen Hochschulen* (Nürnberg, 1877), 10-11; Friedrich W. Ellinger, "Die Juristen der Reichsstadt Nürnberg vom 15. bis 17. Jahrhundert," in *Genealogica, Heraldica, Juridica* : *Reichsstadt Nürnberg, Altdorf und Hersbruck*, Freie Schriftenfolge der Gesellschaft für Familienforschung in Franken, VI (Nürnberg, 1954).

program.⁹ Excommunicated by the pope in 1461 because of his support of Sigismund against Cusanus,¹⁰ Heimburg spent most of his later years in Bohemia in the service of King George of Poděbrady (1458-1471).¹¹ He was not reconciled with the Church until March 19 in 1472, the year of his death which occurred in Dresden in August.¹²

To understand the relations between Heimburg and early humanism, it would be helpful to know clearly what kind of education he received in his youth. Unfortunately, what we know about it is very fragmentary because almost all documents relative to the history of Schweinfurt during this period were destroyed in the Margrave War of 1554 and the Thirty Years' War.¹³ In all probability, Heimburg first went to a Latin school in Schweinfurt whose origins went back to the thirteenth century. The Church of St. Johannis, which maintained the school,¹⁴ had been paying tithes since the Middle Ages to the Stift

---

⁹ Heimburg made three speeches in Mantua : (1) October 29, 1459, for Duke Albrecht of Austria; (2) November 12, 1459, for Duke Wilhelm of Saxony; and (3) November 21, 1459, for Duke Sigismund of Austria. They have been preserved in Munich, Bayerische Staatsbibliothek, Cod. lat. mon. 522 ff. 150-163ᵛ [(1), ff. 156-160ᵛ; (2), ff. 150-155; (3), ff. 161ᵛ-163ᵛ] and are in the legible hand of Hartmann Schedel. Cod. Cent. V. App. 15. of the Stadtbibliothek in Nuremberg also contains these three speeches on ff. 247-253ᵛ. On the Congress of Mantua in general and Heimburg's role in it, see Georg Voigt, *Enea Silvio de' Piccolomini als Papst Pius der Zweite*, III (Berlin, 1863), 59-110; Joachimsohn, *Heimburg*, 144-180; Giovanni B. Picotti, *La dieta di Mantova e la politica de' Veneziani*, Miscellanea di storia Veneta, 3rd ser., IV (Venice, 1912).

¹⁰ Albert Jäger, *Der Streit des Cardinals Nicolaus von Cusa mit dem Herzoge Sigmund von Österreich als Grafen von Tirol*, II (Innsbruck, 1861), 198.

¹¹ Heymann, *George of Bohemia*, 408-620.

¹² Joachimsohn, *Heimburg*, 287, was incorrect in stating that Heimburg was buried in the Kreuzkirche in Dresden. It was in the Sophienkirche that he found his resting place. See Cornelius Gurlitt, *Stadt Dresden*, Beschreibende Darstellung der älteren Bau- und Kunstdenkmäler des Königreichs Sachsen, XXI-XXIV (Dresden, 1903), 96; Gustav Sommerfeldt, "Aus Doktor Gregor Heimburgs letzten Lebensjahren," *Mitteilungen des Vereins für Geschichte der Deutschen in Böhmen* 69 (1931), 46-56.

¹³ Erich Saffert, "Die Schule in der Stadtrechnung : Bemerkungen zu einer Kirchen- und Schulamtsrechnung des 16. Jahrhunderts," in *325 Jahre Gymnasium Schweinfurt 1634-1959* (Schweinfurt, 1959), 13-23; Erich Saffert, "Die Stadtarchiv Schweinfurt im Friedrich-Rückert-Bau," *Archivalische Zeitschrift* 59 (1963), 177.

¹⁴ On the Latin school in Schweinfurt, where the humanists Conrad Celtis and Johann Cuspinian also studied, see V. Völcker, *Geschichte der Studienanstalt Schweinfurt*, I (Schweinfurt, 1882); Karl Ziegler, *Geschichte des humanistischen Gymnasiums in Schweinfurt (1634-1934) und der Lateinischen Schule daselbst* (Schweinfurt, 1934); Friedrich Beyschlag, "Die älteste Geschichte der lateinischen Schule in Schweinfurt (bis 1554)," *Schweinfurter Tagblatt*, Nr. 113, 15 Mai 1905 and Nr. 114, 16 Mai 1905. Joachimsohn (*Heimburg*, p. 2) says : "... gab es damals wohl noch keine städtische Schule."

Haug in Würzburg, the tithe-owner of the whole district of Schweinfurt.[15] The scholastic of the Stift Haug was therefore responsible for the supervision of education in the district. As Schweinfurt became the seat of an archdeaconry in the fourteenth century, the Church of St. Johannis and, as a result, its Latin school acquired more importance in the area.[16] But as far as the educational program of the school is concerned, it must have been traditional in nature and under the influence of scholasticism at the time of Heimburg's entry. The school was probably a "trivial" school where only the elements of the trivium were taught. We know little about its teaching staff in the fifteenth century. Master Friedrich Marquard, who was apparently a supporter of scholasticism, was the head of the school from 1430 to 1440, and among the teachers at the school toward the end of the century, Masters Petrus Popon, Konrad Scheffer and Johann May were more inclined toward humanistic education than Konrad Haug who clung to the traditional approach.[17] By that time there was even in Schweinfurt a controversy between scholasticism and humanism which had first started at the Universities of Heidelberg and Vienna and later spread to many universities in Germany. But Heimburg, who must have entered the Latin school at the beginning of the century, could not have been much influenced by this controversy.

---

[15] Friedrich Schneider, "Neuer Beitrag zur richtigen Erkenntnis des früheren Verhältnisses des Chorherrenstiftes zu Haug in Würzburg zur St. Johanniskirche in Schweinfurt," *Archiv für Stadt und Bezirksamt Schweinfurt* 5 (1907), 46-49; Erich Saffert, "Schweinfurt—Würzburg : Die gegenseitigen historischen Beziehungen," *Veröffentlichungen des Historischen Vereins und des Stadtarchivs Schweinfurt*, Sonderreihe, II (Schweinfurt, 1957).

[16] Erich Saffert, *Im Dienst der Humanitas : Aus der Geschichte des Schweinfurter Gymnasiums* (Schweinfurt, 1959) [Sonderdruck aus dem Schweinfurter Tagblatt vom 5., 6., und 9. Mai 1959].

[17] On Petrus Popon, see *Magistri Petri Poponis colloquia de scholis Herbipolensibus : Ein Beitrag zur Vorgeschichte der Würzburger Hochshule als Festgabe zu deren dreihundertjährigen Jubiläum*, ed. Georg Schepss (Würzburg, 1882), 5-15; [Georg] Schepss, "Die Gedichte des Magisters Petrus Popon : Ein Beitrag zur fränkischen Gelehrtengeschichte des 15. Jahrhunderts," *Archiv des Historischen Vereins von Unterfranken und Aschaffenburg* 27 (1884), 277-300. The former article discusses the *Dictum Magistri Petri Popon contra Herbipolensium scolasticum in Novo Monasterio Herbipolensi*, which is found in Cod. lat. mon. 18910 ff. 26-32. Popon, who taught Cuspinian in Schweinfurt, compiled *Rudimenta Grammaticae ad pueros de Remigio, Donato, Alexandroque studiosissime lecta* (Nürnberg, 1499). See Georg W. Panzer, *Annales Typographici*, II (Nürnberg, 1794), 227; Ludwig F. T. Hain, *Repertorium bibliographicum*, II^2 (Milan, 1948), 235, nos. 14022-14026.

Did Heimburg then go on to the Cathedral school in Würzburg which was so important in the ecclesiastical and cultural development of Schweinfurt? There is no conclusive evidence that he did despite the assertions of many writers in the past.[18] Because of the close relationship between the Latin school in Schweinfurt and the Stift Haug, the young boy could have been sent to either the Cathedral school or the school of the Newminster (Neumünster) in Würzburg where advanced education not available in Schweinfurt could be obtained. It is known that Master Popon, who moved from Schweinfurt to Würzburg toward the end of the century to teach at the Cathedral school, criticized the scholastic curriculum which was in use at the Newminster school.[19] The Cathedral school of Würzburg, which had a long history of education going back to St. Burkard (741-791), the first Bishop of Würzburg, had such high reputation in the tenth century and thereafter that it was no doubt the best cathedral school in Franconia.[20] An examination of the curriculum at the schools of the Cathedral and the Newminster in the fifteenth century shows that while the Newminster school took a rather conservative and cautious attitude toward humanist learning, the Cathedral school was decidedly humanist in orientation and emphasized disputation and reading of poetry.[21] But all these changes took place long after Heimburg left Würzburg even if he actually attended one of the schools there. For we know that he matriculated in the Faculty of Arts of the University of Vienna (founded 1365) on October 13, 1413, as "pauper."[22]

Like the Universities of Erfurt (1392) and Leipzig (1409), the University of Vienna attracted many students from Franconia in the fifteenth century partly because it was by that time a well established

---

[18] Ballenstadius, *Vitae*, 6; Ullmann, *Reformers*, I, 195; Joachimsohn, *Heimburg*, 2.

[19] Ziegler, *Geschichte*, 5; Schepss, "Die Gedichte," 278.

[20] Christian Bönicke, *Grundriss einer Geschichte von der Universität zu Würzburg*, I (Würzburg, 1782), 7; Georg J. Keller, *Die Gründung des Gymnasiums zu Würzburg durch den Fürstbischof Friedrich von Wirsberg* (Würzburg, 1850).

[21] *Magistri Poponis*, 15; Schepss, "Die Gedichte," 279.

[22] *Die Matrikel der Universität Wien*, I (Graz and Cologne, 1956), 99; Albin F. Scherhaufer, "Jung-Schweinfurt auf hohen Schulen," *Schweinfurter Heimatblätter* 26 (1957), 55-56. Joachimsohn, *Heimburg*, 2, n. 10 states: "Eine deutsche Universität hat Heimburg, soweit wir sehen, nicht besucht." Johannes Heymburg de Sweynfurd entered the University of Erfurt in 1409 and Richard Heinberg de Sweynfordia, who is believed to be Gregor's nephew, matriculated at the University of Leipzig in 1441. See Friedrich Beyschlag, "Jung-Schweinfurt auf hohen Schulen," *Archiv für Stadt- und Bezirksamt Schweinfurt* 4 (1906), 41, 66.

school and partly because it was relatively close to Franconia. Konrad von Ebrach from Franconia was active in Vienna as the famous professor of theology after 1384, and Konrad von Rothenburg, another Franconian, had been teaching in the Faculty of Arts probably since 1388.[23] But the dominant trend at the University of Vienna was still scholastic, and it was Aeneas Sylvius Piccolomini who was to become instrumental in fostering humanistic studies in Vienna after he became a member of the Imperial Chancery in 1442 under Kaspar Schlick (d. 1449). Like other faculties of law in the German Empire at that time, the Faculty of Law of the University of Vienna concentrated on the study of canon law rather than civil law; the candidates in the Faculty were nominally required to attend courses in civil law, but these courses were in fact not given.[24] The doctoral graduates of the Faculty were almost without exception called Doctores in Decretis or Decretorum.[25] It remains an open question whether Heimburg was only in the Faculty of Arts or entered the Faculty of Law in Vienna.

Little is known about Heimburg's academic career after his matriculation in 1413, except that he obtained the degree of Doctor in jure canonico in Padua on February 7, 1430, and that when he took an examination in 1430 for the degree, he was already referred to as Legum doctor.[26] In a speech which he made in 1430 to accept the doctorate, Heimburg spoke of many transalpine universities which he had attended.[27] But it is not known which universities besides Vienna

---

[23] J. Abet, "Aus der Geschichte der ersten Würzburger Universität unter Bischof Johann von Egloffstein," *Archiv des Historischen Vereins von Unterfranken und Aschaffenburg* 63 (1923), 4; Joseph Aschbach, *Geschichte der Wiener Universität im ersten Jahrhunderte ihres Bestehens*, I (Vienna, 1865, repr. Farnborough, Hants., 1967), 599-600.

[24] For further discussion on the University of Vienna during the period of early humanism, see Bauch, *Die Reception*; Grossmann, "Die Frühzeit,"; Alphons Lhotsky, *Die Wiener Artistenfakultät 1365-1497* (Graz, 1965); A. Lhotsky, *Aeneas Silvius und Österreich* (Basel and Stuttgart, 1965).

[25] Aschbach, *Geschichte*, I, 101-104. On the study of civil law in fifteenth-century Germany, see Otto Stobbe, *Geschichte der deutschen Rechtsquellen*, II (Braunschweig, 1864), 9; Winfried Trusen, *Anfänge des gelehrten Rechts in Deutschland : Ein Beitrag zur Geschichte der Frührezeption* (Wiesbaden, 1962), 11-33, 106-11.

[26] Arnold Luschin von Ebengreuth, "Quellen zur Geschichte deutschen Rechtshörer in Italien," *Sitzungsberichte der phil.- histor. Klasse der kaiserlichen Akademie der Wissenschaften* [Vienna] 124 (1891), 23; *Acta graduum academicorum Gymnasii Patavini ab anno MCCCCVI ad annum MCCCCL.*, ed. C. Zonta and I. Brotto (Padua, 1922), 166-167.

[27] This speech, *Oratio pro petendis insigniis doctoratus canonici arengata*, is in Cod. lat. mon. 504 ff. 313^v-314 and is printed in Joachimsohn, *Heimburg*, 302-303. This codex

he intended. Various attempts to find a clue to this question by studying the matriculation lists of European universities have not been successful. It is possible that before coming to Padua Heimburg, as some have suggested,[28] studied law or other subjects at the University of Würzburg which had been founded in 1402.[29] But since no one was permitted, under the statute of the University of Padua,[30] to obtain the doctorate in either civil or canon law without studying at least six years in Padua, it is probable that Heimburg's legal studies were done in Padua between 1421 and 1428. He then could complete the requirements for the doctorate in canon law in Padua by 1430. The fact that Heimburg spoke in his doctoral speech of studying grammar and philosophy in transalpine universities[31] seems to indicate that his academic career suggested above is probably correct. Prosdocimus de Comitibus, Heinricus de Alano, Paulus de Dotis, and Jacobus de Zocchis de Ferraria, whom Heimburg mentioned as his law professors, all taught in Padua between 1421 and 1430. We may be certain that Heimburg diligently studied classical authors in Padua as he delved in the fields of civil and canon law. He was in this sense not exceptional because a large number of German students who went to Italy to study law were attracted by classical studies. Heimburg may even have been able to listen to the famous humanist Vittorino da Feltre (1373-1446) who held the chair of rhetoric briefly in 1422 in Padua.

While Heimburg was in Basel, he met many humanists at the council which offered them a good opportunity to search for manuscripts in monasteries and libraries in the North.[32] But contrary to

---

was also copied by Hartmann Schedel. Cf. Richard Stauber, *Die Schedelsche Bibliothek* (Freiburg im Breisgau, 1908, repr. Nieuwkoop, 1969), 32.

[28] [Karl Hagen] in *Braga—Vaterländische Blätter für Kunst und Wissenschaft*, II (Heidelberg, 1839), 416; Ullmann, *Reformers*, I, 195.

[29] Friedrich A. Reuss, *Johann I. von Egloffstein, Bischof von Würzburg und Herzog zu Franken, Stifter der ersten Hochschule in Würzburg* (Würzburg, 1847); Franz X. von Wegele, *Geschichte der Universität Wirzburg* (Wirzburg, 1882, repr. Aalen, 1969); Abet, "Aus der Geschichte," 5-18.

[30] Ebengreuth, "Quellen," 23.

[31] Joachimsohn, *Heimburg*, 302.

[32] Paul Lehmann, "Konstanz und Basel als Büchermärkte während der grossen Kirchenversammlungen," *Zeitschrift des deutschen Vereins für Buchwesen und Schrifttum* 4 (1921), 6-11, 17-27; reprinted in his *Erforschung des Mittelalters*, I (Stuttgart, 1959), 253-280.

the oft-expressed view by many writers,[33] he was not Aeneas Sylvius's secretary at the council, nor was he especially closely associated with Aeneas. His humanistic interest must have been strengthened as he listened to many speeches and talked with learned men from Italy. But there seems to exist no evidence that Aeneas's direct influence on Heimburg began at this time in Basel.

We know, however, that when Heimburg became legal advisor to the city of Nuremberg in 1435 as successor to the famous Dr. Conrad Konhofer,[34] he gradually began to gather around him a group of humanists who paved the way for the future development of humanism in the Imperial City. Nuremberg, which had employed learned lawyers as its legal advisors since the fourteenth century[35] and which, with her central location in the German Empire, was the site of imperial diets many times, held a prominent place among the major German cities.[36] Sigismund, King of the Romans, who liked the city, had moved the royal insignia to Nuremberg in 1424,[37] thereby enhancing its prestige. Nuremberg owed its prosperity in no small degree to the conservative rule of patrician families which strengthened their hold on the city government especially after the unsuccessful rebellion of the city's workingmen in 1348-1349 and which ruled the city sternly, if benevolently, in order to maintain political stability. Little attempt was made by the city council, which consisted exclusively of members of these patrician families, to bring in new ideas from outside. The legal advisors, most of whom were non-Nurembergers, could not exceed their advisory rank. The council never permitted them to participate in decision making. In their education and training, Heimburg's predecessors in the fifteenth century had been little affected by humanism. The learned Dr. Konhofer, for example, was essentially a scholastic as is clear from the one hundred and fifty-one

---

[33] Henricus Pantaleon, *Prosopographiae herorum atque illustrium virorum totius Germaniae*, II (Basel, 1565), 413; Melchior Adam, *Vitae Germanorum Jurisconsultorum* (Heidelberg, 1620), p. 2; Ullmann, *Reformers*, I, 195-196; J. F. von Schulte, *Die Geschichte der Quellen und Literatur des canonischen Rechts von Gratian bis auf die Gegenwart*, II (Stuttgart, 1875), 372, n. 6.

[34] About this learned churchman, see Martin Weigel, *Dr. Conrad Konhofer (†1452): Ein Beitrag zur Kirchengeschichte Nürnbergs* (Nürnberg, 1928).

[35] See above, n. 8; Stobbe, *Geschichte*, II, 59, n. 32; Trusen, *Anfänge*, 222-235.

[36] For a recent treatment of Nuremberg in the fifteenth and sixteenth centuries, see Gerald Strauss, *Nuremberg in the Sixteenth Century* (New York, 1966).

[37] Julia Schnelbögel, "Die Reichskleinodien in Nürnberg 1424-1523," *Mitteilungen des Vereins für Geschichte der Stadt Nürnberg* 51 (1962), 78-159.

manuscripts which he possessed in his library.[38] But in a city which had neither university nor episcopal chancery, the office of legal advisors was probably the only vantage ground from which humanistically inclined lawyers trained in Italy could gradually disseminate the fruits of the new learning.

It is therefore not surprising to note that during his first employment from 1435 to 1440, Heimburg, who was also busy on other missions outside Nuremberg, was unable to do much to promote humanistic studies in this essentially conservative city. But after his return to Nuremberg in 1444 to assume his second term as legal advisor, a small circle of friends of humanistic studies began to gather around him which included Heinrich Leubing (d. 1472), Martin Mair (c.1420-1480), and Niklas von Wyle (d. 1478).[39] Born in Nordhausen, Leubing studied at the Universities of Leipzig, Erfurt, and Bologna, receiving the degree of Legum doctor in 1437 from Bologna.[40] After working in Saxony, Mainz, and the Imperial Court, he came to Nuremberg in 1444 as priest of the Church of St. Sebald and also became legal advisor to the city council as Heimburg's colleague. Mair, who was born in Wimpfen, entered the University of Heidelberg in 1438 and received the Baccalarius in artibus in 1443.[41] He came to to Nuremberg in 1449 as secretary of the council. An admirer of Heimburg, Mair called him "singularis preceptor."[42] Besides becoming the famous chancellor of Mainz, Mair later obtained the degree of Doctor of civil law from the University of Heidelberg. Probably the most literarily inclined of the three was the Swiss Niklas von Wyle from Bremgarten in the Aargau.[43] He had attended the University of Pavia and came to Nuremberg in 1447 to become secretary of the city council.

---

[38] H. Petz, "Urkundliche Beiträge zur Geschichte der Bücherei des Nürnberger Rates, 1429-1538," *Mitteilungen des Vereins für Geschichte des Stadt Nürnberg* 6 (1886), 137-143; Herrmann, *Die Reception*, 5.

[39] Herrmann, *Die Reception*, 5-30.

[40] On Leubing, see Georg A. Will, *Nürnbergisches Gelehrten-Lexicon*, II (Nürnberg, 1756), 432; Joachimsohn, *Heimburg*, 108, 129, 195, 251; Herrmann, *Die Reception*, 9, 26; Lieberich, "Die gelehrten Räte," 170.

[41] On Mair, see *Allgemeine Deutsche Biographie*, XX (Leipzig, 1884), 113-120; Lieberich, "Die gelehrte Räte," 176.

[42] Herrmann, *Die Reception*, 11.

[43] On Niklas von Wyle, see Joachimsohn, "Frühhumanismus," 74-126; Bruno Strauss, *Der Übersetzer Nicolaus von Wyle* (Berlin, 1912).

Unfortunately, Heimburg's friends did not stay very long in Nuremberg, a city which did not enjoy the reputation of being hospitable to the humanists. Limited as their influence might have been, this group around Heimburg did introduce to this Imperial City the discussion of topics which had been debated by literary men in Italy for some time. The city which delighted in being the host to Regiomontanus (1436-1476) and, briefly, to Conrad Celtis (1459-1508) and which later produced such friends of humanism as Hans Tucher (1428-1491), Hartmann Schedel (1440-1514), and Willibald Pirckheimer (1470-1530) had in Heimburg its earliest supporter of the *studia humanitatis*.[44]

Heimburg's competence as a humanist became clear when he discussed humanistic studies at the Imperial Court in Wiener Neustadt in 1449. Aeneas Sylvius, Bishop of Trieste since 1447, had returned to Wiener Neustadt from his see and was in the audience. After listening to Heimburg's speech Aeneas wrote him a letter the same day praising him highly.[45] As Cicero brought eloquence from Greece to Italy, wrote Aeneas, so Heimburg will bring it from Italy to Germany.[46] It seems that Aeneas saw in Heimburg the most promising German humanist of the day. This was indeed a remarkable letter because in describing Heimburg's speech and conduct in Rome as head of the Electors' envoys to Pope Eugenius IV in 1446, Aeneas had drawn a highly critical picture of Heimburg stalking about indignantly at night on Monte Giordano with bare head and breast, denouncing the wickedness of the pope and the curia.[47] Critical as Aeneas was of Heimburg the lawyer-politician, he seems to have appreciated the German humanist in him. But Aeneas's warm appreciation of Heimburg's talent turned into bitter criticism as Heimburg became more involved in ecclesiastical and political events.

---

[44] On the term *studia humanitatis*, see Erich König, "Studia humanitatis und verwandte Ausdrücke bei den deutschen Frühhumanisten," in *Beiträge zur Geschichte der Renaissance und Reformation : Festgabe für J. Schlecht* (Munich, 1917), 202-207; Paul O. Kristeller, *The Classics and Renaissance Thought* (Cambridge, Mass., 1955), 9-12.

[45] The letter is printed in Aeneas Silvius Piccolomini, *Opera* (Basel, 1551, repr. Frankfurt am Main, 1967), 647; *Der Briefwechsel des Eneas Silvio Piccolomini*, ed. Rudolf Wolkan, Fontes Rerum Austriacarum, II, Abt. Diplomataria et Acta, LXII (Vienna, 1912), 79-81.

[46] *Der Briefwechsel*, 79-80.

[47] Aeneas Silvius Piccolomini, *Historia Rerum Friderici III. Imperatoris*, ed. A. F. Kollár, Analecta Monumentorum Omnis Aevi Vindobonensia, II (Vienna, 1761), cols. 123-124.

In some of his speeches, letters, and writings,[48] Heimburg often refers not only to the Bible and Church Fathers, but also to classical writers. In addition to Moses, St. Peter, St. Paul, St. Jerome, St. Augustine, and St. Bernard of Clairvaux, he frequently mentions Socrates, Lactantius, and, of course, Cicero. Other important classical writers and figures whose names Heimburg invoked like other humanists are Homer, Solon, Thales, Zeno, Herodotus, Plato, Diogenes, Aristotle, Terence, Valerius Maximus, Cato, Sallust, Virgil, Horace, Livy, Seneca, Quintilian, and Plutarch. It was his desire, Heimburg stated, not to swerve from the independence of a Diogenes or a Cato.[49] His famous invective against Cusanus, *Invectiva Gregorii Heimburg utriusque iuris doctoris in reverendissimum Patrem Dominum Nicolaum de Cusa*, itself belongs to the genre of writing which humanists like Petrarch, Boccaccio, Poggio, and Valla used to their advantage.[50] It is also worth noting that like Aeneas and other humanists, who were much interested in geography, Heimburg showed a keen awareness of the importance of geographical knowledge. After discussing the *studia humanitatis* in 1449, for example, Heimburg and Aeneas got involved in a detailed discussion on the origin of the Nile.[51] With regard to his writings, it is to be noted that the *Confutatio primatus papae* is a work written not by Heimburg, but by Matthias Döring,

---

[48] Besides the speeches at Mantua, which are mentioned in n. 9 above, the following are the speeches and writings of Heimburg in which he refers to classical writers or has citations from them : (1) Speech before the Council of Basel on November 29, 1432, in *Deutsche Reichstagsakten*, X (Göttingen, 1957), 651-656; (2) Speech in 1453 at the Imperial Court, in Aenas Silvius, *Historia*, ed. Kollár, II, 428-431; (3) Letter of March 6, 1454, to Johannes Rot, in Cod. lat. mon. 518 ff. 103ᵛ-107, Cod. lat. mon. 519 ff. 46-50ᵛ, and printed in Joachimsohn, *Heimburg*, 303-310 and Rupprich, *Die Frühzeit*, 275-282; (4) *Appellatio a papa variis modis ad concilium* (1461), in Melchior Goldast, *Monarchia S. Romana Imperii sive Tractatus de Iurisdictione Imperiali seu Regia et Pontificia seu Sacerdotali*, II (Frankfurt, 1614), 1292[1592]-1595 and Marquard Freher, *Rerum Germanicarum scriptores*, ed. B. G. Struve, II (Strassburg, 1717), 211-214; and (5) *Apologia contra Detractiones et Blasphemias Theodori Laelii Feltrensis Episcopi*, in Goldast, *Monarchia*, II, 1604-1625 and Freher-Struve, *Rerum*, II, 228-255. (4) and (5) are also included in Jurisconsulti acutissimi ... Gregorii de Heimberg ... *Scripta nervosa, iuris iustitiaeque plena* ... (Frankfurt, 1608), which is a collection of his various writings.

[49] Goldast, *Monarchia*, II, 1593.

[50] The text is in Goldast, *Monarchia*, II, 1626-1631 and Freher-Struve, *Rerum*, II, 255-265. On invectives used by humanists, see Voigt, *Die Wiederbelebung*, I, 75, 123, 184, 203, 364, II, 150-153, 448-456.

[51] Joachimsohn, *Heimburg*, 104; *Der Briefwechsel*, 80-81.

although it was once regarded as one of the most remarkable, sometimes infamous controversial works written with Heimburg's pen.[52]

Heimburg, however, was not inclined merely to cite and imitate ancient writers to adorn his speeches or writings. He used them in his practical way. What he appreciated in the new learning was not mere imitation of classical style and rhetoric, but an ability to express one's own thought and feeling in one's own language. He liked Plutarch's statement that Cicero spoke spontaneously,[53] and was opposed to what he considered the thoughtless and often frivolous attitude of Italian humanists. He would therefore not attempt to transport Italian humanist learning indiscriminately into Germany. For all his admiration and love of classical writers, he did not wish to become their slavish follower. He said, as he spoke in Pope Pius II's presence at the Congress of Mantua in 1459, that if his manner of speech was new and different from what the pope was accustomed to at the curia, it was because his was the German way.[54] As his relations with the pope deteriorated, it became increasingly apparent that Heimburg regarded the pope as a paradigm of the superficial imitator of ancient writers.[55] It is perhaps not too far-fetched to see in this conflict between the two, as some have done,[56] a contrast between the Italian and German character, although the real situation was not so simple as to justify the facile analysis.

It seems widely recognized that local circumstances moulded the character of humanism in each country. Humanism in Germany

---

[52] The humanist Matthias Flacius Illyricus (1520-1575) first published the text as *Scriptum contra primatum papae, ante annos 100 compositum* ... (Magdeburg, 1550). MS. Jones 14 of the Bodleian Library, Oxford contains on ff. 315v-327 an English translation (*The confutacion of the popes supremacie wrytten by Gregori of Hemburgh*), done probably in 1590. On the authorship of the *Confutatio*, see Bruno Gebhardt, "Die Confutatio primatus papae," *Neues Archiv der Gesellschaft für ältere deutsche Geschichtskunde* 12 (1887), 517-530; P. Albert, "Die Confutatio primatus papae, ihre Quelle und ihr Verfasser," *Historisches Jahrbuch* 11 (1890), 439-490.

[53] It seems clear from the following that Heimburg liked spontaneous speech. Joachimsohn, *Heimburg*, 304 : "... felicissimum autem est, non quidem apium more sparsa colligere, sed vermium exemplo, quorum ex visceribus sericum prodit, ex se ipso sapere loqui. Quod Ciceronem scisse tradit Plutarcus..."

[54] Joachimsohn, *Heimburg*, 105.

[55] Goldast, *Monarchia*, II, 1594 : "Quod vero me loquacem facit, vir omni pica dicacior, quid dixerim ? ... Fateor quippe me ventositati verborum pro tempore operam dedisse : at non ita ut civilis & Canonicae traditionis praecepta contempserim : quae ille ne unquam quidem olfecit, nuda verbositate contentus."

[56] Ullmann, *Reformers*, I, 196; Voigt, *Die Wiederbelebung*, II, 285-290.

was essentially an outgrowth of humanism in Italy, but it was an intellectual movement among educated persons on a smaller scale than in Italy. It also retained a more traditional and medieval character than the new learning which was pursued by Italian humanists.[57] It was pointed out in 1893 that in Swabia, the Palatinate, and Austria the secular princely courts, the imperial cities, and the universities were the places where humanism first grew, while in Franconia the ecclesiastical princes encouraged the growth of humanism in their courts.[58] This rather simple comparison may no longer be acceptable to recent scholarship. But it did point to the complex nature of the humanist movement in Germany. Heimburg as an early humanist already manifested one of the features of German humanism, that is, to conserve what was native and traditional while accepting from outside the benefits of the new learning. Some humanists in Germany were particularly interested in translating the writings of Italian humanists into German, thereby satisfying not only their thirst for humanist learning, but also their desire to remember their past. Some of Conrad Celtis's works, such as his edition of Roswitha's plays and of the *Ligurinus* of Gunther the Cistercian, and the various translations or Teutschungen of Niklas von Wyle may be mentioned as examples of this romantic, nationalistic feature of German humanism. Heimburg himself seems to have consciously emphasized the importance of this approach, when he translated his own Latin work into German.[59] To see in Heimburg a full-fledged nationalist in the modern sense of the term would be premature and exaggerated. But it cannot be denied that Heimburg was affected by the nationalistic consciousness which was growing in Germany at that time.

To understand the position which Heimburg held in the early development of humanism in Germany, it is best to turn to the much discussed letter of Heimburg to his young friend Johannes Rot (c.1430-1506).[60] It was sent from Nuremberg to Rome on March 6, 1454,

---

[57] A classic statement of this point of view is Gerhard Ritter, "Die geschichtliche Bedeutung des deutschen Humanismus," *Historische Zeitschrift* 127 (1923), 393-453.

[58] Max Herrmann, *Albrecht von Eyb und die Frühzeit des deutschen Humanismus* (Berlin, 1893), 3.

[59] Joachimsohn, *Heimburg*, 197-204. We must note that the vernacular translations of Italian humanist writings were also made outside of Germany. See Kristeller, "European diffusion," 84-86.

[60] See above, n. 48 (3). Cod. lat. mon. 518 was written in its entirety by Hermann Schedel, while some parts of Cod. lat. mon. 519 were written by his cousin Hartmann

in reply to Rot's letter to Heimburg which has been lost. Born in Wemding in Swabia as the son of a shoemaker, the hard-working Rot studied at Italian universities and took the doctorate in canon and civil law at the University of Padua.[61] He is said to have been on friendly terms with humanists like Poggio and Guarino, but we have only evidence of his correspondence with Filelfo.[62] In 1454 Rot was studying rhetoric in Rome under Lorenzo Valla, who was professor of rhetoric there at that time. In the letter to Rot, Heimburg argued that jurisprudence is superior to rhetoric and that Rot should not waste his time studying rhetoric. In his lengthy reply to Heimburg, dated May 16, 1454,[63] Rot strongly defended rhetoric against law and criticized the lawyers for their obscure language. Many humanists since Petrarch and Boccaccio had engaged in a polemic against the lawyers, and Rot's teacher Valla himself wrote in his letter to Candido Decembrio between 1431 and 1433 an incisive attack on lawyers such as Bartolus, Baldus, and Accursius.[64] This exchange of letters between Heimburg and Rot, then, was based on a well established tradition among the humanists.

Besides the difference of their views of humanism, personal factors no doubt played some role in this exchange. Heimburg was by then a strong critic of Aeneas Sylvius, but Rot was desirous of maintaining friendly relations with the future pope, whose help may later have enabled him to obtain a position in the Imperial Chancery. But more important was a battle of principles which was manifested in this

---

Schedel. Hermann used a portion of Heimburg's letter in his own letter to Johannes Ratisbona. See *Hermann Schedels Briefwechsel (1452-1478)*, ed. Paul Joachimsohn (Tübingen, 1893), 76-77.

[61] On Johannes Rot (Rott, Roth), see *Allgemeine Deutsche Biographie*, XIV (Leipzig, 1881), 186-188; Max Herrmann, "Ein Brief an Albrecht von Eyb," *Germania—Vierteljahrsschrift für deutsche Alterthumskunde* 33, n.s. 21 (1888), 499-502; Joachimsohn, *Heimburg*, 19, 99-102, 106-107, 112, 158, 170, 251, 274; Herrmann, *Albrecht*, 127-137.

[62] See Joachimsohn, *Heimburg*, 106, n. 3.

[63] Joachimsohn, *Heimburg*, 310-316. The text is in Cod. lat. mon. 518 ff. 109-121v (*Johannis Rot pro defensione retoricae contra jus civile et jurisperiti et oratoris inter se comparatio*) and Cod. lat. mon. 519 ff. 51-64 (*Johannis Rott pro defensione retorice contra jus civile et jurisperiti et oratoris inter se comparatio*). Joachimsohn, *Heimburg*, 310-316, gave excerpts from the letter and Rupprich, *Die Frühzeit*, 282-289, reprinted them. Hermann Schedel used a portion of this letter in his letter to Heinrich Lur. See *Hermann Schedels Briefwechsel*, 157-158.

[64] For an account of this famous debate, see Myron P. Gilmore, *Humanists and Jurists : Six Studies in the Renaissance* (Cambridge, Mass., 1963), 30-32; Guido Kisch, *Gestalten und Probleme aus Humanismus und Jurisprudenz* (Berlin, 1969), 116-124.

literary exchange. Heimburg, who was after all a lawyer, regarded rhetoric as a means to an end. No matter how attractive and interesting studies of classical writers were, they were significant only as a preliminary step toward the study of law, which was to him nothing less than the true philosophy.[65] Jurisprudence was a more serious subject than rhetoric to him. What is notable, however, is that Heimburg fought for jurisprudence in typically humanistic fashion, using many citations from ancient authors. He felt close to classical writers and often cited them. But he had reservations about those who merely copied and repeated the words of ancient writers. Rot, on the other hand, seems to have been taken in by the new learning. In his letter to Albrecht von Eyb, Rot called himself the first champion of humanistic studies in Germany.[66] His answer to Heimburg is more replete than Heimburg's with references to and citations from classical authors, such as Plato, Aristotle, Seneca, Cicero, Virgil, Pliny, Lactantius, Cato, and Solon, as well as his teacher Valla. Both of these men held a doctorate in canon and civil law from an Italian university. But Heimburg was condemned by Aeneas as a heretic, while Rot paved the way under Aeneas's patronage for future advancement in his ecclesiastical career.[67] The contrast was due not so much to their attitude toward humanism as to their personality and other factors. But it does show that there was a variety of views on humanism among those Germans who were affected by the *studia humanitatis*.[68]

---

[65] In his doctoral speech Heimburg calls the canon law the true philosophy and jurisprudence. Joachimsohn, *Heimburg*, 302.

[66] Joachimsohn, *Heimburg*, 107, n. 1. : "Se fore Germanorum primum, qui artes, que humane intitulantur, amplexus sit." Andreas Bavarus in his letter to Albrecht von Eyb criticized Rot's arrogance. The text of the letter, which is in Cod. lat. mon. 504, f. 2ᵛ (*Andreae Bavari ad Albertum de Eyb epistola de arrogantia Johannis Rottae, qui dicere conatur se esse Germanorum primum, qui artes humanas amplexus sit*), is printed in Herrmann, "Ein Brief," 502-506.

[67] Rot became Bishop of Lavant in 1468 and Bishop of Breslau in 1482. In 1505 he was made Chancellor of the University of Breslau. He was a friend of Rudolf von Rüdesheim, who played an important role in the excommunication of Heimburg. On the later career of Rot, see also Hermann Hoffmann, "Aufzeichnungen des Breslauer Domherrn Stanislau Sauer (†1535) über die Bischöfe Rudolf von Rüdesheim und Johann Roth," *Archiv für schlesische Kirchengeschichte* 13 (1955), 82-137.

[68] From the point of view of ecclesiastical advancement, Nicolaus Cusanus, another contemporary German, resembles Rot. Cusanus was also a friend of Pope Pius II whom Heimburg criticized. This is no doubt the reason why Johannes Kymeus, author of the *Des Babst Hercules wider die Deutschen* (Wittenberg, 1538) which criticized Cusanus, praises Heimburg on ff. ii-iii in his book.

All too often Gregor Heimburg has been either severely criticized as a fanatical enemy of the Church and a "child of the devil" or excessively praised as the "Citizen-Luther before the days of Luther." We have instead proposed to examine his development as a humanist and the position which he held in the early growth of humanism in Germany. It would seem that his exposure to the new learning during his study of law in Padua rather than his education in transalpine schools prepared him as one of the earliest humanists in his country. The loss of documents and archival materials concerning his youth and some of the institutions with which he was associated makes it difficult to have a fuller understanding of his life. Furthermore, his writings, which were almost always responses to particular circumstances, must be used with caution. Due attention must be given to the emotional stress under which he often worked and the humanistic rhetoric which he, like others, utilized. But the available evidence shows that his main concern as a student of humanist learning was not mere imitation of ancient writers and Italian humanists, but the rise of a humanism based on local traditions and circumstances.[69]

C.W. Post Center, Long Island University

---

[69] I am indebted to the American Philosophical Society for a grant which made possible much of the work for this study. While this article was in press, the following study of Heimburg was brought to my notice : Alfred Wendehorst, "Gregor Heimburg," in *Fränkische Lebensbilder*, ed. Gerhard Pfeiffer, IV (Würzburg, 1971), 112-129.

CARDINAL CAJETAN ON "CAMBIUM" OR EXCHANGE DEALINGS

†RAYMOND DE ROOVER

Thomas de Vio (1469-1534), of the Dominican Order, better known as Cardinal Cajetan, scarcely needs an introduction. He is the author of the officially approved Commentaries on the *Summa* of Thomas Aquinas, which are easily available in the magnificent Leonine edition of this *magnum opus*. Cajetan is even more famous as the papal legate whom Leo X (1513-1521) dispatched to Germany in a futile effort to bring Luther back into the Roman fold and to prevent the break that was to tear asunder the unity of the Western Church. In this capacity, Cajetan even made the stage on Broadway and appeared in John Osborne's play, "Luther," as the slippery and worldly cardinal who tried to coax Luther to retract in exchange for a full pardon and release from his vows. Whether or not such a role was in line with Cajetan's character is a different matter. Far from being a slick and wily churchman, Cajetan was a learned theologian, well versed in scholastic dialectics, who was perhaps the most scholarly member of the College of Cardinals during the pontificates of Leo X, AdrianVI, and Clement VII. If his mission proved a failure, probably no one else would have succeeded.

Cajetan was a prolific writer. Besides the Commentaries on the *Summa*, already mentioned, he wrote numerous philosophical and theological works and his advice was often sought on controversial questions. In the last years of his life, he devoted himself entirely to biblical exegesis and came out with interpretations that were often far ahead of his own time. In response to requests for clarification of the issues involved, Cajetan also wrote three short treatises, or opuscules, on socio-economic problems : one on usury, a second on the *montes pietatis* which he bitterly opposed, and a third on *cambium*, or exchange dealings. In a brief study like this, it is impossible to tackle all three of these subjects, and we must therefore strictly confine ourselves to only one of them. We have picked the third because it deals with a topic which involves special difficulties and requires acquaintance with banking practices on which we have written extensively before.

The tract on *cambium* first appeared in 1506 separately; later it was included in several sixteenth-century editions of the *Opuscula omnia* of Cardinal Cajetan. A modern edition, limited to the latter's socio-economic tracts, is now available and should henceforth be used for scholarly purposes in preference to any other.[1]

Contrary to what some believe, *cambium* is not a small and narrow topic, since it involves much more than mere money-changing and embraces the whole question of the development of banking. When Cardinal Cajetan uses the word *campsores*, he refers not only to money-changers but also to exchange-dealers who operated on the money market and would be called "bankers" today. Because of the Church's usury doctrine, bankers were not supposed to charge interest and, consequently, had to look for some other way of lending money at a profit, with the result that banking became tied to exchange: local banking to manual exchange (*cambium minutum*), and foreign banking to "real" exchange or exchange by bills (*cambium per litteras*). Since the discounting of commercial paper was ruled out by the usury prohibition, bankers bought bills of exchange at a price that was determined by the foreign exchange rates. The whole question was whether such transactions were licit or whether they involved usury. It goes without saying that medieval and Renaissance bankers could not afford to lend money gratuitously and that interest was charged surreptitiously by being concealed in the rate of exchange, but the theologians, including Cajetan, were unable to accept this fact without being forced to condemn all banking as usurious and to brand it as a sinful profession, like pawnbroking, histrionics, or prostitution. This was the ticklish problem with which Cajetan came to grips.

Although he was in sympathy with humanism, he approached the issue in scholastic fashion and tried to determine which exchange

---

[1] These three opuscules were written respectively in 1500, 1498, and 1499, but were not published until 1511, except the one on *Cambium* which appeared separately in 1506. I own an edition of these opuscules of Cardinal Cajetan, three volumes in one, bearing the title : *Opuscula omnia Thomae De Vio Caietani, Cardinalis tituli Sancti Xysti, in tres distincta tomos* (Venice, 1588). All the socio-economic writings of Cardinal Cajetan are now available in a modern edition : *Scripta philosophica, Opuscula oeconomico-socialia*, ed. P. P. Zammit, O.P. (Rome, 1934). All references given here are to this modern edition. I also had at my disposal an unpublished English translation of the *Cambium* treatise made by Richard L. Derry, a former student of mine at Boston College, whom I wish to thank.

transactions were licit and which were illicit. In his tract he starts out by dividing exchange transactions into three categories : those that were clearly licit, those that were clearly illicit, and those that were doubtful.[2] Most of his tract is devoted to the difficult task of justifying the latter by emphasizing exchange and downgrading credit as one of the features of an exchange contract.[3]

Among the exchange transactions that were clearly licit, Cajetan mentions first manual exchange in which money-changers charged a fee for changing gold pieces into silver currency, or vice versa. As long as the fee was moderate, such transactions raised no problem, since they were on a cash basis and involved no extension of credit. Next the Cardinal approved of bankers who sold letters of credit and undertook to pay the value thereof abroad. They were obviously entitled to a remuneration for their services, just as the American Express Company rightly charges a commission when issuing travelers checks to tourists. Cajetan did not even question the practice of money-changers who collected certain coins to send them abroad where they would be worth more. In many countries, however, the export of specie was forbidden and punishable by the civil authorities, although such a practice might not have fallen under any ban of the Church.[4]

What Cardinal Cajetan unreservedly condemned was dry and fictitious exchange, whether or not any bills were actually sent abroad, because such transactions were not entered into in order to transfer funds from one country to another, but to derive a profit from a loan disguised under the color of an exchange transaction. This was palliate usury, that is, usury concealed in the form of a contract *in fraudem usurarum*, although he does not state so explicitly.[5] Neither does he attempt to describe dry and fictitious exchange, which involved exchange and re-exchange between two banking places either at current market rates or at rates set in advance by the contracting parties. In the first case, such a transaction still retained its speculative character, since exchange rates fluctuated and the banker did

---

[2] Cajetan, *De Cambiis* (Rome, 1934), 94, cap. I, No. 204. Hereafter cited as Cajetan.

[3] Up to now, the best critical comments are those of Wilhelm Endemann, *Studien in der romanisch-kanonistischen Wirtschafts- und Rechtslehre bis gegen Ende des 17. Jahrhunderts*, 2 vols. (Berlin, 1874-1883; repr. Aalen, 1962), I, 146-151. Cf. Luciano Dalle Molle, *Il contratto di cambio nei moralisti dal secolo XIII alla metà del secolo XVII* (Rome, 1954), 63-66. Dalle Molle's comments are less useful and less reliable.

[4] Cajetan, 94-95, cap. I, Nos. 205-207.

[5] *Ibid.*, 95-96, Nos. 208-209.

not know in advance the rate at which he would be able to make his "returns" or what his profit would be, and he might even lose—but rarely. In the second case, this rate was determined beforehand, so that he knew from the start how much he would earn, and there was no difference between such a contract and a barefaced loan at interest. For example, a banker in Venice who sold Venetian ducats at, let us say, 53 English sterlings per ducat with the understanding that he would repurchase them three months later at the rate of 50 sterlings, would make a profit of 3 sterlings per ducat, whether the ducat in the mean-time went up or down, and it made no difference whether or not bills were actually sent to London for collection.[6] Sending the bills would only have added trouble and expense. Furthermore, such a contract yielded a return of 12 per cent per annum to the lender, which rate was not above normal in the Middle Ages.

The theologians had blinders in this matter and overlooked the fact that such contracts, however damnable from their point of view, had the advantage of shielding both parties against the deleterious effects of erratic exchange fluctuations which could either overburden the borrower or inflict a loss on the lender for the doubtful privilege of lending his money. According to ten cases of exchange and re-exchange recorded among the papers of the Medici Bank, the range of earnings extended all the way from below zero to 26.1 per cent per annum, certainly well beyond the average rate of productivity that could be reaped from business ventures.[7] One may conclude therefrom that the usury prohibition, far from being beneficial to the business community, increased both the risk and the expense of operating in the money market.

What really retains Cajetan's attention and what he discusses at considerable length is the lawfulness of the *cambium reale*, or "real" exchange in which a banker buys a bill of exchange for ready money and expects to collect the value through correspondents in another place and usually, though not always, in another currency.

---

[6] Numerous examples in Rawdon Brown, ed., *Calendar of State Papers, Venetian*, I (1209-1519) (London, 1864), 78, No. 317; 79, No. 321; 88, No. 354; 113, No. 391; 116, No. 400; and *passim*. Thus, for example, a bill bought in Venice at 44 $1/4$ st. per ducat on September 4, 1453, was returned from London on December 4 following at 39 $3/4$ d. st. per ducat.

[7] Raymond de Roover, *The Rise and Decline of the Medici Bank, 1397-1494* (Cambridge, Mass., 1963; corrected 2nd printing, 1968), 120-121, Table 24. See also 117-119, Tables 22-23.

Thus defined, real exchange necessarily involved a credit transaction linked to an exchange transaction, since time elapsed between the conclusion of the contract in one place and its completion in another. To implement a *cambium*, the favorite instrument was the bill of exchange which, as the name implies, was not simply a mandate to pay, similar to the modern check, but was literally a bill of "exchange" payable in another place and in another currency. Even a sight draft was a credit instrument, since it had to travel from the place where it was issued to the place where it was payable, and this took time in an age when communications were so slow.

A *cambium* was thus an ambiguous sort of contract, and its ambiguity gave rise to an endless controversy which started in the thirteenth century in connection with exchange dealings between Genoa and the fairs of Champagne and was still going strong under the pontificate of Benedict XIV (1740-1758), when the last defenders of the traditional usury doctrine took a stand against the insidious attack of Marchese Scipione Maffei (1675-1755).[8] To calm the tempest, Pius V (1566-1572) issued, on January 28, 1571, the bull *In Eam* which, in line with Cajetan's opinion, explicitly condemned all forms of dry and fictitious exchange, but it met with little success.[9] The quarrel, far from being quelled, erupted into a new paroxysm of vehemence as rigorists and latitudinarians joined battle over the interpretation of *In Eam*. The latitudinarians, eager to accommodate the bankers on earth and in heaven, fought tooth and nail to defend the position that all exchanges were licit, provided they were concluded at the just price, that is, at the current rate.

Being eager to uphold real exchange as a licit contract, Cajetan rejects the opinion of early canonists, chiefly Geoffrey of Trani (d. 1245)[10] and Henry of Susa, Cardinal Hostiensis (d. 1271), who claimed

---

[8] On this controversy, see Raymond de Roover, *L'évolution de la lettre de change* (Paris, 1953), which contains a critical bibliography including more than 120 titles of scholastic and legal treatises, 170-216. Cf. Dalle Molle, *Il contratto*.

[9] The text of the bull *In Eam* is available in many publications. I have used the text as published by Sigismondo Scaccia, *Tractatus de commerciis et cambio* (Venice, 1669), § 9, "Constitutiones pontificiae." The date of *In Eam* is Vth Kalend of February 1570, style of Incarnation, hence January 28, 1571. Cf. Giambattista Lupo, *De usuris et commerciis illicitis* (Venice, 1582), Commentarius III, § 2, No. 68.

[10] *Summa super Rubricis Decretalium* (Basel, 1487), rubric *De usuris*, § 33. Geoffrey's text is brief: "What about some one who lends money in order to receive at maturity gold or silver or a different kind of currency? I answer that if he does this in order to gain in the valuation [of the other currency], he is a usurer (*usurarius est*)."

that it was a loan, or *mutuum*, which became usurious once it ceased to be gratuitous.[11] Cajetan's main argument is that profit from exchange transactions is not certain, which is true, although losses occur only in exceptional cases when the money market is seriously disrupted or in disequilibrium, as the economists would say.[12] This argument, therefore, does not carry much weight; however, Cajetan is on firmer ground when he points out that *cambium* is not a loan because it involves an advance which is repayable not in the same but in a different currency and in a distant place.[13] In other words, if a banker disbursed ducats in Venice in order to receive pounds sterling in London at a later date, or the reverse, this was no longer a loan, but an exchange transaction despite the fact that there was a time interval between the advance made in one country and its repayment in another. According to Cajetan, the profits of the exchange-dealers are also condoned on account of *labores et expensae*, since they have to maintain offices and keep clerks to serve their customers.[14]

After questioning whether *cambium est mutuum* or whether *cambium* should be classified as a loan, Cardinal Cajetan also denies that it is either a *permutatio pecuniae pro pecunia* (a commutation of moneys)[15] or a *contractus innominatus do ut des*.[16] In this connection, he mentions the opinion "of a certain illustrious doctor in theology" (*cuiusdam doctoris in theologia*), a reference very probably to Sant'Antonino, archbishop of Florence, one of the very few who regarded *cambium* as a *contractus innominatus*.[17] The reasons given by Cajetan for his rejection are neither convincing nor clear; his main point is, however,

---

[11] *Summa aurea*, Liber V. rub. *De usuris*, No. 8 in fine. Hostiensis quotes Geoffrey of Trani with little change in the text, but he adds that those who lend money from fair to fair at a profit also are usurers, whether or not usury is veiled under the name of a sale, or a commutation, or any other contract.

[12] Cajetan, 99, cap. II, No. 216 : "But it is well known that all bankers practice these exchanges in the hope of gain, so that a profit is likely to result, although this does not always occur (*quamvis non semper eveniat*), as they themselves acknowledge." *Ibid.*, 103, cap. III, No. 226 : "In real exchange the danger of loss is shifted to the money lender, since it occurs that he recovers less than his principal, although such an occurrence is rare."

[13] *Ibid.*, 103, cap. III, No. 227 : "In cambiis autem realibus fit permutatio monetarum diversorum generum et in diversis locis."

[14] Cajetan, 102, cap. II, No. 222.

[15] *Ibid.*, 102, cap. III, No. 224.

[16] *Ibid.*, 107, cap. IV, No. 234.

[17] Sant'Antonino, *Summa theologica* (Verona, 1740), Part III, tit. 8, cap. 3 (col. 299D).

that, in a *cambium*, the foreign currency is not used as a means of exchange—the primary use of money—but as a vendible commodity, which is only a secondary use.[18] Furthermore, Cajetan points out, the exchange-dealers themselves avow that their aim is to make profits, not just to avoid losses, and to meet their pay-roll and other charges; if it were otherwise, why would they stay in business?[19] Thus, he comes to the conclusion that *cambium* is an *emptio venditio* consisting in the purchase and sale of a foreign currency at a price, which like that of any other commodity may fluctuate in accordance with circumstances of time and place.[20]

The purpose of this analysis was to free *cambium* from any suspicion of usury, unless it were grossly misused to cover up a loan, and to make it subject to the rules that governed the just price, especially in the matter of credit sales. According to the norms set down by the canons *Consuluit* and *Naviganti*, the price on future deliveries and on credit sales may differ from the one on cash sales because of the uncertainty as to the behavior of prices and conditions of supply and demand in the near or distant future.[21] This concession, which is called *venditio sub dubio*, was thus extended from commodity sales to *cambium*, provided, of course, that prices were not made to vary solely in response to delayed payment, or *ratione dilatae solutionis*. Still Cajetan betrays his uneasiness because he notes that exchange rates tend to rise in Milan with the approach of the Geneva fairs and that, for instance, the rate of a gold mark payable at the Epiphany fair is lower in October than in November, and in November than in December. He explains this phenomenon by the rather flimsy argument that those operating in the money market rated a gold mark higher when the fair was near and less when it was still remote.[22] True, but is this not the best evidence of the presence of the interest factor as a major cause of exchange fluctuations? Cajetan, however, extricates himself from this difficulty by arguing that the rate, as the fair came close, *sometimes* fell below the one quoted at an earlier date, which is also true, since exchange rates respond to factors other than interest.[23] Never-

---

[18] Cajetan, 107, cap. IV, No. 235; 109, No. 240; 111, cap. V, No. 245; 112, Nos. 246-247.

[19] *Ibid.*, 101, cap. II, No. 220.

[20] *Ibid.*, 107, cap. IV, No. 235.

[21] *Corpus juris canonici, Decretales,* in X, V. 19, 10 and 19. Cf. Cajetan, 120, cap. VI, No. 272.

[22] Cajetan, 108, cap. IV, No. 237.

[23] *Ibid.*, 109, cap. IV, No. 239.

theless, this observation, while correct, does not remove interest from the scene and proves only that at times other factors may be powerful enough to override its action on the money market without eliminating it. Cajetan's argument, therefore, is of questionable validity and rests on faulty analysis because he wants to prove by all means that interest has little influence, if it has any influence at all.

Since, according to Cajetan, *cambium* ought to be regarded as an *emptio venditio*, he makes the most of market valuation and states that the market places a higher value on "expendable" than on "non-expendable" money.[24] So far as I know, he is the first moralist to make this distinction.[25] By "expendable" money he means local or "present" currency, while "non-expendable" money refers to foreign or "absent" currency, that is, to funds available only in a distant place.[26] This distinction between "present" and "absent" money will be taken over by later writers affiliated with the School of Salamanca, namely Martin de Azpilcueta (1492-1586), better known as Dr. Navarrus, and Leonardus Lessius, S.J. (1555-1623).[27]

In one passage, Cajetan states that the speculators operating in the money market value either the foreign currency less than local currency or the local currency more than foreign currency, which is saying the same thing, though in slightly different words.[28] What does he mean exactly by this statement? In my opinion, there seems no doubt that it refers to the way in which the exchanges were quoted, either in local or in foreign currency.[29] Thus, the Venetian ducat was usually worth from three to four sterlings more on the Rialto than in Lombard

---

[24] *Ibid.*, 114-115, cap. VI, No. 253, and pp. 116-117, No. 261.

[25] Sylvester has the same idea and states that a "distant" commodity is worth less than one "present" or readily available. *Summa summarum que Silvestrina dicitur* (Bologna, 1514), rubr. *Usura IV, 5° queritur*.

[26] This meaning is made clear by Cajetan, 124-125, cap. VII, No. 284. Cf. John T. Noonan Jr., *The Scholastic Analysis of Usury* (Cambridge, Mass., 1957), 318.

[27] Azpilcueta, *Comentario résolutorio de cambios* (Salamanca, 1556; modern ed., Madrid, 1965), cap. XIII, No. 62; Lessius, *De justitia et jure* (1st ed., Louvain, 1605), Liber 2, cap, 23, dub. 4, No. 28 ("maior aestimatio pecuniae praesentis quam absentis") and No. 34 ("secundus titulus quo in hoc cambio lucrari potest, est maior aestimatio pecuniae in loco, ubi datur quam ubi redditur"). See Raymond de Roover, "Leonardus Lessius as an Economist," *Mededelingen van de Kon. Vlaamse Academie voor Wetenschappen*, etc., *Klasse der Letteren*, XXXI (Brussels, 1969), fasc. No. 1, p. 27.

[28] Cajetan, 96-97, cap. I, Nos. 210-211.

[29] Noonan (*Scholastic Analysis of Usury*, 318-319) asks himself the same question, but seems to thinks that Cajetan's statement does not make sense. However, it does make good sense, if rightly understood.

Street.[30] In the same way, the écu of 22 groats, Flemish currency, was as a rule rated higher in Bruges, where it was a local money of account, than in Barcelona, where it was a foreign currency. This pattern is corroborated by strong statistical evidence based on actual exchange quotations extending from 1395 to 1406.[31] Thus, in January 1400, the écu was quoted in Bruges 10s. $5^1/_2$d. to 10s. 6d., Barcelona currency, whereas the rate of this same écu in Barcelona never went above 10s., in local money. As long as this condition obtained, the lender or the buyer of bills, whatever his place of residence, whether Barcelona or Bruges, was bound to make a profit on exchange and re-exchange between these two banking centers.

Although "present" money was thus usually more esteemed than "absent" money, it could, and it did, happen—but rarely—that the exchange rates were out of gear; such a situation, however, was not likely to last, since it was not compatible with the equilibrium of the money market : it was altogether unnatural for the bankers to go on indefinitely lending money at a loss. The theologians, however, seized upon this possibility to support their contention that exchange dealings were speculative and not usurious. Among others, Cajetan insists that exchange rates vary with distance in space, overlooking that distance in space was also distance in time, at least before the invention of the telegraph in the middle of the nineteenth century.[32]

All along, Cajetan requires that place difference be respected as an essential feature of the exchange contract and attaches even more importance to it than to observance of the currency difference. He even gives his rather reluctant approval to exchange dealings when the same money is current in the place where the contract originates and where it is carried out.[33] Another requirement which he stresses is that exchange contracts be concluded at the just price, that is, at the rate set by common estimation.[34] This expression in scholastic

---

[30] See above note 6.

[31] Raymond de Roover, "The Bruges Money Market around 1400," *Verhandelingen van de K. Vlaamse Academie voor Wetenschappen*, etc., *Klasse der Letteren*, XXX (Brussels, 1968), 24-25 (Charts 1 and 2), 105-134, 135-154 (Appendices 1 and 2).

[32] Cajetan, 122-123, cap. VI, No. 280 and 124-126, cap. VII, No. 284-285. Cajetan, however, contradicts himself on this crucial point by stating that the exchange-dealers give less and less in local currency or expect to be repaid more and more in foreign currency, depending upon the greater remoteness of the maturity date (p. 97, cap. I, No. 211).

[33] *Ibid.*, 123-124, cap. VII, No. 282.

[34] *Ibid.*, 125, No. 285.

treatises was synonymous with market value in the absence of all fraud and conspiracy.

Cajetan claims that he questioned some business men about their practices. We may well take him at his word. Notwithstanding the fact that his treatise is sometimes tedious, rather pedantic, and indulges too much in scholastic subtleties, it shows evidence of acquaintance with actual practices; although it is questionable how thoroughly Cajetan understood the "ins" and "outs" of the exchange business, the factual information he gives is accurate enough, and I have detected no major mistake. It is also quite possible that Cajetan, on a visit to Florence, had conversations on the subject with Fra Santi Rucellai, who, under the name of Pandolfo, had been a Florentine banker before taking the habit of Saint Dominic at the priory of San Marco. In his treatise on exchange, written for Savonarola, Fra Santi alludes to consultations with a prominent canonist and theologian, also belonging to the Dominican Order. This reference points to Cajetan who, already in 1496, was known as an outstanding canonist and theologian.[35]

By defining the *cambium* contract as an *emptio venditio*, Cajetan subjected it to the rules of the just price, but there is no way of denying that it contained an admixture of elements taken from the *mutuum*. The consequences were not immediately apparent, but they almost inevitably led to laxity and to the approval of all exchanges concluded at the just price, leaving out of the picture only fictitious exchanges, because they were based on fictitious or arbitrary rates instead of on quotations set by market conditions. It is not astonishing, therefore, that Cajetan's definition was later adopted by all theologians inclined towards leniency, including the Neapolitan and Sicilian Theatines, Marco Palescandolo (1542-1622),[36] and Antonio Diana (1585-1663),[37] the Sienese Augustinian, Celestino Bruno (d. 1664),[38] and the Genoese Barnabite, Antonio Benedetto Sansalvatore (ca. 1563-1633),[39] whose work was even put on the Index because of its excessive

---

[35] Raymond de Roover, "Il trattato di Fra Santi Rucellai sul cambio, il monte commune e il monte delle doti," *Archivio storico italiano* 111 (1953), 41.

[36] Giovanni Cassandro, *Un trattato inedito e la dottrina dei cambi nel Cinquecento* (Naples, 1962), cap. 32, 145-147. The author cites Cajetan as his authority.

[37] R. de Roover, *L'évolution*, 181-182.

[38] Domenico Maffei, "Notizie su alcuni trattati cinque-seicenteschi in tema di cambi," *Banca, Borsa e Titoli di Credito : Rivista di dottrina e giurisprudenza* 18 (1965), 309-328.

[39] R. de Roover, *L'évolution*, 200-201. Cf. Ulisse Gobbi, *L'economia politica negli scrittori italiani del secolo XVI-XVII* (Milan, 1889), 249-257.

indulgence towards the Genoese bankers who operated on the so-called fairs of Besançon. Cajetan's treatise helped to lift the barriers which still opposed the march of capitalism.

Brooklyn College, The City University of New York

CONSCIENCE AND PUBLIC FINANCE :
A *QUESTIO DISPUTATA* OF JOHN OF LEGNANO
ON THE PUBLIC DEBT OF GENOA*

JULIUS KIRSHNER

During the late Middle Ages and Renaissance university professors in the faculties of law and theology were constantly asked, or felt self-impelled, to pronounce judgment on whether or not a variety of technical and structural innovations in commerce, industry, and finance were in accord with the prohibition against usury. Their pronouncements are recorded in commentaries on the civil and canon law and on the Sentences of Peter Lombard, and in hundreds of *consilia* and *questiones disputate*. A *questio disputata* of the jurist-statesman, John of Legnano (d. 1383) of the University of Bologna, written in defense of the public debt of Genoa, and critically edited here for the first time, furnishes a typical example of this phenomenon. My interest in his *questio* is non-archeological; it does not rest on the fact it has not been previously edited and combed over by modern scholars. Nor is his work offered as a fulgurating artifact of the Bolognese legal tradition. His *questio* and the doctrinal milieu in which it was written merit attention because they contribute to our understanding of (1) the casuitico-rational system employed by the expert (*peritus, sapiens*) to legitimate a potentially illicit and sinful activity, in this case the central institution of Genoese public finance, and (2) the nodal position of the expert as a mediator between conscience and the impersonal forces of the market place.

From the mid-thirteenth century onward Genoa suffered a series of fiscal crises during which traditional revenues, especially from indirect taxes (*gabelle*) and state monopolies (such as salt), were no longer sufficient to cover outlays for public work projects and govern-

---

* I should like to acknowledge the support of the National Endowment for the Humanities (Grant H5426) and The Institute for Advanced Study, Princeton, New Jersey. All references to the Digest in the *Corpus iuris civilis* will be cited as *D*.

mental administration, expansionist dreams, and, above all, warfare.[1] To augment her revenues, the government initially relied on forced and voluntary contributions from her citizens in the form of short-term loans, pledging to pay citizen-creditors principal plus interest from communal revenues. As fiscal pressures mounted in the mid-thirteenth century, the government of Genoa, like that of Venice[2] and eventually Florence,[3] took the step of consolidating and funding her loan debts, with no obligatory repayment of principal. Instead, it promised creditors an annuity running from 6, 8, 10 to 12%. In the late thirteenth and fourteenth centuries, there were numerous consolidations. These consolidated funds were called *compere*, the creditors, *comperisti*, and the shares which comprised the fund, *luoghi*. Each share was nominally worth a 100 *lire*, and was heritable, mortgageable, and negotiable. Each fund was the proprietor of a *gabella* or several *gabelle* which they had farmed, the proceeds from which provided the *comperisti* with interest (*proventus*). The *comperisti* designated directors (*protectores*) to manage the fund and to make every effort to have interest paid on schedule. If, after interest had been disbursed, there was a surplus, the protectors used the extra revenue to redeem outstanding *luoghi*. But redemption and interest payments were never guaranteed. In times of political difficulties, or when the *gabelle* were not generating sufficient revenue, interest was lowered and even prorogued, while the market price of *luoghi* plummeted.[4] In barest outline, this system of *compere* constitutes, to a large extent, the public debt of Genoa.

Did participation in the *compere*, by necessity or volition, result in mortal sin and eternal retribution? The answer was contingent upon the definition of usury and its applicability to this case.[5] The

---

[1] On the Genoese public debt, see Heinrich Sieveking's classic monograph "Studio sulle finanze genovese nel medioevo e in particolare sulla Casa di S. Giorgio,"*Atti della Società Ligure di Storia Patria* 25 (1905-06), Parts 1 and 2; and the important work of Jacques Heers, *Gênes au XVe siècle : Activité économique et problèmes sociaux* (Paris, 1961), 97-176.

[2] On the development and structure of the Venetian public debt, see Gino Luzzatto, *I prestiti della repubblica di Venezia* (Padua, 1929).

[3] On the origins and creation of the Florentine public debt, see Bernardino Barbadoro, *Le finanze della repubblica fiorentina* (Florence, 1929).

[4] Sieveking, Part 1, 96, 101.

[5] Studies on the usury prohibition and its ramifications are legion, and among them I would recommend Benjamin Nelson, *The Idea of Usury*, 2nd ed. (Chicago, 1971); John T. Noonan, *The Scholastic Analysis of Usury* (Cambridge, Mass., 1957);

classic definition of usury, a most authoratative cliché by the late Middle Ages, derived from Saint Ambrose, and was carried forward in the *Decretum* of Gratian (*ca.* 1140). Ambrose had declared that "whatever is added to the principal is usury" (*quodcumque sorti accedit usura est*).[6] This definition was understood to refer only to loans. In other words, usury was anything demanded or accepted beyond the principal of a loan (*ultra sortem mutui*).[7] Another monument of the usury prohibition was Christ's command "Lend freely, hoping for nothing thereby" (*mutuum date, nihil inde sperantes*, Luc. 6. 35). According to the canonists and theologians, Christ's injunction meant that loans were to be absolutely gratuitous and that the very hope of gain from a loan was to be stigmatized as a sin. In theological terminology, the injunction rested on the criterion of intention, that is, a sin is committed when the desire or will to sin is present, even if the formal act has not followed. As the Franciscan theologian Alexander Lombard (ca. 1268-1314) noted in his *Tractatus de usuris*, "if one originally lent because of hope for profit, his intention is corrupt..."[8]

That the usury prohibition had an indelible impact upon the organization of credit in the late Middle Ages and Renaissance has been forcefully argued and amply documented by Raymond de Roover, in his magisterial studies on banking and exchange.[9] With regard to the public debt of Genoa, Sieveking has observed that the system of *compere*, though animated in the first instance by economic necessity, was favored over straight loans at interest in order to circumvent the prohibition against usury.[10] Sieveking's allegation about the motivation inspiring the *compere*, though possibly correct, raises more questions than it answers. For whom was the strategy of deception intended : citizen-creditors ? professional moralists ? the episcopal

---

Raymond de Roover, *La pensée économique des scolastiques* : *Doctrines et méthodes* (Montreal and Paris, 1971). Noonan's book, however, must be used with caution, because it contains a number of historical inaccuracies.

[6] *Decretum Magistri Gratiani*, C. 14, q. 3, c. 3, *Plerique*; *dicta Gratiani post* C. 14, q. 3, c. 4, in *Corpus iuris canonici*, ed. E. Friedberg, I (Leipzig, 1879), col. 735.

[7] John W. Baldwin, *Masters, Princes and Merchants. The Social Views of Peter the Chanter and His Circle*, I (Princeton, 1970), 271.

[8] Alexander's tract, composed in Genoa or Bologna ca. 1303-07, has been edited by A.-M. Hamelin, *Un traité de morale économique au XIVe siècle* (Louvain and Montreal, 1962). For the quotation, see p. 134.

[9] See, for example, de Roover's *The Rise and Decline of the Medici Bank, 1397-1494* (Cambridge, Mass., 1963), 10-14.

[10] Sieveking, 55-56.

court? God? Were the inaugurators of the public debt self-conscious sinners, resorting to the manipulation of symbols—*luoghi* in place of *mutua*, *comperisti* in place of *mutuarii*, and *proventus* in place of *usura*—to salve their consciences, to satisfy the theoretical demands of canonists and theologians, to evade prosecution in an ecclesiastical court? Addressing himself to this problem, Nelson convincingly argues, on the basis of extensive research in the canonical and theological literature and testamentary documents, that the morality of communal loans and the *compere* were not yet called into question in the twelfth and thirteenth centuries. Nevertheless, echoing Sieveking, Nelson suggests, "that, although no precise decision had come from the doctors or the popes in the twelfth century with reference to interest-bearing communal loans, sufficient doubt attached to these transactions to prompt both prospective creditors and communal officials to give them the form of purchase of town revenues."[11]

Nelson's characterization of the subjective state of both *comperisti* and town officials in this period is, in my view, misdirected. There was nothing unusual about framing the relationship between the commune and its creditors in a contract of sale (*compera*), with the assignment of *gabelle* as interest. The purchase of town revenues was commonplace in the thirteenth century, not just in Genoa, but in all Italian cities, and the *compere* must be seen as a variant of a traditional, and what was popularly imagined as a licit institution. As a strategy of interpretation, the focus on subterfuge—a premeditated attempt to cloak usurious intention and behavior—really distorts our perspective on the workings of the *compere*, because it urges us to think of them in pathological terms. The issue before us is not subterfuge,[12] but one of prophylactic options. Given the options open to the government, it would have been an act of spiritual self-impalement to label the public debt a lending operation, probably inviting charges of usury, when it could just as easily be labeled *compera*, thus probably avoiding trouble with ecclesiastical authorities. Above all else, one

---

[11] "Blancardo (the Jew?) of Genoa and the Restitution of Usury in Medieval Italy," *Studi in onore di Gino Luzzatto*, I (Milan, 1949), 111. Nelson offers no evidence to support his conjecture, and the evidence he does cite (111, n. 2) indicates a glowing moral confidence in the operations of the public debt in the thirteenth and early fourteenth centuries.

[12] On the question of subterfuge in Genoese commercial contracts of the twelfth and thirteenth centuries, see the perceptive article of A. Lattes, "Di una singolare formula genovese nei contratti di mutuo," *Rivista del diritto commerciale* 22 (1924) 542-50.

should not infer from the controversy swirling around the public debt in the fourteenth century,[13] that the members of the government of Genoa and the *comperisti* were spending conscience-stricken and sleepless nights.

Throughout the thirteenth century, theological and juridical analysis of communal loans centered on the issue of the right of the commune and prince to force citizens and subjects to make contributions, in money or in kind, to the city and realm. On the whole, jurists and theologians concurred that if such loans, which they categorized as extraordinary taxation, were levied on behalf of the welfare of the communtity *pro utilitate publica* and *pro necessitate*, then they were justifiable and legitimate.[14] By the second half of the thirteenth century the issue of the right of citizens and subjects to claim compensation on forced loans was beginning to be aired and probed by Franciscan theologians in their general analyses of contracts, usury, and taxation. One of the earliest to treat the lender's claim to compensation was the brilliant Provençal theologian Peter Olivi (d. 1298). He declared in his tract *De contractibus usurariis* that citizens could accept compensation on their loans in the form of damages (*interesse dampni* and *lucrum cessans*).[15] As a legal title to compensation, *lucrum cessans* permitted a lender to claim indemnification if he had forgone an opportunity to invest working capital in an enterprise which, after a period of time, would certainly have yielded a profit and which could be estimated beforehand at the time the loan was contracted. In the same vein, John of Erfurt (or Saxony), in his *Tabula utriusque iuris* (1285), stated that a *civitas*, receiving loans from its citizens, can compensate them from its tax revenues.[16] And compensation, he added, was not to be stigmatized as usury.

---

[13] On which, see my "The Moral Theology of Public Finance : A Study and Edition of Nicholas de Anglia's *Quaestio disputata* on the Public Debt of Venice," *Archivum Fratrum Praedicatorum* 40 (1970), 47-72.

[14] U. Nicolini, *Le limitazioni alla proprietà negli statuti (secoli XII, XIII e XIV)* (Mantua, 1937) and *La Proprietà, il principe e l'espropriazione per pubblica utilità. Studio sulla dottrina giuridica intermedia* (Milan, 1939); G. Post, *Studies in Medieval Legal Thought : Public Law and the State 1100-1322* (Princeton, 1964), 15-21.

[15] Siena, Biblioteca Comunale, MS U.V. 6, fol. 306ᵛ. For a discussion of the MS, see D. Pacetti, "Un trattato sulle usure e le restituzioni di Pietro di Giovanni Olivi, falsamente attribuito a Fr. Gerardo da Siena," *Archivum franciscanum historicum* 46 (1953) 448-57.

[16] Paris, Bibl. Nat. MS lat. 4195, fol. 383. On John's life and writings, see V. Heynck, "Studien zu Johannes von Erfurt," *Franziskanische Studien* 40 (1958), 329-60.

The opinions of Alexander Lombard, minister provincial of the Franciscan province of Lombardy, are more relevant to this paper. For one thing, he devoted a complete section in his *Tractatus de usuris*, probably composed in Genoa or Bologna *ca.* 1303-1307, to the *compere*.[17] For another, his observations on the fiscal and economic practices of the Genoese were textured by first-hand knowledge.

The public debt of Genoa, Alexander observed, was prompted by a frequent need of money to meet various emergencies. Finding themselves in fiscal straits, the Genoese resorted to forced loans, carrying a rate of interest of 6, 8 or 10%, rather than to direct taxes, in order to placate its creditors. Did necessity and public utility give the state the right to compensate its creditors with interest? Did creditors have the right to receive compensation? Alexander answered these questions in the negative, and began his appraisal of the *compere* with a convenient list of arguments presented by those who recognized as licit interest received by the original creditors of the public debt. Some of these we have already noted. Communal loans are forced loans; the community is free to compensate its citizenry in order to lighten the burden of forced levies, a position sustained by Peter Olivi and John of Erfurt. Drawing upon Roman law, another argument focuses on the natural obligation of debtors towards creditors. Thus the community naturally obliges itself to come to the assistance of citizen-lenders. It is maintained that this natural obligation can be reinforced by civil law. The commune, then, may bind itself civilly, that is, by statute, to indemnify or to give a gift to creditors. Communal loans are also viewed as a source of great utility, permitting the commune to function smoothly. Out of gratitude, the commune may wish to pay its debts from available surplus revenues. What could be more equitable, more removed from usury? After all, communal revenues, especially *gabelle*, are indistinguishable from the property

---

[17] Hamelin, *Un traité*, 59. Alexander's analysis of the *compere* is found on pp. 172-75. Noonan's statement that "the Florentine handling of the [government] loan, which was substantially the same as the financial management of the other two cities [Genoa and Venice], was usually taken as a model for theological discussion" (*The Scholastic Analysis of Usury*, 121), is incorrect on two counts. First of all, the system of *compere* was a very different operation from the public debt (*Monte Comune*) of Florence. And secondly the *Monte Comune* did not become a model for theological discussion. Alexander wrote on the *compere*; Gregory of Rimini (d. 1358) wrote on the public debt of Venice; Domenico Pantaleoni (d. 1376) wrote on the *Monte Comune* of Florence (see my "A Note on the Authorship of Domenico Pantaleoni's Tract on the *Monte Comune* of Florence," *Archivum Fratrum Praedicatorum* 43 [1973], 43-81).

of individual citizens. Usury, of course, is not present because citizens accept only what originally belonged to them. It was John of Erfurt who propounded this clever piece of logic.

Unmoved by the logic of his adversaries, Alexander Lombard rejected their arguments without compromise. Lacking the skills of a jurist, his refutation stands on theological precedent. The criterion of intention is his moral guide in judging the actions of the *comperisti*. For Alexander the communal loan was not absolutely voluntary, but mixed-voluntary, containing a blend of coercion and volition. The element of volition is demonstrated by the hope of many Genoese citizens to receive a profitable return on their loans, a profit promised and publicized in the laws authorizing forced loans. Intending to profit, the creditors transform a loan that was not originally voluntary into a voluntary *mutuum*. Even though citizens may be forced to loan, it does not follow that "they are forced to accept *lucrum*."[18] And, Alexander added, the vice of usury is not present in the deed of lending. No, usury arises when a lender, through a prior agreement or corrupt intention, accepts a return beyond what he has loaned.

Alexander did admit that a commune can alleviate the plight of its citizens in a number of ways. It can be achieved if the government offers a spontaneous gift to its creditors. By accepting the gratuity, the lender does not destroy the debtor's act of good will, his spontaneity and generosity, but augments it. Yet the commune may plan to obligate itself by legislation or it may be under compulsion to give a certain amount of interest to citizen-lenders. Now the loan is patently usurious, since once again a desire for profit is present from the beginning of the loan. Alexander also rejected any claim for *lucrum cessans*. The original creditors of the *compere* could not receive profit forgone, Alexander argued, "because just as the lender may profit, he may lose."[19] This argument is similar to that of Saint Thomas, who also stressed the uncertainty of future profits.[20] Alexander denied, moreover, that the commune can bind itself by civil law to pay an increment on a loan. To acknowledge the validity of this proposition "would seem to excuse any usury."[21] It would allow the lender to

---

[18] *Tractatus*, 173.

[19] *Ibid.*, 174.

[20] *Summa theologiae* II-II, q. 78, a. 2, ad 1. Medieval Romanists were, however, favorable to the title *lucrum cessans*. See Hermann Lange, *Schadenseratz und Privatstrafe in der mittelalterlichen Rechtstheorie* (Münster and Cologne, 1955), 32-45.

[21] *Tractatus*, 174.

possess a contractual right to a gift which ought to be given freely and which is an expression of the debtor's natural obligation to his creditor. Accordingly, this argument is false and Alexander declared : "The lender principally ought to lend because of love, although one may have a secondary hope for profit."[22] Supplementing his own position, he quoted Saint Thomas to prove that the loans under analysis are contrary to the principles of justice and in no way could possess the force of a civil obligation.

Furthermore, *utilitas* cannot legitimate usury. Alexander cited the canon, *Super eo*, in which Pope Alexander III prohibited money gained from usury to be used to ransom Christians held captive by the infidel. Paraphrasing this canon, he stated : "Just as one may not cheat to save the life of another, it is not permissible to act usuriously for the utility which will result."[23] Alexander also casts aside the attempt to identify the property of the community with the property of individual citizens. He defined payments of interest based on revenue of the commune as usury.

According to Alexander, the *comperisti* may receive compensation only when the government offers a gift. The gift must represent a spontaneous act of gratitude; and the recipient must have no original hope for profit. Although Alexander did not find it necessary to discuss the trading of shares in the *compere* at market prices, it may be assumed that he would have inveighed against this practice, since in almost all instances he railed against interest payments on Genoese *luoghi*.[24]

Shortly after Alexander's tract appeared, Astesanus (d. 1330), a disciple and successor to Alexander as minister of the Franciscan province of Lombardy, defended the rights of the *comperisti*.[25] He regarded

---

[22] *Ibid.*

[23] *Ibid.*

[24] Though Alexander took a hard line on the *compere*, his position was modulated and lenient with respect to the bill of exchange and the purchase, at a discount, of the rights to the revenue flowing from the government of Genoa's monopoly of salt and bread. See Raymond de Roover, "Les doctrines économiques des scolastiques : à propos du traité sur l'usure d'Alexandre Lombard," *Revue d'histoire ecclésiastique* 59 (1964), 854-66; F. Veraja, *Le origini della controversia teologica sul contratto di censo nel XIII secolo* (Rome, 1960), 158-60.

[25] For what follows, see Astesanus, *Summa de casibus conscientiae* (Rome, 1728) III, XI, 5. An assessment of his *Summa* is given by Pierre Michaud-Quantin, *Sommes de casuistique et manuels de confession du moyen âge (XII-XVI siècles)* (Louvain, 1962), 57-60.

the communal loan as a forced loan which merited compensation. The commune, wishing to relieve the burden placed upon the shoulders of its citizens, can legitimately offer an annual income or interest as compensation. Astesanus also defended the purchase of *luoghi* from the original creditor, with an avowed intention of making a profit due to a change in price. He explained that what was being traded was not money, but only the right (*ius*) to it. This rationale had been used before to justify the *census* contract, but Astesanus appears to have been the first to wield it in support of the developing *borsa* in *luoghi*. While arriving at different conclusions, Astesanus and Alexander were not divided over essentials. He agrees with Alexander that if a lender hopes to profit, he is a usurer. He, too, severs any possible connection between public utility and usury. Nevertheless, if the original creditors prefer to receive the capital of their loans rather than profits, they may accept damages and gifts. What marks Astesanus' treatment is flexibility, a willingness to give the creditors of the public debt the benefit of the doubt that communal loans were not made voluntarily.

John of Legnano entered the lists between 1350-1383, when he was a member of the faculty of law at the University of Bologna.[26] Since his *questio* is highly abstract, with seemingly no specific references to contemporary events, nor to contemporary jurists and theologians, it is impossible at present to assign a precise date for its composition. That John disputed the applicability of the usury prohibition to the public debt is hardly surprising in light of the fact that his contemporaries—Albericus of Rosate (d. 1360), Baldus of Perugia (d. 1400), and Bartholomew of Saliceto (d. 1412), and many other jurists and theologians—were dealing with the same problem.[27] But what motivated the Bolognese jurist to choose as his subject the public debt of Genoa rather than that of Venice and Florence? Alexander Lombard and Astesanus had naturally spoken out on the *compere*, because the center of their world was Genoa. Was John inspired by the moral doubts of an individual or institution, which had investments or was intending to invest in the *compere*? Did an ecclesiastical official or group engage John—the leading canonist at Bologna—to give his

---

[26] On the life and writings of John of Legnano, see S. Stelling-Michaud, "Jean de Legnano," in *Dictionnaire de droit canonique*, VI (Paris, 1957), cols. 111-112; John McCall, "The Writings of John of Legnano with a List of Manuscripts," *Traditio* 23 (1967), 415-437.

[27] On this, see my forthcoming study on the controvery over the public debt.

opinion on this delicate and multi-pronged question ? Did the government of Genoa itself solicit his counsel ? These hypotheses are not imaginary, but are drawn from situations in which such requests were actually made. It appears, however, that his choice of Genoa was arbitrary, made merely for didactic reasons. Structurally and terminologically, his *questio* bears all the marks of a traditional university disputation, whose setting was most likely a hall in the University of Bologna.

To interpret John's *opusculum* with any degree of sophistication, its format and institutional setting (what Kristeller, with characteristic understatement, has called "the modest and prosaic factors" which have an enormous influence upon the course of intellectual history)[28] must be highlighted. In the fourteenth century, the statutes of the University of Bologna prescribed that doctors of law were to engage in a public disputation with their students in the spring, after Lent.[29] The *doctor disputans*, as he was called, was obligated to post, eight days before the disputation was scheduled to occur, the case and problems which would be debated so that his students would have time to prepare their arguments. Since the disputation was a pedagogic exercise through which the student was supposed to acquire the dialectical skills to solve abstract and theoretical questions, the *doctor disputans* selected a problem often relating to a contemporary controversy such as that over the public debt which had not yet been resolved, and whose solution was not contingent upon a concatenation of references to the standard *auctoritates* and *leges*. The student was supposed to learn how to arrive at a solution which was convincing because it was logically appropriate. The student himself did not offer the solution; only the *doctor disputans* had the prerogative of determining the answers to the problems posed at the beginning of the disputation. Now, the *questio disputata*, which is the written expression of a disputation lasting several hours, is never a stenographic account of all the arguments, asides, aggressive displays of erudition, bursts of eloquence, and confusing utterances encountered during the heat of debate. The spontaneity of the actual debate was

---

[28] Paul O. Kristeller, "The University of Bologna and the Renaissance," in *Dissertationes Historicae de Universitate Studiorum Bononiensi*... (Bologna, 1956), 313.

[29] C. Malagola, *Statuti della Università e dei Collegi dello Studio Bolognese* (Bologna, 1888), 107-108. The following discussion of the *questio disputata* is indebted to Hermann Kantorowicz's brilliant article, "The Quaestiones Disputatae of the Glossators," *Tijdschrift voor Rechtsgeschiedenis* 16 (1939), 1-67.

intentionally suppressed, to be replaced by a highly polished condensation of the disputation and solution. Who did the redacting? In fourteenth-century Bologna, it was the *doctor disputans* who was responsible for the redacting. He had to complete this task, under oath and threat of a stiff fine, within one month after the disputation took place.[30] This authorized version was then sold at local shops where university texts were purchased.

John of Legnano's *opusculum* squares almost perfectly with the format of the *questio disputata* delineated above.[31] There is the proponing of the case, which commences with the term *questio* (ll. 1-6). There is the raising of the questions to be disputed, commencing with the term *queritur* (ll. 6-11). There is the disputation consisting of truncated *argumenta* militating against each other in the classical style of *pro et contra* (ll. 12-58). The truncation is signalled by the use of *igitur, etc* (ll. 22, 25 and 30). There is the solution of the *doctor disputans*, commencing with the term *Determinatio* (ll. 59-67). Note that throughout the *questio* there is no mention of specific persons or an actual case. Case, problems, arguments and determination are general and abstract, written throughout in the third person. Note also that there is only one explicit reference to the law (*D.* 32, [1], 38). With regard to the redaction it might be argued that the *questio* at hand is a student's version because (1) the *determinatio* is written in the third person, a characteristic of *questiones reportate*, and (2) the style and grammatical structure of the text are appalling. I would argue that the third-person *determinatio* is too common in legal questions of the fourteenth century to indicate either the redacting hand of a student or doctor;[32] that in general John's style is neither better nor worse than his fellow jurists; and that the text has a definite cogency and coherence, with arguments logically moving toward the solution, suggesting the redaction of the *doctor disputans*. Above all else, I would argue that, given the procedure established at Bologna for the redaction of the *questio disputata*, John himself probably redacted the *questio* on the public debt of Genoa.

On one level, the case and problems which John presented to his students seems, at first glance, bland and academic. The commune of

---

[30] Malagola, *Statuti*, 109.

[31] For the MS and edition, see below, pp. 451-53. The MS I have edited most likely represents a copy of the redaction executed by John.

[32] Note that the *determinatio* ends with John of Legnano's *subscriptio*. Whether this indicates a first-or third-person *subscriptio is* a moot question.

Genoa, in need of funds, forces its citizens to give it money, and provides them with a yearly income of "10% or less" from the receipts of the *gabelle*. Can these creditors licitly receive such income? Assuming that they have a moral as well as a legal right to do so, can a third party purchase and enjoy the original creditor's claim upon communal income. It would be illusory to view John as open-minded about what ought to have been the answers to these questions. After inspecting the terminology and underlying assumptions of both case and problems, it becomes fairly obvious that John was predisposed toward shielding the *comperisti* from the charge of usury. Where Alexander Lombard speaks of citizens who are forced to lend (*ad mutuandum*), John speaks of citizens forced to give (*ad dandum*). For Alexander the creditors of the *compere* are citizen-lenders (*mutuarii*); for John they are citizen-givers (*dantes*). Where Alexander describes profit as *excrescentia ultra mutuum* (a phrase synonymous with usury), John employs the conventional business terms *reditus* and *proventus* (terms for morally acceptable profit). For Alexander the income promised by the commune constitutes a contractual obligation, thus the creditor's profit is assured from the beginning of his loan, a fact tantamount to usury. According to John there is a real but unavoidable risk undertaken by the original creditor, because there is the ever-present danger that the source of income, the *gabelle*, can diminish or dry up altogether. In John's schema, moreover, the investors who voluntarily purchase shares in the public debt are not called lenders but buyers (*ementes*). There is not one term between lines one through eleven which could be used as a peg on which to hang the accusation of usury, or which would even raise the eyebrow of a conscientious rigorist. These symbols and assumptions were deftly orchestrated by John, not with the intention of forestalling an attack against the *comperisti*, which was anyhow contextually imperative, but rather with the intention of incapacitating the arguments which would be used to spearhead that attack and of establishing solid premises upon which a rigorous counter-attack would be launched.

All this is illustrated in the *argumenta*. There is only a single, rather superficial, argument raised against the original creditors (ll. 12-20)· Usury is present, the argument runs, because *proventus* will be given in perpetuity, therefore surging (*ascenditur*) beyond the principal. The principal of what? A loan, indeed a usurious loan, it is asserted, "because something is received beyond the principal." The reasoning here is faulty. If, according to the Ambrosian/Gratianic formula, anything exceeding the principal is usury, it does not logically follow that the relationship between the original creditor and the commune represents a *mutuum*. The lending relationhip is posited but not demonstrated. Furthermore, the attack against the original creditor suffers from a failure to investigate, *inter alia*, the circumstances surrounding the alleged *mutuum*, the intention of both creditors and commune, the nature of the *proventus* (i.e., whether it is paid as mere profit, as a price for the sale of money, as damages, or as a gift), and the alleged uncertainty of the commune's ability to remunerate its creditors.[33]

Each of these variables, on the other hand, is prominently featured in the defense of the original creditor (ll. 20-40). It opens with the premise that a sin (*delictum*) is not committed without intention and an adulterated conscience, that is, an apprehension that one is committing a transgression. This model fact situation applies here, "for neither willingly and intentionally, nor with the hope of profit do the citizens enter into a contract with the commune, but are forced to and unwillingly give money to the commune."[34] The original creditors, therefore, have no intention of receiving anything above the principal of a loan.

There still remains the problem of defining the nature of the contractual relationship between the original creditors and the commune. The problem was exceedingly complicated because the commune was perceived as an extraordinary debtor which possesses the right to seize and detain the property of its citizens *sub necessitate et pro utilitate publica*. An essential element of a loan is the debtor's obligation to return in due time the same quantity of money he borrowed. Here, it is argued, the commune is under no obligation to return the principal (*sors*). Income received by the original creditor is not calculated as *sors* but as *proventus*—a very neat legal fiction. If there is no loan, what kind of contract is it? The answer is: "a contract of sale, which is obvious from the nature of the thing, or an unnamed contract (*contractus innominatus*)." Yet, is a contract of sale as obvious as is claimed? A true contract of sale contained these elements: (1) consent of both parties, (2) what is sold is a thing (*res*), (3) a price which can be measured in money and (4) transfer of ownership to the purchaser.

---

[33] All these variables were probably examined during the actual disputation.

[34] On the relationship between *coactio* and *peccatum* in the canon law, see Stephan Kuttner, *Kanonistische Schuldlehre von Gratian bis auf die Dekretalen Gregors IX* (Vatican City, 1935), 301-07.

It might be argued that elements 2 and 4 are present. In 1303 the Genoese enacted legislation defining *luoghi* as merchandise (*bona mobilia*);[35] and it was taken for granted, even among those who defined *luoghi* as loans, that transfer of ownership occurred. It would require acrobatic talents to demonstrate elements 1 and 3. How could the fact of being forced to give money to the commune be reconciled with the consensual arrangement of the *emptio-venditio*? At least in the text before us, these doubts are not addressed. The assertion of an *emptio-venditio* still stands as an assertion. That these doubts were shared by the defender of the *compere* is underscored by the hedge "or it is an innominate contract." The rationale behind this classification is also missing, though the attempt to assimilate the forced loan to an innominate contract stands on firmer doctrinal grounds. John probably had in mind a type of innominate contract based on the formula *do ut des*, in which one party is obligated to transfer the ownership of something to another who is obligated to give something in return. If the analysis of the contractual nature of the relationship between the original creditor and the commune is non-existent or at best exiguous, the summation of the defense of the original creditors is crisp and forceful. "Therefore, the contract is licit, since there is no intention of the citizens to lend at usury, nor is this the intention of the commune, save that it wishes to remunerate its citizens from its own free and willing solicitude (ll. 38-40)."

Let us turn to the second question—whether or not *luoghi* can be licitly purchased from the original creditors. The attack against them begins with a dialectical maneuver (ll. 41-48). For argument's sake, it is acknowledged that the original creditor, acting under duress, is free from usurious intent and conduct. Citizens who voluntarily invest in the *compere*, however, are not exculpated, because their actions are driven by *voluntas* and not *coactio*. To purchase *luoghi*, therefore, does not seem to be licit. The purchaser's moral footing, it is swiftly rejoined, does not rest on the criterion of intention, but on the formal qualities of the rights of the original creditors. If these *iura* are held to be morally legitimate (as it has been argued), they can be licitly purchased. If these same *iura* are capable of being transmitted to an universal heir, there is no reason why they cannot be transmitted to an individual emptor, who is likened to a *successor*

---

[35] Sieveking, 98-99.

singularis (ll. 48-50).[36] Both casuistic rejoinders meant that the moral and legal content of the original creditor's rights can be and are transmitted at the time of sale to the emptor.

Finally, we arrive at the master's *determinatio*, representing the opinion of John of Legnano. The *determinatio* is presented conditionally rather than apodictically, though all the conditions are assumed to be true and descriptive of the Genoese *compere*. If, acting on its own authority and initiative, the commune forces its citizens to hand over money to the treasury, and if the commune turns over to its citizens receipts from the *gabelle* (considered here as a hypervolatile source of income), there is no usury, because all the constituent elements of that sinful crime are lacking : a loan contract, a stipulation whereby the lender will receive something beyond the principal of his loan, and a corrupt intention with respect to both citizen-creditors and commune. John concludes by defending the *emptores* on the grounds that what is licitly received by the original creditor can be transferred to someone else.

If this determination patently flows from the *argumenta*, it is also guided by a political-economic ideology : That the commune has the moral right and obligation to secure the material well-being of citizens by collecting taxes or forcing citizens to lend to satisfy its legitimate need for credit, though due care had to be taken to soften the burden of taxation lest citizen-creditors be destroyed. Public utility, in this context, included the promotion of the welfare of individual citizens, especially individuals with enough wealth to invest in and profit from the *compere*. That John was guided by this ideology is also seen in his lecture on the decretal *Naviganti*, where he defended the prerogative of the city-state to borrow money by selling rights to a 10% annuity whose source is the "goods of the city" (*sc. gabelle*).[37] What I wish to underline here is that John of Legnano was nourished by a political-economic ideology which he articulated, advocated and perpetuated. He was committed to advising investors and speculators that their own belief in the morality of the operations of the public debt is entirely justifiable.

The material welfare of both creditor and commune, important as it was, remained only half the picture. For every canonist and theologian, the earthly public utility proclaimed by a statute was always

---

[36] A *successor singularis* is an heir to whom is transmitted certain particular rights of a deceased person.

[37] Lucca, Biblioteca Capitolare Feliniana, Cod. 227, fol. 314.

subordinate to a supernatural end : salvation. The citizen-creditor was never simply viewed as a *homo economicus*.[38] He was always a spiritual man, "a pilgrim on his way between this world and the eternal life."[39] Political ideology, juristic conceptions and scholastic dialectics were incapable of being stretched to cover all spiritual contingencies, nor could they account for the presence or absence of purity of the individual investor's conscience *quoad Deum*. All the experts agreed on this fundamental assumption. The limitations of ideology and juristic instrumentalities put the controversy over the public debt beyond definitional solution and apodictic finality. No matter how much one side would emphasize that the conscience of the citizen-creditor was not tainted, the other side (Alexander Lombard, Gregory of Rimini (d. 1358), Saint Bernardine (d.1444), to mention only a few) swiftly condemned citizens of Venice, Florence and Genoa who voluntarily entered the "bond market," or who, though forced to loan to the commune, desired *ab initio* the annuity promised them by statute. To the moralists, such investors were sinful profiteers, a flotilla of contaminated consciences heading straight for the shores of eternal damnation.[40]

How did investors respond to the conflicting interpretations about their spiritual fate ? Some, of course, were bored. Yet to those for whom rigoristic opinions were immediately coercive and glowed with authority, entrance into the market place would now represent a

---

[38] *Contra* the interpretations of John F. McGovern, "The Rise of New Economic Attitudes—Economic Humanism, Economic Nationalism—During the Later Middle Ages and the Renaissance, A.D. 1200-1550," *Traditio* 26 (1970), 217ff. McGovern's portrait of scholastic economic and social doctrines is painted with the colors of *aggiornamento*, and is violently anachronistic (see especially 228-233).

[39] S. Kuttner, *Harmony from Dissonance : An Interpretation of Medieval Canon Law* (Latrobe, 1960), 46; Pierre Michaud-Quantin, "La conscience individuelle et ses droits chez les moralistes de la fin du moyen-âge," in *Universalismus und Partikularismus im Mittelalter*, ed. Paul Wilpert (Berlin, 1968), 54. Although the investor is cast as a male, it should be known that many investors and speculators in this period were women, which is evident from the registers of the public debts of Genoa, Florence, and Venice.

[40] The evidence supporting this interpretation and the statements contained in the next paragraph will be presented in my study of the controversy. I wish to disavow here any intention of establishing a pernicious polarity between rigorists (moralists against some or all the operations of the public debt) and latitudinarians (those who defended these operations). The same moralist often approved one contract, condemned another, expressed particular doubts about another, and so on. If there was a spectrum of diverging interpretations when it came to measuring actual practice against shared verities, there was also a consensus about the validity of many fundamental assumptions.

real spiritual risk. There are well-documented cases of investors who, because of scruples of conscience, were hesitant about purchasing shares in the public debt, and a few isolated cases of investors pulling out of the market altogether. On the other hand, to someone prepared to invest in the public debt because he believed that it was both moral and profitable to do so, an opinion like John of Legnano's was supportive. It gave him the moral territory upon which he could defend himself if necessary. Whatever impact these opinions had upon the operations of the public debt, they did not impede nor spur the actual development of deficit financing and the market in, what we would call today, government bonds. The institutional development of the public debts in Venice, Genoa and Florence was driven by political and economic forces too powerful to be effectively swayed by the *dicta* of theologians and canonists.

The edition of John's *questio* is based on a single copy, the only one which I have been able to locate, housed in the Vatican Library : Vat. lat. 13091, fol. 46ᵛ.[41] This MS dates from the first half of the fifteenth century and its provenance is Genoa.[42] This copy may have been used by the Genoese jurist-statesman Bartholomew Bosco (d. ca. 1437), who, in a *consilium* on the public debt of Genoa, quoted *ad litteram* John of Legnano's *determinatio*.[43] Thus far, Bosco's citation is the only reference to the Bolognese jurist's opinion on the public debt which I have found. In preparing the edition I have emended the MS in several places, and these have been duly noted in the *apparatus criticus*. It should be noted that all the corrections within the MS were made by the original scribe. Since it would not improve upon the meaning of the text, I have seen no advantage in standardizing the following orthographic peculiarities of our single MS : "aditum" = "additum"; "comune" = "commune"; "redere" = "reddere"; "talles" = "tales"; transmituntur" = "transmittuntur"; "vendictio" = "venditio."

---

[41] Cited by McCall, "The Writings of John of Legnano," 434.

[42] On fol. 82ᵛ of the MS, we read : "Explicit sermo beati Francisci ordinatum per fratrem Bartholomeum de Foxano tempore quo erat bachalarius Januae sub anno domini MCCCC XXX II."

[43] *Consilia* (Loano, 1622) *cons.* 262, fol. 419.

Text

Questio talis est : Comune Janue eget pecunia pro neccessariis utilibus civitatis. Cogit cives suos ad dandum eidem certam pecuniam hoc modo, videlicet quia comune dicte civitatis providet recipienda, id est, civibus eisdem; videlicet hoc modo quia assignat eis quasdam gabellas redentes eisdem civibus decem pro centum vel minus, que
5 gabelle possunt deteriorari et minus redere, possent etiam in totum destrui. Queritur, nunquid istis dantibus pecuniam suo comuni sit licitum accipere istos tales reditus vel proventus. Secundo queritur, posito quod istis sit licitum recipere istos proventus talium gabellarum, nunquid sit licitum ementibus dictos proventus recipere vel emere
10 talia iura et ipsis gaudere, videlicet istis qui habuerunt talia iura a dicto communi.

Et circa primum, videtur quod non sit licitum possidere tales reditus tali modo, videlicet primis dantibus, et in primo puncto questionis. Nam non est dubium, quod predicti habent ultra sortem, igitur est
15 usura, *quia quicquid accedit sorti usura est*.[44] Preterea ipsum est mutuum quod patet, quia non potest alius contractus censeri, quia recipit proventus dictarum gabellarum perpetuo et potest ascendere ultra sortem, ymmo ascenditur a predicto contractu circa talles proventus ultra sortem. Igitur est mutuum et usurarium mutuum, quia
20 ultra sortem recipitur. In contrarium videtur, quia delictum non comittitur sine animo et conscientia lesa. Sed ex parte civium non procedit animus delinquendi, nec conscientia lesa, igitur, etc. Et hoc patet quia sunt coacti. Nec sponte et animose, nec sub spe lucri contrahunt cum comuni vel dant eam pecuniam comuni, sed coacti
25 et male libenter dant istam pecuniam comuni, igitur, etc. Deinde ex parte dantium pecuniam non intervenit aliquod pactum ut capiatur aliquid ultra sortem, ergo ex parte comunis provenit talis datio dictorum proventuum. Comune potest providere suis civibus sua volun-

---

11   proventu (*post* dicto) *del. ms.*
14   quod predicti *rep. et del. ms.*
18-19 ymmo - sortem *in marg. inferiore ms.*
21   et *ex* in *corr. ms.*
25   tamen (*post* dant) *del. ms*; istam *ex* istas *corr. ms.*

---

[44] Ambrose, *De Tobia*, c. 13 (PL 14, 773); cf. Gratian (see above, n. 6).

tate spontanea sicut pater filiis et hoc modo non est prohybitum,
30 igitur, etc. Preterea hoc patet quia istud non est mutuum, quia nunquam debent recipere sortem et isti proventus possunt destrui et anichilari, et nichil valere, si dicte gabelle non rederent vel parum rederent prout contingere posset propter causas occurentes. Ergo non est mutuum, cum sors redi non debeat, sed potius erit emptio et vendictio et hoc patet ex natura rei, vel est contractus innominatus. Ergo est licitum, cum non sit intentio civium mutuare sub usuris nec sit intentio comunis, nisi remunerare cives suos ex sua providentia
40 libertatis et voluntatis.

Circa secundum punctum, videtur quod ementibus ab istis civibus non sit licitum tales proventus habere, quia nulla coactio intervenit in casu nostro sed sola voluntas. Sequitur ergo, quod posito quod sit licitum primis civibus qui sunt coacti dicto communi prestare
45 certam pecuniam, talles reditus habere vel tenere, non est tamen licitum emere a predictis civibus talles reditus quia in eis nulla est necessitas. Et ideo si emunt reditus, qui possent ascendere ultra sortem, videtur esse non licitum. In contrarium videtur, quia regulariter attenditur origo et illud quod respicit aliud non terminatur per se,
50 ex quo dependet a certa causa. Emptio que fit de istis gabellis fit respectu iurium que habent primi cives. Igitur ex illo respectu et ex illa causa iudicabatur licitus contractus, si iura sunt licita in primis civibus. Preterea successor singularis et universalis equiparantur et ea que transmituntur ad universalem, transmituntur ad singularem
55 successorem. Sed ad universalem successorem nemo negat quod talles reditus transirent. Preterea illud quod est licitum in persona aliquorum est postea licitum in quoscunque habentes causam ab illis, ut l. pater, de legatis iii.[45]

Determinatio domini Johannis de Lignano iuris utriusque professoris
60 soris excelentissimi.

Responsio secundi (marginal note at lines 47-48)

38-39   civium - intentio *in marg. inferiore ms*; mutare *ms*.
41   secundum *ex* primum *corr. ms*.
45   est *ex* enim *corr. ms*.
47-48   Responsio secundi *in marg. ms*.
50   de *ex* ex *corr. ms*.
51   et illa causa (*post* illo respectu) *del. ms*.
52   sunt *in marg. ms*.

---

[45] *D.* 32, [1], 38.

Si comune cogit cives ad pecuniam tradendam et idem comune tradit gabellas non ex conventione sed auctoritate propria et motu suo, et maxime ubi gabelle possunt deteriorari et anichilari, non est usura, cum deficiat materiale principium, utpote verus contractus
65 mutui, et formale, utpote pactum aditum de plus sorte accipiendo, nec adsit mens depravata tempore tradictionis et si licite sic recipitur, sic licite transfertur in alium.

Jo. de Lignano

University of Chicago

---

66   ne *ms.*
68   Lignagno *ms.*

THE ORIGINS OF THE COLLEGE OF SAINT-RAYMOND AT THE UNIVERSITY OF TOULOUSE

JOHN MUNDY

The document transcribed below is an eighteenth-century archivist's copy of a *vidimus* dated 1524. The *vidimus* reported the contents of act of 1256 which itself contained the text of an earlier act of 1250.[1] The essential contents of this document have been described in a recent history of the university of Toulouse, and this mention, in turn, brought the document to the attention of a recent historian of the inquisition in Toulouse.[2]

The act of 1250 tells us that Bishop William II of Agen, acting as head of the papal inquisition in lands governed by the count of Toulouse, granted to the monastery of the canons-regular of Saint-Sernin a house across the street from the monastery's hospital of Saint-Raymond, where poor students at the university of Toulouse were already being housed.[3] The conditions attached to this grant were that the house be joined to the hospital by a bridge, its street door blocked up, and that it be converted into a dormitory with facilities for study for yet other poor students at the university. The act also tells us that the house had been acquired by the inquis-

---

[1] Departmental Archives of the Haute-Garonne, Series H, Saint-Sernin, liasse 643 with Cresty's archival reference of the eighteenth century cataloguing it as XV, Sac AF, liasse i, tit. 8.

[2] C. E. Smith, *The University of Toulouse in the Middle Ages* (Milwaukee, 1958), 67-68, and Yves Dossat, "Une figure d'inquisiteur : Bernard de Caux," *Cahiers de Fanjeaux* 6 (1971), 259 and note 51. It is to be noted that liasse 643 of the collection of Saint-Sernin is entirely composed of documents dealing with the hospital of Saint-Raymond.

[3] In 1245 Innocent IV wrote the bishop of Toulouse encouraging him to urge the inclusion of poor students in the hospitals of his town. In 1246 the properties and equipment of the hospital of Saint-Raymond were inventoried. It is therefore a good guess that, following the pope's suggestion, Saint-Raymond's was at that time beginning its conversion from a hospital for general service into what was later to become the college of Saint-Raymond. For these documents, see my "Charity and Social Work in Toulouse," *Traditio* 22 (1966), 252-253, nn. 170-175.

itor Bernard de Caux and his associate sometime in the period 1245-1247 for use as a prison for the inquisition,[4] a fact of importance when it is remembered that the inquisitors were afterward hard put to find sufficient prison space for their unhappy clients.[5]

The bishop's act of 1250 appears to reflect the policy of Innocent IV who, in order to win the support of the bishops and representatives of the old monastic orders arrayed in the council of Lyon in 1245 against the Hohenstaufen, had turned somewhat against the new mendicant orders and had attempted to slow their 'reforming,' proselytizing, and inquisitorial activities.[6] A recent historian of the Toulousan inquisition has clearly shown that this pope's policy had, in effect, forced the Dominicans to withdraw from the inquisition in Languedoc, and the pope himself had entrusted that agency to local ordinaries under special commission—hence our bishop of Agen whose activities began early in 1248.[7] And the bishop's act published here provides further evidence that the papal order to go slow was being heard on the local level.

The Dominican inquisition was soon renewed, however. Innocent IV had begun to doubt his own policy, and, when he died and was replaced by Alexander IV in 1254, it was completely overturned.[8] A similar change took place in Languedoc where the last native prince, Raymond VII, died in 1249 and was replaced by the Capetian, Alphonse of Poitiers, the brother of Louis IX. Raymond VII's policies had seemed incoherent : just after the capitulation of the southerners

---

[4] Bernard was an inquisitor on tour from 1243 to 1249, after which he returned to native Agen where he was active in setting up the convent of his order before his death in November, 1522. He and his *socius* were at Toulouse from April, 1245 to May, 1247. For this information see Yves Dossat, *Les crises de l'inquisition Toulousaine* (Bordeaux, 1959), 156-57 and 175.

[5] The matter is discussed by Yves Dossat, 194-95 and 262, n. 49, where we learn that, in 1255, the inquisitors housed their prisoners in the bishop's prison of Saint-Etienne and a few trustees in that of the count in the Narbonese Castle, and that the pressure for prison space was still acute in the late 1260s when the inquisitors were trying to get the castle of Lavaur in order to ease their needs.

[6] Readers will remember that this involved a great deal more than merely the inquisition or the Dominican order, and may also call to mind the celebrated Franciscan Salimbene's hostility to Innocent IV. In his *Cronicon* (*MGH. SS.* XXXII, 419-20) his animus led him to assert that this pope fell sick and died because of his policy towards the mendicants, and that his successor was especially worthy because he rescinded or destroyed the acts of his predecessor.

[7] Dossat, 168-82, an excellent discussion.

[8] Dossat, 182ff. and 276ff.

to the Capetians in 1229, the count's government attacked heresy vigorously; from 1235 to 1243 it fought the Dominican inquisition, thereby protecting heretics; from 1243 on, it supported Innocent IV's localist policy and pursued heretics. The obvious rationale of this policy was that Raymond's government, whatever its second thoughts about the pursuit of heresy may have been, wished to keep the matter in the hands of local lay and ecclesiastical authorities. With Alphonse's accession, things changed. His government, led by officers largely recruited from northern and Atlantic France, consistently worked to integrate and subordinate the new southern domains of the Capetians.[9] Alphonse urged the papacy to re-establish the Dominican inquisition, and his request was answered. Under the general supervision of the house at Paris, new teams were despatched to his domains, Raynald of Chartres and John of Saint-Pierre beginning their very active work early in 1255.[10] In spite of this reversal of policy and in spite of their continuing need for prisons, these inquisitors felt obliged to confirm the bishop's gift to Saint-Sernin, which they did in 1256, and, at that time, also conveyed the property to the abbot and convent. Neither they nor their successors appear to have made use of the clause inserted in the bishop's grant allowing them to use the house if they had need.[11] The ancient monastery of Saint-Sernin and the new university were obviously not without power.

It at first seems curious that a prison for heretics should have been converted into a house for students, the later college of Saint-Raymond. Second thoughts will remind us, however, that this action exemplifies again the often explored theme that the church fought heresy with two weapons, repression and education, and that the Dominicans were the most active of all the new orders in both of those fields. To add to that, the church's proclivity for charity —poor scholars we recall, were to be housed in Saint-Raymond's—attracted the middling folk whose children were especially directed toward careers providing advancement, an attraction that left heresy to the occasional

---

[9] See Dossat's conclusions (322-23) on the policies of Raymond VII and Alphonse of Poitiers. I question only his assertion that, because Alponse did not make money when the costs and profits of the inquisition are balanced, this prince was animated only by the desire to participate in the repression of heresy. The advantages to be derived from dominion cannot be measured by the cash profit or loss occasioned by the actions of one judicial agency.

[10] Dossat, 153, n. 8.

[11] For their need, see n. 5 above.

divagations of the wealthy or to the brief and meaningless rage of the really poor.

Lastly, readers may agree that the differences in the various scribal and juridical protocols of the two *vidimus* are not uninstructive. The easy forms of the thirteenth century sharply contrast with the formalistic rigidity of the phrases penned by the well developed bureaucracy of Renaissance France.

Text

In nomine domini amen.[12] Noverint universi et singuli presentes pariter et futuri presens publicum instrumentum, transsumptum, seu vidimus visuri, lecturi et etiam audituri quod Petrus Galsandi[13] jurium licenciatus subconservator et iudex causarum jurium, rerum, privilegiorum et libertatum universitati venerabilis studii Tholosani studentium [et] membris et suppositis ejusdem, per sanctam sedem apostolicam concessorum per reverendum in Christo patrem et dominum d[ominum] Laurentium Alamandi miseratione divina episcopum et principem Gratianopolis et abbatem incliti monasterii Sanctii Saturnini Tolosae dictorum privilegiorum conservatorem subdelegatus, vidimus, legimus et palpavimus quoddam instrumentum in pergameno descriptum antiquum huiusmodi tenoris :

[Noverint] universi presentes posterique [quod] frater Raynaldus de Carnoto et frater Joannes de Sancto Petro ordinis praedicatorum, inquisitores haeretice pravitatis in civitatibus et terris domini Alfonsi dei gratia comitis Pictaviae et Tholosae a sede apostolica deputati, attendentes quod venerabilis pater dominus episcopus Agennensis olim dum officium inquisitionis haberet in terra domini comitis Tholosani domum quamdam quam emerant inquisitores, scilicet frater Bernardus de Caucio et socius ejus, ut ibi dictum fuit, ad opus carcerum prope ecclesiam Sancti Saturnini Tholosae, ob gratiam et liberalitatem

---

[12] The occasional slips of the eighteenth-century copier have been corrected in this transcription. They are of no philological or historical interest. Spelling variations are retained because they reflect the different styles of the originals and copies. Philippe Wolff kindly aided me by examining the original copy in the archives, my copy being a photograph made in 1946 and insufficiently washed during development so that its chemical surface suffers from crystallization. His assistance was decisive in deciphering several important phrases and also the spelling of several sixteenth-century names. He also saved me from a couple of blunders I could well have avoided myself.

[13] Referred to in the last line of this document as Gaillardi.

p. 2 quam abbas et totus conventus loci ejusdem exibuerunt / inquisitoribus ipsis, contulisset hospitali Sancti Raymundi in quo scolares pauperes commorantur prout in instrumento donationis ejusdem ab ipso domino Agennensi factae continetur quod huic presenti instrumento inferri [mandaverunt] in haec verba :

Noverint universi presentem paginam inspecturi quod dominus Guillermus dei gratia episcopus Agennensis [sciens] labores, afflictationes et taedia quae abbas ecclesie Sancti Saturnini Tholosae et conventus ejusdem loci sustinuerunt multis annis exponendo claustrum [et] domos suas inquisitoribus haereticae pravitatis, volensque ipsis in aliquo satisfacere pro praemissis, domum carceris cum cortili suo quam inquisitores praefati emerant Tholosae, communicato fratris B. de Caucio inquisitoris et aliorum bonorum virorum consilio, auctoritate apostolica sibi commissa in dicto inquisitionis negotio in tota terra illustris viri Raymundi olim comitis Tholosae, contulit hospitali quod dicitur Sancti Raymundi, ubi scolares pauperes commorantur, ita tamen quod, quomodocumque inquisitores praedicti negotii praefata domo pro negotio inquisitionis indiguerint, ipsam possint habere, et ea sine contradictione qualibet possint uti, proprietate ipsius domus hospitali praefato in perpetuum reservata, confrontatur autem predicta domus ab oriente in via publica quae est inter domum et portam ecclesiae supramemoratae, ab austro in via publica quae [est] inter hospitale praedictum et ipsam domum, ab occidente in via publica qua itur ad portam quae dicitur Arnaldi Bernardi. Actum Agenni 14a die introitus Februarii; testes sunt dominus P. officialis Agennensis, frater ordinis praedicatorum B. de Caucio et R. Balairac, Arnaldus de Cassaneli civis Agennensis et ego Aymericus de Casalibus notarius Agennensis qui mandato praedicti domini episcopi hanc cartam scripsi et signum meum apposui in testimonium veritatis anno domini 1249,
p. 3 regnante / domino Alfonso Tholosae comite et praedicto domino Guillermo Agennensi episcopo.

Supradicti vero fratres Rainaldus de Carnoto et Joannes de Sancto Petro inquisitores, pium ejusdem domini Agennensis episcopi considerantes affectum, donationem et concessionem eandem ratam habentes et gratam, ipsam auctoritate apostolica sibi commissa liberaliter approba[ve]runt, adiectis modis, conditionibus et declarationibus infrascriptis, voluerunt tamen et ordinaverunt praefati patres Rainaldus de Carnoto et Joannes de Sancto Petro inquisitores ut domus praedicta cum cortili suo et confrontationibus praedicto hospitali Sancti Raymundi concessa continuetur et contignetur

hospitali praedicto transitu in eum per pontem arcuatum lapideum seu latericium super carreriam publicam praeparato, domus etiam ipsa claudetur inferius, ita quod per hospitale sit ingressus ad illam, et in eis cellae seu competentia loca ad studendum pauperibus scholaribus secundum capacitatem loci superius et inferius aptabuntur, nec licebit alicui domum ipsam vel ejus aliquem partem aliis usibus applicare, [et] reficietur insuper et reparabitur per abbatem Sancti Saturnini cum indiguerit domus ipsa. Si vero quod absit hospitale jamdictum Sancti Raymundi aliquo casu destrueretur vel esse desineret hospitale vel fortasse cessaretur a scolaribus recipiendis in eo, qui sicut dictum est in domo eadem proficerent et studerent, non liceret abbati et conventui Sancti Saturnini aut cuilibet alii domum ipsam sibi appropriare seu aliquatenus retinere, imo praedicta donatio prorsus ipso facto revocaretur et haberetur penitus pro infecta. Has quoque conditiones et declarationes addiderunt memorati inquisi-
p. 4 tores salvis et retentis hiis quae posita fuerant / et concessa superius per dominum episcopum Agennensem, omnia vero perscripta sicut melius superius sunt expressa. Dominus Bernardus abbas et totus conventus Sancti Saturnini Tholosae, videlicet A. Aurioli prior claustralis et A. Bego camerarius et B. de Succo helemosinarius et Vitalis prior de Grisolis[14] et Guillermus Raymundus, Simon prior de Calmonte et P. [de] Rupe cellararius et infirmarius. B. de Prinhaco operarius, Guillermus Teulerius prior de Blanhaco, B. de Martris sacrista, Guilhermus de Lescalar, Maurandus, Ato de Durbano, Magister Petrus Darey, Companhus canonici dictae ecclesiae pro se et omnibus aliis approba-[ve]runt et concesserunt et obligaverunt se bona fide pro se et successoribus suis ad servandum universa et singula quae sunt expressa superius et complenda, domum praefatam claudent inferius, pontem erigent arcuatum super carreriam publicam ut est dictum, et utrumque reparari facient et refici tam ipsi quam successores eorum cum viderint indigere, [et] disponent locum ad cellas et studia scolarium et aptabunt nec contra ordinationem praescriptam ipsi vel successores eorum unquam in aliqua deviabunt. Fecerunt autem inquisitores praefati praedictum dominum abbatem Sancti Saturnini, nomine hospitalis jamdicti, de memorato domo, traditis clavibus, in possessionem corporalem induci, salvis adjectionibus et conditionibus supradictis.

---

[14] All but one of these names (de Lescalar) have been checked against and corrected by means of lists of the members of the chapter of Saint-Sernin in the archives (H. Saint-Sernin, liasse 679 : Cresty XX, lxx, 12, dated May 1249; *ibid.*, liasse 675 : Cresty XIX, lxv, 7, dated March 1256; *ibid.*, liasse 687 : Cresty XX, lxxii, nn, dated March 1262).

Actum fuit hoc Tholosae quarta die introitus mensis Maii, regnante
p. 5 eodem rege Francorum, Alfonso / Tholosano comite, R. episcopo,
anno incarnationis domini 1256. De approbatione dominationis, concessionis et adjectionis modorum, conditionum et declarationum et totius hujus rei a praedictis fratribus inquisitoribus Rainaldo de Carnoto et Joanno de Sancto Petro sic concessae sunt testes frater Raimundus de Fuxo prior praedicatorum Tholosae et frater Guilhermus Arnaldus ordinis praedicatorum et frater Guilhermus Goti gardianus ordinis minorum [Tholosae] et frater Arnaldus de Albia ordinis minorum et Rogerius Convenorum cantor Sancti Stephani Tholosae et Anthonius capellanus Sancti Stephani et Magister Nepos de Montealbano et Guillelmus Petrus de Montibus et Petrus Vasco de Claustro; de approbatione vero et obligatione et totius hujus rei a dicto domino abbate et conventu praedicto sic concessa sunt testes Raimundus de Caucio sacerdos et frater...... Aurioli et Guilhermus Petrus de Monte et Petrus Vasco praedictus et Bernardus Constantius de Capite Denario juvenis et Guilhermus de Mosenquis publicus Tholosae notarius qui de his omnibus testis et in his omnibus presens adfuit et hanc cartam scripsit.

In cujus instrumenti praeinserti visionis et lecturae nobis pro tribunali sedenti in audiencia curiae conservatoriae universitatis praedictae in domo abbatiali Sancti Saturnini Tholosae testimonium atque
p. 6 fidem, nos, subconservator praedictus sedens pro / tribunali ad requisitionem nobilis et discreti viri Magistri Ludovici Guiserandi jurium bachalaurei, collegiati locum tenentis prioris collegii Sancti Raymundi Tholosae ab eodem collegio mandatum habentis ut dixit, transcriptum, transsumptum seu vidimus, unum, duo aut plura in formam publici instrumenti per notarios infrascriptos in scriptis redigi, inscribi et publicari mandavi[mus], sigilloque praedictae curiae jussimus appensione communiri decernentes eidem transcripto, transsumpto seu vidimus tantam fidem adhibendam quantam eidem instrumento praeincerto adhiberetur, in praemissis omnibus interponendo authoritatem nostram judiciariam pariter et decretum, jure nostro et quolibet alieno salvo. Acta fuerunt haec in audientia praedictae curiae hora quae est assueta teneri 17a die mensis Junii, anno incarnationis domini 1524, indictione 12a, pontificatus sanctissimi in Christo patris domini nostri domini Clementis divina providentia papae septimi anno primo, illustrissimo principe et domino nostro domino Francisco dei gratia rege Francorum regnante, presentibus in praemissis discretis viris Magistro Stephano de Frunellis, Petro de Fabro, Geraldo la Ber-

tune[15] jurium bachalaureo, Bernardo Borrilis, et Anthonio Segali notariis praedictae curiae juratis testibus ad praemissa vocatis et nobis
p. 7 Jacobo de Larda/ et Stephano Celeri notariis etiam juratis praedictae curiae qui in vidimatione et transsumpto ac decreti impositione caeterisque aliis praesentes fuimus et de iisdem actum publicum retinuimus et in registro jamdictae curiae regestravimus, et dein[d]e facta collatione cum praedicto originali in aliquibus partibus cassato in primo verbo illegibili, illo et aliis in albo ommissis per alium a nobis fidelem in hanc formam publicam et authentiquam redigere et incrossare fecimus et demum nos hic subsignavimus in fidem praemissorum : P. Gaillardi judex praedictus, J. de Landa, S. Celerii notarius.

Columbia University

---

[15] Mr. Wolff's guess.

GIROLAMO BORRO'S *MULTAE SUNT NOSTRARUM IGNORATIONUM CAUSAE*
(Ms. Vat. Ross. 1009)

CHARLES B. SCHMITT

Though the name of Girolamo Borro (1512-1592) of Arezzo[1] has come up from time to time in a variety of contexts concerning sixteenth-century intellectual life in Italy, no one, to the best of my knowledge, has yet attempted to study his life and works in a comprehensive fashion. Borro had contacts with various eminent figures, including Pietro Aretino, Michel de Montaigne, and Galileo Galilei and taught philosophy for many years in several Italian universities, notably Pisa. Among his works still remaining in manuscript is a brief treatise, *Multae sunt nostrarum ignorationum causae,* which we here propose to edit and study as part of a more comprehensive treatment of Borro and his place in sixteenth-century thought.[2]

This is not the place to deal in great detail with Borro's life and works,[3] but we must briefly sketch what is already generally known about him. He was born, it seems, in Arezzo in 1512 and died in Perugia on August 26, 1592. While we have some information concerning his works and other activities, by no means can we yet reconstruct his life in any detail. He is particularly identified with the University

---

[1] We have decided on the form "Borro," rather than "Borri." Though the name is uniformly written as "Borrius" in Latin, all sixteenth century Italian references which I have found—including the printed editions of his own vernacular works—consistently use "Borro."

[2] Though we shall try to summarize as well as possible in the present paper the previous literature on Borro, limitations of length prevent us from undertaking an analysis of various interesting aspects of his life and thought.

[3] The best article is now by G. Stabile in *Dizionario Biografico degli Italiani,* XIII (1971), 13-17, which has extensive bibliography. A few additions are also made in my forthcoming article on Borro for the *Dictionary of Scientific Biography* (supplementary volume). Of the older literature, the most important sources are U. Viviani, *Medici, fisici e cerusici della provincia aretina vissuti dal V al XVII secolo d. C.* (Arezzo, 1923), 103-09; G. Mazzuchelli, *Gli scrittori d'Italia* ... (Brescia, 1753-63), II, 1789; and A. Fabronius, *Historia Academicae Pisanae* ... (Pisa, 1791-95; repr. Bologna, 1971), II, 281-82, 341-46, 469.

of Pisa, where he taught as professor of philosophy from 1553 to 1559 and again from 1575 to 1586.[4] He also taught at Perugia for a time[5] and, according to the tradition, also at Paris, Rome, and Siena.[6] During the pontificate of Gregory XIII (1572-1585), he fell into difficulty with the Inquisition, but was eventually acquitted.[7] Though a somewhat conservative Aristotelian, he was nevertheless also in correspondence with Pietro Aretino,[8] perhaps coming into contact with the famous *poligrafo* because they shared Arezzo as a birthplace. It is also noteworthy that Montaigne met him in Pisa on July 14, 1581, recording the fact in his *Journal de voyage en Italie*.[9] Borro

---

[4] Fabronius II, 469.

[5] Early in his career, about 1538. G. Ermini, *Storia della Università di Perugia* (Florence, 1947), 580. Borro also returned to Perugia in 1586 after leaving Pisa and died there six years later. See Fabronius II, 343-44 and Viviani (1923), 103.

[6] I have been unable to verify that Borro actually taught at these places. No mention of him could be found in the standard printed works dealing with the history of these universities. The source of this information seems to be the inscription (reproduced in Fabronius II, 344 and Viviani [1923], 103) on the monument dedicated to Borro and written by Laelius Borrius, "suo nipote" according to Viviani. We do know, however, that an attempt was made in 1568 to get Borro to come to the Studio di Siena. See G. Prunai, "Lo studio senese nel primo quarantennio del Principato Mediceo," *Bullettino senese di storia patria* 6 (1959), 79-160, at 89.

[7] On this see C. Dejob, *Marc-Antoine Muret : Un professeur français en Italie dans la seconde moitié du XVIe siècle* (Paris, 1881), 479, which prints a letter written by Borro on November 5, 1583, immediately after his release. See also U. Viviani, *Tre medici aretini* (Arezzo, 1936), 47-52 and Arezzo, Biblioteca della Città d'Arezzo, ms. 38, fols. 122 sg., as well as the text from Montaigne's *Essais* cited below in note 9. See also P. O. Kristeller, "The Myth of Renaissance Atheism and the French Tradition of Free Thought," *Journal of the History of Philosophy* 6 (1968), 233-43, at 240.

[8] For their correspondence see *De Primo* [Secondo, etc.] *libro di lettere di M. Pietro Aretino* (Paris, 1609) II, fols. 158v-159; V, 142-143; *Lettere scritte a Pietro Aretino emendate per cura di Teodorico Landoni* (Bologna, 1873-75) II, parte I, 182-93; and Pietro Aretino, *Il secondo libro delle lettere*, ed. F. Nicolini (Bari, 1916), I, 252, 268; II, 117.

[9] "Mi venne a visitare in casa parecchi volte Girolamo Borro medico, dottor della Sapienza. Et essendo io andato a visitarlo il 14 luglio mi fece presente del suo libro del flusso e riflusso del mare, in lingua volgare : e mi fece vedere un altro libro latino ch'avea fatto, de i morbi de i corpi." *Journal du voyage du* [!] *Michel de Montaigne en Italie...* ed. A. d'Ancona (Città di Castello, 1895), 486-87. Montaigne (492) also mentions Borro by name when he leaves Pisa on July 27.

It is also generally thought that the following text in *Essais* I, 26 (*De l'institution des enfans*) refers to Borro : "Je vy priuéement à Pise un honneste homme, mais si aristotélicien, que le plus general de ses dogmes est: que la touche et regle de toutes imaginations solides et de toute verité, c'est la conformité à la doctrine d'Aristote; que hors de là ce ne sont que chimeres et inanité; qu'il a tout veu et tout dict. Cette

seems to deserve the label *bizzoso* given him by Garin,[10] for he was in frequent dispute with Andrea Camuzzi, Francesco de' Vieri (Il Verino Secondo), and Francesco Buonamico, who were among his colleagues at Pisa.[11]

For a man who lived a life of four score years, many of which were spent in university teaching, Borro's surviving literary output appears remarkably small.[12] His publications consist essentially of three slim volumes : one work on logic,[13] another on motion,[14] and, most popularly, an Italian dialogue dealing primarily with floods.[15] Though he left behind a few manuscripts in addition to the one with which we are here dealing, none of those which have come to light thus far are very substantial.[16] In recent year some attention has been given to his work on motion—along with the much bulkier similar work

---

proposition, pour avoir esté un peu trop largement et iniquement interpretée, le mit autrefois et tint long temps en grand accessoire à l'inquisition à Rome." Montaigne, *Essais*, ed. A.Thibaudet (Bruges, 1950), 183. See also P. Villey, *Les sources et l'évolution des essais de Montaigne* (Paris, 1908) I, 84.

[10] E. Garin, *L'età nuova* (Naples, 1969), 486.

[11] See Fabronius II, 341-43; Viviani (1923), 106-08; Viviani (1936), 47-50. On the sort of disputes between professors—and even personal violence—at the University of Pisa at the end of the sixteenth century see also Dejob, 410.

[12] Much of his work was apparently never published and, indeed, the amount remaining in manuscript seems small. Several of his writings for which we have contemporary evidence have apparently not been recovered. For example, Montaigne (see n. 9 above) mentions a work "de i morbi de i corpi."

[13] *Hieronymus Borrius Arretinus de peripatetica docendi atque addiscendi methodo* (Florence, 1584), hereafter cited as *De methodo*.

[14] *Hieronymus Borrius Arretinus de motu gravium et levium* ... (Florence, 1575; reprinted, 1576), hereafter cited from the 1575 ed. as *De motu*. I should like to underline the fact that this work was first printed in 1575 and not in 1576, as many modern secondary works state. I have examined copies of the 1575 edition at the British Museum [shelfmark : 536.i.2] and at the Biblioteca Nazionale in Florence [shelfmark : Palat. 1.K.6376]. It is regrettably omitted from the list of Borro's works now published in the *Index Aureliensis*.

[15] *Dialogo del flusso e reflusso del mare* ... *Con ragionamento* ... *della perfettione delle donne* (Lucca, 1561). The first part of this edition was reprinted several times in an emended and expanded form, though the *Della perfettione delle donne* was apparently never reprinted. Among the reprints are Girolamo Borro Aretino, *Del flusso et reflusso del mare et dell'inondazione del Nilo* ... (Florence, 1577) and Girolamo Borro Aretino, *Del flusso et reflusso del mare et dell'inondazione del Nilo. La terza volta ricorretto dal proprio autore* ... (Florence, 1583). A further discussion of the various editions of this work must wait for another occasion.

[16] I plan to deal with the other manuscripts of Borro in a future publication.

by his rival Francesco Buonamico[17]—as an example of the sort of Peripatetic treatise on physics being taught at Pisa during Galileo's student days.[18] With the recent upsurge of interest in the logical thought of the Renaissance, Borro's *De peripatetica docendi atque addiscendi methodo* has also gained some attention.[19] Yet no attempt has thus far been made to produce a monographic study on Borro or even to study in a detailed way his relation to Galileo.

Our purpose here is to publish and to give some analysis of a brief work of his, which, to the best of my knowledge, has never been discussed in print and, as far as I have been able to discover, only Kristeller[20] has mentioned the manuscript in connection to Borro's name. Though a brief piece and one which has little, if anything strikingly new, it is not without interest when viewed in relation to Borro's other works and in reference to the intellectual climate of his time. It is closely related to the work on method and seems almost to be a sort of appendix to it. Like that work and Borro's other writings, the *Multae sunt nostrarum ignorationum causae* has the virtue of brevity. It is almost as though the little treatise were meant as a clarification of the following statement in the *De methodo* : "Huius Methodi ignoratio et negligentia monstrorum omne genus omnemque multitudinem generat, necessariamque rerum omnium ignorationem

---

[17] *Francisci Bonamici ... de motu libri X ...* (Florence, 1591).

[18] On Borro's work and its relation to Galileo see P. Duhem, *Études sur Léonard de Vinci* (Paris, 1906-13) III, 205-07; L. Olschki, *Geschichte der neusprachlichen wissenschaftlichen Literatur* (Heidelberg, Leipzig and Halle, 1918-27; repr. Vaduz, 1965) III, 253-56; E.A. Moody, "Galileo and Avempace: The Dynamics of the Leaning Tower Experiment," *Journal of the History of Ideas* 12(1951), 163-93, 375-422, esp. 415-18; T.B. Settle, "Galileo's Use of Experiment as a Tool of Investigation," in E. McMullin, ed., *Galileo, Man of Science* (New York, 1967), 315-27, at 325-26; E. Garin, *Scienza e vita civile nel Rinascimento italiano* (Bari, 1965), 123-26, 141-42; I.E. Drabkin and S. Drake, *Mechanics in Sixteenth Century Italy* (Madison, 1969), 55.

Galileo mentioned Borro twice in his early *De motu* (ca. 1590). See *Le opere di Galileo Galilei*, ed. A. Favaro (Florence, 1890-1909; repr. Florence, 1968) I, 33, 367. Borro was *professor ordinarius* of philosophy at Pisa while Galileo was a student there. The library of Galileo contained both the *De motu* and the *Del flusso e reflusso* (1577 ed.) of Borro. See A. Favaro, "La libreria di Galileo Galilei descritta ed illustrata," *Bullettino di bibliografia e di storia delle scienze matematiche e fisiche* 19 (1886), 219-93, at 268.

[19] N. W. Gilbert, *Renaissance Concepts of Method* (New York, 1960), 186-92 and C. Vasoli, *Studi sulla cultura del Rinascimento* (Manduria, 1968), 341-42. Borro is not mentioned, however, in the comprehensive study of W. Risse, *Die Logik der Neuzeit. 1 Band, 1500-1640* (Stuttgart and Bad Cannstatt, 1964).

[20] *Iter Italicum* (London and Leiden, 1963f.) II, 471. See below, Appendix pp. 471-72, for a fuller discussion.

parit."[21] It gets to the point, makes it, and passes on to something else. As Borro's printed work succinctly outlines the "Peripatetic method of teaching and learning," the one left in manuscript deals with what he considered to be the "causes of our ignorance." Though the title tells us that the causes are many, these reduce to ten, each of which he then treats in turn. These are: (1) ignorance of logic, (2) brief and negligent experience in natural philosophy, (3) negligence of good teachers and books, (4) the subtlety of the Sophists, (5) various defects of nature, (6) bad habits, (7) negligence of the texts, (8) the mixture of doctrines, (9) lack of skill, and (10) love and hatred. After listing these ten, he states clearly that there is not an eleventh one, as some think.[22] His brief discussion of this matter is perhaps worth treating before we turn to his list of the ten genuine causes of ignorance.

According to Borro, some say that corrupt texts are a cause of our ignorance, but they are mistaken, for it is easy to emend them. This seems to be little less than a head-on attack upon the work of the humanists, who placed so much emphasis upon establishing an accurate and readable text. Certainly most humanists of the period would not follow Borro in thinking it a simple matter to emend corrupt texts. Some thinkers, for example Gianfrancesco Pico (1469-1533) and Francesco Patrizi da Cherso (1529-1597), developed this line of approach to such a stage as to call into question the authenticity and validity of many of Aristotle's works.[23] This and other factors—e.g. the lack of any evidence that Borro ever went to the Greek text of Aristotle[24]—make one doubt whether Gilbert's characterization of him as a humanist is entirely accurate.[25]

We do not have the space here for a full analysis of Borro's work. Consequently, we shall limit ourselves to a discussion of several key aspects of it. Our printing of the entire text will make it accessible to other students who may wish to analyze it in greater detail.

More than anything else Borro's treatise illustrates the very conservative and inward looking attitude of many Renaissance

---

[21] *De methodo*, 105.

[22] Appendix, 472.

[23] See my *Gianfrancesco Pico della Mirandola (1469-1533) and His Critique of Aristotle* (The Hague, 1967), 63-69.

[24] Other than an occasional Greek word the writings of Borro betray little attempt to come to grips with the Greek text of Aristotle or of any other Greek author.

[25] *Op. cit.*, 186-92. Duhem (see below, n. 39) seems to go too far in the opposite direction in insisting on his 'Averroism.' One tends to agree more generally with Vasoli's (341, n. 75) judgment.

Aristotelians. His approach is basically scholastic and the only texts cited are those from Aristotle or from Averroes' commentary on Aristotle. This is traditional Aristotelianism betraying little or no influence from the humanist movement. What is more, Aristotle's authority is taken for granted and unquestioned : each of the ten *causae* are backed up by one or more quotation from the Stagirite. Here he puts into practice once again what he had said in the *De methodo* : "... quia nostri instituti non est exponere quid alii vel bene vel male fecerint, sed quid Aristoteles docuerit ac servaverit."[26] Again he stands firm in the conviction : "Extra hanc unam [sc. Aristotelis], nulla est ad philosophandum via."[27] The Aristotelian method of reaching truth is the unique one, and all others end in error. Like Aristotle and most followers of the Aristotelian tradition, Borro emphasized natural philosophy and an experiential, rather than a mathematical, approach to the study of physics. This is evident, for example, in the *De motu*, where he suggests the possibility of dropping balls of different materials to determine whether they fall with equal velocity.[28] Nowhere in the work, however, does he seem to advocate the use of mathematics in natural science. Consequently, the former proclivity has been emphasized by interpreters as a possible influence on Galileo.[29] His attitude toward the matter clearly comes out in the *Multae sunt nostrarum ignorationum causae*. The second of the *causae* is, according to Borro, insufficient attention to the study of natural philosophy.[30] Borro's argument hinges especially on three passages of Aristotle, each of which emphasizes that a theoretical, mathematical approach to natural philosophy is less fruitful than one based on broad experience. He first argues, citing a text from the *De coelo*,[31] that to use the mathematical method of Plato in analyzing nature leads to error. Secondly, he cites a text from the *Nicomachean Ethics*[32] to the effect that while the young can be adept at mathematics,

---

[26] *De methodo*, 39.
[27] *Ibid.*, 18
[28] *De motu*, 214-16. For brief discussions of this passage see W. A. Wallace, *Causality and Scientific Explanation*, I (Ann Arbor, 1972), 149-50 and C. B. Schmitt, "The Faculty of Arts at Pisa at the Time of Galileo," *Physis* 14 (1972), 243-72, at 267-71. I plan to discuss this important text in greater detail on another occasion.
[29] E. Wohlwill, *Galilei und sein Kampf für die copernicanische Lehre* (Hamburg and Leipzig, 1909) II, 290; Olschki, II, 255; Settle, 325-26.
[30] Appendix, 473-74.
[31] Book III, chapter 8.
[32] Book VI, chapter 8, esp. 1142a11-23.

they can hardly do well in natural philosophy which requires φρόνησις and that virtue can be gained only through experience. Thirdly, it is pointed out that Aristotle soundly criticized Plato and Democritus in the *De generatione et corruptione* [33] for their excessively theoretical approach to a subject in which little attention was paid to experience.

It is clear from these passages that for Borro the successful study of natural philosophy depends not upon the application of mathematical methods, but upon long experience and the intensive study of nature. This is brought out even more clearly in the subsequent lines where Borro points out that Aristotle himself spent twenty-seven years as a student and that the two or three years spent by students of his time can hardly be adequate to master this field of enquiry.[34] Finally, he quotes Averroes' censure of Avicenna for not having given adequate attention to the study of natural things.[35] The way to become a good natural philosopher seems therefore to be closely bound up with having experience of the natural world,[36] though the reader of the *Multae sunt nostrarum ignorationum causae* will also note that Borro gives due emphasis to the importance of having good teachers and books as well.[37]

---

[33] Book I, chapter 2, esp. 315a25-316a15.

[34] There is a parallel passage in the Dedicatory Epistle to the *De methodo*, where Borro also complains that students of his own time spend too little time studying in preparation for a life of philosophy. See *De methodo*, Av and the discussion of this text by Gilbert, 187.

[35] In Averroes' commentary on *De coelo*, book III, text 67. *Aristotelis opera cum Averrois commentariis* (Venice, 1562-74; repr. Frankfurt, 1962) V, f. 227.

[36] This is also the force of *causa* 9. See Appendix, 476. For Borro's suggestion that *experimenta* might be used to resolve the problem of falling bodies, see the text cited above in note 28. Drake (55) has noted, after discussing this passage, that : "Perhaps experiment rather than calculation was the tradition at Pisa even among philosophers when Galileo studied there. The suggestion may sound preposterous, but Borro at least seems to have thought that a philosophical problem might be settled by experiment." To the present writer the suggestion sounds commonplace rather than preposterous, for what else would we expect, given the character of sixteenth century Italian Aristotelianism and realizing that Borro's conception of "experiment" is perhaps somewhat different from ours. I have tried to deal with this problem in "Experimental Evidence for and against a Void : the Sixteenth-Century Arguments," *Isis* 58 (1967), 352-66 and "Experience and Experiment : A Comparison of Zabarella's Views with Galileo's in *De motu*," *Studies in the Renaissance* 16 (1969), 80-138. The burden of proof still remains (*pace* Edwards) upon those who wish to show that Italian Aristotelianism of the second half of the sixteenth century was "mathematical" in any way.

[37] Especially in *causae* 3, 6, and 7. See also the Dedicatory Epistle to *De methodo*, especially Aiii, where he decries poor teaching books, and Av, where he discusses both books and teachers.

As will be noted, this express emphasis on experience in the study of natural things is openly anti-Platonic. It reinforces the position stressed elsewhere by Borro in focusing upon those passages of Aristotle where Plato's mathematical approach is rejected. A strong anti-Platonic bent is also evident in other passages. Perhaps nowhere does it come out so openly as in the final *causa*. Here Borro brings forth especially two texts from Aristotle to show his position. The first is the famous text from the *Nicomachean Ethics*,[38] where Aristotle, despite his friendship with Plato and his followers ("the friends of the Ideas"), argues that such a love must not be allowed to stand in the way of his love of truth. The second is a text in Averroes' commentary on the *De coelo* where Plato is criticized for having fallen into error through his excessive love for his master (Socrates) and for geometry.[39] After citing these somewhat flimsy and out of context passages, which are hardly convincing regarding the point at issue, he goes on to draw the additional inference that if love can lead to such ignorance in philosophy, so too must hatred.

Further evidence of Borro's lack of sympathy for the Platonic approach—especially for the type of eclectic Platonism which developed in the Renaissance—is to be found in *causa* eight.[40] He clearly declares his opposition to the syncretic and eclectic tendency of many Renaissance Platonists from Ficino onward.[41] After citing a text where Averroes reproved Avicenna for adopting a conciliatory position between the *philosophi* and the *loquentes*,[42] he launches into a clear polemic against those who wish to combine the doctrines of Plato with those of Aristotle. Even though these syncretically oriented thinkers

---

[38] Book I, chapter 6, esp. 1096a10-18.

[39] Borro refers to text 61 of Book III of the *De coelo*, but the passage he claims to find does not occur in the Aristotelian text. What he seems to have in mind is Averroes' commentary, which reads in part as follows : "Et intendebat [sc. Aristoteles] quod Plato non intendebat facere sermonem falsum, sicut faciunt sophistae, sed accidit ita, quod fecit, sicut illi propter amorem magistri et amorem Geometriae et quia in suo tempore magnificabatur Geometria, credebant Geometrica esse principia rerum sensibilium." Aristoteles-Averroes, V, 223. This is not an isolated instance where Borro attributes to Aristotle the words of Averroes. It happens several times in the *Multae sunt nostrarum ignorationum causae*. Duhem's (III, 206) point about Borro's Averroism, though perhaps overstated and emotionally "loaded," has some element of truth.

[40] See Appendix, 475-76.

[41] For the basic literature on this, see my "Perennial Philosophy : from Agostino Steuco to Leibniz," *Journal of the History of Ideas* 27 (1966), 505-32.

[42] Aristoteles-Averroes, IV, 57.

draw material from several Greek commentators on Aristotle who attempted to combine Aristotelian and Platonic doctrine, Borro feels that such a synthesis cannot be effectively carried out. While they lived, he continues, Plato and Aristotle wished to be *discordes* and if they were to come back to life, they would laugh at the attempt of the Greek commentators ! Such an endeavor merely produces a strange admixture of doctrines, neither Academic nor Peripatetic. Those who attempt such a *concordia* are themselves deceived and contribute to the young being plunged into "the greatest ignorance of all things."[43] In this case one does not have to look far to determine the object of his attack. We know that a chair was established at Pisa in 1576, the incumbents of which were committed to a synthesis of Platonic and Aristotelian philosophy.[44] What is more, we know that one of Borro's chief rivals—one might say "enemies" with some justification—Francesco de' Vieri, the Younger (Il Verino Secondo),[45] was the first holder of the chair. Given (1) Borro's dislike for Verino and (2) his lack of sympathy for a *permistio doctrinarum*, it is highly likely that he had Verino speci-

---

[43] A similar attitude is expressed in *Del flusso* (1577), 36-37, which reads as follows : "Io no ho giurato ne di volere difendere a dritto, et a torto tutta la dottrina di Platone, ne volerlo accordare con Aristotile in quelle parti, nelle quali essi stessi, se ci vivessero, direbbono volere perpetua guerra, come molti altri bene spesso fanno; i quali sono tanto affettionati ad una setta di Filosofi, che anche contro ad ogni debito di ragione, et di dovere per amore, et perforza difendono quello, che fanno non si poter difendere a patto veruno ... Quindi ne nascano le monstrose dottrine, lontane da ogni sentimento humano : Quindi hanno principio et mezzo et fine gli odij, le inimicitie anche mortali, che a tutte l'hore si veggono infra i seguaci di due sette l'una all'altra contraria : Io per me non fui già mai tanto ostinato : Però quando mi pare, che o Platone o gli altri dalla dritta via si partino, non mi vergogno punto à lasciargli ne loro errori : come hora havete udito, che io ho fatto in questo."

[44] P. O. Kristeller, *Studies in Renaissance Thought and Letters* (Rome, 1956), 292-93.

[45] In addition to the reference in the preceding note see also E. Garin, *Storia della filosofia italiana* (Turin, 1966), 586-88, 610-11. Among Verino's works of a concordistic nature might be mentioned especially his *Vere conclusioni di Platone conformi alla dottrina cristiana ed a quella di Aristotile* (Florence, 1590). On the personal disputes between Borro and Verino see the references cited above in n. 11.

Also at Pisa after 1588 was Jacopo Mazzoni of Cesena, a close friend of Galileo much devoted to a syncretic approach to philosophy, who was Verino's successor in the chair mentioned above. Of his works might be mentioned especially *De triplici hominum vita, activa nempe, contemplativa, et religiosa methodi tres ...* (Cesena, 1577) and *In universam Platonis et Aristotelis philosophiam praeludia sive de comparatione Platonis et Aristotelis* (Venice, 1597). On Mazzoni see G. Rossi, "Jacopo Mazzoni e l'ecletticismo filosofico nel Rinascimento," *Rendiconti della R. Accademia dei Lincei, Classe di scienze morali, storiche e filologiche*, 5th ser., 2 (1893), 163-83.

fically in mind when rejecting the syncretic tendency of Renaissance Platonism.[46]

We cannot here go into all of the details of Borro's philosophical position and the disputes which marked his career, but several things of importance do emerge even from our brief analysis. First, we see that one of the most important teachers of Aristotelian philosophy at Pisa, during Galileo's time there[47] as a student, had little sympathy with the sort of eclectic Platonism he saw around him. Secondly, his antipathy for the Platonic tradition in general was particularly deep-seated with regard to the Platonic propensity to employ mathematics in the study of natural philosophy. Thirdly, he vigorously upheld the strong Aristotelian emphasis on the absolute necessity of long experience, if one is to be successful as a natural philosopher. Thus, in some ways, he represents the sort of traditional Aristotelian satirized by Galileo in his dialogues and in no way points in the direction of a mathematical approach to physics, employed so successfully a few years later by Galileo. There are, however, certain similarities between Borro and Galileo, but these must be investigated further and the discussion of them must wait for another occasion.

Appendix

The presumably unique copy of Borro's *Multae sunt nostrarum ignorationum causae* is contained in manuscript Vatican, Rossiano 1009, fols. 20-25. It is written on paper and bound with a fragmentary *Chronicle*, which apparently has no relation to Borro's treatise. In both relevant hand-written inventories of the Rossiana manuscripts[48] the author's name is written as "Hieronymus Borcius." When, in 1967, I came across the manuscript while searching for materials on Borro at the Vatican, I verified the fact that it should actually be assigned to Borro. The author's name, which is to be found at the

---

[46] On the other hand, he accepted the attempt of the Renaissance Platonists to trace the emergence of philosophical truth to pre-Greek times and to connect Greek philosophy with the *prisca theologia* of the ancient Near East. See for example the dedication letter in *De motu*, †2-A, as well as the one in *Del flusso* (1577), †2-†4ᵛ, which at one point (†2ᵛ) says : "... alle colonne di Mercurio Trismegisto, nelle quali, con lettere Hieroglifice, erano scritti i primi principii della Filosofia...."

[47] Galilei, XIX, 32-39.

[48] Aloysii Dichtl, *Codicum Rossianae Bybliothecae index alphabeti ordine digestus*, fol. 11 and *Bybl. Ross. Inventar*, vol. VI.

end of the treatise (fol. 25), should be read as 'Borrius.' In checking this "new discovery" in the *Iter Italicum*,[49] I found that Kristeller had already made the appropriate correction and had assigned the manuscript to Borro. The manuscript itself is neatly written on paper, perhaps by Borro himself, but as yet I have not been able to establish this with certainty. Of its *provenance*, nothing has been learned.[50] Moreover, no evidence, either internal or external, has been uncovered to help us in fixing the date of composition of the treatise.

In establishing the present edition, an attempt has been made to normalize the spelling by introducing the modern distinctions between u and v, i and j; "ę" is consistently expanded to "ae." Otherwise I have printed the text as it is, retaining the orthographical peculiarities. Punctuation has been altered for the sake of clarity and the numbering of the sections has been introduced in brackets to facilitate reference. Additions to the text which have been made for the sake of clarity are enclosed in pointed brackets. I see no need to identify the passages quoted and referred to in the text. Those from Aristotle are always clearly given by work, book, and *particula*, as Borro terms it. The only other writer quoted is Averroes and the precise references can always be easily found in the edition cited in n. 35.

Text

Multae sunt nostrarum ignorationum causae

Prima : ignorantia logicae.
Secunda : brevis et negligens in naturalibus exercitatio.
Tertia : bonorum doctorum et librorum negligentia.
Quarta : sophistarum subtilitas.
Quinta : varius defectus naturae.
Sexta : pessima consuetudo.
Septima : negligentia textuum
Octava : permistio doctrinarum.
Nona : imperitia.
Decima : amor et odium.
Undecima : nonnulli depravatos esse textus inter causas ignorationis redigunt, sed allucinantur, quippe textus mendosi parvo negocio restituuntur. Eam ob rem decem tantum causae sunt nostrae ignorationis.

---

[49] II, 471.

[50] The manuscript is not mentioned, for example, in C. Silva-Tarouca, "La Biblioteca Rossiana," *Civiltà Cattolica*, 18 febbraio 1922, 320-35.

[1] Prima est logicae ignoratio, de qua Aristoteles libro secundo divinorum particula decima quinta, ubi scripsit fieri nulla ratione posse, ut quis et scientiam et capessendae scientiae artem, viam ac 20v logicam et methodum simul addiscat; necesse igitur est, si ad / optatum addiscendi finem pervenire velimus, ut prius quo alium lapidem moveamus, hunc unum, qui ad artem, ordinem, logicam ac methodum pertinet, non tantum moveamus, sed promoveamus etiam : alioquin nec scientias nec artes addiscemus.

Longe absurdius erit addiscendi arte omni ex parte neglecta scientiam capessere velle. Ideo ab Aristotele saepenumero detestantur antiqui, non tantum, ut ignari illarum rerum de quibus sine logica disputabant, sed multo etiam magis, ut audaces ac temerarii, quibus in consilium erat de via eundem, viae terminum non inveniendum temerario abusu quaerere atque invenire audebant; necesse enim erat eos decipi, qui derelicta neglectaque addiscendi arte ad rem aliquam agnoscendam aggrediebantur.

[2] Secundam causam indicavit Aristoteles libro tertio de Coelo particula sexagesima prima, ubi rationem reddidit propter quam erravit Plato in naturalibus et est pauca et brevis exercitatio in illis, versebatur enim in mathematicis et ex illis illarumque principiis falso 21 rebatur demonstranda esse rerum natura / constantium principia, exercitatio enim mathematicarum disciplinarum in quibus semetipsum exercebat eundem induxit in maximum rerum natura constantium errorem; et sexto Ethicorum capite octavo scripsit Aristoteles fieri non posse ut adolescentes naturalium rerum scientiam consequantur prudentiamque assequantur, quod haec illorumque omnium cognitio usu et exercitatione constet; quo usu et qua exercitatione adolescentes non valent, quippe exercitationem et usum temporis diuturnitas faciat, quo qui brevi tempore et cum negligentia semetipsos in Philosophia exercent, eamdem minime addiscunt; et Aristoteles libro primo de ortu et interitu in Platonem et Democritum invehitur, quippe qui aliis in disciplinis occupati non accurate diligenterque naturalia considerarent, sed ad pauca quaedam respicientes facile sententiam ferrent.

Aristoteles septem et viginti annos discipulus extitit, nobis autem duos vel tres annos in perdiscendo ponere nimis longum videtur et 21v id parum temporis, / quod a nobis in perdiscendo ponitur, summa cum negligentia transigitur.

Hanc ob rem ab Averroe Avicenna carpitur libro tertio de Coelo commentatione sexagesima septima. "Paucitas," inquit, "exercitationis istius viri in naturalibus et confidentia in bono ingenio induxit ipsum in multos errores."

[3] Ex hoc libro tertia causa addi potest, quae ad sui ipsius confidentiam pertinet, in quem scopulum impingere non raro solent, qui ingenio valent, putant enim se suo Marte omnia discere posse cum nihil addiscant. Scripsit Aristoteles primo libro Posteriorum oportet addiscentem credere non tantum principiis aut omnibus aut quibusdam, sed et praeceptoribus bonis tamen aliis, qui nihil minus sciunt quam id quod docent, fides habenda non est. Aristoteles haec ad verbum scripsit libro secundo divinorum particula secunda si Timotheus non fuisset, magna musicae caruissemus, si vero Phrinis <non fuisset>, ne Timotheus quidem extitisset. Boni itaque praeceptores
f. 22 bonos discipulos faciunt. Magnus fuit / Theophrastus, quia magnum Aristotelem audivit. Magnus fuit Aristoteles quia[51] magni Platonis discipulus fuit magnusque fuit Plato, quia magnum Socratem sectari voluit.

Nec illorum ratio audienda est, qui dicunt, "ego novus tiro ad rem novam addiscendam aggredior; ille me doctior est, eam ob rem ab illo quantumvis parum doceri tamen possum."

Vera utique dicerentur, si doctor qui parum docet bona et vera etiam doceat; at falsa et mala docet, ideo qui discit et qui docet tempus frustra conterit dediscenda utique sunt, quae ab istis doctoribus addiscuntur.

[4] Huc pertinet bonorum librorum delectus sine quibus frustra laboratur. De omni subtilitate vel etiam Sophistica intelligendum est illud Aristotelis libro secundo divinorum particula decima sexta, dum dixit expectandas non esse in omnibus subtilitates mathematicas, sed prout rei natura postulat; et primo Ethicorum capite tertio, "est
f. 22v hominis eruditi / usuque periti subtilitatem requirere eatenus, quoad rei natura patiatur. Nihil enim interest utrum Mathematicum suadentem probes, an ab oratore necessariam rationem requiras."

[5] Varius defectus naturae est alia ignorationis causa, de qua ab Aristotele libro secundo divinorum particula quinta decima, dum dixit "alii quidem omnia accurate ac subtiliter dici volunt, alios limatum ac subtile dicendi genus offendit, quod illud assequi non possunt," et Aristoteles particula trigesima problematum, problemate primo dixit eos, qui in omnibus bonis artibus excelluerunt, fuisse melancolicos, temperate tamen, nam qui naturae modum excedunt, aut furiunt aut insaniunt.

---

[51] Cod. : qui.

Illi, in quibus pituita redundat, sunt quolibet stipite duriores et quolibet trunco stolidiores, ut nihil aut parum addiscere valeant.

[6] Alia causa est pessima consuetudo de qua / audiri debet illud Aristotelis libro secundo divinorum particula decima quarta, dum dixit, quanta vis sit consuetudinis, leges declarant, in quibus fabularum similia et puerilia plus valent quam cognitio et veritas propter consuetudinem unde qui primo addiscunt falsas doctrinas vix aut ne vix quidem veritatem secundo addiscere possunt.

Caveant quo sibi adolescentes a malis praeceptoribus et a malis libris, ne bona expectatio depravata doctorum et librorum falce secetur. De hac mala consuetudine, de naturae defectu deque brevi et negligenti exercitatione deque harum trium rerum maximo detrimento scripsit Averroes libro primo de Coelo commentatione vigesima secunda.

[7] De negligentia textuum scripsit Averroes tertio de anima commentatione trigesima contra Avicennam et contra semetipsum, dum dixit, "quod fecit istum hominem errare et nos etiam longo tempore fuit,[52] quia moderni dimittunt libros Aristotelis et considerant libros expositorum."/

Idem ego de me ipso dicere possum, qui in mea iuventute ad eundem scopulum alliseram, ad quem alii allidere consueverunt, sed postquam ad hanc ingravescentem aetatem proveni ad memetipsum reversus expositores tamque impostores dereliqui, et unum et solum Aristotelem ex unius et solius eiusdem Aristotelis locorum collationibus explanandum fore constitui.

[8] Permistio doctrinarum est alia nostrae ignorationis causa, propter quam ab Averroe Avicenna carpitur libro secundo de Phisico auditu particula vigesima secunda dum dixit, "via autem qua processit Avicenna in probando primum principium est via loquentium et sermo eius semper invenitur quasi medius inter Peripateticos et loquentes."

In eodem luto haerent fere omnes Graeci expositores, qui Aristotelis doctrinam cum Platonis doctrina permiscent et volunt ipsos fuisse concordes, qui dum vixerunt voluerunt esse discordes, et, si ambo ex inferis ad superos reverterentur, Graecos expositores riderent./

Ex illis nulla una doctrina nascitur, sed permistio quaedam doctrinarum quae non est Accademica [!] nec Peripatetica, unde allucinantur illi, qui hanc concordiam moliuntur, et in causa sunt cur adolescentes in maxima rerum omnium ignoratione versentur.

---

[52] The edition of Averroes, cited above in n. 35, has 'est' in this text (fol. 171).

[9] De peritia vel imperitia, quae est nona causa, audiri debet Aristoteles in hac litera dum dixit particula septuagesima prima veteres Philosophos a vero aberrasse et in viam non rectam deflexisse propter imperitiam; et libro primo de partibus animalium capite primo ex quo loco elicitur doctum perito minorem esse pro eo, quod omnis peritus est doctus multi autem sunt docti, qui non sunt periti, nam doctus est, qui scit per causam, ut scriptum est libro primo posteriorum, contingit non raro, ut qui per causam novit iudicio praeditus non sit et de rebus suis atque alienis praepostere iudicet; verum omnis qui iudicio est praeditus est doctus, nam iudicio praeditus est ille qui postquam rem intus et in cute novit, de ea integre iudicare potest. Est ergo peritus iudex rerum suarum et alienarum integer./

f. 24v Qui imperiti sunt id est qui carent iudicio, a scopo vero aberrant. Hoc iudicium diligenti exercitatione et diuturna auditione et continuata lectione bonorum authorum comparatur, unde falsa est illorum loquendi formula, qui, dum de medicis imperitis verba faciunt, dicunt. Hic est medicus usu peritus, qui in factitanda disciplina excellit, nihil tamen didicit. Nam qui nihil didicit, medicus non potest esse peritus, si vera sunt illa, quae ab Aristotele memoriae tradita fuerunt libro primo de partibus animalium capite primo.

[10] Decima causa est amor et odium. De amore scripsit Aristoteles libro primo Ethicorum capite sexto, dum de felicitate verba fecit et testatus [53] est quaestionem illam difficiles habere explicatus. Causa est quod "amici sint ii, qui Ideas induxerunt. Tamen aequum est veritatis retinendae causa sua, etiam decreta tollere philosophos praesertim et si utrique cari sunt; tamen praeclarum est pluris aestimare veritatem" etc.; et primo Coeli particula centesima prima scripsit

f. 25 Aristoteles arbitri et / non adversarii esse debent ii, qui diligenter quod verum est iudicando volunt invenire; et tertio Coeli particula sexagesima prima scripsit Aristoteles, amor magistri et geometriae induxerunt Platonem in rerum natura constantium gravissimam ignorationem.

Quod si amor tantam ignorationem in Philosophiam induxit [?], dubio procul non minorem odium invehere poterit.

Huius rei hodie testes sunt contrariae disciplinarum sectae, quae se invicem ultro citroque destruunt.

Hieronymus Borrius.

The Warburg Institute, University of London

---

[53] Cod. : textatus.

AN UNPUBLISHED *CONSILIUM* OF
JOHANNES SICHARDUS

GUIDO KISCH

Johannes Sichardus (1499-1552), a representative of humanistic jurisprudence, pupil and protégé of the famous jurist Ulrich Zasius and protagonist of the *mos gallicus* in its fight against the *mos italicus* at the University of Basel in the twenties of the sixteenth century, became an outstanding professor of law and a legal expert at the University of Tübingen where he lived and taught from 1535 until his death. His lectures on the *Codex Iustinianus* were published posthumously in two bulky volumes which appeared in 1565 in Basel. In addition to his academic activities he also served as a counselor in private lawsuits, particularly for the Dukes of Württemberg in their legal controversies mostly deriving from political affairs of which the so-called felony trial instituted against Duke Ulrich by King Ferdinand was the most outstanding. Fifty-three of his far more numerous legal opinions were published posthumously (Frankfurt, 1599). A considerable number of Sichardus' *consilia* still remain unpublished and therefore unknown in the State Archives of Stuttgart and in the University Library of Basel. One of them became known to this writer in connection with his studies on Sichardus as a legal historian.[1]

Professor Kristeller rightfully emphasizes the need for publication of manuscript source material of the sixteenth century : "We need much more research, that is, more monographic studies and more critical editions of rare or unpublished texts, before we can hope to agree on a satisfactory synthesis and interpretation of Renaissance thought." Obviously this also applies to the history of humanistic

---

[1] Guido Kisch, *Johannes Sichardus als Basler Rechtshistoriker*, Basler Studien zur Rechtswissenschaft, XXXIV (Basel, 1952); G. Kisch, *Die Anfänge der Juristischen Fakultät der Universität Basel 1459-1529*, Studien zur Geschichte der Wissenschaften in Basel, XV (Basel, 1962), 358 ff. (bibliography). A detailed historical explanation and juridical analysis of Sichardus' *consilium* as well as of his argumentation is offered with full documentation in G. Kisch, *Studien zur humanistischen Jurisprudenz* (Berlin and New York, 1972), 105-124.

jurisprudence. While publication of the many manuscript *consilia* of Sichardus cannot be expected in the near future, if at all, the presentation of a single interesting example seems appropriate in the context of this Festschrift.

The *consilium* reproduced here in its original wording deserves scholarly attention not only for its interesting legal content but also because it is written in the German language whereas almost all of Sichardus' legal opinions were written in Latin, as was customary in his tlme.

The manuscript deposited in the Stuttgart Hauptstaatsarchiv (A 56. B 8.6) is a rough draft hastily put down and therefore extremely difficult to decipher. It shows no references to Roman law which was at that time the valid common law in most of the national territories of which the Holy Roman Empire of the German Nation was composed. It is in the handwriting of and signed by Sichardus, and is dated by him November 2, 1548.

A twofold legal problem is involved. It was raised by the political and jurisdictional conditions then prevailing in the Duchy of Württemberg. According to old privileges granted to the Dukes by the Emperor, Jews were not allowed to settle, live, or carry on business within the borders of that small country situated in the South of Germany. Only an exceptional special permit, called *Geleitbrief*, to be issued at the discretion of the princely chancery would authorize a temporary sojourn. In January 1548, however, the Emperor granted to all Jews in his Reich the right to travel freely and carry on business safely on all highways and markets of the Empire. He even ordered all secular and ecclesiastical princes to protect the life and property of Jews exercising this prerogative.

The question arose whether the old privileges keeping Jews away from the territory of Württemberg had been abrogated by the issue of the new imperial law which was more liberal and favorable to the Jews, because it would be applicable to the whole Roman-German Empire.

Sichardus' decision denied such abrogation. The basis of his opinion was the fact that the new general imperial privilege did not include a *clausula derogatoria* explicitly abolishing all older privileges.

This reasoning of Sichardus seems to legal-historical judgment an unconvincing oversimplification. It does not do justice either to the wording or to the spirit of the Emperor's liberal general privilege of January 30, 1548.

Of even more interest is Sichardus' decision of the second legal question. A lawsuit which an unnamed Jew had legitimately brought before the imperial lawcourt at Rottweil was "avocated," *i. e.*, called away by the Duke of Württemberg to be tried at the princely tribunal in his residence in Stuttgart. Legally this was legitimate and the prince was entitled to withdraw that lawcase to his own lawcourt. His action necessitated an answer to the question whether the Jew had the right to stay on Württemberg territory without a special permit in order to attend to his interests in the lawsuit.

Sichardus argues thus : The Jew did not enter or does not wish to enter the princely territory by his own free will. Rather he was or is compelled to do so because of the "avocation" of his lawsuit before the princely court. Hence, he did not make himself punishable for having entered Württemberg. He even can rightfully claim a princely permit, a *Geleitbrief*, and the Duke is obligated to issue it.

From this legal opinion and its author's argumentation it is clear that Sichardus strictly adhered to the rules of law. Like his great contemporary Johannes Reuchlin, he did not allow his reasoning to be influenced and marred by extra-legal considerations or sentiments, and in this case of a Jew, by religious prejudice. This is remarkable indeed in a time when the popular feeling aroused by the Church generally turned against the Jews.

This *consilium*, like his numerous other legal opinions, testifies to the correctness of the characterization of Sichardus by one of his modern biographers : "Righteous, reliable and of moral integrity, judicious and considerate, free of any bias in secular as well as religious matters, able to weigh and evaluate all aspects of a problem, also to harmonize conflicting interests, Sichardus was entrusted with the solution of all kinds of problems involving great responsibility. He was always successful in solving them in an impartial and conscientious manner."

Text

Edel, ehrwirdig, ernvest, hochgebort, gunstig, gebittend hern ! Ewr V., Wurde und gunst sye myn willig dinst zuvor!

Eurs eur V. wurd und gunst vermog ains furstlichen bevelchs deshalb an mich jungst gesunnen hab ich alles inhalts vernommen und neben den fhall, der sich diser zeyt in der judschen remission zutregt, dises furstenthumbs Wirtenbergs und dan der juden fryhytten auch volgends ewer myner hern der furstlichen rhatten bedencken erwogen. Und wiewol dasselbig zerthylt und nit eynhellig gewest, so ist es doch dermassen gestelt, das ich es in synem fhall nit wuste zu verbessern.

Dan so sich uff disen tag begebe, das ein jud wolte im furstenthumb und sunderlich daren wandren, so hett ich gentzlich darfur, er muste darzu sonderlich geleyt und sicherheyt haben. Und werden inen die gemeyne fryheyten, so erstlich zue Regenspurg und dan wider dises furstenthumbs alte und special fryhytten uff verschynem rychstag zue Augspurg der Judenschaft sein gegeben worden, nit furtragen, dan die selbige der Juden genant fryhyten haben khein clausulam derogatoriam specialium precedentium privilegiorum. Aber hynwyder findt ich wol, das die special fryheytten, so dem furstenthumb sein vor vyl jaren geben worden, alle noturftige clausulas motus proprii... und darzu derogatorias habe aller gemyne und sondrliche p. 2 itziche und khunfftige satzungen, ordnungen / alt fryhyt anbedacht der judschn fryhytten, auch alles anders, das wyder dise fryhyt, begnadigung und gabe im gemynen oder sonderlich von romischen khysern erlangt, geordnet oder furgewendt mochte werden. Deshalb dunkt mich, obglych die kheyserliche Majestät, unser allergnedigster herr, die judischyt mit eynem gemynen privilegio begapt, also das sie furohin durch alle furstenthumb sicher mit iren lyben, haben und guttern wandren mogen, dass solchs verstanden worden von den furstenthumben, die nit darfur sonderlich und in specie von alter her gefryet. Wa aber ain furstenthumb zuvor darfur were in specie gefryet, wie das furstenthumb wirtenberg ist, das dise Judischet general fryhyt derwydr nichs wircken und vyl weniger dasselbig uffheben möge, und bleibt also dis furstenthumbs special alt fryhyt anbedacht dr judschen general nuw fryhyten in allen crefften und wird, wie weyt sich aber gemelt dises furstenthumb fryhyt streck, ... dan allain das wandren den juden verbotten, idest ne versentur in ducatu. Und ob damit auch ain schlichter durchzug inen den juden verbotten sein, ist von unnotten itzundt zue disputiren, und erfundt sich auch aus gemelts privilegii praefatione, quae plerumque causam finalem privilegii ostendit, erschynt.

Und ist uff diesen tag nit die frag, wie es soll mit den juden, so im furstenthumb vermög irer benempten fryheytten wandren wolten, gehalten werden, sonder so ain rechtliche juden handlung were von Rotwyl durch meynen gn.f. und h. avocirt, und das rotwylisch hoffgericht deferirte der avocation mit geburlicher remission, wie itzundt geschehen, und solchs die fryheytten und verträg vermogen. Ob

man dan in disem fhall den remittirten juden sicherung und gelyt
uff sein person zue und von dem rechten zu geben schuldig, oder ob
p. 3 es genug syhe, das man / am ehesten an syner stat als syne anwaldt
verglytte, und muste der jud daran hebig und benugig sein etc. Und
wie wol es uff bydt wese allerly bedencken hat, wie solichs myne h.
die furstliche rhate wol bedacht, so lass ich mir doch der hern rhatten
meynung gefhallen, die dahin geschlossen, das mein g.f.u.h. dem recht
nach schuldig seyhe, den juden für sein person zue und von dem rechten gnugsam zu verglytten. Den das vermag das gemyn recht, das
menglichem, er syhe Christ oder Jud, erlaubt ist, das er moge allent-
halb sicher und seyner gelegenheyt nach wandren. So nun dis furstenthumb wyder gemyne recht vor den juden gefreyet, also das sie one
verglyttens drynen nit sollen noch dorfen wandren, so muss volgen,
dass solche fryhytt musse eingezogen und restringirt werden; also
das es allein werdt verstanden von den juden, die freywillig und nach
irem gefhallen, idest voluntarie wolten in disem furstenthumb wandren,
das solchs inen verbotten, und das alsdan solchs ine verbotten werte.
Aber denjhenigen, so auss getrungner not uff anrufen meins g.f. und
h. und volgends iussu iudicis remittierten, musten im furstenthumb,
idest in loco remisso wandren, were mit disem privilegio nichs benom-
men. Ne secundum unum privilegium oponentur duo specialia, contra
ius idest, quod non est dicendum.

Es ist auch sonst dem rechten und billikhyt gemess, do so ain sache
werdt vor aynem gerichtstab abgefordert, und es volge daruff ein
remission, das dieselbig remission geschehe cum omnibus circumstantiis et qualitatibus, wie sie zuvor were angefengt. Nun ist aber zwischen
4 dem / juden selbs personlich und Hansen Kolblin die rechtvertigung
zu Rotwyl angefangt und getryben worden, eben die selbig ist uff
meins g.f. und h. avocation remittirt worden, so muss ja volgen, dass
wie der jud legitimam personam standi in iudicio zu Rotwyl gehept,
also muss er itzundt propter remissionem factam cum omnibus suis
circumstantiis, qualitatibus et appendicibus in furstenthumb auch
legitimam personam standi in iudicio nit von syner person wegen,
sonder propter remissionem petitam et obtentam. Et ideo iudicium,
quod nunc coram illustrissimi principis mei consiliariis Stutgardie
vel alibi in ducatu celebrabitur, vocabitur surrogatum iudicio Rot-
wylensi, quo casu ortum est, surrogatum debere sapere naturam et
conditionem surrogantis.

Ich hette auch darfur, so diser jud uff die geschehen remission
khains gelyts begert het und doch were der remission personlich noch-
khummen, im furstenthumb und vor der furstlichen cantzly erschy-

nen, er het nichts wyder des furstenthumbs fryhyt gehandlet, man mochte inen darumb vermog der fryhyt nit straffen. Diewyl aber auch der jud in sua et propria persona und zu Uberfluss, wie mich dunkt, ains glydes begert, khan mans ime mit fugen nit wol abschlagen und tregt dis sein beger so nit uff ime, das er andern zum exempell damit konte bekhomen, das der juden jungst ausgepracht privilegium gegen disem furstenthumb und des alte fryheytten.

Dis hab ich Ewer v. erw. und gunst uff derselben begern gutter meynung et salvo iudicio rectiore nit verhalten sollen, denen ich zu dienen nach allen mynem vermogen alzyt willig und bereyt bin. Datum 2. Novembr. An. (15)48. Ewer v., eerw. und gunst williger Joh. Sichardus.

University of Basel

THE LAST WILL OF A VENETIAN PATRICIAN (1489)

PATRICIA H. LABALME

On March 10, 1489, Bernardo Giustiniani, Venetian patrician, statesman, and man of letters, died at the age of eighty-one. Five days earlier, "sound in mind although weighed down by bodily infirmity," he had made his last will and testament. Disposing of his earthly goods, according to conscience and custom, he bequeathed at the same time to the historian a document of considerable interest. A man of wealth and prominence, belonging to one of the oldest Venetian families, famous, after his death, as the first able historian of his city's past, his final words, couched in the legal formulae and careful script of the notary, outline the possessions and preoccupations of an unusual human being.[1]

Yet Bernardo Giustiniani's will reveals more than the material, religious, and intellectual concerns of his life. It suggests much about the Venetian world he inhabited. His chosen executors included men of importance. His religious bequests are a partial guide to the monasteries and churches of fifteenth-century Venice. The division of his real estate outlines the property holdings and the industrial enterprise of a rich Venetian concerned for his family's future. Particularly interesting are the provisions he made for the manuscript of his *History of Venice*, his selection of scholars who were to edit it and supervise its publication. It was upon this work, appearing three years after his death, that his later reputation would rest, long after the ducats had been dissipated and the palazzi converted into civic offices and museums and the will itself folded, filed, executed and forgotten.

The will exists in two copies, not identical but alike in their principal dispositions. One is presently in the Archivio di Stato, part of the original notary's collection of wills, written on paper;[2] the other is among the "manuscripts of diverse provenance" in the Biblioteca

---

[1] For Bernardo Giustiniani's life, see Patricia H. Labalme, *Bernardo Giustiniani : a Venetian of the Quattrocento* (Rome, 1969).

[2] Archivio di Stato di Venezia, Notarile, Testamenti, b. 1203, n. 33.

Museo Correr, written on a large sheet of parchment.[3] Both are dated March 5. The notary, Nicolò Rosso, parish priest of the church of San Gemignano, is the same, as are the two witnesses, but whereas the two witnesses signed both copies, the notary signed only the Correr.[4] This and other dissimilarities argue that the Correr copy was the later, more elegant and refined copy, presented to the family, whereas the Archivio copy was only a notebook draft, preserved among the notary's own papers and, upon his death, given, as was customary, to the appropriate officials. What was inserted in the Archivio copy is fully entered into the lines of the parchment; what was cancelled in the Archivio copy does not appear in the Correr manuscript. Abbreviations of *et* in the first have been written out in the second. A passage added at the end in the Correr version affirms and increases the executors' powers of agency. And there are words written large in the Correr manuscript to indicate the various sections of the will: the first marking religious bequests, specific minor legacies to servants, friends, unwed granddaughters, and the payment or forgiveness of debts owed and outstanding; the next indicating the major division of property between son and grandchildren; a third preceding real estate arrangements; a fourth introducing the testator's literary bequest; a fifth accounting for what he might have neglected to mention. There are, in the margin of this same Correr copy, faint markings of A, B, and C, to distinguish certain sections, and there are lines drawn under the date, indiction, name and titles of the testator and his father, his parish and further on, half-way through the will, certain properties bequeathed to his son. It seems likely that the Correr parchment was that son's own copy in which he marked and from which he must have made his claims.[5]

---

[3] Biblioteca Museo Correr, MS. P. D. c. 751/83. The text of this will is published below.

[4] On Nicolò Rosso and the notarial office in Venice, see Andrea da Mosto, *L'Archivio di Stato di Venezia* (Rome, 1937), I, 226 and 232. The Church of San Gemignano as it existed in Bernardo's time is described by Francesco Sansovino, *Venetia citta nobilissima et singolare* (Venice, 1581), ff. 42-44ᵛ.

[5] Venetian testamentary practice at the time of Bernardo's death is clarified by a directive of the Maggior Consiglio dated December 2, 1474 (see Antonio Pinelli, *Parti Veneziani*, ff. 544-545ᵛ, an eighteenth-century collection of official documents in the Biblioteca Nazionale Marciana). Here three copies are mentioned. The first, which was the draft read aloud to the testator and accepted and signed by the witnesses, remained in the notary's possession as the "prothocolo"; a second and third (*cedulae*) were copied forthwith, signed by the witnesses, and one of these copies was sealed and deposited with

This same son, Lorenzo, the only survivor of his father's three sons, was the principal heir and among the most important executors of his father's estate. Lorenzo shared his legal task with his sister and brother-in-law, Orsa and Andrea Dandolo; his own wife Eleanora (originally of the Contarini family); his four nephews and Bernardo's grandsons by the deceased Marco : Luigi, Pietro, Leonardo, and Nicolò Giustiniani; and Bernardo's two brothers-in-law, Constantino and Francesco Priuli. Such family participation was normal. More selective were the two men named as executors who did not belong by blood or marriage to the Giustiniani. One was Ser Antonio Errizo (Ençio in the text), formerly a "gastaldo" or appellate judge of civil sentences attached to the Procurators *de citra* and thus a man experienced in the administration of legacies and judgments arising from disputes between heirs.[6] The other was Domenico Morosini, first named among the executors and himself a major figure in the political and cultural affairs of Venice.

Born in 1417 and ten years Bernardo's junior, Domenico Morosini led a life equally long and active.[7] He served in various governmental positions which must, at times, have coincided with those of Bernardo. Certainly he shared a similar interest in the cultural progress of the

---

the Cancelleria Inferiore, the other remaining with the notary, "acciò che con il protho-colo, et con l'una, et l'altra cedula l'autentico, che poi diè trar fuora, et roborare, se possa sempre conferire." The Archivio copy appears to be the drafted version, "il protho-colo." The Correr copy, to which was added then the final standard section giving larger powers of agency to the executors, because of its full complement of signatures, its marginal markings, its eventual arrival among the Correr collections, and because of its elegance, would appear to be a fourth copy belonging to the family. This would mean that the second and third copies, the Chancery copy, sealed as neither of the two extant copies are, and the extra notarial copy have disappeared. For additional information on Venetian testamentary law, see G. Pedrinelli, *Il notaio istruito nel suo ministero* (Venice, 1768).

[6] For this office, see da Mosto, I, 102-103, and G. Rezasco, *Dizionario del linguaggio italiano storico ed amministrativo* (Florence, 1881), 170-171.

[7] On the life of Domenico Morosini, see Claudio Finzi's edition of and introduction to the *De bene instituta re publica* (Milan, 1969), 1-56. It appears that by the time Bernardo's *History* was published in 1492, there was a family connection. Lorenzo's daughter Elisabetta had married a Morosini and Brognoli in his letter of dedication to Lorenzo refers to Domenico Morosini as "affine tuo." For the marriage see P. Litta, *Famiglie celebri italiane* (Milan, 1819-1902), "Giustiniani," Tavola X, and for the dedicatory letter see note 20. Morosini's material worth was noted by Marino Sanudo and provides some indication, lacking to us in Bernardo's case, of the wealth of a rich Venetian : "Era gran richo, lassò facultà per ducati 80 milia, contadi 20 milia e più." *I Diarii* (Venice, 1879-1903), VIII, 27.

city. We know that in 1487, Morosini as ducal councillor was instrumental in more than doubling the salary of Giovanni Calfurnio, professor of rhetoric in Padua, a man whom Bernardo was to propose, only two years later, as one of his literary executors. Morosini appears to have inspired a work *De verbo civiltate* dedicated to him by Matteo Colacio in 1486 and he himself, probably in the last years of the Quattrocento, wrote a treatise *De bene instituta re publica* which remained unfinished at the time of his death. Although Bernardo's correspondence contains no reference to Morosini, the families were close enough for Morosini to undertake a written description of the Blessed Lorenzo Giustiniani's miracles which would serve later in the process of sanctification of Bernardo's uncle.[8] Bernardo esteemed him sufficiently to constitute him along with his son Lorenzo and son-in-law Andrea Dandolo "the greater part" of his executors, and he gave him the power of final decision in the emendation of his *History of Venice*. A man of stature, his authority must have helped to validate Bernardo's every intention for the disposing of his last remains and the distribution of his wordly goods.

Bernardo's first concern in his will was his place of burial. He chose not the church on the Lido where his father lay, but the Patriarchal Church of San Pietro di Castello where his holy uncle had been buried thirty years before. He arranged for a marble tomb and composed its inscription : "Bernardus Iustinianus Leonardi procuratoris filius Beati Laurentii patriarche nepos miles orator et procurator"; and he left instructions and funds for a more suitable and ornate tomb for his uncle than that which had previously existed. At the same time, he contributed to the endowment of a benefice, established by his uncle's will but still inoperative because of the failure of the Venetian Camera degli Imprestiti regularly to meet its obligations : "And because the Blessed Lorenzo Giustiniani, my uncle, established with his ducats a *mansionaria* in the cathedral church at the altar of San Michele for masses to be celebrated in perpetuity, as may be found in his will, and because due to the failure of the Camera the money was not wholly forthcoming, I therefore will and ordain that what is lacking should be supplied to the sum of thirty ducats every year." This money was to come from the profits of Bernardo's soap workshop or from his own income from investments in the Monte Vecchio.[9]

---

[8] The *Miracula B. Laurentii Iustiniani Venetiarum patriarchae* are discussed by Finzi, 7, and E. A. Cicogna, *Delle inscrizioni veneziane*, II (Venice, 1827), 96.

[9] The income from the soap workshop is called "refusuris saponorum." J. F.

What was this soap workshop which is mentioned twice in Bernardo's will but nowhere else in his writings? Later in the will he refers to it as an *apotheca saponarie* and *fabrica*, attached to his house in San Fantin. He must have owned one of the many small domestic soap workshops which, by the fifteenth century, provided a major product for Venice's export trade and which, only a few months after Bernardo's death, were to be protected by a statute forbidding production outside the city in the Terra Ferma.[10] The industry depended on the arrival of soda, in the form of ashes from Egypt and Syria obtained by burning plants rich in alkaline substance, and oil from Apulia, and it flourished until the seventeenth century, when the difficulty of obtaining these necessary ingredients by sea encouraged the rise of competition elsewhere.[11] But at the time of Bernardo's death, revenue from this source was still certain enough to provide prayers for his uncle "in perpetuity" and on behalf of Bernardo's own soul, *pro anima mea*.

The benefice established for his uncle was followed, in the will, by a long list of bequests *pro anima mea*. There were thirty-five in all, sometimes in the form of a forgiveness of debt, sometimes with words specifying the relationship of a particular church or *scuola* to Bernardo and his family. The largest bequest went to the Monastery of Santa Croce "de scopulo" on the Giudecca and consisted of 1,000 ducats in shares of the Monte Nuovo to be given within one month of Bernardo's death.[12] It was to this monastery that three of Bernardo's daughters had gone as nuns, bringing with them already a considerable

---

Niermeyer defines "refusio" as a restitution or refund (*Media Latinitatis Lexicon Minus*) and Rezasco defines "refusura" as a "pagamento d'Imposta anticipato." A *mansionaria* was an endowment which supported a chapelry.

[10] "Per la parte 1489, 9 ottobre ... fu vietato la fabbrica dei savoni fuori della Dominante, stante la floridezza nella quale all'hora si atrovava." The law is quoted by Domenico Sella, *Commerci e industrie a Venezia nel secolo XVII* (Venice, 1961), 132. See also Gino Luzzatto, *Storia economica di Venezia dall'XI al XVI secolo* (Venice, 1961), 187-88, 197, and F. Lane, *Venice and History* (Baltimore, 1966), 261.

[11] Sella, 80. On Venetian soapmaking, see F. Lane, *Venice : A Maritime Republic* (Baltimore, 1973), 160.

[12] This forced loan for the funded public debt had been established in April of 1482 at a time when the Monte Vecchio was many years in arrears with its interest payments. See G. Luzzatto, *Il debito pubblico della Repubblica di Venezia dagli ultimi decenni del XII secolo alla fine del XV* (Milan, 1963), 229-65; Finzi, 40, n. 122. Gino Luzzatto in *Studi di storia economica Veneziana* (Padua, 1954), 169-70, has provided figures for similar bequests of shares in the public debt made by Girolamo Querini in 1457.

sum of money as dowries for their spiritual marriages.[13] And it was in this monastery that the Blessed Eufemia Giustiniani had lived and had died, two years prior to the will. One can only speculate on her relationship to Bernardo, but it is possible that she was his sister. Bernardo's exeptional generosity to this foundation argues the closest of ties.[14] It also seems possible that the current abbess of Santa Croce was one of his daughters, for to the abbess' care and accountancy were committed all the other pious bequests, amounting to about five hundred ducats, that they might be more swiftly fulfilled and distributed.

Other churches received lesser amounts. The Monastery of San

---

[13] A. Stella, *Bernardi Iustiniani Patritii Veneti Senatoris, Equestris, Procuratoriique ordinis viri ampliss[imi] Vita* (Venice, 1553), f. 10ᵛ.

[14] Litta, *Famiglie*, "Giustiniani," Tavola X, suggests that Eufemia was Bernardo's sister, explaining the uncertainty surrounding her as due to a Venetian indifference to cloistered females : "I veneziani erano si rigorosi nel loro oligarchico isolamento, che non si curavano di conservar memoria delle donne passate ne' chiostri." Da Mosto, II, 129, records the same relationship. On the history of the Church of Santa Croce see Flaminio Corner, *Notizie storiche delle chiese e monasteri di Venezia e di Torcello tratte dalle chiese veneziane e torcellane illustrate* (Padua, 1758), 534-544; da Mosto, II, 129, "Archivi degli istituti religiosi"; and Giulio Lorenzetti, *Venezia e il suo estuario* (Rome, 1956), 757. Earlier members of the Giustiniani family had been associated with many of the churches mentioned in this will, but the proof that Santa Croce on the Giudecca had a special connection with the family lies in its archives which contain a collection of Giustiniani documents, mostly property deeds and wills dating from the fifteenth and sixteenth centuries (Archivio di Stato di Venezia, Santa Croce alla Giudecca, Busta 6). Particularly interesting among this collection are nos. 338 and 339, two very partial copies of Bernardo's will, one of which is in Nicolò Rosso's hand (no. 339), an account of that will's pious bequests probably kept by the abbess as Bernardo instructed (see below), a series of notes sent the abbess by Bernardo's son Lorenzo and his grandsons Leonardo and Luigi concerning the writings of Bernardo and his father Leonardo, the distribution of legacies to individuals and institutions named in the will, and payments for the work done on the marble altar in San Pietro di Castello. One of the notes from Lorenzo dated August 28, 1490, requests thirty ducats "per conto di castelo" and the abbess' prayers on behalf of her relative ("cugnia") : "confesso le forze non son da tanto, che'l non basteria diexe, non che eser solo." But the specific problem Lorenzo faced is not made clear. Another note asks for a disbursement of ten ducats "da dar a maestro Zorzi che è sta' soprastante a Castel dei lavorieri fatti." The marble tomb, not yet visible to Sanudo in 1493 when he began his *Vite dei Dogi* (ed. Monticolo, *RIS*, Città di Castello, 1900), 76, was completed by the time of Sansovino's *Venetia citta nobilissima* (1581) when an "oratorio del Beato Lorenzo Giustiniano" existed with altar, chapel, and marble statue, containing also Bernardo's tomb, inscribed as he had instructed (f. 5ᵛ). One sees here how the grandeur of family monuments was already of considerable importance in the late fifteenth century.

Domenico di Castello was to have sixty ducats, the Scuola Santa Maria di Carità in Padua fifty ducats. Several foundations received thirty ducats, the great majority only five ducats. A number of charities caring for the poor received bequests of ten to fifty ducats, including the "poveri carceratis," the indigent of the prisons, perhaps debtors for whom such charity was the only means of recourse.[15] What proportion of the estate such bequests represented is hard to estimate, but, for all the devotion they indicate, it is doubtful that they signified, as according to St. Augustine they should, a share equal to that bestowed on every heir, or even the tenth part as seems to have been customary a century earlier.[16]

Following the religious bequests came the gifts to servants, artisans, and friends, each individually named and some distinguished by receiving their legacies "in signum amoris." Then there was allowance for a granddaughter's dowry, the sum to be the same as Bernardo had given previously for the marriage of another granddaughter. He stipulated that if this girl Cecilia should die before her marriage, then her oldest sister should receive it, and so successively; if all the sisters should die, then the sum, never mentioned, was to be divided equally among her brothers. A debt of fifty ducats, borrowed towards a dowry for Maria Dandolo, another granddaughter, and still owed Bernardo by his son-in-law, Andrea Dandolo, was to be forgiven *in signum dilectionis*.[17] A sentence authorized the estate's repayment of monies owed "for uncertain matters," matters which the testator may have neglected and which he wanted settled before the major division of his goods. And then he proceeded to that major division,

---

[15] Brian Pullan, "The Relief of Prisoners in Sixteenth-Century Venice," *Studi Veneziani* 10 (1968), 221-29.

[16] Enrico Besta in *Le successioni nella storia del diritto italiano* (Milan, 1961), 119-20, cites St. Augustine, Sermo 86, cap. 11, nr. 13 (Migne, *PL*, XXXVIII, col. 529) : "Fac locum Christo cum filiis tuis, accedat familiae tuae Dominus tuus... Duos filios habes, tertium illum computa; tres habes, quartus numeretur; quintum habes, sextus dicetur; decem habes, undecimus sit." For the tenth part given by Bernardo's grandfather, amounting to 300 ducats, see below. Bernardo's religious bequests totalled 1532 ducats.

[17] It would seem that Andrea Dandolo's debt had been largely paid off, for the entire dowry towards which Bernardo had contributed must have been much greater. Dowries in Venice were, by this time, reaching such proportions (5,000 to 10,000 ducats) that in 1505 a legal limit of 3000 ducats was set. See F. Lane, "Naval actions and fleet organization" in *Renaissance Venice*, ed. J. R. Hale (London, 1973), 166 and G. Priuli, *I Diarii*, R. I. S, XXIV, Part 3, II, 392-93.

marked by a faint "B" in the margin of the Correr parchment, the most significant section of the will :

> Furthermore, I leave all my goods, movable and immovable, to be divided equally between the aforesaid Lorenzo Giustiniani, my son and executor, and Luigi, Pietro, Leonardo, and Nicolò Giustiniani, my grandsons and executors, ordaining that one part belong to the aforesaid Lorenzo Giustiniani, my son and executor, and the other part belong to Luigi, Pietro, Leonardo, and Nicolò, my grandsons and executors. I wish, moreover, that Lorenzo Giustiniani... may, in life as in death, dispose of his share in whatever way he might wish or that it should please him. However, my grandsons may not alienate any portion of the aforesaid goods bequeathed by me, but in the event of any heir's death, the portion of the deceased should go to the living heirs as long as the line shall last... and should the line of the aforesaid grandsons die out, those goods should go to the heirs of the aforesaid Lorenzo Giustiniani, if any remain... If, however, no heirs of the aforesaid Lorenzo Giustiniani remain, then the Lord Procurators of San Marco should sell those goods and dispense the proceeds of the sale *pro anima mea*.

So the family wealth was to be protected and preserved. Of the grandsons by Marco, only Luigi's line would survive through the sixteenth century, dying out in 1601. But Lorenzo's line survived his father's death by three hundred years, the last direct heir dying in 1792, only a few years before Napoleon's destruction of the Venetian Republic. To Lorenzo also went the important real estate properties, to be distributed before the division of goods, the home at San Fantin (with soap storehouse and workshop) and the home in Murano with its gardens and outbuildings, to go from oldest son to oldest son, "so that both house and garden may be maintained more elegantly," because these had been committed to Bernardo by his father Leonardo, "who greatly loved that home." In compensation, the grandsons received the "great house" built on the Grand Canal, unless Lorenzo preferred to exchange with them his house in San Fantin for this property; and in compensation for the Murano property the grandsons were to receive four other houses near the great house on the Grand Canal together with a boat-shed. These four houses and boat-shed were to be appraised "by common friends" and if found to be worth less than one thousand ducats, Lorenzo was to make good the difference in cash. No heir, at the risk of forfeiting his share, was in any way to infringe upon these arrangements.[18]

---

[18] The Giustiniani had been associated with property in San Moisè since the early fourteenth century, although the "great house" is referred to in the will as newly built, "novam positam," on the Grand Canal. G. Fontana in his *Venezia Monumentale* : *i*

Having divided and disposed of his liquid capital and his property, Bernardo turned to that which he had specially treasured in his later years, his work on the *History of Venice*. He had already much revised the work, as the Cicogna manuscript bears witness,[19] and in his will he spoke of having given his *Historia* "a final polish." He thought, nevertheless, that it would require an editor's touch, and so he appointed Benedetto Brognoli da Legnano as his principal editor who together with another (whom he hoped would be Giovanni Calfurnio of Padua) should examine and emend the work as necessary, with Domenico Morosini to arbitrate any disputes which might arise between the two.

His choice of editor was fortunate. Benedetto Brognoli was well-known as a scholar and widely experienced as an editor of the classics, having seen many works of Cicero through the press as well as the writings of contemporaries such as Giorgio da Trebisonda, the printing of whose *Rettorica* Brognoli had supervised in 1472.[20] A teacher of grammar, rhetoric, and philosophy in Venice for over forty years, he was honored at his death in 1502 with an oration, a tomb in the Church of the Frari, and an inscribed monument, still visible today.

Palazzi (Venice, 1967), 237, mentions a document stating that in 1474 the mason, Master Paolo da Bergamo, acquired stones and little columns for the restoration of the palazzo, at that time the property of Franceso Giustiniani, first cousin of Leonardo, Bernardo's father. There is also a document among the Commissarie of the Procuratori di San Marco, Citra, 115 (Archivio di Stato di Venezia), listing expenses for the restoration of the Casa Grande in 1477, still in Francesco's possession. When Bernardo acquired the palazzo is not certain, but a property deed of 1485 in the Archives of Santa Croce (Busta 6, no. 348) and the record of a lawsuit brought by Bernardo against Francesco's will in 1486 (Procuratori di San Marco, Citra, 115, no. 14) indicate that these years mark the date of Bernardo's claim and imminent possession. Lorenzo, Bernardo's son, evidently exercised his option, since in 1506 Priuli records that he was rebuilding "il palazzo che al presente si vede a S. Moisè dietro la chiesa sopra il Canal Grande, antiche habitazioni de' suoi maggiori" (Giuseppe Tassini, *Alcuni palazzi ed antichi edifici di Venezia* [Venice, 1879], 206-207). The Murano house is now the Museo Vetrario di Murano. Both this country home and the "great house" were labelled "astacio" indicating that they were "abitazione del padrone, la casa padronale o domenicale" (Rezasco, "stazio").

[19] The Cicogna MS. 1809, now in the Biblioteca Museo Correr, contains many additions, corrections, and cancellations, some of which are undoubtedly the author's.

[20] On Benedetto Brognoli, see G. Mazzuchelli, *Gli scrittori d'Italia*, II (Brescia, 1753-63), 2134-36, and Bruno Nardi, "Letteratura e cultura veneziana del Quattrocento," in *La Civiltà veneziana del Quattrocento* (Florence, 1957), 120 and 142, n. 53. For Brognoli's connection with Giorgio da Trebisonda, see G. Castellani, "Giorgio da Trebisonda, maestro di eloquenza a Vicenza e a Venezia," *Nuovo Archivio Veneto* 11 (1896), part 1, 138.

This erudite man found little to change in Bernardo's history, as he wrote in a dedicatory letter to Bernardo's son, Lorenzo.[21] Even those narrative descriptions of the Goths and Lombards, which Bernardo himself had recognized as perhaps too lengthy, Brognoli left essentially untouched. And in effect the work was published within four years of Bernardo's death, soon earning interest and acclaim.

What part was played by the second editor, Calfurnio of Padua, is hard to say. He was also an able scholar, originally from Bergamo, whose abilities as a teacher of rhetoric so commended him to the Venetian authorities that his salary at Padua was raised from to 100 fiorini in 1487 and to 120 fiorini by 1500. He, too, had edited Latin authors for the press, adding commentaries to the works of Terence, Vergil, and Ovid. But except for his appearance in Bernardo's testament, there is no indication that he actually participated in the publication of Bernardo's *History*.[22] Nor is there much likelihood that Domenico Morosini's arbitration between the two scholars was ever necessary. The historical and literary problems which had presented themselves so forcibly to Bernardo as he wrote must have seemed minor to his editor, not worth learned argument or academic consultation.

Two further sections concluded the will. One was a restatement of the division between son and grandsons of all "present and future goods," including whatever was left unordered and undescribed, with the same distinction between Lorenzo's freedom of action and the limitations placed on what the grandsons might do. But here a further division was made among the grandsons : Luigi and Pietro could do what they pleased, but Leonardo, while he himself could sail and traffic freely with his goods, could not give his share to others to trade for him, and the same restriction would apply to the youngest brother Nicolò when he reached the age of eighteen.[23]

---

[21] "Praeter paucula quaedam quae vel rudia vel inchoata relicta fuerant, quibus manum imposuimus extremam, nihil prorsus reperri, quod ut in opera cuius auctor prius extinctus esset, quam ederetur non magnopere probandum esse censerem." The letter was printed with the work itself in Venice in 1493 : Bernardo Giustiniani, *De origine urbis Venetiarum rebusque eius ab ipsa ad quadringentesimum usque annum gestis Historia*, A2-A4.

[22] For Calfurnio see Vittorio Cian, "Un umanista bergamesco del rinascimento, Giovanni Calfurnio," *Archivio Storico Lombardo*, 4th ser., 37 (1916), 221-48. Finzi (8, n. 27) cites the decision of the Venetian Senate in 1487 to raise the salary of Calfurnio from 40 to 100 fiorini.

[23] Such precautions show Bernardo's care to have his grandchildren experienced

The last passage in the will affirmed the powers of the executors to settle debts, make agreements, ask for receipts from debtors, establish power of attorney, appear in court and swear upon the soul of the testator, as he himself might do were he still alive. A curse and monetary fine were placed on any who dared to violate this will. So devised, the document was ratified by the signatures of the witnesses and the notary and entrusted to its executors and the legal processes of the city.

One hundred years earlier, another Bernardo Giustiniani, who was grandfather to the later one, wrote a will which provides significant contrast. That fourteenth-century Bernardo had faced an untimely death during a visit to Chioggia. He had written his own will in that city and given the Italian text to a notary who introduced it and concluded it with the customary Latin formulae and had it witnessed by three other men.[24] In this will of 1388, the religious bequest of 300 ducats is made without further specification, simply as a "dreto diexemo per anima mia." 400 ducats went to his wife, still young, her third child not yet born. This would be Leonardo, father of the later Bernardo. Servants were remembered with ten, twenty, and fifty ducats; one bondsman was to be freed after five more years of service. The estate was to be divided between his sons, and should his wife be pregnant with a daughter, a suitable dowry was to be provided for her. His sons, upon reaching the age of eighteen, were each to be given 1000 ducats "per merchadezar," and when they were twenty should become their own masters if that should seem proper to the executors. There were a number of family loans and debts to be regulated, assets to be disposed of, relatives to be provided for. So much was in the vernacular. Then, in Latin, there were bestowed upon the executors the same full powers of acting on behalf of the testator, and a similar curse called upon any who violated the will plus the identical fine of five pounds of gold.

---

in commercial affairs, mindful perhaps of the many young men in this time who sought to make their fortunes otherwise, in political careers or Terra Ferma investments, precautions which his grandfather, a century earlier, did not find necessary (see below).

[24] The will, dated October 8, 1388, was published by M. Dazzi in the *Archivio Veneto* 15 (1934), 312-19, along with other "Documenti su Leonardo Giustinian." This fourteenth-century Bernardo did not die until a few years after he made his will, since he mentions only three children (two born, one perhaps *in utero*) and his grandson records in his *Vita Beati Laurentii* that his grandmother Quirina was left with five children to raise after her husband died "iuvenili aetate" (*Acta sanctorum*, I [Antwerp, 1643], 552).

No real estate was specified, nor was there any literary work to provide for. Here was a man contemplating death in the very midst of an active commercial career, with his children not even fully born. What was potential for him appears realized in his fifteenth-century namesake who lived out his full measure of years and gave to his final dispositions more order and more definition. Long after 1489, the family would survive and flourish. There would be other Giustiniani of prominence and power in later centuries. But one catches here, in 1489, a clear portrait of an unusual member of this line, glimpsing in such concrete and formalized arrangements a particular human being in the final allotment of his material substance, in order to promote the spiritual health of his soul, the publication of his *History* in which his city's destiny was magnified, and the honor, progression, and profit of his patrician descendants.

Text

In nomine dei eterni amen. Anno ab incarnatione domini nostri Iesu christi Millesimo quadrigentesimo octuagesimo nono, mensis marcii, die quinto, Inditione septima Rivoalti.[25]

Solicite unusquisque vivere debet et Iuxta salomonis dictum sua semper novissima cogitare ne in caute occumbat et sua bona indisposita derelinquat, Quapropter Ego Bernardus Iustinianus procurator miles et orator filius quondam magnifici domini leonardi procuratoris de ultra de confinio sancti geminiani dei gratia sanus mente licet infirmitate corporea sim pregravatus cogitans quod premissum est et nolens abintestato decedere sed de bonis meis dum mihi facultas suppetit condere testamentum et anime mee saluti providere desiderans, Accersito ad me presbitero nicolao rubeo ecclesie sancti geminiani plebano et venetiarum notario Ipsum diligenter rogavi ut hoc meum ultimum scriberet testamentum pariter et compleret cum clausulis et additionibus consuetis et opportunis salvis semper statutis consiliis ordinibus et consuetudinibus communis Venetiarum. In quo quidem meo testamento constituo et esse volo meos fidei commissarios et huius mee ultime voluntatis exequtores Magnificum

---

[25] The text of the will is given as found in the Biblioteca Museo Correr manuscript. Abbreviations have been written out and the use of u/v and i/j follows modern typographical conventions. Punctuation and paragraphing have been added for clarity.

dominum dominicum maureçenum quondam domini petri Magnificos dominos constantinum et franciscum de priolis quondam magnifici domini Ioannis olim procuratoris cognatos meos dilectissimos dominum andream dandulo generum meum amantissimum dominam ursiam dandulo uxorem predicti domini andree filiam meam amantissimam Laurentium Justinianum filium meum amantissimum dominam helenam Iustiniano nurum meam amantissimam Aluisium petrum leonardum et nicolaum Iustiniano fratres et filios quondam marci Iustiniano nepotes meos amantissimos et Ser Antonium ençio olim magnificorum dominorum procuratorum de citra gastaldionem amicum meum carissimum qui omnes seu eorum maior pars post mei obitum adimplere facere et exequtioni mandare teneantur sive teneatur declarando illam esse maiorem partem inqua erit voluntas Magnifici domini dominici maureçeno domini andree dandulo generi mei et Laurentii Iustiniani amantissimi filii mei.

In primis namque recomendans animam meam creatori altissimo ordino corpus meum sepeliendum in ecclesia sancti petri de castello cohopertum sepultura marmorea convenienter in terra posita inter altare sancti michaelis et sepulcrum beati laurentii Iustiniani olim patriarche venetiarum et patrui mei colendissimi. Inqua sepultura marmorea volo me sculpiri debere in hec verba Bernardus Iustinianus leonardi procuratoris filius beati Laurentii patriarche nepos miles orator et procurator. Et quoniam illud altare sancti michaelis in predicta ecclesia sancti petri de castello positum non est bene ornatum pro ut de Iure deberet et pro simili sepulcrum beati laurentii Iustiniani volo quod de bonis meis sint de novo constructa et exornata marmoribus et picturis condecentibus ita quod ille locus pulcer et ornatus haberi possit.

Item volo ad sepulturam meam capitulum sancti marci cui dari volo pro ut moris est. Item volo quod structura seu laborerium suprascriptum ordinetur et compleatur per magnificum dominum dominicum maureçeno et laurentium Iustinianum commissarios meos suprascriptos et si aliquis eorum decederet antequam laborerium predictum fuisset expletum quod deus advertat, tunc volo quod loco decedentis sit et esse debeat dominus andreas dandulo suprascriptus commissarius meus.

Item quia beatus laurentius Iustinianus patruus meus dimissit unam mansionariam in ecclesia cathedrali ad altare sancti michaelis celebrandam in perpetuum de ducatis pro ut in eius testamento apparet et propter defectum camere ipsi denarii totaliter exigi non possunt,

Ideo volo et ordino quod illud quod deficeret ad sumam ducatorum triginta omni anno solvendam dicto masionario [*sic*] sicut ipse voluit de bonis meis videlicet refusuris saponorum seu montis veteris suppleatur et adiungetur tantum quod ascendat ad sumam ducatorum triginta omni anno pro dicta mansionaria pro anima mea. Item dimicto capitulo sancti petri de castello ducatos tres omni anno ut ipsi celebrare debeant unum anniversarium pro anima mea. Item dimicto monasterio sancte crucis de scopulo a Iudaica ducatos mile in prestitorum montis novi quos dari volo infra terminum unius mensis post mei obitum. Item dimicto suprascripto monasterio sante crucis ducatos tres omni anno in perpetuum ut moniales teneantur facere omni anno unum anniversarium pro anima mea. Item quia habere debeo a monasterio sancte marie ab angelis de muriano pro ut apparet in libris meis et domus hec decha Iustiniano cum maioribus meis habuerit sumam devotionem monasterio predicto et expendiderit temporibus elapsis maiorem sumam denariorum pro fabrica ipsius monasterii, Ideo ego volo quicquid dictum monasterium apparebit debitor totum libere dono ipsi monasterio pro eius fabrica ut ipse moniales teneantur orare pro anima mea. Item dimicto scole sancte marie de caritate de padua ducatos quingentos prodium imprestitorum montis veteris ut orent deum pro anima mea et defunctorum meorum. Ipsi et enim scole multum debeo pro caritate quam erga me declaraverunt. Item dimicto monasterio sancti dominici de castello ducatos sexaginta auri ut celebrent et orent pro anima mea. Item dimicto monasterio sancti petri Martiris de Muriano ducatos quadraginta auri ut celebrent et orent pro anima mea. Item dimicto pauperibus Iesuatis ducatos triginta auri ut orent pro anima mea. Item dimicto monasterio sancti andree de littore ducatos triginta auri ut celebrent pro anima mea. Item dimicto monasterio sancti Iacobi a Iudaica ordinis servorum ducatos decem ut celebrent pro anima mea. Item dimicto monasterio sancti sebastiani ducatos decem ut celebrent pro anima mea. Item dimicto monasterio sancti bernardi de muriano ducatos quinque auri ut moniales orent pro anima mea. Item dimicto monasterio sancti Iacobi de muriano ducatos sex auri ut moniales orent pro anima mea. Item dimicto monasterio sancti mathie de muriano ducatos quinque auri ut celebrent pro anima mea. Item dimicto monasterio monasterio[*sic*] sancti michaelis de muriano ducatos quinque auri ut celebrent pro anima mea. Item dimicto monasterio corporis christi ducatos quinque auri ut moniales orent pro anima mea. Item dimicto monasterio sancte catherine asaccis ducatos sex auri ut moniales orent pro anima mea. Item dimicto monasterio anuntiate ducatos viginti auri ut moniales orent pro anima mea. Item dimicto monasterio sancti francisci astigmatibus apud sanctam crucem de venetiis ducatos decem auri ut moniales orent pro anima mea. Item dimicto monasterio sancti ludovici ducatos quinque auri ut moniales orent pro anima mea. Item dimicto monasterio sancte marie ab orto ordinis sancti georgii in alega ducatos decem auri ut celebrent pro anima mea. Item dimicto monasterio sancti andree de çirada ducatos quinque auri ut moniales orent pro anima mea. Item dimicto monasterio sancti antonii ducatos quinque ut celebrent pro anima mea. Item dimicto monasterio sancti servuli ducatos quinque auri ut moniales orent pro anima mea. Item dimicto monasterio sanctorum cosme et damiani ducatos quinque ut moniales orent pro anima mea. Item dimicto monasterio spiritus sancti ducatos quinque ut moniales orent pro anima mea. Item dimicto monasterio sante marie de gratia ducatos quinque ut celebrent pro anima mea. Item dimicto capitulo sancti geminiani ducatos quinque omni anno imperpetuum ut celebrent pro anima mea. Item dimicto capitulo sancti moisi ducatos quinque omni anno in perpetuum ut celebrent pro anima mea. Item dimicto capitulo sancti fantini ducatos quinque omni anno imperpetuum ut celebrent pro anima mea. Item dimicto ecclesie sancti fantini pro resto omnium rationum ducatos quadraginta quatuor auri pro anima mea. Item dimicto pauperibus sancti geminiani ducatos viginti auri pro anima mea. Item dimicto pauperibus sancti moysi ducatos viginti auri pro anima mea. Item dimicto pauperibus sancti fantini ducatos decem auri pro anima mea. Item dimicto pauperibus carceratis ductos quinquaginta auri pro anima mea.

Item dimicto sebastiano servitori meo ducatos triginta quinque auri pro suo fideli servire. Item dimicto ludovico straçarolo servitori meo ducatos duodecim auri. Item dimicto magdalene furlane ducatos decem auri pro suo psalario et legato semel tantum. Item dimicto victori de Ioane servitori meo ducatos vigintiquinque auri in signum amoris. Item dimicto hieronimo bondi servitori meo ducatos vigintiquinque auri in signum amoris. Item dimicto presbitero philippo firmano canonico venetiarum ducatos sex ut oret pro anima mea. Item dimicto helene famule ducatos quatuor auri. Item dimicto capellanis et clerico sancte crucis a Iudaica id quod videbitur domine abbatisse. Item dimicto magistro tomasio de brisio familiari meo ducatos triginta auri in signum amoris et fidelitatis. Item dimicto magistro Ioanni dominico familiari meo ducatos decem auri in signum caritatis. Item dimicto domine riche de alberto ducatos quatuor auri pro anima mea. Item volo et ordino quod post obitum meum quam primum fieri poterit ponatur totum illud quod dispensari volo pro anima mea in monasterio sancte crucis a Iudaica ut cito expleatur voluntas mea et teneatur computus per dominam abbatissam et aliam ut sibi videbitur omnium dispensationum ad pias causas ultra particularia legata monasterii.

Item dimicto de bonis cecilie Iustiniano nepti mee et filie laurentii Iustiniani suprascripti filii et commissarii mei pro suo maritare tantum quantum habuit Ursia neptis mea et filia quondam marci olim filii mei, et si dicta cecilia decederet ante suum maritare tunc volo quod illud quod sibi dimicto deveniat in aliam sororem suam et sic successive. Et si omnes decederent ante suum maritare tunc volo quod illud quod sibi dimicto deveniat inter fratres suos equaliter. Item quia habeo unum scriptum manu domini andree dandulo generi mei de ducatis quingentis auri quos exbursavi pro dotte marie filie sue nupte in dominum hieronimum bembo quos ipse mihi promissit restituere, Nolo ut commissarii mei ullo umquam tempore molestent ipsum dominum andream sed ipsi domino andree dandulo libere remicto et ipsos ducatos quingentos dono in signum dilectionis. Et quoniam superius ordinavi depositum in monasterio sancte crucis a Iudaica poni debere pro rebus ad pias causas dimissis et posset esse quod aliquod restituere neccesse esset pro in certis que mihi essent obscura volo quod ille peccunie sint obligate pro incertis que fortasse reperirentur, et que super essent alegatis superius specificatis id quod supererit suppleatur.

Item dimicto omnia mea bona In mobilia seu stabilia equaliter dividenda in duas partes inter suprascriptum laurentium Iustinianum filium et commissarium meum et aluisium petrum leonardum et nicolaum Iustiniano nepotes et commissarios meos videlicet quod una pars sit suprascripti laurentii Iustiniano filii et commissarii mei, Altera vero sit aluisii petri leonardi et nicolai Iustiniano nepotum et commissariorum meorum. Volo autem quod laurentius Iustinianus suprascriptus filius et commissarius meus possit tam in vita quam in morte disponere de parte sua quicquid voluerit seu sibi placuerit, Nepotes autem mei non possent alienare quidpiam de dictis bonis meis per me sibi dimissis sed deficientibus aliquibus eorum vadat pars decedentis inter super viventes de heredibus in heredes quousque durabit stirps et descendentes ipsorum meorum nepotum semper in propinquiores, deficientibus autem omnibus destirpe predictorum meorum nepotum,

Vadant ipsa bona in stirpem suprascripti laurentii Iustiniani si qua remaneret, si autem stirps suprascripti laurentii filii mei nulla remaneret tunc domini procuratores sancti marci vendant ipsa bona et dispensent tractum pro anima mea.

Verum ante divisionem predictorum meorum bonorum stabilium fiendam volo quod sit in libertate suprascripti laurentii Iustiniani filii et commissarii mei accipere pro sua parte domum sancti fantini astacio cum apotheca saponarie et cum omni et toto eo quod comprehendit dicta fabrica et ad incontrum dimictere nepotibus meis suprascriptis domum magnam astacio novam positam in confinio sancti moisi super canale magnum cum omni et toto eo quod comprehendit ipsa domus tam inferius quam superius. Sed si dictus laurentius suprascriptus filius et commissarius meus velet ipsam domum magnam astacio novam positam in predicto confinio sancti moisi ut supra, volo quod in sua libertate sit Ipsam domum accipere et libere possidere demictendo domum sancti fantini cum apotheca ut supra suprasscriptis nepotibus meis conditionatam sicut superius conditionavi bona stabilia nepotibus meis. Item dimicto laurentio Iustiniano suprascripto filio et commissario meo domum meam astacio positam muriani in confinio sancti stephani cum orto et domuncula vinearii que vadat de heredibus in heredes predicti laurentii filii mei de singulo in singulum heredem ut teneatur ornatior tam domus quam ortus quoniam hoc habui in precepto amagnifico genitore meo qui maxime domum illam dilexit. Volo autem ut pro compenso nepotes mei suprascripti habeant illas quatuor domus cum squaro quas habeo Iuxta predictam domum magnam et estimentur per communes amicos, et si extimate fuerint minoris precii ducatorum mille addantur per laurentium Iustiniano filium meum tot denarii qui ascendant ad sumam ducatorum mille et sint conditionate ut supra in divisione. Item volo et ordino quod si laurentius Iustinianus suprascriptus filius et commissarius meus et aluisius petrus leonardus et nicolaus nepotes mei et commissarii in aliquo molestarent commissariam meam tunc volo et ordino quod illud totum quod sibi dimicto tam stabile quam mobile deveniat et devenire debeat in commissariam meam cassando et anullando legata ipsi filio seu nepotibus dimissa deveniendo ipsa legata parentibus et obedientibus in totum testamento et voluntati mee.

Erit autem mihi per quam gratissimum ut quandocumque videbitur tempus Magnifico domino dominico maureçeno suprascripto commissario meo et laurentio Iustiniano suprascripto filio et commissario meo dent operam ut magister benedictus lignacensis qui nunc tenet ludum venetiis adhibito alio qui magis sibi placeret mihi autem non displiceret caphurnius patavii rhetoricam legens ambo vel separatim percurrent et examinent quindecim libros ame compositos et ad ultimam limam reddactos et quicquid illis quoquomodo mutandum aut demendum videatur mutent et demant, et si illi discreparent Iudicet inter eos magnificus dominus dominicus maureçenus et emendent ut ipse Iudicabit.

Residuum vero omnium aliorum meorum bonorum mobilium presentium et futurorum mihi quocumque modo Iure forma causa titulo et colore aut commissarie mee spectantium et pertinentium et omne caducum inordonatum et pro non scriptum et id quod ad caducum in ordinatum et pro non scriptum posset quomodolibet devenire dimicto dividendum in duas partes, Quarum una sit laurentii Iustiniani suprascripti filii et commissarii mei libera possendi eam alienare et quicquid sibi placuerit de ea facere. Alia vero medietas sit aluisii petri leonardi et nicolai Iustiniano suprascriptorum nepotum et commissariorum meorum inter eos equaliter dividenda hac tamen conditione quod aluisius et petrus possint facere de suis partibus quicquid sibi placuerit leonardus vero in omnibus bonis per eum acquisitis liber dominus sit et posset partem suam ipse met navigare et trafficare non dando partem suam adtrafficandum aliis neque bona sua et mercantias aliis comendare. Illud idem dico de parte spectante nicolao suprascripto nepoti et commissario meo cum fuerit perventus ad etatem decem octo annorum. Notario vero dimicto ducatos decem pro anima mea et pro labore suo. Interogatis interogandis dixit nil aliud ordinare vele.

Preterea plenissimam virtutem et potestatem do tribuo confero penitus et concedo suprascriptis commissariis meis seu maiori parti eorum post mei obitum meam intromictendi administrandi seu furniendi commisariam. Et in super perectendi exigendi et recipiendi sive recuperandi denarios res bona et havere quodlibet a cunctis mihi et dicte mee commissarie nunc et in futurum qua vis ratione modo iure forma et causa dare debentibus ac ubicumque et apud quoscumque ea vel ex eis poterunt quomodolibet reperiri. Item cum quibuslibet meis et dicte mee commissarie debitoribus presentibus et futuris paciscendi concordandi et pacta quelibet faciendi. Item cartulam securitatis et omnes alias cartulas rogandi et fieri faciendi. Item procuratorem costituendi et etiam revocandi et cum pleno mandato substituendi et si opus fuerit in iudicio quolibet comparendi, agendi, defendendi nec non in animam meam iurandi sicut egomet facere possem si viverem. Et generaliter omnia et singula pro dicta mea commissaria faciendi quequilibet verus et legiptimus procurator facere potest et debet. Statuens firmum et ratum quicquid predictos meos commissarios seu per maiorem partem eorum factum fuerit seu gestum. Siquis vero hoc meum ultimum testamentum seu meam hanc ultimam voluntatem infringere seu violare presumpserit omnipotentis Dei se noverit in cursurum et componat se omnibus suis heredibus soluturum auri libras quinque. Et hec mei testamenti carta in sua nihilominus firmitate perduret. Signum suprascripti clarissimi viri domini Bernardi Iustiniani qui hec fieri rogavit.

Ego presbiter Hieronymi Boneto ecclesie Sancti Gemianani iuratus testis subscripsi.

Ego Franzesco dezuane deiveri sartor insanziminian iurado testis subscripsi.

Ego presbiter Nicolaus rubeus ecclesie sancti geminiani plebanus et venetiarum notarius Complevi et Roboravi.

Barnard College, Columbia University

THE LAST WILL OF A VENETIAN
GRAND CHANCELLOR

FELIX GILBERT

Why the last will of Gianpietro Stella deserves publication needs some explanation. There is nothing particularly unusual about this last testament of 1522. Like most of his contemporaries Stella begins with some remarks about man's uncertainty about the time of his death and about the need to make arrangements about one's property in good time. After an appeal to God for clemency, Stella named those whom he wanted to be his executors, and he gave instructions for his funeral and burial. Then Stella gave directions for the disposal of his possessions. First he settled the legacies of a religious and benevolent character, then gifts and legacies to relatives and servants; he also explained that some of his relatives had not been mentioned in his will because they were well off; his sisters had been omitted because, after the death of their parents, he had provided them with dowries. After these bequests he desired the remainder of his estate be used to buy land, and the income from this land should go to a priest who should celebrate daily masses for the salvation of the souls of his father, mother, and his own. Certainly such a last testament is in conformity with the custom of the time.

But Stella was a Venetian Grand Chancellor and as such a figure of some importance. And if one looks more closely at his will in connection with what one knows about his career, it becomes of some significance for the understanding of the role of the Chancellory in sixteenth-century Venice.[1] When Stella established his last will, he had been

[1] A succinct description of the functions of the Venetian Cancelliere Grande will be found in Andrea da Mosto, *L'Archivio di Stato di Venezia*, 219; till da Mosto's discussion of this issue, Horatio F. Brown, "The State Archives and the Constitution of the Venetian Republic," *Venetian Studies* (London 1887), 204-206 was the best short treatment. An interesting report about the work of the Venetian Chancellory, composed in the early sixteenth century, can be found in the "Traité du Gouvernement de Venise," published in P. M. Perret, *Histoire des relations de la France avec Venise*, II (Paris 1896); the chancellory is treated in chapter XVI of this treatise, pp. 277-280. The treatment of the Venetian Chancellory in the historical literature is unsatisfactory; if mentioned at all, the remarks are full of errors.

Grand Chancellor for five years, since January 25, 1517.[2] The Grand Chancellor of Venice was elected by the Great Council and undoubtedly Stella's election was due to the political services which he had rendered to the Republic in the course of many years.

Prior to the election of a Grand Chancellor a list of candidates and their qualifications was read out to the Great Council. Stella, it was stated, had taken part in twelve diplomatic missions in the suite of an ambassador and had been sent out on nine other diplomatic missions alone, "solo."[3] It was customary, or at least very frequent, that an ambassador was accompanied by a secretary, taken from the staff of the Chancellory, but it was rare that a secretary of the Chancellory was sent out "solo," i.e., headed a diplomatic mission. Indeed, although several of Stella's competitors for the office of Grand Chancellor were members of the Chancellory with diplomatic experience, he was the only one of whom it was stated that he had been "solo" on a mission. Stella had the advantage that he was fluent in German,[4] and the most important missions which he conducted "alone" were to German speaking countries. In the early spring of 1509, Stella was sent to Maximilian who was then in Flanders;[5] Stella's task was to find out whether there was a chance to separate the German king from his allies, the French king and the Pope, and to persuade him to desist from making war on Venice. Stella's mission was exploratory because, if he should find Maximilian favorably inclined, his mission was to be followed by that of an ambassador; but it did not come to this. Stella's mission was a failure. After his return to Venice at the beginning of July, Stella said that he had been sent "too late" ("tardi, tardi");[6] he had not even succeeded in getting an audience with Maximilian. His reports, however, had raised no false hopes, and

---

[2] For Stella's election, see *I Diarii di Marino Sanuto* (in future quoted as *Sanuto*), XXIII, 528-530. In the following, two other elections of Grand Chancellors will be frequently mentioned, that of Alvise Dardani, elected on December 22, 1510 (see *Sanuto*, XI, 687-688), and that of Francesco Fasiol on March 13, 1511 (see *Sanuto*, XII, 76).

[3] See preceding note.

[4] See *Sanuto*, XXX, 356 etc.

[5] *Sanuto*, VIII, 10 reports about Stella's first letter from this mission, and then mentions frequently (34, 69, 154, 247) letters received from Stella; about the aims of the mission, see the dispute about the instruction to be given to Stella in *Archivio di Stato di Venezia*, Senato Secreta, Reg. vol. 41, ff. 183-186v, and for the further policy of Venice towards Maximilian, vol. 42, ff. 37-38.

[6] See Sanuto, VIII, 483.

the failure of his mission therefore did Stella no harm. Shortly after his return to Venice in July 1509, he became the secretary of Andrea Gritti,[7] who, as Provveditore Generale, supervised, for the Venetian government, military operations in northern Italy. Before departing again from Venice Stella received assurances that his position in the Chancellory, namely, as secretary to the *Auditori Nuovi*, would be reserved for him.[8] Stella's stay in the military camp ended in 1512 when, in the struggle between the Venetians and the French for Brescia, Gritti became a prisoner of war and was brought to France.

After a few months back in Venice, Stella was sent to Switzerland to arrange the payments which Venice would make to the Swiss if they could prevent Milan from falling into French hands.[9] Again, Stella's mission was unsuccessful, but again this was not his fault. For while Stella was in Switzerland, Venice changed sides, from an alliance with the Pope against the French to an alliance with the French king against the Pope. The reason for this reversal of alliances was that the Venetians were unable to come to any agreement with Maximilian when the Pope decided to align against the French. Since the Swiss regarded the French as their chief enemies and were anxious to keep on good terms with Maximilian, Stella's mission was doomed.[10] On his way back to Venice Stella passed through an area controlled by the Germans and his safe-conduct was disregarded; he became a prisoner of the Germans for two and a half years during which he suffered hardships and illness.[11] Only in December 1515 did he return to Venice and was he able to resume work in the Chancellory.[12]

Unquestionably these political misadventures were a great advantage to Stella when in 1517 the position of the Grand Chancellor became vacant. Along with his qualifications for this position read to the Great Council it was stated that Stella "è stà mexi 30 in prexon con pericolo di la vita e ruina di la facoltà sua."[13] Twice before Stella had aspired to the position of Grand Chancellor: in 1510, after the death of the Grand Chancellor Dedo, he had been almost at the bottom of

---

[7] See *Sanuto*, VII, 529.

[8] See *Sanuto*, X, 124.

[9] See *Sanuto*, XIV, 480; in the following, Sanuto remarks frequently (XIV, 521, 637; XV, 118, 125, 276, 315) on Stella's mission and his reports.

[10] See *Sanuto*, XVI, 143, 324.

[11] See *Sanuto*, XVII, 125, 377.

[12] See *Sanuto*, XXI, 349, 461.

[13] See *Sanuto*, XXIII, 529.

the vote, and in 1511, after the death of Dedo's successor, he did not even find anyone who would nominate him.[14] The great majority with which he was elected in 1517 indicated a new evaluation of his capabilities; Stella's strength clearly was his political ability and the ensuing contacts with influential Venetians. A passage in Stella's last will confirms his concern with being close to power. Sanuto, in recording Stella's death, wrote—clearly he found this fact striking, if not shocking—that Stella had appointed the Doge to be one of his executors.[15] It is true, indeed, that Stella requested that in case trouble developed over the settlement of his affairs three Venetian patricians—Andrea Gritti, Giorgio Corner, and Luca Tron—ought to be consulted for a final decision. But Sanuto seems not to have taken in account that in 1522, when Stella made his last will, Antonio Grimani was Doge; Gritti followed him only in 1523, a few months before Stella died. At the time when the testament was composed the three men whom Stella mentioned were the favorites for the succession of Grimani, who was old and sick. Clearly Stella did everything he could to make sure that he would have a Doge as his executor.

The importance of political contacts and connections in Stella's career should be mentioned because members of the Chancellory were considered to be experts, possessors of a particular skill, but politically neutral or unpolitical. It is true that the Venetian Grand Chancellor was an outstanding figure among the Venetian magistrates. Like the Doge, once elected, he held his position for life. In solemn processions he walked directly ahead of the Doge, clad in a long red robe lined with fur, similar to that worn by the head of the Council of Ten. He ranked directly behind the Procurators of San Marco and the Savi, ahead of the members of the Senate.[16] Sanuto's careful descriptions[17] of the elections of a Grand Chancellor whenever the office fell vacant show the prestige which the office enjoyed: the hall of the Great Council was crowded, filled by many nobles who did not ordinarily bother to show up for the Great Council, eminent foreigners came to observe the proceedings, relations and friends of the various candidates jammed the courtyard of the Ducal palace, and excitedly

---

[14] See n. 2.

[15] See *Sanuto*, XXXIV, 355.

[16] For statements on the position of the Grand Chancellor in the Venetian hierarchy, see the literature, mentioned in note 1, and also Pompeo Molmenti, *Venice*, trans. Horatio F. Brown (Chicago, 1906), Part I: The Middle Ages, vol. I, 170-171.

[17] See n. 2.

pressed up the staircase to the hall. Nevertheless, in Renaissance Italy the Chancellor and the members of the Chancellory were not expected to make policy, and although there were exceptions—as the example of Niccolò Machiavelli shows—the members of the Chancellory were expected to serve the policy of any regime or any group in power. In Venice, the rule that the Chancellor had no place in the policy making group was constitutionally anchored. In 1268, when the office of the Grand Chancellor was created, it had been decreed that the holder of this office must always be a Cittadino, a citizen. A Venetian noble—i.e., a member of the Great Council and as such of the ruling group—was not allowed to hold this position. The subordinate position of the Grand Chancellor appears clearly at the occasion of an election to the office because the various candidates, accompanied by one or two nobles who favored them, walked around in the city soliciting the votes of the members of the Great Council.[18] The reservation of this office to a Cittadino was meant—as political writers liked to explain—to assure that the people had a part in the government. According to Contarini, the Cancellarius was the "dux ex populo."[19] Actually this was an idealized picture of the function of the Chancellor. In the course of the Quattrocento, the Chancellory, comprising the ducal secretaries, the secretaries who worked in the Pregadi, the Ten, and other high offices and a number of extraordinary secretaries,[20] gradually became a closed professional guild which the average citizen could hardly aspire to enter. It is true that this development stood in contrast to the liberal terms in which the Venetians liked to think about the structure of their society, and far into the sixteenth century the development of the Chancellory into an exclusive guild was bitterly fought. When in 1517 the death of the Grand Chancellor Fasiol created a vacancy, the Doge Loredan insisted that

---

[18] See *Sanuto*, XXIII, 523.

[19] In book 5 of his *De magistratibus et republica Venetorum*, Gasparo Contarini discusses the chancellory and the importance of the Grand Chancellor "qui in maximo est honore"; there also the expression "quasi Cancellarius ducem ex populo referat" (in Contarini, *Opera Omnia* [Paris, 1571], 323-324).

[20] In the contemporary treatise, published by Perret (277), the figures given are fifty secretaries and fifty extraordinary secretaries, but they are probably exaggerated. The yearly salary of the Grand Chancellor was then 300 ducats, the most important secretaries—primarily the ducal secretaries—received 200 ducats; income from perquisites was distributed among all members of the Chancellory. The Grand Chancellor held his position for life, the secretaries for five years, although prolongation was customary.

the choice should be limited to the secretaries of the Chancellory.[21] His view was eagerly supported by the members of the Chancellory who even presented historical proof that, from the fourteenth century on, all Grand Chancellors had been members of the Chancellory. But this thesis encountered considerable opposition; although in the election of Stella a member of the Chancellory became Grand Chancellor, the question in principle remained unsolved, and the conflict broke out again after Stella's death in 1523. Gritti who was then Doge promoted a law according to which the Grand Chancellor must be elected from among the secretaries, but this was voted down.[22] As it happened this made no difference because again a member of the Chancellory was elected Grand Chancellor. However, the issue is of some significance because it shows the extent to which the requirements of practical politics had outrun traditional political concepts. The view of the Grand Chancellor as a kind of "tribune of the people," justifying the notion that the Venetian government realized the classical notion of a "mixed government," might remain dear to humanists and to men who cared about the image that Venice showed to the outside world, but in the autocratic oligarchy which Venice had become in the sixteenth century, the people had no voice and were not wished to be heard; what was needed in the Chancellory was a corps of specialists.

Distinct from the rest of the population by possessing a particular skill as well as by being the only existing group of permanent government employees, the members of the Chancellory had no ties other than those to the city they served. They became bound to Venice by an ethos of state service.[23] Some such attitude seems reflected in the

---

[21] The words of the Doge were : "Era mal non far di la Canzelaria," see *Sanuto*, XXIII, 495.

[22] See *Sanuto*, XXXIV, 362.

[23] Of course, there is a similar situation all over Europe. The secretaries of the rulers became the representatives of "the interests of the state," in contrast to the advocacy of partial interests by single groups of society. Yet the situation in republican Venice is somewhat unique. In monarchical countries, secretaries could become confidants of princes and even leading ministers. In Venice, the members of the ruling oligarchy not only determined policy, but were also its executors, and the members of the chancellory could neither determine policies nor become instruments in carrying them out. On the other hand, this outsider role might have reinforced the tendency to look upon politics from the point of view of the "interest of the state" and might have nourished a "civil-service-ethos." A comparative study of the political ideology in the various European chancellories should be worthwhile.

moving words in which Stella expressed his wish to be buried in the church of San Geminiano which stood on the west side of the Piazza San Marco facing the Basilica—so that "cussì come in vita la me ha honorato, cussì post mortem io sia cum el corpo in loco propinquo a ley in signo de reverentia, chè se in vita non ho punto integre satisfar al debito mio, almeno morto supplisca a tanta obligatione."

Belonging to a special and distinct group of society provided the members of the Chancellory not only with the feeling of a particularly close relation to the city of San Marco, it made them also feel entitled to obtain the customary advantages of exclusiveness. Like any guild or closed group in society the members of the Chancellory wished to be masters in their own house and to determine whom to admit to their circle. We find an indication of this in Stella's last will; in explaining why he left no money to one of his sisters, he wrote that he had provided her son, his nephew Giorgio Dario, with government employment as notary and secretary. Many members of the Chancellory were related to each other; there seem to have been families in which a position in the Chancellory became hereditary. Stella himself was the son of a secretary of the Council of Ten; his brother-in-law was a secretary in the Chancellory,[24] and when Stella was elected Grand Chancellor in 1517, the other candidates, with one exception, all were sons of secretaries in the chancellory, one of them even of a Grand Chancellor. Of the Grand Chancellors succeeding Stella, one was the son of a former member of the Chancellory, the other son of a Grand Chancellor.[25] One would expect that nepotism would seriously affect the quality of the service in the Chancellory, but the profession contained an inbuilt counterweight against the dangers arising from nepotism. Service as secretary required special skills which could be obtained only by training and it would have been extremely risky to propose for such training a son or a nephew who was intellectually unsuited.

In Venice the training of officials of the Chancellory took place at the School of San Marco which, in 1443, had been founded by the Venetian government with the express purpose of preparing a number of young men for service in the Chancellory.[26] But the School of San

---

[24] Francesco Dario, mentioned sometimes by *Sanuto*, for instance, XXIV, 674.

[25] 1523 Niccolò Aurelio, son of a secretary of the Ten; 1524 Gerolamo Dedo, son of the Grand Chancellor who died in 1510.

[26] See my article "Biondo, Sabellico, and the Beginnings of Venetian Official Historiography," in *Florilegium Historiale*, ed. Rowe and Stockdale (Toronto, 1971), particularly p. 279.

Marco was also a chief center of humanistic studies in Venice, and as such it served to maintain a link between Italian humanism and the work in the Venetian Chancellory. The important role which the chancellories of the Italian city-states play in the development of humanism is well-known and almost obvious. Although in the course of time work in the Chancellory extended into different areas—filing, keeping records of discussions, registering votes, employment in diplomatic missions—, a Chancellory was an assembly of scribes and its basic task was to compose documents in the right script and correct Latin. Interest in the Latin language established a natural bond between humanism and the scribes of the Chancellory, and made the chancellories crucial agencies in the development of humanism. In the second part of the fourteenth century in the early stages of humanism the Venetian Chancellory, like that of other Italian city-states, had been an important factor in the promotion of humanistic studies.[27] The Grand Chancellor of this time, Benintendi di' Ravegnani, was a close friend of Petrarch and a literary figure of some significance; he was regarded as master and teacher by all those working under him. But the somewhat striking fact which has contributed to the erroneous view of a lack of humanist interest in Venice is that none of Benintendi's successors made a contribution of significance to humanism.[28] In explanation of this lack of literary interest and productivity of the members of the Venetian Chancellory one might point to the complex structure of the Venetian government which made the presence of record keeping secretaries at many councils and offices necessary and required from the Grand Chancellor the direction and supervision of an extended staff; it left little time for activities outside the officially assigned tasks. Nevertheless, the work that was done in the Chancellory—concerned as it was with the linguistic, legal and even ideological aspects of the drafting of documents—made

---

[27] The basic work for the relation of the Chancellory to the beginnings of humanism in Venice is Lino Lazzarini, *Paolo de Bernardo e i primordi dell' Umanesimo in Venezia* (Geneva, 1930). For the role of Petrarch in Venice, see Paul Oskar Kristeller, "Il Petrarca, l'Umanesimo e la Scolastica a Venezia," in *La Civiltà veneziana del Trecento* (Florence, 1956), 149-178. But see also the article by Lino Lazzarini, "Francesco Petrarca e il primo Umanesimo a Venezia," in *Umanesimo europeo e Umanesimo veneziano*, ed. Vittore Branca (Florence, 1964), 63-92; this article also emphasizes that, in the Quattrocento, the Venetian chancellory no longer remained a center of humanistic studies.

[28] 1390, Pietro Rossi; 1396, Giovanni Vido; 1402, Niccolò Gherardo; 1405, Giovanni Piumazzo; 1428, Francesco Beaciano; 1439, Francesco della Siega; 1470, Alessandro dalle Fornaci; 1482, Giovanni Dedo.

contact with the world of humanism a necessity, and, even if, in contrast to Florence, the roster of secretaries in the Venetian Chancellory did not contain names with a reputation as humanist writers, a basically humanist attitude remained alive in the Venetian Chancellory. To a large extent this was the result of the establishment of the School of San Marco. Since its foundation the School of San Marco always had prominent humanists as Professors.[29] We find as teachers in this School Perleo, Mario Filelfo, George of Trebizond, Benedetto Brognoli, Merula, Giorgio Valla, Sabellico, Leonico. We have no proof that Stella was a student at the School of San Marco but this seems a most justifiable assumption; it would have been the time when Brognoli and Sabellico taught there. The oration at his funeral was to be given by Marino Becichemo who during the years of the war of the League of Cambrai had been a lecturer at the School of San Marco and became then Professor at the University of Padua. But the strongest proof for the role which a humanist education played in Stella's life are the titles of the books of his library and the evident pride which he took in them. Although it might be hazardous to draw many conclusions from the titles listed in Stella's last will, there are a few points which perhaps deserve attention. His reliance, in many cases, on classical texts in printed form might be an indication of the flowering of book printing in Venice. Although Stella appears to have had equal interest in Greek and Roman authors, the list of his books seems to show a certain preference for historical writers; this corresponds to the prevailing mood of humanistically inclined Venetians since the fifteenth century. The appearance of contemporary authors—like Marsilio, Valla, or even Sebastian Brant—is remarkable especially if one considers that religious and theological authors are unrepresented.[30] In its entirety Stella's library reveals a man in whom a humanist education had developed many intellectual interests but for whom humanistic knowledge was a practical necessity and an adornment rather than stimulus to pursue intensive studies in a particular field. Stella was a man who lived in the present rather than in the past.

One can only assume that the connections with powerful Venetians of his time assured that the instructions of Stella's last will were carefully carried out. His funeral was arranged as Stella had wished.

---

[29] See my article, referred to in n. 26.

[30] This is speculative because his last will indicates that he possessed books beyond those which he mentioned by title.

We know that from the report which Sanuto has left us.[31] Becichemo was proud of the speech he made at the funeral and had it printed.[32] Behind its easily rolling passages which build up a picture of awe-inspiring virtue all individuality is lost. It is good, therefore, that we know from other sources[33] that Stella was an enormously fat man who loved to eat well, that he was pompous and concerned about his own comfort and that when he had received the high dignity of Grand Chancellor he used the harm which imprisonment had done to his health and the gout which he had inherited to stay frequently away from his office and to spend his days at home with his "good, loyal and patient Maria."

Text

Iesus Christus, Virgo Maria

MDXXII, die primo mensis Decembris, in contrata Sancti Gregorii.[34]

In Christi nomine amen. Cum nil certius in hoc seculo sit morte, magisque dubium et incertum hora, providendum est saluti animae prius, deinde regulationi pauperis facultatis meae, ut id quod cum sudore acquisivi, post mortem non dilapidetur, sicut fieri solet, immo pie et religiose administretur, prout a sapientissimis

---

[31] See *Sanuto*, XXXIV, 362-363.

[32] Marini Becichemi *Orationes Duae Prima est gratulatio ad ... Andream Grittum... altera est funebris laudatio ... de meritis Joannis Petri Stellae, magni Venetiarum cancellarii ... Venetiis 1524.* Becichemo's speech lists the various embassies in which Stella was employed but—beyond praise—adds nothing to our knowledge of Stella's training, thought and achievements. The first part of the speech discusses the history of chancelleries and is of some interest as a testimony for the close relation between humanism and chancelleries.

[33] See *Sanuto*, XXVII, 238, 307, 647; XXXIV, 362.

[34] Stella's last will can be found in the *A.S.V.*, Archivi notarili, Testamenti, among the papers of the notary Francesco dal Pozzo (Puteolanus), who was active as notary from 1486-1529. In addition to the testament and the codicil which are both published here, these papers contain a first version of Stella's last will, which is identical with the final version—with exception of two, brief, unimportant passages which are crossed out and corrected; the final version gives these passages in the corrected form.—The parish of San Gregorio, in which Stella lived, was in the sestiere of Dorsoduro, close to what is now Santa Maria della Salute.

viris fieri consuetum est. Ego vero Ioannespetrus Stella eques,[35] magnus Venetiarum cancellarius, quondam domini Dominici, excelsi Consilii Decem Secretarii, haeres fidei tantum paternae, presens conditum testamentum statui. Voglio adunque che questo sia el mio ultimo testamento et voluntà, et se alcuno altro havesse facto, sia nullo, irrito et casso. Ordino che dapoi la mia morte, dicto testamento sia levato in publica forma per uno notario de Venetia, secundo li ordini et leze de questa cità. Primo racommando l'anima mia al summo creator miser Iesu Christo et ala sua matre Virgine Maria, mia devotissima, che in tute le mie adversità mai non me ha abandonato, et a tuti li Sancti et Sancte de vita aeterna, che me concedino che ala mia morte me acceptino in la sua gratia. Lasso mei commissarii miser Patre Piero, presente plebano[36] de San Zuane de Rialto, miser Hector Ottobon, scrivan al Sal, et miser Zuan Regolino, scrivan ali Signori gubernatori, cum admonitione che in li bisogni occorrenti dimandino el suffragio deli Magnifici et Clarissimi miser Zorzi Corner Cavalier procurator, miser Andrea Gritti procurator, et miser Luca Trun, nei quali ho firma speranza, et supplico che cussì come in vita me sono sta' protectori, cussì in morte se degnino cum iusticia favorir dicti mei executori. Deinde voglio che'l mio corpo sia sepulto in San Geminiano, in capo dela piaza del glorioso miser San Marco protector de questa Ser.^{ma} republica, aziò che cussì come in vita la me ha honorato, cussì post mortem io sia cum el corpo in loco propinquo a ley in signo de reverentia, chè se in vita non ho possuto integre satisfar al debito mio, almeno morto supplisca a tanta obligatione. L'arca mia sarà, piacendo a Dio, davanti la porta dela Frezaria,[37] in dicta ecclesia, in terra. Poi, sopra dicta porta, sarà una memoria dela fede mia, come neli instrumenti celebrati in questa materia per el Rev.^{do} Domino Ionnefrancesco Puteolano notario Veneto appar. Nel qual acto ce intervien la auctorità del Rev.^{mo} patriarcha de questa cità, el Rev.^{do} plebano de San Geminiano, capitolo etc. Item ordino che in le mie exequie, apresso el corpo siano do-

---

[35] A Grand Chancellor was automatically made "eques."
[36] Identical with piovane, parish priest.
[37] The name of the street at the back of San Geminiano is still the same today, although the church was destroyed in 1807, in order to make place for the Napoleonic wing of the Piazza San Marco.

pieri[38] vinti,[39] de lire diexe l'uno, diexe di quali siano portati da tanti marinari, et li altri da X Iesuati. Et perchè la luce che va avanti conferisse più ala veduta del'homo che quella da drieto, ho facto dir in vita le messe de San Gregorio, le messe dela Madona et mandato a Sisa,[40] factum etiam tuor le sagre. Voglio praeterea che, separata l'anima dal mio corpo, sia tolto el mio anello da bolla cum el qual sum consueto sigillar, et quello destructo, adeo che cum epso non se possi più sigillar. Et cum quel'oro et ducati quatro apresso, sia facta una corona d'arzento dorata ala gloriosissima Verzene Maria da San Fantin, la qual sia posta ogni festa solenne sopra el capo de epsa gloriosissima Matre, in singular mia devotione. Ordino insuper che ali poveri de San Lazaro siano dati ducati do, ali poveri puti dela Pietà ducati do, a Madona Santa Maria de Gratia ducati tre, che facino dir tante messe per l'anima mia. Ali poveri dela contra' de Sancto Geminiano ducati quatro. Ala mia scolla de miser San Marco[41] ducati diexe, i quali siano dati ali più poveri fratelli de dicta scolla. Item lasso a mio cugnato Benedeto Girardello, citadin Bergomense, uno quadro novo cum una testa de Christo passo, cum el suo timpano, uno robon zambelloto negro imbordado de veludo negro, et uno robon paonazo imbordado de damaschin negro. Preterea non se maravigli alcuno se non lasso cossa alcuna al mio nepote Marco Antonio di Zentili, perchè per la Dio gratia el non ha bisogno. Item lasso a Zuan Antonio Dario, fiol de miser Francesco mio cugnato, li volumi infrascripti, videlicet. Aulo Gelio in carta bona a stampa.[42] Duo vocabulista[43] in carta bambasina,[44] scripti a pena. Valerio

---

[38] Doppiere is a cross of wax candles.
[39] Identical with venti, 20.
[40] Assisi.
[41] The "Scuola Grande di San Marco" (not to be confused with the "School of San Marco," the center of humanistic studies) had a particularly large number of professional men—higher civil service and university graduates—among its members. See Brian Pullan, *Rich and Poor in Renaissance Venice* (Oxford, 1971), 95. The Scuola Grande di San Marco, now the Ospedale Civile, close to the Church San Giovanni e Paolo, had been completed in its present form—with the famous frescoes of Carpaccio and Bellini, now in the Accademia—by the beginning of the sixteenth century.
[42] Aulus Gellius, *Noctes Atticae*, first printed in 1469, first Venetian edition 1472, followed by several other Venetian editions. Stella's copy might be the Aldus edition of 1515, which Egnatius, the well-known Venetian scholar and humanist, professor at the School of San Marco, had prepared.
[43] Dictionary.
[44] Carta bambasina, or carta bombicina,—a specially good, heavy paper,—had its

Maximo a stampa in carta bambasina.[45] Prisciano in carta bona a stampa.[46] De finibus bonorum et malorum, Tusculane a stampa in carta bona.[47] Speculum iudiciale in carta bona a pena.[48] La Instituta, Marsilio Facino, Valla in volume picolo in carta bambasina a pena,[49] et le tre Deche de Livio.[50] Item lasso a Nicoleto, fiol de dona Maria che me governa, oltra che li ho facto le spexe et vestito, per l'anima mia, de mio patre et matre, i volumi infrascripti videlicet. Aretino cum el compendio rerum graecarum, in carta bona scripto a pena.[51] Epistole de Phalaris grece, in carta bona scripte a pena.[52] Plinio, De naturali historia.[53] Terentio in carta bona scripto a pena. Iustino historico a stampa in carta bambasina.[54] Le elegantie del Valla, grande.[55] Lucano in carta

---

name from the ancient Bambyke (the Arab el-Mambay), where paper was manufactured. The derivation from bambagia (cotton) is considered to be erroneous.

[45] Valerius Maximus, *Dictorum factorumque memorabilium libri novem*, first printed in 1470, first Venetian edition in 1471, followed by several other Venetian editions; first Aldus edition 1502, reprinted in 1514.

[46] Priscianus, *Opera*, first printed in 1470, several Venetian editions, one in 1485, prepared by Benedetto Brognoli, professor at the School of San Marco.

[47] Only a Paris edition of 1477 had these two works (and no other) by Cicero together in one volume; single editions of these two works, of course, were very frequent.

[48] Since this is a handwritten manuscript, identification seems impossible.

[49] See previous note about these three manuscripts; but the following might be said: Facino is misspelled for Ficino, Valla could be Lorenzo or Giorgio Valla, although Lorenzo seems more likely because, when, at a later place, Stella writes Valla, it is evident that he means Lorenzo Valla.

[50] It is not clear whether this is a manuscript or a printed edition. There were many Venetian editions of Livy, since the first edition of 1470, some of them with annotations by Sabellico, a professor at the School of San Marco; but Stella might have possessed the Aldus editions (1518-20, 1521).

[51] Probably Leonardo Bruni Aretino's *Commentaria rerum graecarum*, which were printed only in 1539.

[52] A Greek edition of *Phalaridis tyranni epistola* was printed in Venice in 1498.

[53] Plinius Secundus, C., *Historiae naturalis libri XXXVII*, was first printed in Venice in 1469, but there are two later Venetian editions—one with comments by Ermolao Barbaro, and the other prepared by Alessandro Benedetti—which might have interested a Venetian, because these two men were famous figures in Venetian intellectual life. Benedetti's *Diaria de Bello Carolino* has been the first volume in the Renaissance Text Series, initiated by the Renaissance Society of America, published in 1967.

[54] Justinus' well-known historical compendium was first printed in Venice in 1470, but there are several other Venetian editions. The Aldus edition is of 1522.

[55] The first Folio edition of Lorenzo Valla, *De elegantia latinae linguae libri sex* is of 1471, but there are several others.

bambasina a stampa.⁵⁶ Navis Stultorum, sono duo volumi in bambasina a stampa, cohoperti de bianco.⁵⁷ Et tuti altri mei libri excepti li publici, si in carta bona come bambasina, che se ritrovano over se ritroverano. Item lasso al dicto Nicoleto ducati diexe amore Dei. A dona Maria veramente sua matre, lasso per suo salario et mercede per anni sete ducati otantaquatro, a ducati 12 al'anno. Ala qual dona Maria oltra quelli, me reservo per carità rimunerar de maior premio, per molte fatiche havute in caxa mia, per sua sola bontà, fede et pacientia. De tuto el residuo veramente deli mei beni mobili de qualumque conditione et sorte se sia, excepto tamen le cosse suprascripte le qual ho donato et donate, voglio siano inseme cum quelle nel mio inventario signate, sotoscripto manu propria et sigillato, exceptuando etiam da questo residuo tute quelle cosse che de mia mano sarano notade in uno inventario over memoriale, scripto de mia mano et sotoscripto dapoi questo testamento, da esser distribuite secondo come in epso inventario ordinerò. Voglio che Anzola, fiola natural del quondam Aluvise mio fratello, la qual ho tenuto ad imparar in monasterio già anni octo del mio, habbi per suo maridar over monachar ducati ducento, over la valuta de quelli. Il che facto, voglio et ordino che tuto el mio residuo predicto sia per li mei commissarii, over maior parte de loro, venduto, et del tracto comprato tanti campi, dico campi et non altro, che rendino più se potrà. La intrata di quali haver debi uno mansionario⁵⁸ devoto, bon et catholico, da esser electo per dicti Commissarii, over la mazor parte de quelli, nei quali habbi ad intervenir etiam el Rev.ᵈᵒ plebano de San Geminiano, el qual dove inclinerà, quella sia la maior parte. El qual mansionario sia obligato ogni giorno dir messa davanti l'altar dela glorississima Verzene Maria, per l'anima deli mei patre et matre et mia.

Et perchè è honesto che, cussì come solo ho portato grandissimo pexo sopra le spalle, de tre sorelle da marito, senza esser dotate

---

⁵⁶ Marcus Annaeus Lucanus, *Pharsalia* was first printed in Venice in 1470, followed by several other Venetian editions; the Aldus edition is of 1502.

⁵⁷ I was unable to identify this item. There can be little doubt that the work Stella lists is Sebastian Brant's *Narrenschiff*. There were many editions of Latin translations of this book. However, they were always entitled *Stultifera Navis*, never "Stultorum Navis"; moreover, editions in two volumes do not exist. Did Stella have two copies?

⁵⁸ Mansonario, Mass-priest, who earned according to the number of Masses celebrated or corpses buried.

nè da patre nè da matre nè altri, ma lassate nude a speranza dela divina clementia, quale me ha concesso tanta gratia che deli mei beni castrensi, chè mai altri beni non ho havuti nè da patre nè da matre, cum el mio sudor solo, fatiche et pericoli nei quali me son posto a servitio de questo Ill.mo Stato : cussì, aziò appari che quello ho acquistato non lo habbi convertito, salvo in bone et laudabile opere, dichiarirò quello ho dato a cadauna de epse tre sorelle in dote. Primo, a Madalena, la mazor, relicta de miser Francesco di Zentili, ducati 600. A Veronica, moglie de Benedeto Girardello, citadin Bergomense, ducati 400. A Marieta, moglie de miser Francesco Dario, ducal Secretario, ducati mille, amorevolmente satisfacti, oltra la qual dote me ho affaticato darli et ho dato molto maior dono nela persona de Zorzi Dario suo fiolo, mio nepote, dotato de uno deli do notariati del iudicato de proprio, de valuta de ducati 200 vel circa al'anno, a supplicatione mie per li meriti mei per lo Excellentissimo Conseio di X concesso. Dele qual dote voglio che tute habbino a restar contente et pregar el nostro Signor Dio per l'anima mia, perchè me par haver facto più del possibile, non da fratello ma da patre, a laude de Dio quale sempre sia ringratiato. Nè se meravigli alcuno che habbi dato più al'una che al'altra, amandole tutte in uno grado, perchè le condition deli tempi et le commodità me ho ritrovato, nec non li meriti de cadauna me hano astricto far cussì, come soleno far quelli che viveno in questo misero mundo, da diversi corsi dela fortuna necessitati.

Et perchè io havea dato un'altra cedula testamentaria in mano del suprascripto Domino Ioannefrancesco Puteolano, clerico et nodaro da Venetia, confesso haver rehavuto dicta polliza sigilata, et factone la mia voluntà, perchè voglio che questo sia el mio ultimo testamento.

Idem Ioannespetrus Stella
manu propria

Iesus Maria - 1522[59] primo Ianuarii

Havendo testato io Zuanpiero Stella cavallier, cancellier de Venetia, et ordinato le cosse mie per mano del Rev.do Domino Ioanfrancesco Puteolano, nodaro Veneto, adi primi decembre 1522 et facto mentione dele cosse ho donato de mano propria et nel'inventario

---

[59] 1522 according to the Venetian calendar, actually 1523.

notate, come per epso inventario de tuto el mio mobile appar, sotoscripto manu propria et sigillato consueto annulo, cum la clausula etc., per el presente inventario dele cosse non contenute nel mio testamento dechiarisco et voglio che quello in questa cedula sarà annotato vaglia tanto quanto el mio proprio testamento, quale mente mia è sia inviolabelmente observato, et similiter quello che ala giornata sarà qui annotato manu propria.

Primo adonque, dapoi el mio testamento ho comprato tre tapedi Rodiani grossi, uno di qual voglio sia de dona Maria di Doctori che me governa, inseme cum una capsa nova facta al modo dele altre sono in la camera longa. La qual capsa ha sopra el converchio depicta una testa granda de vechio, et la capsa de azuro et bianco. Li altri do tapedi vadino cum li altri.

Item s'el occorresse, il che sia in piacer del nostro Signor Dio, che io venisse a manchar nel tempo la caxa è fornita de legne, vino, frumento, oglio et altro, dechiarisco et ordino che le dicte cosse siano fidelmente per li mei commissarii vendute et posto el danaro in comprar terre per la mansionaria, come ho ordinato nel mio testamento, pagando honestamente quelli se affaticherano.

La turchese io porto in dedo in effeto è de dona Maria, et cussì viglio [*sic* = voglio] la ge sia restituita casu quo io avanti non l'havesse facto.

Institute for Advanced Study

GIOVANNI GARZONI (1419-1505) TO ALESSANDRO ACHILLINI (1463-1512): AN UNPUBLISHED LETTER AND DEFENSE*

HERBERT S. MATSEN

As is well known, Alessandro Achillini was an important Bolognese Aristotelian philosopher and physician who earned degrees in philosophy and medicine at the University of Bologna on September 7, 1484.[1] He taught philosophy and medicine at that same University from September, 1484 until early in 1512, the year of his death,[2] except for two academic years, 1506-1508, when he 'read' philosophy at the University of Padua.[3] As one can determine by studying extant archival documents pertaining to the University of Bologna for the period of Achillini's activity, which records are preserved in the Bolognese Archivio di Stato, there is scant reference to Achillini outside an academic context.[4] Thus far, I know of only one document

---

* This paper is a by-product of work undertaken while on a Fulbright Scholarship in Italy, 1958-1960. I am also indebted to the Committee on Research and Productive Scholarship of the University of South Carolina for a grant which made further study and completion possible. The following offered valuable suggestions or corrections: Professors P. O. Kristeller, Patricia F. Paden, Charles B. Schmitt, Roger Sullivan, F. Edward Cranz and Edward P. Mahoney.

[1] Giovanni Bronzino, ed., *Notitia doctorum sive catalogus doctorum qui in Collegiis Philosophiae et Medicinae Bononiae laureati fuerunt ab Anno 1480 usque ad Annum 1800*, Universitatis Bononiensis Monumenta, IV (Milan, 1962), 1.

[2] On Achillini's career and doctrine, most important are Ladislao Muenster, "Alessandro Achillini, Anatomico e filosofo, professore dello Studio di Bologna (1463-1512)," *Rivista di storia delle scienze mediche e naturali*, 4th ser., 24 (1933), 7-22, 54-77; and Bruno Nardi, *Saggi sull'Aristotelismo padovano dal secolo XIV al XVI* (Florence, 1958), 179-279. See also my doctoral dissertation (Columbia University, 1969), now revised and published as *Alessandro Achillini (1463-1512) and His Doctrine of "Universals" and "Transcendentals"* : *A Study in Renaissance Ockhamism* (Lewisburg, Pa., 1974).

[3] Documentary justification can be found in Herbert S. Matsen, "Alessandro Achillini (1463-1512) as Professor of Philosophy in the 'Studio' of Padua (1506-1508)," *Quaderni per la storia dell'Università di Padova* 1 (1968), 91-109, republished as "Appendix I" in my book on Achillini (cited in previous note).

[4] The kinds of documents pertaining to the University of Bologna in which Achillini's name appears are seven : (a) Copies of letters from the Commune of Bologna, including

of consequence in addition to those just mentioned in note four in which Achillini appears, viz., in a letter written to him by a famous contemporary, who was a physician, historian and orator, Giovanni Garzoni (1419-1505).[5]

---

letters to professors; for example, copies of two sent to Achillini in 1507 (Archivio del Comune, "Litterarum." See my paper cited in the previous note to illustrate this and other documents mentioned in this note); (b) Volumes containing salary authorizations of Professors of the University, among others (in Archivio del Comune, "Libri Partitorum"; for example, the official reappointment of Achillini as Professor of Philosophy and of Medicine, dated September 14, 1508); (c) Quarterly records (Riformatori dello Studio, "Quartironi degli stipendi"), which are proof of salary authorizations and usually actual disbursements for the Professors of the University, Achillini included, with the tax, if any, each had to pay; (d) Notices of official doctoral-conferring meetings of the College of Medicine and Arts (Archivio dello Studio, "Registri d'atti dei Collegi, 1481-1500" and "Libro segreto del collegio di medicina e d'arti dall'anno 1504 a tutto il 1575"); (e) The "Rotuli" or faculty lists for the 'Arts' professors for each year (Archivio dello Studio, "I rotuli dello Studio Bolognese, 1484-1512"), published by Umberto Dallari: *I Rotuli dei lettori, legisti e artisti dello Studio Bolognese dal 1384 al 1799*, 4 vols. (Bologna, 1888-1924), I, 1384-1513; (f) One carton of 'penalties,' called "Puntazioni," issued every three or four months which recorded infractions of those professors who either did not 'read' on an assigned day or who did not have the requisite number of students (Riformatori dello Studio, "Puntazioni dei lettori, 1463-1513"); and, (g) One carton of "Disputes of Scholars" (Riformatori dello Studio, "Dispute di Scolari, 1462-1527") which indicates on one sheet for each disputation the philosophical and medical questions which will be or which have been disputed either by one of the professors or by a student under his direction. See Giorgio Cencetti, *Gli archivi dello Studio Bolognese* (Bologna, 1938).

[5] Although Garzoni would seem an interesting subject for monographs, references to him are scattered. The most extensive account of his life and works with which I am familiar is Giovanni Fantuzzi, *Notizie degli scrittori bolognesi*, IV (Bologna, 1784), 78-100; IX (1794), 115-128. Cf. Ulysse Chevalier, *Répertoire des sources historiques du Moyen Age: Bio-bibliographie*, I, col. 1658. More recent contributions include : (a) on the polemic between Garzoni and Benedetto Morandi, Lodovico Frati, "Le polemiche umanistiche di Benedetto Morandi," *Giornale storico della letteratura italiana* 75 (1920), 32-39; (b) on two short political opuscula, Lynn Thorndike, "Giovanni Garzoni on Ruling a City," *Political Science Quarterly* 46 (1931), 277-280, and "Giovanni Garzoni on the Office of Prince," *ibid.*, 589-592; (c) concerning an unpublished work by Vincenzo Fassini on Garzoni, Florio Banfi (i.e. the Hungarian Ladislao Holik Barabàs), "Un umanista bolognese e i domenicani. A proposito dell'opera inedita su Giovanni Garzoni del P. Vincenzo Domenico Fassini O. P. contenutasi nel Codice Vat. Lat. 10686," *Memorie Domenicane* 52 (1935), 365-378; 53 (1936), 14-25, 69-80; (d) on Garzoni and a Cardinal of Hungary, idem, "Giovanni Garzoni ed il Cardinale Tommaso Bakócz [Bakacs, d. 1521] Primate d'Ungheria," *L'Archiginnasio* 31 (1936), 120-139; (e) an important study on his library by Guglielmo Manfré, "La Biblioteca dell'umanista bolognese Giovanni Garzoni (1419-1505)," *Accademie e biblioteche d'Italia* 27 (1959), 249-278 (especially 250, n. 1); 28 (1960), 17-72; (f) on Garzoni's medical and especially astrological opus-

According to Fantuzzi, Garzoni while still young studied Latin letters for four years in Rome at the school of Lorenzo Valla.[6] This must have been during the period 1449-1456.[7] After the death of his father Bernardo, ca. 1456,[8] he returned to his city of origin and continued his studies with Antonio Urceo called 'Codro';[9] he was also a student of Guarino of Verona (d. at Ferrara December 4, 1460).[10] Later, he studied medicine and received a degree in that subject in 1466.[11] Then, claims Fantuzzi, he was promoted by the 'Senate' to a chair *first of philosophy* and then of medicine in the public schools, i.e., in the communal University; his name begins to appear as one of those professors inscribed on the 'Roll of the University' in 1468 (sic) and ceases to appear there in 1504.[12]

---

cula, Pearl Kibre, "Giovanni Garzoni of Bologna (1419-1505), Professor of Medicine and Defender of Astrology," *Isis* 58 (1967), 504-514; and, finally (g) on the polemic between Garzoni and Morandi concerning the condition of man, Charles Trinkaus, *In Our Image and Likeness : Humanity and Divinity in Italian Humanist Thought*, I (Chicago, 1970), 177-78, n. 13 (pp. 389-390) and Chapter 7.

[6] On Valla, see the pioneer study by Remigio Sabbadini, "Cronologia documentata della vita di Lorenzo della Valle, detto il Valla," in Luciano Barozzi and R. Sabbadini, *Studi sul Panormita e sul Valla* (Florence, 1891), 49-148, and L. Barozzi, "Lorenzo Valla," *ibid.*, 149-265. Cf. Girolamo Mancini, *Vita di Lorenzo Valla* (Florence, 1891).

[7] See Sabbadini, 123, 125, 131-2.

[8] On his father Bernardo, also a famous physician, see Fantuzzi, 75-77.

[9] At least Garzoni was indebted to Codro for assistance in studying Latin letters, whether or not he was a student in a formal sense. See Garzoni's letter to Codro in Antonio Urceo (Codro), *Orationes ... epistolae ...* (Bologna, 1502), Tii. (Cf. Fantuzzi, 79; Carlo Malagola, *Della vita e delle opere di Antonio Urceo detto Codro* [Bologna, 1878], 63, 223-225; and Ezio Raimondi, *Codro e l'Umanesimo a Bologna* [Bologna, 1950], 71, 83-85). Also contained in the same volume (Tii^v-Tiiii) is Codro's long reply to Garzoni's letter in which the main issue is the nature of *persona*, specifically whether it is a substance or a quality.

[10] Kibre (505, n. 4) quotes from a Garzoni manuscript on Juvenal, 876 : "Ego a disertissimo omnium Veronensium Guarino praeceptore meo..." For the contents of MS. 876, see n. 11.

[11] Fantuzzi, 79. For justification, Fantuzzi refers to no earlier works than G. N. P. Alidosi (*I dottori bolognesi di teologia, filosofia, medicina, e d'arti liberali, dall' anno 1000 per tutto marzo del 1623* [Bologna, 1623], 92) and I. B. Cavazza (*Catalogus omnium doctorum collegiatorum in artibus liberalibus et in facultate medica ... ab anno ...1156* [Bologna, 1664], 21).

[12] Fantuzzi, 79 : "Indi promosso dal Senato ad una Catedra *prima di Filosofia*, poi di Medicina nelle pubbliche Scuole, il suo nome comincia a vedersi descritto ne[i] Rotoli dello Studio l'anno 1468 (sic), e termina d'esservi l'anno 1504" (emphasis added). Trinkaus on two occasions (I, 271; 390, n. 13), perhaps depending on Fantuzzi, says that Garzoni was appointed to teach both medicine *and philosophy*, but I know of no good

Fantuzzi is a valuable work, but one does, on occasion, find difficulties. In the first place, he does not document his claim that Garzoni was first appointed to a chair of philosophy.[13] Although it is possible that the Commune made such an appointment, it seems doubtful in the light of the following evidence : in the 'Rotuli' or lists of faculty appointments, one for each year for the 'Legisti' and one for the 'Artisti,' one finds Garzoni listed only as a 'professor of practical medicine' from the academic year 1466-67 to 1504-05, inclusive.[14] Incidentally, the full title was "Ad lecturam Pra[c]ticae medicinae in tertiis" and the first time that Garzoni's name appears in the 'Rotuli,' viz., for the academic year 1466-67, dated October 18, we find indicated the medical subject matter that he and two other professors named to the same 'chair' were supposed to 'read,' i.e., teach, that year. The work in question consisted of four treatises (*fens*) of the famous mediaeval medical textbook, Avicenna's *Canon*, Book III.[15] Book III of Avicenna's *Canon* concerns diseases affecting all parts of the body, described in order from the head to the feet (*a capite ad calcem*), together with their treatment. *Fens* 9-12 treat of the throat, lungs and chest, heart and mammary glands, respectively.[16] A second obvious slip of Fantuzzi involves the beginning of

contemporary evidence; on this matter, Kibre (505), referring only to his medical appointment, is more accurate, I believe.

[13] Dr. Benedetto Nicolini, formerly Director of the Archivio di Stato, Bologna, has kindly informed me that there is no notice concerning any appointment, medical or philosophical, for Giovanni Garzoni during the year 1466 (in VI [1466-1470], "Libri Partitorum").

[14] See Dallari, I, 73 for the first entry (1466-1467) and 188 for the last (1504-1505). However, in candor one must say that appearing on the 'Rotulus' for a given year does not prove that the person whose name is so inscribed actually taught at the University that academic year. For, although Achillini's name continued to appear in the 'Rotuli' for the years 1506-1507 and 1507-1508, it is well known that during that two-year period he was actually 'reading' at the University of Padua. But the main point is that Garzoni is listed in the 'Rotuli' only as a teacher of 'practical' medicine and never of philosophy, which conflicts with Fantuzzi's claim that he was appointed first to a chair of philosophy.

[15] Dallari, I, 73 : "Ad lecturam Pra[c]ticae medicinae in tertiis. (Legatur tertius [*Canonis*] Avicenn[a]e, nona fen, decima, undecima, decimasecunda.) D[ominus] M[agister] Iohannes (sic) de Gozadinis, D. M. Baldassar de Iohannittis, D. M. Iohannes de Garzonibus."

[16] For an edition, see Avicenna, *Liber Canonis* ... translated by Gerard of Cremona (Venice, 1507) : "Fen 9 : de dispositionibus gutturis," ff. 234^{v}b-239; "10 : de dispositionibus pulmonis et pectoris...," 239-256^v; "11 : de dispositionibus cordis," 257^{v}b-264; and "12 : de mammilla et dispositionibus eius...," 264-265b. Cf. Kibre, 505, n. 7.

Garzoni's professorship. If the 'Rotulus' for 1466-1467 is correct, he began to teach in that year (1466) and not in 1468, as Fantuzzi claims.[17]

In addition to his fame as a professor of 'practical medicine' at the University, Garzoni was also widely known for his historical works, for his numerous lives of saints and for his oratorical skills. Among his historical writings, one might note his history of Saxony,[18] and his work in praise of the city of Bologna.[19] There are also some lives of saints attributed to Garzoni, for example, of St. Antonio abbot,[20] St. Dominic, St. Peter and St. Thomas Aquinas.[21] Furthermore, there are many manuscripts of these and other works, particularly of orations of various kinds and letters.[22] For another indication of his importance as an orator, we have the obituary notice of Garzoni by the prior of the College of Medicine for the first three months of 1505, viz., Clarus Franciscus de Genulis, [23] according to whom "he [scil. Garzoni] was beyond dispute in our time the most famous

---

[17] See n. 12 above.

[18] *Ioannis Garzonis Bononiensis de rebus Saxoniae, Thuringiae, Libonotriae, Misnae et Lusatiae libri duo* (Basel, 1518). This work was reprinted in Joannes Burchardus Menkenius (ed.), *Scriptores rerum Germanicarum praecipue Saxonicarum...*, II (Leipzig, 1728), cols. 999-1056. Cf. Fantuzzi, 83. For more details on Garzoni's library, see Manfré.

[19] See his *De dignitate urbis Bononiae commentarius*, ed. Ludovicus Antonius Muratorius, in *Rerum Italicarum scriptores*, XXI (1732), 1141-1142 (Muratori's preface), 1143-1168 (Garzoni's text). Cf. Fantuzzi, 82.

[20] ...*in Vitam divi Antonii abbatis* (Bologna, 1503). Cf. Fantuzzi, 82.

[21] Garzoni's lives of these three saints are included in the work edited by Leandro Alberti, *De viris illustribus Ordinis Praedicatorum libri sex* (Bologna, 1517). For the life of St. Dominic, see Book I, ff. 7-22v; for that of St. Peter, II, ff. 52v-55v; and for that of St. Thomas, IV, ff. 130v-135.

[22] For manuscripts of Garzoni's Latin works the obvious starting point is Fantuzzi, whose work has been made more precise by Manfré. Also see Lodovico Frati, "Indice dei Codici Latini conservati nella R. Biblioteca Universitaria di Bologna," in *Studi italiani di filologia classica* 16 (1908), 103-142 and 17 (1909), 1-171. For "Garzoni," see "Indice" in 17 (1909), 154. For corrections and addenda, see Paul Oskar Kristeller, *Iter Italicum*, I (London and Leiden, 1963), 19, 20, 23 and 24. For a more extensive list of Garzoni manuscripts, see Kibre, 504-507, nn. 1-29. But Miss Kibre does not mention Manfré's detailed analysis of Garzoni's library. Also, see Trinkaus, II, 891-2.

[23] On the first of January 1505, Clarus Franciscus de Genulis wrote (Archivio dello Studio, "Libro segreto del Collegio," c. 3): "1505 Kallendis Januarii : Quae in collegio medicinae peracta fuerint dum trimestri sequenti prioratus officium exercerem ego clarus franciscus de genulis in sequentibus manu propria annotantur." On Clarus Franciscus de Genulis (d. 1524), who was on the faculty of the University of Bologna from 1498-99 to 1510-11 and 1512-13 to 1524-25, see Dallari, I and II and Alidosi, 41 (F).

orator of all ages."[24] Even allowing for some exaggeration, it would seem that Garzoni, in the opinion of a contemporary, was of some importance as an orator. The obituary note is interesting for a number of other reasons. In the first place, it gives the exact date of death, January 28, 1505, and not 1506 as some later scholars inferred from the date inscribed on the gravestone set up by Garzoni's heirs in the Chiostro of San Domenico in Bologna.[25] Second, the prior suggests that Garzoni died at the time when many subterranean winds (i.e., earthquakes) were terrorizing the citizens of Bologna.[26] Third, the writer refers to Garzoni's history of his native city and to his medical accomplishments.[27]

Garzoni's letter is preserved, at least in part, in three manuscripts, two in the University Library of Bologna and one in the Vatican. The first Bolognese University manuscript, which Frati thinks is fifteenth century and autograph, is MS. 750.[28] Unfortunately, the letter is incomplete; in fact, the one-half page which should have contained the last lines seems to have been torn out.[29] Furthermore, since the paper has blotted the ink, it is difficult to read. Fortunately, however, in the same library there is a later copy in MS. 1896, late sixteenth century, formerly in the library of San Domenico in Bologna.[30]

---

[24] *Libro segreto del Collegio* [note 23], carta 3 : "Erat enim garzo[nus] citra contentionem omnium aetatis nostrae oratorum eminentissimus" (Obituary notice published by Malagola, 224-225, n. 1).

[25] Fantuzzi, 79-80.

[26] *Libro segreto*, c. 3 : "Magister Johannes (sic) de garzonibus 28ª Januarii mortuorum numerum anxit dum urbs nostra subterraneis ["sobterraneis"; Malagola] ventis agitata et cives metu perculsi maximo tremore tremerunt." See Corrado Ricci, "La Madonna del Terremoto dipinta dal [Francesco] Francia," *La vita italiana*, n.s., 3 (1897), 881-886·

[27] For details, see the obituary notice printed by Malagola, 224.

[28] Bologna, Biblioteca Universitaria, MS. 750 (Lat. 442), f. 68ᵛ. See Frati (above, n. 22), *Studi italiani di filologia classica* 16 (1908), 263, (Lat.) n. 442 : " 'Ioannis Garzoni orationes ... cum epistolis aliquot Io. Garzonis.' Cart., sec. XV... prov. 'Ex Biblioth. Io. Garzoni.' Autogr." Cf. Manfré (above, n. 5), 28 (1960), 45.

[29] Why was the remainder of the letter in this manuscript (cited below as B1) torn out ? One may be permitted to speculate that it was because the rest of the letter does not show Cicero in the most favorable light, which might have been painful for a committed Ciceronian. On the other hand, the end of the letter reveals Achillini in a rather favorable light, which one of his detractors could have found offensive.

[30] Bologna, Bibl. Univ., MS. 1896 (Lat. 842, Vol. I), f. 274-274ᵛ. Frati (1908), 367 (Lat. 842, Vol. I). Cf. Manfré, 27 (1959), 259 and Kristeller, *Iter Italicum*, I, 24b. Frati says : "sec. XVI... prov. da Giovanni Garzoni." Cf. Fantuzzi, 95-98. This volume is one of

This book, along with many other treasures, was transferred, probably in 1837, to the Biblioteca Comunale in the Palazzo dell'Archiginnasio.[31] However, it is possible that the volume was one of the seventy-one given by the eighteenth-century canonist, also named Giovanni Garzoni, to the library of the University of Bologna.[32] With respect to the date of this manuscript, we are more fortunate. Frati does give the date of the MS. as supplied in a letter of dedication, but he omits much interesting information which can be supplied by Fantuzzi.[33] Fantuzzi provides the letter of dedication of one Fabritius Garzonus (or Garzonius), son of Marcellus and grandson of Giovanni, to the Dominican Antonius Balducius of Forlì.[34] As I understand Fabritius, he says that in accordance with his father's (Marcellus') wishes he is presenting works of Giovanni, his (Fabritius') grandfather, which he has collected in three volumes, to the library of the monastery of San Domenico. He enumerates the contents of the three volumes which include, among other items, many lives of saints and martyrs, histories of numerous cities of Gaul, Spain and Saxony, opuscula on friendship, on princes and their duties, on the highest good, orations and, finally, letters, of which many are addressed to brothers of Antonius' religious order. He concludes with the city and the date, which corresponds to the eighth of February 1568.[35] On f. 185 of MS.

---

three, containing treatises, letters and orations, which have survived, it would seem, in a damaged condition. See Fantuzzi, 95.

[31] See P. Alfonso d'Amato, "Il patrimonio librario dell' antica Biblioteca [di San Domenico]," in P. Michele Casali, ed., *La Biblioteca di S. Domenico in Bologna* (Bologna, 1959), 67-113.

[32] Lodovico Frati, "Bologna. R. Biblioteca Universitaria," in Giuseppe Mazzatinti, *Inventari dei manoscritti delle biblioteche d'Italia*, XV (1909), 6.

[33] Fantuzzi, 95. Cf. Manfré, 27 (1959), 259, and Kristeller, *Iter*, I, 24b.

[34] MS. 1896 (Lat. 842, Vol. I), f. III^v; in Fantuzzi, 95 : "Illustri Viro ac merito Venerando Patri Fratri Antonio Balduccio Foroliviensi apud D. Dominicum Bonon. Priori dignissimo ... Fabritius Garzonius S. P. D." Cf. Manfré, 27 (1959), 259. On Fabritius Garzonius (d. 1574), see Dallari, II, 135; Fantuzzi, 77-78; and Luigi Ferrari, *Onomasticon* (Milan, 1947), 339. On Antonius Balducius Foroliviensis (d. 1580), see Ferrari, 66. For help with a number of manuscript problems, I am grateful to Dott. ssa Luigia Risoldi, formerly Director of the Bolognese Biblioteca Universitaria.

[35] MS. 1896 (Fantuzzi, 95, as corrected, and Manfré [1959], 259) : "Cum quotidie varia opera Joannis Garzonis Avi mei sua tempestate eloquentissimi a variis iisque ingenuis Viris petantur, quin in lucem etiam me inscio prodeant, meminerimque Marcellum Patrem meum statuisse Coenobio isti amplissimo omnia offerre, proximis diebus, quo voluntati ipsius etiam mortui satisfacerem, quotquot potui collegi, in triaque volu-

1896, and not f. 184 as Frati says, we read : "Epistolae (sic) Familiares Ioannis Garzonis divise in X libros," and Fantuzzi lists Garzoni's letter to Achillini as appearing in the fourth book.[36]

The third version of the letter is in Vat. Lat. 10686, which contains an eighteenth-century collection of Garzoni's letters and also a life of Garzoni prepared by the Dominican Vincentius Dominicus Fassinus.[37] According to a note near the beginning of the manuscript, Fassini says that he prepared his selection of Garzoni's letters from a manuscript belonging to the library of San Domenico in the year 1761.[38] This same Fassini (1738-1787),[39] under the pseudonym 'Dionysius Sandellius,' prepared in 1765 a life of Garzoni and intended to publish it together with a selection of his letters, but only the biography appeared, in 1781.[40]

As far as the actual date of Garzoni's letter to Achillini is concerned, the evidence is not conclusive. The first and obvious indication is the fact that Frati dates MS. 750 as fifteenth century.[41] Second, in Book IV, sixty-ninth letter of the collection in the second Bolognese University manuscript named, I did see a date, viz., October 26, 1504; this was the only date seen in Book IV.[42] Perhaps the best

---

mina digessi ... Haec sunt in iis Voluminibus multa Sanctorum, Patrum et Martyrum Vitae, plurium Civium Historiae, Galliae, Hispaniarum, Pannoniae, Saxonia[e], Libelli de Amicitia, de Principe, de officio Principis, de summo bono. Quamplures Orationes et Epistolae (sic) Familiares ex quibus multae ad clarissimos quosque istius Ordinis Viros inscriptae ... Vale. Bononiae sexto Idus Februarias MDLXVIII."

[36] Fantuzzi, 96. In fact, in Book IV, there are seventy letters, of which the one to Achillini is number sixty-seven. Book IV begins on f. 252 and ends on f. 279.

[37] Biblioteca Apostolica Vaticana, Vat. Lat. 10686, p. 106-107.

[38] *Ibid.*, p. 3. See Marcus Vattasso in Vattasso and Henricus Carusi, *Codices Vaticani Latini* [10301-10700] (Rome, 1920), p. 659 : "Joannis Garzonis Bononiensis selectae epistolae nunc primum e manuscripto codice bibliothecae S. Dominici erutae ["editae": MS.] et auctoris vita illustratae a F. Vincentio Dominico Fassini O[rdinis] P[raedicatorum] anno 1761."

[39] See Ferrari, 296b.

[40] See Fantuzzi, 82 (cf. Vattasso [above, n. 38] : "Fassini Domenicano sotto nome di Dionisio Sandelli con questo titolo *De Vita et Scriptis Joannis Garzonis Bononiensis Commentarius Dionysi Sandelli, praemissus Epistolarum selectarum eiusdem Garzonis Collectioni quas anno 1765 cum praefatione Auctor ipse Commentarii edere cogitaverat*. Brixiae 1781 ex typographia Petri Vescovi.") There is a copy of this rare work in the Biblioteca Comunale dell'Archiginnasio in Bologna.

[41] See n. 28 above.

[42] MS. 1896 (Lat. 842, Vol. I), f. 279 : "VII Kalendas Novembres 1504."

that one can do is suggest that the letter was written in the late fifteenth century, probably about the year 1500.[43]

What does Garzoni's letter to Achillini tell us about the relationship between the two writers, their respective interests and Achillini's impact upon a distinguished contemporary? For a number of reasons, we can say that Garzoni is more interested in the *studia humanitatis*, viz., in grammar, rhetoric, history, poetry and moral philosophy, particularly as studied by the contemporary Florentine humanists;[44] of these subjects, most obvious is his interest in oratory. For one thing, he studied under Lorenzo Valla and Antonio Urceo (Codro), both of whom were interested in these subjects. For another, Garzoni cites specific texts of Cicero on two occasions (although one of them does not seem to be Ciceronian). Third, we know about Garzoni's importance as an orator, which would also suggest his interest in Cicero as a model. On the other hand, I know of no such interest on Achillini's part in such oratorical and literary subjects as treated by Cicero and by the late fifteenth-century humanists.[45] From the letter, Garzoni seems to be defending Achillini against attacks of contemporaries; it is also clear that he considers Achillini to be an important philosopher.

The occasion for Garzoni's support appears to have been an oration or speech Achillini gave for which, apparently, he was taken to task. At the beginning of the letter, Garzoni says that for a long time he has considered Achillini's high reputation among their contemporaries to be well deserved. Garzoni suggests that some of his contemporaries

---

[43] On the other hand, there is a clue in lines 14-15 of the letter, where Garzoni says that on the previous day the [papal?] legate had found Achillini's oration to be elegant and profound. If the legate had been present at the general congress of the Franciscan Order held in Bologna on June 1, 1494, it is possible that Garzoni's letter was written to Achillini on the day after Achillini had delivered the substance of his first printed work, *Quodlibeta de intelligentiis*, to the Franciscan Congress. That he did present his work to the Franciscan Congress, meeting at Bologna on June 1, 1494, is proved by the explicit of the printed edition, also dated 1494, f. 35b : "Expliciunt quolibeta de intelligentiis ... ab Alexandro de Achillinis ... Anno Domini Mccccxxxxiiii Kalendis Iuniis *in capitulo generali minorum edita* ..." (emphasis added). Cf. Nardi, *Saggi*, 179-180.

[44] On the expression *studia humanitatis*, see Paul Oskar Kristeller, *Renaissance Thought : The Classic, Scholastic and Humanist Strains* (New York, 1961), 9-10, nn. 6-8.

[45] Still, Achillini had some interest in at least one of the *studia humanitatis*, viz., rhetoric, as reflected in the fact that he helped prepare for publication Aegidius Romanus' (i.e., Colonna, also called Giles of Rome) commentary on Aristotle's *Rhetoric*. Achillini wrote an introductory letter for the edition but it was not published until 1515, in Venice, three years after his death.

are critical of Achillini because, paraphrasing a text attributed to Cicero (falsely, it would seem), they are envious of him. What Garzoni seems to find fault with is what appeared to him to be an intemperate objection to Achillini. One of his contemporaries criticized Achillini because of his uneasiness in speaking before a multitude, especially at the beginning of his speech. This we may infer from the letter. But that should surprise no one, Garzoni says in effect. Even Cicero had the same anxiety when he began to speak, and surely you, least of all, Alexander, should be compared with him. From this remark it is clear that although Garzoni admires Achillini as a philosopher, he is not blind to the fact that Achillini's discourse is somewhat less than Ciceronian in style; I suspect that he is also referring to Achillini's prose style.

In substance, Garzoni's attitude substantiates another near contemporary view of Achillini, viz., that of Paolo Giovio. Among other things, Giovio says that Achillini was an accurate interpreter of Averroes and solid in doctrine. But, he implies, although Achillini was formidable in debate, he was less successful in class lecturing. For this reason, and because of his marked ambition, his 'concorrente' at Padua, the famous Pietro Pomponazzi of Mantua (1462-1525), was able to depopulate his lectures.[46] But, Garzoni says near the end of his letter, "we must leave those [who criticize you] to their ignorance (*sed relinquamus eos cum ignorantia sua*)." He also says that he considers himself to be one of Achillini's best friends.

In sum, then, the letter makes clear that Garzoni and Achillini are on good terms and that Garzoni is interested in and concerned for Achillini's welfare. Secondly, it seems just as obvious that their interests

---

[46] Paolo Giovio, *Elogia veris clarorum virorum imaginibus apposita* (Venice, 1546), f. 36 (*Opera*, vol. VIII : *Elogia virorum illustrium*, ed. R. Meregazzi [Rome, 1972], 84) : "Alexander Achillinus Bononiensis accuratus Averrois interpres, quum Patavii Philosophiam profiteretur, solidae, constantisque doctrinae famam obtinuit, vel ipso Pomponatio acri aemulo insidiosa ambitione, scholam eius depopulante." That Achillini was a colleague of Pomponazzi during the academic year 1506-1507 can be proved by the beginning of Gregorio da Lucca's 'reportatio' of Pomponazzi's commentary on Averroes' *De substantia orbis* (Vat. Regin. Lat. 1279, f. 3, in *Pomponazzi : Corsi inediti dell' insegnamento padovano*. I. *Super libello de substantia orbis*, ed. Antonino Poppi [Padua, 1966], p. 1) : "Expositio Libelli De Substantia Orbis Excellentissimi ... Magistri Petri Pomponacci Mantuani Patavii. M.DVII.XX. Mensis Februarii dum Primum Locum Ordinarie Philosophiae ad concurrentiam excellentissimi Allexandri Achellini (sic) Bononiensis publice profiteretur." This evidence should have been included in my paper on Achillini's two-year sojourn at Padova (see n. 3 above).

do not coincide; Garzoni is more interested in the *studia humanitatis* whereas, by inference, Achillini finds the traditional Aristotelian and Averroistic doctrines more to his liking. Nevertheless, it is clear that Garzoni respects Achillini while not being blinded to the limitations of his style. Finally, Achillini's impact on Garzoni had been noticeable and marked. As suggested, what Garzoni seems to be doing is taking to task contemporaries who had been criticizing Achillini's delivery and, I suspect, prose style; he is saying that they should be more reflective and temperate in their attacks. These facts and inferences help account for Garzoni's defense of Achillini.

As stated, Garzoni's letter to Achillini is found in three manuscripts :

- B1 Bologna, Biblioteca Universitaria, MS. 750 (Lat. 442), Fifteenth century, f. 68ᵛ (incomplete);
- B2 Bologna, Biblioteca Universitaria, MS. 1896 (Lat. 842, Vol. I), dated 1568, f. 274-274ᵛ; and
- V Biblioteca Apostolica Vaticana, Lat. 10686, dated 1761, pp. 106-107.

Since B1 is blotted and consequently difficult to make out, I have had to depend more on B2 than I would have liked. But I did determine that the differences between B1 and B2 are, for the most part, trivial. For the part of the letter not contained in B1, I have usually chosen the reading of B2 over V unless the sense required otherwise.

Text

Ioannes Garzo[nus] Alexandro Achillino Bonon[iensi] S[alutem] P[lurimam] D[icit] : Dignitatem tuam, mi Alexander, diu statui mihi tecum habere communem. Nulla enim pars corporis tui vacat officio. Addo, quam calleas philosophiam, quae quantum tibi laudis afferat, re ipsa
5 docet, ut ex omnibus philosophis, quos mea vidit aetas, tibi principatus deferri possit. Sed cum invidia, teste M[arco] Tullio, comes sit virtutis,[47] nulla me admiratio tenet, si a quibusdam minus liberalis

---

1 *P. D.*] omitted B2 and V. 4 *calleas*] calles B1, B2. *re*] res B1, B2, V. 6-7 *comes sit virtutis*] virtutis sit comes B2, V. 7 *tenet*] tenit B1, tenuit B2.

---

[47] *invidia, teste Marco Tullio, comes sit virtutis*. Not found in Cicero's writings. See the *lexica* of a) philosophical works (Merguet, I-II [1887-1892]); b) speeches (*ibid.*, I-II [1877-1880]); c) rhetorical works (Abbott, Oldfather and Canter, 1964); and d) letters (Oldfather, Canter and Abbott, 1938). See also *Thesaurus Linguae Latinae*, III (1906-1912), cols. 1769-1780 [*comes*] and VII, 2 (1959), cols. 199-206 [*invidia*]. However, see Cornelius Nepos (d. 44 B. C.), *Chabrias*, 3, 3; [*Opera*] *quae exstant* ..., ed. Henrica Mal-

de te prolatus est sermo; satius illis fuisset, si cogitationes suas in melius retulissent. Nam quod nonnullos qui tibi virtutem invident,
10 ingenio tuo et industria fregisti, aequo animo ferre non possunt. Flores tu eo tempore in quo videre hominem philosophum habendum est loco miraculi. Non fero etiam graviter exardeo, cum quosdam animadvertam qui virtute et scientia tecum volunt in contentionem venire honoris. Pridie apud legatum et elegans et gravis abs te habita
15 est oratio. Admirabatur asellus, quod dicere inciperes cum timore.[48] Quotienscu[m]que M[arcus] Tullius dicebat, totiens ei videbatur venire in iudicium, non ingenii solum sed virtutis atque officii.[49] Eo fiebat ut magna sollicitudine animi et magno timore diceret.[50] Nulli mirum videri debet si tibi, qui cum Cicerone minime [sic] conferendus es,
20 dicenti eadem acciderunt. Sed relinquamus eos cum ignorantia sua.

---

10 *fregisti*] fregeris B1, B2, V.   11 *videre*] videndo B2.   12 *etiam*] at B2, V.
13 *virtute et scientia*] scientia, virtute B2, V.   *tecum*] et tecum B2.   *volunt*] nolunt B1, B2.   15 *inciperes*] inciperet B1, B2.   16 *Quotienscu[m]que*] Quotiescunque B2, Quotiescumque V.   16 *totiens*] totens B1, toties B2, V.   17 *atque*] et B2, V. *officii*] B1 ends.   18 *timore*] timore timore B2.   20 *dicenti*] dicendi B2, V.   21 *deseram*] deferam B2.

---

covati, 2d ed. (Turin, 1960 [1944]), p. 71, lines 9-11 : "est enim hoc commune vitium in magnis liberisque civitatibus, *ut invidia gloriae comes sit ...*" (See A. Otto, *Die Sprichwoerter und sprichwoerterlichen Redensarten der Roemer* [Leipzig, 1890; repr. Hildesheim, 1962], p. 176.) Cf. Sallustius Crispus (d. 35 B.C.), *Bellum Iugurthinum*, 55, 3; ed. P. H. Damsté, 3rd ed. (Leiden, 1950), p. 64, lines 3-4 : "*meminisse post gloriam invidiam sequi*" (Otto, *ibid.*). Cf. St. Hieronymus (d. 420), *Regula Monachorum*, Caput 19, 'De laude et detractione vitanda, et periculis huius vitae'; *Patrologia Latina* 30 (1865), col. 379A [ed. 1846, col. 367B] : "Qui invidus est, aliena felicitate torquetur, quoniam *virtus semper invidiae patet.*"

[48] *Admirabatur asellus, quod dicere inciperes cum timore.* I am indebted to Professor F. Edward Cranz for the following suggestions : either 'Asellus' is a contemporary name (Asellius, Asellio ?) or 'asellus' may not be a proper name at all, but may simply mean 'some ass,' i.e., 'some ass marvelled.'

[49] Cicero, *Pro A. Cluentio oratio* 18, 51; *Orationes* I : *Pro Sex. Roscio, Pro Cluentio ... Pro Caelio*, ed. Albert Curtis Clark (Oxford, 1905) : "Semper equidem *magno cum metu incipio dicere; quotienscumque dico, totiens mihi videor in iudicium venire non ingeni solum sed etiam virtutis atque offici* (sic), ne aut id profiteri videar quod non possim, quod est impudentiae, aut non id efficere quod possim, quod est aut perfidiae aut neglegentiae." Cf. E. G. Sihler, *Cicero of Arpinum* ... (New Haven, 1914), 108-113, at 111-112, and H. J. Rose, *Handbook of Latin Literature* ... 2nd ed. (London, 1949), 174.

[50] See the text in the previous note, first sentence : "Semper equidem magno cum metu incipio dicere." The most striking example was Cicero's unsuccessful attempt in 52 B. C. to defend T. Annius Milo, accused of killing Clodius, both candidates for the consulship. According to three writers, viz., Asconius in his commentary on Cicero's

Quantum in me fuerit, non te deseram, presertim cum me optimum tibi esse Amicum profitear. Non te fugiat, mi Alexander, me existimationis tuae procurationem suscepisse. Vale.

University of South Carolina

---

21 *presertim*] omitted V.   23 *procurationem*] procuratorem B2.   *suscepisse*] suscaepisse B2.

Pro Milone, Dio Cassius and Plutarch, Cicero spoke feebly in Milo's defense and afterwards wrote the more highly regarded *Pro Milone* which, they say or imply, he should have delivered. But there seem to have been compelling political circumstances which may have helped to account for Cicero's 'timidity.' For Cicero's *Pro Milone* and Asconius' commentary, see *Orationes* II : *Pro Milone* ... *Philippicae* I-XIV, ed. A. C. Clark, 2nd ed. (Oxford, 1918), in particular, Asconius (d. 88 A.D.), *In Milonianam* (sic), 36. Cf. Cassius Dio (Second-Third Centuries A.D.), 40, 54, 2; *Dio's Roman History*, with English translation by Earnest Cary, III (London, 1914), 468-69 and Plutarch (d. ca. 120 A. D.), *Cicero*, 35; *Plutarch's Lives*, trans. Bernadotte Perrin, VII (London and New York : Loeb edition, 1919), 170-73. On this matter, see Jérôme Carcopino, *Cicero : The Secrets of His Correspondence*, trans. E. O. Lorimer, I (New Haven, 1951), 257, n. 3, and H. J. Rose, 182.

A FRAGMENT OF *AN EXPOSITION OF THE FIRST LETTER OF SENECA TO LUCILIUS* ATTRIBUTED TO PETER OF MANTUA

THEODORE E. JAMES

Very little is known about the circumstances of the life and of the academic career of Peter Alboini of Mantua (Petrus Mantuanus). The earliest reference to him that I was able to find is contained in the records of the University of Padua where, under the date of Sept. 3, 1389, he is said to be the son of Giovanni and a student of philosophy and logic.[1] In 1392 he is teaching natural philosophy at the University of Bologna along with Jacobus de Armis and Franciscus de Camerino.[2] In the early part of the first semester he wrote a letter to his former friend at Padua, Pietro Tomasi, which gives us some insight into his personal and academic interests.[3] He sends his regards to Petrus Paulus (Vergerius), Bartholomeus de Comitibus, Petrus Choco, Bartholomeus de Mantua, Baldassarus, Johannes de Janua, Antonius de Monte, Jacobus de Coracis, Almericus and Laurentius. In the spirit of Seneca's *First Letter to Lucilius* Alboini advises Tomasi to give himself in earnest to study, to avoid idleness and unfruitful friendships, and to develop his great potential in intellectual matters.

---

[1] A. Gloria, *Monumenti della Università di Padova (1318-1405)*, I (Padua, 1888), 512. See C. Vasoli, "Pietro degli Alboini da Mantova 'scolastico' della fine del Trecento e un'epistola di Coluccio Salutati," *Rinascimento*, 2nd ser., 3 (1963), 3-21. Though Vasoli does not refer to Alboini's *Expositio*, I am indebted to him for much information about Peter.

[2] U. Dallari, *I rotuli dei lettori, legisti e artisti dello Studio Bolognese dal 1384 al 1799*, IV (Bologna, 1924), 16-17.

[3] R. Cessi, "La giovinezza di Pietro Tomasi erudito del secolo XV," *Athenaeum* 1 (1913), 131; A. Segarizzi, "La corrispondenza familiare d'un medico erudito del Quattrocento (Pietro Tomasi)," *Atti dell'I. R. Accademia di scienze, lettere ed arti degli agiati in Rovereto*, 3rd ser., 13 (1907), 220, n. 2. Both articles are based on a manuscript in the Archivio di Stato in Venice : Procurator di S. Marco di Citra, Atti Congregazione di Carità, Busta 120. Professor Kristeller checked the manuscript for me and found that the letter is no longer in that manuscript.

Peter probably continued to teach Natural Philosophy at the University of Bologna until 1395.[4] From this time until 1399, perhaps the year of his death, his name appears on the university records as a teacher of moral philosophy, and also natural philosophy in the last year. It is quite possible that the *Expositio* was part of the content of his courses in moral philosophy.[5]

The reputation of Peter as a humanist-philosopher and the esteem in which he is held by his contemporaries are well known from the eulogies of Socino Benzi and Coluccio Salutati.[6] According to the latter, Peter has become proficient in grammar and rhetoric, he is an "illustrious dialectician" in the areas of Aristotelian and terminist logic, he is outstanding as a teacher of natural and moral philosophy, and he has a special love for Seneca. The latter alone would assure him of a welcome among his humanist contemporaries. However Peter still has not mastered the art of writing verse, in the opinion of Salutati, and is not completely enamored with the poets. Yet there is some hope for him to become a full-fledged humanist and Salutati volunteers to help Alboini understand the poets, especially Vergil.[7]

---

[4] Dallari (*loc. cit.*) mentions no teachers for the years 1393-95. Socino Benzi mentions in his *Life of Ugo Benzi* that Hugo studied under Peter at Bologna in 1393. See D. P. Lockwood, *Ugo Benzi, Medieval Philosopher and Physician 1376-1439* (Chicago, 1951), 23-24.

[5] The format in which the matter is treated is representative of a classroom "explication du texte" rather than a letter like the ones written by C. Salutati to G. Quatrario, Bernardo da Moglio and Antonio da Scarperia (F. Novati, ed., *Epistolario di Coluccio Salutati*, vol. I, Bk. 2. Letter V; vol. II, Bk. 7, Letter IIII; vol. III, Bk. 10, Letter VIIII; vol. IV, Ep. Agg. I, in *Fonti per la storia d'Italia*, vols. 15-18, Rome, 1896). In the same series, vol. 74, L. Smith, ed., *Epistolario di Pier Paolo Vergerio* (Rome, 1934), Letter XXXVII, Vergerio discusses some of the contents of Seneca's *First Letter*. Uberto Decembrio discusses the same letter in his *Moralis philosophiae dialogi*, according to F. Novati (I, 65, n. 3), who refers to cod. Ambr. B, 123 sup. f. 109. Domenico de'Peccioli, *Commentarium in epistolas Senecae ad Lucilium*, in cod. Paris. Lat. 5815, is mentioned by J. Quétif and J. Echard, *Scriptores Ordinis Praedicatorum*, I (Paris, 1719, repr. New York, 1959), 771. F. Novati (III, 250, n. 1) gives the number of 8555 to this manuscript. The present shelf number is 8555. If Peter used Seneca's *Letters* as the basis of a course in moral philosophy it would be indicative of an interest that is distinctively humanistic and quite different from "scholastic" courses which were usually based on Aristotle's *Ethics*.

[6] Lockwood, 23-24; F. Novati, III, Letter XXII.

[7] Novati, *ibid*. A poem entitled *Carmina Petri Mantuani* is found in Venice, Biblioteca Marciana, Marc. lat. XI 59 (4152) ff. 166-167ᵛ, inc. cognite vir Musis priscis neque

The reputation of Peter in the fifteenth and sixteenth centuries is well documented by the many manuscripts and printed editions of his *Logica* and *De primo et ultimo instanti*, by four commentaries on the latter and by many references made to them by the philosophers, logicians and scientists of those times.[8]

The fragment printed here for the first time contains an explicit attribution of the work to Peter of Mantua. There is no historical evidence connecting it with Peter Pomponazzi (1462-1525), who also was known as Peter of Mantua. Although the date assigned to the manuscript does not make it impossible to allot the *Expositio* to Pomponazzi, the rest of the contents of the manuscript make such an attribution highly improbable. Peter Alboini did teach moral philosophy; the *Expositio* is in the format of a classroom analysis and commentary; Alboini did have a high regard for Seneca as Salutati witnesses; Novati attributes to Peter a letter treating of the same materials;[9] he was friendly with the humanists for whom the under-

---

vatibus impar. At end : Petrus de Mantua salutem et sincerum animum serviendi. (P. O. Kristeller, *Iter Italicum*, II [Leiden, 1967], 253). I was unable to secure a copy of this poem to check whether it could be the one read by Salutati which he says he could not understand. (Cf. Novati, *loc. cit.*, Letter XXII).

[8] There are at least seven manuscripts of the *Logica*, fifteen of the *De instanti* and five of the three different commentaries on the latter : three of that of Apollinaris Offredus, one of that by Giovanni Marliani and one by an Anonymous Commentator. The commentary by Mengo Bianchelli is found in a printed edition of Venice, 1507. Printed editions of the *Logica* and *De instanti* appeared in either Padua ca. 1475 or Venice 1480 (according to two different bibliographers), Pavia 1483 and Venice 1492 (two editions). References to Peter's works are found in Ermolao Barbaro (See C. Dionisotti, "Ermolao Barbaro e la fortuna di Suiseth," *Medioevo e Rinascimento, Studi in onore di Bruno Nardi*, I [Florence, 1955], 232 and 234. Dionisotti remarks that there are other references "che per tutto s'incontrano..."). Bassiano Politi da Lodi in his dedicatory letter to Rodrigo Carvajal in the 1505 edition of a collection of works by Suiseth, Bradwardine, Biagio Pelacani *et alii* refers to the *De instanti* and to Giovanni Marliani's commentary on it (Dionisotti, 238-9). Gaetanus de Thienis refers to Peter in his commentary on the "De incipit et desinit" of Heytesbury and in his commentary "super primum sophisma" of the same (G. Hentisberus, *Regulae solvendi sophismata, de incipit et desinit* [Venice, 1494], ff. 27b, 28^{v}b, 82b, 82^{v}b). Simon de Lendenaria mentions Peter several times in his *Recollectae supra sophismatibus Hentisberi* (*ibid.*, ff. 171b, 175b, 180). Alessandro Achillini and Pietro Pomponazzi also refer to him (A. Achillini, *Opera omnia in unum collecta* [Venice, 1551], f. 74^{v}b; Pomponazzi, *De intensione et remissione formarum*, 1525], f. 12a). Pomponazzi calls Peter of Mantua a "vir certe acutissimi ingenii."

[9] Novati, I, p. 64, n. 3 : "cod. Vatic. 5122, c. 59 B." Novati's reference to a "Letter" on the subject by Peter may actually be the *Expositio* which Novati refers to in a note to Salutati's Letter to Peter Alboini, vol. III, Letter XXII, p. 319. The folio reference

standing of the *First Letter* was such a challenge and source of lively debate because the words are expressed "dubio et obscuro et abdito sensu."[10] A topic which challenged the minds of Petrarch, Giovanni Dondi, Lazzaro da Cornigliano, Gasparino Barzizza, Domenico de' Peccioli, Marsilio di Santa Sofia, Alberico da Rosciate, Donato da Compostella, Piero Paolo Vergerio, Martin Recco, Uberto Decembrio, Coluccio Salutati, Giovanni Quatrario, Bernardo da Moglio, Antonio da Scarperia, *et alii* would be an important and popular one to discuss in the university course in moral philosophy as well as in private letters.[11] A combination of evidence presented here with the date and explicit reference in the manuscript may be sufficient for the time being to allow us to accept the *Expositio* as the work of Peter Alboini of Mantua.

According to Alboini the purpose of this *First Letter* is to persuade Lucilius to gather time and use it so that no part of life may slip away unprofitably. In a fashion that was customary among humanists he gives an elaborate exposition of the first paragraph, which may have been his first lecture on the *Letters* themselves. He divides it into two parts, the first about the ways in which time passes unprofitably and is lost by us, and the second about the ways in which a man's life flows away and is lived badly. It is in the second part that Peter devotes a great deal of space to the textual problem about the correct wording of the passage and to the meaning of several of the terms employed in the different divisions of the life of man.[12] Peter prefers the reading which contends that the greatest part of life is lost to those acting evilly, i.e. acting with a bad intention; that a great part of life is lost to those doing nothing either good or evil,

---

is the same as Vat. lat. 5223, and Vat. lat 5122 does not contain such a Letter according to P. O. Kristeller, *Iter Italicum*, II, 331.

[10] C. Salutati, Letter to G. Quatrario, in Novati, I, Bk. 2, Letter V, p. 63.

[11] Novati; Smith; B. L. Ullman, *The Humanism of Coluccio Salutati*, Medioevo e Umanesimo, IV (Padua, 1963), 21. The interpretation of the words and contents of Seneca's *First Letter* was a subject of lively discussion and controversy at the time of Salutati. Ullman does not make any reference to the *Expositio* itself by Peter of Mantua.

[12] Judging from the *Letters* of Salutati the problem of the appropriate reading here was one of serious import and was discussed widely. Salutati prefers the reading of *magna pars ... male agentibus, maxima ... nichil, tota vita ... aliud*. He mentions some other opinions which have been identified as those of Domenico de'Peccioli, Alberico da Rosciate, Petrarch, Uberto Decembrio and Gasparinus Barzizza. Salutati makes no mention of Alboini or of his opinion in this place. See F. Novati. *loc. cit.*, notes.

because life is more unprofitable to one acting evilly than to one doing nothing good or evil; and that the whole of life is lost when one neither lives evilly nor does anything good or bad. Space does not permit me to go into greater detail about the variety of opinions expressed on these problems. I hope to be able to write a follow-up article to discuss this very interesting and widely debated issue. Peter thinks that his version of the text is more consistent with the rest of the *First Letter* and with the other works of Seneca which treat of the same topic, such as the *De brevitate vitae*.

Text

Expositio prime epistole Senece ad Lucilium quam edidit Magister Petrus de Mantua[13]

Ita fac. Seneca in hac prima epistola intendit suadere Lucilio quod ipse tempus suum coligat, et ita exigentibus rebus adaptet quod nequa de parte eius vita inutiliter elabatur. Dividitur autem hec epistola in partes duas quoniam in prima parte ortando quod tempus coligat et bene disponat, ostendit Lucilio quot modis a nobis tempus inutiliter effluat et perdatur ut illos modos ad posse devitet, malum enim non vitatur nisi cognitum. In secuda parte ostendit quot modis vita hominis inepte effluat et male ducatur comparandos[14] illos malos vite lapsus ad invicem. Pars ibi secunda, *Et si volueris.* Prima in duas, in prima namque parte ortatur Lucilium facere ea que scribit ipse se facere suadens quod coligat illa tempora que solebant ab eo Lucilio inaniter effluere cum ipse minor et impotentior esset. In parte secunda enumerat et declarat modos quibus a nobis tempora illa perduntur, pars ibi secunda, *Persuade tibi.* De prima dicit ortando Lucilium *Ita fac mi Lucili,* suple sicut facere te scribis, quia ista est epistola responsiva.

Vendica te tibi, id est, acquire te tibi. Collige tempus quod adhuc auferebatur, scilicet, per impotentiam cum ipse minor esses et nondum ad tantos labores aptus ad quantos nunc es. Super qua parte inteli-

---

[13] Città del Vaticano, Biblioteca Apostolica Vaticana, Vat. lat. 5223, ff. 59ᵛ, 60, 61, 61ᵛ. See P. O. Kristeller, *Iter Italicum*, II, 372. All quotations of the actual wording of Seneca's text of the *First Letter* will be italicized even though some are not underlined in the manuscript. I follow the spelling of the autograph.

[14] *comparando* ?

gendum primo quia dixi quod in hac prima parte ortatur Lucilium etc. quod ille imperativus potest ibi stare persuasive et preceptive, quia infra dicet se precipere, iuxta illos versus,

> Imperat, ortatur, permittit, consulit, orat,
> Temptat, et applaudit, solet irridere secundus.[15]

Inteligendum secundo quia dicit *vendica te tibi*, quod tunc homo se sibi vendicat cum ipse se a passionibus liberat iuxta illud Ciceronis quarto *Rhetoricum* [16] Liber est is qui nulli turpitudini servit. Et in quinto *Paradoxo* [17] inquit solum sapientem esse liberum, ceteros esse servos. Passiones autem sunt quas enumerat Boetius,[18] scilicet, spes, dolor, timor et gaudium, et plures enumerat Aristoteles,[19] scilicet, iram, concupiscentiam, invidiam, tristitiam, etc. Cum igitur homo se ab istis liberaverit, se sibi vendicaverit et liber et sui iuris erit. Tertio inteligendum quod a nobis tempora tripliciter effluunt in quibus nullum opus virtutis exercemus. Quedam auferuntur per impotentiam puta ea in quibus comedere, dormire et alia corporis comoda exercere oportet que tempora sunt dimidium vite vel plus. Unde Aristoteles primo *Ethicorum*[20] ait proverbium antiquorum fuisse quod nichil differe videntur felices a miseris secundum dimidium vite, quia dum dormiunt, dum comedunt, dum ventri intenti sunt non differunt, sed alio tempore maxime differunt, quia hi bonas, illi malas operationes exercent. Quedam igitur tempora a nobis auferuntur. Quedam surripiuntur per delectationes. Unde Ovidius *de Fastis*,[21] Vivimus indocti, placidisque senescimus annis. Et currunt, freno non remorante, dies. Et in nono [decimo] *Methamorphoseos*,[22] Labitur oculte

---

[15] H. Walther, *Carmina medii aevi posterioris latina*. I : *Initia carminum ac versuum medii aevi posterioris latinorum* (Gottingen, 1959), p. 444, 8778 : Imperat, hortatur : Berlin, lat. qu. 699 (s. XII.), f. 42ᵛ. *Die Handschriften-Verzeichnisse der Preussischen Staatsbibliothek zu Berlin*, XIV, *Verzeichnis der lateinischen Handschriften*, III : *Die Görreshandschriften von Fritz Schillmann* (Berlin, 1919), p. 157a : "Bl. 42ᵛ Istud folium tractat de prisciano maiori"; p. 158a : "Imperat, hortatur, predicit, consulit, orat/ Permittit, temptat, irascitur inperativus."

[16] *Rhetorica ad Herennium*, IV, 17, 4-5.

[17] *M. T. Ciceronis paradoxa Stoicorum*, V, 33, 17-18; 35, 3-4.

[18] *Philosophiae consolationis libri quinque*. Lib. I, meter lines 8-11 : gaudia pelle/ pelle timorem / spemque fugato / nec dolor adsit.

[19] Cf. *Nicomachean Ethics*, II, 5, 1105b21-23; *Rhetoric*, II, 1378a20ff.

[20] *Nicomachean Ethics*, I, 13, 1102b6.

[21] Ovid, *Fasti* VI, 771-772 : "Tempora labuntur, tacitisque senescimus annis, et fugiunt freno non remorante dies."

[22] Ovid, *Metamorphoses*, X, 519-20.

fallitque volatilis etas. Et nichil est annis velotius. Et Aristoteles quarto *Physicorum*,[23] Gaudentes modicum considerant de tempore, et ideo eis effluit ipsis non percipientibus quia delectationes eorum animum tantum aliciunt ut ad alia animum non extendant. Tristantes autem e converso animum in diversa revolvunt et inquirunt qualiter a tristitia liberentur et expectant unde et tempus considerant, et hinc est quod hyemales dies aliquando apparent longiores quam sint propter eorum tedium. Et quedam effluunt per negligentiam seu per accidiam. Ultimo notatur quod ibi est relatio simplex, colige tempus quod auferebatur, sicut mulier damnavit que salvavit. Et zephirus
f. 60 revehit frondes[24] / quas boree spiritus aufert.[25] Et expectantibus cum cupiditate magna videtur tempus longum quia multum de eo considerant, ideo omnis mora torquet amantem.[26]

Exinde cum inquit *Persuade*, in ista parte enumerat et declarat et quot modis et quibus antedicta tempora perdantur, et post hoc, secundo comparat membra ad invicem. Ibi secunda, *Turpissima*. De prima dicit quod iam tactum est per alia vocabula, tamen cum prioribus tribus convertibilia, respondendo singula singulis. Exinde ait *Turpisima tamen iactura est*. Comparat membra dicens quod temporis amissio que est per negligentiam est molestius ferenda quam temporis ereptio et quam temporis subductio per delectationes, quod elapsum est, nam temporis ablatio vel ereptio est fere tota tollerabilis. Si enim somno et comestioni tantum solum tempus impendatur quantum oportet, tunc tota temporis ereptio toleratur. Temporis quoque subductio interdum tolerari debet si ipsa fuerit quando oportet et ubi oportet et quantum oportet. Temporis vero amissio que per negligentiam est tolleranda non videtur, quia unum de capitalibus

---

[23] Aristotle, *Physics*, IV, 11, 218b21-31.
[24] At the bottom of f. 59ᵛ is found this note :
"Tempora a nobis tripliciter *effluunt* [suprascr. labuntur]
Quedam auferentur per impotentiam.
Quedam surripiuntur per delectationes.
Quedam effluunt per negligentiam.
Sed statim insurgit dubium numquid tantum tripliciter a nobis effluant tempora. Et arguitur quod tantum uno modo quia aut aliquid agimus aut nichil; si aliquid agimus, non amittimus tempus iuxta communem modum loquendi; si nichil, tunc unico modo amittitur quia nichil agendo. Oppositum arguitur quod plipliciter [dupliciter ?] quia per malas et vitiosas operationes."
[25] Boethius, I, V, meter lines 14-15 : "quas Boreae spiritus aufert / revehat mites zephyrus frondes."
[26] Marginal note : "Expectatio supplicium est, franciscus petrarcha."

peccatis est. Ex accidia alia plurima peccata oriuntur ut luxuria. Unde Ovidius *de Remedio*,[27] Otia si tollas, periere cupidinis arcus, et idem in eodem, [28] Queritur Egistus quare sit factus adulter. Causa est in promtu, desidiosus erat. Oriuntur etiam male et varie cogitationes multe. Unde Lucanus,[29] Variam semper dant otia mentem. Est igitur molestius ferenda temporis iactura que fit per negligentiam quam aliqua aliarum duarum.

Exinde dicit, *Et si volueris attendere*. In parte ista ostendit, presupposita divisione de vite lapsu inutili, [et ?] membra comparat; et dividitur hec in duas partes, quia in prima facit quod dictum est, in parte secunda probat, ibi secunda, *quem michi dabis*. Pro primo intelectu est advertendum quod duplex litera hic invenitur,[30] *magna pars vite elabitur male agentibus, maxima nichil agentibus*. Pro cuius expositione, si litera sic legatur, intelligendum quod hominum quidam agunt bonum imperfecte sicut aliqui qui vadunt ad eclesiam propter vitare infamiam, vel qui dant elimosynam propter inanem gloriam. Alii sunt qui nichil boni faciunt. Alii sunt qui simpliciter agunt malum. Dicatur igitur quod primis, scilicet, male agentibus, id est, imperfecte bonum agentibus magna pars vite labitur. Unde accipitur ibi male agere pro imperfecte agere, sicut solemus dicere, equus male curit, id est, tarde et imperfecte, ita dicitur male agere, id est, imperfecte agere. Secundis maxima pars labitur, scilicet, nichil agentibus, id est, nichil boni nec mali agentibus. Terciis vero tota vita labitur, scilicet, simpliciter malum agentibus. Sed iste textus cum eius expositione non videtur conformari sequenti litere illi, scilicet, *quem michi dabis* etc., quia Seneca ibi probat dictum suum et ultimo vult concludere quod nullus est qui consideret tempus, tamquam in illa divisione innuerit omnibus vitam labi. Illa autem expositio solum loquitur de quibusdam etc. Alia vero litera est, *Maxima pars vite labitur male agentibus, magna nichil agentibus* etc. Pro cuius litere expositione inteligendum primo, quod refert inter male agere et malum agere. Male enim agere est cum mala intentione agere, sed malum agere est rem malam facere etiam licet sit cum bona intentione, sicut frequenter accidit quod volens bene facere malum facit preter intentionem. Ex quo patet quod ceteris paribus peius est male facere quam malum facere et ideo non potest

---

[27] Ovid, *De remedio amoris*, 139.
[28] *Ibid.*, 161-2.
[29] Lucan, *Pharsalia*, IV, 704.
[30] See n. 12 above.

f. 61 accipi [31] / ibi li *aliud* pro malo quia plus de vita elabitur male agentibus quam malum agentibus. Unde scribitur circa tertium *Ethicorum* quod Deus est considerator adverbiorum et non nominum,[32] quia connumerat plus qualiter agas et quali intentione quam quid agas licet agas male. Secundo patet etiam quod inutilius vita labitur male agenti quam nichil agenti, scilicet, nec bonum nec malum, ideo ibi bene dicitur *magna*, ibi *maxima*. Ulterius inteligendum quod eorum quibus inutiliter vita labitur quidam male agunt, quidam nichil agunt et quidam dant se delectationibus. Et nulli tantum perseverant in suo proposito sicut tercii, quia difficile nimis est a delectationibus abstinere. Unde dicit infra Seneca[33] quod quidam sunt qui ante moriuntur quam ipsi coincipiunt vivere, quia ipsi continue dant se delectationibus mundanis, non tamen alios ledendo sed suum expendendo etc. Et ideo dicitur *male agentibus maxima, nichil agentibus magna*, delectationibus se prebentibus tota vita labitur, et scias quod hec distinctio nuper data sumpta est ab ipsomet Seneca in principio libelli de *Brevitate Vite*[34] ubi sic loquitur, Satis longa vita et in maximarum rerum consumatione large data est, si tota bene colocaretur. Sed ubi per luxum, ubi per negligentiam defluit, ubi nulli bone rei impenditur, (...) quam ire non inteleximus, transisse sentimus. In quibus verbis tangit luxum qui triplex est, ut inquit Ysidorus,[35] scilicet, in victu, coitu et vestitu, per quem luxum inteligit delectationes. Tangit aliud membrum cum dicit, *Ubi nulli rei bone impenditur*, sed male, tangit male agentes. Sed adhuc ista expoxitio licet ipsa sit satis prope veritatem tamen non videtur probari per textum sequentem immediate nec illi textui est conformis sicut enim patet per textum sequentem, in hac distinctione vult innuere quod nullus est cui non labatur vita inutiliter, prout dicit Seneca, *quem michi dabis qui aliquod precium tempori ponat, qui diem extimet*, etc., quasi dicat nullum.

Dicendum igitur quod maxima pars vite labitur male agentibus,

---

[31] At bottom of f. 60 : "volve cartam ubi tale signum ◻ ."
At top of f. 61 : "supra volve cartam ubi tale signum ◪ ."

[32] D. Du Cange, *Glossarium mediae et infimae latinitatis*, rev. ed., ed. L. Favre, I (1883), 98 : "Adverbium est pars orationis quo recta forma clauditur operis, ut Deus non est remunerator nominum sed adverbiorum. Melberi Vocabularius praedicantium." This is the closest I could find to the actual text.

[33] *Epist.* XXIII, 11. There are many different versions of this text. See Salutati, III, Bk. 10, Letter VIIII, p. 253, lines 25-26 and Loeb ed. Seneca, Letter XXIII, 11.

[34] *Dialogorum liber X ad Paulinum de brevitate vitae*, 1. 3.

[35] I was unable to locate this in any of the consulted writings of Isidore of Seville, Isidor Pacensis or Isidor Mercator.

inteligendo ut in secunda expositione, et magna nichil agentibus, et tota labitur aliud agentibus de quibus minus videretur quicquid agant, sive dent se delectationibus sive dent se artificiis vel cuivis alteri rei, quia ut ipsemet Seneca dicit *ad Paulinum de Brevitate Vite*,[36] Exceptis admodum paucis, ceteros in ipso vite apparatur vita destituit, dum autem parant vivere, dicit eos Seneca non vivere. Unde dicit etiam paulo post principium[37] quod omnes homines sunt inquieti, quia alius spe lucri condendi cupidine captus trans maria ducitur, alium in supervacuis laboribus tenet operosa sedulitas, alius avaricia torquetur, et sic discurit ostendendo omnibus vitam labi. Unde ad hoc ut Seneca bene affirmaret vitam omnibus inutiliter labi, dixit vitam totam labi illis de quibus minime videretur, puta agentibus aliud a male agere et a nichil agere quicquid agant, ut ipse innuat omnibus vitam labi quod statim ipse probat, quod scilicet, omnibus vita labatur, quia dicit, *quem dabis michi qui aliquid precium tempori ponat, qui diem extimet* etc., quasi dicat nullum.

Sed statim occurit dubium contra istam expositionem quia videtur quod adhuc equaliter labatur, vel plus, de vita et male agentibus quam artificibus et vite apparatui intendentibus, nam male agunt simpliciter, igitur non bene dicitur quod tota vita labitur istis et maxima pars illis, sed pocius dicendum fuit e converso. Ad quod dicendum est quod ad hoc, ut Seneca penitus innueret, quod nulli sunt quibus non inepte
61ᵛ vita labatur, dixit totam / vitam labi illis quibus non ita videtur vita labi, non quia Seneca neget etiam male agentibus vitam totam labi, immo in tertio membro innuit argumentum per locum a minori, ut si de quo minus videtur inesse et inest, ergo de quo magis; sed minus videtur inesse de intendentibus apparatui vite, qui etiam non videntur male agere, quod scilicet eis tota vita labatur, et tamen labitur, igitur multo magis labitur aliis quibus videtur.[38]

This *Expositio* by Peter Alboini of Mantua is significant in that it points up the interest of a so-called scholastic logician and natural and moral philosopher in the humanism of the fourteenth century. In this treatise we see something of Peter's humanistic background

---

[36] *Op. cit.*, 1.1.
[37] *Ibid.*, 2.1.
[38] Rest of folio blank. I am indebted to Professor Paul O. Kristeller for the reference he gave me to this work attributed to Peter of Mantua. He has assisted me in ways too numerous to mention in regard to the completion of my study of Peter Alboini's *De primo et ultimo instanti* and of the final version of the *Expositio. Ad multos annos.*

in the classical poets such as Ovid and Lucan as well as the expected acquaintance with Aristotle, Cicero and Boethius. More than that his knowledge of the *Dialogues* of Seneca and the fact that he probably used Seneca's *Epistulae Morales* as the basis of his course on moral philosophy definitely make him one of the propagators of the humanist tradition.

Manhattan College

BIBLIOGRAPHY OF THE PUBLICATIONS OF
PAUL OSKAR KRISTELLER
FOR THE YEARS 1929-1974

MAJOR PUBLICATIONS

1929

1 *Der Begriff der Seele in der Ethik des Plotin.* Heidelberger Abhandlungen zur Philosophie und ihrer Geschichte, 19. Edited by Ernst Hoffmann and Heinrich Rickert. Tübingen : Verlag von J. C. Mohr (Paul Siebeck), 1929. viii+110 pp.

1933

2 "La posizione storica di Marsilio Ficino," *Civiltà Moderna* 5 (1933), 438-45. Translated by Melisenda Codignola. Reappeared in 20, 47 and 141 as the second part of Chapter II.

1934

3 "L'unità del mondo nella filosofia di Marsilio Ficino," *Giornale critico della filosofia italiana* 15 (1934), 395-423. Reappeared in 20, 47 and 141 as Chapter VII.

1936

4 "Un uomo di Stato e umanista fiorentino : Giovanni Corsi," *La Bibliofilia* 38 (1936), 242-57. Reprinted in 60 as Chapter VIII.

1937

5 *Supplementum Ficinianum : Marsilii Ficini Florentini Philosophi Platonici Opuscula Inedita et Dispersa.* Florence : Leo S. Olschki, 1937. 2 vols. clxxxii, 142 and 384 pp. Reprinted in 1973. See 145.
6 "La teoria dell'appetito naturale in Marsilio Ficino," *Giornale critico della filosofia italiana* 18 (1937), 234-56. Reappeared in 20, 47 and 141 as Chapter X.

1938

7 "Volontà e amor divino in Marsilio Ficino," *Giornale critico della filosofia italiana* 19 (1938), 185-214. Reappeared in 20, 47 and 141 as Chapter XIII.
8 "Per la biografia di Marsilio Ficino," *Civiltà Moderna* 10 (1938), 277-98. [Signed "Platonicus"]. Reprinted in 60 as Chapter IX.
9 "Nuove fonti per la storia dell'umanesimo italiano," *Civiltà Moderna* 10 (1938), 299-321. [Signed "P.O."]. Reprinted in 60 as Chapter XVIII.
10 "Marsilio Ficino e Lodovico Lazzarelli : Contributo alla diffusione delle idee ermetiche nel Rinascimento," *Annali della R. Scuola Normale Superiore di Pisa, Lettere, Storia e Filosofia*, Ser. II, vol. 8 (1938), 237-62. Reprinted in 60 as Chapter XI.

1939

11 "Un documento sconosciuto sulla Giostra di Giuliano de' Medici," *La Bibliofilia* 41 (1939), 405-17. Reprinted in 60 as Chapter XXI.
12 "Florentine Platonism and Its Relations with Humanism and Scholasticism," *Church History* 8 (1939), 201-11. Presented as a lecture at the meeting of the American Society for Church History, Princeton Theological Seminary, April 28, 1939, and also at the Casa Italiana, Columbia University, May 11, 1939.

1940

13 "The Theory of Immortality in Marsilio Ficino," *Journal of the History of Ideas* 1 (1940), 299-319. Reappeared in 20, 47 and 141 as Chapter XV.

1941

14 "Ancora per Giovanni Mercurio da Correggio," *La Bibliofilia* 43 (1941), 23-28. Reprinted in 60 as Chapter XII.
15 "Augustine and the Renaissance," *International Science* 1 (1941), 7-14. Originally a paper read before the Augustinian Society in Cambridge, Mass., on January 16, 1941. For fuller, documented version see 21.

16 (With John H. Randall, Jr.) "The Study of the Philosophies of the Renaissance," *Journal of the History of Ideas* 2 (1941), 449-96. Given in a briefer form as a lecture at the New England Renaissance Conference, Brown University, April 13, 1940.

1942

17 "An Unpublished Description of Naples by Francesco Bandini," *Romanic Review* 33 (1942), 290-306. Reprinted in 60 as Chapter XIX.

1943

18 (With Lincoln Reis) "Some Remarks on the Method of History," *The Journal of Philosophy* 40 (1943), 225-45.
19 "The Place of Classical Humanism in Renaissance Thought," *Journal of the History of Ideas* 4 (1943), 59-63. Reprinted in 60 as Chapter II and in 65. See 128 for a German version.
20 *The Philosophy of Marsilio Ficino.* Translated by Virginia Conant. Number Six of the Columbia Studies in Philosophy. Edited under the Department of Philosophy, Columbia University. New York: Columbia University Press, 1943. 441 pp. There are sixteen chapters which we shall refer to as I-XVI. Reprinted in 1964. See 94. For the Italian and German versions see 47 and 141. Chapters II and XIII were presented as lectures at the University of Michigan, August 7 and 8, 1939. Chapter VII was presented as a lecture at Harvard University, on April 14, 1939, and also at Yale University, on May 18, 1939. Chapter XIII was presented again as a lecture to the Department of Philosophy, Columbia University, on November 10, 1939.

1944

21 "Augustine and the Early Renaissance," *Review of Religion* 8 (1943-1944), 339-58. This is a revised version of 15 with footnotes added. Reprinted in 60 as Chapter XVII.
22 "Ficino and Pomponazzi on the Place of Man in the Universe," *Journal of the History of Ideas* 5 (1944), 220-6. Reprinted in 60 as Chapter XIV.

23 "The Scholastic Background of Marsilio Ficino : With an Edition of Unpublished Texts," *Traditio* 2 (1944), 257-318. Reprinted in 60 as Chapter IV.

1945

24 "Humanism and Scholasticism in the Italian Renaissance," *Byzantion* 17 (1944-1945), 346-74. Given as a lecture at Connecticut College, New London, on March 9, 1944 and also at Brown University on December 15, 1944. A German version was presented as a lecture at Freiburg im Breisgau to the Philosophische Fakultät der Universität and the Deutsch-Italienische Gesellschaft on June 30, 1952 and also at Heidelberg to the Historisches Seminar der Universität on July 1, 1952. The article was reprinted in 60 as Chapter XXV and in 80. See 38 and 110 for an Italian version. See 149 for a German version.
25 No. 16 reissued in *Surveys of Recent Scholarship in the Period of Renaissance Compiled for the Committee on Renaissance Studies of the American Council of Learned Societies*. First Series, 1945.
26 "The School of Salerno : Its Development and its Contribution to the History of Learning," *Bulletin of the History of Medicine* 17 (1945), 138-94. Reprinted in 60 as Chapter XXIV. See 56 for an Italian version.

1946

27 "The Philosophical Significance of the History of Thought," *Journal of the History of Ideas* 7 (1946), 360-366. Reprinted in 60 as Chapter I. Presented as a paper to the Annual Meeting of the American Philosophical Association, Eastern Division, Sarah Lawrence College, on February 22, 1946.
28 "The Origin and Development of the Language of Italian Prose," *Word* 2 (1946), 50-65. This is a slightly abridged version. Reprinted in its full form in 60 as Chapter XXIII and in 104. Presented in the full form as a lecture to the Linguistic Circle of New York (Ecole Libre) on April 13, 1946 and again to the Linguistic Circle of Columbia University on March 4, 1950. See 39 for an Italian version of the full text as it appeared in 60.
29 "Francesco da Diacceto and Florentine Platonism in the Sixteenth Century," in *Miscellanea Giovanni Mercati, Volume IV :*

Letteratura classica e umanistica. Studi e Testi, 124. Vatican City : Biblioteca Apostolica Vaticana, 1946, 260-304. Reprinted in 60 as Chapter XV.

1947

30 "Music and Learning in the Early Italian Renaissance," *Journal of Renaissance and Baroque Music* [*Musica Disciplina*] 1 (1946-1947), 255-74. Reprinted in 60 as Chapter XXII and in 104.

31 "The Philosophy of Man in the Italian Renaissance," *Italica* 24 (1947), 93-112. Reprinted in 60 as Chapter XIII and also in 80. Presented as a lecture to the Friends of Italy, New York, on April 10, 1946. See 110 for an Italian version and 149 for a German version.

1948

32 *The Renaissance Philosophy of Man : Selections in Translation.* Edited by Ernst Cassirer, Paul Oskar Kristeller, and John H. Randall, Jr. Chicago : The University of Chicago Press, 1948. Especially : General Introduction (with J. H. Randall, Jr.), 1-20; Introduction to Giovanni Pico della Mirandola, 215-22; Footnotes to Pietro Pomponazzi, 280 ff.; Selective Bibliography, 397-400.

33 "Latin Manuscript Books before 1600 : A Bibliography of the Printed Catalogues of Extant Collections," *Traditio* 6 (1948), 227-317. See 48, 72 and 108.

34 "Un codice padovano di Aristotele postillato da Francesco e Ermolao Barbaro : il manoscritto Plimpton 17 della Columbia University Library a New York," *La Bibliofilia* 50 (1948), 162-78. Reprinted in 60 as Chapter XVI.

1950

35 "Un nuovo trattatello inedito di Marsilio Ficino," *Rinascimento* 1 (1950), 25-42. Reprinted in 60 as Chapter VII-A.

36 "Renaissance Philosophies," in *A History of Philosophical Systems.* Edited by Vergilius Ferm. New York : Philosophical Library, 1950, 227-39.

37 "Movimenti filosofici del Rinascimento," *Giornale critico della filosofia italiana* 29 (1950), 275-88. Presented as a lecture at the

Scuola Normale Superiore, Pisa, on February 5, 1949, and again to the Facoltà di Magistero dell'Università di Roma and the Istituto di Studi Filosofici on March 29, 1949. It was also given as a lecture that same year at the Villa Fabbricotti, Florence (April 23); the Centro Italiano di Relazioni e di Cultura Internazionali, Bologna (May 3); the Accademia dei Sepolti, Volterra (May 15); the Università Popolare, Siena (May 17); and the Circolo di Cultura e delle Arti, Trieste (May 24). See 60, Chapter III, for an English version of this article.

38 "Umanesimo e Scolastica nel Rinascimento italiano," *Humanitas* 5 (1950), 988-1015. Given as a lecture at the Università di Trieste, May 23, 1949. Italian version of 24.

39 "L'origine e lo sviluppo della prosa volgare," *Cultura neolatina* 10 (1950), 137-56. See 28 and 60.

1951

40 "A New Manuscript Source for Pomponazzi's Theory of the Soul from his Paduan Period," *Revue internationale de philosophie*, 5 (1951), N° 16 : *Renaissance italienne*, 144-57. Also presented as a lecture at the New England Conference of Renaissance Studies, Smith College, October 30, 1953.

41 "Umanesimo e filosofia nel Rinascimento italiano," in *Umanesimo e scienza politica, Atti del Congresso Internazionale di Studi Umanistici: Roma-Firenze, 1949*. Edited by Enrico Castelli. Milan : Carlo Marzorati, 1951, 507-16.

42 "Matteo de'Libri, Bolognese Notary of the Thirteenth Century, and his Artes Dictaminis," in *Miscellanea Giovanni Galbiati*. vol. 2 Fontes Ambrosiani, 26. Milan : Biblioteca Ambrosiana, 1951, 283-320.

1952

43 "The Modern System of the Arts : A Study in the History of Aesthetics," *Journal of the History of Ideas* 12 (1951), 496-527 ; 13 (1952), 17-46. Reprinted in 104 and 136. This article was given in an earlier, shorter form as lectures at the American Society for Aesthetics, New York Chapter, Hunter College, on February 6, 1948; at St. John's College, Annapolis, on March 12, 1948; to the French Graduate Union, Columbia University, on Novem-

ber 8, 1950; and to the Department of Romance Languages, Harvard University, on March 16, 1951. It was also given as a lecture during 1951 at Northwestern University, on June 26; the University of Wisconsin at Madison, on June 28; the University of Minnesota, on July 2; the University of Portland, on July 9; Reed College, on July 10; the University of Utah on August 1; and the University of Colorado, on August 2.

44 "Petrarch's 'Averroists': A Note on the History of Aristotelianism in Venice, Padua and Bologna," in *Mélanges Augustin Renaudet, Bibliothèque d'Humanisme et Renaissance* 14 (1952), 59-65.

1953

45 *Die italienischen Universitäten der Renaissance*. Schriften und Vorträge des Petrarca-Instituts Köln, 1. Krefeld: Scherpe-Verlag, 1953. 30 pp. Presented as a lecture at the Petrarca-Institut (Universität), Cologne, July 10, 1952.

45 "El Mito del Ateismo Renacentista y la tradición francesa del librepensiamento," *Notas y Estudios de Filosofía* vol. 4, No. 13 (1953), 1-14. Translated from an unpublished French version by Maria Elena Vela. The French version was originally presented as a lecture at the Université de Fribourg, Faculté des Lettres, on June 27, 1952, and again at the French Graduate Union, Columbia University, on March 8, 1961. See 124 for a revised and enlarged English version.

47 *Il pensiero filosofico di Marsilio Ficino*. Biblioteca Storica del Rinascimento, New Series 3; Florence: G. C. Sansoni, 1953. xix +492 pp. This book is not a translation of 20, but is the actual manuscript of 1938 brought up to date by Professor Kristeller. The Italian version was revised from the German original (see 141) with the help of Professor Alessandro Perosa. Both the footnotes and the bibliography were brought up to date. The distinctive advantages that this Italian edition has over the American edition (see 20) are (1) that all the original quotations are given in Latin and (2) that two additional indices have been added, one for the authors who are cited in the works of Ficino and the other for passages cited in the volume from all authors.

48 "Latin Manuscript Books before 1600, Part II: A Tentative List of Unpublished Inventories of Imperfectly Catalogued

Extant Collections," *Traditio* 9 (1953), 393-418. See 33, 72 and 108.

1954

49 "Relazione sulla edizione di scrittori umanisti," in *La Pubblicazione delle Fonti del Medioevo Europeo negli ultimi 70 anni (1883-1953), Relazioni al Convegno di Studi delle Fonti del Medioevo Europeo in occasione del 70° della fondazione dell'Istituto Storico Italiano (Roma, 14-18 aprile 1953)*. Rome: Istituto Storico Italiano per il Medio Evo, 1954, 323-26.
50 "Tasks and Experiences in the Study of Humanist Manuscripts," *Renaissance News* 7 (1954), 75-84.

1955

51 "Ficino and Renaissance Platonism," *The Personalist* 36 (1955), 238-49.
52 "Two Unpublished Questions on the Soul by Pietro Pomponazzi," *Medievalia et Humanistica* 9 (1955), 76-101. "Errata Corrigenda," *ibid.*, 10 (1956), 151.
53 "A Philosophical Treatise from Bologna Dedicated to Guido Cavalcanti: Magister Jacobus de Pistorio and His 'Questio de felicitate'," in *Medioevo e Rinascimento, Studi in onore di Bruno Nardi*. vol. 1. Pubblicazioni dell'Istituto di Filosofia dell'Università di Roma, 1. Florence: G. C. Sansoni, 1955, 425-63.
54 *The Classics and Renaissance Thought*. Martin Classical Lectures, 15. Cambridge, Mass.: Harvard University Press, 1955. xiii+106 pp. Originally presented as the Charles Beebe Martin Lectures at Oberlin College, February 22-26, 1954. See 80 and 119. See 110 for an Italian version and 149 for a German version.
55 "Il Petrarca, l'umanesimo e la scolastica," *Lettere Italiane* 7 (1955), 367-88. Originally given as a lecture. See 59.
56 "La Scuola di Salerno: Il suo sviluppo e il suo contributo alla storia della scienza." Translated by Antonio Cassese. Centro Salernitano di Studi di Medicina Medioevale. 2. Appendice alla *Rassegna storica Salernitana* 16 (1955), 1-68. [New pagination after the regular pagination]. Translation of 26.

1956

57 "The University of Bologna and the Renaissance," *Studi e memorie per la storia dell' Università di Bologna*, New Series 1. Institutum Memoriae Universitatis Studiorum Bononiensis pervestigandae. *Dissertationes historicae de Universitate Studiorum Bononiensi ad Columbiam Universitatem saecularis ferias iterum sollemniter celebrantem missae*. Bologna, 1956, 313-23.

58 "Una novella latina e il suo autore Francesco Tedaldi, mercante fiorentino del Quattrocento," in *Studi Letterari: Miscellanea in onore di Emilio Santini*. Palermo: U. Manfredi, 1956, 159-80.

59 "Il Petrarca, l'Umanesimo e la Scolastica a Venezia," in *La civiltà veneziana del Trecento*. Florence: G. C. Sansoni, 1956, 147-78. Given as a lecture at the Fondazione Giorgio Cini, San Giorgio Maggiore, Venice, on June 1, 1955.

60 *Studies in Renaissance Thought and Letters*. Storia e Letteratura, 54. Rome: Edizioni di Storia e Letteratura, 1956. xvi+680 pp. This volume reprints various previously published articles, some of which were revised. The following list indicates the chapter number in the volume and the entry number of the article in this bibliography. Ch. I (pp. 3-9) = 27; Ch. II (pp. 11-15) = 19; Ch. IV (pp. 35-97) = 23; Ch. VI (pp. 123-38) = a portion of 5 ("De traditione operum Marsilii Ficini," vol. I, pp. clxviii-clxxxi); Ch. VII, section A (pp. 139-50) = 35; Ch. VIII (pp. 175-90) = 4; Ch. IX (pp. 191-211) = 8; Ch. X (pp. 213-9) = entry 7 from the list of Minor Publications; Ch. XI (pp. 221-47) = 10; Ch. XII (pp. 249-57) = 14; Ch. XIII (pp. 261-78) = 31; Ch. XIV (pp. 279-86) = 22; Ch. XV (pp. 287-336) = 29; Ch. XVI (pp. 337-53) = 34; Ch. XVII (pp. 355-72) = 21; Ch. XVIII (pp. 373-94) = 9; Ch. XIX (pp. 395-410) = 17; Ch. XXI (pp. 437-50) = 11; Ch. XXII (pp. 451-70) = 30; Ch. XXIII (pp. 473-93) = 28; Ch. XXIV (pp. 495-551) = 26; Ch. XXV (pp. 553-83) = 24. The volume also contains the following previously unpublished essays: Ch. III (pp. 17-31), "Philosophical Movements of the Renaissance" (English version of 37); Ch. V (pp. 99-122), "Lay Religious Traditions and Florentine Platonism"; Ch. VII, section B (pp. 150-4), "Due lettere inedite al Ficino"; section C (pp. 154-8), "Sei poesie inedite riguardanti Marsilio Ficino"; section D (pp. 158-74), "Nuovi appunti su codici, edizioni e documenti del Ficino"; and Ch. XX (pp. 411-35), "Francesco

Bandini and His Consolatory Dialogue upon the Death of Simone Gondi." The bibliography and the indices of the volume (pp. 589-680) were prepared by Maria Laura De Nicola. Chapter III was given as a lecture at Indiana University on April 23, 1948; at Princeton University on December 9, 1948; at the Leopoldskron Student Rest Center, Salzburg, on May 27, 1949; at Pennsylvania State College on May 12, 1950; at the University of Washington on July 5, 1951; at the University of Oregon on July 11, 1951; at Stanford University on July 16, 1951; at the University of Southern California on July 24, 1951; at Claremont College on July 27, 1951; and at Queens College, New York, on February 26, 1953; and to the University Seminar on the Renaissance, Columbia University. It was also given in Italian as a lecture to the Associazione Filosofica Ligure at Genoa on April 16, 1952, and to the Facoltà di Lettere and the Società Filosofica at Turin on April 24, 1952. Chapter V was originally given as a lecture at Connecticut College on January 22, 1950; at the University of Oregon on July 11, 1951; and again at Wellesley College on November 18, 1952. It was also given in Italian as a lecture at the Istituto Nazionale di Studi sul Rinascimento, Palazzo Strozzi, Florence, on March 13, 1952.

1957

61 "Renaissance Research in Vatican Manuscripts," *Manuscripta* 1 (1957), 67-80. Presented as a paper to the Annual Meeting of the American Historical Association, Saint Louis, December 28, 1956.

62 "Nuove fonti per la medicina salernitana del secolo XII," *Rassegna storica Salernitana* 18 (1957), 61-75. Given as a lecture in English to the History of Science Society, Metropolitan New York Section, at Hunter College, on March 8, 1954; to the Medieval Club of New York on December 14, 1955; at Claremont College on May 23, 1956; to the Annual Meeting of the Mediaeval Academy of America, Cambridge, Mass., on April 26, 1957; to the University Seminar on Classical Civilization, Columbia University, on November 20, 1958; and to the Society for Ancient Greek Philosophy, University of Vermont, on December 27, 1958.

1958

63 "Moritz Steinschneider as a Student of Medieval Europe," *American Academy for Jewish Research: Proceedings* 27 (1958), 59-66. Given as a lecture to the Annual Meeting of the American Academy of Jewish Research, Jewish Theological Seminary of America, New York, on December 29, 1957.

1959

64 "Beitrag der Schule von Salerno zur Entwicklung der scholastischen Wissenschaft im 12. Jahrhundert: Kurze Mitteilung über handschriftliche Funde," in *Artes Liberales: Von der Antiken zur Wissenschaft des Mittelalters*. Edited by Josef Koch. Studien und Texte zur Geistesgeschichte des Mittelalters, 5. Leiden and Cologne: E. J. Brill, 1959, 84-90. A slightly revised German version of 62. It was a communication submitted to, but not personally read at, the VI. Mediaevistentagung at the Thomas-Institut der Universität Köln, October 7, 1955.
65 No. 19 reprinted in *The Renaissance: Medieval or Modern?* Edited by Karl H. Dannenfeldt. Boston: D. C. Heath, 1959, 75-78.
66 "Renaissance Manuscripts in Eastern Europe," *Renaissance News* 12 (1959), 83-90. Originally read as a paper to the New England Conference of Renaissance Studies, Dartmouth College, on October 11, 1958, and to the University Seminar on the Renaissance, Columbia University, on December 16, 1958.
67 "Renaissance Platonism," in *Facets of the Renaissance*. The Arensberg Lectures, First Series. Edited by William H. Werkmeister. Los Angeles: University of Southern California Press, 1959, 87-107. Given as a lecture at the University of Southern California on May 22, 1956.
68 "Die Platonische Akademie in Florenz," *Agorà: Eine Humanistische Schriftenreihe*, No. 12, Fifth year (1959) *Studia Humanitatis: Beiträge und Texte zum italienischen Humanismus der Renaissance*, 35-47. This article is a revised version of a lecture given at the Centre d'Études Supérieures de la Renaissance, Tours, on July 29, 1958. The translation from the French is by Renate Lieser and Manfred Schlösser. See 83 for an English version.

69 "Renaissanceforschung und Altertumswissenschaft," *Forschungen und Fortschritte* 33 (1959), 363-69. Given as a lecture at the Institut für Griechisch-Römische Altertumskunde, Deutsche Akademie der Wissenschaften, Berlin, on August 30, 1958. Reprinted in 149.

1960

70 (Editor in Chief). Union Académique Internationale. *Catalogus Translationum et Commentariorum : Mediaeval and Renaissance Latin Translations and Commentaries*; Annotated Lists and Guides. vol. 1. Washington, D.C. : The Catholic University of America Press, 1960. xxiii+249 pp. See especially the Preface (ix-xiv) and the Bibliography (xv-xxiii). See 138 below.

71 "Humanist Learning in the Italian Renaissance," *The Centennial Review* 4 (1960), 243-66. Based on a lecture given at Syracuse University on March 18, 1959. Reprinted in 104.

72 *Latin Manuscript Books before 1600 : A List of the Printed Catalogues and Unpublished Inventories of Extant Collections.* New edition, revised. New York : Fordham University Press, 1960. xxii+234 pp. In addition to the "Preface to the First Edition" (xiii-xxii) there is also a "New Preface" (vii-xii). See 33 and 48 for the first edition and 108 for the third edition. This second edition is a complete revision and a considerably enlarged version of 33 and 48. It includes references to printed and unprinted manuscript catalogues not mentioned in them.

73 "Paduan Averroism and Alexandrism in the Light of Recent Studies," in *Aristotelismo Padovano e Filosofia Aristotelica*. Atti del XII Congresso Internazionale di Filosofia (Venice and Padua, 1958), vol. 9. Florence : G. C. Sansoni, 1960, 147-55. Reprinted in 104. For a shorter published version of this paper, see Minor Publications entry 127. Given as a paper at the Annual Meeting of the American Philosophical Association, Eastern Division, Harvard University, on December 28, 1957, and also to the University Seminar on the Renaissance, Columbia University, on April 21, 1959.

74 "Der Gelehrte und sein Publikum im späten Mittelalter und in der Renaissance," in *Medium Aevum Vivum : Festschrift für Walther Bulst*. Edited by Hans Robert Jauss and Dieter Schaller. Heidelberg : Carl Winter Universitätsverlag, 1960, 212-30. Presented in an English version as a lecture to the University

Seminar in Medieval Studies, Columbia University, on April 14, 1959. For an English translation from the German original, see 146. The footnotes of this English translation have been brought up to date.

75 "Ludovico Lazzarelli e Giovanni da Correggio, due ermetici del Quattrocento, e il manoscritto II. D. I. 4 della Biblioteca Comunale degli Ardenti di Viterbo," in *Biblioteca degli Ardenti della Città di Viterbo : Studi e Ricerche nel 150º della fondazione.* Viterbo : Agnesotti, 1960, 13-37.

1961

76 "A New Work on the Origin and Development of Humanistic Script," *Manuscripta* 5 (1961), 35-40. This is a review article of Berthold L. Ullman, *The Origin and Development of Humanistic Script.* Rome : Edizioni di Storia e Letteratura, 1960.
77 "Some Problems of Historical Knowledge," *The Journal of Philosophy* 58 (1961), 85-110. Originally presented as two lectures to the New York Philosophy Club, at Columbia University, on February 17, 1956 and November 21, 1958, and again as a paper to the University Seminar on Hermeneutics, Columbia University, on November 7, 1960.
78 "Two Unpublished Letters to Erasmus," *Renaissance News* 14 (1961), 6-14.
79 "Changing Views of the Intellectual History of the Renaissance since Jacob Burckhardt," in *The Renaissance : A Reconsideration of the Theories and Interpretations of the Age.* Edited by Tinsley Helton. Madison : The University of Wisconsin Press, 1961, 27-52. Originally given as a lecture at the University of Wisconsin at Milwaukee on November 13, 1959. Reprinted in 96, the paperback edition. See 139 for an Italian version.
80 *Renaissance Thought : The Classic, Scholastic, and Humanistic Strains.* New York : Harper and Brothers (Harper Torchbooks, The Academy Library), 1961. xi+173 pp. A slightly revised reprinting of 54 along with 24 and 31, both of which had already been reprinted in 60 as Chapters XXV and XIII. See 149 for a German version.
81 "The Moral Thought of Renaissance Humanism," in *Chapters in Western Civilization.* Edited by the Contemporary Civilization Staff of Columbia College, Columbia University. vol. 1, Third

Edition. New York and London: Columbia University Press, 1961, 289-335. Reprinted in 104.

82 "Sebastiano Salvini: A Florentine Humanist and Theologian, and a Member of Marsilio Ficino's Platonic Academy," in *Didascaliae: Studies in Honor of Anselm M. Albareda Prefect of the Vatican Library Presented by a Group of American Scholars*. Edited by Sesto Prete. New York: Bernard M. Rosenthal, 1961, 205-243 plus 4 plates.

83 "The Platonic Academy of Florence," *Renaissance News* 14 (1961), 147-59. This article is a modified English version of 68. Reprinted in 104. Given as a paper at the Annual Meeting of the Renaissance Society, Middle Atlantic Section, Free Library of Philadelphia, on October 29, 1960; at the University of California at Los Angeles on May 8, 1961; at the University of Oregon as the Failing Distinguished Lecture on May 23, 1961; at the City College of New York on February 28, 1962; at the Hebrew University, Jerusalem, on May 3, 1962; and at Bard College on November 12, 1962.

84 "Un 'Ars Dictaminis' di Giovanni del Virgilio," *Italia medioevale e umanistica* 4 (1961), 181-200.

1962

85 "The European Diffusion of Italian Humanism," *Italica* 39 (1962), 1-20. Reprinted in 104. Given as a paper at the Annual Meeting of the Modern Language Association, Philadelphia, on December 27, 1960, and as a somewhat longer lecture at the Casa Italiana, Columbia University, on February 23, 1961.

86 "Studies on Renaissance Humanism during the Last Twenty Years," *Studies in the Renaissance* 9 (1962), 7-30. Based on a paper given at the New England Renaissance Conference, Brown University, on October 17, 1959.

87 No. 43 reprinted in *Ideas in Cultural Perspective*. Edited by Philip P. Wiener and Aaron Noland. New Brunswick: Rutgers University Press, 1962, 145-206.

88 *La tradizione aristotelica nel Rinascimento*. Saggi e Testi, 2. Edited jointly by the Centro per la Storia della Tradizione Aristotelica nel Veneto of the University of Padua and by the University Seminar on the Renaissance of Columbia University. Padua: Editrice Antenore, 1962. 38 pp. See 109 for an English version. Given as a lecture at the Università Cattolica del Sacro

Cuore, Milan, on April 10, 1962 and at the University of Padua on April 13, 1962.

89 "Umanesimo filosofico e umanesimo letterario," *Lettere Italiane* 14 (1962), 381-94. Given as a lecture at the Fondazione Giorgio Cini, Venice, on April 14, 1962. It was also given as a paper in an earlier, English version at Skidmore College on February 29, 1960; at the University of British Columbia as the Koerner Lecture on May 2, 1960; and at the University of California at Berkeley on May 15, 1961.

1963

90 "Aufgaben und Probleme der Handschriftenforschung," in *Wort und Text : Festschrift für Fritz Schalk*. Frankfurt : Vittorio Klostermann, 1963, 1-13. Given as a lecture at the Romanisches Seminar der Universität, Freiburg im Breisgau, on June 28, 1962. Reprinted in 149.

91 No. 67 reprinted by Harper and Row as a Harper Torchbook, The Academy Library, New York, 1963, 103-23.

92 "Giovanni Pico della Mirandola and his Sources," in *L'opera e il pensiero di Giovanni Pico della Mirandola nella storia dell'umanesimo : Convegno Internazionale, Mirandola 15-18 settembre. Relazioni*. Florence : Istituto Nazionale di Studi sul Rinascimento, and Mirandola : Comitato per le Celebrazioni Centenarie in Onore di Giovanni Pico, 1963, 43-96. This is a preliminary, incomplete version of 106 lacking the plates and bibliography of the final version and containing only four of the fourteen Latin poems. Given as a lecture at Mirandola on September 17, 1963, and again to the University Seminar on the Renaissance, Columbia University, on December 17, 1963 and at the North Central Renaissance Conference, Victoria College, University of Toronto, on May 15, 1964.

93 *Iter Italicum : A Finding List of Uncatalogued or Incompletely Catalogued Humanistic Manuscripts of the Renaissance in Italian and Other Libraries. Volume I : Italy, Agrigento to Novara*. London : The Warburg Institute, and Leiden : E. J. Brill, 1963. xxviii+533 pp. See 123 below.

1964

94 No. 24 reprinted in *Academic Discourse*. Edited by John J. Enck. New York : Appleton-Century-Crofts, 1964, 245-74.

95 No. 20 reprinted. Gloucester, Mass. : Peter Smith, 1964.
96 No. 79 reprinted in a Paperback edition. Madison : The University of Wisconsin Press, 1964.
97 "Umanesimo italiano e Bisanzio," *Lettere Italiane* 16 (1964), 1-14. Reprinted in 115. This article is based on a lecture given at the Fondazione Giorgio Cini, Venice, on September 13, 1963. For an English version, see 142; for a German version, see 149.
98 "An Unknown Humanist Sermon on St. Stephen by Guillaume Fichet," in *Mélanges Eugène Tisserant*, vol. 6. Studi e Testi, 236. Vatican City : Biblioteca Apostolica Vaticana, 1964, 459-97 and 1 plate.
99 "History of Philosophy and History of Ideas," *Journal of the History of Philosophy* 2 (1964), 1-14. Reprinted in 142. Given as a paper at the New York Philosophy Club on March 15, 1963.
100 "An Unknown Correspondence of Alessandro Braccesi with Niccolò Michelozzi, Naldo Naldi, Bartolommeo Scala, and Other Humanists (1470-72) in Ms. Bodl. Auct. F. 2. 17," in *Classical Mediaeval and Renaissance Studies in Honor of Berthold Louis Ullman*. Edited by Charles Henderson, Jr., vol. 2. Storia e Letteratura, 94. Rome : Edizioni di Storia e Letteratura, 1964, 311-63 plus 4 plates.
101 *Eight Philosophers of the Italian Renaissance*. Stanford : Stanford University Press, 1964. xiv+194 pp. Chapters I to VIII were given as the Arensberg Lectures at Stanford University under the auspices of the Francis Bacon Foundation during May, 1961. The precise dates were May 2 (Petrarch), 4 (Valla), 5 (Ficino), 9 (Pico), 11 (Pomponazzi), 12 (Telesio), 16 (Patrizi), 18 (Bruno). The Appendix, entitled "The Medieval Antecedents of Renaissance Humanism," contains a lecture which was given on several other occasions, but not during the Arensburg series at Stanford. It was presented separately at Stanford to the Graduate Program in the Humanities on May 4, 1961; at Cornell University on October 31, 1961; at the Dumbarton Oaks Research Library, Washington, on January 15, 1962; and at the University of Illinois, Urbana, on October 18, 1962. See 122, 129 and 130.
102 "Some Original Letters and Autograph Manuscripts of Marsilio Ficino," in *Studi di Bibliografia e di Storia in onore di Tammaro De Marinis*, vol. 3. Verona and Vatican City : 1964, 5-33. Printed by G. Mardersteig in Verona and distributed by the Vatican Library.

1965

103 No. 31 reprinted in *Intellectual Movements in Modern European History*. Edited by Franklin L. Baumer. New York: Macmillan, 1965, 12-28.
104 *Renaissance Thought II: Papers on Humanism and the Arts*. New York, Evanston and London: Harper and Row (Harper Torchbooks, The Academy Library), 1965. x+234 pp. This is a collection of previously published papers. Ch. I = 71, Ch. II = 81, Ch. III = 85, Ch. IV = 83, Ch. V = 22, Ch. VI = 73, Ch. VII = 28, VIII = 30, and IX = 43. Chapters V, VII and IX had also been reprinted in 60.
105 "The Humanist Bartolomeo Facio and His Unknown Correspondence," in *From the Renaissance to the Counter-Reformation: Essays in Honor of Garrett Mattingly*. Edited by Charles H. Carter. New York: Random House, 1965, 56-74.
106 "Giovanni Pico della Mirandola and His Sources," in *L'opera e il pensiero di Giovanni Pico della Mirandola nella storia dell'umanesimo: Convegno Internazionale (Mirandola: 15-18 Settembre 1963), vol. I: Relazioni*. Florence: Istituto Nazionale di Studi sul Rinascimento, 1965, 35-133, and discussion, 134-42. This is the final version of 92.
107 "A Thomist Critique of Marsilio Ficino's Theory of Will and Intellect: Fra Vincenzo Bandello da Castelnuovo O. P. and His Unpublished Treatise Addressed to Lorenzo De' Medici," in *Harry Austryn Wolfson Jubilee Volume on the Occasion of His Seventy-Fifth Birthday, English Section*, vol. 2. Jerusalem: American Academy for Jewish Research, 1965, 463-94. Given as a lecture to the University Seminar on the Renaissance, Columbia University on March 20, 1962.
108 No. 72 reprinted in a Third Edition. New York: Fordham University Press, 1965. xxvi+284 pp. This edition is identical with the second edition except for the Preface to the Third Edition (vi-x) and Supplementary Material (pp. 233-84). See 33, 48 and 72.
109 "Renaissance Aristotelianism," *Greek, Roman and Byzantine Studies* 6 (1965), 157-74. This is an English version of 88. Given in an earlier form as a lecture to the History of Ideas Colloquium, Brandeis University, on April 11, 1956; at the University of Southern California on May 24, 1956; and to the Graduate

Philosophy Club, Yale University, on February 10, 1960. It was presented in its final form as a paper to a joint colloquium of the Philosophy departments of Duke University and the University of North Carolina at Chapel Hill held at Duke on October 10, 1964.

110 *La tradizione classica nel pensiero del Rinascimento.* Translated by Fabrizio Onofri. Florence : La Nuova Italia, 1965. x+199 pp. This is a translation by F. Onofri of 80 except for Chapter V, for which the translation in 38 was used.

111 "Der Nachlass Ludwig Bertalots," *Quellen und Forschungen aus italienischen Archiven und Bibliotheken* 45 (1965), 429-33.

112 "An Unknown Letter of Giovanni Barbo to Guarino," *Italia medioevale e umanistica* 8 (1965), 243-48.

1966

113 "Pier Candido Decembrio and His Unpublished Treatise on the Immortality of the Soul," in *The Classical Tradition : Literary and Historical Studies in Honor of Harry Caplan.* Edited by Luitpold Wallach. Ithaca : Cornell University Press, 1966, 536-58.

114 "Philosophy and Humanism in Renaissance Perspective," in *The Renaissance Image of Man and the World.* Edited by Bernard O'Kelly. Columbus : Ohio State University Press, 1966, 29-51. Given as a lecture at the Fourth Annual Conference on the Humanities, Ohio State University, on October 27, 1961 and as a paper to the New York Renaissance Club, New York University, on February 14, 1963.

115 "Umanesimo italiano e Bisanzio," in *Venezia e l'Oriente tra tardo medioevo e Rinascimento.* Edited by Agostino Pertusi. Civiltà europea e civiltà veneziana, 4. Florence : G. C. Sansoni, 1966, 19-33. A reprinting of 97 but without the notes and bibliographical references. For an English version, see 142.

116 "Platonismo bizantino e fiorentino e la controversia su Platone e Aristotele," *ibid.*, 103-116. Given as a lecture at the Fondazione Giorgio Cini, Venice, on September 14, 1963. A German version was given as a lecture at the University of Münster on July 8, 1968. For an English version, see 142; for a German version, see 149.

117 *Renaissance Philosophy and the Medieval Tradition.* Wimmer Lecture, 15. Latrobe : The Archabbey Press, 1966. x+120 pp. Reprinted in 142. Given in a briefer form as the Wimmer Lecture

at St. Vincent College, Latrobe, Pa., on October 25, 1961. It was also presented as a lecture to the University Seminar in Medieval Studies, Columbia University, on December 11, 1962; at the Medieval Club of New York, New York University, on March 1, 1963; as the Class of 1902 Lecture at Bryn Mawr College on October 17, 1963; and at the Renaissance Seminar of the University of Chicago on January 21, 1964; and at the New York Philosophy Club, Columbia University, on October 15, 1965. It was also presented in a German version as a lecture at the University of Freiburg im Breisgau on June 28, 1962 and again at the Freie Universität, Berlin on June 28, 1966. For a German version, see 149.

118 "Marsilio Ficino as a Beginning Student of Plato," *Scriptorium* 20 (1966), 41-54 plus 4 plates.

119 "Classical Antiquity and Renaissance Humanism," in *The Renaissance Debate*. Edited by Denys Hay. New York : Holt, Rhinehart and Winston, 1966, 106-110. Reprinted from 54 (pp. 5-13).

1967

120 *Le Thomisme et la pensée italienne de la Renaissance*. Conférence Albert-Le-Grand 1965. Montreal : Institut d'Études Médiévales, and Paris : Libraire J. Vrin, 1967. 291 pp. plus 8 plates. Given as the Conférence Albert-Le-Grand at the Institut d'Études Médiévales, Montreal, on November 15, 1965. For an English version, see 146. The two supporting Latin texts have been omitted in the English version. See 147 for an Italian version.

121 "John H. Randall, Jr., and Renaissance Philosophy," in *Naturalism and Historical Understanding : Essays on the Philosophy of John Herman Randall, Jr*. Edited by John P. Anton. Albany : State University of New York Press, 1967, 35-41.

122 Articles in *The Encyclopedia of Philosophy*, edited by Paul Edwards. New York : The Macmillan Company and the Free Press, 1967. "Ficino, Marsilio," vol. 3, 196-201; "Florentine Academy," 206-7; "Petrarch," vol. 6, 126-8; "Pico della Mirandola, Count Giovanni," 307-11; and "Pomponazzi, Pietro," 392-6. These articles are substantially identical with the presentation to be found in 101.

123 *Iter Italicum : A Finding List of Uncatalogued or Incompletely Catalogued Humanistic Manuscripts of the Renaissance in Italian*

and Other Libraries. Volume II : Italy, Orvieto to Volterra; Vatican City. London : The Warburg Institute, and Leiden : E. J. Brill, 1967. xv+736 pp. See 93 above.

1968

124 "The Myth of Renaissance Atheism and the French Tradition of Free Thought," *Journal of the History of Philosophy* 6 (1968), 233-43. Revised and enlarged English version of 46. Originally read in an earlier form as a paper at the New England Conference on the Renaissance, Brown University, on April 28, 1951.

125 "The European Significance of Florentine Platonism," in *Medieval and Renaissance Studies : Proceedings of the Southeastern Institute of Medieval and Renaissance Studies, Summer 1967*. Edited by John M. Headley. Chapel Hill : University of North Carolina Press, 1968, 206-29. Originally given as a lecture at the Southeastern Institute of Medieval and Renaissance Studies, Chapel Hill, on August 22, 1967. It was also presented as a lecture at Rutgers University on December 11, 1967 and at Vassar College on April 11, 1968. See 134 for an Italian version.

1969

126 No. 60 reprinted. Rome : Edizioni di Storia e Letteratura, 1969.

127 *Der italienische Humanismus und seine Bedeutung.* Vorträge der Aeneas-Silvius-Stiftung an der Universität Basel, 10. Basel : Helbing and Lichtenhahn, 1969. 35 pp. Given as a lecture at the Aeneas-Silvius-Stiftung, Basel, on May 20, 1969 and again at the University of Frankfurt, Frankfurt am Main, on June 6, 1969. See 133 for an Italian version and 140 for an English version.

128 "Die Rolle des klassischen Humanismus in der Wissenschaft der Renaissance," in *Zu Begriff und Problem der Renaissance.* Edited by August Buck. Darmstadt : Wissenschaftliche Buchgesellschaft, 1969, 222-27. German translation of 19. Translated by Marie-Luise Gutbrodt.

1970

129 *Ocho filosofos del Renacimiento italiano.* Translated by Maria Martinez Peñaloza. Mexico City : Fondo de Cultura Económica, 1970. 223 pp. Spanish translation of 101.

130 *Otto pensatori del Rinascimento Italiano*. Translated by Renzo Federici. Milan and Naples : Riccardo Ricciardi, 1970. x+ 195 pp. Italian translation of 101.
131 "The Contribution of Religious Orders to Renaissance Thought and Learning," *The American Benedictine Review* 21 (1970), 1-55. Based on a lecture at the Monastic Manuscript Microfilm Library, Saint John's University, Collegeville, Minn., on October 15, 1968. The lecture was given again to the University Seminar on the Renaissance, Columbia University, on October 7, 1969. This essay was reprinted with some revisions and additions in 146.
132 "Erasmus from an Italian Perspective," *Renaissance Quarterly* 23 (1970), 1-14. Given as a lecture at the Erasmus Quinquecentennial, Grand Valley State College, Allendale, Mich., on February 24, 1967; at Wayne State University on February 5, 1968; at Brown University on May 11, 1968; and at the University of Notre Dame on December 13, 1969.
133 "L'influsso del primo umanesimo italiano sul pensiero e sulle scienze," in *Il pensiero italiano del Rinascimento e il tempo nostro, Atti del V Convegno Internazionale del Centro di Studi Umanistici, Montepulciano—Palazzo Tarugi 8-13 agosto 1968*. Centro di Studi Umanistici "Angelo Poliziano," Fondazione Secchi Tarugi. Florence : Leo S. Olschki, 1970, 1-21. Italian version of 127. Given as a lecture at the Centro di Studi Umanistici "Angelo Poliziano," Montepulciano, on August 8, 1968.
134 "La diffusione europea del platonismo fiorentino," *ibid.*, 23-41. Italian version of 125 slightly revised. Given as a lecture at the Sezione Lombarda, Istituto Nazionale di Studi sul Rinascimento, Milan, on June 24, 1968.
135 "A Latin Translation of Gemistos Plethon's 'De fato' by Johannes Sophianos Dedicated to Nicholas of Cusa," in *Nicolò Cusano agli inizi del mondo moderno : Atti del Congresso internazionale in occasione del V centenario della morte di Nicolò Cusano, Bressanone, 6-10 settembre 1964*. Facoltà di Magistero dell'Università di Padova : Pubblicazioni, 12. Florence : G. C. Sansoni, 1970, 175-93. Given as a lecture at The Mediaeval Institute, University of Notre Dame, on January 31, 1967, and at the Center for Medieval and Renaissance Studies, Ohio State University, on May 1, 1967.
136 No. 43 reprinted in *Problems in Aesthetics : An Introductory Book*

of Readings. Second edition. Edited by Morris Weitz. New York : The Macmillan Company, 1970, 108-163.

1971

137 "A Little-Known Letter of Erasmus, and the Date of His Encounter with Reuchlin," in *Florilegium Historiale : Essays Presented to Wallace K. Ferguson.* Edited by J. G. Rowe and W. H. Stockdale. Toronto : University of Toronto Press in association with The University of Western Ontario, 1971, 52-61 plus 2 plates.

138 (Editor in Chief). Union Académique Internationale. *Catalogus Translationum et Commentariorum : Mediaeval and Renaissance Latin Translations and Commentaries ; Annotated Lists and Guides.* vol. 2. Washington, D.C. : The Catholic University of America Press, 1971. xv+440 pp. See especially the Preface (ix-xii) and the Bibliography (xiii-xv) as well as the Addenda to vol. 1 (423-6). Co-author with Aubrey Diller of the articles on Stephanus Byzantius (221-3) and Strabo (225-33). See 70 above.

139 "Le interpretazioni della civiltà del Rinascimento dopo Burckhardt," in *Interpretazioni del Rinascimento.* Edited and translated by Alfonso Prandi. Bologna : Società Editrice Il Mulino, 1971, 165-84. Italian translation of 79.

1972

140 "The Impact of Early Italian Humanism on Thought and Learning," in *Developments in the Early Renaissance.* Edited by Bernard S. Levy. Albany : State University of New York Press, 1972, 120-157. English version of 127. Given as a lecture at the Second Annual Conference on Problems in Medieval and Early Renaissance Studies, State University of New York at Binghamton on May 4, 1968 and also at the Folger Library, Washington, D.C., on March 6, 1970.

141 *Die Philosophie des Marsilio Ficino.* Frankfurt am Main : Vittorio Klostermann, 1972. xi+452 pp. See 20 and 47 for the English and Italian versions. This edition contains a new Preface ("Vorrede") dated February 2, 1972 (pp. vii-xi). Professor Kristeller began the writing of the book in 1933 in Berlin and completed the work in Italy in 1937. The manuscript was the

basis of the Italian version which he composed with the help of Alessandro Perosa in 1938 and of the English version which was translated with the aid of Virginia Conant and others. This edition has the same indices as the Italian version but it gives all the quotations from Ficino in German translation.

142 *Renaissance Concepts of Man and Other Essays.* New York: Harper and Row (Harper Torchbooks), 1972. viii+183 pp. Several chapters of this book were published earlier. Ch. 4 is an English version of 97 and 115, while Ch. 5 is a revised English version of 116, with footnotes added. Ch. 6 = 117 and Ch. 7 = 99. Ch. 1 ("The Dignity of Man"), Ch. 2 ("The Immortality of the Soul") and Ch. 3 ("The Unity of Truth"), which have not been published previously, were given as the Arensberg Lectures, under the auspices of the Francis Bacon Foundation, at the Claremont Graduate School and University Center on May 17, 19 and 21, 1965 under the general title of "Renaissance Concepts of Man." The first chapter was also presented as a lecture under the title "Renaissance Concepts of Man" at Columbia College, N.Y., as part of the Contemporary Civilization Lecture Series on November 19, 1963; at the Shakespeare Renaissance Festival sponsored by the Department of History, University of Chicago, on January 20, 1964; at Wheaton College on March 23, 1964; at a joint Duke-UNC Philosophy Colloquium, University of North Carolina at Chapel Hill, on October 9, 1964; under the auspices of the History Department, Harvard University, on December 4, 1964; at Smith College, on March 12, 1965; and at the University of California at Davis on May 14, 1965. The last lecture at Davis was also part of a meeting of the Renaissance Conference of Northern California. Ch. 5 was presented as a lecture at the University of California at Los Angeles on May 20, 1965.

143 "Buoninsegni (Boninsegni), Giovambattista," in *Dizionario biografico degli Italiani,* vol. 15. Rome, 1972, 255-256.

1973

144 "Francesco Patrizi da Cherso, *Emendatio in libros suos novae philosophiae,*" *Rinascimento* 21 (1970), 215-218. This volume was published at Florence in 1973.

145 No. 5 reprinted. Florence: Leo S. Olschki, 1973.

1974

146   *Medieval Aspects of Renaissance Learning. Three Essays.* Edited and translated by Edward P. Mahoney. Duke Monographs in Medieval and Renaissance Studies, 1. Durham, N.C. : Duke University Press, 1974. xii+175 pp. The three chapters of this book are English versions of 74 (= Ch. I, pp. 1-25) and 120 (= Ch. II, pp. 27-91) and an expanded version of 131 (= Ch. III, pp. 93-158). All three of the essays have been revised and the footnotes throughout have been brought up to date. In the third essay, many additions have been made to Appendix B : Humanists and Scholars of the Religious Orders (pp. 126-158).

147   "Il tomismo e il pensiero italiano del Rinascimento," *Rivista di filosofia neo-scolastica* 66 (1974), 841-96. Italian version of 120 without the modifications to be found in the English version in 146. Name of translator not given.

148   "The Use of Mediaeval and Renaissance Manuscripts," in *Seventh International Congress of Bibliophiles, 29 September-13 October 1971, Boston, Philadelphia, New York : Acts.* Edited by Gabriel Austin. London : William Clowes and Sons, 1974, 31-42.

149   *Humanismus und Renaissance, I : Die antiken und mittelalterlichen Quellen.* Edited by Eckhard Kessler and translated by Renate Schweyen-Ott. Humanistische Bibliothek, Abhandlungen und Texte; Reihe I : Abhandlungen. Band 21. Munich : Wilhelm Fink Verlag, 1974. 259 pp. The eleven chapters of this book have appeared before, mostly in English, but also in Italian and German. Ch. I-IV (pp. 11-86) = 54; Ch. V (pp. 87-111) = 24; Ch. VI (pp. 112-144) = 117; Ch. VII (pp. 145-160) = 97; Ch. VIII (pp. 161-176) = 116; Ch. IX (pp. 177-194) = 31; Ch. X (pp. 195-209) = 69; Ch. XI (pp. 210-221) = 90. The footnotes are grouped together (pp. 222-259). The translation for chapters VII and VIII was based on the English versions to be found in 142 (Ch. 4 and Ch. 5). In the "Vorrede," Professor Kristeller indicates the various former appearances of the different chapters. The publisher promises (p. 5, note) a second volume of collected papers, entitled *Philosophie, Bildung und Kunst,* to be published in 1975 as volume 22 in the same series.

MINOR PUBLICATIONS

1931

1 Review of *Plotins Schriften*, translated by Richard Harder, Bd. I : *Die Schriften 1-21 der chronologischen Reihenfolge*. Leipzig : Verlag von Felix Meiner, 1930, in *Deutsche Literaturzeitung* 52 (1931), cols. 57-61.

1932

2 Review of Willy Theiler, *Die Vorbereitung des Neuplatonismus*. Berlin : Weidmannsche Buchhandlung, 1930, in *Deutsche Literaturzeitung* 53 (1932), cols. 438-45.

1936

3 Review of Lamberto Borghi, "La dottrina morale di Coluccio Salutati," *Annali della R. Scuola Normale Superiore di Pisa : Lettere, storia e filosofia*, Serie II, vol. 3, 1934, pp. 75-102 and 469-92, in *La Nuova Italia* 7 (1936), 53-54.
4 "Il Platonismo nella letteratura francese" [Review of Walter Mönch, "Marsilio Ficino und die Nachwirkung Platons in der französischen Literatur und Geistesgeschichte," *Kant-Studien*, Band 40, Heft 4 (1935), pp. 165 ff.], *Giornale critico della filosofia italiana* 17 (1936), 190-92.

1937

5 Review of *Humanismus und Renaissance in den deutschen Städten und an den Universitäten*. Edited by Hans Rupprich. Leipzig : Reclam, 1935, in *La Nuova Italia* 8 (1937), 52-3.
6 Review of Walter Mönch, *Die italienische Platonrenaissance und ihre Bedeutung für Frankreichs Literatur und Geistesgeschichte (1450-1550)*, Romanische Studien, Heft 40. Berlin : Emil Ebering, 1936, in *Giornale critico della filosofia italiana* 18 (1937), 205-7.

1938

7 Review of August Buck, *Der Platonismus in den Dichtungen Lorenzo de' Medicis*, Neue Deutsche Forschungen, Abteilung Romanische Philologie, Band 3. Berlin : Junker und Duennhaupt, 1936, in *Giornale critico della filosofia italiana* 19 (1938), 149-53. Reprinted in entry 60 of the Major Publications as Chapter X : "Lorenzo de' Medici platonico."

8 Review of Eugenio Garin, *Giovanni Pico della Mirandola, Vita e dottrina*. Florence : Le Monnier, 1937, in *Giornale critico della filosofia italiana* 19 (1938), 374-78.

9 Review of Pearl Kibre, *The Library of Pico della Mirandola*. New York : Columbia University Press, 1936, in *Giornale critico della filosofia italiana* 19 (1938), 378-81.

10 Review of Eugenio Anagnine, *G. Pico della Mirandola, Sincretismo religioso-filosofico*. Bari : Laterza, 1937, in *Civiltà Moderna* 10 (1938), 331-35. [Signed "Lector"].

11 Review of Bohdan Kieszkowski, *Studi sul Platonismo del Rinascimento in Italia*. Florence : Sansoni, 1936, in *Annali della R. Scuola Normale di Pisa; Lettere, Storia e Filosofia*, Serie II, vol. 7 (1938), 341-49.

1939

12 Review of *Beiträge zur Inkunabelkunde, Neue Folge im Auftrage der Gesellschaft für Typenkunde des XV. Jahrhunderts und der Kommission für den Gesamtkatalog der Wiegendrucke*, volumes I and II. Edited by Carl Wehmer. Leipzig : Harrassowitz, 1935 and 1938, in *Maso Finiguerra : Rivista della stampa incisa e del libro illustrato* 4 (1939), 165-68.

1940

13 Review of Pilo Albertelli, *Gli Eleati, Testimonianze e frammenti*. Bari : Laterza, 1939, in *Philosophic Abstracts* No. 1 (Winter, 1939-40), 18.

14 Review of Augusto Guzzo, *Sic vos non vobis*, vol. 1. Naples : Luigi Loffredo, 1939, in *Philosophic Abstracts* No. 1 (Winter, 1939-40), 19.

15 Review of Enrico Turolla, *Vita di Platone*. Milan : Bocca, 1939, in *Philosophic Abstracts* No. 1 (Winter, 1939-40), 20.
16 Review of Giovanni Gentile, *Opere complete di Giovanni Gentile*, vol. XI. *Il pensiero italiano del Rinascimento*. Florence : Sansoni, 1940, in *Philosophic Abstracts* No. 3 (Fall, 1940), 19.
17 Review of Augusto Guzzo, *Sic vos non vobis*, vol. 2. Naples : Luigi Loffredo, 1940, in *Philosophic Abstracts* No. 3 (Fall, 1940), 19-20.
18 Transcription and translation of a Michelangelo poem from a manuscript in the Huntington Library, in Charles de Tolnay, "Michelangelo Studies," *The Art Bulletin* 22 (1940), 127.
19 Review of Raymond Klibansky, *The Continuity of the Platonic Tradition during the Middle Ages. Outlines of a "Corpus Platonicum Medii Aevi."* London : The Warburg Institute, 1939, in *The Journal of Philosophy* 37 (1940), 409-11. Hereafter this journal will be cited as *JP*.
20 Review of Johannes Hessen, *Platonismus und Prophetismus. Die antike und die biblische Geisteswelt in strukturvergleichender Betrachtung*. Munich : Ernst Reinhardt, 1939, in *JP* 37 (1940), 586-7.
21 Review of Sofia Vanni Rovighi, *La filosofia di Edmund Husserl*. Milan : Società Editrice "Vita e Pensiero," 1939, in *JP* 37 (1940), 587.
22 Review of *Plato Latinus*, edidit Raymundus Klibansky. Volumen I. *Meno*, interprete Henrico Aristippo, edidit Victor Kordeuter, recognovit et praefatione instruxit Carlotta Labowsky. London : Warburg Institute, 1940, in *JP* 37 (1940), 695-97. See also 43, 119 and 178.

1941

23 Review of Erwin Panofsky, *Studies in Iconology : Humanistic Themes in the Art of the Renaissance*. New York : Oxford University Press, 1939, in *Review of Religion* 5 (1940-41), 81-86.
24 Review of John O. Riedl, *A Catalogue of Renaissance Philosophers*. Milwaukee : Marquette University Press, 1940, in *Philosophic Abstracts* No. 5-6 (Summer, 1941), 17.
25 Review of Gordon H. Clark, *Selections from Hellenistic Philosophy*. New York : F. S. Crofts and Co., 1940, in *JP* 38 (1941), 26.
26 Review of Charles Trinkaus, *Adversity's Noblemen : The Italian*

Humanists on Happiness. New York: Columbia University Press, 1940, in *JP* 38 (1941), 81-84.

27   Review of Whitney J. Oates, *The Stoic and Epicurean Philosophers.* New York: Random House, 1940, in *JP* 38 (1941), 446-47.

28   Review of Marshall Clagett, *Giovanni Marliani and Late Medieval Physics.* New York: Columbia University Press, 1941, in *JP* 38 (1941), 643-44.

29   Review of Lynn Thorndike, *A History of Magic and Experimental Science.* Volumes V and VI: *The Sixteenth Century.* New York: Columbia University Press, 1941, in *JP* 38 (1941), 690-92.

1942

30   Review of *Iohannis Dominici Lucula Noctis.* Edited by Edmund Hunt. Notre Dame: Publications in Medieval Studies, The University of Notre Dame, 1940, in *Review of Religion* 6 (1941-42), 79-80.

31   Review of *Johannis Scotti Annotationes in Marcianum.* Edited by Cora E. Lutz. Cambridge, Massachusetts: The Mediaeval Academy of America, 1939, in *The American Journal of Philology* 63 (1942), 480-83.

32   Review of Richard W. Emery, *Heresy and Inquisition in Narbonne.* New York: Columbia University Press, 1941, in *Church History* 11 (1942), 70-71.

33   Review of Desiderius Erasmus, *The Praise of Folly.* Translated with an essay and commentary by Hoyt H. Hudson. Princeton: Princeton University Press, 1941, in *JP* 49 (1942), 445-46.

34   Review of *Renaissance Studies in Honor of Hardin Craig, Philological Quarterly,* vol. XX, No. 3, pp. 193-531. Iowa City: University of Iowa, 1941, in *JP* 46 (1942), 530-31.

35   Review of Roy W. Battenhouse, *Marlowe's Tamburlaine, A Study in Renaissance Moral Philosophy.* Nashville: Vanderbilt University Press, 1941, in *JP* 46 (1942), 556-58.

36   Articles on "Ficino, Marsilio" and "Renaissance" in *The Dictionary of Philosophy.* Edited by Dagobert D. Runes. New York: Philosophical Library, 1942, 109 and 270-71.

1943

37 Review of *Four Treatises of Theophrastus von Hohenheim called Paracelsus*. Edited by Henry E. Sigerist. Baltimore : The Johns Hopkins Press, 1941, in *JP* 40 (1943), 109-110.
38 Review of *The Rhetoric of Alcuin and Charlemagne*. A Translation, with an introduction, the Latin text and notes by Wilbur S. Howell. Princeton : Princeton University Press, 1941, in *JP* 40 (1943), 166.
39 Review of Victor L. Dowdell, *Aristotle and Anglican Religious Thought*. Ithaca : Cornell University Press, 1942, in *JP* 40 (1943), 362.
40 Review of William K. Prentice, *Those Ancient Dramas Called Tragedies*. Princeton : Princeton University Press, 1942, in *JP* 40 (1943), 419.
41 Review of Gershom G. Scholem, *Major Trends in Jewish Mysticism*. Published for the Jewish Institute of Religion, New York. Jerusalem : Schocken Publishing House, 1941, in *JP* 40 (1943), 474-75.
42 Review of *The Vita Sancti Malchi of Reginald of Canterbury*. Edited by Levi R. Lind. Urbana : The University of Illinois Press, 1942, in *JP* 40 (1943), 526-7.

1944

43 Review of *Corpus Platonicum Medii Aevi. Plato Arabus*, Vol. II : *Alfarabius, De Platonis Philosophia*. Edited by Franz Rosenthal and Richard Walzer. London : The Warburg Institute, 1943, in *JP* 41 (1944), 164-65. See also 22, 119 and 178.
44 Review of James J. Donohue, *The Theory of Literary Kinds : Ancient Classifications of Literature*. Dubuque : Loras College Press, 1943, in *JP* 41 (1944), 446-47.
45 Review of Charles N. Cochrane, *Christianity and Classical Culture : A Study of Thought and Action from Augustus to Augustine*. New York : Oxford University Press, 1944, in *JP* 41 (1944), 576-81.

1945

46 Co-editor (with James Gutmann and John Herman Randall,

Jr.) of Ernst Cassirer, *Rousseau, Kant, Goethe: Two Essays*. The History of Ideas Series, 1. Princeton : Princeton University Press, 1945. v+98 pp.

47 Review of Walter Pagel, *The Religious and Philosophical Aspects of Van Helmont's Science and Medicine*. Baltimore : The Johns Hopkins Press, 1941, in *Review of Religion* 9 (1945), 325.

48 Review of Dionysius Pseudo-Areopagita, *Theologia Mystica, Being the Treatise of Saint Dionysius Pseudo-Areopagite on Mystical Theology, Together with the First and Fifth Epistles*. Translated by Alan W. Watts. West Park : Holy Cross Press, 1944, in *Review of Religion* 9 (1945), 426.

49 Review of *Dunchad : Glossae in Martianum*. Edited by Cora E. Lutz. Philological Monographs, American Philological Association, 12. Lancaster : Lancaster Press, 1944, in *American Journal of Philology* 66 (1945), 423-25.

50 Review of *The Autobiography of Giambattista Vico*. Translated by Max H. Fisch and Thomas G. Bergin. Ithaca : Cornell University Press, 1944, in *The Philosophical Review* 54 (1945), 428-31.

51 Review of Pico della Mirandola, *Of Being and Unity (De Ente et Uno)*. Translated by Victor M. Hamm. Milwaukee : Marquette University Press, 1943, in *JP* 42 (1945), 77-80.

52 Review of Plato, *The Timaeus and the Critias or Atlanticus : The Thomas Taylor Translation*. Foreword by R. Catesby Taliaferro. New York : Pantheon Books (The Bollingen Series), 1945, in *JP* 42 (1945), 474-75.

53 Review of *Marsilio Ficino's Commentary on Plato's Symposium*. The text with a translation and introduction by Sears R. Jayne. The University of Missouri Studies, 19. Columbia : University of Missouri, 1944, in *JP* 42 (1945), 586-88.

1946

54 Review of Juan Urriza, *La preclara Facultad de Artes y Filosofia de la Universidad de Alcala de Henares en el Siglo de Oro : 1509-1621*. Madrid : Consejo Superior de Investigaciones Cientificas, 1941 (1942), in *Hispanic Review* 14 (1946), 80-81.

55 Review of Harold Cherniss, *Aristotle's Criticism of Plato and the Academy*. vol. I. Baltimore : The Johns Hopkins Press, 1944, and of Harold Cherniss, *The Riddle of the Early Academy*. Berkeley

and Los Angeles : University of California Press, 1945, in *JP* 43 (1946), 163-66.
56 Review of *MAPKOY ANTΩNINOY AYTOKPATOPOΣ TA EIΣ EAYTON. The Meditations of the Emperor Marcus Antoninus*. Edited with translation and commentary by Arthur S. L. Farquharson. 2 volumes. Oxford : Clarendon Press, and New York : Oxford University Press, 1944, in *JP* 43 (1946), 250-51.
57 Review of Ermolao Barbaro, *Epistolae, Orationes et Carmina*. Edited by Vittore Branca. 2 volumes. Florence : Bibliopolis (L. S. Olschki), 1943, in *JP* 43 (1946), 419-20.
58 Review of G. Pico della Mirandola, *De Hominis Dignitate, Heptaplus, De Ente et Uno, e scritti vari*. Edited by Eugenio Garin. Florence : Vallecchi, 1942, in *JP* 43 (1946), 586-87.
59 Review of J. H. Whitfield, *Petrarch and the Renascence*. Oxford : Basil Blackwell, 1943, in *The Romanic Review* 37 (1946), 94-95.

1947

60 Review of Otto Benesch, *The Art of the Renaissance in Northern Europe : Its Relations to the Contemporary Spiritual and Intellectual Movements*. Cambridge, Massachusetts : Harvard University Press, 1945, in *The Art Bulletin* 29 (1947), 60-61.
61 "Bruno's Trial," *Journal of the History of Ideas* 8 (1947), 240. This is a review of Angelo Mercati, *Il Sommario del Processo di Giordano Bruno, con appendice di documenti sull'eresia e l'inquisizione a Modena nel secolo XVI*. Studi e Testi, 101. Vatican City, Biblioteca Apostolica Vaticana, 1942.
62 Review of Eugenio Garin, *Filosofi italiani del quattrocento*. Florence : Le Monnier, 1942, in *JP* 44 (1947), 669.

1948

63 Review of Augustus Pelzer, *Addenda et Emendanda ad Francisci Ehrle Historiae Pontificum tum Bonifatianae tum Avenionensis. vol. I*. Vatican City : Biblioteca Apostolica Vaticana, 1947, in *Traditio* 6 (1948), 390.
64 Memorial Notice on Edgar Zilsel, *Proceedings and Addresses of the American Philosophical Association* 1947-48, vol. XXI : *The Philosophical Review* 57 (1948), 375.

65 Review of *Asclepius: A Collection and Interpretation of the Testimonies*. Edited by Emma J. Edelstein and Ludwig Edelstein. Baltimore : The Johns Hopkins Press, 1945, in *JP* 45 (1948), 613.

66 Review of Bruno Switalski, *Plotinus and the Ethics of St. Augustine*. New York : Polish Institute of Arts and Sciences in America, 1946, in *JP* 45 (1948), 613-14.

67 Review of Cecil Roth, *The History of the Jews in Italy*. Philadelphia : The Jewish Publication Society of America, 1946, in *Review of Religion* 13 (1948), 102.

1949

68 Review of *The Correspondence of Sir Thomas More*. Edited by Elizabeth F. Rogers. Princeton : Princeton University Press, 1947, in *JP* 46 (1949), 51-52.

69 Review of Eugenio Garin, *La filosofia*. 2 volumes. Milan : Francesco Vallardi, 1947, in *JP* 46 (1949), 160-61.

70 Review of Harry A. Wolfson, *Philo : Foundations of Religious Philosophy in Judaism, Christianity and Islam*. Cambridge, Massachusetts : Harvard University Press, 1947, in *JP* 46 (1949), 359-63.

71 Review of Frederick Copleston, *A History of Philosophy*. Vol. I : *Greece and Rome*. Westminster, Maryland : The Newman Bookshop, in *JP* 46 (1949), 872. See 128.

72 Review of Culbert G. Rutenber. *The Doctrine of the Imitation of God in Plato*. New York : King's Crown Press, 1946, in *JP* 46 (1949), 873-74.

73 Review of Simone Pétrement, *Le dualisme dans l'histoire de la philosophie et des religions : Introduction à l'étude du dualisme platonicien, du gnosticisme et du manichéisme*. Paris : Gallimard, 1946, in *JP* 46 (1949), 874.

74 Review of W. H. S. Jones, *Philosophy and Medicine in Ancient Greece*. Baltimore : The Johns Hopkins Press, 1946, in *JP* 46 (1949), 874-75.

75 Review of Sofia Vanni Rovighi, *Introduzione allo studio di Kant*. Milan : Carlo Marzorati, 1945, in *JP* 46 (1949), 875.

76 [Report on project:] "Medieval and Renaissance Latin Translations and Commentaries," *Renaissance News* 2 (1949), 37-40. See also 81, 109, 116, 123 and 135.

77 Review of George Boas, *Essays on Primitivism and Related Ideas in the Middle Ages*. Baltimore : The Johns Hopkins Press, 1948, in *Isis* 40 (1949), 377.
78 Article on "Bruno, Giordano" in *Collier's Encyclopedia*, vol. 4. New York : P. F. Collier and Son, 1949, 152-53.

1950

79 Articles in *Collier's Encyclopedia*. New York : P. F. Collier and Son, 1950. "Cusanus, Nicolaus," vol. 6, 190-91; "Ficino, Marsilio," vol. 8, 29-30; and "Pico della Mirandola, Count Giovanni," vol. 16, 45.
80 [Note on some recent Italian books], *Renaissance News* 3 (1950), 32.
81 "Mediaeval and Renaissance Latin Translations and Commentaries," *Renaissance News* 3 (1950), 75. See also 76, 109, 116, 123 and 135.
82 Report : "A Catalogue of Renaissance Manuscripts in Italian Libraries" (1948), *The American Philosophical Society, Year Book 1949* (Philadelphia : The American Philosophical Society, 1950), 236.
83 Review of Ernst R. Curtius, *Europäische Literatur und lateinisches Mittelalter*. Bern : A. Francke, 1948, in *Annali della R. Scuola Normale Superiore di Pisa : Lettere, storia e filosofia*, Serie II, vol. 19 (1950), 205-8.
84 Review of Giovanni Di Napoli, *Tommaso Campanella filosofo della restaurazione cattolica*. Padua : Cedam, 1947, in *The Philosophical Review* 59 (1950), 250-1.
85 Review of Mario Santoro, *Uno scolaro del Poliziano a Napoli : Francesco Pucci*. Naples : Libreria Scientifica Editrice, 1948, in *The Romanic Review* 41 (1950), 132-33.
86 Review of Wallace K. Ferguson, *The Renaissance in Historical Thought : Five Centuries of Interpretation*. Boston : Houghton Mifflin, 1948, in *JP* 47 (1950), 129-32.
87 Review of Eugenio Garin, *Der italienische Humanismus*. Bern : A. Francke, 1947, in *The Romanic Review* 41 (1950), 218-19.
88 Review of Eugenio Garin, *Der italienische Humanismus*, in *JP* 47 (1950), 222-23.

1951

89 "Latin Translations and Commentaries : Medieval and Renaissance," *Progress of Medieval and Renaissance Studies in the United States and Canada*, Bulletin No. 21 (Boulder, 1951), 76-84. See 104 and 124.

90 [Note on recent Italian publications], *Renaissance News* 4 (1951), 56-57.

91 Review of Hiram Hayden, *The Counter-Renaissance*. New York : Charles Scribner's Sons, 1950, in *Journal of the History of Ideas* 12 (1951), 468-72.

92 Review of Ernst Hoffmann, *Platon*. Zürich : Artemis-Verlag, 1950, in *JP* 48 (1951), 619-21.

93 Review of Josef Staudinger, *Das Schöne als Weltanschauung im Lichte der Platonisch-Augustinischen Geisteshaltung*. Vienna : Herder, 1948, in *JP* 48 (1951), 621-22.

94 Review of *Volumen Medicinae Paramirum of Theophrastus von Hohenheim called Paracelsus*. Translated by Kurt F. Leidecker. Baltimore : The Johns Hopkins Press, 1949, in *JP* 48 (1951), 763-64.

95 Review of Giuseppe Saitta, *Il pensiero italiano nell'Umanesimo e nel Rinascimento*. Vol. I : *L'Umanesimo*. Bologna : Cesare Zuffi, 1949, in *JP* 48 (1951), 764-65.

96 Review of Heinrich Fichtenau, *Askese und Laster in der Anschauung des Mittelalters*. Vienna : Herder, 1948, in *JP* 48 (1951), 790-91.

97 Review of Bert Mariën, *Bibliografia critica degli studi Plotiniani*. Bari : Laterza, 1949, in *JP* 48 (1951), 791.

1952

98 Review of Vernon Hall, Jr., *Life of Julius Caesar Scaliger (1484-1558)*. Transactions of the American Philosophical Society. New Series, vol. XL, Part 2. Philadelphia : The American Philosophical Society, 1950, 85-170, in *The American Historical Review* 57 (1951-52), 394-96.

99 Letter to Alessandro Perosa (on problems of research in Italian archives and libraries) in *Il Ponte* 8 (1952), 442-44.

100 Review of Tommaso Campanella, *Opuscoli inediti*. Edited by Luigi Firpo. Florence : Leo S. Olschki, 1951. in *JP* 49 (1952), 25.

101 Review of Marcus Tullius Cicero, *Brutus*; *On the Nature of the Gods; On Divination; On Duties*. Translated by Hubert M. Poteat with an introduction by Richard McKeon. Chicago: The University of Chicago Press, 1950, in *JP* 49 (1952), 198-99.
102 [List of some recent books of interest published in Italy and Switzerland], *Renaissance News* 5 (1952), 39-40.

1953

103 Annual report on the *Catalogus translationum et commentariorum* in *Union Académique Internationale, Compte rendu* 27 (1953), 51-53. Hereafter this publication will be cited as *UAICR*.
104 "Medieval and Renaissance Latin Translations and Commentaries: Second and Third Annual Reports of Progress," *Progress of Medieval and Renaissance Studies in the United States and Canada*, Bulletin No. 22 (Boulder, 1953), 52-55. See 89 above and 124.
105 Report: "Handlist of Uncatalogued Renaissance Manuscripts in Italian and Some Other European Libraries" (1951), *The American Philosophical Society, Year Book 1952* (Philadelphia: The American Philosophical Society, 1953), 239-240.
106 Letter dated August 29, 1951 concerning Codex Estensis latinus 1080 (Alpha J. 5, 19) at Modena, in Baccio Ziliotto, "Chiose zovenzoniane," *Archeografo Triestino*, Series IV, vol. 28-29 (1952-53), 218.
107 "Giovanni Pico, Count of Mirandola (1463-94)," in *Ioannes Picus Mirandulanus Comes Concordiae Oratio de Hominis Dignitate*. With English translation by Elizabeth L. Forbes. Lexington, Ky.: The Anvil Press, 1953, 48-49.

1954

108 Annual report on the *Catalogus* in *UAICR* 28 (1954), 58.
109 "Mediaeval and Renaissance Translations and Commentaries," *Renaissance News* 7 (1954), 114-15. Report on same project. See also 76, 81, 116, 123 and 135.
110 [Report as Secretary:] "Advisory Committee on Medieval and Renaissance Texts," *American Council of Learned Societies, Bulletin* No. 47 (1954): *Proceedings Number*, 37-38.
111 Review of Wit Stwosz, *Le Rétable de Cracovie*. Warsaw: Panst-

wowy Instytut Wydawniczy, 1953, in *Renaissance News* 7 (1954), 119-20.

112 Review of *Plotini Opera*, vol. I : *Porphyrii Vita Plotini, Enneades I-III*. Edited by Paul Henry and Hans-Rudolf Schwyzer. Paris : Desclée de Brouwer, and Brussels : L'Edition Universelle, 1951, in *JP* 51 (1954), 74-75. See 148 below.

1955

113 Annual Report on the *Catalogus* in *UAICR* 29 (1955), 47-48.
114 Letter on Hans Nachod, in *To Hans Nachod on the Occasion of his Seventieth Birthday May 31, 1955, Greetings and Tributes from Friends and Colleagues*. (A pamphet of 20 pages which was privately printed by Mr. Hans P. Kraus. Professor Kristeller's letter is dated January 16, 1955 and is found on pages 7 and 8.)

1956

115 Annual report on the *Catalogus* in *UAICR* 30 (1956), 58-59.
116 "Mediaeval and Renaissance Latin Translations and Commentaries," *Renaissance News* 9 (1956), 20-21. Report on same project. See also 76, 81, 109, 123 and 135.
117 Report : "Handlist of Uncatalogued Renaissance Manuscripts in Italian and Other European Libraries" (1954), *The American Philosophical Society, Year Book 1955* (Philadelphia : The American Philosophical Society, 1956), 290-291.
118 "Supplementary Booklist" ["A List of Books published 1948-56 which have not been noticed in the *RN* bibliographies"], *Renaissance News* 9 (1956), 241-46.
119 Review of *Corpus Platonicum Medii Aevi. Plato Latinus*, edidit Raymundus Klibansky. Volumen II. *Phaedo*, interprete Henrico Aristippo, edidit et praefatione instruxit Laurentius Minio-Paluello... adiuvante H. J. Drossaart-Lulofs. London : Warburg Institute, 1950; and of Volumen III. *Parmenides usque ad finem primae hypothesis nec non Procli Commentarium in Parmenidem, Pars ultima adhuc inedita, interprete Guillelmo de Moerbeka*, ediderunt...Raymundus Klibansky et Carlotta Labowsky. London : Warburg Institute, 1953, in *JP* 53 (1956), 196-201. See also 22, 43 and 178.
120 Articles in *Encyclopaedia Britannica*. Chicago : Encyclopaedia

Britannica, 1956. "Ficino, Marsilio," vol. 9, 217-18; "Pico della Mirandola, Giovanni, Count," vol. 17, 912; and "Pomponazzi, Pietro," vol. 18, 206-7.

121 [Annotated bibliography :] "Philosophy," in *A Critical Bibliography of French Literature*. D. C. Cabeen, General Editor. Vol. II : *The Sixteenth Century*. Edited by Alexander H. Schutz. Syracuse : Syracuse University Press, 1956, Entry nos. 187-311, pp. 23-34.

1957

122 Annual report on the *Catalogus* in *UAICR* 31 (1957), 66-68.
123 "Medieval and Renaissance Latin Translations and Commentaries; Catalogus Translationum et Commentariorum (CTC)," *Renaissance News* 10 (1957), 225-26. Report on same project. See also 76, 81, 109, 116 and 135.
124 "Medieval and Renaissance Latin Translations and Commentaries," *Progress of Medieval and Renaissance Studies in the United States and Canada*, Bulletin No. 24 (Boulder, 1957), 34-36. This is a presentation of the fourth, fifth and sixth annual reports, that is, 1954-56. See above 89 and 104.
125 "Additional Notes on Publications," *Renaissance News* 10 (1957), 117-18 and 170-71. These lists contain comments by Professor Kristeller.
126 Review notes of Roberto Weiss, *Humanism in England during the Fifteenth Century*. 2nd. ed. Oxford : Basil Blackwell, 1957, and Henri Busson, *De Pétrarque à Descartes*. I : *Le rationalisme dans la littérature française de la Renaissance (1533-1601)*. Paris : Vrin, 1957, in *Renaissance News* 10 (1957), 241-42.
127 "Paduan Averroism and Alexandrism in the Light of Recent Studies," *JP* 54 (1957), 774-75. Abstract of paper read at the Annual Meeting of the American Philosophical Association, Eastern Division, Harvard University, on December 28, 1957. See Major Publications entry 73.
128 Review of Frederick Copleston, *A History of Philosophy*. Vol. III : *Ockham to Suarez*. Westminster, Maryland : The Newman Press, 1953, in *JP* 54 (1957), 565-67. See 71 above.

1958

129 Annual report on the *Catalogus* in *UAICR* 32 (1958), 61-62.
130 Report : "Microfilming of the Inventario Ceruti of the Biblioteca Ambrosiana in Milan, Italy" (1953), *The American Philosophical Society, Year Book 1957* (Philadelphia : The American Philosophical Society, 1958), 438-439.
131 Review of André Chastel, *Marsile Ficin et l'art*. Geneva : Librairie E. Droz, 1954, in *The Art Bulletin* 40 (1958), 78-79
132 Review of Philip Merlan, *From Platonism to Neoplatonism*. The Hague : Martinus Nijhoff, 1953, in *Journal of the History of Ideas* 19 (1958), 129-133.
133 Review of A. J. Festugière, *La Révélation d'Hermès Trismégiste*. vol. III : *Les doctrines de l'âme*; vol. IV : *Le Dieu inconnu et la Gnose*. Paris : Librairie Lecoffre, J. Gabalda et Cie, 1953-54, in *JP* 55 (1958), 1110-14.

1959

134 Annual report on the *Catalogus* in *UAICR* 33 (1959), 67-68.
135 ["Annual Report" :] "Catalogus Translationum et Commentariorum," *Renaissance News* 12 (1959), 65-67. See also 76, 81, 109, 116 and 123.
136 Review of Georg Luck, *Der Akademiker Antiochos*. Bern and Stuttgart : Paul Haupt, 1953, in *JP* 56 (1959), 425-27.
137 Review of Paul van Schilfgaarde, *Geschiedenis der Antieke Wijsbegeerte*. Leiden : A. W. Sijthoff, 1952, in *JP* 56 (1959), 427.
138 Review of Galvano della Volpe, *Eckhart o della filosofia mistica*. Rome : Edizioni di Storia e Letteratura, 1952, in *JP* 56 (1959), 427.
139 Review of Herman Baeyens, *Begrip en Probleem van de Renaissance*. Université de Louvain, Recueil de Travaux d'Histoire et de Philologie, 3e série, 48e fascicule, 1952, in *JP* 56 (1959), 427-28.
140 Review of *Offener Horizont : Festschrift für Karl Jaspers*. Munich : R. Piper, 1953, in *JP* 56 (1959), 428.
141 Review of François Masai, *Pléthon et le Platonisme de Mistra*. Paris : Les Belles Lettres, 1956, in *JP* 56 (1959), 510-12.
142 Letter in Italian, dated January 7, 1959, to Dott. Barrera, which serves as an Introduction to Marsilio Ficino, *Opera Omnia*, vol. I.

Turin: Bottega d'Erasmo, 1959, p. iii. Also "Nota bibliografica," pp. ix-xii. This is a photographic reprint of the Basel edition of 1576. It was edited by Mario Sancipriano.

1960

143 Annual Report on the *Catalogus* in *UAICR* 34 (1960), 91.
144 Report: "Handlist of Uncatalogued Renaissance Manuscripts in Italian and Other European Libraries" (1958), *The American Philosophical Society, Year Book 1959* (Philadelphia: The American Philosophical Society, 1960), 600.
145 Obituary of Ludwig Bertalot, *Renaissance News* 13 (1960), 338.
146 "Ludwig Bertalot†," *Archiv für Kulturgeschichte* 42 (1960), 388-89. See 151 for an Italian version.
147 "Ludwig Bertalot†," *Gnomon* 32 (1960), 676-77. Same as 145.
148 Review of *Plotini Opera*. vol. II: *Enneades IV-V*. Edited by Paul Henry and Hans-Rudolf Schwyzer. Paris: Desclée de Brouwer et Cie, and Brussels: L'Edition Universelle, 1959, in *JP* 57 (1960), 771-73. See 112 above.
149 Review of Emile Bréhier, *The Philosophy of Plotinus*. Translated by Joseph Thomas. Chicago: The University of Chicago Press, 1958, in *JP* 57 (1960), 774-75.

1961

150 Annual report on the *Catalogus* in *UAICR* 35 (1961), 70-71.
151 "In memoria di Ludovico Bertalot," *Lettere Italiane* 13 (1961), 108-9. Italian version of 146.
152 "Leonardo Olschki, Writer, Scholar, 76," *The New York Times*, December 12, 1961 (vol. 111), p. 57. Obituary notice on Olschki.
153 Review of D. P. Walker, *Spiritual and Demonic Magic from Ficino to Campanella*. London: The Warburg Institute, 1958, in *Speculum* 36 (1961), 515-17.
154 Review of Michele Schiavone, *Problemi filosofici in Marsilio Ficino*. Milan: Marzorati, 1957, in *JP* 58 (1961), 51-53.

1962

155 Annual report on the *Catalogus* in *UAICR* 36 (1962), 84-85.
156 "ACLS," *Renaissance News* 15 (1962), 55-56. Report on the

Annual Meeting of the American Council of Learned Societies to the Council of the Renaissance Society of America, hereafter referred to as RSA.

157 "In Memoriam Leonardo Olschki (*Verona 1885, †Berkeley 1961)," *Romanische Forschungen* 74 (1962), 109-10.

158 "Ludwig Bertalot (1884-1960) ['Bibliographie']," *Scriptorium* 16 (1962), 102-4.

159 Review of Erwin Panofsky, *Renaissance and Renascences in Western Art*. Stockholm : Almquist and Wiksell, 1960, in *The Art Bulletin* 44 (1962), 65-67.

160 Review of Richard Newald, *Nachleben des antiken Geistes im Abendland bis zum Beginn des Humanismus*. Tübingen : Niemeyer, 1960, in *Gnomon* 34 (1962), 220-22.

161 Review of *Procli Diadochi Tria Opuscula (De Providentia, Libertate, Malo) Latine Guilelmo de Moerbeka Vertente et Graece ex Isaacii Sebastocratoris Aliorumque Scriptis Collecta*. Edited by H. Boese. Berlin : W. de Gruyter, 1960, in *JP* 59 (1962), 74-78.

162 Review note of M.A. Goukovsky, "Issledovanija o zhisni i tvorchestve Leonardo da Vinci," *Trudy Gosurdarstvennovo Ermitazha, Zapadnoevropejskoe Iskusstvo* 6 (1961), 22-50, in *Renaissance News* 15 (1962), 68.

163 Review note of *Akty Kremony XIII-XVI Vekov v Sobranii Akademii Nauk SSSR*; *Atti di Cremona dei sec. XIII-XVI nell'Archivio dell'Istituto di Storia, Sezione di Leningrado, dell' Accademia delle Scienze dell'URSS*. Edited by V. Rutenburg and E. Skrzynskaia. Moscow and Leningrad : Akademia Nauk SSSR, 1961, in *Renaissance News* 15 (1962), 70.

164 Review note of *Drammaturgia di Lione Allacci accresciuta e continuata fino all'anno MDCCLV*. Turin : Bottega d'Erasmo, 1961, in *Renaissance News* 15 (1962), 74.

165 Review note of *Mediaeval and Renaissance Studies* 5 (1961). Edited by Richard Hunt, Raymond Klibansky and Lotte Labowsky. London : Warburg Institute, 1961, in *Renaissance News* 15 (1962), 181.

166 Review note of Alberto Chiari, *Indagini e letture*. Terza serie. Florence : Le Monnier, 1961, in *Renaissance News* 15 (1962), 184.

1963

167 Annual report on the *Catalogus* in *UAICR* 37 (1963), 85-86.
168 "ACLS," *Renaissance News* 16 (1963), 55. Report to RSA.
169 "Recollections of Don Giuseppe De Luca," in *Don Giuseppe De Luca : Ricordi e testimonianze*. Edited by Mario Picchi. Brescia : Casa Editrice Morcelliana, 1963, 227-31.
170 Review of C. C. Bayley, *War and Society in Renaissance Florence : The 'De Militia' of Leonardo Bruni*. Toronto : University of Toronto Press, 1961, in *The Canadian Historical Review* 44 (1963), 66-70.
171 Review of Ernst Hoffmann, *Platonismus und Christliche Philosophie*. Zurich and Stuttgart : Artemis-Verlag, 1960, in *Journal of the History of Philosophy* 1 (1963), 99-102.

1964

172 Annual report on the *Catalogus* in *UAICR* 38 (1964), 119-20.
173 "ACLS," *Renaissance News* 17 (1964), 51. Report to RSA.
174 Review of *Supplement to the Census of Medieval and Renaissance Manuscripts in the United States and Canada*. Originated by C. U. Faye, continued and edited by W. H. Bond. New York : The Bibliographical Society of America, 1962, in *Renaissance News* 17 (1964), 317-20.
175 "Necrology : Dr. Beatrice Reynolds," *Renaissance News* 17 (1964), 356-57.

1965

176 Annual report on the *Catalogus* in *UAICR* 39 (1965), 86-87.
177 "ACLS," *Renaissance News* 18 (1965), 71-72. Report to RSA.
178 Review of *Corpus Platonicum Medii Aevi. Plato Latinus*. ed. Raymundus Klibansky. Volumen IV. *Timaeus a Calcidio translatus commentarioque instructus*, in societatem operis coniuncto P. J. Jensen edidit J. H. Waszink. London : Warburg Institute, and Leiden : E. J. Brill, 1962, in *JP* 62 (1965), 14-17. See also 22, 43 and 119.

1966

179 Annual report on the *Catalogus* in *UAICR* 40 (1966), 83-84.
180 "ACLS," *Renaissance News* 19 (1966), 70-71. Report to RSA.

181 Review of Frederick R. Goff, *Incunabula in American Libraries: A Third Census of Fifteenth-Century Books Recorded in North American Collections*. New York: The Bibliographical Society of America, 1964, in *Renaissance News* 19 (1966), 133-35.
182 "On Humanistic Scholarship" [Letter to Henry Allen Moe], *ACLS Newsletter* vol. 17, No. 3 (March, 1966), 10-12.

1967

183 Annual report on the *Catalogus* in *UAICR* 41 (1967), 86.
184 "ACLS," *Renaissance Quarterly* 20 (1967), 76-78. Report to RSA. (The *Renaissance News* was renamed *Renaissance Quarterly* in 1967.)
185 Editor of Ernst Cassirer, *Dall'Umanesimo all'Illuminismo*. Florence: La Nuova Italia, 1967. Also author of preface (pp. v-viii).
186 Review of Norman P. Zacour and Rudolf Hirsch, *Catalogue of Manuscripts in the Libraries of the University of Pennsylvania to 1800*. Philadelphia: University of Pennsylvania Press, 1965, in *Renaissance Quarterly* 20 (1967), 480-81.
187 Review of Endre von Ivanka, *Plato Christianus : Übernahme und Umgestaltung des Platonismus durch die Väter*. Einsiedeln, Switzerland: Johannes Verlag, 1964, in *Speculum* 42 (1967), 374-75.
188 Review of Philip Merlan, *Monopsychism, Mysticism, Metaconsciousness: Problems of the Soul in the Neoaristotelian and Neoplatonic Tradition*. International Archives of the History of Ideas, 2. The Hague: Martinus Nijhoff, 1963, in *JP* 64 (1967), 124-25.

1968

189 Annual report on the *Catalogus* in *UAICR* 42 (1968), 89.
190 "ACLS," *Renaissance Quarterly* 21 (1968), 96-97.
191 Address at the University of Padua: "I discorsi di B. L. Ullman, P. O. Kristeller e B. Nardi Dottori 'Honoris Causa' dell'Università di Padova," *Quaderni per la Storia dell'Università di Padova* 1 (1968), pp. ix-xiii. The address and the awarding of the honorary degree took place on November 22, 1962.

192 Foreword to Quirinus Breen, *Christianity and Humanism: Studies in the History of Ideas*. Edited by Nelson Peter Ross. Grand Rapids : William B. Eerdmans, 1968, pp. v-vi.
193 Editor (with Philip P. Wiener) of *Renaissance Essays from the "Journal of the History of Ideas."* New York : Harper Torchbooks, 1968. Also author of Introduction (pp. 7-9).
194 Review of Agostino Pertusi, *Leonzio Pilato fra Petrarca e Boccaccio : Le sue versioni omeriche negli autografi di Venezia e la cultura greca del primo Umanesimo*. Venice and Rome : Istituto per la Collaborazione Culturale, 1964, in *Romanic Review* 59 (1968), 125-26.
195 Review of Helmut Boese, *Die lateinischen Handschriften der Sammlung Hamilton zu Berlin*. Wiesbaden : Otto Harrassowitz, 1966, in *Renaissance Quarterly* 21 (1968), 179-82.
196 Review of Ludwig Edelstein, *The Meaning of Stoicism*. Martin Classical Lectures, 21. Cambridge, Massachusetts : Harvard University Press, 1966, for Oberlin College, in *JP* 65 (1968), 79-80.

1969

197 Annual report on the *Catalogus* in *UAICR* 43 (1969), 95-96.
198 "American Council of Learned Societies," *Renaissance Quarterly* 22 (1969), 85. Report to RSA.
199 "Catalogus Translationum et Commentariorum," *Renaissance Quarterly* 22 (1969), 304.
200 Discussion talks in *Arts Libéraux et philosophie au moyen âge, Actes du Quatrième Congrès International de philosophie médiévale*. Montreal and Paris : Vrin, 1969, 69-70, 154-55 and 263.
201 Foreword to Siegfried Kracauer, *History : The Last Things before the Last*. New York : Oxford University Press, 1969, pp. v-x. See 208 for a German version.
202 Review of *The Cambridge History of Later Greek and Early Medieval Philosophy*. Edited by A. H. Armstrong. Cambridge and New York : Cambridge University Press, 1967, in *JP* 66 (1969), 221-24.

1970

203 "American Council of Learned Societies," *Renaissance Quarterly* 22 (1970), 103-04. Report to RSA.

204 Review of John W. O'Malley, *Giles of Viterbo on Church and Reform: A Study in Renaissance Thought*. Leiden: E. J. Brill, 1968, in *The Catholic Historical Review* 55 (1969-70), 85-86.

1971

205 "American Council of Learned Societies," *Renaissance Quarterly* 24 (1971), 117-119. Report to RSA.
206 [Memorial notice:] "Roberto Weiss" (with Astrik Gabriel and Kenneth Setton), *Speculum* 46 (1971), 574-575.
207 "Notice" (committee report on the discovery of the Leonardo manuscripts in the Biblioteca Nacional in Madrid, with Theodore S. Beardsley, Jr. and Carlo Pedretti), *Renaissance Quarterly* 24 (1971), 430-431.
208 "Vorwort" to Siegfried Kracauer, *Geschichte-Vor den letzten Dingen*. Frankfurt: Suhrkamp, 1971, 7-12. German version of 201.

1972

209 "American Council of Learned Societies," *Renaissance Quarterly* 25 (1972), 124. Report to RSA.
210 Foreword to Thomas Carson Mark, *Spinoza's Theory of Truth*. New York and London: Columbia University Press, 1972, pp. v-vi.
211 Short testimony, in *Prezzolini 90*, Quaderni dell'Osservatore, No. 13 (Milan, 1972), 65.
212 Review note of *Bibliografia filosofica Italiana 1850-1900*. Rome: Edizioni Abete, 1969, in *Renaissance Quarterly* 25 (1972), 158. This book was published by the Istituto di Studi Filosofici.

1973

213 "American Council of Learned Societies," *Renaissance Quarterly* 26 (1973), 111-12. Report to RSA.
214 [Memorial minute:] "John Berberelly," *Proceedings and Addresses of the American Philosophical Association* 46 (1972-1973), 173.

1974

215 "ACLS," *Renaissance Quarterly* 27 (1974), 134-35. Report to RSA.

216 "The Validity of the Term 'Nominalism'," in *The Pursuit of Holiness in Late Medieval and Renaissance Religion. Papers from the University of Michigan Conference.* Edited by Charles Trinkaus and Heiko A. Oberman. Leiden : E. J. Brill, 1974, 65-66.
217 "The Role of Religion in Renaissance Humanism and Platonism," *ibid.*, 367-70.
218 "Additional on 'Preaching for the Popes'," *ibid.*, 440-43.
219 Foreword to Herbert S. Matsen, *Alessandro Achillini (1463-1512) and His Doctrine of "Universals" and "Transcendentals" : A Study in Renaissance Ockhamism.* Lewisburg, Pa. : Bucknell University Press, 1974, 9-11.
220 "Scholarship and the Humanistic Tradition," in *The Idea of a Modern University.* Edited by Sidney Hook, Paul Kurtz and Miro Todorovich. Buffalo : Prometheus Books, 1974, 255-56.

INDEX

All proper names and major subjects mentioned in the Festschrift, as well as in Professor Kristeller's Bibliography, are included in the Index, with the exception of those which appear in the *Tabula Gratulatoria* or in titles cited in footnotes. Manuscripts and institutions are indexed under their geographical locations, e.g. "Oxford" entries include, without distinction, all references to the city Oxford, to Oxford University or its individual Colleges, and to manuscripts held in Oxford libraries. An "n" is appended to the number of a page on which a reference appears only in the footnotes.

INDEX

Aargau, 415
Abbott, Kenneth M., 528n
Abelard, Peter, 245n
Abet, Josef Friedrich, 412n, 413n
Abubacer (Ibn Tufayl), 96
Abydenus, 51n
Academy, New, 248n
Academy, Platonic, 258, 259, 260, 265, 266, 270, 272n, 273, 274, 574
Academy, Platonic (Florentine), 8, 395, 396n, 555, 558, 563. *See also* Platonism, Florentine
Acakia, Martinus, 285n
Accursius, Franciscus, 33n, 420
Achillini, Alessandro, 518, 519, 521n, 523n, 525, 526, 527, 528, 530, 533n, 589
Adam, 51, 52, 53, 54, 55, 56, 57, 58, 61, 63, 66, 67, 379
Adam of Balsham, Bishop of Saint Asaph, 237
Adam, Melchior, 414n
Adams, Marilyn McCord, 101n, 102, 103, 104, 108n, 109n, 110n, 114
Addison, Joseph, 376
Adrian VI, Pope (Adrian Floresnz Dedal), 423
Aelfric, Abbot of Eynsham, 373
Aeneas Sylvius Piccolomini. *See* Pius II, Pope
Aeschlimann, Erhard, 393n
Africa, 175, 176
Agen, 454, 455, 457, 458, 459
Agricola, Rudolf, the Elder, 408
Agrigento, 11, 559
Alamand, Laurens, Bishop of Grenoble and Abbot of Saint-Sernin of Toulouse, 457
Albany, New York, 50n
Albareda, Anselm M., 558
Alberico da Rosate, 442
Albert of Saxony, 149n
Albert, Peter Paul, 418n
Albertelli, Pilo, 570

Alberti, Leandro, 522n
Alberti, Leon Battista, 195, 196, 197, 198, 199, 203, 212, 223, 393, 401, 402
Albertus Magnus, Saint, 92, 95n, 119, 120, 133, 146, 151, 153, 155, 156, 158, 159, 160n, 245, 246, 247, 400n
Alboini, Giovanni degli, da Mantova, 531
Alboini, Pietro degli, da Mantova, 531, 532, 533, 534, 535, 540
Albrecht of Habsburg, Archduke of Austria, 408, 409n
Albrecht of Hohenzollern, Margrave of Brandenburg, 408
Albumasar (Abu Mashar), 93
Alcalá de Henares, 574
"Alchindo," 76, 87
Alciato, Andrea, 35, 36, 47n
Alcinous, 293
Alcuin, 573
Aldus. *See* Manutius, Aldus
Alessio, Franco, 245n
Alexander III, Pope (Orlando Bandinelli), 335, 441
Alexander IV, Pope (Rainaldo dei Conti di Segni), 455
Alexander VII, Pope (Fabio Chigi), 65n
Alexander of Aphrodisias, 80, 81, 82, 84, 85, 91, 93, 94, 95, 96, 97, 146, 147, 152, 153, 162, 163, 262n, 277, 293
Alexander the Great, 94n, 176, 260n, 323
Alexander of Hales, 240, 247
Alexander Lombard, 436, 439, 440, 441, 442, 445, 449
Alexandrism, 7, 80, 81, 93, 556, 581
Alexinus, 248, 249n
Alfarabi (al-Farabi), 118, 153, 573
Alfonso V of Aragon (Alfonso I of Naples, called "the Magnanimous"), 136, 137, 397
Alfred, King of England, 371
Algazel (al-Ghazali), 153
'Ali ibn al-Abbas, 284, 285, 286
'Ali ibn Ridwan, 281, 284, 286, 287, 288, 289, 290, 292

Alidosi, Giovanni Niccolò Pasquali, 520n, 522n
Aliotti, Girolamo, 137, 138
Alkindi (al-Kindi), 76n
Allacci, Lione, 584
Allen, Don Cameron, 57n
Allen, Percy S., 355n
Allen, Reginald E., 262n
Allendale, Michigan, 565
Allison, Anthony F., 366n
Almandal, 93
Almerico da Seravalle, 531
Alphonse of Poitiers, Count of Toulouse, 455, 456, 457, 458, 460
Altadell, Gabriel, 136, 139
Altomonte, 168
Amabile, Luigi, 168n, 173n, 178n, 179n, 183, 184, 185n, 186n, 187n
Amann, Émile, 229n
Amboise, 20n
Ambrose, Saint, 38, 90n, 436, 445, 451n
America, 57, 66, 175, 176, 177
Amerio, Romano, 183n, 184n
Amidei, Girolamo, 76, 88
Ammonius Hermiae, 293
Amoenus, Gervasius (Drocensis), 355
Anagnine, Eugenio, 570
Anaxagoras, 150, 195, 262n
André, Bernard, 354, 355
Andreas Bavarus, 421n
Ann Arbor, Michigan, 547
Annandale-on-Hudson, New York, 558
Annapolis, Maryland, 550
Anne of Brittany, 20n
Anselm, Saint, Archbishop of Canterbury, 92
Anstey, Henry, 241n, 242n
Antella, 404
Antiochus of Ascalon, 582
Anton, John P., 281n, 287n, 563
Antonelli, Giuseppe, 118n
Antoninus, Saint, Archbishop of Florence, 428
Antoninus, Marcus Aurelius, 575
Antonio, Saint, Abbot, 522
Apelles of Colophon, 24
Apollodorus of Athens, 308n
Apollonius the Egyptian, 51

Apollonius Pergaeus, 269n, 270, 271n, 273n
Apuleius, Lucius Madaurensis, 344
Apulia, 487
Aquilecchia, Giovanni, 60n
Aquileia, 74
Aquinas, Thomas. *See* Thomas Aquinas
Aragon, 135n, 136, 137
Archimedes, 24, 269
Archipoeta, 320, 321, 322, 323, 324, 325, 326, 327, 330, 331, 332, 334, 335, 337, 338
Archytas of Tarentum, 196, 270, 271, 272n
Aretino, Pietro, 462, 463
Arezzo, 137, 138, 139n, 462, 463
Argentré. *See* D'Argentré, Bertrand
Argyropoulos, Joannes, 117, 126, 395, 396, 400n
Ariostea di Ferrara, 118n
Ariosto, Ludovico, 166n, 351
Aristides of Thebes, 24
Aristippus, Henricus, 571, 580
Aristocles of Messene, 95
Aristotelianism, 6, 70, 76, 87, 99, 101, 102, 103, 109, 115, 116, 127, 133, 148, 150, 151, 153, 154, 161, 162, 165n, 166, 176, 192, 193, 236, 238, 247, 253n, 275, 276, 277, 278, 280, 281, 282, 288, 289, 291, 293, 294, 295, 296, 301, 302, 303, 307, 308, 309, 376, 377, 465, 467, 468n, 470, 471, 473, 475, 528, 532, 551, 558, 561
Aristotle, 1, 6, 13, 19n, 20, 31, 39, 70, 74, 77n, 87, 88, 89n, 93, 94, 95, 96, 97, 100, 101, 102, 110, 112, 114, 116, 117, 118, 119, 120, 121, 122, 123, 124, 125, 126, 127, 128, 131, 133, 144, 145, 146, 147, 148, 149, 150, 151, 152, 153, 154, 155, 156, 157, 158, 159, 160, 161, 162, 163n, 166, 174, 191, 192, 193, 194, 202, 203, 204, 213, 223, 226, 234, 235n, 239, 241, 244n, 247, 248, 251, 252, 253, 254, 255, 256, 258, 260, 262, 263, 264, 265, 266, 267, 268, 269n, 272, 273, 274, 276, 278, 284, 288n, 291, 292, 296, 297, 300, 301, 304, 305, 318, 375, 377, 395, 403, 417, 421, 466, 467, 468, 469, 470, 472, 473, 474, 475, 476, 526n, 532n, 536, 537, 541, 549, 562, 573, 574

Armagh (County, Ireland), 368
Armstrong, Arthur Hilary, 101n, 587
Armstrong, Charles Arthur John, 354n
Arnim, Hans F. A. von, 248n
Arthur, King of Britain, 385
Arundel, Earls of. *See* Fitzalan, William *and* Howard, Thomas
Aschbach, Joseph, 412n
Asclepius, 576
Asconius Pedianus, Quintus, 529n, 530n
Asellius (Asellio), 529n
Asia, 63, 175
Assisi, 513
Astesanus (de Ast), 441, 442
Aston, Margaret E., 309n
Athens, 33, 36, 39, 250, 398
Attica, 33
Augsburg, 480
Augustine, Saint, Bishop of Hippo, 7, 51, 56, 90n, 93, 215n, 223, 226, 247, 251, 252, 417, 489, 546, 547, 573, 576
Augustinian Hermits, Order of, 71, 72n, 75, 140, 432
Augustinianism, 247, 256, 578
Augustus Caesar, 327, 332, 333, 334, 335, 337, 338, 573
Aulus Gellius, 37n, 193, 198, 199, 513n
Aurelianus, Johannes Philippus, 118n
Aurelio, Niccolò, 508n
Aureoli, Petrus, Archbishop of Aix, 108
Austen, Jane, 375
Austin, Gabriel, 568
Austria, 187, 407, 419
Avempace (Ibn Badjdja), 96, 123n
Averroes (Ibn Rushd), 78n, 93, 94, 95, 116, 117, 118, 119, 120, 121, 122, 123, 124, 125, 126, 127, 128, 144, 146, 147, 148, 149, 150, 151, 152, 153, 154, 155, 156, 157, 159, 160, 162, 229, 277, 281, 284, 286n, 288n, 292, 297, 301, 467, 468, 469, 472, 473, 475, 527
Averroism, 6, 7, 55, 62n, 119, 123, 124, 127, 144, 146, 148, 149, 277, 278, 284, 292, 302, 466n, 469n, 528, 551, 556, 581
Avicenna (Ibn Sina), 93, 97, 147, 151, 153, 156, 157, 162, 468, 469, 473, 474, 475, 521

Avignon, 231, 234, 251n, 256, 257
Aztecs, the, 56, 60

Babylon, 51, 54
Bacon, Francis, 64, 167
Bacon, Roger, 232n
Baconthorp, John, 95n
Bacquet, Jean, 44n
Baethgen, Friedrich, 1
Baeyens, Herman, 582
Bagenal, Philip H. D., 366n
Bagnoll, Dudley, 367
Bagnoll, Nicholas, 366, 367, 368
Bagolini, Giovanni Francesco, 126
Bagolini, Girolamo (da Verona), 124, 126
Baiae, 24
Baine, Rodney M., 370n
Baines, Richard, 61, 62
Bainton, Roland H., XXV, 5
Baldo degli Ubaldi (Baldo da Perugia), 420, 442
Balducius, Antonius, 524
Baldwin, John W., 436n
Bale, John, 353
Ballenstadius, Joannes A., 407n, 411n
Bambrough, Renford, 262n
Bambyke (el-Mambay), 514n
Bandello, Matteo, 393
Bandello, Vincenzo, 7
Bandello da Castelnuovo, Vincenzo, 561
Bandini, Francesco, 547, 553-554
Banfi, Florio, 519n
Baptista de Avolio, 121
Baptista Mantuanus, 84n
Barabàs, Ladislao Holik. *See* Banfi, Florio
Barbadoro, Bernardino, 435n
Barbaro, Ermolao, 20, 40, 81, 152, 162, 514n, 533n, 549, 575
Barbaro, Francesco, 549
Barbet, Jeanne, 240n
Barbo, Giovanni, 562
Barcelona, 431
Barclay, Alexander, 384
Barnes, Jonathan, 262n
Baron, Eguinaire, 35
Baron, Hans, 4, 399n
Barozzi, Luciano, 520n
Barozzi, Pietro, 149

Barrera, Angelo, 582
Bartholomeus de Mantua, 531
Bartolo da Sassoferrato, 420
Bartolomeo da Saliceto, 442
Barzizza, Gasparino, 534
Basel, 70n, 116, 117, 124, 318n, 352, 387, 389, 392, 408, 413, 414, 417n, 477, 564
Basil the Great, Saint, Archbishop of Caesarea, 138
Baskervill, Charles Read, 383n
Basset, Bernard, 358n
Bateson, Mary, 353n
Bathsheba, mother of Solomon, 385
Battenhouse, Roy W., 572
Bauch, Gustav, 407n, 412n
Baudouin, François, 33, 34, 35, 36, 41, 42n
Baugh, Albert C., 372n
Baumer, Franklin L., 561
Baumgardt, Carola, 315n
Baur, Ludwig, 199n
Bayley, Charles C., 585
Bazan, Bernard, 84n
Beaciano, Francesco, 509n
Beardsley, Theodore S., Jr., 588
Beauvais, 21
Beccadelli, Antonio (Panormita), 136, 137, 214n, 221n
Becichemo, Marino, 510, 511
Becker, Felix, 118n
Bede, the Venerable, Saint, 399
Belgium, 65n
Bellantius, Lucas, 90n
Bellini, Giovanni, 513n
Belt, Elmer, XXV
Bembo, Pietro, 74, 75n
Bendyshe, Thomas, 57, 58n, 64n
Benedetti, Alessandro, 514n
Benedict, Saint, Abbot of Monte Cassino, 340
Benedict XIV, Pope (Prospero Lorenzo Lambertini), 427
Benedictines, 137, 240, 244n
Benesch, Otto, 575
Ben Israel, Manasseh, 53n
Bennett, Josephine Waters, XXV
Bentworth, Richard, Bishop of London, 238

Benz, Meinrad, 104n
Benzi, Socino, 532
Benzi, Ugo, 278, 287, 532n
Berberelly, John, 588
Bergamo, 4, 55, 492
Bergfeld, Christoph, 44n
Bergin, Thomas G., 574
Berkeley, California, 559
Berlin, 1, 2, 3, 4, 389n, 536n, 556, 563, 566, 587
Bernard de Caux, 455, 457, 458
Bernard of Clairvaux, Saint, 138, 366, 417
Bernardine of Siena, Saint, 449
Bernardini, Antonio, 41n
Berners, John Bourchier, second Baron, 371, 376
Bernstein, Eduard, 178n
Bertalot, Ludwig, 5, 562, 583, 584
Berthelet, Thomas, 365, 366
Bertola, Ermanegildo, 118n
Besançon, 433
Bessarion, Cardinal, Archbishop of Nicaea, 33, 125, 162n, 396
Besta, Enrico, 489n
Bethlehem, 335
Beyschlag, Friedrich, 409n, 411n
Beza, Theodore, 307n, 309n
Biagio da Parma. See Pelacani, Biagio
Bianchelli, Mengo, 533n
Biese, Nicolas, 286n
Bigongiari, Dino, 6
Billanovich, Giuseppe, 4, 395n
Binghamton, New York, 566
Biondo da Forlì, Flavio, 132, 399
Blackwell, Constance T., XXV
Blanchet, Léon, 165n, 184n
Blois, 43
Bloomington, Indiana, 554
Blount, William, fourth Lord Mountjoy, 355
Blumenau, Laurentius, 407
Boas, George, 51n, 577
Boccaccio, Giovanni, 138, 339, 340, 341, 342, 343, 344, 345, 346, 347, 348, 349, 350, 351, 399, 417, 420
Bodemann, Eduard, 139n, 142
Bodin, Jean, 31, 36, 42, 44, 47, 48
Boehner, Philotheus H., 108n, 236n

Bönicke, Christian, 411n
Boese, Helmut, 584, 587
Boethius of Dacia, 223-224
Boethius, Anicius Manlius Severinus, 101, 102, 103, 104, 105, 109, 111, 112, 114, 151, 223, 247n, 253n, 255, 536, 537n, 541
Bohemia, 19n, 407, 409
Boileau, Daniel, 375
Bologna, 7, 72, 73, 74, 75, 76, 140n, 275, 352, 415, 434, 439, 442, 444, 518, 519n, 521n, 522, 523, 524, 525, 526n, 528, 531, 532, 550, 551, 552, 553
Bombe, Walter, 402n, 403
Bonansea, Bernardino M., 165n, 168n, 172n, 183n, 185n
Bonaventure, Saint (Giovanni di Fidanza), 240, 245n, 247
Bond, William H., 585
Bonitz, Hermann, 248n
Borcius, Hieronymus. *See* Borro, Girolamo
Bordeaux, 65
Borghi, Lamberto, 569
Borgnet, Auguste, 151n
Borro (Borrius), Girolamo, 462, 463, 464, 465, 466, 467, 468, 469, 470, 471, 472, 476
Borro, Laelio, 463n
Borst, Arno, 53n
Bosco, Bartolomeo, 450
Boston, Massachusetts, 568
Botero, Giovanni, 175n, 177n
Boulder, Colorado, 551
Bourges, 21, 35, 37, 44
Bovelles, Charles de, 21, 26
Braccesi, Alessandro, 560
Bradner, Leicester, 12
Bradwardine, Thomas, 235, 237, 238n, 533n
Brahe, Tycho, 309
Branca, Vittore, 4, 74n, 347n, 509n, 575
Brandenburg, Margrave of. *See* Albrecht of Hohenzollern
Brant, Sebastian, 510, 515n
Bray, William, 359n
Breen, Quirinus, 41n, 587
Bréhier, Emile, 583
Bremgarten, 415

Brescia, 504
Breslau, 421n
Bressanone (Brixen), 408, 565
Brewer, John Sherren, 232n
Briçonnet family, 21
Brisson, Barnabé, 32n, 44n, 46
Brockhaus, Clemens, 407n
Brognoli da Legnano, Benedetto, 485n, 491, 492, 499, 510, 514n
Bronxville, New York, 548
Bronzini, Giovanni, 518n
Brotto, Augusto Giovanni, 412n
Brower, Reuben, 381n
Brown, Horatio F., 502n, 505n
Brown, Malcolm, 266n, 271n, 272n
Brown, Rawdon, 426n
Brucker, Jacob, 229n
Bruges, 235n, 237n, 431
Brunelleschi, Filippo, 402, 403, 404
Brunet, Jacques Charles, 52n
Bruni, Leonardo (Aretino), 120, 129, 130, 131, 132, 133, 134, 135, 136, 137, 138, 139, 140n, 141, 142, 214n, 223, 224, 226, 227, 399, 514, 585
Bruno, Celestino, 432
Bruno, Giordano, 59, 60, 61, 62, 63, 64, 166, 560, 575, 577
Brussels, 19
Bryn Mawr, Pennsylvania, 563
Buck, August, 564, 570
Buda, 400n
Budé, Guillaume, 30n, 36, 38
Bühler, Curt, XXV
Buffon, Count de. *See* Le Clerc, Georges Louis
Bulan II, King of the Khazars, 52
Bullinger, Heinrich, 306
Bulmer-Thomas, Ivor, 271n
Bulst, Walther, 556
Buonamico, Francesco, 464, 465
Buoninsegni (Boninsegni), Giovambattista, 567
Burana, Johannes Franciscus, 124, 126
Burckhardt, Jacob, 387, 388, 389, 390, 391, 392, 393, 394, 396, 397, 400, 401, 402, 403n, 404, 557, 566
Buridan, John, 97, 242n
Burkard, Saint, Bishop of Würzburg, 411

598   INDEX

Burkhardt, Frederick, XXV
Burley (Burleigh), Walter, 235n, 236, 238, 254, 288n
Burlington, Vermont, 554
Burnyeat, Myles, 262n
Busson, Henri, 581

Cabala, 27, 53, 59, 179n
Cabeen, David C., 581
Cagni, Giuseppe Maria, 393n, 394, 395, 396n, 398, 399, 400n, 403
Cain, 66
Cajetan, Cardinal (Tommaso de Vio), 74, 77n, 78, 88, 89, 92, 96, 97, 423, 424, 425, 426, 427, 428, 429, 430, 431, 432, 433
Calabria, 165, 166, 169n, 173, 176, 178n, 179, 180, 181, 184
Calcidius, 585
Calfurnio, Giovanni, 486, 491, 492, 500
Callus, Daniel A. P., 245n
Calvin, John, 35, 38
Calvinism, 65, 308
Cambridge (England), 130, 353
Cambridge, Massachusetts, 546, 547, 551, 554, 556, 567, 581
Camden, Carroll, 309n
Camerini, Paolo, 125n
Campana, Augusto, 4
Campanella, Tommaso, 64, 164, 165, 166, 167, 168, 169, 170, 171, 172, 173, 174, 175, 176, 177, 178, 179, 180, 181, 182, 183, 184, 185, 186, 187, 188, 189, 276, 577, 578, 583
Campbell, William Edward, 356, 357n
Campion, Thomas, 376
Camuzzi, Andrea, 464
Cange, Dominus du. *See* Du Fresne, Charles
Canozi, Lorenzo (da Lendinara), 117, 118
Canter, Howard V., 528n
Canterbury, 135, 237n, 246, 247n
Capelli, Luigi M., 195n
Capetians, 455, 456
Capellanus, Andreas, 349
Capivaccio, Girolamo, 302
Capizzi, Antonio, 191n, 193n, 194n, 208n
Caplan, Harry, 562
Caprin, Giulio, 394n

Carcopino, Jérôme, 530n
Careggi, 396n
Carlos, Don, Prince of Viana, 136n
Carlow (County, Ireland), 367
Carolus-Barré, Louis, 34n
Carpaccio, Vittore, 513n
Carter, Charles H., 561
Carthage, 63
Cartwright, Julia, 71n, 73n, 85n
Carusi, Henricus, 525n
Carvajal, Rodrigo, 533n
Cary, Earnest, 530n
Casali, Michele, 524n
Casaubon, Isaac, 128
Cassandro, Giovanni, 432n
Cassese, Antonio, 552
Cassirer, Ernst, 2, 6, 38n, 165n, 195n, 275, 279, 280, 549, 574, 586
Cassuto, Umberto, 119n
Castellani, Giorgio, 491n
Castelli, Enrico, 550
Castelvetro, Lodovico, 375
Castiglione, Baldassare, 73n, 85
Castleisland (County Kerry, Ireland), 367
Cato, Marcus Porcius, 417, 421
Cavalcanti, Guido, 346, 552
Cavazza, Giovanni Battista, 520n
Cecioni, Cesare G., 384n
"Celestino," 76, 87
Cellius, Erhard, 311n
Celtis, Conrad, 409n, 416, 419
Cencetti, Giorgio, 519n
Cesalpino, Andrea, 59
Cesena, 470n
Cessi, Roberto, 531n
Ceylon, 180
Chaignet, Antelme-Édouard, 156n
Chaldeans, the, 21, 52, 56, 66
Chambers, Raymond W., 361, 372n
Champagne, 427
Champier, Symphorien, 27n
Chapel Hill, North Carolina, 564, 567
Chapelain, Jean, 375
Chapman, George, 376, 384, 385
Charles I (Charlemagne), Emperor, 328, 330, 334, 573
Charles V, Emperor, 478
Charles VIII, King of France, 20n

INDEX

Charles IX, King of France, 45
Charles, Duke of Bourbon, Constable of France, 86
Charles-Orland (son of Charles VIII, King of France), 20n
"Charondas." *See* Le Caron, Louis
Chartres, 244n
Chastel, André, 582
Chatelain, Émile, 245n
Chaucer, Geoffrey, 349, 371, 373, 382
Cherniss, Harold F., 258n, 574
Cherso, 466
Chesterfield, Earl of. *See* Stanhope, Philip Dormer
Chevalier, Ulysse, 519n
Chiari, Alberto, 584
Chicago, Illinois, 563, 567
Chilmead, Edmund, 178n
China, 57, 63
Chioggia, 493
Choco, Petrus, 531
Cholmley, Richard, 61n
Choppin, René, 44n
Christina, Queen of Sweden, 19, 65
Chrysippus, 196, 248, 249, 251
Church Fathers, the 29, 51, 90n, 224, 236n, 251, 350, 417
Chwolson, Daniel, 54n
Cian, Vittorio, 492n
Cicero, Marcus Tullius, 2, 33, 37, 41, 93, 157, 191, 192, 193, 194, 195, 205, 220, 223, 226, 248, 249, 323, 333, 373, 376, 377, 399n, 416, 417, 418, 421, 491, 514n, 523n, 526, 527, 528, 529, 530n, 536, 541, 579
Cicogna, Emmanuele A., 486n
Cino da Pistoia (Guittone dei Sighibuldi), 346
Cinque Chiese (Pecs), 400n
Cipelli, Giovanni Battista (*pseud.*: J. B. Egnatius), 513n
Cittadino, Antonio, 285n
Clagett, Marshall, 572
Claremont, California, 554, 567
Clark, Albert Curtis, 529n, 530n
Clark, Gordon H., 571
Claymond, John, 353
Clement VI, Pope (Pierre Roger), 231, 239, 240, 241, 242, 247n, 253, 254, 255, 256, 257
Clement VII, Pope (Giulio de' Medici), 71n, 73n, 79, 85, 86, 423
Clement VIII, Pope (Ippolito Aldobrandini), 169
Clement of Alexandria, 350
Clermont (Beauvaisis), 45
Clichtove, Josse, 21, 26
Clodius, Publius, 529n
Cocchi, Donato, 395n
Cochrane, Charles N., 573
Codignola, Melisenda, 545
Coimbra, 128
Colacio, Matteo, 486
Colet, John, 352, 353n
Collegeville, Minnesota, 565
Colocza, 400n
Cologne, 19n, 132, 133, 551, 555
Colonna, Egidio. *See* Egidio Romano
Colorado Springs, Colorado, 272n
Colt, Jane. *See* More, Jane
Columbus, Christopher, 57
Columbus, Ohio, 562, 565
Comin de Tridino, 127
Commandino, Federigo, 280
"Commentator, the" *See* Averroes
Commentators, Greek, 100, 123, 125, 144, 145, 152, 153, 154, 155, 156, 157, 158, 159, 161, 162, 163, 253, 470, 475
Conant, Virginia, 567
Condé, Prince of. *See* Henry II de Bourbon
Connan, François, 36, 44
Constance, 244n
Constantine I, Emperor of Rome, 334, 335, 390
Constantinople, 187
Contarini, Gasparo, 88, 506
Contarini, Marcantonio, 74
Conyngton, Agnes, 360
Copenhagen, 66
Copernicus, Nicolaus, 50, 99, 174
Copinger, Walter A., 353n
Copleston, Frederick, 576, 581
Corner, Flaminio, 488n
Corner, Giorgio, 505, 512
Corneus, Andrew, 356, 362
Corsano, Antonio, 214n

Corsi, Giovanni, 545
Cosenza, Mario Emilio, 137n, 139n
Cosenza, 166
Cosmati, the, 391n
Costil, Pierre, 19n
Cotroneo, Girolamo, 48n
Counter-Reformation, 164, 165, 166, 177, 184, 188, 189
Courthope, William J., 370
Coxe, Henry O., 131n, 132n, 134n, 142, 143, 149n
Cracow, 19, 579
Craig, Hardin, 572
Cranmer, Thomas, Archbishop of Canterbury, 353
Cranz, F. Edward, XXIII, 10, 81n, 152n, 518n, 529n
Crellius, Johannes, 59n
Cremona, 584
Crescini, Angelo, 278n, 286n
Cresty, Claude, 454n, 459n
Croce, Benedetto, 179n
Crusius, Martinus, 311, 312, 313, 314, 315, 316, 317, 318, 319
Cruz Hernández, Miguel, 123n
Cujas, Jacques, 36
Curtius, Ernst Robert, 190n, 577
Cusanus. *See* Nicholas of Cusa
Cuspinian, Johannes (Spieshaymer), 409n
Cyprian, Saint (Thascius Caecilius Cyprianus), 365
Cyrus, King of Persia, 176
Czechoslovakia, 19

D'Abano, Pietro, 276, 277, 278, 281, 284, 286, 287, 288n, 289, 290, 292, 293n, 296, 297, 298, 301
D'Ableiges, Jacques, 42n, 45
Da Compostella, Donato, 534
Da Cornigliano, Lazzaro, 534
Dactylomelos, Vitalis, 123n
Da Diacceto, Francesco, 548
Da Feltre, Vittorino (Vittorino de' Rambaldoni), 413
Da Fiano, Francesco, 223
Da Forlì, Melozzo, 403
D'Ailly, Pierre, 95n

Dallari, Umberto, 519n, 521n, 522n, 524n, 531n, 532n
Dalle Fornaci, Alessandro, 509n
Dalle Molle, Luciano, 425n, 427n
Dall'Orologio, Francesco Scipione Dondi, 149n
Dal Pozzo, Gianfrancesco (Puteolanus), 511n, 512, 516
Da Lucca, Gregorio, 527n
D'Amato, Alfonso, 524n
Da Moglio, Bernardo, 532n, 534
Da Mosto, Andrea, 484n, 485n, 488n, 502n
Damsté, Pieter H., 529n
Danchin, F.-C., 61n
D'Ancona, Alessandro, 175n, 183n, 463n
D'Ancona, Paolo, 393n
Dandolo, Andrea, 485, 486, 489, 495, 498
Dandolo, Maria, 489
Dandolo, Orsa (*née* Giustiniani), 485, 495, 498
Daniel, the Prophet, 329, 330
Daniel, Samuel, 376, 386
Dannenfeldt, Karl H., 555
Dante Alighieri, 177, 346, 347, 349, 351, 393, 399, 400
Da Piglio, Benedetto, 407
Dardani, Alvise, 503n
D'Argentré, Bertrand, 44n
Dario, Francesco, 508n, 513, 516
Dario, Giorgio, 508, 516
Dario, Giovanni Antonio, 513
Da Rosciate, Alberico, 534
Da Scarperia, Antonio, 532n, 534
Daun, 408
David, King of Israel, 224, 226, 227, 323, 385
Davidsohn, Robert, 400n
Davis, Walter R., 374n
Davis, California, 567
Dazzi, Manlio, 493n
De Acosta, Joseph, 63
De Alano, Heinricus, 413
Dean, Ruth, XXV
De Angleria, Pedro Martir, 57
De Armis, Jacobus, 531
De Azpilcueta, Martin (Dr. Navarrus), 430
De Balmes, Abram 123, 124, 126
De'Bardi, Alessandra, 397

De'Bardi, Roberto, 400n
De Beaumanoir, Philippe (de Remi), 45
De Camerino, Franciscus, 531
De Caprariis, Vittorio, 42n
De Castellanos, Juan, 63n
Decembrio, Pier Candido, 420, 562
Decembrio, Uberto, 532n, 534
De Chambre, William, 235n
De Chasseneux, Barthélemy, 31
De Comitibus, Bartholomeus, 531
De Comitibus, Prosdocimus, 413
De Coracis, Jacobus, 531
Dedo, Gerolamo, 508n
Dedo, Giovanni, 504, 505, 509n
De Dotis, Paulus, 413
De Dryvere, Jérémie, 286n, 304
Deferrari, Roy Joseph, 253n
Defoe, Daniel, 371, 372
De Genulis, Clarus Franciscus, 522
De Ghellinck, Joseph, 236n, 251n, 254n
Dei Bardi, Ruberto. *See* De'Bardi, Roberto
Deism, 50
De Janua, Johannes, 531
Dejob, Charles, 463n, 464n
De La Mare, Philippe, 67n
De Lendenaria, Simon, 533n
De'Libri, Matteo, 550
Delius, Walter, 122n
Della Fonte, Bartolommeo, 191n
Della Francesca, Piero, 403
Della Robbia, Luca, 404
Della Siega, Francesco, 509n
Della Torre, Arnaldo, 395n
Della Volpe, Galvano, 582
Del Medigo, Elia, 119, 120, 121, 127
Del Nero, Bernardo, 396n
Delphini, Giulio, 286n
Del Torre, Maria Assunta, 278n
De Luca, Giuseppe, 5n, 585
Del Virgilio, Giovanni, 558
De'Maffei, Timoteo, Bishop of Ragusa, 402n
De Marinis, Tammaro, 135, 136n, 143, 560
De Mario, Antonio, 139n
De Mattei, Rodolfo, 175n
De'Medici. *See* Medici
Democritus of Abdera, 168n, 213, 468, 473

De Monte, Antonius, 531
De Mornay, Philippe, 56
De'Negri, Enrico, 339n
Denholm-Young, Noel, 232n
De Nicola, Maria Laura, 554
Denifle, Heinrich S., 245n
Denmark, 243n
Denzer, Horst, 44n
De Odis, Marcus, 126
De'Peccioli, Domenico, 532n, 534
De Rijk, Lambertus M., 236n, 243n, 244n, 245n, 256n
De Roover, Raymond, 426n, 427n, 430n, 431n, 432n, 436, 441n
Derry, Richard L., 424n
De Sanctis, Francesco, 339, 341n
Descartes, René, 13, 31, 280, 284
Desmarets, Samuel, 59
De Solcia, Zaninus, 54-55
D'Este, Isabella, 71n, 73, 75n, 85
De Thiart. *See* Tyard, Pontus de
De Thou, Christofle, 44n
De Tolnay, Charles, 571
De Toulouse, Grégoire, 31
Detroit, Michigan, 565
De Valles, Francisco, 286n
De'Vieri, Francesco, the younger (Il Verino Secondo), 464, 470
De Vio, Thomas. *See* Cajetan
De Worde, Wynkyn, 356, 357
De Zerlis, Lancillotus, 118n
De Zocchis, Jacobus (de Ferraria), 413
Diacceto, Francesco da, 8
Diagoras of Melos, 205
Diana, Antonio, 432
Di Bozzolo, Federico, 72
Di Cesinge (Csezmicze), Giovanni (Janus Pannonius), Bishop of Cinque Chiese, 400n
Dichtl, Aloysius, 471n
Diels, Herman, 156n
Diether of Isenburg, Archbishop of Mainz, 408
Digard, Anicet, 34n
Di Gentili, Francesco, 513
Di Gentili, Marcantonio, 513
Diller, Aubrey, 566

Di Napoli, Giovanni, 71n, 75n, 76n, 77n, 83n, 88n, 92, 144n, 149n, 183n, 215n, 577
Dio Cassius, 530n
Diodorus Cronus, 248, 249n
Diodorus Siculus, 51n
Diogenes, 417
Diogenes Laertius, 51n, 194, 199, 223, 248
Dionisotti, Carlo, 533n
Dionysius the Areopagite, 205, 574
Dionysius Sandellius (*pseud.*). *See* Fassini, Vincenzo
Di'Ravegnani, Benintendi, 509
Di Zentili. *See* Di Gentili
Döring, Matthias, 417
Domat, Jean, 45
Dominic, Saint, 432, 522
Dominicans, 55n, 74, 88, 89, 166, 168, 172, 179, 237, 245, 246, 423, 432, 455, 456, 524
Dominicus, Johannes, 572
Donatello (Donato di Niccolò de' Bardi), 224, 403, 404
Donato, Girolamo, 146n, 152, 162
Dondi, Giovanni, 534
Doneau, Hugues, 36, 44
Doni, Anton Francesco, 180n
Donno, Elizabeth Story, XXII, XXIII, 384n
Donohue, James J., 573
Dossat, Yves, 454n, 455n, 456n
Douglas, Gavin, 376
Douie, Decima L., 247n
Dowdell, Victor L., 573
Drabkin, Israel E., 305n, 465n
Drake, Stillman, 465n, 468n
Dresden, 409
Dreux, 355
Drossaart-Lulofs, Hendrik Joan, 580
Drusianus. *See* Torrigiano dei Torrigiani
Dryden, John, 375, 376
Du Bellay, Joachim, 37n, 38
Dudith, Andreas, 19
Düring, Ingemar, 262n
Du Fresne, Charles, Seigneur du Cange, 539n
Du Haillan, Bernard de Girard, Sieur, 44n
Duhem, Pierre, 237n, 246n, 276, 278, 465n, 466n, 469n

Dukas, Jules, 121n
Dumoulin, Charles, 44n, 45
Dunchad of Rheims, 574
Dunleckney (County Carlow, Ireland), 367
Duns Scotus, John, 92, 93, 95, 96, 101, 106, 107, 108, 109, 113, 114, 146, 147, 148, 155, 156, 157, 158, 160, 245n, 256
Durand d'Auvergne, 129, 138n
Durand de Saint Pourçain, 95n
Durham (England), 235
Durham, North Carolina, 164n, 562
Du Tillet, Jean (Greffier), 44n
Dyce, Alexander, 354n

Ebrach, Konrad von, 412
Ebrard, Friedrich, 44n
Echard, Jacques, 532n
Eckhart, Meister, 582
Edelstein, Emma J., 576
Edelstein, Ludwig, 576, 587
Edridge, T. A., XXIV
Edwards, Paul, 563
Edwards, William F., 279, 280, 281, 282, 468n
Effler, Roy R., 89n
Egidio Romano, 95n, 121n, 240, 526n
Egidio da Viterbo, 92, 588
Egnatius, Joannes Baptista (*pseud.*). *See* Cipelli, Giovanni Battista
Egypt, 487
Egyptians, the, 51, 66
Ehrle, Franz, 233, 243n, 257, 575
Elias Cretensis. *See* Del Medigo, Elia
Eliot, George (Mary Ann Evans), 375
Elizabeth I, Queen of England, 61, 359, 370n
Ellinger, Friedrich W., 408n
Ely, 131, 132, 133n
Elyot, Thomas, 352, 363, 365, 366, 368
Emden, Alfred B., 134n, 235n, 238n, 241n
Emery, Richard W., 572
Ençio, Antonio. *See* Errizo, Antonio
Enck, John J., 559
Endemann, Wilhelm, 425n
Engel, Friedrich, 178n
England, 11, 62, 63, 130, 131n, 132, 134, 135, 178, 234, 241, 243n, 245, 246n, 254, 256, 352, 354, 355, 367

Epicureanism, 214n, 215n, 225, 226, 227, 228, 250, 572
Epicurus, 55, 195, 205, 215n, 218, 220, 221, 226, 227
Erasmus, Desiderius, 135, 172, 353, 354, 355, 358, 359, 375, 557, 565, 566, 572
Erfurt, 235n, 236n, 237n, 238n, 406, 411, 415
Erigena, John Scotus, 572
Erikkson, Leif, 66
Ermini, Giuseppe, 463n
Errizo (Ençio), Antonio, 485, 495
Eskimos, the, 66
Este family, 141
Ethiopians, the, 59, 64
Euclid, 260, 261, 266n, 267n, 269n, 279, 289
Eudoxus of Cnidos, 260n, 262n, 270, 272n, 273n, 274
Eugene, Oregon, 554, 558
Eugenius IV, Pope (Gabriele Condulmieri), 131n, 416
Eunomius, Bishop of Cyzicus, 251
Europe, XXI, XXII, XXIV, 11, 12, 15, 56, 66, 169, 171n, 176, 177, 178n, 182, 187, 308, 390, 400, 507n
Eusebius Pamphili, Bishop of Caesarea, 95
Evans, Robert O., 372n
Evanston, Illinois, 551
Eve, 56, 57, 63
Eyb, Albrecht von, 408, 421
Eyssell, Aernout Philip Theodoor, 44n
Ezekiel, the Prophet, 220, 329, 330

Fabius Maximus, Quintus (Cunctator), 397
Fabroni, Angelo, 462n, 463n, 464n
Facio, Bartolommeo, 218, 561
Fahd, Toufic, 54n
Fano, 139
Fantuzzi, Giovanni, 519n, 520, 521, 522, 523n, 524, 525
Farquharson, Arthur S. L., 575
Fascism, 3, 342
Fasiol, Francesco, 503n, 506
Fassini, Vincenzo (*pseud.* : Dionysius Sandellius), 519n, 525
Fauchet, Claude, 37, 44n

Favaro, Antonio, 465n
Favre, Léopold, 539n
Faye, Christopher U., 585
Federici, Renzo, 565
Federigo di Montefeltro, Duke of Urbino, 397, 401, 402, 403, 404
Felici, Giovanni Sante, 100n
Ferdinand I, King of the Romans, Emperor, 477
Ferdinand I, King of Naples (Don Ferrante of Aragon), 137
Ferguson, Wallace K., XXV, 391n, 392n, 394n, 399n, 566, 577
Ferm, Vergilius, 549
Ferrante of Aragon. *See* Ferdinand I, King of Naples
Ferrante, Joan M., XXIII
Ferrara, 75n, 90, 132, 141, 400n, 520
Ferrari, Luigi, 524n, 525n
Festugière, André Marie Jean, 582
Fichet, Guillaume, 560
Fichtenau, Heinrich, 578
Ficino, Marsilio, 2, 3, 4, 6, 7, 8, 20, 21, 24, 26, 74n, 151, 158n, 159n, 194, 205, 206, 207, 208, 209, 210, 211, 212, 395, 396, 398n, 469, 510, 514, 545, 546, 547, 548, 549, 551, 552, 553, 558, 560, 561, 563, 566, 567, 569, 572, 574, 577, 581, 582, 583
Fielding, Henry, 375
Fiesole, 402n, 403
Filelfo, Francesco, 226, 227, 420
Filelfo, Mario, 510
Filippo di Pietro, 116
Finland, 243n
Finzi, Claudio, 485n, 486n, 487n, 492n
Fiocco, Giuseppe, 118n
Fiorentino, Francesco, 59n, 101n, 214n, 275
Firpo, Luigi, 166n, 167n, 168n, 169n, 172n, 174n, 178n, 180n, 181n, 183n, 184, 188n, 578
Fisch, Max H., 574
Fishacre, Richard, 245n, 246n
Fitzalan, William, eleventh Earl of Arundel, 353
Fitzralph, Richard, 236
Flacius, Mathias (Illyricus), 418n

Flanders, 243n, 503
Flandinus, Ambrosius, 70, 71, 72, 73, 74, 75, 76, 77, 78, 79, 80, 81, 82, 83, 84, 85, 86, 87, 88, 89, 90, 91, 92, 93, 94, 95, 96, 97, 98, 99
Florence, 3, 4, 13, 132, 135, 136, 137, 140n, 143, 168, 224, 345, 393, 395n, 396n, 398, 399, 400, 403, 404n, 432, 435, 439n, 442, 449, 450, 464n, 510, 550, 554, 555, 558, 585
Fois, Mario, 215n, 223n
Fontana, Benedictus, 117, 124
Fontana, Gianjacopo, 490n
Forbes, Elizabeth L., 579
Forlì, 524
Forshall, Josiah, 131n
Fournol, Étienne, 48n
Fraenkel, Peter, 38n
France, 11, 27, 30, 31, 43, 45, 46, 86n, 169, 178, 185, 186, 187, 188, 189, 456, 457, 504
Francis I, King of France, 85, 86, 303
Francis of Meyronnes (Mayronis), 95n, 133, 240
Franciscans, 55n, 245, 247n, 359, 455n, 526n
Franconia, 407, 411, 412, 419
Frankfurt, 477
Frankfurt am Main, 312, 564
Frati, Lodovico, 393n, 519n, 522n, 523n, 524, 525
Freeman, Kathleen, 191n
Freher, Marquard, 417n
Freiburg im Breisgau, 1, 3, 548, 559, 563
Freudianism, 97
Fribourg, 551
Friedberg, Emil Albert von, 436n
Friedlein, Gottfried, 258n
Friedrich I (Barbarossa), Emperor, 324, 325, 326, 328, 330, 331, 332, 333, 334, 335, 336, 337, 338
Friedrich of Hohenzollern, Duke of Saxony, 408
Frisch, Christian, 317n
Frizzi, Enrico, 394n
Froissart, Jean, 371, 376
Fueter, Eduard, 394n
Fugger family, 371n

Gabriel, Astrik, 588
Gadol, Joan. *See* Kelly-Gadol, Joan
Gaedertz, Karl Theodor, 310n
Gaeta, Franco, 214n
Gaetano di Thiene, 533n
Gafsa, 343
Gaillardi (Galsandi), Petrus, 457, 461
Galbiati, Giovanni, 550
Galen of Pergamum, 121, 125, 248, 281, 283, 284, 285, 288, 289, 291, 292, 293, 296, 297, 298, 299, 300, 302,
Galileo Galilei, 168, 276, 277, 278, 279, 280, 281, 282, 284, 298, 304, 305, 462, 465, 467, 468n, 470n, 471
Gallop, David, 262n
Galsandi, Petrus. *See* Gaillardi, Petrus
García, Gregório, 63
Gardner, Edmund, 184n
Garin, Eugenio, 4, 22n, 117n, 144n, 154n, 215n, 464, 465n, 470n, 570, 575, 576, 577
Garzoni, Bernardo, 520
Garzoni, Fabrizio, 524
Garzoni, Giovanni, 519, 520, 521, 522, 523, 524, 525, 526, 527, 528
Garzoni, Giovanni (18th century), 524
Garzoni, Marcello, 524
Gascoigne, George, 380n, 386
Gassendi, Pierre, 65
Gaul, Leopold, 151n, 153n
Gaul, 524
Gay, Peter, 48n
Geanakoplos, Deno J., 152n
Gebhardt, Bruno, 418n
Geiger, Ludwig, 407n
Geminus, 293
Geneva, 429
Genoa, 79, 427, 434, 435, 436, 437, 438, 439, 441n, 442, 443, 444, 445, 449, 450, 554
Gentile da Foligno, 287
Gentile, Giovanni, 3, 4, 60n, 571
Genua, Marcantonio. *See* Passeri, Marcantonio
Geoffrey of Trani, 427, 428n
George of Poděbrady, King of Bohemia, 408, 409
George of Trebisond. *See* Giorgio da Trebisonda

Georgi, Anette, 328n
Gerard of Cremona, 521n
Gerlach, Walter, 311n
Germain de Ganay, 21
Germany, 4, 15, 138n, 170, 177, 178, 187, 243n, 406, 407, 410, 412, 414, 416, 418, 419, 421, 422, 423, 478
Gersonides. *See* Levi ben Gershon
Getto, Giovanni, 347n
Geyer, Bernhard, 151n
Ghent, 402
Gherardo, Niccolò, 509n
Ghiberti, Lorenzo, 404
Giele, Maurice, 84n
Gilbert de la Porrée, 120
Gilbert, Felix, XXI, XXV, 508n, 510n
Gilbert, Neal W., XXII, 257n, 278n, 279, 280, 283n, 465n, 466, 468n
Giles of Rome. *See* Egidio Romano
Giles of Viterbo. *See* Egidio da Viterbo
Gilmore, Myron P., XXI, 42n, 47n, 362, 387, 388, 420n
Gilson, Etienne, 74, 77n, 82n, 88, 95, 106n, 107
Gilstrap, William J., 180n
Giorgia, Hasnoz, 400n
Giorgio da Trebisonda, 396, 491, 510
Giovanni da Correggio, 557
Giovio, Paolo, 527
Girardello, Benedetto, 513, 516
Giuncta. *See* Junta family
Giustiniani, Bernardo, 483, 484, 485, 486, 487, 488, 489, 490, 491, 492, 493, 494, 495, 501
Giustiniani, Bernardo (grandfather), 493
Giustiniani, Cecilia, 489, 498
Giustiniani, Eleanora Contarini, 485, 495
Giustiniani, Elisabetta. *See* Morosini, Elisabetta
Giustiniani, Eufemia, Blessed, 488
Giustiniani, Francesco, 491n
Giustiniani, Leonardo (elder), 486, 488n, 490, 491n, 493, 494, 495
Giustiniani, Leonardo (younger), 485, 488n, 490, 492, 495, 498, 499, 500
Giustiniani, Lorenzo, Blessed, 486, 488n, 495

Giustiniani, Lorenzo, 485, 486, 488n, 490, 491n, 492, 495, 498, 499, 500
Giustiniani, Luigi, 485, 488n, 490, 492, 495, 498, 499, 500
Giustiniani, Marco, 485, 490, 495
Giustiniani, Nicolò, 485, 490, 492, 495, 498, 499, 500
Giustiniani, Orsa. *See* Dandolo, Orsa
Giustiniani, Pietro, 485, 490, 492, 495, 498, 499, 500
Giustiniani, Quirina, 493n
Gloria, Andrea, 531n
Glucker, John, 128n
Gobbi, Ulisse, 432n
Goethe, Johann Wolfgang von, 574
Goetz, Walter, 387n
Goetze, Albrecht, 5
Goff, Frederick R., 121n, 287n, 586
Gohin, Ferdinand, 34n
Goldast, Melchior, 417n, 418n
Goldbrunner, Hermann, 140n
Golding, Arthur, 384
Goliath, the Philistine, 224
Gomperz, Heinrich, 191n, 192
Gondi, Simone, 554
Gonzaga, Ercole, Cardinal, 71n, 73, 124
Gonzaga, Federico II, Marquess, then Duke, of Mantua, 73n, 85, 86n
Gonzaga, Francesco, Cardinal (d. 1566), 72, 73n, 85, 127
Gonzaga, Sigismondo, Cardinal, 71n, 73, 74
Gonzaga family, 72, 73
Googe, Barnabe, 384
Gordan, Phyllis Goodhart (Mrs. John D.), XXI, XXIV, XXV
Gorgias of Leontini, 191n, 192, 195
Gossembrot, Sigismund, 407-408
Gottfried IV, Bishop of Würzburg, 408
Goukovsky, Matvei Aleksandrovich, 584
Grabmann, Martin, 243n, 245n, 246n, 256n
Grammaticus, Joannes. *See* Philoponus, Joannes
Grataroli, Guglielmo, 70n
Gratian (Franciscus Gratianus), 236n, 436, 445, 451n
Gray, William, 131, 132, 133, 135

Grayson, Cecil, 195n, 196n
Graz, 312, 313
Greco, Aulo, 393n
Greece, 33, 39, 45, 398, 416
Greene, Robert, 386
Greenland, 66
Gregory XIII, Pope (Ugo Buoncompagni), 463
Gregory XV, Pope (Alessandro Ludovisi), 186
Gregory Nazianzen, Saint, 96
Gregory of Nyssa, Saint, 96
Gregory of Rimini, 95n, 439n, 449
Greville, Fulke, 376
Grillo, Francesco, 186n
Grimani, Antonio, 505
Grimani, Domenico, Cardinal, 74, 119, 120, 121, 123, 149
Gritti, Andrea, 504, 505, 507, 512
Groblicki, Julian, 104, 105
Grossmann, Karl, 407n, 412n
Grossmünster, 307n
Grotius, Hugo, 47, 65, 66
Gruner, Carl, 310n
Grynaeus, Simon, 124
Gualter (Walther), Rudolph, 306, 307n, 308, 309
Guarini, Battista, 138
Guarino Veronese, 132, 140, 141, 400n, 420, 520, 562
Guilmart, Kenneth, XXIII
Gunther the Cistercian, 419
Gurlitt, Cornelius, 409n
Gutbrodt, Marie-Luise, 564
Guthrie, William Keith Chambers, 191n, 192, 208n
Gutmann, James, 573
Guzzo, Augusto, 570, 571

Hagen, Karl, 413n
Hain, Ludwig F. T., 286n, 353n, 410n
Hale, John R., 489n
Halevi, Judah, 52, 54n, 65, 67
Hall, Vernon, Jr., 578
Halliday, Thomas W., 180n
Halm, Carl Felix von, 140n, 142
Haly. See 'Ali ibn Ridwan
Hamelin, Alonzo M., 436n, 439n

Hamm, Victor M., 574
Hammond, Joseph Samuel, XXIV
Hampe, Karl, 1
Hannibal, 397
Hanover (Germany), 139, 142
Hanover, New Hampshire, 555
Hapsburg family, 169, 170, 176, 186, 187, 188
Harder, Richard, 569
Hardison, Osborne Bennett, Jr., XXV, 381n
Harpsfield, Nicholas, 372n
Harriot, Thomas, 61, 62
Haug, Konrad, 410
Hault, Henry, 355
Haréau, Bernard, 253n
Haute-Garonne, 454n
Hawes, Stephen, 365
Hay, Denys, 563
Hayden, Hiram, 578
Hayduck, Michael, 153n
Hazlitt, William C., 370n
Headley, John M., 564
Healey, John, 51n
Hearn, Thomas, 131n
Heath, Thomas L., 269n, 270
Hédelin, François, 59n
Heers, Jacques, 435n
Hegel, Georg Wilhelm Friedrich, 13
Heiberg, Johan L., 269n
Heidegger, Martin, 1, 3
Heidelberg, 1, 4, 7, 13, 406, 410, 415, 548
Heimburg, Gregor, 406, 407, 408, 409, 410, 411, 412, 413, 414, 415, 416, 417, 418, 419, 420, 421, 422
Heimburg, Hans, 408
Heinberg, Richard, 411n
Heinze, Richard, 156n
Heller, Josef, 123n
Helton, Tinsley, 557
Henderson, Charles, Jr. 560
Heninger, Simeon K., Jr., 384n
Henry VII, King of England, 354, 355
Henry VIII, King of England, 131n, 359, 367
Henry II de Bourbon, Prince de Condé, 65
Henry of Ghent, 95n

INDEX 607

Henry of Susa. *See* Hostiensis
Henry, Paul, 580, 583
Hentisberus, Gulielmus. *See* Heytesbury, William of
Heraclitus, 206
Hermannus Alemannus, 118
Hermes Trismegistus, 20, 26, 29, 39, 62, 95, 201, 202n, 211n, 471n, 582
Herodotus, 51n, 417
Heron, the Engineer, 266
Heron, Henry, 366, 367
Heron, John, 368
Heron, Nicholas, 367
Heron, William, 367, 368, 369
Herrmann, Max, 407n, 415n, 419n, 420n, 421n
Herveus Brito, 95n, 96
Hessen, Johannes, 571
Heusler, Andreas, 389n
Heymann, Frederick G., 406n, 409n
Heymburg, Johannes, 411n
Heynck, Valens, 438n
Heyse, Paul, 393n
Heytesbury, William of, 92, 533n
Hieatt, A. Kent, 215n, 216n
Highet, Gilbert, 190n
Hippasus, 271
Hippias of Elis, 195
Hirsch, Elizabeth, XXV
Hirsch, Felix, XXV
Hirsch, Rudolf, 586
Hispaniola, 57
Hispanus (Peter of Spain?; Giovanni Montesdoch?), 126
Hitchcock, Elsie Vaughan, 358n, 372n
Hobbes, Thomas, 50, 65, 189
Hochstein, Natalia, 141n
Hodgkin, Thomas, 187n
Hoffmann, Ernst, 1, 2, 545, 578, 585
Hoffmann, Fritz, 237
Hoffmann, Hermann, 421n
Hog, Thomas, 246n
Hohenburg, Herwart von, 317
Hohenstaufen family, 455
Holcot, Robert, 232n, 237, 238, 250n
Holland, 170, 177, 178n, 187, 243n, 407
Holt, John, 358n
Home, Henry, Lord Kames, 58

Homer, 3, 311, 312, 313, 314, 315, 316, 317, 318, 319, 325, 375, 417
Hook, Sidney, 589
Horace (Quintus Horatius Flaccus), 321, 323, 417
Hostiensis, Cardinal, 427, 428n
Hotman, François, 43, 45
Howard, Henry, Earl of Surrey, 373, 386
Howard, Thomas, second Earl of Arundel, 130n
Howell, Wilbur S., 573
Huddleston, Lee Eldridge, 57, 63, 64n
Hudson, Hoyt H., 572
Hugh of Saint Victor, 92
Hultsch, Friedrich, 271n
Humanism, 6, 7, 8, 9, 11, 30, 31, 32, 35, 37, 39, 47, 48, 56, 69, 116n, 120, 121, 124, 125, 126, 127, 128, 132, 133, 135, 137, 140, 145, 163, 190, 191n, 211, 254, 276, 283, 373, 375, 376, 396, 398, 399n, 400n, 406, 407, 408, 409, 410, 411, 412, 414, 415, 416, 418, 419, 420, 421, 422, 424, 467, 477, 478, 509, 510, 511n, 513n, 532, 540, 541, 546, 547, 548, 550, 552, 553, 555, 556, 557, 558, 559, 560, 561, 562, 563, 564, 565, 566, 568, 569, 571, 577, 578, 581, 584, 586, 587, 589
Humanists, the, 4, 8, 9, 11, 35, 36, 37, 73, 92, 117, 124, 133, 162, 163, 190, 191, 192, 193, 194, 212, 215n, 223, 224, 227, 235, 239, 241n, 283, 284, 301, 375, 393, 397, 398, 399, 404, 407, 409n, 413, 414, 416, 417, 418, 419, 420, 422, 466, 507, 526, 532, 533, 534, 568, 572
Hume, David, 241
Humfrey (Humphrey), Duke of Gloucester, 134
Hungary, 243n, 400n
Hunt, Edmund, 572
Hunt, Richard W., 134n, 584
Hurter, Hugo, 72n
Hus, Jan, 92
Husserl, Edmund, 571
Hussite heresy, 78, 82, 97
Hussites, 82, 97
Hyginus, 308n
Hyllyngworth, Kateryn, 360

Iamblichus, 95, 270, 271
Ibn Wahshiyya, 54
Iceland, 66
Imerti, Arthur D., 60
Immortality controversy, 144, 163
India, 54, 180
Indians (American), 57, 58, 59, 60, 61, 62, 63, 64, 175
Indies, the, 170
Ingrassia, Giovanni Filippo, 286n
Innocent IV, Pope (Sinibaldo de' Fieschi), 454n, 455, 456
Innocent VIII, Pope (Giovanni Battista Cibo), 136
Ireland, 178n, 366, 367, 368
Isaac, Jean, 101n
Isidorus, Saint, Archbishop of Seville, 539n
Isidorus (Pacensis), Bishop of Beja, 539n
Isidorus Mercator, 539n
Isleworth, 353
Isocrates, 192
Italy, 3, 4, 6, 8, 9, 10, 11, 20, 31, 71, 85, 86n, 132, 135, 139, 144, 149n, 165, 169, 170, 171, 173, 175, 178, 179, 184, 187, 243n, 275, 276, 280, 283, 324, 328, 334, 335, 337, 355, 387, 391, 400, 402, 406, 407, 408, 413, 414, 415, 416, 419, 462, 504, 506, 509, 518n
Ithaca, New York, 560
Ivanka, Endre von, 586
Ivry, Alfred L., 148n

Jacob, Ernest Fraser, 354n
Jacobus de Pistorio, 552
Jacopo da Forlì, 278, 287, 293n, 296n
Jacopo of Portugal, Cardinal, 404n
Jacquot, Jean, 56n, 61
Jäger, Albert, 409n
Jaeger, Werner, 2, 3, 190n, 192
Jakob I of Sirk, Archbishop of Trier, 408
Jandun. *See* John of Jandun
Janos, Vitez, 400n
Janson, Horst W., 224n
Jaspers, Karl, 1, 582
Jauss, Hans Robert, 556
Javelli, Giovanni Crisostomo, 88, 95, 96, 99

Jayne, Sears R., 353n, 370n, 574
Jensen, Povl Johannes, 585
Jeremiah, the Prophet, 329, 330
Jerome, Saint (Eusebius Hieronymus), 90n, 93, 251, 350, 417, 529n
Jerusalem, 67, 558
Jesuits, the, 128, 185, 308n
Jesus Christ, 28, 55, 67, 168n, 182, 210, 222, 224, 225, 226, 250, 306, 308, 327, 330, 331, 332, 333, 335, 376, 385, 436, 512
Jews, the, 55, 60, 66, 67, 68, 119, 124, 250n, 478, 479, 480, 481
Joachimsohn, Paul, 406, 407, 409n, 411n, 412n, 413n, 415n, 417n, 418n, 419n, 420n, 421n
Joannes Canonicus, 95n, 97
Johann II, Bishop of Würzburg, 408
Johann III, Bishop of Würzburg, 408
John XXI, Pope (Petrus Hispanus), 245n
John XXII, Pope (Jacques Duèse of Cahors), 251n
John the Baptist, Saint, 336, 337
John of Damascus (Damascene), Saint, 293
John of Erfurt (or Saxony), 438, 439, 440
John of Jandun, 153, 154
John of Legnano, 434, 442, 443, 444, 445, 447, 448, 450, 452, 453
John of Saint-Pierre, 456, 457, 458
John of Salisbury, 244n, 245n
Johnson, Samuel, 375
Jonathan, Prince of Israel, 224, 226
Jones, William Henry Samuel, 576
Jordanus Nemorarius, 20
Joseph, the Patriarch, 94
Josse of Ghent. *See* Justus of Ghent
Judaea, 335
Junta, Thomas, 125, 126, 127
Junta family, 123, 125, 127
Justinian I (Flavius Anicius Justinianus), Emperor, 36n, 44
Justinus, Marcus Junianus, 514
Justus of Ghent, 402
Juvenal (Decimus Junius Juvenalis), 321

Kaegi, Werner, 388, 389n, 390n, 391n, 392, 400n, 405n

INDEX 609

Kames, Lord. *See* Home, Henry
Kampschulte, Franz W., 407n
Kant, Immanuel, 1, 2, 13, 574, 576
Kantorowicz, Hermann U., 443n
Kaphahn, Fritz, 389n, 390n
Kardos, Tiberio, 400n
Karl of Hapsburg, Archduke of Styria, 169
Karoch, Samuel, 408
Kautsky, Karl, 178n
Kavanagh, Art, 367
Kavanagh, Murlough, 367
Kedirmystir, Richard, Abbot of Wynchcombe, 357
Keeler, Leo W., 154n
Keller, Georg J., 411n
Kelley, Donald R., 37n, 44n
Kelly-Gadol, Joan, 401n, 402, 404n
Kent, 361
Kepler, Johannes, 280, 310, 311, 312, 313, 314, 315, 316, 317, 318, 319
Kessler, Eckhard, 568
Khazars, the, 52
Kibre, Pearl, 243n, 520n, 521n, 522n, 570
Kieszkowski, Bohdan, 119n, 570
Kilvington, Richard, 237, 254
Kilwardby, Robert, Archbishop of Canterbury, 245n, 246, 247n, 253, 256
Kincaid, Gwen, XXIII
Kirkwood, Patricia Frueh, 318n
Kirshner, Julius, 438n, 439n
Kisch, Guido, 420n, 477n
Klein, Edward J., 366n
Klibansky, Raymond, 571, 580, 584, 585
Kliem, Fritz, 260, 269n
Koch, Josef, 555
Kocher, Paul H., 51n, 61
König, Erich, 416n
Kolblin, Hansen, 481
Kollár, Adám Ferencz, 416n, 417n
Konhofer, Conrad, 414
Konrad III of Daun, Archbishop of Mainz, 408
Kordeuter, Victor, 571
Kracauer, Siegfried, 587, 588
Kraus, Hans P., 580
Kraus, Martin. *See* Crusius, Martinus
Krefeld, Heinrich, 322n, 324, 327, 330n

Kress, Georg von, 408n
Kretzmann, Norman, 108n, 110n
Kristeller, Edith (*née* Lewinnek), 15
Kristeller, Paul Oskar, XXI, XXII, XXIII, XXIV, 1, 2, 3, 4, 5, 6, 7, 8, 9, 10, 11, 12, 13, 14, 15, 16, 19, 20, 31, 71, 77, 78, 79, 81n, 84n, 101n, 116n, 119n, 130, 135n, 136n, 137n, 138n, 139n, 143, 144n, 145n, 152n, 154n, 163n, 165n, 166n, 190n, 191n, 194n, 195n, 206n, 209n, 258, 259n, 275, 306, 396, 398n, 400n, 407n, 416n, 419n, 443n, 463n, 465, 470n, 472, 477, 509n, 518n, 522n, 523n, 524n, 526n, 531n, 533n, 534n, 535n, 540n
Krofta, Kamil, 406n
Kroner, Richard, 1
Kühn, Carl Gottlob, 248n, 285n, 298n
Kugler, Franz, 389n
Kurtz, Paul, 589
Kuttner, Stephan G., XXV, 446n, 449n
Kyd, Thomas, 386
Kymeus, Johannes, 421n

Labalme, George, Jr., XXV
Labalme, Patricia H., XXV, 483n
Labowsky, Carlotta, 571, 580, 584
Lacombe, George, 116n
Lactantius Firmianus, Lucius Caelius, 199, 223, 226, 417, 421
Ladislaus Posthumus, King of Hungary and of Bohemia, 408
Lafargue, Paul, 178n, 179n
Lambert of Auxerre, 245n
Lambeth, 361
Lamocensis (Lamosen), 72, 73n, 75
La Mothe le Vayer, François de, 65, 66n
Lana, Italo, 205n
Landino, Cristoforo, 4, 377
Lane, Frederic C., 487n, 489n
Lange, Hermann, 440n
Languedoc, 455
La Peyrère, Isaac, 50, 52, 53, 54, 57, 59, 62, 64, 65, 66, 67, 68, 69
Latrobe, Pennsylvania, 7, 563
Lattes, Alessandro, 437n
Laubmann, Georg von, 142
Lauchert, Friedrich, 71n, 72n, 73n
Laurana, Luciano da, 402

Lavant, 421n
Lavaur, 455n
Lazzarelli, Ludovico, 546, 557
Lazzarini, Lino, 509n
Leahy, Louis, 89n
Lear, John, 310n, 311n, 318n
Le Caron, Louis, 30n, 31, 32, 33, 34, 35, 36, 37, 38, 39, 40, 41, 42, 43, 44, 45, 46, 47, 48, 49
Le Clerc, Georges Louis, Count de Buffon, 58n
Le Douaren, François, 35, 36, 44
Lee, Edward, Archbishop of York, 360, 361
Lee, Geoffrey, 360
Lee, John, 360
Lee, Sister Joisse (Joyeuce Leigh, younger), 359, 360, 361
Lee, Joysse (elder), 359
Lee, Leticia, 361
Lee, Rensselaer W., XXV, 198n, 374n
Lee, Richard (grandfather), Mayor of London, 360
Lee, Richard (elder), 360, 361
Lee Richard (younger), 360, 361
Lee, Sidney, 131n
Lefèvre d'Etaples, Jacques (Faber Stapulensis), 19, 20, 21, 22, 23, 24, 25, 26, 27, 28, 29, 122
Lefranc, Pierre, 60n, 61, 62
Legh, Rauff, 360
Lehmann, Paul, 328n, 406n, 413n
Lehmberg, Stanford E., 362
Lehnerdt, Max, 137n
Leibniz, Gottfried Wilhelm von, 13, 167, 273n
Leidecker, Kurt F., 578
Leigh, Joyce, 359
Leipzig, 406, 411, 415
Leland, John, 131, 353
Lemay, Richard, XXII, 100n, 114
Leningrad, 584
Leo X, Pope (Giovanni de' Medici), 74, 75n, 82, 123, 371n, 423
Leonardo da Vinci, 584, 588
Leoniceno, Niccolò, 283, 284, 285, 286, 287, 288, 290, 291, 292, 293, 294, 295, 296, 297, 298, 299, 300, 301, 302, 303, 304, 305
Leowitz, Cyprian, 309n
Le Roux de Lincy, Antoine Jean Victor, 20n
Le Roy, Louis, 39n
Lessius, Leonardus, 430
Leubing, Heinrich, 415
Levi ben Gershon (Gersonides), 126
Levi, Carlo, 342
Levy, Bernard S., 566
Lewis, Clive Staples, 370, 371, 375, 376, 380n, 382
L'Hôpital, Michel de, 44n
Lhotsky, Alphons, 412n
Liddell, Henry G., 242n
Lieberich, Hans, 406n, 415n
Lieser, Renate, 555
Lilith, wife of Cain, 66
Lily, William, 359
Lind, Levi R., 573
Lisbon, 55n
List, Martha, 311n
Litta, Pompeo, 485n, 488n
Little, Andrew G., 234n, 246n
Livy (Titus Livius), 417, 514
Lockwood, Dean P., 5, 532n
Lodge, Thomas, 384
Loisel, Antoine, 37, 46
Lombards, the, 333
Lombardy, 439, 441
London, 60, 62, 130, 135, 136n, 137, 138, 142, 236n, 238, 354, 355, 360, 366, 426, 428, 430, 464n
Lorch, Maristella de Panizza, 214n, 216n, 217n, 218n
Loredan, Leonardo, Doge of Venice, 506
Lorenzetti, Giulio, 488n
Lorimer, Emily Overend, 530n
Los Angeles, California, 554, 555, 558, 561, 567
Lost Tribes, the, 57
Louis IX, King of France, 455, 460
Louis XIII, King of France, 187
Louis XIV, King of France, 65n, 169
Lovejoy, Arthur O., 51n
Lucan (Marcus Annaeus Lucanus), 317, 325, 514, 515n, 538, 541

Lucca, 448n
Lucian of Samosata, 310, 311, 318, 359
Lucilius (Iunior), 249, 250, 534, 535, 536
Luck, Georg, 582
Lucretius (Titus Lucretius Carus), 208, 364
Luder, Peter, 408
Luke, Saint, Evangelist, 328, 334n, 335, 336n
Lull, Ramón, 21, 26, 29
Lumiansky, Robert M., XXV
Lupo, Giambattista, 427n
Lupset, Thomas, 365, 366
Lur, Heinrich, 420n
Luschin von Ebengreuth, Arnold, 412n, 413n
Luther, Martin, 38, 78, 92, 422, 423
Lutherans, the 82, 97, 172
Lutz, Cora E., 572, 574
Luzzatto, Gino, 435n, 487n
Lydgate, John, 386
Lyly, John, 385
Lyons, 123, 303, 304, 352, 455
Lysippus of Sicyon, 24

McCall, John Patrick, 442n, 450n
McGovern, John F., 449n
Machiavelli, Niccolò, 62n, 164, 171, 178, 189, 506
Machiavellianism, 41, 170, 171, 184, 187, 188
McKee, David Rice, 65n
McKeon, Richard, 579
McKerrow, Ronald Brunlees, 61n
McMullin, Ernan, 465n
Macrobius, Ambrosius Theodosius, 151, 157
Madison, Wisconsin, 551
Madius, Vincentius, 126
Madrid, 588
Maestlin, Michael, 313, 314, 315, 316, 317
Maffei, Domenico, 432n
Maffei, Scipione, 427
Magellan, Ferdinand, 57
Magi, 21, 23, 25, 26, 27, 28
Mahoney, Edward P., XXII, 77n, 99n, 100n, 121n, 145n, 154n, 166n, 518n, 568

Mai, Angelo, Cardinal, 390n
Maier, Anneliese, 235n, 238n, 240n, 242n
Maier, Ernst, 100n
Maimonides (Moses ben Maimon), 52, 53, 54, 59
Mainz, 408, 415
Maiolus, Laurentius, 121
Mair (Mayr, Mayer, Meyer), Martin, 408, 415
Malagola, Carlo, 443n, 444n, 520n, 523n
Malcolm, John, 245n
Malcovati, Henrica, 529n
Mallé, Luigi, 196n
Malory, Thomas, 376
Manardi, Giovanni, 285n, 301, 304
Manasse, Ernst, XXIII
Mancini, Girolamo, 214n, 520n
Mandonnet, Pierre, 243n, 246n
Manetti, Gianozzo, 395
Manfré, Gulielmo, 519n, 522n, 523n, 524n
Manicheanism, 251
Manilius, Marcus, 308n
Manning, Owen, 359n
Mansion, Auguste, 116n
Mantinus, Jacob, 123, 124, 126
Mantua, 71, 72, 73, 74, 75, 76, 85, 91, 408, 409n, 417n, 418, 527
Manutius, Aldus, 121
Marburg, 1
Marcel, Raymond, 206n, 207n
Mardersteig, Giovanni, 560
Marguerite de France, 32n
Maria of Hapsburg, Archduchess of Styria, 169
Mariën, Bert, 578
Mark, Saint, Evangelist, 332n
Mark, Thomas Carson, 588
Marliani, Giovanni, 533n, 572
Marlowe, Cristopher, 61, 62, 64, 375, 384, 386, 572
Marquard, Friedrich, 410
Marranos, 65n, 66, 67, 69
Marrou, Henri-Irénée, 190n, 252n
Marsili, Luigi, 399
Marsilio Ficino. *See* Ficino, Marsilio
Marsilio di Santa Sofia, 534
Martel, Charles, 389n

612 INDEX

Martin V, Pope (Ottone Colonna), 131n, 214n
Martin of Tours, Saint, 323
Martin, Charles Trice, 247n
Martinez-Gomez, Luis, 199n
Martinez Peñaloza, Maria, 564
Martinozzi, Galeozzi, da Fano, 139
Martinozzi, Pietro, da Fano, 139
Marxism, 179n
Masai, François, 582
Matsen, Herbert S., 518n, 519n, 527n, 589
Matthew, Saint, Evangelist, 328, 329, 331
Mattingly, Garrett, 561
Maudith, John, 236
Maximilian I, Emperor, 503, 504
Maximilian II, King of Bavaria, 392n
Maximilian of Hapsburg, Archduke of Austria, 172
May, Johann, 410
Mazzacane, Aldo, 44n
Mazzatinti, Giuseppe, 524n
Mazzolini, Silvestro, da Prierio, 430n
Mazzoni, Jacopo, 163n, 470n
Mazzuchelli, Giovanni Maria, 123n, 124n, 462n, 491n
Medici, Cosimo de', 131, 141, 396, 397, 400n, 402n, 403
Medici, Cosimo II de', Grand Duke of Tuscany, 277
Medici, Ferdinand I de', Grand Duke of Tuscany, 168
Medici, Giovanni de'. *See* Leo X, Pope
Medici, Giuliano de', 546
Medici, Lorenzo de', 561, 570
Medici family, 403
Megarics, 249
Meiss, Millard, XXV
Meisterlin, Sigismund, 408
Melanchthon, Philipp, 38, 40
Melissus of Samos, 150
Menaechmus, 259, 260, 261, 262, 263, 264, 265, 266, 267, 268, 269, 270, 271, 272, 273, 274
Mencke, Johann Burchard, 522n
Menéndez Pelayo, Marcelino, 55n
Menzies, Robert, 406n
Mercati, Angelo, 575
Mercati, Giovanni, Cardinal, 5, 548

Mercurio, Giovanni, da Correggio, 546
Meregazzi, Renzo, 527n
Merguet, Hugo, 249n, 528n
Merk, Augustin, 251n
Merlan, Philip, 148n, 582, 586
Mersenne, Marin, 65
Merula, Giorgio, 510
Michaud-Quantin, Pierre, 441n, 449n
Michelangelo Buonarroti, 571
Michelozzi, Niccolò, 560
Middleburg, Paul von, 398n
Middletown, Connecticut, 164n
Migne, Jacques-Paul, 245n, 252n, 489n
Milan, 3, 4, 122, 170, 187, 324n, 332, 333, 393n, 395n, 429, 504, 532n, 559, 565, 582
Milan, Duke of (unidentified), 141
Milo, Titus Annius, 529n, 530n
Milton, John, 375, 376, 381
Milwaukee, Wisconsin, 557
Miner, Earl, 372n
Minio-Paluello, Lorenzo, 116n, 248n, 256n, 580
Minneapolis, Minnesota, 551
Minturno, Antonio, 375
Mirandola, 559, 561
Modena, 4, 575, 579
Moe, Henry Allen, 586
Mönch, Walter, 569
Mohammed, the Prophet, 168n
Mohler, Ludwig, 162n
Molho, Anthony, 21n
Molmenti, Pompeo, 505n
Momigliano, Attilio, 341, 344
Mommsen, Theodor E., 194n
Monachus. *See* Torrigiano dei Torrigiani
Mondolfo, Rodolfo, 191n
Montagu, M. F. Ashley, 279n
Montaigne, Michel de, 41, 462, 463, 464n
Montanari, Fausto, 215n
Montano, Giovanni Battista, 286n, 301
Montepulciano, 565
Montesdoch, Giovanni. *See* Hispanus
Montesquieu, Charles, Baron de, 31, 45, 47, 48
Montils-lez-Tours, 20n
Montreal, 563
Moody, Ernest A., 6, 230n, 465n

Moore, John D., XXIV
Morandi, Benedetto, 519n, 520n
More, Cresacre, 357
More, Henry, 376
More, Jane (*née* Colt), 358
More, Thomas, Saint, 164, 180, 183, 189, 352, 354, 356, 357, 358, 359, 360, 361, 362, 363, 364, 365, 366, 368, 369, 373, 380n, 576
Morosini, Domenico, 485, 486, 491, 492, 495, 499, 500
Morosini, Elisabetta (*née* Giustiniani), 485n
Morrow, Glenn R., 258n, 259n, 260n, 261, 262n, 266n, 269n
Mortagh Oge (Kavanagh), 367
Mortari, Vincenzo Piano, 47n
Moser, Johann Jacob, 316n
Moses, the Lawgiver, 39, 62, 67, 168n, 210, 417
Moses Maimonides. *See* Maimonides
Mountjoy. *See* Blount, William
Muenster, Ladislao, 518n
Münster, 562
Muir, Kenneth, 370n
Mundy, John, 454n
Munich, 4, 139, 140, 141, 142, 244n, 317, 409n, 412n, 417n, 419n, 420n, 421n
Murano, 490, 491n
Muratori, Lodovico Antonio, 522n
Muscati, Jehudae, 52n
Mynors, Roger A. B., 131n, 132n, 133n
Mystakidès, Basileios Athanasiou, 318n

Nabateans, 52, 54
Nachod, Hans, 580
Nahum, the Prophet, 251n
Naldi, Naldo, 560
Naples, 4, 71, 72, 76, 136, 137, 168, 170, 173, 179, 185, 187, 547, 577
Napoleon I, Emperor of the French, 490
Narbonne, 572
Nardi, Bruno, 144n, 148n, 150n, 158n, 162n, 275, 491n, 518n, 526n, 552, 586
Nashe, Thomas, 61, 62
Naudé, Gabriel, 188n
Navarrus, Doctor. *See* De Azpilcueta, Martin
Neckham, Alexander, 243n

Neidhart, Carl, 394n
Nelson, Benjamin, 435n, 437
Nelson, John Charles, XXI
Nelson, William, 354n, 355n
Neoplatonism, 27, 34, 37, 40, 43, 95, 101, 103, 109, 111, 112, 114, 202, 205, 376, 377, 400n, 569, 582, 586
Neopythagoreanism, 27, 43
Nepos, Cornelius, 528n
Netherlands. *See* Holland
Neumann, Carl Woldemar von, 310n
New Brunswick, New Jersey, 564
New Haven, Connecticut, 164n, 547, 562
New London, Connecticut, 548, 554
New York City, 5, 164n, 546, 547, 548, 549, 550, 551, 554, 555, 556, 557, 558, 559, 560, 561, 562, 563, 565, 567, 568
Newald, Richard, 584
Newry (County Down, Ireland), 367
Newton, Francis, XXIII
Newton, Isaac, 284
Niccoli, Niccolò, 214n, 395n, 399, 404
Nicholas V, Pope (Tommaso Parentucelli), 132, 133n, 397, 399, 401
Nicholas of Autrecourt, 255, 256
Nicholas of Cusa, Cardinal, 2, 26, 29, 95n, 199, 200, 201, 202, 203, 204, 205, 206, 207, 212, 408, 409, 417, 421n, 565, 577
Nicolaus Trivetus. *See* Trivet, Nicholas
Nicoli, Nicolò. *See* Niccoli, Niccolò
Nicolini, Benedetto, 521n
Nicolini, Fausto, 30n, 463n
Nicolini, Ugo, 438n
Niermeyer, Jan Frederik, 486n-487n
Nifo, Agostino (Suessanus), 72, 76, 78, 88, 120, 126, 145, 154n, 157n, 160, 161, 162, 163
Nigidius Figulus, Publius, 317
Nissus, Vitalis, 125, 126
Noah, 52, 57, 64
Noland, Aaron, 558
Nominalism, 193, 207, 229, 232, 233, 243, 244n, 246n, 256, 257, 589
Noonan, John T., Jr., 430n, 435n, 436n, 439n
Norden, Eduard, 2
Nordhausen, 415

Noreña, Carlos G., 56n
North, Thomas, 385
Northampton, Massachusetts, 550, 567
Norton, Massachusetts, 567
Norway, 57, 66, 243n
Novara, 11, 324n, 559
Novati, Francesco, 532n, 533n, 534n
Novatianus (Novatus), Antipope, 251
Nuremberg, 408, 409n, 414, 415, 416, 419

Oates, Whitney J., 572
Oberlin, Ohio, 552
Oberman, Heiko A., 589
Ockham, William of, 101, 102, 108, 109, 110, 114, 229, 230, 231, 233, 238, 239, 245, 246n, 251n, 253, 254, 256, 257, 581
Ockhamism, 229, 230, 233, 239, 240, 257, 589
Oddo degli Oddi, 286n, 301
Oddos, Jean-Paul, 69n
Odo of Morimond, 26
Offredi, Apollinare, 533n
O'Kelly, Bernard, 224n, 562
Oldfather, William A., 528n
Olivi, Peter, 438, 439
Olomouc, 19
Olschki, Leo S., 4
Olschki, Leonardo, 465n, 467n, 583, 584
O'Malley, John W., 588
Ong, Walter J., XXV, 300n, 304n, 380n
Onofri, Fabrizio, 562
Ophir, 57
Orleans, 21
Orvieto, 11, 564
Osborne, John, 423
Ossinger, Joannes Felix, 72n
Ostia, 172
Otto, August, 529n
Ovid (Publius Ovidius Naso), 23n, 139n, 308n, 335, 384, 385, 386, 492, 536, 538, 541
Owen, Gwilym E. L., 261, 262n
Oxford, 130, 131, 132, 133, 134, 135, 142, 143, 235n, 236, 237, 238, 239, 241, 242, 243, 245, 246, 247, 253, 255, 256, 257, 353, 361, 418n, 560

Pacetti, Dionisio, 438n

Pacioli, Lucas, 118
Paden, Patricia F., 518n
Padua, 7, 15, 117, 119, 126, 132, 133, 145, 149, 154n, 162, 163, 168, 169, 186, 237n, 275, 276, 278, 279, 281, 408, 412, 413, 420, 422, 486, 489, 491, 492, 500, 510, 518, 521n, 527, 531, 551, 556, 558, 559, 565, 586
Pagallo, Giulio F., 145n, 149n, 150n
Paganinus de Paganinis, 121
Pagel, Walter, 59, 574
Palatinate, the, 407, 419
Palescandolo, Marco, 432
Palestine, 63
Palmieri, Matteo, 223
Palo Alto, California, 554, 560
Pandolfo. See Rucellai, Santi
Pannonius, Janus. See Di Cesinge, Giovanni
Panofsky, Erwin, 571, 584
Panormita. See Beccadelli, Antonio
Pantaleon, Henricus, 414n
Pantaleoni, Domenico, 439n
Pantin, William Abel, 235n
Panzer, Georg W., 410n
Paolo da Bergamo, 491n
Pappus of Alexandria, 271
Papuli, Giovanni, 278n
Paqué, Ruprecht, 230n
Paracelsus (Theophrastus Bombastus von Hohenheim), 54, 57, 58, 59, 60, 62, 63, 573, 578
Paris, 20, 21, 26, 36n, 39, 46n, 65, 124n, 229, 230, 231, 232, 233, 234, 235, 236n, 238, 239, 240, 242, 243, 244n, 245, 246, 247, 251n, 253, 255, 256, 257, 276, 303n, 307n, 352, 400, 438n, 456, 436, 532n
Parker, Henry, Lord Morley, 362
Parks, George B., 130n
Parma, 4
Parmenides of Elea, 40n, 150, 205n
Parnassus, Mount, 345, 346
Parron, William, 354n
Paschal III, Antipope (Guido da Crema), 330, 336
Paschini, Pio, 119n
Pasquier, Étienne, 37, 44n, 45, 46
Pasquier, Étienne Denis, Duke, 46n

Passeri, Marcantonio (Genua), 126
Pastor, Ludwig von, 214n, 387, 388, 390
Patch, Howard Rollin, 103n
Patrick, J. Max, 372n
Patrizi, Francesco, da Cherso, 466, 560, 567
Patteta, Federico, 136n
Paucidrapius, Jacobus, 122
Paul, Saint, Apostle, 28, 65, 66, 219, 233n, 250, 251, 252, 331, 417
Paul V, Pope (Camillo Borghese), 186
Paulus (Correspondent of Seneca), 540
Paulus Israelita (Riccius), 122, 123, 126
Pauly, August Friedrich von, 260n
Pavia, 86, 122, 214, 221, 334, 415
Peckham, John, Archbishop of Canterbury, 247n
Pedretti, Carlo, XXV, 588
Pedrinelli, Giovanni, 485n
Pelacani, Biagio, 533n
Pelagio, Alvaro, 55
Pélicier, Paul, 21n
Pelster, Franz, 234n, 244n, 246n
Pelzer, Auguste, 5, 575
Perini, David Aurelio, 72n, 73n
Perleo (Perleone), Piero, 510
Perosa, Alessandro, 4, 5n, 551, 567, 578
Perotti, Niccolò, 132, 138
Perret, Paul Michel, 502n, 506n
Perrin, Bernadotte, 530n
Persiani, R., 144n
Persians, 176
Persius Flacus, Aulus, 23
Pertusi, Agostino, 562, 587
Perugia, 462, 463
Pesaro, 397, 402n
Peter, Saint, Apostle, 28, 330, 417, 522
Peter Lombard, 92, 237n, 434
Peter Martyr. See De Angleria, Pedro Martir
Peter of Spain. See Hispanus and John XXI, Pope
Peterson, Douglas L., 373n
Petrarca, Francesco, 6, 8, 117n, 138, 192, 193, 195, 239, 349, 351, 365, 371, 373, 382, 383, 399, 417, 420, 509n, 534, 537n, 551, 552, 553, 560, 563, 575, 581
Petrarchism, 369, 373

Pétrement, Simone, 576
Petrus Blesensis. See Pierre de Blois
Petrus Cellensis. See Pierre de Celles
Petrus Chrysologus, Saint, Archbishop of Ravenna, 250n
Petrus Mantuanus. See Alboini, Pietro degli
Petrus Paulus Vergerius. See Vergerio, Pietro Paolo
Petrus Ravenensis. See Petrus Chrysologus
Petz, Hans, 415n
Pfeiffer, Gerhard, 422n
Phaer, Thomas, 386
Pharisees, 226
Pheidias (Phidias), 24, 377
Philadelphia, Pennsylvania, 558, 568, 586
"Philaletes," 76n, 77n, 78, 79, 80, 81, 82n, 83, 85, 87, 88, 89, 90, 91n, 93, 94, 95, 97, 98
Philip III, King of Spain, 176, 188
Philip of Opus, 260n, 266, 267
Philo Judaeus, 576
"Philoplato," 76, 87
Philoponus, Joannes, of Alexandria, 95, 146, 293
Phoenicia, 57
Piacenza, 72
Picchi, Mario, 585
Piccolomini, Enea Silvio. See Pius II, Pope
Pico della Mirandola, Gianfrancesco, 194, 352, 356, 362n, 366, 466
Pico della Mirandola, Giovanni, 8, 20, 21, 22n, 38, 90n, 119, 120, 121, 165n, 352, 353, 354, 355, 356, 357, 358, 359, 360, 361, 362, 363, 365, 366, 367, 368, 369, 549, 559, 560, 561, 563, 570, 574, 575, 577, 579, 581
Picotti, Giovanni B., 409n
Pierre de Blois, 244n, 250n
Pierre de Celles, Abbot of Saint Remi, Bishop of Chartres, 244n, 245n
Pietro da Stilo, 174, 175
Pilato, Leonzio, 587
Pinborg, Jan, 236n, 238n, 256n
Pindar, 37n
Pine, Martin, XXIII
Pinelli, Antonio, 484n

Pines, Shlomo, 54n
Pintard, René, 65n
Pinvert, Lucien, 34n
Pirckheimer, Thomas, 407
Pirckheimer, Willibald, 416
Pisa, 3, 4, 5, 15, 161, 168, 462, 463, 464, 465, 468n, 470, 471, 550, 570, 577
Pithou, François, 37
Pithou, Pierre, 37, 44n
Piumazzo, Giovanni, 509n
Pius II, Pope (Enea Silvio Piccolomini), 393, 407, 408, 412, 414, 416, 417, 418, 420, 421
Pius V, Pope, Saint (Antonio Ghisliere), 427
Plato, 1, 2, 6, 13, 27, 31, 32, 35, 36, 37, 38, 39, 40n, 41, 42, 46, 48, 51n, 71n, 73, 76n, 87, 88, 91n, 93, 95, 103, 144, 145, 146, 150, 151, 153, 154, 155, 157, 158, 159, 160, 161, 162, 163n, 180, 190n, 191, 192, 193, 194, 196, 197, 200, 202, 203, 205, 206, 207, 208, 209, 210, 211, 212, 213, 223, 241n, 247, 248, 251n, 258, 259, 262, 263, 267, 270, 272, 273, 274, 291n, 349, 371n, 377, 378, 395, 403, 417, 421, 467, 468, 469, 470, 473, 474, 475, 476, 562, 563, 569, 571, 573, 574, 576, 578, 580, 585, 586
Platonism, 2, 7, 8, 32, 34, 35, 39, 40, 41, 44, 48, 76, 87, 91, 176, 190, 193, 203, 205, 207, 277, 280, 291, 293, 302, 395, 399n, 400n, 469, 470, 471, 475, 555, 562, 569, 570, 571, 576, 578, 582, 585, 586, 589
Platonism, Florentine, 7, 8, 276, 546, 548, 553, 562, 564, 565. *See also* Academy, Platonic (Florentine)
Platonists, the, 29, 159, 160, 192, 293, 294, 469
Pléiade, the, 37
Plethon, Gemistos, 565, 582
Pliny the Elder (Gaius Plinius Secundus), 23, 24, 421, 514n
Plotinus, 1, 2, 5, 6, 13, 159n, 375, 377, 400n, 545, 569, 576, 580, 583
Plusquam Commentator. *See* Torrigiano dei Torrigiani

Plutarch of Chaeroneia, 140, 318, 382, 417, 418, 530n
Poggio Bracciolini, Giovanni Francesco, 132, 141, 218, 399, 407, 417, 420
Polain, Louis, 352n
Poliakov, Léon, 53n
Politi da Lodi, Bassiano, 533n
"Polixenus," 75n, 76, 77, 78, 80, 83, 87, 88, 89, 90, 91, 93, 94
Poliziano, Angelo Ambrogini, detto il, 30n, 577
Polka, Brayton, 215n, 227n
Polybius, 42, 43n
Polyhistor, Alexander, 51n
Pomponazzi, Pietro, 6, 7, 8, 70, 71, 72, 73, 74, 75, 76, 77, 78, 79, 80, 81, 82, 83, 84, 86, 87, 88, 89, 90, 91, 92, 93, 95, 96, 97, 98, 99, 100, 101, 111, 112, 113, 114, 115, 126, 144, 160, 163, 275, 277, 278, 527, 533, 547, 549, 550, 552, 560, 563, 581
Pomponius Mela, 51n
Pomponius, Sextus, 33, 36n
Pontano, Giovanni Giovano, 136, 137
Poole, Reginald Lane, 132n, 133n
Poor Clares, 359
Pope, Alexander, 375, 376
Popkin, Richard H., 67n, 68n, 194n
Popon, Petrus, 410, 411
Popper, Karl R., 266n
Poppi, Antonino, 155n, 278n, 527n
Porphyry, 253, 255, 580
Portland, Oregon, 551
Post, Gaines, 438n
Postel, Guillaume, 65, 67
Poteat, Hubert M., 579
Poughkeepsie, New York, 564
Powicke, Frederick M., 241n
Prague, 19n, 310
Prandi, Alfonso, 566
Prantl, Carl, 246n, 252n
Praxiteles, 24
Preen, Friedrich von, 389n
Premuda, Loris, 283n
Prentice, William K., 573
Prete, Sesto, 558
Princeton, New Jersey, 262n, 434n, 546, 554

Prisca theologia, 21, 28, 210, 212, 471n
Priscian (Priscianus Caesariensis), 234n, 514
Priuli, Constantino, 485, 495
Priuli, Francesco, 485, 495
Priuli, Girolamo, 489n, 491n
Proclus Diadochus, 95, 205n, 258, 260, 261, 266, 267, 269n, 272n, 273n, 293, 580, 584
Procopius, 3
Proctor, Robert G. C., 352n
Prodicus of Ceos, 193
Protagoras, 190, 191n, 192, 193, 194, 195, 196, 197, 198, 199, 200, 201, 202, 203, 204, 205, 206, 207, 208, 209, 210, 211, 212, 213
Protestant Reformers, 38, 308
Protogenes of Caunus, 24
Providence, Rhode Island, 547, 548, 558, 564, 565
Prunai, Giulio, 463n
Prynne, William, 178n
Pseudo-Clement, 28
Ptolemy (Claudius Ptolemaeus), 174, 403
Publicio, Jacopo, 407
Pucci, Francesco, 577
Pufendorf, Samuel von, 45
Pullan, Brian, 489n, 513n
Purnell, Frederick, XXIII, 163n
Puteolano, Ioannefrancesco. *See* Dal Pozzo, Gianfrancesco
Puttenham, George, 374
Pygmies, 59
Pyrgoteles, 24
Pythagoras, 24, 26, 29, 34, 151, 195, 199, 209
Pythagoreanism, 26, 205n, 206, 271, 402n. *See also* Neopythagoreanism

Quatrario, Giovanni, 532n, 534
Querini, Girolamo, 487n
Quétif, Jacques, 532n
Quintilian (Marcus Fabius Quintilianus), 37n, 417

Rabelais, François, 41
Radetti, Giorgio, 214n, 215n
Raggio, Olga, 210n
Ragnisco, Pietro, 144n, 149n, 162n, 275

Ragusa, 402n
Raimondi, Cosma, 226, 227
Raimondi, Ezio, 520n
Ralegh (Raleigh), Sir Walter, 59, 60, 61, 62, 64
Ramus, Peter, 284, 300, 303, 304
Randall, Sir Alec, 65n
Randall, John Herman, Jr., 6, 12, 16, 195n, 278n, 280n, 547, 549, 563, 573
Ranke, Leopold von, 389n
Ransom, John Crowe, 342
Raphael (Raffaello Sanzio), 389
Rashdall, Hastings, 241n
Rastell, John, 57, 356, 357
Rastell, William, 356, 357
Ratisbona, Johannes, 420n
Raymond VII, Count of Toulouse, 455, 456, 458
Raymond, Marcel, 37n
Raynal, Louis, 35n
Raynald of Chartres, 456, 457, 458
Recco, Martin, 534
Reed, Arthur William, 352, 356, 357, 358, 359
Reese, Gustave, XXV
Reformation, the, 124
Regensburg, 480
Reggio, 352
Reginald of Canterbury, 573
Regiomontanus, Joannes, 416
Reinald von Dassel, Archbishop of Cologne, Chancellor to Emperor Friedrich I, 320, 321, 323, 324, 325, 326, 327, 328, 330n, 334, 336, 337
Reis, Lincoln, 547
Reitlinger, Edmund, 310n, 311n
Renan, Ernest, 116n
Renaudet, Augustin, 19n, 21n, 551
Reuchlin, Johannes, 479, 566
Reumont, Alfredo, 400n
Reuss, Friedrich A., 413n
Reynolds, Beatrice, 585
Reynolds, Leighton D., 250n
Rezasco, Giulio, 485n, 487n, 491n
Ribner, Rhoda M., 385n
Ricci, Corrado, 523n
Riccioli, Giovanni Battista, 308n
Riccius. *See* Paulus Israelita

Rice, Eugene F., Jr., XXI, XXII, XXIII, 19n, 21n, 33n, 38n
Richard, the Sophist. *See* Fishacre, Richard
Richard de Bury, Bishop of Durham, 231, 232, 233, 234, 235, 236, 237, 238, 239, 253, 254, 256, 257
Richelieu, Armand Jean du Plessis, Cardinal, Duc de, 65, 169, 186, 187, 188, 189, 375
Rickert, Heinrich, 545
Riedl, John O., 571
Rigg, James Macmullen, 356, 366
Righi, Gaetano, 41n
Rinuccini, Alamanno, 395n
Risoldi, Luigia, 524n
Risse, Wilhelm, 278n, 465n
Ritter, Gerhard, 419n
Robinson, Forrest G., 377n
Robson, John A., 236n
Roger, Pierre. *See* Clement VI, Pope
Rogers, David Morrison, 366n
Rogers, Elizabeth F., 358n, 576
Rohr, Michael, 263n
Rollenhagen, Gabriel, 310, 311, 318
Rollenhagen, George, 310, 311
Rollins, Hyder, 373
Rome, 3, 4, 5, 8, 36, 39, 43, 45, 72, 75, 85, 132, 138, 139, 143, 166, 168, 169, 170, 172, 174, 179, 181, 182n, 184, 186, 187, 188, 214n, 223, 333, 335, 336, 387, 389, 398, 399, 416, 419, 420, 463, 464n, 520, 550, 552
Ronsard, Pierre, 37
Roper, William, 358n
Rose, Herbert J., 529n, 530n
Rosen, Edward, 311n, 318n
Rosenthal, Bernard, XXV
Rosenthal, Franz, 573
Ross, Nelson Peter, 587
Ross, Richard, 26n
Ross, William David, 260n, 266n, 267n, 272n
Rossellino, Antonio, 404n
Rossi, Giuseppe, 470n
Rossi, Pietro, 509n
Rossi, Vittorio, 394n, 404n
Rossmann, Fritz, 318n

Rosso, Nicolò, 484, 488n, 494, 501
Roswitha (Hroswitha of Gandersheim), 419
Rot (Roth, Rott), Johannes, 417n, 419, 420, 421
Roth, Cecil, 576
Rothenburg, Konrad von, 412
Rottweil, 481
Rouen, 366
Roure, Marie-Louise, 235n, 236n
Rousseau, Jean Jacques, 574
Roussell, Gérard, 26
Rowe, Bryan, 353
Rowe, John Gordon, 508n, 566
Rubinstein, Nicolai, 328n
Rucellai, Santi (Pandolfo), 432
Rudolph II of Hapsburg, Emperor, 172
Rüdesheim, Rudolf von, 421n
Runes, Dagobert D., 572
Rupprich, Hans, 407n, 417n, 420n, 569
Russell, Bertrand, 273n
Russell, John, 134
Russia, 11
Russo, Luigi, 341, 344, 347n
Rutenber, Culbert G., 576
Rutenburg, Viktor I., 584
Ryan, John K., 172n
Ryle, Gilbert, 261, 262n
Rymer, Thomas, 375

Sabbadini, Remigio, 520n
Sabians (Sabeans), 53, 54
Sacchetti, Francesco, 395
Sacrobosco, Joannes de, 20
Saffert, Erich, 409n, 410n
Saffron, Morris, XXV
Saint Louis, Missouri, 554
Saitta, Giuseppe, 100n, 214n, 578
Salerno, 7, 548, 552, 554, 555
Salimbene da Parma (Balien Adam), 455n
Salinger, Gerard, 54n
Salloch, William, XXV
Sallust (Gaius Sallustius Crispus), 141, 417, 529n
Saloman, Herman P., 50n
Salt Lake City, Utah, 551
Salutati, Coluccio, 140n, 193n, 399, 532, 533, 534, 539n, 569

Salvini, Sebastiano, 558
Salzburg, 554
Sambin, Paolo, 144n
San Diego, California, 54n
San Marino, California, 571
Sánchez Reyes, Enrique, 55n
Sancipriano, Mario, 583
Sandellius, Dionysius (*pseud.*). *See* Fassini, Vincenzo
Sangodenzo, 4
Sansalvatore, Antonio Benedetto, 432
Sansovino, Francesco, 484n, 488n
Santangelo, Vincenzo, 215n
Santinello, Giovanni, 199n, 203n
Santini, Emilio, 553
Santoro, Mario, 577
Sanudo, Francesco, 119
Sanudo, Marco, 119
Sanudo, Marino, 485n, 488n, 503n, 504n, 505, 506n, 507n, 508n, 511
Sapellico, Marcantonio, 510, 514n
Saratoga Springs, New York, 559
Sardinia, 170
Sarsa, Samuel, 55
Saul, King of Israel, 333
Saumaise, Claude, 57, 66, 67
Savonarola, Girolamo, 432
Saxl, Fritz, 11
Saxony, 408, 409n, 415, 522, 524
Scaccia, Sigismondo, 427n
Scaglione, Aldo, 341n
Scala, Bartolommeo, 560
Scaliger, Julius Caesar, 375, 377, 578
Scepticism, 248n
Schab, William H., 135n, 143
Schaffhausen, 307n
Schalk, Fritz, 559
Schaller, Dieter, 556
Schedel, Hartmann, 409n, 413n, 416, 419n-420n
Schedel, Hermann, 408, 419n, 420n
Scheffer, Konrad, 410
Schepss, Georg, 410n, 411n
Scherhaufer, Albin F., 411n
Schiavone, Michele, 583
Schickard, Wilhelmus, 55n
Schilling, Jan, of Cracow, 19n
Schlick, Kaspar, 412

Schlösser, Manfred, 555
Schmitt, Charles B., 195n, 278n, 466n, 467n, 469n, 518n
Schneider, Friedrich, 410n
Schnelbögel, Julia, 414n
Schnurrer, Christian Friedrich, 311n
Schoeps, Hans Joachim, 53n, 65n
Scholasticism, 6, 7, 8, 9, 36, 40, 89, 92, 94, 98, 133, 192, 241n, 410, 411, 412, 414, 424, 431, 432, 467, 532n, 540, 546, 548, 550, 552, 553, 555, 557
Scholem, Gershom G., 573
Schulte, Johann Friedrich von, 414n
Schutz, Alexander H., 581
Schwamm, Hermann, 106n, 107, 108
Schweinfurt, 408, 409, 410, 411
Schweyen-Ott, Renate, 568
Schwyzer, Hans-Rudolf, 580, 583
Scipio de Gabiano, 123
Sclano, Salvo, 286n
Scotism, 108, 109, 115, 147, 240, 251n, 256, 257
Scotland, 178n
Scoto, Girolamo, 125
Scoto, Ottaviano, 120, 122
Scoto, Tomás, 55
Scott, Robert, 242n
Scott, Theodore K., 242n
Scotus, John Duns. *See* Duns Scotus, John
Seattle, Washington, 554
Sebastocrator, Isaac, 584
Séché, Léon, 38n
Secret, François, 27n
Segarizzi, Arnaldo, 531n
Segrave, Walter, 236n, 238
Seigel, Jerrold E., 191n, 215n
Selby-Bigge, Lewis A., 241n
Sella, Domenico, 487n
Seneca, Lucius Annaeus, 97, 193, 195, 226, 249, 250, 372, 386, 417, 421, 531, 532, 533, 534n, 535, 538, 539, 540, 541
Sermoneta, Alessandro, 92
Servites, Order of, 88
Settle, Thomas B., 465n, 467n
Setton, Kenneth, 588
Sextus Empiricus, 194, 248
Sextus, Rufus, 138

Sforza, Alessandro, Lord of Pesaro, 397, 402n
Sforza, Costanzo, 402n
Shakespeare, William, 374, 375, 376, 385, 386
Shapiro, Marianne Goldner, 351n
Sharpe, Reginald Robinson, 361n
Sherburn, George W., 372n
Sherwood (Shirwood), William of. See William of Shyreswood
Sichardus, Johannes, 477, 478, 479, 482
Sicily, 170, 335
Sidney, Philip, 374, 376, 377, 378, 379, 380, 384, 385
Siena, 139, 168, 278, 438n, 463, 550
Sieveking, Heinrich, 435n, 436n, 437
Siger of Brabant, 243n, 255
Sigerist, Henry E., 58n, 573
Sigismund, Bishop of Würzburg, 408
Sigismund of Hapsburg, Duke (later Archduke) of Austria and Count of the Tyrol, 408, 409
Sigismund of Luxemburg, King of the Romans, Emperor, 408, 414
Sihler, Ernest G., 529n
Silva-Tarouca, Carlo, 472n
Silvestre, Hubert, 234n
Simon Magus, 28
Simon of Mephan, Archbishop of Canterbury, 237n
Simon, Richard, 50, 53, 56, 65, 68
Simplicius, 145, 146, 149n, 150, 152, 153, 155, 156, 159, 162, 163
Skelton, John, 354, 374, 382
Skrzynskaia, Elena C., 584
Slonimsky, Henry, 52n
Slotkin, James Sydney, 55n, 58n, 60n, 64n
Smalley, Beryl, 232n
Smith, Cyril E., 454n
Smith, Hallett, 370n, 384n
Smith, Hilary, XXIII
Smith, Leonard, 532n, 534n
Smith, Preserved, 354n
Socialism, 164, 169, 178, 179, 181, 183, 184
Society of Jesus. See Jesuits
Socinians, 59

Socrates, 41, 113, 114, 190n, 191, 192, 193, 206, 212, 251n, 417, 469, 474
Solomon, King of Israel, 57, 385
Solon, 417, 421
Sommerfeldt, Gustav, 409n
Sophianos, Johannes, 565
Sophianus, Michael, 127
"Sophista," 75n, 76, 78n, 80, 81, 84, 85, 87, 89n, 90, 94, 96, 98
Sophists, 190, 191n, 192, 241, 466, 472
Soudek, Josef, 130, 133, 135, 138, 139, 140n, 141
South Bend, Indiana, 565
Spain, 11, 170, 171, 173, 175, 176, 177, 178, 186, 188, 367, 524
Spampanato, Vincenzo, 165n
Spencer, John R., 198n
Spenser, Edmund, 376, 381, 384, 385
Speusippus, 272n
Spiazzi, Raimondo, 253n
Spina, Bartolomeo, 74, 75n, 76, 77n, 82n, 83, 87n, 88, 89, 90, 91, 94n
Spinoza, Benedictus de, 13, 50, 68, 276, 588
Spiriti, Lorenzo, 359
Spitz, Lewis W., 406n
Sprat, Thomas, Bishop of Rochester, 372n
Stabile, Giorgio, 462n
Stagninus, Bernardinus, 120
Stanhope, Philip (1732-1768), 375
Stanhope, Philip Dormer, fourth Earl of Chesterfield, 375
Stapleton, Thomas, 357n
Stapulensis, Fabrus. See Lefèvre d'Etaples, Jacques
Stauber, Richard, 413n
Staudinger, Josef, 578
Steinhöwel, Heinrich, 407
Steinschneider, Moritz, 116n, 123n, 555
Stella, Alvise, 515
Stella, Angela, 515
Stella, Antonio, 488n
Stella, Gianpietro, 502, 503, 504, 505, 507, 508, 510, 511, 512, 513n, 514n, 515n, 516
Stelling-Michaud, Sven, 442n
Stephanus Bohemus (Stephanus Martini de Tyn), 19n

Stephanus Byzantius, 566
Stephen, Saint, Protomartyr, 560
Stephen of Tournai, 245n
Stewart, Hugh Fraser, 102n
Stillingfleet, Edward, Bishop of Worcester, 56
Stilo, 165, 173
Stilpo (Stilpon), 248, 249n
Stintzing, Roderich von, 44n
Stobaeus, 260n
Stobbe, Otto, 412n, 414n
Stockdale, W. H., 508n, 566
Stoicism, 70, 82, 84, 97, 99, 176, 193, 214n, 223, 224, 225, 227, 241, 247, 248, 252n, 587
Stoics, the, 84, 97, 99, 191, 193, 225, 248, 249n, 250, 252, 263n, 269n, 572
Stolpe, Sven, 65n
Strabo, 566
Strassburg, 352
Strathmann, Ernest A., 56n
Strauss, Bruno, 415n
Strauss, Gerald, 414n
Strauss, Leo, 54n, 65n
Strigonia (Esztergom), 400n
Strittmater, Anselm, 5
Struever, Nancy S., 191n
Struve, Burcard Gotthelff, 417n
Stucki, Johann Wilhelm, 306n, 307, 308, 309
Studia humanitatis, 9, 30, 132, 391-392, 396, 399, 400, 416, 417, 421, 526, 528
Stufler, Johann, 89n, 104n
Sturm, Johann, 304
Stuttgart, 312, 478, 479
Stwosz, Wit, 579
Styria, 169, 314
Suarez, Francisco, 581
Sudhoff, Karl, 58n
Suessanus. *See* Nifo, Agostino
Suiseth. *See* Swineshead, Richard
Sullivan, Roger, 518n
Surrey, Earl of. *See* Howard, Henry
Swabia, 407, 419, 420
Sweden, 19, 187, 243n
Swift, Jonathan, 375
Swineshead, Richard, 533n
Switalski, Bruno, 576

Switzerland, 170, 307n, 308, 504
Sylvester. *See* Mazzolini, Silvestro
Symonds, John Addington, 173n, 178n, 179n
Syracuse, New York, 556
Syria, 487
Syrianus, 262n

Tacitus, Cornelius, 372
Taddeo degli Alderotti, 286
Tagliacozzo, Giorgio, 48n
Taliaferro, Robert Catesby, 574
Tanswell, John, 360n
Taprobane, 180
Tartars, 180
Tassini, Giuseppe, 491n
Taylor, Thomas, 574
Tedaldi, Francesco, 553
Tedeschi, John, 21n
Telesio, Bernardino, 166, 168, 174, 176, 276, 560
Terence (Publius Terentius Afer), 141, 376, 417, 492, 514
Tetzel, Johann, 371n
Thales, 150, 417
Theiler, Willy, 569
Themistius, 145, 146, 149n, 152, 153, 155, 156, 159n, 162, 163
Theophilus of Antioch, 51
Theophrast von Hohenheim. *See* Paracelsus
Theophrastus of Eresos, 153, 156, 474
Thibaudet, Albert, 464n
Thieme, Ulrich, 118n
Thienis, Gaetanus de. *See* Gaetano di Thiene
Thillet, Pierre, 81n
Thomas Anglicus. *See* Wilton, Thomas
Thomas Aquinas, Saint, 84n, 85, 88, 89, 92, 93, 96, 97, 101, 103, 104, 105, 106, 109, 111, 112, 113, 119, 128, 146, 147, 148, 154, 156, 158, 165n, 240, 241, 246, 247, 253, 256, 400n, 423, 440, 441, 522
Thomas de Vio. *See* Cajetan
Thomas, Ernest C., 232n, 233n
Thomas, Ivor. *See* Bulmer-Thomas, Ivor
Thomas, Joseph, 583

Thomism, 7, 8, 96, 106, 113, 115, 147, 157, 165n, 166, 184n, 561, 563, 568
Thorndike, Lynn, 19n, 283n, 519n, 572
Thucydides, 33
Timanthes of Cythnus, 24
Timmermans, B. J. H. M., 214n
Tinello, Francesco, 137n
Tiraboschi, Girolamo, 72n, 73n, 77n
Tisias (Teisias) of Syracuse, 192
Tissard, François, 27n
Tisserant, Eugène, Cardinal, 560
Todorovich, Miro, 589
Toeplitz, Otto, 272n
Tomacello, Marino, 136, 137
Tomasi, Pietro, 531
Tomeo, Niccolò Leonico, 510
Tomitano, Bernardino, 128
Toronto, 559
Torrigiano dei Torrigiani (Drusianus; Monachus; Trusianus), 281, 286, 287, 288, 290, 292, 294, 296
Tottel, Richard, 373, 385
Toulouse, 454, 455n, 457, 458, 459, 460
Tours, 555
Trapezuntius. *See* Giorgio da Trebisonda
Traversari, Ambrogio, 194, 223
Tribonian, 36
Trier, 408
Trieste, 416, 550
Trinkaus, Charles, XXI, XXIII, 9n, 14n, 193n, 207n, 215n, 520n, 522n, 571, 589
Trithemius, Joannes, 21
Trivet (Triveth), Nicholas, 246n
Troilo, Erminio, 275
Troje, Hans, 44n
Trombetta, Antonio, 154n, 160
Tron, Luca, 505, 512
Troy, 333
Trusen, Winfried, 412n, 414n
Trusianus (Turisanus). *See* Torrigiano dei Torrigiani
Tucher, Hans, 416
Tübingen, 310, 311, 312, 313, 315, 318, 319, 477
Tunisia, 343
Turin, 554
Turks, the, 170, 173, 176, 187
Turolla, Enrico, 571

Tuscany, 391
Twyne, Thomas, 386
Tyard, Pontus de, 37n

Ullman, Berthold Louis, 140n, 534n, 557, 560, 586
Ullmann, Carl (Karl), 406n, 411n, 413n, 414n, 418n
Ulpianus, Domitius, 32, 33n, 36, 42, 46
Ulrich, Duke of Württemberg, 477
Ulster, 368
United States of America, XXI, XXII, 1, 3, 5, 7, 8, 11, 12, 14, 15
University Park, Pennsylvania, 554
Untersteiner, Mario, 191n, 192, 205n
Urban VIII, Pope (Maffeo Barberini), 179, 186
Urbana, Illinois, 560
Urbino, 397, 401, 402, 403n
Urceo, Antonio ("Codro"), 520, 526
Urriza, Juan, 574

Valentinelli, Giuseppe, 55n
Valerius Maximus, 417, 513-514
Valla, Giorgio, 510, 514n
Valla, Lorenzo, 30, 47n, 132, 191n, 198, 199, 214, 215n, 216, 217, 218, 219, 221, 222, 223, 224, 225, 226, 227, 417, 420, 421, 510, 514, 520, 526, 560
Valton, Philip, 35
Vancouver, British Columbia, 559
Van Helmont, Jean Baptiste, 574
Vanini, Lucilio, 64
Vanni Rovighi, Sofia, 144n, 571, 576
Van Schilfgaarde, Paul, 582
Van Steenberghen, Fernand, 84n
Vasari, Giorgio, 392, 404
Vasoli, Cesare, 124n, 215n, 278n, 283n, 465n, 466n, 531n
Vatican City, 11, 19, 73n, 136, 143, 178, 235n, 237n, 240n, 244n, 401, 450, 462, 471, 523, 525, 527n, 528, 533n, 534n, 535n, 554, 560, 564
Vattasso, Marco, 525n
Vela, Maria Elena, 551
Venice, 4, 55n, 77, 117, 118, 120, 123n, 125, 127, 145n, 152n, 170, 235n, 276, 277, 284, 352, 426, 428, 435, 439n, 442,

INDEX 623

449, 450, 483, 485n, 487, 488n, 489n, 490, 491, 492n, 502, 503, 504, 506, 507, 508, 509, 510, 511n, 512, 514n, 515n, 526n, 531n, 532n, 551, 553, 556, 559, 560, 562
Veraja, Fabiano, 441n
Verene, Donald, 48n
Vergerio, Pietro (Pier) Paolo, the elder, 140, 407, 532n, 534
Verino, Il Secondo. *See* De Vieri, Franceso
Vernia, Nicoletto, 118, 119, 144, 145, 146, 147, 148, 149, 150, 151, 152, 153, 154, 155, 156, 157, 158, 159, 160, 161, 162, 163
Verona, 560
Vespasiano da Bisticci, 132, 387, 388, 389, 390, 392, 393, 394, 395, 396, 397, 398, 399, 400, 401, 402, 403, 404
Vespucci, Amerigo, 57
Viana, 136n
Vico, Giovanni Battista, 30, 31, 40, 45, 47, 50, 68, 574
Victor IV, Antipope (Ottaviano de Frascati), 330
Vida, Marco Girolamo, 375
Vido, Giovanni, 509n
Vienna, 141, 314, 406, 410, 411, 412
Villani, Filippo, 400
Villani, Giovanni, 400
Villey, Pierre, 464n
Vintimiglia, 79
Virgil (Publius Vergilius Maro), 325, 335, 373, 417, 421, 492, 532
Vitaliani, Domenico, 283n
Viterbo, 557
Vives, Juan Luis, 56, 375
Viviani, Ugo, 462n, 463n, 464n
Völcker, Valentin, 409n
Voigt, Georg, 137n, 214n, 407n, 409n, 417n, 418n
Volterra, 11, 550, 564

"W. H." *See* Heron, William
Walker, Daniel Pickering, 583
Wallace, John M., 372n
Wallace, William A., 467n
Wallach, Luitpold, 562
Waltham, Massachusetts, 561

Walther, Hans, 536n
Walther, Rudolph. *See* Gualter, Rudolph
Walzer, Richard, 573
Warham, William, Archbishop of Canterbury, 135
Warton, Thomas, 370
Washington, D. C., 560, 566
Waszink, Jan Hendrik, 585
Watenphul, Heinrich, 322n, 335
Waters, Emily, 387n
Waters, William G., 387n
Watkins, Renée N., 195n, 196n
Watson, Thomas, 384
Watts, Alan W., 574
Wegele, Franz X. von, 413n
Wehmer, Carl, 570
Weigand, Herman J., 5
Weigel, Martin, 414n
Weigenmaier, Georg, 311
Weimann, Karl-Heinz, 140n
Weisheipl, James A., 235n, 241n
Weiss, Roberto, 31, 352n, 406n, 581, 588
Weitz, Morris, 565
Wellesley, Massachusetts, 554
Wemding, 420
Wendehorst, Alfred, 422n
Werkmeister, William H., 555
West Indies, 64
Whitacre, Alfred E., 104n
White, Hayden V., 48n
White, Henry J., 251n
Whitfield, John Humphreys, 575
Whitford, Richard, 366
Wieacker, Franz, 406n
Wiener, Philip P., 558, 587
Wiener Neustadt, 416
Wieruszowski, Helene, XXII
Wilhelm, Duke of Saxony, 409n
Will, Georg A., 415n
William II, Bishop of Agen, 454, 455, 457, 458, 459
William I, King of Sicily, 335
William of Moerbeke, 580, 584
William of Shyreswood (Sherwood, Shirwood), 232n, 245n
Williamson, George, 372n
Wilpert, Paul, 199n
Wilson, Cook, 266n

Wilson, Curtis, 237n
Wilton, Thomas (Anglicus), 108
Wimpfen, 415
Windet, John, 366
Winstanley, Gerrard, 189
Winter, Eduard, 407n
Winwar, Frances, 340n, 344
Wissowa, Georg, 260n
Witt, Ronald G., XXIII
Wölfflin, Heinrich, 392n
Wohlwill, Emil, 467n
Wolfenbüttel, 4
Wolff, Philippe, 457n, 461n
Wolfson, Harry Austryn, 116n, 127, 561, 576
Wolkan, Rudolf, 416n
Woodbridge, Frederick J. E., 276
Wordsworth, John, 251n
Worm, Ole, 66n
Wühr, Wilhelm, 388n
Württemberg, 477, 478, 479
Würzburg, 408, 410, 411, 413
Wyatt, Sir Thomas, the elder, 370n, 373, 382, 383, 385
Wycherley, William, 376
Wyclif, John, 244n
Wyle, Niklas von, 407, 415, 419
Wynchcombe, Abbot of. *See* Kedirmystir, Richard

Xenophanes of Colophon, 150
Xenophon, 194

York, 360

"Z. A.," Mr., 65n
Zabarella, Francesco, Cardinal, 215n, 227
Zabarella, Jacopo, 275, 277, 278, 279, 280, 291, 295, 299, 301, 302
Zacour, Norman P., 586
Zalmoxis (Salmoxis), 26
Zammit, Paul, 424n
Zara, 402
Zasius, Ulrich, 35n, 36, 477
Zedler, Johann Heinrich, 306n, 307n
Zeno of Elea, 417
Ziegler, Karl, 409n, 411n
Ziliotto, Baccio, 579
Zilsel, Edgar, 575
Zimara, Marcantonio, 121, 126
Zöckler, Otto, 54, 55n
Zonta, Gasparo, 412n
Zoroaster, 26
Zorzi, Maestro, 488n
Zurich, 4, 307n
Zwinger, Theodor, 286n
Zwingli, Ulrich, 306